The historiography of eighteenth and early nineteenth century campaigns is dominated by operational narratives and biographies of senior officers. How armies were staffed, fed and medically provisioned was critical to their successful performance in the field, yet much less is known of these key issues. Eyewitness accounts highlight instances of mismanagement, but by ignoring the ordinary they can provide a distorted view of reality, while published information on the organisation of the British Army at this period is confined to home administration, not that of an expeditionary force overseas. By using predominantly unpublished sources, including the general orders issued by the Duke of York's headquarters, it has been possible to provide considerable detail on the structures necessary for the daily functioning of an army on campaign. Integral to this were the men engaged in staff positions, the commissariat and the medical department, their suitability, how they were appointed, and their day-to-day responsibilities.

The internal organisation of the British Army's fighting units is often taken for granted, but the start of any war during the eighteenth century inevitably led to rapid expansion and major developments in recruiting methods. As the proportion of recruits increased, unit cohesion and experience declined for both officers and men, affecting discipline, operational capability, and health; all factors which tend to be overlooked in standard campaign narratives. A key component of the fighting troops in Flanders were the Ordnance units, comprising the artillery and engineers, which are so often neglected but so critical in providing firepower support and technical expertise. Similarly forgotten are the considerable numbers of women and children who officially accompanied forces in the field, all of whom came under military discipline and received their subsistence from the army. Their numbers, the roles they fulfilled and their experiences in Flanders are discussed in detail.

Underpinning the entire administrative structure of the army on campaign was its relationship with corresponding organisations at home. Performance in the field was heavily dependent on the effectiveness of working relationships on both sides. Structures evolved throughout the eighteenth century, becoming gradually more formalised with increased definition of the duties performed in each role, a process that was to continue until the defeat of Napoleon in 1815. The Flanders campaign represented a key point in this evolutionary process at the start of the French Wars.

R.N.W. Thomas has a PhD in Archaeology from Southampton University. He is a contributor to the Oxford Dictionary of National Biography and has published a number of papers on the Flanders campaign in conference proceedings and academic journals. He edited the letters of Daniel George Robinson for the Army Records Society. He works in the shipping industry.

No Want of Courage

The British Army in Flanders, 1793–1795

R.N.W. Thomas

Helion & Company

Helion & Company Limited
Unit 8 Amherst Business Centre
Budbrooke Road
Warwick
CV34 5WE
England
Tel. 01926 499619
Email: info@helion.co.uk
Website: www.helion.co.uk
Twitter: @helionbooks
Visit our blog at http://blog.helion.co.uk/

Published by Helion & Company 2022
Designed and typeset by Mach 3 Solutions Ltd (www.mach3solutions.co.uk)
Cover designed by Paul Hewitt, Battlefield Design (www.battlefield-design.co.uk)

Text © R.N.W. Thomas 2022
Cover: Soldiers of the 11th Light Dragoons and 33rd Foot by Guillaume Auguste de Willermin, dated Capellen, October 1795. (Anne S.K. Brown Military Collection)
Illustrations © as individually credited.
Maps by George Anderson © Helion & Company 2022

Every reasonable effort has been made to trace copyright holders and to obtain their permission for the use of copyright material. The author and publisher apologise for any errors or omissions in this work, and would be grateful if notified of any corrections that should be incorporated in future reprints or editions of this book.

ISBN 978-1-915070-40-1

British Library Cataloguing-in-Publication Data.
A catalogue record for this book is available from the British Library.

All rights reserved. No part of this publication may be reproduced, stored in a retrieval system, or transmitted, in any form, or by any means, electronic, mechanical, photocopying, recording or otherwise, without the express written consent of Helion & Company Limited.

For details of other military history titles published by Helion & Company Limited, contact the above address, or visit our website: http://www.helion.co.uk

We always welcome receiving book proposals from prospective authors.

Contents

List of Maps and Illustrations		vi
Acknowledgements		vii
Notes		viii
Introduction		xi
1	The British Army and the Campaign in the Low Countries	15
2	The Staff	52
3	The Commissariat	97
4	The Medical Services	130
5	The Regiments	172
6	The Ordnance	217
7	Conclusion	260
Notes on the Appendices		270
I	Strength Returns	271
II	Casualty Returns	282
III	Magazine States	294
IV	March Discipline	297
V	Dispositions for Opening the First Parallel at Valenciennes	300
VI	Field Train of Artillery Ordered to attend the British Troops in the Low Countries, exclusive of the Battalion Guns now there	305
Bibliography		308
Index		316

List of Maps and Illustrations

Maps
1	Flanders: the area of operations.	22
2	The fortresses of Flanders.	32
3	Siege of Valenciennes.	249
4	Dunkirk.	254

Illustrations
Henry Dundas, 1st Viscount Melville, by Johann Friedrich Bolt, 1796.	19
The Right Honourable Lord Grenville, by Samuel William Reynolds.	19
The Earl of Moira, by Joshua Reynolds.	48
Lieutenant General Sir William Erskine, Bt, by Richard Cosway and Samuel Reynolds.	58
Schuit, by Jan Weissenbruch.	75
Lieutenant General the Hon Henry Edward Fox, by Charles Turner.	81
A bilander, by Pearson Scott Foresman.	117
John Gunning, Surgeon General.	138
Sir Lucas Pepys, Physician General, by J. Godby after H. Edridge.	139
Embarkation of Lord Moira's Troops at Southampton, 20 June 1794 (Preliminary Study).	194
'Vue de l'Assaut du chemin couvert de Valenciennes 25/26 Juli 1793', by J. Petrich.	253

Colour Plates
His Royal Highness the Duke of York, by John Hoppner.	i
Sir James Henry Craig, by Thomas Lawrence.	ii
Jeffery Amherst, 1st Baron Amherst, 1784, by Robert Edge Pine.	ii
Friederich Josias, Prinz von Sachsen Coburg.	ii
Marquis Cornwallis landing at Ostend in June 1794.	ii
'Watson and the Shark', by John Singleton Copley.	iii
John Hunter (1728–1793), surgeon and anatomist.	iii
William Pitt, Studio of Thomas Gainsborough RA, 1727–1788.	iii
'The Grand Attack on Valenciennes', Philip James de Loutherbourg.	iv
'Flannel coats of mail against the cold', by Isaac Cruikshank.	vi
'An early lesson of marching', by George Woodward, and Thomas Rowlandson.	vi
British Army baggage wagon and escort, by Thomas Rowlandson.	vii
'Recruits', by Henry William Bunbury.	vii
The Duke of Richmond, by Isaac Cruikshank.	viii
'Royal British Artillery', unknown artist, 1795.	viii
'The Artillery Driver', by Robert Dighton Snr. and Carington Bowles.	viii

Acknowledgements

This book could not have been written without the help and assistance of many people, and it gives me great pleasure to have this opportunity to express my thanks to them.

I would like to record my sincere gratitude to Terese Austin, Head of Reader Services at the William L. Clements Library, University of Michigan, for her very prompt assistance with providing copies of the Henry Clinton Papers and the James Moncrieff Papers. Ursula Ackrill and Jayne Amat at the University of Nottingham Libraries, Manuscripts and Special Collections, were also extremely helpful in copying the Papers of Lord William H. Cavendish Bentinck. At the University of Manchester Library, I am sincerely grateful to Dr James Peters, Archivist at the University Archive Centre, for his help in identifying relevant material and in obtaining copies of it from the uncatalogued Clinton Papers and to Angie McCarthy for copying services. I am greatly in debt to the archivists, librarians and staff of the following institutions: The National Archives, Kew, where the overwhelming bulk of primary source material utilised for this study is held, the Departments of Western Manuscripts and India Office Records at The British Library, London, and the National Army Museum, London.

I am most grateful to a number of friends and acquaintances for the help they have given during the writing of this book. These include Dr Rory Muir for information regarding Assistant Commissary Benjamin Mee, Stephen Wood and René Chartrand regarding illustrations and Dr John Houlding for assistance and references regarding regimental officers.

I received considerable help from Helion during the production phase of this book, and especially from Dr Andrew Bamford and Rob Griffith, who ensured that everything was done with efficiency and the minimum of fuss.

I am greatly indebted to Dr Alan Guy, former Director of The National Army Museum, London, who has provided ongoing support and advice during the writing of this book. His extensive knowledge of the eighteenth century British Army has been of great assistance.

Needless to state, all faults of error or omission lie with the author.

Notes

Abbreviations

AO	Audit Office Papers, The National Archives, Kew
BL	British Library
GO	General Order
HO	Home Office Papers, The National Archives, Kew
NAM	National Army Museum, London
ODNB	Oxford Dictionary of National Biography
PRO	Public Record Office Papers, The National Archives, Kew
T	Treasury Papers, The National Archives, Kew
TNA	The National Archives, Kew
UML	The University of Manchester Library, The Clinton Papers (uncatalogued)
UNL	University of Nottingham Libraries, Manuscripts and Special Collections
WLCL	William L. Clements Library, The University of Michigan
WO	War Office Papers, The National Archives, Kew

Measurements

Measurements of weight are expressed in pounds avoirdupois (lb), hundredweight (cwt) or long tons, as follows: 1 ton = 20 hundredweight = 2,240 pounds. In the interests of readability, many of the measurements expressed in pounds in the original documents, most of which are in the millions, have been converted into tons.

Money

Sterling currency is expressed in whole pounds (e.g. £10), whole shillings (e.g. 5/–) or whole pence (e.g. 9d). Pounds, shillings and pence are separated by commas (e.g. £2,10,0). Shillings and pence are separated by an oblique (e.g. 7/6). One pound consisted of 20 shillings, each of 12 pence. Occasional mention is made of guineas, which comprised 21 shillings, and are not abbreviated in this book.

Place Names

Place names are as written in the original sources. The modern equivalents are:

Arnheim	Arnhem
Baiseaux	Baisieux
Baseele	Bruyelle
Berlikom, Berlicom	Berlicum
Burlon	Bourlon
Cateau	Le Cateau-Cambrésis
Contigh, Contick, Conteig	Kontich
Courtrai, Courtray	Kortrijk
Dordt	Dordrecht
Estrew	Estreux
Gent	Ghent
Grammont	Geraardsbergen
Grosbeck, Groesweek, Grossbeek	Groesbeek
Kelemhoute, Calnhoot	Kalmthout
Klingerbeck	Klingelbeek
Lannoi	Lannoy
Lis	Lys
Nymeguen	Nijmegen
Oosterhoute, Oosterhoot	Oosterhout
Osnabruck	Osnabrück
Pittehem	Pittem
Rhené	Rheine
Roosendael, Rosendale, Roosendale, Rosindael	Roosendaal
St. Amand	Saint-Amand-les-Eaux
Tournay	Tournai
Turcoing	Tourcoing
Tuyl	Tuil
Veaux	Vaux-Andigny
Wicken, Wichen	Wijchen

The area in which the British expeditionary force was engaged comprised the Austrian Netherlands and the United Provinces of the Netherlands, which conformed approximately to modern day Belgium and The Netherlands respectively. The eighteenth century designations are used in this book.

Ranks

Many British Army officers had both regimental and army ranks, which could be different. Regimental rank was based on the date on which the individual received a commission in his unit, whereas army rank could result from a number of factors, such as previous good services, length of service or the date at which the same rank had been achieved in another regiment. Promotions in army rank could be made 'by brevet', for men holding the rank of captain and upwards, though came without any additional pay. The higher, or 'brevet', rank took precedence when troops from more than one unit were brigaded together, while seniority within the regiment was determined solely by the individual's regimental rank, regardless of whether he also held a higher rank in the army.[1]

As with many issues, the Foot Guards differed from the remainder of the Army when it came to rank designations, as all except ensigns held dual regimental and army rank. Lieutenants were designated captains in the Army and captains were lieutenant colonels. This took effect when officers transferred between guards and line units, when guardsmen took the senior of their two ranks with them. Foot Guards officers could also have army rank acquired on the same basis as already described, so Henry, Lord Mulgrave, for example, was a captain and lieutenant colonel (i.e. a company commander) in the 1st Foot Guards dating to 6 June 1783 yet held the army rank of colonel dating to 18 November 1790. Officers serving in a Foot Guards regiment at the time they are referred to in the text have their dual rank noted when serving in a regimental or a staff capacity (in other words, when not commanding troops from units other than their own), for example, Captain and Lieutenant Colonel James Perryn of the 1st Foot Guards.

Regimental Designations

Regiments of cavalry are referred to by their numerical designation followed by the type of regiment. For example, the 1793 *Army List* designation of the Fifteenth (or the King's) Regiment of (Light) Dragoons has been rendered as the 15th Light Dragoons in the text. The three regiments of foot guards are referred to as the 1st Foot Guards, Coldstream Guards and 3rd Foot Guards; the regimental motto of the Coldstream Guards, *'nulli secundus'*, has been respected. The full titles of regiments of the line have been omitted and instead they are referred to by their numerical designation. For example, the Fourteenth (or the Bedfordshire) Regiment of Foot is shortened to the 14th Regiment.

---

1   The annual printed Army Lists can be downloaded from The National Archives <https://discovery.nationalarchives.gov.uk/details/r/C14273>.

Introduction

This book is about the administration of an eighteenth century British army in the field. It is about organisations and structures, how they functioned, their roles and responsibilities, who populated them and how they performed on campaign. Above all, it is about people, because people, with all their talents and shortcomings, are the basis of any organisation. The subject of this book is the British army serving in Flanders between 1793–1795 commanded, until the last weeks of 1794, by Frederick, Duke of York (1763–1827), second son of King George III.

The Flanders campaign has attracted remarkably little attention from the British perspective compared to other conflicts in the long eighteenth century. Defeat in Flanders ensured that the campaign was largely consigned to obscurity after the biographies and memoirs of the participants had been completed by the mid-nineteenth century. As far as operational histories are concerned, over 100 years elapsed from the end of the campaign before the appearance of Sir John Fortescue's narrative, which made use of several published accounts from participants together with a selection of the more important British documents, though it was written in a highly opinionated style perhaps more acceptable to readers of the time.[1] Aside from a short account of the battle of Tourcoing (17–18 May 1794) by Hilaire Belloc published in 1912,[2] over another century passed before two narrative operational accounts of the campaign were published in 2018 and 2020, both primarily based on printed sources.[3] Two useful personal accounts were published in 2013 and 2018 respectively, both from officers, one of the 1st Dragoon Guards and the other the Coldstream Guards.[4] Defeats rarely attract interest from military historians. From the British viewpoint, the Flanders campaign was overshadowed by more successful operations later in the French Wars, but this relative flurry of publishing activity suggests renewed interest in what has been an otherwise neglected area of Britain's military involvement on the continent of Europe.

Before proceeding further, it would be worth setting out the content of this book. Although the structure of the British military at home is outlined for the purposes of context, the core

---

1 J.W. Fortescue, *A History of the British Army* (London: Macmillan, 1899–1930).
2 H. Belloc, *Tourcoing* (London: Stephen Swift, 1912).
3 S. Brown, *The Duke of York's Flanders Campaign. Fighting the French Revolution 1793–1795* (Barnsley: Frontline Books, 2018) and P. Ball, *Neither Up Nor Down. The British Army and the Flanders campaign 1793–1795* (Warwick: Helion, 2020).
4 P. Duckers (ed.), *A Diary of the Flanders campaign 1793–1796. Lt. Col. James Russell 1st (King's) Dragoon Guards* (Shrewsbury: Spink & Son, 2013) and P. Harrington (ed.), *With the Guards in Flanders. The Diary of Roger Morris 1793–1795* (Warwick: Helion, 2018).

of the book aims to address how this translated into the structure of an expeditionary force in the field. Chapter 1 traces developments in the political and administrative structures responsible for the deployment and organisation of the British Army during the eighteenth century. The second half of this chapter further sets the scene with an outline of the diplomatic and operational details of the campaign in the Low Countries, also addressing issues concerned with the leadership of the allied Combined Army and perceptions of the Duke of York as commander of the British expeditionary force. Chapter 2 examines the various departments comprising the headquarters staff. Little work relating to eighteenth century armies has been undertaken in this area, so this chapter seeks to trace developments from the War of the Spanish Succession (1701–1713) to see how these structures evolved over time. It examines who the individual members of the staff in Flanders were, how they were appointed, their experience, and the functions they performed. It is heavily based on the orderly books of the Duke of York's army, a source which has not previously been used. These records exist for the entirety of the campaign, apart from the final four months of 1793. Given that officers would transcribe general orders into notebooks for their own reference, it is possible that the missing months lie in some personal archive yet to be discovered. An indication that this remains a possibility lies in a newspaper article from 1915 in which was discussed: '... a pocket-book once belonging to Captain M. Crawford, of the Royal Horse Guards'.[5] This apparently contained general orders issued between 10 August and 1 October 1793, which would have provided material for one of the missing months. Unfortunately, no individual of this rank and name served in the Army at the time in question, suggesting the identity of the owner is either incorrect or the officer was a subsequent custodian of the document.

Chapter 3 examines the Commissariat, a civilian department acting under the directions of the Treasury. Commissaries were men of business, employed for their commercial knowledge, and thus contrasted with the uniformed military personnel whom it was their job to subsist. Much of the work already undertaken in this critical area for the entire period of the French Wars is in the form of unpublished university theses, but the primary source material for this chapter comprises the correspondence between the War Office and the commissary-general in Flanders. Chapter 4 turns to another civilian department, by examining the provision of medical facilities accompanying the army. Military medicine has attracted considerable interest in recent years, but relatively little of this attention has been directed specifically at the Flanders campaign of 1793–1795. The chapter examines who the medical personnel were, their qualifications, their effectiveness on campaign, their interactions with each other and with government agencies in London. Official correspondence between the medical personnel in Flanders and the authorities at home comprises much of the source material on which this chapter is based.

Chapters 5 and 6 focus on the fighting units comprising the Duke of York's army. Chapter 5 examines the regiments of cavalry and infantry, their composition, state and condition. It provides a detailed analysis of the officer corps, its experience and training, in order to gain insight into the performance of individual units on campaign. The role of women, who were integral to each unit, is also discussed. Chapter 6 performs a similar analysis for

---

5 'The old fighting in Flanders. Officer's diary of 1793', *The Mail*, 10 September 1915, p.6.

that 'army within an army', the artillery, engineers and artificers belonging to the Board of Ordnance. Although small in number, their role in the field, during siege operations and in the construction of static defences was critical for the success, or otherwise, of armies on campaign. The Board's responsibilities were wide ranging, but have received relatively little attention from historians, despite its key role in arming the military forces of the Crown, together with fixed defences located at home and overseas. Although the Board's internal organisation at home has been covered in discussions of army administration, much still needs to be done on the day-to-day management of its operations, especially regarding the functioning of ordnance troops and equipment on campaign. This chapter seeks to redress that balance.

Finally, the appendices. The business of managing an army in the field involved increasing levels of bureaucracy during the eighteenth century. This served two purposes: first, so that commanders on the spot received information regarding the state and condition of the forces under their command, both to plan operations and put resources in place to bring them about and, secondly, to assist the authorities at home in their higher direction of the war and to account for its financial cost. Inevitably, much of this huge mass of returns, many of which are mentioned in Chapter 2, has not survived the passage of time. This particularly concerns those containing information passed no further than army headquarters. Much of this information was relevant only to a particular point in time – such as lists of qualified bakers or men fit to work in the trenches at Dunkirk – so was most likely disposed of even before the campaign ended. Most of what has survived consists of material forwarded to the authorities at home, most notably to the Home Office (and after July 1794, the War Office) for army strength and casualty returns, and to the Treasury for magazine states and other commissariat matters. All the returns discovered that touch upon these issues have been included in Appendices I to III.

Matters of operational procedure, providing some insight into the business of actually managing a field army, comprise Appendices IV and V covering march discipline and the mechanism for opening the trenches before Valenciennes. Both marches and sieges occupied considerable amounts of the soldiers' time in Flanders, yet the detail of how these important activities were actually conducted is usually overlooked in campaign narratives. These appendices also aim to illustrate the degree of administrative planning necessary for headquarters staff to carry out operational tasks common to armies of the period.

Finally, Appendix VI provides a breakdown of the equipment comprising that critical element of a field army – the ordnance train. The appendix aims to show that the artillery accompanying the army consisted of somewhat more than just guns and gunners; considerable resources in support personnel, equipment and spare parts were all required. The appendix outlines the types of artillery piece comprising the ordnance park, together with an insight into the scale of the enterprise, with obvious implications for logistics within the theatre of operations.

As the Flanders campaign wore on, the burden of bureaucracy placed on both the headquarters staff and regimental officers increased. Some of this was undoubtedly due to differences in the management style of successive adjutants-general, but also reflected the increased size of the forces commanded by the Duke of York from mid-1794. The scale of this bureaucratic task was all the greater, given that it was undertaken by hand, since little evidence has been found of standardised forms, let alone printing facilities to produce them.

One may conclude that military bureaucracy imposed a growing burden on the individuals so employed, especially as the composition of the headquarters staff was also evolving at this period. The examples that follow serve to illustrate some aspects of its nature and extent.

It is inevitable that several fruitful subjects for research remain unaddressed. These fall into three main areas. The first consists of a matter close to the heart of each individual soldier – pay and remuneration. This is mentioned only in the context of additional pay granted for work that lay outside the soldiers' normal duties, such as constructing batteries and field works, serving as drivers for wagons and artillery, or working in hospitals. Army pay was complex at this period and it is unlikely that the men of any two regiments received the same remuneration, since much depended on the price of certain uniform or equipment items dictated by regimental colonels. The second area that would benefit from considerably greater attention is military discipline. The experience of the officer corps, the ratio of recruits to trained soldiers and the effectiveness of mechanisms to supply the men with pay and sustenance may go far to explain why certain units had an enviable disciplinary record and others did not. This, however, is beyond the scope of the present book. The final area omitted here consists of tactics and operations. Although fundamental to the very being of an army in the field, these matters have little place in what is essentially an administrative study. Devotees of the flashing sabre and the plunging bayonet should therefore look to the operational narratives mentioned above.

Chronologically, this administrative analysis of the Duke of York's army ends at the close of 1794, by which time the campaign was effectively over. What remained was the defence of the River Lek and the withdrawal of the army from Amerongen to the Dutch border, which was reached on the last day of January 1795. This period was marked by several minor actions and a most harrowing retreat, in conditions of great hardship during the coldest winter for 30 years.

1

The British Army and the Campaign in the Low Countries

Before looking in detail at the various components of the British expeditionary force, it would be as well to place it in the context both of administrative developments during the eighteenth century and of the field operations in which it participated in the Low Countries.

Army Administration in the Later Eighteenth Century

No perfect understanding of the British Army of the eighteenth century can be gained without first discussing the manner in which it was administered at the highest level, including why and how the structures developed in the way they did.

The Monarch and Parliament
Perceptions of the Army and how it should be managed originated in the late seventeenth century, especially in the aftermath of the English Civil War (1642–1651), when it had deposed and executed King Charles I. There followed a period of military rule after a failed royalist uprising in 1655, when the country was governed by 10 (later 12) major generals, backed by the militia. They combined the defence of the realm with policing and various administrative functions, resulting in the blurring of any distinction between the civil and military administration. The Restoration of the Stuart monarchy in 1660 led to the disbandment of the Army, with the only troops permitted being those guarding the person of the King or as garrisons in the various fortified places ensuring the security of the kingdom. The number of armed men in guards and garrisons was limited by the ability of the King to pay them. However, soldiers became increasingly involved in maintaining public order and upholding the rule of law, the authority for which came from Royal Warrants that made soldiers answerable only to the King rather than the jurisdiction of magistrates, except in extreme cases according to the Articles of War. At the same time, the civilian population considerably resented having soldiers quartered on them which, coupled with the soldiers' lack of discipline, made troops increasingly unpopular. Against a background of the growing fear and distrust with which the Army was regarded, its role in national defence also developed during the late seventeenth century. Once troops had been raised, it proved less easy to disband them after overseas threats receded. Hence, Parliament failed to persuade the

King to reduce additional troops raised during the Second Dutch War (1665–1667) since the Third Dutch War (1672–1674) and the threat of war with France in 1677 ensured that existing forces were augmented, rather than demobilised. Parliament eventually succeeded in exerting a measure of control as by 1699, the Army was reduced to an establishment of 7,000 men in England with a further 12,000 in Ireland, funded from local resources.[1]

The growing presence of a regular standing army in Britain fostered tension between the King and Parliament, since neither wished the other to have absolute control; the King because of what had happened to Charles I and Parliament due to fears of Royal suppression. The role of Parliament was strengthened following the so-called 'Glorious Revolution' of 1688, when the pay of the Army was placed under its control, and by 1697 the practice was established of voting annually on its exact composition. Parliament also assumed control over military discipline, following a mutiny at Ipswich in 1689, by annually voting on the Mutiny Act, which ensured that a standing army in time of peace was illegal without its consent. The concept of private funds being used for the purchase of officers' commissions and funding what was a semi-privatised military force also developed at this time, allowing the state to earn a financial return by avoiding the use of public money and ensuring that men who had invested their personal assets would be reluctant to lose them by stirring up rebellion. A creative balance was hereby created, as respect for private property usually prevented the monarch from dismissing officers who had caused offence.[2]

It was only from the 1750s that the presence of a standing army was grudgingly accepted, even though its unpopularity remained undiminished. The French invasion threats of 1744 and 1756, together with the successful landing of Prince Charles Edward Stuart in Scotland in 1745 clearly demonstrated that the Army's numbers were barely adequate for Britain's defence, let alone sufficient for overseas commitments. Government initiatives to reduce manpower were thereafter primarily focused on cost savings, as we shall see in more detail in Chapter 5, rather than from an inherent dislike of a standing army *per se*.[3]

In theory, the monarch commanded the British Army in person, together with the Royal Navy and Board of Ordnance. In reality, the amount of work involved made this impractical, so day-to-day management was conducted by the Admiralty and the Ordnance while that of the Army was in the hands of the commander-in-chief. This last position existed only in wartime due to the fear of having military men in charge for longer than was necessary, issues of cost, and because the administrative load in peacetime did not justify the presence of a commander-in-chief with a supporting staff. The Crown's role was therefore confined to approving or rejecting decisions made by the Admiralty and Ordnance, or the Commander-in-Chief of the Army – when one was appointed, usually only in wartime. The honorary title of 'Captain-General' was sometimes attached to this office, as when John, Duke of Marlborough commanded in the field in lieu of Queen Anne, or when William Augustus, Duke of Cumberland, favourite son of King George II, had held it in the

---

1 C.M. Clode, *The Military Forces of the Crown; their Administration and Government* (London: John Murray, 1869), vol.1, pp.52–66 and A. Guy, *Œconomy and Discipline. Officership and Administration in the British army 1714–63* (Manchester: Manchester University Press, 1985), pp.4–6.
2 J.A. Houlding, *Fit for Service. The Training of the British Army, 1715–1795* (Oxford: Clarendon Press, 1981), p.153 and Guy, *Œconomy and Discipline*, pp.5–6.
3 C. Barnett, *Britain and Her Army* (London: Cassell, 2000), pp.165–170.

1740s–1750s. The title fell somewhat into disrepute under Cumberland, and was not given to Frederick Duke of York in Flanders, or indeed at any time in his later period as commander-in-chief.[4] Mention should be made of the Board of General Officers, which was also involved with the administration of the Army. Although initially formed to advise on recruiting, it quickly assumed responsibility for matters relating to uniform and clothing (which it subsequently delegated to the Clothing Board), and thereafter concentrated on various matters of Army administration, disputes and the provision of opinions on draft regulations.[5]

The Secretary-at-War

The role of Secretary-at-War was not precisely defined during the eighteenth and nineteenth centuries. It originated as military secretary in attendance on the king in his capacity as head of the Army, and in the case of William III, accompanying him abroad on campaign. Almost all issues connected with the daily administration of the Army, both in peace and war, were overseen by the King and Secretary-at-War. The latter was also responsible for matters such as recruitment and discipline, for issuing instructions to regimental agents (civilian bankers and go-betweens appointed by proprietary colonels on a personal basis) countersigning letters of service appointing general officers to their commands and for receiving reports from the Board of General Officers and presenting them to the King. In the absence of a commander-in-chief, he was also responsible for issuing marching orders to regiments and thus held a leading police function in the suppression of riots and civil disturbances. Many of these functions were conducted via a senior officer, the Adjutant-General who, since 1781, was Lieutenant General Sir William Fawcett.[6] Despite the diversity of tasks handled by his office, the Secretary-at-War's primary role was concerned with finance and especially for the pay, allowances and composition of regimental establishments. His office was responsible for the preparation of annual army estimates and, once agreed by the Treasury, he presented them to Parliament. This raised an important issue, since the Secretary-at-War was not a minister of state, and therefore had none of the responsibilities to Parliament that this entailed, yet was in charge of a considerable portion of national expenditure. This issue was addressed in 1782–1783 when legislation was passed transferring the entire responsibility for financial and administrative business previously held by regimental agents to the War Office.[7] Previously, agents had received the pay of regiments for which they acted and were in charge of issuing it to officers and men, accounting (often long after the fact) to the Auditors of Imprest. Now, this role was gradually assumed by the War Office through

---

4　J.L. Pimlott, *The Administration of the British Army 1783–1793* (Unpublished PhD thesis. Leicester University, 1975), p.34 and Clode, *The Military Forces of the Crown*, vol.2, pp.335–340.

5　This was composed of senior officers holding the rank of major general or above who were chosen each October. Approximately 70 men served on the Board at any one time, with 25 being a quorum. Pimlott, *Administration of the British Army*, pp.42–45 and Guy, *Œconomy and Discipline*, pp.30–32.

6　Clode, *The Military Forces of the Crown*, vol.2, pp.253–258; T. Hayter (ed.), *An Eighteenth Century Secretary-at-War. The Papers of William, Viscount Barrington* (London: The Bodley Head, 1988), pp.13–14; Guy, *Œconomy and Discipline*, pp.29–30 and Houlding, *Fit for Service*, pp.61–62.

7　An Act for the better regulation of the office of Paymaster General of His Majesty's forces, 22 Geo.3, c.81 and 23 Geo.3, c.50, in Anon., *The Statutes at Large of England and of Great-Britain: from Magna Carta to the Union of the Kingdoms of Great Britain and Ireland* (London: Eyre and Strahan, 1811), vol.15, pp.350 and 450.

the appointment of regimental paymasters.[8] The nature of the Secretary-at-War's duties changed on the appointment of Jeffrey, Lord Amherst as Commander-in-Chief in 1793, since the channel for communicating the King's orders to the Army moved from the former to the latter. However, the relationship between the two appointments caused friction since, on the one hand, the Secretary-at-War was answerable to Parliament for Army expenditure and on the other, a military commission directed him to follow the directions of the Commander-in-Chief. This raised a constitutional issue, as it could not be permitted for the Army to control its own expenditure; this matter was not resolved until 1812.[9]

The Secretary-at-War for the majority of the Flanders campaign was Sir George Yonge, who had held the position since July 1782, with a gap of eight months between April and December 1783. Yonge previously served as a Lord of the Admiralty between 1766–1770, was appointed a Privy Councillor in April 1782, and had been the Member of Parliament for Honiton since 1754, with a short break between 1761–1763. Thus, he was well-connected at the highest level and had amassed plenty of political know-how by 1793, even if he was not always popular.[10] Yonge was replaced as Secretary-at-War by William Windham in July 1794 in a piece of political manoeuvring that bolstered support for the Government in Parliament. In this manoeuvre, Windham was given a seat in the Cabinet – a position which Yonge had not enjoyed. Windham had been Member of Parliament for Norwich since 1784, but he lacked his predecessor's years of experience in political office, having only very briefly served as Chief Secretary to the Lord Lieutenant of Ireland in 1783, and he was known to be indecisive.[11]

The Secretary for War

In this summary of the Army's administrative structure it may appear curious to find the role of the Secretary for War, a minister of state, placed after that of a more junior official, the Secretary-at-War. The reason for this is that the appointment did not exist until 11 July 1794 and functioned only during the final six months of the Flanders campaign. There had only been two ministers of state since the abolition of the Secretary for the Colonies in 1782, these being for the Home and Foreign Departments. Henry Dundas was the first incumbent of this new position, being replaced at the Home Department by the Duke of Portland as part of the musical chairs that resulted in Windham taking the role of Secretary-at-War.

Dundas was a highly experienced political operator, having held office in various capacities for over a quarter of a century prior to the outbreak of war in 1793. His appointments had included Solicitor General for Scotland (1766–1775), Lord Advocate (1775–1783), Treasurer of the Navy (1782–1800, with a break between April 1783 and January 1784) and Home Secretary (1791–1794). He had been a Member of Parliament, mainly for Scottish

---

8   Clode, *The Military Forces of the Crown*, vol.2, pp.259–263.
9   Clode, *The Military Forces of the Crown*, vol.2, pp.264–265.
10 'YONGE, George (1733–1812), of Colyton, Devon', *History of Parliament Online*, <https://www.historyofparliamentonline.org/volume/1754-1790/member/yonge-george-1733-1812>, accessed 20 April 2021.
11 'WINDHAM, William (1750–1810), of Felbrigg Hall, Norf', *History of Parliament Online*, <https://www.historyofparliamentonline.org/volume/1754-1790/member/windham-william-1750-1810> and <https://www.historyofparliamentonline.org/volume/1790-1820/member/windham-william-1750-1810>, accessed 20 April 2021.

Henry Dundas, 1st Viscount Melville, by Johann Friedrich Bolt, 1796. (Rijksmuseum, Amsterdam, RP-P-1910-1064)

The Right Honourable Lord Grenville, by Samuel William Reynolds, 1773–1835, after John Hoppner, 1758–1810. (Yale Center for British Art, Paul Mellon Fund, B1977.14.9968)

constituencies, since 1774 and had served as a Privy Councillor between 1782–1789. Using his position as Lord Advocate, Dundas effectively created a role for himself as the political manager of Scotland, thus becoming the source of vast patronage for his fellow countrymen. As Home Secretary, he had been a key man in the formulation of British war strategy with the Prime Minister, William Pitt, and the Foreign Secretary, Lord Grenville. His move to the newly created War Office cemented this role.[12] The Secretary for War, being a minister of state, was responsible for the Army both to the King and Parliament, whereas the Commander-in-Chief was responsible for its administration and discipline. Matters such as finance, arming and deployments, as we have already seen, were administered through the Secretary-at-War.

The Board of Ordnance
The Board of Ordnance was confirmed as a civil department of state by Royal Warrant in 1683, at the end of King Charles II's reign, and therefore was not part of the fighting army as such. It was headed by a Master-General of the Ordnance whose orders, in the form of warrants, came only from the King, the Privy Council and secretaries of state,

---

12 'DUNDAS, Henry (1742–1811), of Melville Castle, Edinburgh', *History of Parliament Online*, <https://www.historyofparliamentonline.org/volume/1790-1820/member/dundas-henry-1742-1811>, accessed 21 April 2021 and M. Fry, 'Dundas, Henry, first Viscount Melville (1742–1811)', *ODNB*, <https://doi.org/10.1093/ref:odnb/8250>, accessed 21 April 2021.

not from the Secretary-at-War. It was primarily associated with the Royal Navy, whose requirements for ships' guns and warlike stores far exceeded that of the Army and whose activities pre-dated the formation of a standing army.[13] After 1688, the Board was effectively split into the military branch under the Master-General, which included the Royal Regiment of Artillery and what later became the Royal Engineers, and the civil branch headed by the Surveyor-General which administered the military branch, acted as the custodians of state assets (including real-estate and moveable property) and as contractors for the supply of munitions and equipment to the Navy and Army. The Master-General was a political appointment, although the incumbent could be a military officer, holding a seat in the Cabinet and serving as its military advisor. This arrangement was deemed politically acceptable since his department was a civil one, not being part of the Army, and the soldiers belonging to it made up only a relatively small number of technical specialists. The civilian world of the Board was apparent in its staffing, since officers could be appointed from the Navy, Army or civilian life. Like any other department of state, the Board submitted its estimates to the Treasury for approval, subsequently laying them before Parliament.[14] The Duke of Richmond, a combative and sometimes controversial political heavyweight, who was also Colonel of the Royal Regiment of Artillery, had been appointed Master-General in 1782. Much of his correspondence was sent via his secretary, Captain James Murray Hadden, who served as adjutant of one of the parks of artillery from 4 April 1783, but was replaced by First Lieutenant Joseph Heaven on 15 March 1793, probably because Richmond relied more heavily on his services after the outbreak of war. Hadden subsequently served as Surveyor-General between November 1804 and July 1810.[15]

The day-to-day administration of the Board of Ordnance was managed by five 'principal officers', who met three times a week in winter and twice in summer at the Ordnance Office in Westminster. These men were the Lieutenant General of the Ordnance, the Surveyor-General, the Clerk of the Ordnance, the Storekeeper, and the Clerk of the Deliveries, all of whom were responsible to Parliament. The duties of each of these men were numerous and will only be briefly described here. The Lieutenant General was a military appointment, the most senior in peace time due to the absence of a commander-in-chief, and was the Master-General's deputy. In the absence of a Master-General, for example after the death of the Duke of Montagu in 1749 until a replacement was appointed in 1756, the Lieutenant General was responsible for managing the affairs of the Board.[16] He received and distributed all incoming warrants, orders and other correspondence to the appropriate members of the Board, reviewed and discussed with the Board all requests for stores or repairs to property, maintained the ordnance train and had responsibility for discipline and training. Lieutenant

---

13 Clode, *The Military Forces of the Crown*, vol.1, p.74.
14 Clode, *The Military Forces of the Crown*, vol.2, pp.204–207; Anon., *The Thirteenth Report of the Commissioners of Military Enquiry. The Master General and Board of Ordnance* (London: House of Commons, 1811), pp.11 and 53 and H.C.B. Rogers, *The British Army of the Eighteenth Century* (London: George Allen & Unwin, 1977), p.36.
15 Anon., *The Thirteenth Report*, pp.105 and 131.
16 Anon., *The Thirteenth Report*, pp.11–12 and 53 and R. Whitworth, *Field Marshal Lord Ligonier. A Story of the British Army, 1702–1770* (Oxford: Clarendon Press, 1958), pp.180 and 183.

General the Hon William Howe was appointed to the post in March 1782, having served as Commander-in-Chief in North America between 1775–1778.[17]

The Surveyor-General was primarily responsible for engineering services, ensuring the adequate storage of all stores, the supervision of labour and the preparation of estimates for works and repairs. In 1793, the post was held by Captain the Hon George Cranfield Berkeley RN, who had been appointed in 1789 and was Member of Parliament for Gloucestershire.[18] The Clerk of the Ordnance was the Board's record keeper, having responsibility for ledgers containing all the warrants, orders, patents and grants, together with lists of all personnel and their remuneration. This position was filled by John Sargent, a political ally of the Duke of Richmond and Member of Parliament for Seaford since 1793.[19] The Storekeeper, as the title suggests, ensured the safe storage of all ordnance, munitions and stores, according to the regulations specifying what could be accepted and delivered from storage. John Clater Aldridge, a friend of the Duke of Richmond and Member of Parliament for New Shoreham, held this post from December 1783 until his death in April 1795.[20] Finally, the Clerk of the Deliveries was responsible for issuing ordnance and *matériel* to those authorised to receive it, while keeping complete records of his authority for doing so.[21] The holder of this position in 1793 was Captain Thomas Baillie RN, who was appointed in 1782 by the Duke of Richmond.[22] Aside from matters associated with stores, the Board also had powers to acquire land to be used for the defence of designated locations, it was responsible for the Survey of Britain, for the care and maintenance of all buildings connected with the defence of the realm and for undertaking contracts for the supply of goods and services.[23] Many of the Board's decisions were communicated via their secretary, Augustus Rogers, who was appointed in 1784 and briefly served as the Member of Parliament for Queenborough between December 1793 until his death in February 1794. He was replaced as secretary by Robert H. Crew in May 1794, both operating from the Board's office in Westminster.[24]

---

17 'HOWE, Hon. William (1729–1814)', *History of Parliament Online*, <https://www.historyofparliamentonline.org/volume/1754-1790/member/howe-hon-william-1729-1814>, accessed 29 March 2021.
18 Anon., *The Thirteenth Report*, pp.12–13 and 53 and 'BERKELEY, Hon. George Cranfield (1753–1818)', *History of Parliament Online*, <https://www.historyofparliamentonline.org/volume/1754-1790/member/berkeley-hon-george-cranfield-1753-1818>, accessed 29 March 2021.
19 Anon., *The Thirteenth Report*, pp.13 and 53–54 and 'SARGENT, John (1750–1831), of Woolavington, Suss.', *History of Parliament Online*, <https://www.historyofparliamentonline.org/volume/1790-1820/member/sargent-john-1750-1831>, accessed 29 March 2021.
20 Anon., *The Thirteenth Report*, pp.13 and 54 and 'ALDRIDGE, John Clater (?1737–95), of New Lodge, St. Leonard's Forest, Suss.', *History of Parliament Online*, <https://www.historyofparliamentonline.org/volume/1754-1790/member/aldridge-john-clater-1737-95>, accessed 29 March 2021.
21 Anon., *The Thirteenth Report*, pp.13 and 54. A detailed explanation of the roles of the Principal Officers may be found in Clode, *The Military Forces of the Crown*, vol.1, pp.457–461 and in Anon., *The Thirteenth Report*, Appendix 1.
22 R. Cock, 'Baillie, Thomas (c.1725–1802)', *ODNB*, <https://doi.org/10.1093/ref:odnb/1069>, accessed 29 March 2021.
23 Clode, *The Military Forces of the Crown*, vol.2, pp.216–219 and Rogers, *British Army*, p.36.
24 'ROGERS, Augustus (d.1794), of Turnham Green, Mdx.', *History of Parliament online*, <https://www.historyofparliamentonline.org/volume/1790-1820/member/rogers-augustus-1794> and Anon., *The Thirteenth Report*, p.106.

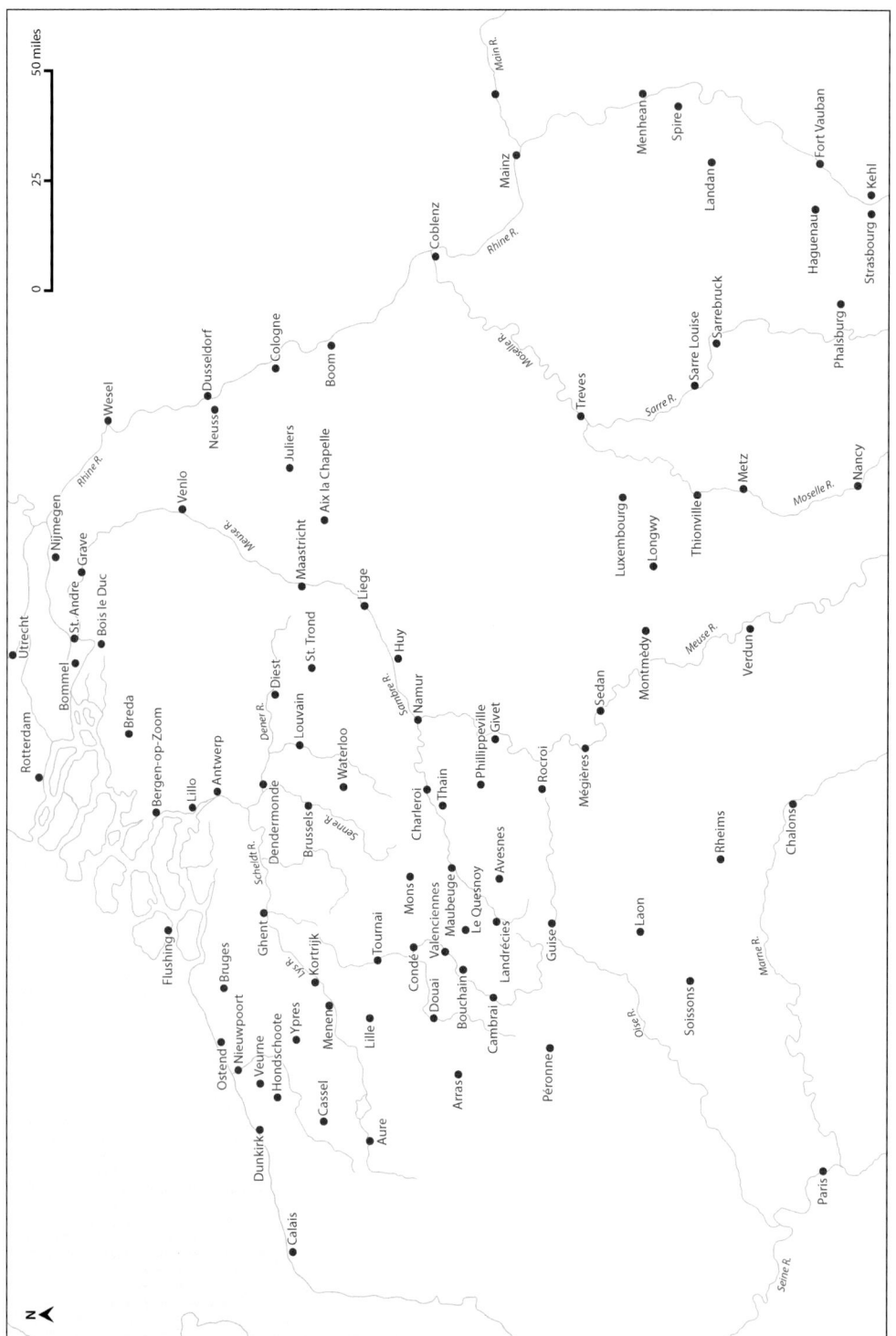

Map 1 Flanders: the area of operations.

The Board of Ordnance was also an important manufacturer through its facilities at Woolwich Arsenal and elsewhere. Not the least of these was the Royal Brass Foundry for the production of cannon. Iron guns were produced under contract by private suppliers, but officers of the Royal Artillery had the responsibility for proving both brass and iron ordnance. A 'laboratory' also existed at Woolwich under a comptroller reporting to the Board of Ordnance and staffed by civilian artificers, which conducted experiments in armament developments. The third production facility at Woolwich was the Royal Carriage Department under the control of a civilian 'constructor of carriages'. Outside London, the Board had powder mills at Faversham and Waltham. Small arms were contracted from private suppliers until the early nineteenth century, but the Board was responsible for arranging their manufacture, storage and issue, maintaining standards of manufacture and proving. Aside from ordnance and related materials, the Board was also a significant supplier of clothing, primarily for its own troops, but also of greatcoats to the Army together with some items of camp necessaries.[25]

Mention should also be made of the Board of Ordnance in Ireland, not least because several companies of artillery from this establishment served in Flanders. The Irish Board was amalgamated with that in England in 1674, though continued to maintain separate accounts. It had its own Master-General and principal officers, the full apparatus of an ordnance train, and was responsible for the defence of fortifications and coastal batteries in a similar way to its sister organisation in Britain. A battalion of artillery was first formed in 1755 from men sent from Woolwich, and by 1783 this consisted of six marching companies and one invalid company, with a combined establishment of 701 men. Severe cuts followed, however, and the establishment was reduced to 386 men from late 1783 until large scale recruitment took place in 1793. This resulted in the battalion expanding to 20 marching and one invalid company, with an establishment of 2,069 by October 1794; the battalion was subsequently split into two in May 1795.[26]

The Campaign of 1793

So much for the organisational structure of the Crown's land forces at home. It now remains to look at the diplomatic and operational context of the British expeditionary force sent to Flanders.

The French Revolutionary government declared war on Austria on 20 April 1792. French troops attempted invasions of the Austrian Netherlands at the end of that month but fled in panic after scarcely meeting any opposition. Another French incursion led to the capture of both Menen and Kortrijk on 19 June, only for them to scuttle back over the border to Lille for no obvious reason. Whilst the first four months of war had been uneventful, this would change in September with the arrival in theatre of a Prussian army, led by the Duke of

---

25 Clode, *The Military Forces of the Crown*, vol.2, pp.224–236.
26 F. Duncan, *History of the Royal Regiment of Artillery Compiled from the Original Records* (London: John Murray, 1874), vol.1, pp.162–163; K.P. Ferguson, *The Army in Ireland from the Restoration to the Act of Union* (Unpublished PhD thesis. University College Dublin, 1980), pp.119–120 and Guy, *Œconomy and Discipline*, p.34.

Brunswick. But the Prussians made a dismal effort in the weeks that followed, and after the desultory combat at Valmy (20 September 1792) shuffled off in retreat. It was once more the turn of the French to go on the attack. Their invasion of the Austrian Netherlands began in great numbers on 3 November 1792. Three days later the Austrians were beaten at Jemappes (6 November 1792), and by the close of the year the allies were back at the Dutch border.[27] In a fit of revolutionary enthusiasm, on 1 February 1793 France declared war on Great Britain.

The direct threat posed to the United Provinces had been met with alarm in London, for not only was there a strong possibility that the country would be overrun, but that the victorious French would go on to commandeer Dutch naval assets and thus pose a grave threat to Britain and its commerce. Their assumption of control over the entrance to the River Scheldt, an international hot-spot since the sixteenth century, added to these fears. There was also alarm and much revulsion at home over the guillotining of King Louis XVI in Paris on 21 January.

On 16 February 1793, the French launched their invasion of Dutch territory. The fortress of Breda fell on the 25th, Klundert on the 28th, then Gertruidenberg on 4 March, after which the attackers sat down before the walls of Willemstad.[28] It was as these dire events were unfolding that King George III issued orders for the Guards Brigade to embark for the United Provinces (20 February 1793).[29]

The British Expeditionary Force Embarks

The early hours of Monday, 25 February 1793 witnessed the commencement of Britain's military involvement in the French Wars. The Guards Brigade, comprising the first battalions of each of the three regiments, had been ordered to parade at St James's Park and Sir Gilbert Elliot, the future Lord Minto, witnessed the occasion:

> I got up at half after five yesterday morning to see the three battalions of Guards march off to Greenwich, where they embarked for Holland. It answered perfectly, and I felt much pleasure and interest in the scene. They are about 2,000 men, all young, and almost all fine men; some uncommonly so. They were all animated by a spirit natural on the occasion, not to mention spirits of a different sort, of which they had more than one could wish. Many of them were too drunk to walk straight. On the whole, however, their zeal and eagerness to go on service, which does not promise to be child's play, was very striking. The regret and dejection of those who were left was no less so.[30]

---

27 J.A. Lynn, *The Bayonets of the Republic. Motivation and Tactics in the Army of Revolutionary France 1791–94* (Urbana and Chicago: University of Illinois Press, 1984), pp.4–12.
28 T.C.W. Blanning, *The French Revolutionary Wars 1787–1802* (London: Hodder Headline, 1996), pp.90–93 and C.J. Esdaile, *The Wars of the French Revolution 1792–1801* (Abingdon: Routledge, 2019), pp.96–97.
29 George III to Pitt, 20 February 1793, in A. Aspinall (ed.), *The Later Correspondence of George III* (London: Cambridge University Press, 1968), vol.2, p.9.
30 Countess of Minto (ed.), *Life and Letters of Sir Gilbert Elliot, First Earl of Minto from 1751 to 1806* (London: Longmans Green & Co, 1874), vol.2, p.118.

Given the early hour, at least some of the guardsmen cannot have enjoyed much sleep the previous night, preferring to appear on parade: 'Prim'd with WHITBREAD'S entire, and their bosom-friend gin'[31] in front of their sovereign and the entire royal family, who had assembled to witness their departure. The men proceeded to Greenwich in scenes that can only be described as utterly chaotic and on arrival at the square of Greenwich Hospital:

> A grenadier drunk, from the centre rank reel'd,
> And hiccupping, up to his Majesty wheel'd,
> 'Never mind all these Jacobins, G–e, rest in quiet,
> We'll quell them my Hearty! As quick as a riot,'
> The King was delighted, and laughed out aloud;
> While the fellow was hail'd by three cheers from the crowd.[32]

The men completed their embarkation from the hospital stairs before nightfall, suggesting that at least some order at last prevailed.[33] While most of the troops got on board safely, the same did not necessarily apply to their equipment, as Lieutenant and Captain Henry Clinton of the 1st Foot Guards wrote to his father:

> To be sure there never was half so many blunders as were committed yesterday. The D[uke] of R[ichmond] neglected to give proper orders for the embarkation of the artillery in consequence of which the guns will not be on board the same ships as the Companies ... He put the mortars & guns here aboard one transport & the ammunition another.[34]

So began Britain's military involvement in the French Wars. Chaotic, comic and, for those dependents left behind, sad and tragic. Although none of the participants could possibly have known it, the embarkation of the regiments of Foot Guards at Greenwich was but the opening step in a conflict that was to last for over 22 years.

War Aims

Before proceeding further, it would be worth pausing to consider the initial aims of the expeditionary force sent to the United Provinces and how these were amended as events unfolded.

The Duke of York was presented with two sets of instructions on being appointed commander of the expeditionary force sent to the United Provinces. The first of these stated that his role was: '... to command Our Forces that are intended to serve in the United Provinces ... for the defence of the said United Provinces, and for acting against the Enemy'. Two of the three articles in the Duke's 'separate instructions' concerned arrangements for

---

31 Anon., *An Accurate and Impartial Narrative of the War by an Officer of the Guards* (London: Cadell & Davies, nd), vol.1, p.1.
32 Anon., *Officer of the Guards*, vol.1, pp.2–3.
33 R. Brown, *An Impartial Journal of a Detachment from the Brigade of Foot Guards, Commencing 25th February, 1793, and Ending 9th May, 1795* (London: Stockdale, 1795), pp.2–3.
34 UML: The Clinton Papers (uncatalogued): Henry Clinton to Sir Henry Clinton, 26 February 1793.

mobilising the Hanoverian contingent and for liaising with the Dutch regarding its deployment. He was ordered to: '… endeavour as far as you can, to avoid dividing Our said Troops, or placing them in the Frontier Garrisons of the said Provinces. Nevertheless in this respect you are at liberty to act as you shall judge best for the defence of the said Provinces'. The third article confirmed the Duke of York's position at the head of the chain of command for the Brigade of Guards, commanded by Major General Gerard Lake, and ordered the Duke to conform himself: '… as exactly as possible to the tenor of Our Instructions given to the said Major General Lake'. As curious as it might seem to make a force commander subject to the instructions given to his subordinate, Lake's orders were to take: '… the Detachment of Our British Foot Guards … and employ the same, either separately or in conjunction with the Forces of the United Provinces, or those of their Allies, in any measure for repelling a Foreign Enemy, or for maintaining the authority of the Government and the internal security of the said Provinces'.[35] Lake was separately sent a letter marked 'secret' of the same date as his instructions that added further conditions regarding the deployment. These severely restricted his movement, and it is worth quoting the relevant paragraph in full:

> You must however observe, that it is not His Majesty's intention that you should without further Instructions from hence, suffer any part of the force under your command to be moved to any place, from which you could not maintain a communication with the Port of Helvoet, or the distance of which would prevent you from returning thither in four and twenty hours after receiving an order for that purpose, if any occasion should arise which might make it appear necessary to His Majesty to direct your speedy return to England.[36]

Lake was further ordered only to tell the Prince of Orange, the Grand Pensionary[37] and the British ambassador to The Hague, Lord Auckland, of these provisions. Major General Ralph Abercromby, appointed to command a brigade comprising the 14th, 37th and 53rd Regiments, was issued with the same instructions in a letter dated 9 March.[38]

The Duke of York and his suite disembarked from the frigate *Syren* at Helvoetsluys on the morning of 27 February, the same day that the transport ships with the Brigade of Guards departed from the Nore. Their arrival was eagerly anticipated, as Henry Clinton informed his father the following day:

---

35 TNA: WO 6/7: Part A, pp.1–3, 'Instructions for Our most dearly beloved son His Royal Highness Frederick Duke of York, Knight of the Most Noble Order of the Garter, Lieutenant General of Our Forces. Given at Our Court of St. James's the Twenty third day of February 1793, in the Thirty third year of Our Reign'; 'Separate Instructions for …' and 'Instructions for our Trust and Wellbeloved Gerard Lake Esquire, Major General of Our Forces whom we have appointed to command a Detachment of Our British Foot Guards to serve in the United Provinces. Given at Our Court of St. James's the Twenty third day of February 1793, in the Thirty third year of Our Reign'.
36 TNA: WO 6/7: Part A, p.4, Dundas to Lake, 23 February 1793.
37 The most senior civil official in the United Provinces after the Stadtholder. The office was held by Laurens Pieter van de Spiegel (1736–1800) between 1787–1795.
38 TNA: WO 6/7: Part A, pp.6–8, Dundas to Abercromby, 9 March 1793.

The arrival of the Transports is of the greatest consequence at this very critical moment, not so much on account of the forces they contain as from the effect our assistance has on the minds of the panic struck Hollanders who look upon the English as their guardian angels. Through all the towns the Duke passed last night he was rec'd with the most hearty & universal acclamations of joy from all ranks of people who turned out with torches to receive him.[39]

Events, however, were to overtake the instructions issued to the senior British commanders. On 1 March, an Austrian army of 40,000 men under Prince Friedrich Josias von Coburg-Saalfeld crossed the River Roer at Düren and Jülich, defeating the French at Aldenhoven, where they inflicted some 2,000 casualties and took 300 prisoners. Coburg crossed into the Austrian Netherlands the following day, forcing the French to abandon their siege of Maastricht and allowing Coburg's forces to enter the town on 3 March. The considerable loss of men and *materiél* sustained by the French during the Austrian advance led Paris to order Dumouriez to return to the Austrian Netherlands immediately. Leaving some 20,000 men in the United Provinces, he travelled south, reaching the army at Leuven on 13 March before marching east towards the Austrian position at Sint-Truiden. The Battle of Neerwinden was fought on 18 March and ended in disaster for the French, with their repeated assaults on the Austrian positions being bloodily repulsed.[40] The subsequent retreat caused mass desertions from the French army, with Dumouriez's continued attempts to halt the Austrian advance resulting in a further defeat at Pellenberg on 23 March. The position was hopeless and led the French commander to arrange a settlement allowing his forces to withdraw to their own borders unmolested.[41]

The instructions issued to the British commanders had quickly become outdated in the light of these events. They were amended on 19 March when Henry Dundas wrote to Colonel Sir James Murray, the expeditionary force's adjutant-general, stating that the troops commanded by the Duke of York could now be:

> ... employed in such manner as he judges may be most expedient, for co-operating either with the Dutch troops, or with such Imperial[42] and Prussian troops as are acting in the Low Countries, for the purpose of embarrassing the retreat of the French Army from the Territories of the Republic of Holland, or the Low Countries, and of promoting the success of the Confederate Armies.

Lest this could be considered as offering too much latitude, Dundas added that the troops should not be diverted from their original purpose, the defence of the United Provinces,

---

39 WLCL: Henry Clinton Papers: vol.235, Henry Clinton to Sir Henry Clinton, 28 February 1793.
40 A. von Witzleben, *Prinz Friedrich Josias von Coburg-Saalfeld, Herzog zu Sachsen* (Berlin: R. Decker, 1859), vol.2, pp.99–103 and 114–144.
41 Blanning, *The French Revolutionary Wars*, pp.98–99 and Esdaile, *The Wars of the French Revolution*, pp.96–97. The number of French killed and wounded during the brief campaign was estimated at 20,000, compared to Austrian casualties of 2,600 killed and 2,400 wounded. Auckland to Grenville, 11 April 1793 in W. Auckland (ed.), *The Journal and Correspondence of William, Lord Auckland* (London: Richard Bentley, 1862), vol.3, p.17.
42 Imperial, i.e. Austrian.

since the British Government still retained the option to withdraw them for any alternative use they might determine. Accordingly, the Duke of York extended the contractual termination date for the transports utilised for conveying the two brigades of infantry to the United Provinces by six months, instead of releasing them from their engagement at Helvoetsluys.[43]

Measures taken by the British Government in late February and repeated the following month, together with the extended hire of the transport vessels, amply demonstrated that the defence of the United Provinces remained the objective, while the expeditionary force could yet be withdrawn altogether, for some other purpose to be determined. Dundas also showed signs in two letters addressed to Sir James Murray on 19 March of thinking in terms of advantages to be gained from post-war peace talks by encouraging the Duke of York to consider occupying coastal ports such as Antwerp or Ostend. This may appear premature with the benefit of hindsight, but all the participants could see at the time was the rapid collapse of French forces and their precipitate withdrawal. As if matters were not bad enough for the French, Dumouriez defected to the Austrians on 6 April, undertaking to lead his army in a march on Paris to overthrow the Jacobin government. Assurances were given to Coburg that his supporters in Valenciennes and Lille would declare in his favour but, as Henry Clinton informed his father: 'He got as far as Courtray when he found his men were not to be trusted & accordingly made his escape with 1000 horse & young Egalité who has resumed the title of duc de Chartres'.[44] In the meantime, the French minister of war, the Marquis de Beurnonville, was sent by the Convention to assume command of the *Armée du Nord*. He was accompanied by four deputies tasked with arresting Dumouriez and bringing him to Paris for trial, but they themselves were arrested on 1 April on appearing at his headquarters and all were handed over to Coburg.[45]

Aside from providing the British expeditionary force with greater liberty of movement, the French retreat prompted a discussion in allied ranks of what to do next, since their initial objectives – the defence of the United Provinces and the recovery of the Austrian Netherlands – had been achieved within the space of some three weeks. Considerable allied armies had been mobilised and were now located in the regained territory with neither orders nor objectives. Coburg, as commander of the largest military force then present in the theatre of operations, determined in late March on arranging a conference to discuss the strategic direction of the war; this was held at Antwerp on 7 April.[46] Aside from Coburg, the British attendees were the Duke of York and William Eden, Lord Auckland, who had served as ambassador at The Hague since 1789. Prussia was represented by *Generalleutnant* Alexander von Knobelsdorf, commanding the Prussian forces (the Duke of Brunswick having departed sick), and Count von Keller, ambassador at The Hague since 1790. Aside

---

43   TNA: WO 6/7: Part A, pp.8–11, Dundas to Murray, 19 March 1793.
44   UML: The Clinton Papers (uncatalogued): Henry Clinton to Sir Henry Clinton, 8 April 1793. Louis Philippe, Duc de Chartres (1773–1850), subsequently King of France, 1830–1848.
45   Auckland to Grenville, 5 April 1793, in Auckland (ed.), *William, Lord Auckland*, vol.3, p.10; Pitt to Grenville, 8–13 April 1793, in Historical Manuscripts Commission (ed.), *Report on the Manuscripts of J.B. Fortescue Esq., preserved at Dropmore* (London: HMSO, 1905), vol.2, pp.390–392 and Lynn, *The Bayonets of the Republic*, pp.10–11.
46   Auckland to Grenville, 31 March 1793, in Auckland (ed.), *William, Lord Auckland*, vol.3, pp.3–4.

from Coburg, the Austrian representatives were Count Franz von Metternich, Minister Plenipotentiary of the Austrian Netherlands, and Count Louis Stahremberg, soon to be appointed ambassador to London. The Prince of Orange attended for the Dutch.[47]

The British objectives were laid out by Lord Grenville, the Foreign Secretary, in a letter to Lord Auckland of 3 April. These comprised two over-arching issues, being the conduct of future operations and: '… the advantages to which the powers at war may respectively look'. The taking of Valenciennes and Lille – the latter supposedly facilitated by the prior capture of Dunkirk – formed the principal objectives of the former, while the latter meant persuading Austria not to pursue its interest in swapping the Austrian Netherlands with the Electorate of Bavaria (the so called 'Bavarian Exchange'), a policy that had been pursued without success by the Austrians since the 1770s.[48] Were this to take place, the British feared the removal of Austrian interests immediately to the north of the French border would encourage a continuation of the war by placing what Lord Grenville termed: '… a dependent and weak power on the frontier of France'.[49] Fortunately for the British, capturing the border fortresses was regarded with favour by Austria, since it was unlikely that the Bavarian Exchange could be effected without the security they provided and, if that goal was not pursued, they would still provide a safeguard against a further French invasion. As far as military operations were concerned, the Antwerp conference decided to position 8–10,000 British, Hanoverian and Dutch troops in West Flanders at Ostend, Veurne and Menen while they prepared for the campaign, with a similar number of men forming a 'moveable corps' in the same area. Meanwhile, the main army of 48,000 men under Coburg would attempt to capture Valenciennes, Maubeuge, Condé and, if possible, Lille.[50]

The British Expeditionary Force

So much for the events preceding the departure of the expeditionary force and the diplomatic background leading to its deployment, but what of its context within the large allied army now assembling on the border of France?

The major allied powers, Austria and Prussia, fielded armies that dwarfed the British contingent, which numbered only 7,959 all ranks on 15 October 1793 (see Appendix I, Table I.1). At the same time, the Austrian army comprised 73 companies, 102 battalions and 145 squadrons which, using the notional strength of each unit type provided by Sir James Murray in his letter to Henry Dundas of the same date, was the equivalent of 104,850 rank-and-file. The size of the British contingent was similar to the 11,580 Hanoverian and 7,082 Hesse Cassel all ranks with the allied army on 7 October 1793 and militarily can be regarded as of an equivalent value, but no more.[51] The British expeditionary force was

---

47 Auckland to Grenville, 5 April 1793, in Auckland (ed.), *William, Lord Auckland*, vol.3, p.10.
48 For a fuller discussion of this, see J. Black, *British Foreign Policy in an Age of Revolutions 1783–1793* (Cambridge: Cambridge University Press, 1994), pp.82–93.
49 Grenville to Auckland, 3 April 1793 and Auckland to Grenville, 9 April 1793, in Auckland (ed.), *William, Lord Auckland*, vol.3, pp.5 and 14.
50 Auckland to Grenville, 9 April 1793 and Bentinck to Auckland, 10 April 1793, in Auckland (ed.), *William, Lord Auckland*, vol.3, pp.13–14 and 15–16.
51 TNA: WO 1/167: pp.321–330 and 337–343, enclosures in Murray to Dundas, 15 October 1793. These figures comprise the full establishment minus killed, died or wanting to complete. An Austrian company was reckoned at 100, each battalion at 700 and each squadron at 130 rank and file.

fighting on behalf of the host nations, the Dutch in the United Provinces and Austria in the case of the Austrian Netherlands.

None of the separate contingents fought as national entities in Flanders until June 1794. As far as operations (but not administration) were concerned, brigade-level formations often existed on an ad hoc basis, with units being intermingled within the same force and commanded by general officers of any nationality as circumstances required. As examples, the British cavalry were assigned to the covering army at Hondschoote commanded by the Hanoverian *Feldmarschall* Wilhelm von Freytag in August–September 1793, whereas the 8th Light Dragoons, 12th, 38th and 55th Regiments all served with the Hanoverian *Generalmajor* von Hammerstein, himself under Austrian command, between April and June 1794. The Duke of York commanded a large corps of Austrian troops comprising 18,291 of all ranks in mid-October 1793. This blurring of identities makes any judgement of performance on national lines problematic, since no commander could be held responsible for the condition, training, or equipping of foreign units under his command. It also bound the national contingents together in a manner that made it extremely difficult for subsidiary commanders to conduct operations that did not meet with agreement from the Austrian leadership. Both the British and Dutch forces, together with their auxiliaries, were either numerically too small or lacked the necessary *matériel* to strike out alone, requiring strong Austrian support to do so. This meant that the decisions taken by Coburg and his staff had a marked bearing on both the tactical and strategic aspects of the war. A key example of this concerned the siege of Valenciennes, which Coburg appointed the Duke of York to command. Naturally, the Duke's plan was to have his own chief engineer, Colonel James Moncrieff, to conduct the siege, but when a difference of opinion arose regarding the methods to be adopted the Austrians very quickly assumed control by appointing their own engineer instead. It could hardly be otherwise, since they supplied the largest contingent of men employed in the siege works, and nearly all of the ordnance and equipment. While this may only have resulted in British embarrassment, the slow and methodical manner with which the Austrians conducted all of their military operations did have one very marked outcome. Although the siege of Valenciennes was concluded successfully, the significant time it had taken – 57 days – enabled the French time to assemble an overwhelming force that managed to defeat the army covering the siege of Dunkirk at Hondschoote.[52] The Austrians were also capable of amending the tactical plans of subsidiary commanders as they saw fit. William Bentinck, one of the Duke of York's aides-de-camp, noted in connection with the planned approach march to Dunkirk that the: 'Plan projected by the D[uke] of Y[ork was] rejected by the P[rince] of C[obourg] to march from Tourcoin in the rear of the enemy [where] they would have enleved[53] all the posts between Lille & the Lis.'[54]

Conversely, requests by the British to amend Austrian plans fell on deaf ears – especially after the defeat at Tourcoing, when an over-complicated scheme formulated by the Austrian staff came to nothing, resulting in considerable losses to York's column.

So it was that the modest size of the British expeditionary force, and its subordinate place in the allied order of battle, left the Duke of York with few options for any independent

---

52   Lynn, *The Bayonets of the Republic*, pp.226–227.
53   A corruption of the French 'enlever' meaning to remove.
54   UNL: Pw Ja 446: Memorandum on the lines of communication in Flanders, nd. Bentinck Papers.

action. Worse, the objectives given him by his own government had changed even before his troops had disembarked. A new mission was unfolding, and it was not one for which his army was prepared. So long as the task was limited to the defence of the United Provinces, it had been assumed that soldiers and their equipment could be moved in locally-sourced water transport. Wheeled transport did not seem to be required. But now it was needed urgently for a projected advance via the Austrian Netherlands to the French border. This was a big problem, since a large number of wagons, horses and drivers were all required immediately, at a time when exactly the same resources were also in demand from other armies in the field. Sir James Murray wrote to Henry Dundas on 26 March highlighting the difficulties with transportation: 'The want of every thing requisite for that purpose has of course occasioned delay, nor is it possible even in a longer period, to be provided with what would be essentially necessary, for operating at any considerable distance from Water Carriage'.[55] Practical issues included 14 battalion guns serving with the two brigades of infantry, which had no associated equipment enabling them to proceed by land. Nor was there the means to transport reserve ammunition for the artillery and infantry – not to mention the considerable resources required to move commissariat supplies for both man and beast. It was hardly surprising that one of the very first tasks undertaken by Brook Watson, the commissary-general, was to appoint two Dutchmen to be in charge of procuring wagons and horses. Initially at least, the Duke of York's army was immobile until these important matters could be resolved.

Aside from the lack of transportation, the expeditionary force was also deficient in its composition compared to what might be expected for a field army. The only artillery comprised the light 6-pounder battalion guns, used for close infantry support, and it was not until the ordnance park arrived in mid-May that the Duke of York was adequately supplied in this area. The same issue applied to cavalry, since the first regiments comprising a combined total of 12 troops, did not arrive until the end of April, with more arriving in theatre between May and September. Although not the subject of this study, the same piecemeal approach was also apparent with the assembly of auxiliary troops from various German states. The Hanoverian contingent joined the army in stages between 29 April and 24 May, the Hesse Cassel troops between 10–19 July with a second contingent arriving on 16 November, while the men from Hesse Darmstadt reached the army on 22 November and a battalion from Baden on 1 December.[56] The gradual build-up of the original expeditionary force and its German auxiliaries therefore continued throughout 1793, since treaties had to be negotiated and men supplied only after the commencement of hostilities. As may be surmised, preparations within Britain itself were not much further forward. There was no field-ready, all-arms strike force for despatch overseas. Individual units, and everything needed to keep them in the field, such as commissariat and medical support services, had suddenly to be brought together, as had civilian shipping assets. Nor should it be assumed that qualified men were ready and waiting to provide these essential requirements. The army's first commissaries did not arrive in the United Provinces until a fortnight after the Guards Brigade had landed, and the medical staff not until late-April.

---

55 TNA: WO 6/7: Part B, pp.11–12, Murray to Dundas, 26 March 1793.
56 P. Demet, *'We are Accustomed to do Our Duty.' German Auxiliaries with the British Army 1793–95* (Warwick: Helion, 2018), pp.25, 28 and 57.

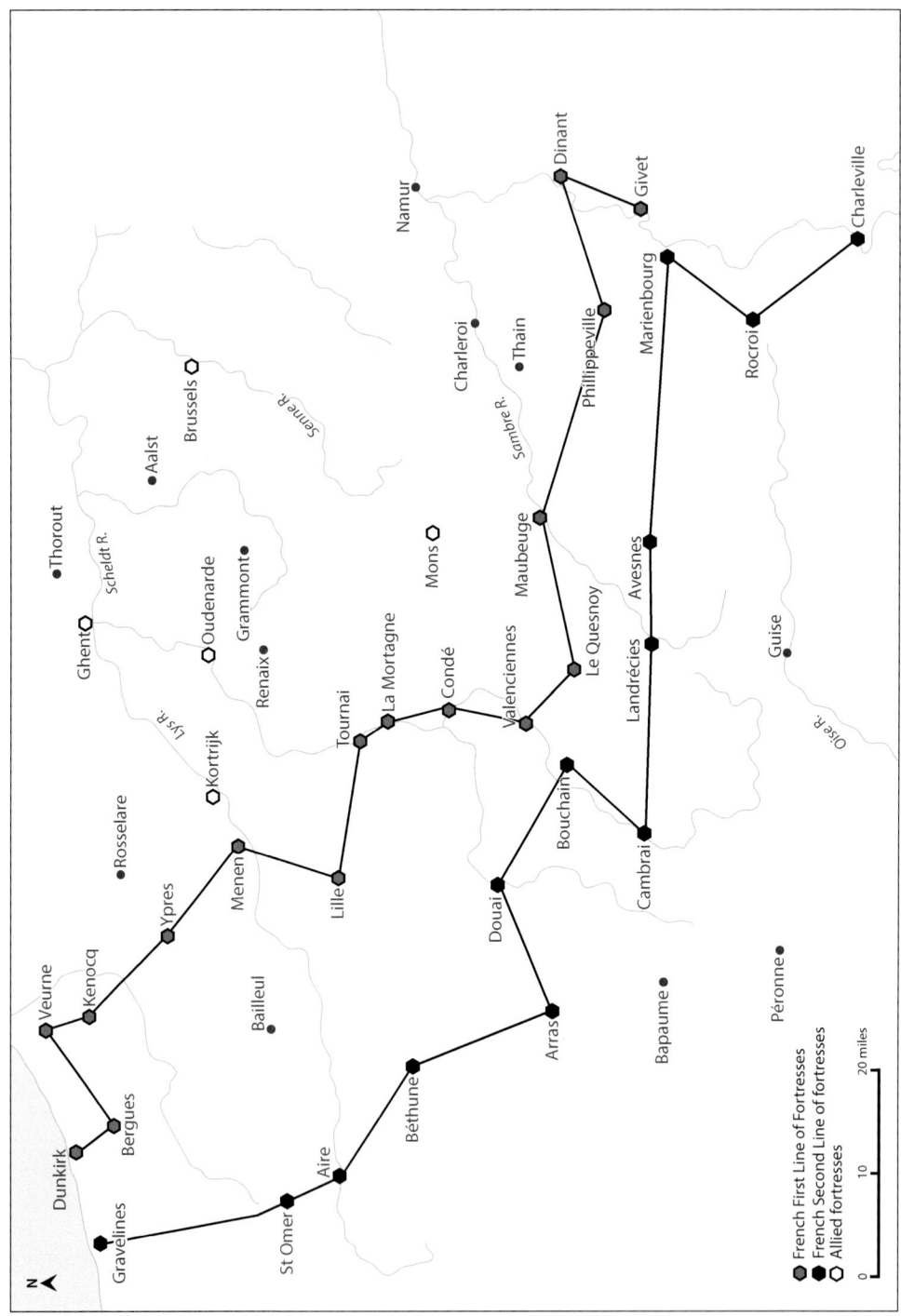

Map 2 The fortresses of Flanders.

Siege Warfare

In late March 1793 the allies had arrived at the French border. This frontier zone was possibly the most heavily defended area in Europe, protected by numerous fortifications, many of which had been erected or improved by the celebrated engineer, *Maréchal* Sébastien Le Prestre de Vauban (1633–1707) during the late seventeenth and early eighteenth centuries. Vauban had created what he termed a *'pré carré'* (square meadow) comprising the figurative fences defining France's borders. The northern border facing the Austrian Netherlands consisted of a double line of fortifications, with each belt consisting of 13 fortresses between the Channel coast and the River Meuse, all designed to be mutually supporting. The northern belt commenced with Dunkirk in the west, continuing through Bergues, Ypres, Menen, Lille, Tournai, Condé, Valenciennes, Le Quesnoy, Maubeuge and ending at Dinant and Givet, both on the River Meuse. The southern belt started at Gravelines on the Channel coast, extending through Aire, Arras, Bouchain, Cambrai and Landrécies to Rocroi and Charleville in the east. According to eighteenth century military convention, it was accepted that a fortress would surely fall at some point, but a resolute governor should be able to hold out long enough for relief forces to arrive or, if forced to it, to withstand at least one direct assault. Such a sacrificial resistance would blunt any offensive, and limit the number of other places that an enemy could hope to lay siege to in the normal spring to autumn campaigning season.[57] It was this double fortress barrier that dictated the conduct of operations until the French became strong enough to push the allies away from it following the Battle of Fleurus (26 June 1794). One can only speculate whether the French could have invaded the Austrian Netherlands quite so easily in 1792 and 1794 had the Austrian Emperor Joseph II not practically demolished his fortifications in 1781 in order to remove the Dutch garrisons that had been in occupation since 1715 under the terms of the Third Barrier Treaty.[58]

We have already noted one of the key decisions of the Antwerp conference, which was to continue allied efforts at besieging various fortified towns in northern France. The remainder of the 1793 campaign was spent with this in mind. Condé-sur-l'Escaut was blockaded by the Austrians from 30 March, but the town did not fall until 10 July, after a notable 102 days resistance. Meanwhile, on 14 April the Prussians besieged Mainz, in what was to prove another protracted operation. The city did not fall until 23 July, having held out for 100 days. Next was Landrécies, besieged on 20 April by the Dutch, in what was the shortest investment of all, lasting only 10 days before the town fell on 30 April. None of these operations involved the Duke and the British expeditionary force directly, but this was to change with the investment of Valenciennes, where the formal siege commenced on 2 June. With the Duke of York nominally in command, the technical aspects of the attack were masterminded by Austrian engineers, who also supplied the siege train and nearly half of the troops engaged in the trenches. Although the siege lasted only 57 days, fairly short in comparison to Condé-sur-l'Escaut and Mainz, it was long enough to delay subsequent operations against Dunkirk. While York marched west in late August, the Austrians invested

---

57 C. Duffy, *Fire and Stone. The Science of Fortress Warfare 1660–1860* (Newton Abbot: David & Charles, 1975), pp.11–13 and P. Griffith, *The Vauban Fortifications of France* (Oxford: Osprey Publishing, 2006), pp.4–5, 12–13 and 36.
58 C. Duffy, *The Fortress in the Age of Vauban and Frederick the Great, 1660–1789* (London: Routledge & Kegan Paul, 1985), pp.106 and 166.

the next fortress on their list, Le Quesnoy, though this was fortunately a short affair lasting just over three weeks and ending with the town's capitulation on 11 September. They then invested Maubeuge, located on the River Sambre, on 30 September before being driven away following a ferocious two-day engagement at Wattignies (15–16 October). Outnumbered, the Austrians had valiantly beaten off a series of French attacks until their left wing was overwhelmed in a manner reminiscent of Hondschoote fought the previous month. In both cases, the governors of the besieged towns had held out long enough to allow a relieving army to arrive.

The abortive siege of Dunkirk should be discussed in more detail, since this event was key to the experience of the British expeditionary force, and to the views of contemporaries and subsequent commentators on the Duke's capabilities as a general. The idea of taking the town had originated with George III, who told Pitt in late March 1793 that:

> ... the most advantageous step that can be taken and most conducive to shorten both the sea and land operations of France would be the English and combined forces, with some addition from the Dutch, getting possession of Dunkirk, as this would enable battering trains of artillery to be embarked in Holland and landed in the most advantageous situation for the Austrians to carry on regular sieges.[59]

The idea was adopted with relish by the men formulating British strategy – Pitt, Dundas and Grenville. Dundas urged Sir James Murray on 16 April to ensure that Coburg understood the importance to the British of taking the town, adding on 1 August that the anticipated capture should be by the Duke of York in the King's name, since by doing so: '... we should participate in that Indemnification which the Belligerent Powers have just reason to expect'.[60] The British Government's decision to make Dunkirk a war aim antagonised the Dutch, since the Prince of Orange wished to undertake the operation himself and tried to persuade the Duke of York to abandon the project. This, of course, he could not do since it had been ordered by the King and the British Government.

At least some in the army thought the expeditionary force should undertake an operation by itself, which might serve to quiet those in Britain who objected to the war, even though Dunkirk itself offered few actual advantages.[61] Naturally, when the siege did not go as expected, one-and-all in the army blamed the Government. One of the Duke of York's aides-de-camp, William Bentinck, was typical of many, stating: '... that the siege of Dunkirk was contrary to the opinion of all the Generals & military people, but solely the plan of the ministry of England'.[62] His disgust was echoed by Henry Clinton, who wrote to his father: 'I understand the whole of this move has been undertaken in direct opposition to the opinion

---

59 George III to Pitt, 29 March 1793, in J. Holland Rose (ed.), *Pitt and Napoleon: Essays and Letters* (London: G. Bell & Sons, 1912), p.224.
60 Dundas to Murray, 16 April 1793, in *William, Lord Auckland*, vol.3, pp.23–24; TNA: WO 6/7: pp.139–140, Dundas to Murray, 1 August 1793 and York to George III, 31 August 1793, in Aspinall (ed.), *Later Correspondence*, vol.2, p.83.
61 WLCL: Henry Clinton Papers: vol.235, Henry Clinton to Sir Henry Clinton, 2 August 1793.
62 UNL: Pw Ja 612: nd. Journal of William Bentinck.

of the Prince of Cobourg, P[rince] Hohenloe, in short the whole of that Counsil, Merely because it was thought it would please at home'.[63]

It is not the purpose of an administrative analysis of the expeditionary force to examine its operational progress in detail, other than to observe that the slowness in prosecuting the siege of Valenciennes gave valuable time for the French *Armée du Nord* to assimilate its new recruits and rebuild formations shattered in March and April 1793. British observers were far from happy with what they regarded as the dilatory nature of the siege, with Major Harry Calvert of the Coldstream Guards writing to his sister on 23 July: '… for in regard to time or probability I never will again venture to form a conjecture when an Austrian engineer is concerned'.[64] Further delays were experienced from a subsequent demonstration against Cambrai, where intelligence reports had suggested the population would not long endure a siege, followed by an operation to take the Camp de César to facilitate the siege of Le Quesnoy. However, the principal cause of failure lay with delays in sending out from Britain the heavy ordnance necessary to undertake the siege of Dunkirk, meaning that for the time being the expeditionary force had to rely totally on Austrian resources. By the time it did arrive, the French had gathered in overwhelming force and the Duke of York's corps was simply too weak to maintain its position.

'Systematic' or 'methodical' are the most apt characteristics of Austrian war-making in Flanders. Besieging fortress after fortress best utilised the technical skills and vast *matériel* at their disposal, which none of the other allied armies possessed. As we have seen, the defeats inflicted on the *Armée du Nord* during the Austrian advance of March and early April 1793 led to its near disintegration, but were not exploited. With hindsight, this was the moment the allies could have invaded France, which was indeed suggested by elements at Austrian headquarters, notably by Coburg's chief of staff, *Oberst* Karl Mack von Lieberich. But the idea was nullified by the determination of the British Government to besiege Dunkirk (which had been seen as a potential threat to national security for a century), indecision on Coburg's part and squabbles within his own staff.[65] Instead, the allies spent months besieging no less than seven fortresses distributed along the frontier, and by so doing handed their enemy the best opportunity available to shelter behind strong walls while rebuilding their shattered units. This sluggish approach could be ascribed to an over-reliance on system and method, bordering, some might say, on timidity. Conversely, it seemed hardly sensible for the allies to venture deep into enemy territory without eliminating hostile elements in their rear. Such, at least, were the conventions of the day, and the allies acted in accordance with them. But the result was that the *Armée du Nord* was allowed to expand from some 150,000 men on 1 March 1793 to about 225,000 men in December, and these men were given time to train and become assimilated into their units. Much of the French army was based in three

---

[63] UML: The Clinton Papers (uncatalogued): Henry Clinton to Sir Henry Clinton, 2 September 1793. The same sentiments were expressed by Harry Calvert in his diary entry for 8 September. H. Verney (ed.), *The Journals and Correspondence of General Sir Harry Calvert* (London: Hurst & Blackett, 1853), p.121.

[64] WLCL: Henry Clinton Papers: vol.235, Henry Clinton to Sir Henry Clinton, 7 June 1793; UML: The Clinton Papers (uncatalogued): Henry Clinton to Sir Henry Clinton, 9 and 23 July 1793 and Calvert to his sister, 23 July 1793, in Verney (ed.), *Calvert*, p.89.

[65] E. Taylor (ed.), *The Taylor Papers, Being a Record of Certain Reminiscences, Letters, and Journals in the Life of Lieut.-Gen. Sir Herbert Taylor* (London: Longmans, Green, & Co., 1913), p.39.

massive camps, at La Madeleine near Lille, Famars near Valenciennes (before moving to the Camp de César near Paillencourt in May) and at Maubeuge. By the late summer of 1793 the new recruits had been training for some four months and acquitted themselves with great credit against the Hanoverians at Hondschoote and the Austrians at Wattignies. By this time, the allies' great opportunity had been missed and the forces ranged against them were now much larger and better trained.[66]

On the eastern front, Prussian efforts markedly slowed after the fall of Mainz on 23 July, though French attempts to shift them met with conspicuous failure at Pirmasens on 14 September and then at Kaiserslautern on 28–29 November. Meanwhile, the Austrians under Würmser broke through the formidable Wissembourg Lines on 13 October, but failed to exploit their success until lethargy and mutual suspicion between the allies prevented any significant further activity.[67]

Perceptions of the Duke of York

The Duke of York was a popular commander and impressed those around him. Lord Borringdon, a visitor to the army during the siege of Valenciennes, wrote to his friend Lord Granville Leveson Gower:

> I assure you it gave me infinite pleasure to see the manly and gentlemanlike way, and at the same time the very great precision, clearness and quickness with which he gave his orders upon all occasions. One cannot indeed fail to consider him as an ornament and blessing to his country, and the very flattering way in which persons of all countries and descriptions make mention of him must be highly grateful to every Englishman.[68]

Although Dunkirk represented the first major allied reverse in 1793, the Duke of York's reputation as a field commander suffered little harm, as Henry Clinton observed that: 'The Duke bears this very severe stroke with wonderfull fortitude. He says himself he expects to be obliged to live on a strict defensive for a few days when he proposes again to advance. Whether he thinks so or not he does well to say so.'[69]

His father, General Sir Henry Clinton, agreed that: 'HRH has lost no credit. Those who form the plans with means inadequate & tardy are alone to blame', while Harry Calvert wrote to his father that: '… the Duke's character rises very much by this reverse of fortune. His good humour and spirits never forsake him, and he meets the unfortunate events that have happened with a degree of constancy and resolution that do him infinite honour'.[70] The prominent Whig Member of Parliament Charles James Fox informed the House

---

66 Lynn, *The Bayonets of the Republic*, pp.226–234.
67 Blanning, *The French Revolutionary Wars*, pp.110–111 and Esdaile, *The Wars of the French Revolution*, p.109.
68 C. Granville (ed.), *Lord Granville Leveson Gower (First Earl Granville). Private Correspondence 1781 to 1821* (London: John Murray, 1916), vol.1, p.67.
69 WLCL: Henry Clinton Papers: vol.235, Henry Clinton to Sir Henry Clinton, 9 September 1793.
70 WLCL: Henry Clinton Papers: vol.235, Sir Henry Clinton and Harriet Clinton to William Henry and Henry Clinton, 28 September 1793; Calvert to John Calvert, 10 September 1793 in Verney (ed.), *Calvert* pp.126–127.

of Commons on 10 April 1794 he: '… rejoiced that no insinuation had been made in the smallest degree disrespectful to the character or conduct of the Duke of York; and that, after the raising of the siege, West Flanders had been recovered under the Prince's immediate orders. What man could do, he had done'.[71] Lest it be thought that only the Duke's staff and personal connections expressed praise for him, First Lieutenant Thomas Fenwick of the Royal Artillery wrote to his wife on 2 October 1793: 'No Commanding Officer ever succeeded in gaining the love (I may with propriety say) so completely as His Royal Highness has done.'[72]

Lord Malmesbury passed through Ghent in November 1793 en route to Berlin for a diplomatic mission to the Prussian court and met Colonel the Hon Henry Fox, the newly appointed quartermaster-general to the expeditionary force, who: '… spoke most highly of him [the Duke of York] as a man, and able general', a view that was echoed by the Dutch quartermaster-general, *Generaal-Major* Volkier Rudolf, Baron Bentinck, at a meeting in The Hague.[73] Another visitor to the army in 1793, William Windham, soon to be appointed Secretary-at-War in 1794, wrote:

> These clamours against the Duke of York are for the most part utterly without foundation and in all very nearly so.
>
> They originate in the mere licentiousness of the officer part of the army. The Duke of York is, I believe, a most respectable character; his conduct is, I am sure, in many respects perfectly exemplary. Nothing material in the campaign has suffered from him, if anything at all has; and all the latter part has been of a sort to do him the highest honour. Both the court of Vienna and the Austrian army are full of his praises.[74]

Despite these glowing testaments of the Duke of York, it is clear that some in the army held alternative views. Colonel John St Leger, the deputy adjutant-general, informed Lord Malmesbury in early December that Sir James Murray was unpopular, and this reflected adversely on the Duke of York; Murray was to be recalled to London just over a fortnight after this conversation so, if this was a cause of unpopularity, it was swiftly removed.[75] Another possible cause were the high spirits characterising the Duke of York's suite, as recounted by William Elliot of Wells[76] who visited headquarters at Tournai on 2 November, remarking:

---

71   Verney (ed.), *Calvert* pp.127–128.
72   J.H. Leslie (ed.), 'Campaigning in 1793-Flanders', *Journal of the Society for Army Historical Research*, vol.8, 1929, p.29.
73   Earl of Malmesbury, *Diaries and Correspondence of James Harris, First Earl of Malmesbury* (London: Richard Bentley, 1844–1845), vol.3, p.9.
74   William Windham to Mrs Crewe, 26 December 1793, in H. Baring (ed.), *The Diary of the Right Hon. William Windham, 1784–1910* (London: Longmans Green and Co, 1866), p.299; this is reproduced in W. Windham, *The Windham Papers* (London: Herbert Jenkins, 1913), vol.1, p.193.
75   Malmesbury, *Diaries and Correspondence*, vol.3, p.15.
76   'ELLIOT, William (1766–1818), of Wells, nr. Jedburgh, Roxburgh and Reigate, Surr.', *History of Parliament Online*, <https://www.historyofparliamentonline.org/volume/1790-1820/member/elliot-william-1766-1818>, accessed 28 September 2020.

Almost all the persons immediately about the Duke are very young men, and as they live at head-quarters, they fill his table, and prevent him from inviting the general officers and colonels of regiments as frequently as it is usual for a commander-in-chief to do. This is one source of disgust. The youth of the circle which surrounds him occasions also a levity of manners at head-quarters, hence arises a lamentable deficiency of discipline among the officers. The Duke feels this, and sometimes *expresses* himself harshly, when he ought to *act* with severity. His own deportment is perfectly steady and unexceptionable, and the stories which are spread of his drinking are absolutely false; but he has not had the training or military education required for a commander.[77]

Just over one month later, in early December, Lord Malmesbury advised the Duke to invite senior officers to dine at headquarters more often, as this would encourage them to speak well of him when writing home.[78] The issue was still relevant on 21 January 1794, shortly after Colonel Sir James Craig reached headquarters to assume the role of adjutant-general, when he wrote to Henry Dundas that the only aspect he wished to change of the Duke's treatment of the officers was: '… with respect to the invitations to his table; in this it appears to me that sufficient attention is not paid to the Field officers and those of higher rank'.[79] The available evidence in fact shows that the Duke of York did invite commanding officers to dine, most notably on 4 June, the King's birthday, in both 1793 and 1794. Nor was this hospitality limited to commanding officers, for a general order dated 16 January 1794, proclaimed: 'H.R.H. the Commander in Chief desires the pleasure of the Company of the officers of the Garrison to a Ball at the Town House at 7 o'clock on the Evening of the 18th'. The general officers of the army arranged a birthday dinner for the Duke on 16 August 1794 at which 130 guests were invited, and Lieutenant General the Hon William Harcourt was at least one military officer attending a dinner with the Duke on 3 September. An explanation for the apparent lack of dinner invitations during the winter of 1793–1794 could be due to the Duke's physical condition. He wrote to his father on 8 November 1793 that his health: '… has been very much deranged for some time, having had a violent bilious complaint in my stomach for these last four months, for which it has not been in my power as yet to do anything'.[80] Although not possible to be conclusive, it is likely that the Duke had contracted either dysentery or typhoid, with the 'bilious' description referring to yellow-green vomit and watery stools.[81] He may have considered the consequences of revealing his poor state of health to senior officers outweighed the benefits of inviting them to dine.

The principal croakers were officers of the Foot Guards, which is curious given that the Duke had been Colonel of the Coldstream Guards since 27 October 1784 and several

---

77 Minto (ed.), *Lord Minto*, vol.2, p.185.
78 Malmesbury, *Diaries and Correspondence*, vol.3, pp.18–19.
79 TNA: WO 1/168: p.189, Craig to Dundas, 21 January 1794.
80 Harcourt (ed.), *The Harcourt Papers*, vol.4, part 2, p.496; Calvert to his sister, 4 June 1793 in Verney (ed.), *Calvert*, p.80; Brown, *Impartial Journal*, p.159; NAM: 1985-12-15-5: GO, Ghent, 16 January 1794; Baring (ed.) *William Windham*, p.316 and York to George III, 5 November 1793, in Aspinall (ed.), *Later Correspondence*, vol.2, p.118.
81 P. Lenihan, *Fluxes, Fevers and Fighting Men. War and Disease in Ancien Regime Europe 1648–1789* (Warwick: Helion, 2019), p.24.

members of his immediate staff were Foot Guards officers. The likely source of this friction was identified by Mrs Mary Harcourt on 24 November: '... there is a positive order from England for no leave of absence to be granted to any officer at present, which makes the Guards grumble not a little'.[82] In response, Lieutenant and Captain John Gage of the 1st Foot Guards, serving in the Guards Flank Battalion, requested leave to sell his commission and quit the army immediately, a request which was referred directly to the King. Gage was an equerry to the Duke of Gloucester, so was permitted to depart, though the Duke urged his father to refuse leave for him to sell out. This affair became known to the army at large and was mentioned by Colonel George, Lord Herbert, commanding the 2nd Dragoon Guards, who stated to Lord Malmesbury on 7 December that he: '... condemned the conduct of Gage'.[83] Another likely source of discontent was Captain and Lieutenant Colonel Lowther Pennington, commanding the Coldstream Guards, who unsuccessfully tried his adjutant at a court martial, only to have the Duke of York rescue the officer by appointing him deputy judge advocate on 15 November 1793. Both incidents took place in November, and may explain some of the increased negative perception of the Duke as the year drew to a close.

In addition to his links with the unpopular Murray, and the alleged failure to invite senior officers sufficiently often to dine at headquarters, it was possible that York was disapproved of as a consequence of his youthfulness, and hence his lack of command experience. Born in August 1763, the Duke was only 29 when he was sent overseas in command of the expeditionary force – admittedly several years older than the Duke of Cumberland, another prince of the blood, but no-one could claim that York shared Cumberland's forceful personality. His two infantry brigadiers in 1793 were Gerard Lake and Ralph Abercromby, aged 43 and 53 respectively. His cavalry commander was Lieutenant General Sir William Erskine, aged 65, and the senior artillery officer was 50. York's ranking engineer (and adjutant-general to the expeditionary force) was Sir James Moncrieff, aged 48 or 49. It would have been strange indeed if at least some of these veterans did not look on their young general with disquiet, perhaps even with disloyalty. After all, they had their own reputations to protect. To be fair, no direct evidence of this tendency has yet come to light, but the suspicion lingers.

The Campaign of 1794

Allied Strategy
From the British perspective, one of the principal difficulties faced by Pitt, Dundas and Grenville was the multiplicity of perceived opportunities, with insufficient means to realise them. They were not always in agreement in 1793, expeditions were launched to Flanders, Toulon and the West Indies, while considerable resources were also allocated to La Vendée. The traditional British loathing of standing armies meant that it always took time for the

---

82 Harcourt (ed.), *The Harcourt Papers*, vol.4, part 2, p.413. This order originated from the King. TNA: WO 6/8: p.97, Dundas to Murray, 9 November 1793.
83 York to George III, 15 and 19 November 1793, in Aspinall (ed.), *Later Correspondence*, vol.2, pp.120, 127 and Malmesbury, *Diaries and Correspondence*, vol.3, p.19. The Marquis of Buckingham informed Lord Grenville on 6 January 1794 that 'near 50 officers have got leave of absence'. Historical Manuscripts Commission (ed.), *Dropmore*, vol.2, p.491.

country to mobilise in strength at the beginning of a war, so it was unrealistic to think of using a home-grown military force to turn back the tide of the French Revolution. To resolve the competing claims for military resources – whilst at the same time satisfying the King's insistence that his son must not be left with a command incommensurate with his royal status, the Marquess of Buckingham (Grenville's brother) suggested that all the British infantry should be withdrawn from Flanders and assigned to Toulon, thus affording the Duke a *de facto* recall, but without any implied loss of face. Under this scheme, the cavalry would remain in Flanders under Sir William Erskine, but reporting to *Feldmarschall* Wilhelm von Freytag commanding the Hanoverian contingent.[84]

Whilst the British were juggling their limited resources, the Austrians stayed focused on the higher direction of the Flanders campaign, especially with questions regarding the command of the allied army that emerged in late 1793. Major Charles Craufurd, one of the Duke of York's aides-de-camp, was sent to Vienna in November at the request of Coburg to report on the military situation. While there, he held conversations with Franz Maria, Baron von Thugut, the Austrian Foreign Minister, and subsequently on his return, with Count Florimund Mercy d'Argenteau, the Austrian Minister at Brussels. Both Thugut and Mercy concluded that the 1793 campaign had been hindered by insufficiently rapid preparation, the want of a properly conceived operational plan, insufficient troop numbers and, most alarmingly, because: 'That there was not an officer at the head of the Austrian army capable of conducting the operations'. A key prerequisite for 1794 was: 'Either a Commander-in-Chief, or an executive person in the entire confidence of the Commander-in-Chief, who is capable of conducting the operations in chief'.[85] So it came about that the former Austrian Quartermaster-general, *Oberst* Karl Mack von Lieberich, was reinstated and reached Brussels at the end of January 1794. The prospect of his imminent arrival prompted the Duke of York to tell his father: 'The return of General Mack to his former situation about the Prince of Cobourg will, I am sure, restore that spirit and confidence to the Austrian troops which I am sorry to say the misfortunes and faults committed at the end of the last campaign have greatly destroyed.'[86]

A conference was held at Brussels on 2 February to discuss Mack's campaign plan, with both York and the Hereditary Prince of Orange attending.[87] York then brought Mack to London for two meetings, the first with Pitt, Dundas, Grenville and the Austrian ministers in London, Count Stahremberg and Count Meraeldt, and the second attended additionally by York and Lord Amherst, the British Army's Commander-in-Chief. Mack made it clear to the Prime Minister that he regarded Coburg as 'wholly insufficient' for field command;

---

84 Buckingham to Grenville, 16 October 1793, in Historical Manuscripts Commission (ed.), *Dropmore*, vol.2, pp.445–446 and M. Duffy, *Soldiers, Sugar and Seapower. The British Expeditions to the West Indies and the War against Revolutionary France* (Oxford: Clarendon Press, 1987), p.49.
85 York to George III, 29 November 1793, and 'The substance of the conversation that was held by the Baron de Thougout, Minister for Foreign Affairs at Vienna, to Major Craufurd, Aid de Camp to H.R.H. the Duke of York, as well as from Count de Merci, which Major Craufurd was desired to repeat to his Royal Highness', in Aspinall (ed.), *Later Correspondence*, vol.2, pp.131 and 138–141.
86 Aspinall (ed.), *Later Correspondence*, vol.2, p.148.
87 TNA: WO 1/168: pp.255–256 and 259–282, Craig to Nepean, 3 February 1794 enclosing 'Considerations sur l'ouverture et les operations de la campagne prochaine de l'annee 1794, Bruxelles le 4 Fevrier 1794'.

moreover, that he, Mack, had only agreed to return to the army if either Emperor Francis II, or the Emperor's brother the Archduke Karl took personal control. The fortuitous return from India of General Charles, Marquis Cornwallis on 3 February led to Pitt, Dundas and Grenville proposing to the King that this highly distinguished officer should take command of the British troops and their German auxiliaries in the West Flanders sector. King George did not disagree in principle but insisted that his son the Duke of York should retain a command at the very least equivalent to the one he had been sent out with in 1793. The King's underlying fear was that the Austrians would frustrate this latest plan, as they would always want one of their own generals to have supreme authority.[88] The proposal to employ Cornwallis was thus stymied, and York rejoined his army at Kortrijk on 5 March.

Final dispositions for the campaign were settled at a conference at Valenciennes on 17 March. The Duke of York's force was to form the right flank of Coburg's main army, numbering some 67,000 men based around Valenciennes. The Austrian *Feldzeugmeister* François de Croix, Count von Clerfayt with 30,000 men was to be positioned in West Flanders with garrisons at Nieuwpoort, Ostend, Ypres and Menen, while on the opposite flank *Feldmarschall-Lieutenant* Count Franz von Kaunitz with some 27,000 Austrians was located on the River Sambre. It had been King George's wish that the Hanoverian contingent should come under his son's command, but this was frustrated by their high sickness levels, which confined them to garrison duties in West Flanders, and hence under Austrian command until such time as they could participate in the campaign. The elderly *Feldmarschall* von Freytag was recalled and replaced as commander of the Hanoverians by *General der Cavallerie* Count Ludwig von Wallmoden-Gimborn.[89] Supreme command of the combined army was assumed by the Austrian Emperor Francis II. His presence with the troops had been mooted since late 1793 and his brother, Archduke Karl, had continually urged him to go in person to inspire his subjects, improve inter-allied relations and encourage the troops. Coburg added his voice to this appeal, stating in particular that only the presence of the Emperor could improve co-operation with the Prussians. Francis reached Valenciennes on 14 April, and reviewed the army on the heights overlooking Le Cateau-Cambrésis two days later.[90]

Triumph and Disaster, April–June 1794

The 1794 campaign was fought along two main river axes – the Sambre to the south and the Scheldt and Lys to the north. The French *Armée du Nord* numbered about 207,000 men at the start of the campaign, with its subsidiary, the *Armée des Ardennes* providing a further 36,000 men, though both formations contained significant numbers of new recruits. The French plan was for their commander-in-chief, Jean-Charles Pichegru, to advance along the northern axis with 70,000 men, taking Ypres and Tournai. A force of 24,000 men in the centre under *Général de division* Jean-Henri-Becays Ferrand, formerly the commandant of Valenciennes, was tasked with holding his position, while 60,000 men forming the

---

88 Lord Grenville to George III and reply, 16 and 17 February 1794, in Historical Manuscripts Commission (ed.), *Dropmore*, vol.2 pp.505–507.
89 York to George III, 8 March 1794, in Aspinall (ed.), *Later Correspondence*, vol.2, pp.183–184.
90 Blanning, *The French Revolutionary Wars*, p.112; K.A. Roider, *Baron Thugut and Austria's Response to the French Revolution* (Princeton: Princeton University Press, 1987), pp.148–149.

right wing of the French army under *Généraux de division* Louis Charbonnier and Jacques Desjardins would cross the River Sambre and advance on Mons.⁹¹

The allies moved first, with Coburg's army advancing all along its front on 17 April in order to facilitate the investment of Landrécies on the River Sambre, a continuation of their 1793 strategy. The only part of the army to meet with French resistance was commanded by the Duke of York, who inflicted over 2,000 casualties and took 24 guns at Vaux and Prémont before taking up positions to the west of Le Cateau-Cambrésis to cover the siege.⁹² A subsequent build-up of French forces in the vicinity of Cambrai, at Villers-en-Cauchies, was dispersed following a spectacular Anglo-Austrian cavalry action on 24 April. This was followed by a three-pronged French attack as a final attempt to shift the allies from Landrécies, one element of which – 28,000 men and 79 guns under *Général de brigade* René-Bernard Chapuis – issued forth from Cambrai and the Camp de César on 26 April to attack the Duke of York. Seeing the mass of French infantry advancing unsupported, the Duke launched his cavalry at their flank, capturing *Général* Chapuis, 22 canon and 350 of all ranks while the cavalry of the left wing were no less successful, inflicting 1,200 casualties and taking 10 guns with 11 ammunition tumbrels.⁹³ With the French attack defeated by the combined army, there was nothing else to hinder the siege of Landrécies, which fell on 30 April.

The allies' bright start to the campaign was not to last, however. Having failed to dislodge Coburg and the Duke of York from their positions covering Landrécies, Pichegru decided to achieve his object by launching an offensive in West Flanders. This consisted of three divisions, the whole under the command of *Général de division* Joseph Souham, who aimed to take Menen and Kortrijk. The French advanced on 27 April, defeating Clerfayt at Mouscron the next day and capturing both towns soon after. Immediately following the fall of Landrécies, Coburg ordered the Duke of York to proceed immediately to West Flanders and co-operate with Clerfayt to repair the situation. The two generals agreed a plan on 3 May, only for Clerfayt to declare two days later that he had insufficient troops to execute it. A further French attack on 10 May was again crushed by the Duke of York's cavalry at Willems, inflicting 2,000 casualties and taking 450 prisoners and 13 guns, while Count Kaunitz defeated another French thrust aimed at Mons on 14 May, inflicting 5,000 casualties and taking three guns. Having made his eastern flank secure, the Austrian Emperor ordered Coburg to West Flanders with the bulk of the army. Here, the allied solution was to envelop Souham's forces by using six widely dispersed columns, according to a plan formulated by Mack, but his over-complex manoeuvre resulted in disaster, as several of the columns, notably including those commanded by the Duke of York, were isolated and defeated at Tourcoing on 17–18 May. The French continued their advance but were temporarily halted at Tournai on 22 May.⁹⁴

In the light of these discouraging events, Emperor Francis summoned a conference at Tournai, which took place on 24–25 May. The mood amongst the Austrian generals was one

---

91   Lynn, *The Bayonets of the Republic*, p.15 and Blanning, *The French Revolutionary Wars*, pp.112–113.
92   TNA: AO 16/53/1: GO, Bermerain, 16 April and Cateau, 19 April 1794.
93   TNA: WO 1/168: pp.741–743 and 789–793, York to Dundas, 25 and 28 April 1794.
94   York to George III, 6, 13 and 16 May 1794, in Aspinall (ed.), *Later Correspondence*, vol.2, pp.202–203, 205 and 206–207 and Lynn, *The Bayonets of the Republic*, pp.16–17.

of dejection and defeatism, with only Coburg and the Duke of York expressing any optimism. This represented a signal moment in the campaign of 1794, as it marked the genesis of Austria's belief that the forces ranged against the allies were simply too overwhelming. It is perhaps wrong to suggest that the Emperor thereafter lost interest in the Austrian Netherlands. Rather, his departure from Vienna to join the army had coincided with an uprising in occupied Poland, which foreign minister Baron Thugut was convinced had revolutionary overtones imported from France. On a personal note, the Empress was soon to give birth, and he was anxious to be at her side, so he departed the army for Vienna on 13 June. In the meantime, the situation on the ground continued to deteriorate. Reinforced by 40,000 men of the *Armée de la Moselle*, the French attacked on 16 June, were defeated, but attacked again two days later. The struggle reached its conclusion at Fleurus on 26 June, when Coburg failed in an ambitious attempt to envelop the French positions and was forced to retreat. The loss of the Austrian Netherlands now became inevitable. Brussels fell on 10 July and the French were poised on the Dutch border by the end of the month.[95]

The effectiveness of the *Armée du Nord* had been significantly boosted by this time, both in numbers, the habituation of its soldiers to war and in the breadth of its operational thinking. In June, Harry Calvert confided to his friend Sir Hew Dalrymple: 'I have observed with great concern, and mentioned to other people besides yourself, that the enemy's plan of operations is materially different from that of last year. It is more united, has more consistency, and bears no longer the marks of the irruption of banditti.'[96]

The *Armée du Nord* was subsumed on 29 July 1794 by the newly constituted *Armée de Sambre et Meuse*, and it was this formation that provided the core of the ongoing French offensive.

But before continuing with operational matters, we should pause for a moment to consider in more depth two issues that had become of ever greater concern to the allies during 1794 – changes in the army's leadership, and inter-allied relations.

The Allied High Command
As we have seen, Coburg's position at the head of the combined army was being questioned by Vienna since late 1793. The defeats of May and June 1794 did nothing to enhance his reputation and any confidence in his abilities drained until the inevitable conclusion was reached at the end of August when he resigned and the Austrian command devolved on the next senior officer, *Feldzeugmeister* Clerfayt. This, however, was only intended to be an interim solution, since the Austrian Ministers in London, Counts Stahremberg and Mercy, informed William Pitt that: '... there is no Austrian General whom his Court can name in whom it would have entire confidence' and therefore suggested that the Marquis Cornwallis assumed command of the combined army with the local rank of field marshal. This plan was dismissed by Cornwallis, who thought it highly unlikely that either the court at Vienna or the Duke of York would agree. There then followed a discussion in Government circles of replacing the Duke of York with Cornwallis, so William Windham, the newly appointed Secretary-at-War, was sent to the Duke's headquarters to broach the subject. He conceded

---

95 Blanning, *The French Revolutionary Wars*, pp.113–115; Esdaile, *The Wars of the French Revolution*, p.125 and Roider, *Baron Thugut*, pp.149–152.
96 Calvert to Dalrymple, 20 June 1794, in Verney (ed.), *Calvert*, p.257.

that complaints of the Duke from a section of the officer corps had diminished, while an appreciation of his qualities had increased: '… yet a confidence is not felt in his capacity to conduct an army'.[97] Matters conspired against the plan due to the reluctance of Cornwallis, the strategic situation in the United Provinces, and the need to persuade the King, which included arranging a *douceur* for the Duke of York. It was perhaps naïve of ministers to believe that Cornwallis would accept command of the British contingent only, when he had all but refused that of the combined army, including the Austrians.[98] The Duke of Brunswick, a Prussian officer, was subsequently offered command of the combined British and Dutch forces but declined, citing a want of common purpose among the allies and excusing himself by pointing out that his participation would in any case require the permission of his king, Frederick-William II. Discussions between these two in October concluded that without sufficient means, the mission could not succeed. That Brunswick's outlook coincided with that voiced by Lord Cornwallis came as no surprise to Harry Calvert: 'The Prince of Brunswick has declined the command that was offered. I concluded he would; for I think no officer with a grain of character to lose, would risk it on the co-operation of the Prussians and Austrians.'[99]

Inter-Allied Relations
The 1793 campaign had been conducted with reasonable harmony between the allies, all of whom had contributed at one time or another to the military successes of that year. Yet competing aims and priorities had always simmered below the surface, and which French successes brought into sharper focus. It was in any case true that whilst in every eighteenth century war the British had cooperated with, or even hired continental auxiliary forces *en bloc*, often in large numbers, relations with their foreign comrades-in-arms had frequently been difficult. Some of this dissension was rooted in national prejudice, which may have led British officers to stereotype their Hanoverian and Hesse Cassel allies in Flanders as a set of ill-organised plunderers.[100]

Against this chequered backdrop, it is also necessary to mention Britain's controversial role in Dutch politics. Britain had long been in favour of the Orangeist faction and in the years prior to 1793 this policy, which involved support for the Stadtholder, Willem V, and the centralisation of power in his hands, had been implemented by the British ambassador to the United Provinces, Lord Auckland. Orangeists formed the majority in the provinces of Friesland and Gelre, on the eastern shores of the Zuiderzee, and of Zeeland on the North Sea coast, but the remaining provinces supported the Patriot faction, which sought

---

97 Windham to Pitt, 16 September 1794, in Windham, *The Windham Papers*, vol.1, p.240.
98 Pitt to Cornwallis, 24 August, Cornwallis to Pitt, 25 August, Cornwallis to Colonel Ross, 28 August 1794, in C. Ross (ed.), *Correspondence of Marquis Cornwallis* (London: John Murray, 1859), vol.2, pp.259–260, 261–262 and 263–264 and Pitt to Windham, 10 and 25 September 1794, Windham to Pitt, 16 and 19 September 1794, in Windham, *The Windham Papers*, vol.1, pp.231–233, 239–246 and 253–256. The position of the Duke of York is discussed extensively in A. Burne, *The Military life of Frederick Duke of York and Albany* (London: Staples Press, 1949), pp.184–189.
99 Calvert to Dalrymple, 9 November 1794 (postscript dated 10 November 1794), in Verney (ed.), *Calvert*, p.388.
100 S. Conway, *The British Army, 1714–1783. An Institutional History* (Barnsley: Pen & Sword, 2021), pp.73–74 and Demet, 'We are Accustomed to do Our Duty', pp.140–141 and 170.

greater representation and political reform. The polarisation of Dutch politics had led to the Prussian invasion of 1787, triggered by the detention of Willem's consort, the sister of King Frederick-William of Prussia, by Patriot forces who were nominally (but, as it turned out, not militarily) supported by France. The fact that units of the Dutch regular forces fought on both sides of this brief conflict may partly explain their subsequent poor performance against the French in 1793–1795. Britain had provided substantial funding for the Orangeist cause and, as we shall see further in Chapter 5, commenced military preparations in the event that France sought to support the Patriots. Britain had also guaranteed the position of Stadtholder remaining with the House of Orange in a defensive alliance signed at The Hague on 15 April 1788.[101] Given the factional nature of Dutch politics, and Britain's overt support for the Orangeist cause, it is hardly surprising that friction occurred when British soldiers came into contact with those holding different views.

Adverse comments by British soldiers about the Dutch appeared almost immediately the troops disembarked. Captain Thomas Powell of the 14th Regiment noted in March 1793 that the civilian population of Brielle stole his men's cooking equipment and locked the doors of their houses, all at a time when the French were bombarding Willemstad only 20 miles away.[102] Major Jesse Wright of the Royal Artillery wrote to his wife on 22 March 1793 from Dordrecht, which was: '… one of the most disaffected towns in all Holland; they hate the Prince of Orange, who is here just now. He is a poor-looking creature, and not at all to be compared to the Duke of York, who is also here present.'[103]

The mood of the civilian population seemed to change for the better as the expeditionary force entered the Austrian Netherlands, with First Lieutenant Thomas Fenwick writing to his wife that the inhabitants of Lokeren: '… came out to receive the Duke with a Band of Music, all the Bells in the Town began chiming and the music continued all the time the Troops remained on the Parade'. A very similar reception met the Duke at Bruges.[104] But would this hold firm in times of adversity?

British accounts of the Flanders campaign make frequent references to the poor fighting qualities of the Dutch troops. For example, Captain Thomas Powell wrote in his diary that on 18 August 1793 the 14th Regiment encountered them fleeing from Menen in 'the greatest confusion' such that he was: '… obliged to make our men make use of their arms to prevent ourselves from being trod to death'.[105] Lieutenant Charles Stewart of the 28th Regiment was

---

101 Black, *British Foreign Policy*, pp.138–149 and 151–153; S. Schama, *Patriots and Liberators. Revolution in the Netherlands 1780–1813* (London: Collins, 1977), pp.126–132; H.L. Zwitzer, 'The British and Netherlands Armies in Relation to the Anglo-Dutch Alliance, 1688–1795', in G.J.A. Raven and N.A.M. Rodger (eds), *Navies and Armies: The Anglo-Dutch Relationship in War and Peace, 1688–1988* (Edinburgh: John Donald, 1990), pp.44–46 and 'Defensive Alliance between His Majesty the King of Great Britain, and their High Mightinesses the States General of the United Provinces', in Anon., *Journal of the House of Commons*, vol.43 (London: House of Commons, 1795), pp.500–501. Prussia signed a similar treaty with the United Provinces in Berlin, also on 15 April, while Britain and Prussia signed a defensive alliance on 13 August 1788, the whole being known as the 'Triple Alliance'.
102 NAM: 1976-07-45: Diary of Captain Thomas Powell, 14th Foot, March 1793–March 1796.
103 Leslie (ed.), 'Campaigning in 1793-Flanders', p.10.
104 Leslie (ed.), 'Campaigning in 1793-Flanders', p.16 and NAM: 1994-03-129: Dalrymple's diary for 16 April 1793, Papers and correspondence associated with General Sir Hew Dalrymple.
105 NAM: 1976-07-45: 'Diary of Captain Thomas Powell'.

disparaging about the Prince of Orange, who had inspected the army at Oosterhout on 24 August 1794 as he seemed: '... to possess a cold indifference for every object around him, one would think nature had formed their constitutions to look only with pleasure on the dreary prospects of their bogs & mists'.[106]

The Duke of York noted the practical difficulties in obtaining transport for food and forage as the population turned against the British during the retreat of 1794 and considered this lack of co-operation stemmed from the highest levels. He ascribed it to the Prince of Orange's attempts to deflect attention from himself for the defenceless state of the Dutch fortresses by blaming all reverses on the British, his displeasure at not having them under his command and King George III's orders not to place British troops in Dutch fortresses.[107] Relations with the Dutch deteriorated markedly towards the end of 1794, and William Windham wrote to the Prime Minister in September that: 'The conduct of the Dutch is such as to create every day new resentment. Anything so brutish, stupid, and selfish, was never seen'.[108]

While British participants often wrote admiringly of Austrian regiments, this was far from the case regarding the strategy dictated by their senior commanders. We have already mentioned the failure to take opportunities and a penchant for method. One other key area of disagreement concerned tactics and especially the dispersal of troops over wide areas, making them weak everywhere and hence vulnerable to attack. This was succinctly expressed by the Duke of York in a letter to his father: 'I humbly agree with your Majesty that the system of cordons into which the Austrians have fallen ever since the beginning of this war, is exceedingly pernicious as well as dangerous, and has been the real origin of all the misfortune to which they have been subject.'[109]

Relations with the Austrians were sometimes challenging. Polite but forceful exchanges of view between York and Coburg continued right up until the latter's departure from the army at the end of August 1794 and thereafter with his successor, *Feldzeugmeister* Clerfayt, as also at the higher diplomatic level. Given that the main theatre of operations until mid-1794 lay for much of the time within Austrian territory, the British envoy to Brussels, Lord Elgin, was a key participant. Matters became more difficult in May 1794, when the Austrian Emperor banned all foreign ministers at Imperial headquarters, greatly reducing information about what was passing there at times when the British did not form a part of the main army. As the Duke of York wisely remarked: '... to say the truth, it wants a great deal of steadiness and prudence to keep well with the Austrians'.[110]

But the worst diplomatic breakdown was between Austria and Prussia. It must be considered very doubtful whether York or the British ministers could have done anything to prevent it. Although Prussian troops had launched the initial military effort into northern

---

106 R.M. Grazebrook, 'The campaign in Flanders of 1793–1795. Journal of Lieutenant Charles Stewart, 28th Foot', *Journal of the Society for Army Historical Research*, vol.29, 1951, p.11.
107 TNA: WO 1/171: pp.597–613, Observations of His Royal Highness the Duke of York, undated but received 24 December 1794.
108 Windham to Pitt, 19 September 1794, in Windham, *The Windham Papers*, vol.1, p.245. Windham renewed his complaints about Dutch 'stupidity and brutality' in a letter to Pitt of 21 September.
109 York to George III, 13 May 1794, Aspinall (ed.), *Later Correspondence*, vol.2, p.205.
110 York to George III, 16 May 1794, Aspinall (ed.), *Later Correspondence*, vol.2, p.207.

France in 1792 before spending April-July 1793 in the successful siege of Mainz, their forces did not participate in any significant manner thereafter. Shortly after conducting unsuccessful peace negotiations with the French after the failure at Valmy, Prussia participated in the second partition of Poland with Russia in early 1793, annexing territory as compensation for costs incurred during the invasion of France. This was done without consulting Austria and was the direct cause of a further cooling in relations. Austrian attitudes towards Prussia had in any case hardened with the appointment of Baron Thugut as foreign minister on 27 March 1793, when his predecessors, Count Louis Cobenzl and Anton Spielmann, both of whom had promoted co-operation, were side-lined. The Prussians delivered a heavy blow when on 22 September 1793 they informed the Austrians that King Frederick-William urgently needed to attend to affairs in Poland, and would scale back his military contribution accordingly. In 1794, the Prussians declined to cooperate with the coalition forces unless provided with the means to do so. In Berlin, Frederick-William frankly admitted to Lord Malmesbury that he lacked the cash for another campaign in the west, and cited this as a cause of Prussian inactivity since 1793. The result of this virtual ultimatum was a tripartite treaty, signed on 19 April 1794, stipulating that Prussia would furnish an army 62,000 strong from 24 May to cooperate with either the British or the Dutch, or indeed both combined, in return for a subsidy of £50,000 per month, with an additional £100,000 to be paid on demobilisation. Little or nothing came of this initiative however, as Prussia continued to be embroiled militarily in Poland throughout 1794. Subsequent pleadings by Malmesbury and Cornwallis were met with procrastination or downright refusals to act. Lieutenant Colonel George Don, York's deputy-adjutant-general, was sent in October with a final plea to *Generalfeldmarshall* Möllendorff, commanding Prussian forces on the Rhine, only to be brusquely informed that any thought of Prussian co-operation with either the British or the Austrians must be put aside.[111]

Defeat and Withdrawal, July – December 1794

The operational events of May and June 1794 largely ended any allied belief that the French could be defeated. As far as the British were concerned, at the end of May the King (at the urging of the Duke of York and Coburg) stated that all troops in the pay of Great Britain should be gathered into a single formation, this being the first time that they served together. Allied efforts in the Low Countries would now be prosecuted by three armies for the remainder of the campaign, consisting of the British and their German auxiliaries commanded by the Duke of York, the Austrians under Coburg (until late August, and thereafter under *Feldzeugmeister* Clerfayt) and lastly the Dutch commanded by the Hereditary Prince of Orange. The Austrian army drifted eastwards until a conference held at their

---

111 'Treaty between His Britannic Majesty, the King of Prussia, and the States General of the United Provinces', in Anon., *A Collection of State Papers Relative to the War Against France* (London: Debrett, 1795), vol.2, pp.9–12; Malmesbury to Grenville, 3, 5, 9, 21 and 28 June 1794, in Historical Manuscripts Commission (ed.), *Dropmore*, vol.2, pp.565–566, 577–578 and 592; Malmesbury to Grenville, 23 October 1794, in Malmesbury, (ed.), *Diaries and Correspondence*, vol.3 pp.145–147 and Cornwallis to Dundas, 21 June 1794, in Ross (ed.), *Marquis Cornwallis*, vol.2, pp.253–255. Don's appointment as Deputy Adjutant-General was not announced in GO until 21 November, but it is clear he was performing these duties prior to that date.

The Earl of Moira, by Joshua Reynolds. (Anne S.K. Brown Military Collection)

headquarters decided on a complete separation from the British and Dutch with a retreat on Maastricht, a fact that the Duke of York discovered on 20 July.[112]

In the meantime, the Duke of York received a considerable reinforcement on 9 July, comprising 6,760 all ranks under the command of Lord Moira (see Appendix I, Table I.3). This force had been intended to serve in La Vendée in late 1793, but arrived off the coast too late to assist the Royalists. It had since been stationed in the Channel Islands and the Isle of Wight, so was conveniently placed when Henry Dundas wished to reinforce Ostend in June 1794, which both Moira and the Duke of York viewed as impractical. The retirement of Coburg at the end of July had a domino effect on the other allied armies, since it forced the Dutch to retreat and the Duke, whose headquarters were close to Antwerp, had to conform by crossing into the United Provinces on 24 July. The southern part of the country was, in theory, protected by a line of fortresses running from Bergen-op-Zoom in the west to Nijmegen in the east, though their poor condition and weak garrisons inspired little confidence. The allies were granted a degree of breathing space during August as the French focused their attention on retaking various towns in their rear, including Niuewpoort, Le Quesnoy, Condé and Valenciennes. Once released from these operations, they were able to muster significantly greater numbers than the allies, with an estimated 80,000 men opposing the British in mid-September compared to 58,900 all ranks (of whom 7,300 were sick) under the Duke of York.[113]

The French were now free to turn their attention to the United Provinces and clashed with the allied outposts on 10 September. The outpost line was breached at Boxtel on 14 September with a failed counter-attack by Lieutenant General Abercromby the following day. The result was a retreat from the line of the River Aa to positions defending the River Meuse. This was a severe reverse, but in the words of William Windham, who was with the army at the time, it was 'wholly unavoidable'.[114] It was at this time that the British regiments faced their harshest test so far, for in retreat before a numerically superior enemy, discipline slumped and sickness rates surged. As will be seen in due course, York's army now contained a high proportion of recruits, lacking in training and equipment – with predictable impacts on discipline, health and morale. The French were in a similar state, but ruthlessness at the top, a potent ideology, and sheer numbers gave them the cutting edge. The army moved to defend the line of the River Waal on 22 October, where the key point was the town of Nijmegen which the French commenced to attack within the week. A heroic sortie by the garrison on 4 November did not alter the fact that the town was indefensible, and it was evacuated three days later.

As the military situation imploded, plans for the Duke of York's future crystallised at home and he was recalled to London, departing on 2 December. Many felt genuine regret at his leaving: 'Here the British army lost a father and a friend, who had endeared himself to them by his humanity, justice, and benevolence. The army felt themselves very much

---

112 George III to Grenville, 25 May 1794 enclosing York to George III, 23 May 1794, in Historical Manuscripts Commission (ed.), *Dropmore*, vol.2, pp.558–560; and Calvert's diary, 20 July 1794, in Verney (ed.), *Calvert*, p.279.
113 Calvert's diary, 15 September 1794, in Verney (ed.), *Calvert*, p.325 and TNA: WO 1/170: pp.551–563, enclosures in Craig to Nepean, 26 September 1794.
114 Windham to Pitt, 16 September 1794, in Windham, *The Windham Papers*, vol.1, p.235.

obliged to their commander, and his Royal Highness had every reason to be so to them, and expressed himself so in the handsomest manner on taking his leave.'[115]

The command now devolved on the Hanoverian *General der Cavallerie* Wallmoden as the next senior officer, with Lieutenant General Harcourt commanding the British troops.[116]

A severe frost set in on 18 November and unseasonably cold weather led to the River Waal, otherwise a formidable obstacle, freezing over on 22 December. The temperature on Christmas Day dropped to 8°F (-13°C), but this did not stop the French attacking the Dutch sector across the ice two days later. They were driven back, but a further attack on 3 January succeeded, by which time it was clear that the allied position was untenable. The final retreat towards the River Rhine began four days later.

Fighting the Revolution

The campaign in the Low Countries ended in failure for the allies. France was politically and militarily stronger at the end of 1794 than it had been two years previously, whereas the allied powers lacked focus, lost territory and failed to reverse the political or military threats posed by France. Britain was distracted by numerous projects generated by the fertile minds of Pitt, Dundas and Grenville; the Austrians and Prussians by the perception of easier pickings closer to home, and by depleted financial resources that made them pause their efforts against France. The question then remains, could anything have been done differently to ensure success in 1793 or 1794?

It is clear that the French were militarily weak during the first half of 1793. As John Lynn has shown, the massive influx of recruits had to be trained, assimilated and equipped before they could be launched at the allies. The Revolutionary government in Paris, and successive French commanders on the spot, assessed the situation far more realistically than the leaders of the combined army. At first, they gained sufficient respite behind the fortress belt to mould a flood of recruits into a dynamic fighting force. For what seemed the best of reasons the allies had played into their hands by devoting what resources they possessed to siege warfare, which was ongoing from the investment of Condé-sur-l'Escaut in March 1793 to the fall of Landrécies at the end of April the following year. By this long drawn out resistance, the chain of fortresses had performed exactly as intended.[117] Subsequently, the hammer-blows inflicted on the allies at Hondschoote, Wattignies, Tourcoing and Fleurus all showed that the French were well able to match the combined army in open battle, indicating that the war was effectively lost by the late summer of 1793, when the superior military resources and skills enjoyed by the allies were outweighed by the numbers, determination and intensive training exhibited by the revolutionaries.

---

115 L.T. Jones, *An Historical Journal of the British Campaign on the Continent, in the Year 1794; with the Retreat Through Holland, in the Year 1795* (Birmingham: Swinney & Hawkins, 1797), p.144. Jones served as a lieutenant in the 57th Regiment in 1794 but was subsequently promoted captain in the 14th Regiment on 28 January 1795.
116 TNA: WO 16/53/7: GO, Arnhem, 2 December 1794.
117 Duffy, *Fire and Stone*, pp.19–20 and Duffy, *The Fortress in the Age of Vauban*, pp.85 and 87.

The allies lacked the boldness and capability to push on through the fortress belt in the early summer of 1793, and perhaps it was not worth the risk. In any case, the decision clearly rested with the lead coalition partner in theatre, and that was the Austrians, not Frederick, Duke of York. His expeditionary force was a small component of a much greater whole, upon which he was dependent for many important military functions, as will be seen in detail below. Only from June 1794 were his British troops and their German auxiliaries gathered into a single formation, by which time the die was cast. Retreat and evacuation were the only options left.

2

The Staff

Ensuring that fighting men may be directed to the desired point in sufficient numbers, suitably equipped, fed and clothed, implies the existence of a centralised function able to identify objectives and co-ordinate resources. It may seem obvious to state that the role of a fighting man in the ranks of a regiment of cavalry or infantry, or manning an artillery piece, was to do just that – to fight – but enabling him to do so was the job of the staff of the army.

Relatively little attention has been paid to the actual mechanisms by which British eighteenth century armies moved around their theatres of operations, though a recent exception is a detailed study of the staff during the War of the Spanish Succession (1701–1713) by Stewart Stansfield.[1] This represents a marked contrast to extensive operational studies of the major wars on the continent of Europe during the period, including the War of the Austrian Succession (1740–1748) the global Seven Years' War (1756–1763) and the intercontinental War of American Independence (1775–1782).[2] When the subject of administration has been addressed it is generally from a peacetime perspective when affairs were controlled from offices in London or Dublin, rather than by the army in the field.[3] The historian has to wait until the Peninsular War in the early years of the nineteenth century for S.G.P. Ward's seminal study of the staff under the future Duke of Wellington before this important subject is again addressed in detail.[4]

An exception to this trend has been research into one aspect of the staff's work, the Commissariat, which has been addressed at length in the context of America,[5] and forms the subject of Chapter 3. This chapter will examine in more detail the composition of the

---

1   S. Stansfield, *Early Modern Systems of Command. Queen Anne's Generals, Staff Officers and the Direction of Allied Warfare in the Low Countries and Germany, 1702–1711* (Solihull: Helion, 2015). See also: Rogers, *British Army*, pp.82–108.
2   The 'War of American Independence' of 1775–1782 is abbreviated to the 'American War' in the remainder of this book.
3   E.E. Curtis, *The Organization of the British Army in the American Revolution* (New Haven: Yale University Press, 1926, reprinted by EP Publishing, 1972), pp.33–50.
4   S.G.P. Ward, *Wellington's Headquarters. A Study of the Administrative Problems in the Peninsula* (Oxford: Oxford University Press, 1957).
5   N. Baker, *Government and Contractors. The British Treasury and War Supplies 1775–1783* (London: The Athlone Press, 1971); R.A. Bowler, *Logistics and the Failure of the British Army in America 1775–1783* (Princeton: Princeton University Press, 1975) and D. Syrett, *Shipping and the American War 1775–83* (London: The Athlone Press, 1970).

staff in Flanders, the functions of the various departments, the roles they fulfilled and their effectiveness in the field.

Eighteenth century armies generally lacked the formal organisational structures familiar to students of later conflicts. Individual units tended to be placed in ad hoc formations that could be relatively fluid in both their size and composition. Brigade groupings could achieve some permanence during a campaign, but aggregations of units were usually formed for a particular task in hand and could include mixed arms, while semi-permanent formations of larger than brigade strength were rare. General officers often formed a pool of individuals who were allocated to formations of a size appropriate to their rank, rather than being permanently in command of designated groups of units.

There was no formal education provided for officers in the British service, other than for those employed by the Board of Ordnance, and whatever military knowledge they acquired resulted from private reading or residences at military seminaries in Europe. At the time of the Flanders campaign, the foundation of a staff college at High Wycombe was still some years in the future, developed under the sponsorship of the Duke of York and the immediate direction of the émigré French *Général* Francis Jarry (1733–1807). It commenced operation in May 1799 with an initial intake of 30 students, being renamed The Royal Military College by royal warrant in June 1801. Given this lack of formal training, it would be worth reviewing how troops were administered on campaign during the earlier years of the eighteenth century.

Scouller has noted that British armies serving in Europe during the War of the Spanish Succession did not require large numbers of staff, since warfare involved relatively shorter distances, lower levels of complexity and higher standards of comfort. The overall commander personally exercised many of the duties that in subsequent wars would be undertaken by subordinates and, importantly, the transmission of orders tended to be by word of mouth and undertaken personally by the individuals to whom they were given.[6]

At the head of an army in the field was the then captain-general, John Churchill, Duke of Marlborough, who commanded the troops in the absence of the sovereign. His deputies were the generals of horse and foot with responsibility for their arm of service. Under them were the lieutenant generals and major generals who commanded formations of differing sizes in the order of battle. Semi-permanent brigades comprising varied numbers of battalions or squadrons were commanded by brigadiers. All of these general officers were confined to their own arm of service – horse, dragoons or foot – as were their aides-de-camp to which officers of major general or above were entitled in varying numbers.[7]

The principal staff officer was the quartermaster-general, who had the brevet of colonel if he did not already hold that rank. He was responsible for quartering on campaign and on the march, for routeing and for supplying the troops. Either he or the captain-general issued orders to both the generals of the day (as Stansfield has termed them, the 'first generals on call') and the wagonmaster-general every morning and evening regarding the next day's movements. Men, vehicles, and animals were thereby deployed by subordinate generals and the wagonmaster's deputies and, through them, to each unit. The quartermaster-general

---

6 R.E. Scouller, *The Armies of Queen Anne* (Oxford: Oxford University Press, 1966), pp.53–54 and Stansfield, *Early Modern Systems*, p.194.
7 Stansfield, *Early Modern Systems*, pp.31–33 and 36.

also held the responsibility for reconnaissance, finding suitable locations for camps and the gathering of intelligence. The wide nature of his duties meant that he was assisted by a deputy quartermaster-general.[8]

The other principal staff officer in the field was the adjutant-general. His responsibilities were mainly for the tactical movement of troops and their discipline, with similar roles at brigade level being performed by a brigade major or the town major when in garrison.[9] His role later in the century for receiving and issuing orders from the force commander was not immediately apparent at this period since generals of the day assumed responsibility for undertaking whatever duties were required at any particular time. As we shall see below, the adjutant-general's important role later in the century of monitoring unit strengths was at this period undertaken by a muster master, whose responsibility was to ensure that regiments were kept up to their establishment strength, equipment was kept in good order, and that leave periods were not exceeded. Since many of these functions had a direct bearing on pay and expenditure, his presence could be regarded as more of a Treasury watchdog than an integrated member of the army staff.[10]

Also at headquarters was the judge advocate general, responsible for the execution of the Crown's powers under the Mutiny Act, including the organisation of courts martial. Much of the administration of these powers was undertaken by the provost marshal, who was responsible for the apprehension and custody of prisoners, the execution of military justice, details of courts martial (including warning witnesses and the preparation of accommodation), the maintenance of order in camps, quarters and on the march and for ensuring that the prices charged by sutlers were fair. He usually had three or four other ranks as assistants. Finally, headquarters also included a deputy paymaster who, as the title suggests, paid the army and provided any extraordinary sums required.[11]

Aside from the relative lack of staff officers, it is important to note that a captain-general (when someone was given this exalted title), or in most cases the Commander-in-Chief of the British Army, had little control over some of his subordinate officers. The commissary general and deputy paymaster both reported to the Treasury, the Ordnance was a department of state and not of the Army, while the judge advocate was also independent of the army commander. It is also worth noting that some potentially lucrative military appointments were sold to civilians, or else presented as rewards to courtiers.

Some of these features, especially regarding the separation of powers, continued for over another century, though there was a noticeable increase in the definition of the roles and responsibilities of the different staff members with time. Humphrey Bland's eighth and revised edition of his *Treatise on Military Discipline*, published in 1759, enumerated the quartermaster-general's responsibility for laying out camps to take account of security from

---

8   Scouller, *Armies of Queen Anne*, pp.64 and 170; Stansfield, *Early Modern Systems*, pp.34–35 and 194–225 and R.Molesworth, *A Short Course of Standing Rules, for the Government and Conduct of an Army, Designed for, or in the Field* (London: Dodsley, 1744), pp.66–70.
9   Scouller, *Armies of Queen Anne*, pp.54, 62 and 66–67 and Stansfield, *Early Modern Systems*, pp.34 and 140.
10 Scouller, *Armies of Queen Anne*, p.60.
11 Scouller, *Armies of Queen Anne*, pp.63–64, 90 and 263 and Stansfield, *Early Modern Systems*, pp.35 and 213–221.

surprise attacks by the enemy, the proximity of wood, water and forage and, in terms of unit distribution, to the line of battle.[12] As previously, the commander-in-chief issued instructions to the lieutenant generals and major generals of horse and foot appointed for each 24 hour period (the lieutenant generals and major generals of the day). The latter then transmitted these at orderly time at headquarters to the brigade majors of the day, who communicated them to their formations. In this, the involvement of the quartermaster-general had by now given way to the adjutant-general, who maintained a record of all the orders given and issued them himself should the generals of the day be absent from headquarters or during combat, when he assumed responsibility for communicating them to subsidiary commanders, ensuring that important messages were not lost in transmission.

As during the War of the Spanish Succession, the adjutant-general also had responsibility for discipline in the army and for correctly positioning or withdrawing outposts as necessary. Aside from their role in transmitting daily orders, brigade majors also ensured that officers and men were detailed to the various duties required and detachments paraded.[13] Bland ended his career as a lieutenant general, having first served under Marlborough and then during the Jacobite rebellions in 1715 and 1745 (in the latter commanding the British cavalry at Culloden) and during the War of the Austrian Succession, where he served as quartermaster-general and aide-de-camp to King George II.[14] Bland wrote with the benefit of long years of active service during which his wealth of experience indicated an increased professionalism in the higher direction of armies on campaign. It is therefore no surprise that his book went through nine editions by the time of his death in 1763 and was one of the most widely read military works in Britain during the eighteenth century.

The key role of the adjutant-general in the transmission of orders continued during the Seven Years' War. Lieutenant Colonel Charles Hotham, adjutant-general to the British forces in Prince Ferdinand of Brunswick's army, confirmed in his testimony during the trial of Lord George Sackville in 1760 that he received them direct from the adjutant-general of the allied army.[15] Aside from issuing orders, the adjutant-general was also responsible for preparing strength returns, rosters of duty and for the maintenance of discipline.[16] This higher degree of control became necessary due to the larger size of armies by the mid-eighteenth century. Whilst the basic formation during the War of the Spanish Succession had been the brigade (the composition of which could be fluid), the Seven Years' War saw groupings of brigades into larger aggregations that could contain a mixture of cavalry, artillery and infantry according to circumstances. However, it is important to stress that these higher formations were not permanent and could change with each operation.[17]

The size of forces during the American War also justified the use of higher 'all-arms' formations. It also meant the quartermaster-general's department became the largest

---

12 H. Bland, *A Treatise on Military Discipline: In Which is Laid Down and Explained the Duty of the Officer and Soldier, Through the Several Branches of the Service* (London: Johnston, 1759), pp.297–303.
13 Bland, *Treatise*, pp.334–339.
14 I. Gruber, *Books and the British Army in the Age of the American Revolution* (Chapel Hill: University of North Carolina Press, 2010), pp.70–71 and Houlding, *Fit for Service*, pp.182–184.
15 Anon., *The Proceedings of a General Court Martial held at the Horse Guards … upon the trial of Lord George Sackville* (Cork: Bagnell and Swiney, 1760), p.183.
16 Ward, *Wellington's Headquarters*, pp.11–12
17 Rogers, *British Army*, pp.101–102.

service department in the army. Duties comprised the ordering, issuing, care and maintenance of camp and field equipment, the supply of forage during the first year of hostilities and its most extensive duty; the provision of land transport comprising both wagons and horses. Its wider responsibilities included the acquisition of intelligence, planning the army's movements, and the selection and layout of camp sites. The department was also heavily engaged with other matters that would not normally be associated with an army on campaign, including the provision of municipal services in New York and Philadelphia (maintaining roads, dykes, bridges, lights and fire-engines), managing a number of vegetable gardens and operating a large fleet of sea-going vessels.

Despite these extensive and diverse roles, it is somewhat surprising that the quartermaster-general was also a formation commander, so the actual management of the department was undertaken by deputies since it was impossible for one man to administer the whole. Indeed, the department contained some 1,100 people at headquarters in New York, with an additional 230 in the southern theatre. Of these, up to 16 were deputy or deputy assistant quartermaster-generals seconded from their regiments and many of the remainder were civilians comprising clerks, storekeepers, wagonmasters, drivers, sailors and tradesmen (including collar makers, carpenters, farriers and blacksmiths).[18]

There are several conclusions from the above. Firstly, the increasing size and complexity of land operations as the eighteenth century progressed required similarly enhanced capabilities for the staff function. The diverse operations undertaken by the quartermaster-general's department in America, together with the number of personnel involved, would have been unthinkable during the War of the Spanish Succession. Secondly, roles often lacked clear definition, either for individuals or formations. Staff sometimes acquired multiple, possibly conflicting, responsibilities, whilst formations had not assumed the degree of permanence associated with the nineteenth and twentieth centuries. They were often fluid in nature and designed for a particular task in hand rather than as relatively fixed administrative structures. Thirdly, there was an almost total absence of individual training in staff duties. Personnel having staff responsibilities were often appointed for reasons of patronage or kinship and had to learn by doing. Some may also have possessed personal attributes, such as language skills or an aptitude for conducting business. Due to the absence of sufficient specialist personnel in the army, civilians were employed in significant numbers to perform important functions, especially in the medical services or commissariat. It now remains to examine the staff during the Flanders campaign in more detail.

Perceptions of the Staff in Flanders

We have already seen that the allied combined army spent until mid-1794 operating along the French border, often within France itself. Staff work usually passes without comment when matters go smoothly, so it is perhaps unsurprising that the few mentions we have of it were mostly written after the close of the campaign, while memories of hardships endured during the final six months remained vivid, and their tone may not reflect operations as a

---

18 Bowler, *Logistics*, pp.21–27.

whole. One example is a letter written by Lieutenant Colonel Charles Craufurd to Lieutenant Colonel Denis Le Marchant at the end of 1795 or early 1796:

> As we stand at present, when an army goes upon service, we are so destitute of officers qualified to form the Quarter-Master-General's department, and an efficient corps of Aids-de-camp, and our officers in general have so little knowledge of the most essential parts of their profession, that we are obliged to have recourse to foreigners for assistance, or our operations are constantly liable to failure in their execution. The getting officers from the allies, that you may be acting with for the most confidential situations in your army, is subject to very serious political objections, as well as highly disgraceful and injurious to the service from the jealousies and dissensions which it naturally excites.[19]

These comments are by implication remarkably self-critical, since Craufurd was himself an aide-de-camp during the first 12 months of the campaign, one of only six attached to the Duke of York. He then served as a deputy adjutant-general from February 1794 until the end of the year.

On the same theme, Richard Glover referred to the campaign of 1794 when he wrote of: '… the absence of a single English officer of any consequence among the staff serving under [Major General the Hon Henry] Fox in the Quartermaster-general's department'.[20] This was hardly fair, since the deputy quartermaster-general during Fox's tenure was Lieutenant Colonel Robert Brownrigg who had been commissioned in 1774 and served as a deputy adjutant-general during the so-called Spanish Armament of 1790. He subsequently served as quartermaster-general at the Horse Guards between 1803–1811 and ended his career as a full general. Professor Glover's assertion that the bulk of the work was performed by foreign officers drafted in due to their staff expertise also bears further examination. From 1793 until the close of 1794, both men who served as quartermaster-general, their two deputies and 12 of the 17 assistants traced as part of this study were from Britain or Ireland, indicating that this was not the case.

A young participant attached to the staff from early 1793, Herbert Taylor, wrote in 1838, 43 years after the campaign ended:

> Zeal and gallantry were conspicuous on all occasions, but could not make up for all deficiencies. We were, in fact, 'in leading strings,' and except when opposed to the enemy in the field, the laughing stock of our allies. This remark applies more particularly to the staff arrangements and the outpost duties, of which at first we betrayed great ignorance.[21]

---

19   D. Le Marchant (ed.), *Memoirs of the late Major–General Le Marchant* (London: Samuel Bentley, 1841), p.83.
20   R. Glover, *Peninsular Preparation. The Reform of the British Army 1795–1809* (Cambridge: Cambridge University Press, 1963, republished by Ken Trotman, 1988), p.197.
21   Taylor (ed.), *Taylor Papers*, pp.27–28.

Lieutenant General Sir William Erskine, Bt, by Richard Cosway and Samuel William Reynolds. (Anne S.K. Brown Military Collection)

Taylor spent his first year on the staff in Flanders as a civilian, until appointed cornet in the 2nd Dragoon Guards on 25 March 1794, so one might well question his professional judgement during this period. The great expansion of the Army following the outbreak of war in 1793 meant that officers were granted commissions as a result of raising men for rank, so these individuals were unlikely to have undergone appropriate levels of training prior to finding themselves on active service in Flanders (see Chapter 5). The careers of all individuals who served on the Duke of York's staff have been analysed for this study, and there is no evidence to suggest that such men served in anything other than regimental employ.

The only major study of the staff during the French Wars by S.G.P. Ward is equally disparaging of the Duke of York's headquarters in Flanders. Ward contends that the lessons learned during the Seven Years' War and in America had largely been forgotten and highlights the detrimental effects of Fox's dual role as quartermaster-general and brigade commander without acknowledging that this was common eighteenth century practice. Ward concludes by quoting the renowned Prussian general and military reformer Gerhard von Scharnhorst (who had served as a captain in the Hanoverian contingent in Flanders) to the effect that: 'We can almost say that the Duke of York and General Wallmoden possessed no General Staff'.[22]

Far from past lessons being forgotten, it is interesting to note that two officers who had headed the quartermaster-general's department in America also served under the Duke of York in Flanders. The senior of these was Sir William Erskine who, when a lieutenant

---

22 Ward, *Wellington's Headquarters*, pp.20–21.

colonel in the 1/71st Regiment and a local brigadier general, was appointed quartermaster-general by Lord Howe in September 1776, serving as such for three years. He was heavily engaged in operations during this period, participating in the Monmouth campaign of June-July 1778 and subsequently commanding the eastern district of Long Island during the winter of 1778-1779. The additional responsibility of supervising his department led to weakened health and a return to England in September 1779.[23] As a lieutenant general, Erskine was appointed the Duke of York's cavalry commander in May 1793 and took charge of the army during his absence in England in early 1794 before departing for home later that year. His successor in America, albeit temporarily, was Major Lord Cathcart who was quartermaster-general between September 1779 and March 1780.[24] As a local brigadier general, he arrived in Flanders in late June 1794 and was promoted to major general four months later, serving as an infantry brigade commander until May 1795 and then commanding the cavalry remaining in Germany until December. Both Erskine and Cathcart had spent their careers as regimental officers, subsequently commanding formations on active service. Both men would have been ideally situated to provide guidance or advice if asked.

A third senior officer in Flanders with staff experience was Major General David Dundas, the author of the *Principles of Military Movements* published in 1788, who served briefly as a brigade commander at Ostend and Nieuwpoort between September and November 1793. He returned to Flanders in May 1794, being promoted local lieutenant general on the continent on 1 December that year and commanding a cavalry brigade. Dundas had extensive staff experience, having served as assistant quartermaster-general to his uncle, General David Watson, between 1756-1758 and then in the same capacity with Prince Ferdinand of Brunswick's army between 1758-1759. He combined this last appointment with that of a lieutenant in the 56th Regiment and a practitioner engineer, having originally attended the Royal Academy, Woolwich. He subsequently served as quartermaster-general in Ireland between 1778-1789 and then adjutant-general, also in Ireland, until 1792.[25]

With regard to these three senior officers with staff experience, it should be noted that only Erskine served during the campaign of 1793 (leaving aside the few weeks that Dundas was at Ostend and Nieuwpoort), with Dundas reaching Flanders in May 1794 and Cathcart in late June. Indeed, Cathcart's brigade was a part of Lord Moira's force, which did not join the main army until July, so any help or guidance provided by Cathcart would have been subsequent to that. Erskine left Flanders in late 1794 and died the following March, though one or more of these officers was present in Flanders from May 1793 until the end of 1794.

---

23 M.M. Boatner, *Cassell's Biographical Dictionary of the War of American Independence 1763-1783* (London: Cassell, 1963), p.349.
24 M. Eddy, 'Cathcart, William Schaw, first Earl Cathcart (1755-1843), army officer and politician'. *ODNB*, <https://doi.org/10.1093/ref:odnb/4889>, accessed 5 June 2020.
25 J. Houlding, 'Dundas, Sir David (1735?-1820), army officer and military writer', *ODNB*, <https://doi.org/10.1093/ref:odnb/8247>, accessed 5 June 2020.

The Commander-in-Chief's Department

The Commander-in-Chief

Any survey of the Duke of York's staff must commence with the Commander-in-Chief himself, before turning to the functions undertaken by the two principal departments under the adjutant-general and quartermaster-general.

There were several reasons behind the Duke of York's appointment. It owed much to the priorities of coalition warfare, since the British expeditionary force acted as part of the allied combined army, dominated by the Austrians but also containing a sizeable Dutch component. Perhaps most importantly, the Duke was a Prince of the Blood, and could therefore speak on equal terms with the other national commanders, who at various times comprised the Austrian Emperor, the King of Prussia and the Hereditary Prince of Orange. According to the norms of the day, it would not have been easy for an individual of lesser social standing to have participated on an equal footing with coalition partners of this status at councils of war where campaign strategy was decided. Furthermore, the Duke had been groomed for a military life from an early age. He lived in Hanover between 1780–1787 studying the Prussian military system under his uncle, the Duke of Brunswick. Indeed, he met Frederick the Great in 1783 and 1785, attending the Prussian military reviews in those years. Compared to the lack of training available to all officers at this period, the Duke of York's experience would have been very much out of the ordinary at a time when men could rise to relatively senior command at a young age, wealth or connections permitting.[26] According to Herbert Taylor, the Duke was more effective than his staff when he assumed the role of quartermaster-general following the death of Colonel James Moncrieff on 7 September 1793 until the arrival of his successor, Colonel the Hon Henry Fox, at headquarters on 8 October: 'The Duke of York himself, although inexperienced, had more turn for business, and was more capable of directing arrangements in their various detail than most of those about him.'[27] The Duke also took over Sir James Murray's correspondence with Government ministers from his departure in December 1793 until the arrival of Sir James Craig the following month.

Also important were language skills. The Duke was fluent in German, the language of the great majority of troops he would serve with in Flanders, and in French. This was important, since for the greater part of the campaign he directly commanded significant numbers of Austrians and Hanoverians, together with contingents from Hesse Darmstadt, Hesse Cassel, Baden and Brunswick.

The Duke of York was officially appointed: 'Commander in Chief of all our Forces as well horse as Foot that are intended to serve in the United Provinces' by the King on 23 February 1793.[28] Given the discussion above regarding the role and responsibilities of a commander-

---

26 R.N.W. Thomas, 'Command and Control in the First Coalition: The Duke of York in the Low Countries, 1793–1794'. In K.A. Roider, & J.C. Horgan, (eds) *The Consortium on Revolutionary Europe 1750-1850, Proceedings, 1991* (Florida State University: Institute on Napoleon and the French Revolution, 1992), pp.267–273.
27 Taylor (ed.), *Taylor Papers*, p.28.
28 TNA: HO 51/147: pp.28–29, Commission appointing the Duke of York as Commander in Chief, 23 February 1793.

in-chief, it would be worth enumerating what powers were given him by this commission. The Duke was authorised to prepare whatever rules and ordinances he considered necessary for the officers and soldiers under his orders, to hold courts martial and to award the death penalty, or whatever other punishments were deemed fit. He also had the authority to appoint a provost marshal, a judge advocate and to take musters of the troops from which he could sign warrants for their pay according to the establishment level. Officers up to the rank of captain could be appointed to fill vacancies when serving overseas until the King's pleasure was known. The commission covered '… our British and Hanoverian Forces …' and therefore did not encompass Austrian units or those from the other German states that were to come under the Duke's orders. Matters concerning pay and discipline were handled by the respective staff structures of those contingents, meaning that his authority over them was limited to operational dispositions.

Aides-de-Camp

As commander-in-chief, the Duke of York was able to make personal appointments to his immediate staff, the most numerous of which were his aides-de-camp. He commenced the 1793 campaign as a lieutenant general and was therefore entitled to two, these being Captains Henry Clinton and Charles Craufurd, who both reached the army on 23 February 1793.[29] According to Herbert Taylor, these men spoke and wrote German well,[30] probably a criterion for selection. The older of the two was Charles Craufurd, who was born on 12 February 1763 and had just celebrated his thirtieth birthday when appointed. He had been an equerry to the Duke since his return from Hanover in 1787, when he established his own household, remaining as such until 1813. He would have known the Duke well and also corresponded regularly with the Prince of Wales during the campaign. Craufurd was commissioned cornet in the 1st Dragoon Guards in 1778 and promoted lieutenant on 25 April 1781 before transferring on promotion to captain in the 2nd Dragoon Guards on 1 April 1783; he had therefore been in this rank for nearly 10 years when he proceeded to Flanders. It was during this time that he and his younger brother translated an important study on the Seven Years' War by Johann Gottlieb Tielke, formerly a captain in the Saxon artillery, from the original German. The work examined the battles of Zorndorf and Maxen in great detail to illustrate the influence of topography on tactics.[31] Craufurd's relatively slow rate of promotion quickened considerably once he was on campaign and had opportunities of distinguishing himself. These were not long in coming, since he was sent home with despatches reporting the victory at Famars on 23 May 1793, for which he received the brevet of major in his regiment four days later. The Duke thanked the King for this mark of esteem, stating: '… he is a most deserving officer and has been of the greatest service to me.' He further distinguished himself on 27 October 1793 when: 'One squadron of the Queen's

---

29 TNA: AO 16/52: p.98, enclosure in Murray to Watson 16 July 1793 and C. James, '*An Universal Military Dictionary, in English and French; in Which Are Explained the Terms of the Principal Sciences that are Necessary for the Information of an Officer*' (London: T. Egerton, 1816), p.8.
30 Taylor (ed.), *Taylor Papers*, p.28.
31 J.G. Tielke, *An Account of Some of the Most Remarkable Events of the War Between the Prussians, Austrians, and Russians, from 1756 to 1763: and a Treatise on Several Branches of the Military Art* (London: J. Walter, 1787–1788).

Dragoon Guards under Major Craufurd had the advantage of cutting off a French piquit of about two hundred men of whom not one single man escaped.' Both of these events clearly show that Craufurd adopted a dual role, that of aide-de-camp to the commander-in-chief in addition to duties with his regiment. He also had a third responsibility, for occasional diplomatic and other missions. The first of these was during the second half of March 1793 when he was sent for consultations with Coburg and the Duke of Brunswick; a second occurred at the end of the year when he travelled to Vienna. After an active first campaign in Flanders, Craufurd was promoted to lieutenant colonel in the 2nd Dragoon Guards on 1 February 1794 and appointed deputy adjutant-general 12 days later. Charles Craufurd was the elder brother of the more well-known Robert 'Black Bob' Craufurd killed at the head of the Light Division in the Peninsular War.[32]

The majority of the Duke's personal staff served in the Foot Guards, and Henry Clinton was no exception. He was born on 9 March 1771, so had his twenty-second birthday a matter of days after his arrival in Flanders. He was first commissioned into the 11th Regiment in 1787 but transferred to the 1st Foot Guards two years later and, aside from brief interludes with the 15th and 66th Regiments, remained with them during his career. Like Craufurd, Clinton assumed multiple roles in Flanders, being sent to deliver despatches to the Duke of Brunswick one week after his arrival, despite his youth, possibly because he had served as a lieutenant in the Brunswick forces in 1788 (his father had been aide-de-camp to Prince Charles of Brunswick during the Seven Years' War).[33] He also participated in action, serving as a volunteer in the assault on the hornwork at Valenciennes on 26 July 1793 and was shot through the thigh at Willems on 10 May 1794, shortly after receiving promotion to major, having taken home the Duke's despatches following the action at Vaux on 17 April. He was a lively soul and Harry Calvert wrote on 28 August 1794: '... my friend Clinton has been all the time chattering at my elbow'[34] whilst the anonymous 'Officer of the Guards' described him as:

> HAL CL–NT–N, that noisy that venturesome boy,
> Whose sprightliness tends cank'ring care to destroy;[35]

Clinton was subsequently a division commander in the Peninsula where he served at Salamanca, Vittoria, Orthes and Toulouse before commanding the 2nd Division at Waterloo.[36]

---

32 York to George III, 15 March, 31 May, 27 October and 29 November 1793, in Aspinall (ed.), *Later Correspondence*, vol.2, pp.21, 45, 113–114 and 131; 'CRAUFURD, Charles Gregan (1763–1821), of Clumber Park, Notts.', *History of Parliament Online*, <https://www.historyofparliamentonline.org/volume/1790-1820/member/craufurd-charles-gregan-1763-1821>, accessed 11 July 2021 and TNA: HO 51/147: pp.204–205, Commission appointing Major Charles Craufurd deputy adjutant-general, 12 February 1794.
33 WLCL: Henry Clinton Papers: vol.235, Henry Clinton to Sir Henry Clinton, Dordrecht, 9 March 1793.
34 Calvert to his sister, 19 August 1794, in Verney (ed.), *Calvert*, p.309; WLCL: Henry Clinton Papers: vol.235, Sir Henry Clinton to William Henry & Henry Clinton, [8] August 1793.
35 Anon., *Officer of the Guards*, vol.2, pp.42–43.
36 'CLINTON, William Henry (1769–1846), of Foley Place, Marylebone, Mdx.', *History of Parliament Online*, <https://www.historyofparliamentonline.org/volume/1790-1820/member/clinton-william-

York was promoted full general on 12 April 1793 and was thus entitled to four aides-de-camp. The first of these additional men was Lieutenant and Captain Harry Calvert, appointed on 27 April 1793.[37] He was the same age as Craufurd and had spent his early career in the 23rd Regiment, seeing extensive service in America, including at Yorktown, following which he had been a prisoner until 1783. Calvert transferred to the Coldstream Guards on 19 February 1790 and accompanied the regiment to Flanders before subsequently being appointed aide-de-camp. The Duke sent him to summon the fortress of Valenciennes on 27 April 1793 and he was sent home with despatches announcing its capture, being promoted captain and lieutenant colonel in his regiment on Christmas Day that year. As with Craufurd and Clinton, Calvert was also employed on liaison missions to allied headquarters, visiting the Austrians in September 1794 and Brunswick and Berlin in April 1795.[38]

The final aide-de-camp to serve in the 1793 campaign was Captain Lord William Bentinck, whose appointment was announced in general orders on 7 May 1793.[39] He was a younger son of the Duke of Portland, who had briefly served as Prime Minister in 1783 and then Home Secretary from July 1794. Bentinck had been born on 14 September 1774, so at 18 was the youngest of the four aides-de-camp. He was first commissioned into the Coldstream Guards on 27 January 1791, promoted to captain lieutenant in the 2nd Dragoons the following year and then captain in the 11th Light Dragoons in February 1793, the capacity in which he proceeded to Flanders. His swift promotion continued when he was appointed major in the 28th Regiment on 23 February 1794 and then lieutenant colonel in the 24th Light Dragoons on 14 March the same year. There is no record of Bentinck being employed on any diplomatic or liaison mission, which is perhaps unsurprising given his age, though he was noted for having an abundance of energy. He left for England on 10 November 1793, on appointment as an extra aide-de-camp to Lord Moira, but this was cancelled in February 1794 on his promotion to major.[40]

Two further aides-de-camp were appointed prior to the start of the 1794 campaign, taking the places of Craufurd and Bentinck. These were Captains John Walbanke Childers and William Wynyard. Childers, whose appointment was announced in general orders on 6 March 1794, was born in about 1767, so would have been aged 27.[41] He was commissioned

---

henry-1769-1846>, accessed 11 July 2021.
37 NAM: 1985–12–15–4: GO, Tournay, 27 April 1793 and James, *An Universal Military Dictionary*, p.8.
38 H. Chichester and J. Sweetman, 'Calvert, Sir Harry, first baronet (bap. 1763, d. 1826), army officer', *ODNB*, <https://doi.org/10.1093/ref:odnb/4422>, accessed 5 June 2020.
39 NAM: 1985–12–15–4: GO, Tournay, 7 May 1793.
40 BL: Add Ms 37,874: pp.144–145: Calvert to Windham, 10 November 1794, Windham Papers, vol.33; NAM: 1985–12–9: GO, Guernsey, 18 December 1793 and Headquarters, 23 February 1794, and 'CAVENDISH BENTINCK, Lord William Henry (1774–1839)', *History of Parliament Online*, <https://www.historyofparliamentonline.org/volume/1790-1820/member/cavendish-bentinck-william-henry-1774-1839>, accessed 11 July 2021. Aspects of Bentinck's life and career may be found in: C.E. Barrett, *Lord William Bentinck in India, 1828–1835* (Oxford, Oxford University Press, 1954), J. Rosselli, *Lord William Bentinck and the British occupation of Sicily, 1811–1814* (Cambridge: Cambridge University Press, 1956), J. Rosselli, *Lord William Bentinck: The Making of a Liberal Imperialist, 1774–1839* (Sussex: Sussex University Press, 1974), C.H. Phillips (ed.), *The Correspondence of Lord William Cavendish Bentinck: Governor-General of India 1828–1835* (Oxford: Oxford University Press, 1977).
41 NAM: 1985–12–15–5: GO, Harlebeke, 6 March 1794.

into the 11th Light Dragoons, the same regiment as Bentinck, on 20 January 1783 and spent his entire career with them, being promoted major on 1 March 1794 and lieutenant colonel on 2 April 1795.

William Wynyard was another guardsman and, as with Charles Craufurd, was made an equerry to the Duke in 1787. He was born on 20 June 1759, so at 34 was the oldest of all the aides-de-camp to serve in Flanders. He was commissioned into the 30th Regiment in 1771 before transferring to the 64th in 1777, seeing active service in America where he was seriously wounded at Brandywine (11 September 1777) and served as an extra major of brigade in 1781.[42] He transferred to the Coldstream Guards in 1782 and was adjutant during the 1793 campaign when he was placed under arrest by his commanding officer for allegedly failing to report the absence from parade of a brother officer. The case was found unproven at the subsequent court martial and the Duke subsequently told the King that Wynyard's commanding officer, Captain and Lieutenant Colonel Lowther Pennington, was 'perfectly mad'.[43] It may have been as a result of this incident that Wynyard was appointed deputy judge advocate on 15 November 1793 (an appointment he retained until at least March 1795), shortly before he was appointed aide-de-camp on 17 April 1794; this is another example of one man holding multiple roles.[44]

Private Secretary to the Commander-in-Chief

So much for the aides-de-camp. The Duke was also provided with a private secretary, Captain Edwin Hewgill, another Coldstreamer. He was born in 1761, and aged 31 on joining the army in February 1793. He was first commissioned on 19 March 1782, being appointed adjutant in 1787 before promotion to lieutenant and captain on 13 January 1790. Herbert Taylor remarked that Hewgill spoke and wrote German well, a distinct advantage in coalition warfare, and his record of service stated that he also knew French.[45] He had translated from the German the important work on field engineering by the aforementioned Captain J.G. Tielke, published in the English version in 1789.[46] Hewgill was not the only secretary employed by the Duke, since Sir James Murray was also appointed as such 'during the present campaign' for a salary of £300 per annum.[47] As we shall discuss shortly below, Murray was also adjutant-general to the army in Flanders, and his appointment as secretary encompassed correspondence with Government ministers. Herbert Taylor has already been mentioned several times in the context of his pen-portraits of colleagues at headquarters. He was not commissioned (into the 2nd Dragoon Guards) until 25 March 1794, so spent the

---

42 W.C. Ford, *British Officers Serving in the American Revolution 1774–1783* (Brooklyn: Historical Printing Club, 1897), p.186.
43 York to George III, 19 July 1793 in Aspinall (ed.), *Later Correspondence*, vol.2, p.61.
44 TNA: HO 51/147: p.163 and WO 25/41: p.250, commission appointing Capt. William Wynyard as Deputy Judge Advocate and AO 16/53/1: GO, Cateau, 17 April 1794.
45 TNA: WO 25/746/1: pp.20–21, Returns of officers' services: Maj. General Edwin Hewgill and Taylor (ed.), *Taylor Papers*, p.28.
46 J.G. Tielke, *The Field Engineer; or Instructions Upon Every Branch of Field Fortification; Demonstrated by Examples which Occurred in the Seven Years War between the Prussians, the Austrians, and the Russians* (London: J. Walter, 1789).
47 TNA: HO 51/147: p.72, Dundas to Amherst, 15 April 1793. The recipient of this letter is unidentified, but Amherst appears most likely.

campaign of the previous year as a civilian having joined the army as a *protégé* of Sir James Murray whom he had accompanied on a diplomatic mission to Frankfurt in March 1793. He received an appointment as under-secretary for foreign correspondence on 12 April 1793 before becoming Murray's secretary.[48] He evidently made himself useful at headquarters, as on his chief's departure at the end of the year the Duke wrote to the King: 'I shall be very glad to be allowed to keep Mr. Taylor with me to copy for me as he is really a very good young man and very desirous to be of use'.[49] As with all of the Duke's retinue, his promotion was rapid and Taylor progressed to lieutenant in his regiment in July 1794 and captain the following year.

Ancillary Staff

Headquarters also contained various ancillary staff, perhaps the foremost of whom was Dr Richard North, the Duke's personal surgeon. He commenced his career as a hospital mate at Dominica in 1787 before accompanying the army to Flanders in February 1793, being officially appointed staff surgeon on the continent on 18 March. Taylor stated: 'The Duke of York's personal surgeon was very unfit for the post, being negligent and drunken'.[50] Perhaps surprisingly, North was appointed by the Army Medical Department in London, rather than by the Duke of York himself, as an aggrieved Harry Calvert complained to Sir Hew Dalrymple on 28 September 1794: 'A notable instance we have of their discernment and impartiality is the person of the gentleman who has the care of the lives and limbs of his Royal Highness and his family'.[51]

A chaplain appears to have been absent from headquarters in 1793, but the Reverend Mr. Gamble joined at some point prior to January 1794. It is possible that he was the same John Gamble serving as chaplain to the 37th Regiment until 4 April 1793 before transferring to the 11th Light Dragoons on the same date.[52] A post master was also added to the staff when John Neville was announced in general orders on 14 March 1794; he had previously been appointed deputy provost marshal on 28 January.[53] By December that year there were also a number of other individuals on the headquarters staff, comprising the French émigré *Colonel* H.R.N. Anaudin and Messers Nowille, Boulton, Lawson and Spicer together with four orderly dragoons, two orderly sergeants from the heavy cavalry, a sutler, two messengers and 14 dragoons, who comprised an escort. The headquarters baggage was pulled by 44 commissariat horses together with a further 16 more under contract.

In summary: of the six aides-de-camp and two secretaries, four were Guardsmen (of whom three were from the Coldstream Guards) and the remainder cavalrymen, with two men each from both the 2nd Dragoon Guards and 11th Light Dragoons. Two aides-de-camp had also been royal equerries. The Duke was appointed colonel of the Coldstream Guards

---

48 TNA: AO 16/52: p.98, enclosure in Murray to Watson 16 July 1793 and AO 16/52: p.232, enclosure in Watson to Rose, 22 September 1794.
49 York to George III, 15 January 1794, in Aspinall (ed.), *Later Correspondence*, vol.2, p.146.
50 NAM: 1985-12-15-4: GO, 18 March 1793 and Taylor (ed.), *Taylor Papers*, p.28.
51 Calvert to Dalrymple, 28 September 1794, in Verney (ed.), *Calvert*, p.338.
52 BL: Add Ms 46,711: p.88, Bread and forage return for HRH the Commander in Chief & Suite, 31 December 1794 to 2 January 1795, Don Papers, vol.10 and Anon., *A List of the Officers of the Army and Marines with an Index*, (London: War Office, 1793 and 1795).
53 NAM: 1985-12-15-5: GO, Ghent, 28 January 1794 and Courtrai, 14 March 1794.

on 27 October 1784, thus explaining the number of men from this regiment on his personal staff. In terms of age, the Duke was born on 17 August 1763, so was 29 at the start of the 1793 campaign; leaving the teenagers Bentinck and Taylor aside, the remaining six aides-de-camp and secretaries were aged between 22 (Clinton) and 33 (Wynyard) in 1793. Taken together, these men could be seen as a group of friends, many of whom would have known each other and the Duke for some years prior to the Flanders campaign.

Some idea of the group's military experience can also be made by looking at the dates of their first commissions, but these must be used with caution due to the practice of children being given commissions in order to boost their seniority prior to actually joining a unit. This was certainly the case for Wynyard, who on paper had 22 years service at the start of the 1793 campaign. However, he was aged only 12 when commissioned ensign in the 30th Regiment in 1771, so one assumes that his actual service commenced when he was promoted to lieutenant in the 64th in 1777 at age 18. On this basis he would still have had nearly 16 years' service prior to Flanders and, importantly, had served during the American War. Both Craufurd and Calvert were similar, having been commissioned 15 years prior to 1793. The difference between them was that Calvert had seen service in America, during the campaign in the Carolinas ending at Yorktown. Hewgill and Childers had 11 and 10 years' service respectively, but both had been commissioned too late to participate in the American War. Of the remainder, Clinton had seen five years' service, Bentinck two and Taylor none. Taken as a group, the mean number of years' service was just over nine, though five of the eight individuals had 10 years or more. Despite being relatively young, the group as a whole was composed of experienced regimental soldiers, with two having already seen extensive active service.

Before concluding this review of the Commander-in-Chief's Department, some mention should be made of intelligence matters. Perhaps unsurprisingly, references to this subject are relatively sparse in the available documents, but a letter from Sir James Craig to Henry Dundas of 16 February 1794 stated that Harry Calvert: '… has the charge of the department of intelligence & keeps copies of every thing which we receive of that nature'.[54] The memoir of Lieutenant General Samuel Graham, serving as a captain in the 19th Regiment in 1793, makes a direct reference to the 'secret intelligence department' also stating that it was headed by Calvert.[55] Intelligence networks produced reports on the numbers and disposition of enemy troops that were summarised into reports for the Duke of York.[56] Some of the Duke of York's foreign staff also bore some of the responsibility: 'H.R.H. the Commander in Chief orders that all Prisoners & Deserters taken or coming from the enemy and all suspected persons may be taken to Major Hardenberg his aide de camp who will examine them properly.'[57]

---

54 TNA: WO 1/168: p.283, Craig to Dundas, 16 February 1794.
55 J.J. Graham, *Memoir of General Graham with Notices of the Campaigns in which he was Engaged from 1779 to 1801* (Edinburgh: R. & R. Clark, 1862), p.176.
56 For example, TNA: WO 1/168: pp.317–326 and 327–336, 'Extracts of Reports of Secret Intelligence For His Royal Highness the Commander in Chief From Saturday 8th February to 11th inclusive' and 'Substance of Reports for His Royal Highness the Duke of York From the 9th February to the 13th both days inclusive'. Both of these reports relate to 1794.
57 TNA: AO 16/53/1: GO, 29 April 1794.

Major von Hardenburg of the Hanoverian 10th Light Dragoon Regiment was appointed a Hanoverian aide-de-camp to the Duke after his predecessor was killed at Hondschoote on 8 September 1793. There were thought to be spies operating in and around the allied army in March, October and December 1794, but apart from general orders requesting the army to remain vigilant, it is unknown what countermeasures were taken against them, if any.[58] Calvert's intelligence gathering role is also mentioned in his correspondence in September 1794 with Lord St Helens, ambassador at The Hague, when he lamented the absence of an intelligence network in the United Provinces and asked for assistance in establishing one.[59]

The Adjutant-General's Department

Personnel

The relative stability in terms of personnel numbers in the Commander-in-Chief's Department was not the case in either of the other two main headquarters departments of the army. Both the adjutant-general's and the quartermaster-general's underwent a significant enhancement during 1794, as a result of the multifarious functions they were now expected to perform.

Colonel Sir James Murray received a commission from the King on 25 February 1793 appointing him: '… to be Adjutant General to our Forces serving on the Continent under the Command of our most dearly beloved Son His Royal Highness the Duke of York'.[60] As has already been mentioned, Murray also acted: '… during the Continuance of the present Campaign as Secretary to His Royal Highness for the purpose of carrying on his Royal Highness's official Correspondence'.[61] The role of adjutant-general was a key one, so what experience did Murray have to fulfil this demanding position?

Murray was born in 1751, so was aged 42 at the start of the 1793 campaign. He was first commissioned in 1762, at the age of 11, but his actual service would most probably have commenced in 1770 when he was appointed lieutenant in the 19th Regiment. He saw active service in America and the West Indies between 1776 and 1780, ending the American War as a lieutenant colonel. After some years on half pay,[62] he received promotion to colonel and was appointed aide-de-camp to the King on 18 November 1789. Aside from his Royal connection, Murray also had diplomatic experience, being sent to the allied headquarters at Koblenz in 1792. A further mission in January 1793 saw him despatched to The Hague, where he consulted Lord Auckland, the British ambassador, and then to the Prussian headquarters at Frankfurt, from where he returned in March.[63] By the start of 1793 Murray

---

58 Demet, 'We are Accustomed to do Our Duty', p.135; NAM: 1985-12-15-5: GO, Courtrai, 15 March 1794 and TNA: AO 16/53/6: GO, Arnheim, 27 October 1794.
59 Calvert to Lord St. Helens, 13 September 1794, in Verney (ed.), *Calvert*, p.324.
60 TNA: HO 51/147: pp.71–72 and WO 25/41 p.61: Commission appointing Sir James Murray adjutant-general, 25 February 1793.
61 TNA: HO 51/147: p.72: Dundas to Amherst, 15 April 1793.
62 Unemployed commissioned officers were entitled to receive half pay as a retainer for future services.
63 R.N.W. Thomas, 'Pulteney, Sir James Murray, seventh baronet (c. 1755–1811), army officer', *ODNB*, <https://doi.org/10.1093/ref:odnb/19620>, accessed 5 June 2020 and 'MURRAY (afterwards PULTENEY), Sir James', 7th Bt. (c.1755–1811), of Park Lane and Marble Hall, Twickenham, Mdx.'

therefore had over 25 years' service, five years of which had been spent in active theatres of operations, and possessed useful diplomatic experience. However, Murray's tenure as adjutant-general lasted only until the close of the 1793 campaign when he was recalled. What had gone wrong?

The clue to Murray's failure as adjutant-general lay in his character, which was perhaps best described by Henry Bunbury, who served with him in the Helder Expedition of 1799. He noted that Sir James (who changed his name to Pulteney in 1794) was 'a very odd man' and 'In point of natural abilities he was of a high rank.' He was 'Remarkably good-tempered, cool, unpretending, utterly indifferent to danger or to hardships,' but he continued:

> Sir James was dreamy, and he liked better to amuse his mind with doubts and varied trials of a problem than to end it by a decision. His view of a subject was nine times out of ten right; but he had no confidence in his own opinion, and he lazily surrendered his better judgement on matters which demanded action. Pulteney had awkward manners; he received officers uncouthly; did not know, or seem to care, how to put them at their ease; and till one came to know him in intimacy, as I did a few years afterwards, the kindness of his nature, the extent of his knowledge, and the largeness of his views remained hidden under a grotesque and somewhat repulsive exterior.[64]

The anonymous 'Officer of the Guards' provided a vignette of him as 'Sir Jamie' at a headquarters dinner just after the Dutch had abandoned the fortified town of Menen on 12 September 1793:

> The – smil'd applause: and Sir J–m–ie demanded
> Permission to speak, which was not countermanded.
> ' 'Twas a pity,' he said, 'it appear'd to him plain,
> Our Allies were unable their post to maintain:
> But, we sure might retake it, or let it alone,
> He was much at a loss which was best to be done;
> In short, what the –, might think proper to do,
> Was surely the properest plan to pursue.'
> And J–hn–t–ne, Pr–ce J–hn,[65] nay we all, to a man,
> Declar'd he had struck out a wonderful plan.
> The — then triumphantly rose from his seat,
> And said, ' 'tis resolv'd – we'll the enemy meet'.[66]

History of Parliament Online, <https://www.historyofparliamentonline.org/volume/1790-1820/member/murray-%28afterwards-pulteney-%29-sir-james-1755-1811>, accessed 11 July 2021.

64 H. Bunbury, *Narratives of some Passages in the Great War with France (1799–1810)* (London: Peter Davies, 1927), pp.30–31.

65 Colonel Robert Johnstone, deputy quartermaster general; 'Prince John' was Captain John Murray. S.G.P. Ward, The author of the 'Accurate and Impartial Narrative', *Journal of the Society for Army Historical Research*, vol.70, 1992, pp.211–223.

66 Anon., *Officer of the Guards*, vol.1, p.96.

Murray was not to remain in post for much longer. He was recalled to London for consultations and interviewed by Henry Dundas on 20 December. He was persuaded to relinquish the adjutant-generalship and instead assume command of the Scotch Brigade.[67] This did not go down well, as Dundas reported to the King: 'He did not say a great deal but seemed much hurt, and pressed much that Mr Dundas would give the reasons which had induced your Majesty to take this determination.' Dundas replied that the King thought: '… his talents were more calculated for the field than the desk'.[68]

The sacking of Murray was done as if by the King, thus shielding Government ministers and the Duke of York from embarrassment in any future dealings with him. This was just as well, since he was one of the Duke's formation commanders at the Helder in 1799. The Duke expressed his considerable relief to his father, also providing further details of Murray's failings:

> I trust that your Majesty is thoroughly sensible of the extreme delicacy I felt concerning Sir James Murray who is without doubt a perfectly good man, and has very good military talents, but unfortunately is not endowed with that spirit of exactness and order which are absolutely necessary in an Adjutant General, besides that he certainly does not possess that manner of writing which is requisite for his publick correspondence.[69]

Despite being his *protégé*, Herbert Taylor noted that Murray: '… wanted the official habits and the method required for the duties of Adjutant-General' and the Duke, in another expression of thanks to the King concluded that Murray was: '… a very worthy man and a very good officer, yet was by no means fit for the office of Adjutant-General'.[70]

So much for Murray. The other members of the adjutant-general's department in 1793 included his two deputies, John Hayes St Leger, appointed on 30 March, and *Oberstleutnant* Hacke, subsequently replaced by *Major* Löw of the Hanoverian Light Battalion on 17 August.[71] St Leger, otherwise known as 'Handsome Jack,' was born on 23 July 1756, so was aged 36 at the commencement of the campaign. He served in the 55th, 90th and 65th Regiments before transferring to the 1st Foot Guards as captain and lieutenant colonel on 5 September 1787. He was one of the Prince of Wales' boon companions and appointed to his household in 1784 and again in 1787 after a break when he lived in Ireland recouping his finances. His presence in Flanders was in fact fortuitous, as he was only ordered on service due to the illness of Captain and Lieutenant Colonel Charles Talbot, who was: '… confined

---

67 Originally formed in the sixteenth century from Protestants volunteering to serve the Dutch Republic. This spelling is taken from the 1795 *Army List* after the unit transferred to the British Army.
68 Henry Dundas to George III, 21 December 1793, in Aspinall (ed.), *Later Correspondence*, vol.2, pp.136–137.
69 York to George III, 3 December 1793, in Aspinall (ed.), *Later Correspondence*, vol.2, p.131.
70 York to George III, 31 December 1793, in Aspinall (ed.), *Later Correspondence*, vol.2, pp.141–142 and Taylor (ed.), *Taylor Papers*, p.28.
71 TNA: HO 51/147: p.97 and WO 25/41: p.146: Commission appointing Lieutenant-Colonel John St Leger deputy adjutant-general, 30 March 1793 and NAM: 1985-12-15-4: GO, Turcoing, 17 August 1793.

by illness at Gravesend'.[72] Once in theatre, his appointment must, at least in part, have been the result of his royal connections. Herbert Taylor stated that: 'Colonel St. Leger, was quick and intelligent, but equally had not acquired official habits'.[73] St Leger was appointed a brigadier on the continent of Europe on 20 November 1793 and removed from his post of deputy adjutant-general when appointed deputy barrack master-general on 22 January 1794.[74] Löw was selected by the Duke as a replacement for *Oberst-Lieutenant* Hacke who: '… has the misfortune of being already laid up near six weeks with a violent fit of ghout, in consequence of a very bad fall from his horse.' He is referred to as '… the eldest Captain Löw of the Foot Guards…' in the Duke's letter to the King requesting both him and his promotion to major as: '… there would be great difficulties if the officer who acts as my German Adjutant-General had not the rank of a field officer'.[75] The final member of the department was Captain Thomas Carteret Hardy who was appointed at an unknown date in 1793 as assistant deputy adjutant-general. Like Craufurd, he was an officer in the 2nd Dragoon Guards, but left the department at the start of 1794 to become St Leger's assistant barrack master-general on 5 February.[76]

As far as the British members of the department were concerned, the 1794 campaign witnessed a new team with all three of its former occupants removed and a new set of men installed. The principal conundrum was to where find a new adjutant-general, but the Duke had already written to the King on 3 December, more than two weeks before Murray's fateful interview with Henry Dundas, with his own suggestion: 'I really know no one officer who I could wish to propose to your Majesty as Adjutant General, but from everything which I have heard, for I am very little acquainted with him, Colonel Craig is a very exact officer and one who is thoroughly fit for that office.'[77]

Craig was appointed adjutant-general on 20 December, the same day that Murray resigned, and reached headquarters at Ghent by 13 January 1794.[78] One week later, the Duke was glad to report: 'Colonel Craig has now begun to do the duty of Adjutant-General; he appears to me to be a very clear headed man, and very exact in his business, and he already relieves me from a great deal of trouble.'[79]

James Henry Craig was born in 1748, so was aged 45 at the time of his appointment. He was commissioned into the 30th Regiment in 1763, before promotion to captain in the 47th in 1771. He saw extensive service in America, being present at Bunker Hill (17 June 1775)

---

72 NAM: 1985-12-15-4: GO, 11 March 1793.
73 'TAYLOR, Sir Herbert (1775-1839), of Fan Court, Chertsey, Surr. and Little Camden House, Kensington, Mdx.', *History of Parliament Online*, <https://www.historyofparliamentonline.org/volume/1820-1832/member/taylor-sir-herbert-1775-1839>, accessed 11 July 2021 and Taylor (ed.), *Taylor Papers*, p.28.
74 TNA: HO 51/147: pp.199-200, Commission appointing Colonel John St. Leger Barrack Master, 22 January 1794.
75 York to George III, 2 August 1793, in Aspinall (ed.), *Later Correspondence*, vol.2, p.69.
76 NAM: 1985-12-15-4: GO, Ghent, 5 February 1794.
77 York to George III, 3 December 1793, in Aspinall (ed.), *Later Correspondence*, vol.2, p.131.
78 TNA: HO 51/147: p.172 and WO 25/41: p.267, Commission appointing Colonel James Henry Craig adjutant-general, 20 December 1793 and York to George III, 15 January 1794, in Aspinall (ed.), *Later Correspondence*, vol.2, p.146.
79 York to George III, 22 January 1794, in Aspinall (ed.), *Later Correspondence*, vol.2, p.148.

where he was severely wounded, Ticonderoga (5–6 July 1777) and Saratoga (19 September 1777) where his distinguished services resulted in him being sent home with the dispatches; for this he was promoted major in the 82nd Regiment on Christmas Day 1777. He spent February until November 1781 commanding at Wilmington, being promoted to lieutenant colonel in his regiment on the last day of that year. Craig transferred to the 16th Regiment on 30 June 1783, when the 82nd was reduced, and was promoted colonel in the Army on 18 November 1790. He spent much time on the continent studying Prussian military tactics and it was his regiment that was used to trial David Dundas' *Principles of Military Movements* published in 1788. At the time of his appointment, Craig was serving as lieutenant governor of Jersey.[80]

Regarding the remaining members of the department, we have already noted Charles Craufurd's switch from aide-de-camp to deputy adjutant-general on 12 February 1794, replacing St Leger. Craufurd became unwell in October 1794 and returned home, being replaced by Lieutenant Colonel George Don on 21 November; Don became the *de facto* adjutant-general during Craig's absences from headquarters.[81] Captain George Gordon was appointed deputy assistant adjutant-general on 11 March 1794 joined on 2 April by Lieutenant William Eden in the same appointment, though he only stayed until July before transferring to the quartermaster-general's department.[82] Eden is likely to have owed this to his uncle, Lord Auckland, who was ambassador at The Hague, whereas Gordon was another 11th Light Dragoon (together with the Duke's aides-de-camp Bentinck and Childers) and was transferred from the quartermaster-general's department with responsibility for inspecting all foreign corps raised for the service of Great Britain.

The increased number of British troops in theatre led to the appointment of two more deputy assistant adjutants-general in June and July 1794; these were Captain Robert Anstruther and Lieutenant Robert Brinley respectively.[83] Brinley had actually been in post since 25 November 1793, but with the force commanded by Lord Moira whilst Anstruther could have owed his appointment to being an officer of the 3rd Foot Guards.

In summary, the department consisted of an adjutant-general with two deputies (one British, one Hanoverian) and a deputy assistant during the 1793 campaign. This was increased by the addition of two deputy assistants in 1794 after all of the British members had been replaced. As we have seen, the principal activities undertaken related to the administration of discipline, the preparation of all orders and regulations and the collection and formulation of strength returns. It now remains to see how these functions were exercised in practice.[84]

---

80   J. Sturgis, 'Craig, Sir James Henry (1748–1812), army officer and governor-in-chief of British North America', *ODNB*, <https://doi.org/10.1093/ref:odnb/6572>, accessed 5 June 2020.
81   TNA: AO 16/53/7: GO, Arnhem, 21 November 1794; Calvert to Dalrymple, 12 October 1794, in Verney (ed.), *Calvert*, p.359 and S.G. Benady, 'Don, Sir George (1756–1832)', *ODNB*, <https://doi.org/10.1093/ref:odnb/7791>, accessed 26 February 2021.
82   Gordon – NAM: 1985-12-15-5: GO, Courtrai, 11 and 25 March 1794. Eden – NAM: 1985-12-15-5: GO, St Amand, 2 April 1794 and Kelemhoute, 23 July 1794.
83   Anstruther – TNA: AO 16/53/3: GO, 9 June 1794. Brinley – NAM: 1985-12-9: GO, 25 November 1793 and TNA: AO 16/53/4: GO, Kelemhoute, 23 July 1794.
84   Although dating from a slightly later period, the following are useful: Anon., *The Eleventh Report of the Commissioners of Military Enquiry. Departments of the Adjutant-General and Quarter-Master*

Discipline

A thorough survey of discipline during the Flanders campaign would require a complete series of records for both regimental and general courts martial. Unfortunately, these do not exist at a regimental level, and would take more space than could be warranted in this analysis of the disciplinary function of the adjutant-general's department. What will be discussed here are the various categories of case that came before general courts martial, which, by definition, tended to be of a more serious nature.

Theft and plundering represented the single greatest cause of disciplinary breaches and were a feature from the start of 1793 until 1795 when the army departed Germany. Typically, complaints would be received from local inhabitants, which filtered up to headquarters, the Duke would publish a general order about plundering, a court martial would be held and the offenders punished; the process would then be repeated. The first admonition on this subject was issued on 23 May 1793:

> H.R.H. the Commander in Chief is much concerned at the repeated Complaints, that are made of the Scandalous practice of plundering and Marauding.
>
> H.R.H. finds it therefore necessary to inform the troops that he has therefore Given orders, to the Provost Martial, to use every Exertion towards apprehending all Plunderers & Marauders, as His Royal Highness is determined to use the most serious measures, to put a Stop to such disgraceful Behaviour.[85]

Officers may have been complicit in this, knowingly or otherwise, since a general order of 30 August 1793 warned that any who had purchased plundered articles must return them at once, with no refund.[86]

Stringent orders against plundering multiplied during 1794, probably due to the significant influx of recruits. The first of these was issued in the general orders of 20 May following a request from the Austrian Emperor on the subject, from which it is reasonable to conclude that looting was not solely a British problem but one affecting the combined army as a whole. General officers and officers commanding regiments were urged to get the problem under control.[87] This appears to have had little effect, as a more strongly worded order was issued two months later on 24 July: 'It is with the utmost concern that H.R.H. the Commander in chief has perceived the very Scandalous height to which plundering and meroding [sic] of every Species has gotten into the army under his Command.'[88]

The failure was attributed to: '... the inattention of the Officers Commanding Regiments.' The Duke threatened two measures should a continuation occur. First, 'H.R.H. will put in arrest the first Officer Commanding their Reg'ts in which any disobedience of Insubordination to order is perceiv'd' and second, as far as the culprits were concerned: '... two Drum'rs & a Trumpeter are continually to attend the provost Guard to execute

---

General (London: House of Commons, 1810) and Anon., *A Collection of Orders, Regulations, and Instructions for the Army; on Matters of Finance and Points of Discipline* (London: T. Egerton, 1807).
85 NAM: 1985–12–15–4: GO, Famars, 23 May 1793.
86 NAM: 1985–12–15–4: GO, Camp before Dunkirk, 30 August 1793.
87 TNA: AO 16/53/2: GO, Tournay, 20 May 1794.
88 TNA: AO 16/53/4: GO, Calnhoot, 24 July 1794.

such punishment as the due discharge of the duty of that Officer may Oblige him to inflict.' Once again, this failed to achieve the desired result and a general order of 23 September stated that five men belonging to the 38th Regiment were to be executed for being caught plundering but a stay had been given in the hope that this would encourage the men to desist.[89] It did not, and things worsened as the army retreated through the United Provinces into Germany. One variation on plundering occurred in February 1795 when men from the Hanoverian *jäger* shot many deer in a park, leading Wallmoden to order their commanding officer to pay compensation.[90]

Churches were a particular target, with a reward of 20 crowns being offered to anyone informing on the culprits who plundered the church at Aulnois on 25 May 1793. The church at Saultain was robbed on 21 July 1793 of a silver ball, a small silver cup and a large silver chalice, for which a reward of 40 crowns was offered to anyone providing information together with a free pardon to any offender who turned in his accomplices. Incidents continued, however, with the magistrates of Kortrijk complaining of criminal behaviour in churches in the town. Commanding officers were instructed to let their men know that anyone offending in this way would be severely punished.[91]

Another form of indiscipline noticed in general orders was drunkenness – a besetting sin of the British military. The first recorded instance was on 12 March 1793 when Sergeant Moore and Corporal Laurence of an unidentified Guards regiment were demoted to private for '… Irregular & Unsoldierlike Behaviour while on duty,' which appears to have been due to: '… neglect of duty and Drunkenness in particular'.[92] Far more serious was the case of David Cogan of the 14th Regiment, who deserted to the enemy on 5 July 1793 from the trenches before Valenciennes. He was recaptured when the town fell and executed on 5 August.[93] Two of the most notorious incidents occurred within 10 days of each other. The first formed the subject of a general order dated 31 March 1794, after three men plundered a property in the village of Warlem and shot the householder when he offered resistance; the second was outlined in the general order of 10 April when two men of the 14th Regiment attempted the same crime, shooting a mother and mortally wounding her baby.[94]

The orders and instructions issued from the commander-in-chief, via the adjutant-general's department, applied both to soldiers and female camp followers. Rose Archer and Sarah Cotton attached to the Guards Flank Battalion were pardoned for theft following the earnest entreaties of the inhabitants of Pittehem but they were no longer permitted to remain with the army. A general order dated 16 July 1793 stated that: 'Any Women Employed in the Hospital who may be Guilty of any improper Conduct will not be suffered to remain with the army, nor will they be allowed for their passage to England.' [95]

---

89   TNA: AO 16/53/6: GO, Grosbeck, 23 September 1794.
90   TNA: AO 16/53/7: GO, Osnabruck, 20 February 1795.
91   NAM: 1985-12-15-4: GO, Estreux, 29 May 1793 and 22 July 1793 and NAM:1985-12-15-5: GO, Courtrai, 21 March 1794.
92   NAM: 1985-12-15-4: Brigade Orders, 8 March 1793.
93   NAM: 1985-12-15-4: GO, Estrew, 4 August 1793.
94   NAM: 1985-12-15-5: GO, St Amand, 31 March 1795 [*sic* 1794] and 10 April 1794.
95   NAM: 1985-12-15-4: GO, Courtray, 21 April 1793 and Estreux, 16 July 1793.

Oversight of military justice, including the infliction of punishments lay with the judge advocate general and the provost marshal.

Issuing Orders

A critical function of the adjutant-general's department was the transmission of orders. A general order of 10 April 1793 stated: '… the Majors of Brigade & the Adjutants of Regiments are to be every day at Head Quarters for orders.' This was in accordance with a routine chain of command, as set out in a general order dated 28 August 1793 whilst the army was besieging Dunkirk:

> The General Officers of the Day are to attend at orderly time, the days they come on duty.
>
> An orderly officer from each Corps on duty, to attend on the Lieutenant Gen'l of the Day, to carry his orders to the different Corps.
>
> The Lieutenant Gen'l of the Day will station himself, at the first House, on the right of the Canal, going towards the Town near the Pontoon Bridge.
>
> The General Officers of the Day, are to be at 5 o'Clock in the Evening, at their respective posts and Enable themselves to make the distribution of the Troops immediately on their arrival.[96]

Force commanders also aimed to improve communications by embedding personnel in other contingents of the allied army as liaison officers. For example, Major General Lake appointed *Kapitein* Fagel of the Dutch Guards as his aide-de-camp in March 1793. British orderly officers were required to attend every day at Cobourg's headquarters from May 1793 onwards and at *Feldzeugmeister* Alvinczi's during the siege of Dunkirk. Meanwhile, Lieutenant Henry George Johnston of the 6th Dragoons was attached to the Archduke Karl's headquarters and Lieutenant and Captain John Murray of the 3rd Foot Guards was appointed aide-de-camp to *Feldmarschall* von Freytag. When Freytag was recalled in March 1794, Murray was made an additional aide-de-camp to the Duke of York, though no official notification of this has yet been found. York referred to '… my Aide de Camp Captain Murray…' in his letter of 28 April 1794 to Henry Dundas, also sending him home with the official despatch reporting the victory at Beaumont fought two days previously.[97]

The campaign of 1794 witnessed a change in the system of passing orders with the generals of the day assuming a less prominent role. Instead, orders were passed direct to formation commanders and individual units. A general order of 25 February required all cavalry regiments to send a 'very careful' orderly-man to headquarters to attend constantly on Lieutenant General Sir William Erskine, whilst the major of brigade and an orderly officer from each regiment were to attend for orders at headquarters every morning at 10:00

---

96 NAM: 1985-12-15-4: GO, Antwerp, 10 April 1793 and 1985-12-15-4: GO, Camp before Dunkirk, 28 August 1793.

97 NAM: 1985-12-15-4: GO, 11 March 1793 and Baiseaux, 21 May 1793 and Camp before Dunkirk, 27 August 1793; TNA: AO 16/53/3: GO, Tournay, 15 June 1794 and WO 1/168: p.789: York to Dundas, 28 April 1794.

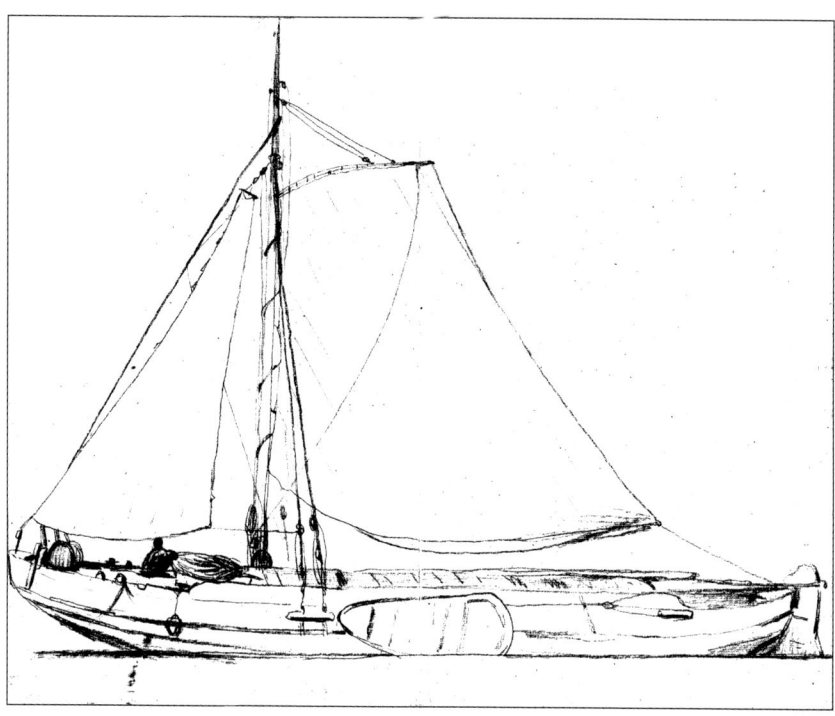
Schuit, by Jan Weissenbruch. (Rijksmuseum, Amsterdam, RP-T-1938-80)

a.m., though this was changed to 6:00 a.m. on 1 August. By June 1794, it was decreed that an orderly officer from each brigade must be permanently at headquarters where a room was to be provided for them, with a daily changeover of personnel at 10:00 a.m. They were instructed not to absent themselves under any circumstances, as they were regarded as being on guard.[98] During the second half of 1794, new formalities were imposed. Brigade-majors were to ensure that non-commissioned officers sent to headquarters were there by 9:00 a.m. and were 'perfectly uniformly dressed'. The senior sergeant was to command, and to give the aide-de-camp in waiting a list of their names, regiments and the brigades to which they belonged. Orderly officers were also instructed to hand their names to the adjutant-general, together with the brigades to which they were attached; relieving officers likewise. If they did not already have their horses standing by, orderly officers were to send for them at once.[99]

Once orders had been passed down to the formation level, staff work was undertaken by brigade majors together with unit quartermasters. An example concerned the Brigade of Guards at the end of March 1793: 'The Baggage of the Brigade to be embarked on Board

---

98 NAM: 1985-12-15-5: GO, Harlebeke, 25 February 1794; TNA: AO 16/53/3: GO, 20 June 1794 and AO 16/53/4: GO, Roosendael, 2 August 1794.
99 TNA: AO 16/53/5: GO, Oosterhout, 17 August 1794 and AO 16/53/7: GO, Arnhem, 29 December.1794.

the Schutes, as soon as possible. The Major of Brigade will shew the Quartermasters the different schutes appointed for them.'[100]

Unfortunately, brigade orderly books do not appear to have survived, so the only insight we have regarding the transmission of orders from the brigade level downwards is for the first three weeks of the 1793 campaign when the Foot Guards were the only British troops present in theatre.

Aside from operational matters, one other category of orders issued by the adjutant-general concerned tactics. All of these were from 1794, with the first, on 26 February for the cavalry to saddle-up at daybreak and to remain so for a period of two hours. Interesting information is sometimes conveyed in passing, as on 28 June, during the march of Lord Moira's force from Ostend to join the army: 'The 87th Regiment which by his Majesty's permission is to serve as a Light Corps under Lieutenant Col. Doyle will head the column of infantry.'[101]

A long section on battalion formation and tactics, especially relating to the use of a third rank, was contained in a general order of 27 July, whilst considerable detail was provided on 5 August regarding the composition and posting of picquets.[102]

Strength Returns

In addition to discipline and orders, the third main function of the adjutant-general's department was to maintain as near constant a record of the effective strength as possible. The principal method was to compile weekly and monthly returns from each regiment. Both the number and variety of these rose significantly almost as soon as Sir James Craig took over the role of adjutant-general, indicating an increased desire on the part of headquarters to have detailed and regular information regarding both men and equipment.

According to a general order dated 17 February 1794, weekly reports were submitted every Monday, but by 18 July the need for up-to-date information was clearly more urgent. From now on, unit returns were to be made daily at morning roll-call and sent to brigade majors. Each brigade state was then to be forwarded to the adjutant-general's office, where they were consolidated in a morning report submitted to the Duke of York in person.[103]

Specific returns were often demanded. For example, on 14 July 1793 all units were asked to list officers entitled to receive bât and forage money, including their dates of joining the army on the continent.[104] On the same date, a return of men fit for duty in the trenches at Dunkirk was to be sent to the deputy adjutant-general by 6:00 p.m.[105] Regiments were asked on 25 April 1793 to send returns listing the name of the baker in each unit, and on 9 June 1794 the names of each unit's surgeon and surgeon's mate, including their commission dates

---

100 NAM: 1985–12–15–4: GO, 31 March 1793. A Schuyt, or schuit, is a Dutch boat with a flat bottom. The major of brigade was Lieutenant and Captain Lloyd Hill, 1st Foot Guards.
101 NAM: 1985–12–15–9: GO, 28 June 1794.
102 NAM: 1985–12–15–5: GO, Harlebeke, 26 February 1794 and TNA: AO 16/53/4: GO, Rosendale, 27 July 1794 and Oosterhoute, 5 August 1794.
103 NAM: 1985–12–15–4: GO, 2 March 1793; 1985–12–15–5: GO, Ghent, 7 February 1794; TNA: AO 16/53/2: GO, Tournay, 23 May 1794 and AO 16/53/4: GO, Contigh, 18 July 1794.
104 Bât and forage money was paid to captains of companies and other officers authorised to purchase and maintain bât horses used for carrying camp equipage.
105 NAM: 1985–12–15–4: GO, Estreux, 14 July 1793.

where known.[106] Another general order (10 August 1794) requested the names and ranks of each regiment's officers and their seniority dates, with immediate effect.[107] The army's going into winter quarters invariably resulted in many officers departing on home leave, with others intending to do so as soon as possible. As part of preparations for the 1794 campaign, regiments were required to make returns of officers currently absent, how long their leave had been granted for, and when they were expected back. Before an officer went on leave, details were to be entered in a passport, to be shown to Major General Stewart, commanding at the embarkation port of Ostend.[108] Other forms of losses also had to be recorded. These included returns listing the names of men captured, sick in hospital, killed and wounded, or otherwise missing from their units together with the dates thereof and the reason.[109] The adjutant-general's department was also responsible for combing units to find drivers for the artillery due to the greatly increased number of guns joining the army during the summer of 1794, an issue that is discussed further in Chapter 6.

Weapons, Clothing and Equipment

In addition to its main involvement with personnel, the adjutant-general's office was also responsible for the supply of arms, clothing and equipment. The first mention of the subject in general orders was on 8 January 1794 concerning articles of clothing donated to the army by well-wishers in Britain, which were considered as part of the men's regimental equipment. They were not under any circumstances to be disposed of by the troops, who would be made accountable at the regimental inspection. A general order of 20 March 1794 requested all units to complete a return signed by the commanding officer and brigade commander listing the number of arms existing in each regiment. Proformas were used to specify the number of each item that was serviceable, unserviceable, wanting to complete (by which is meant completing the regimental inventory) and alterations since the last return (lost in action or accidentally damaged) before submitting to the adjutant-general's office on the last day of every month. A similar return was requested by each unit showing the state of its clothing.[110]

The department was also engaged during 1794 in compiling returns of equipment losses suffered by individuals and units. A general order of 7 February required all regiments to submit claims to brigade majors, enabling them to be settled by the adjutant-general during his time in London. Repeat requests were made 10 days later, and in May and June for losses sustained in the new campaign.[111]

---

106 Bakers – NAM: 1985-12-15-4: GO, Tournay, 25 April 1793. Surgeons – TNA: AO 16/53/3: GO, 9 June 1794.
107 TNA: AO 16/53/5: GO, Oosterhout, 10 August 1794.
108 NAM: 1985-12-15-5: GO, 1 January 1794 and Ghent, 4 and 10 February 1794.
109 Prisoners – NAM: 1985-12-15-5: GO, Ghent, 28 January and 17 February 1794. Sick – NAM:1985-12-15-5: GO, Ghent, 7 February 1794. Killed and wounded – TNA: AO 16/53/2: GO, Tournay, 11 May 1794 and AO 16/53/7: GO, Deventer, 19 January 1795. Missing – TNA: AO 16/53/7: GO, Rhené, 15 February 1795.
110 NAM: 1985-12-15-5: GO, Ghent, 8 January 20 March 1794; TNA: AO 16/53/2: GO, Tournay, 3 June 1794; AO 16/53/5: GO, 9 August 1794 and AO 16/53/7: GO, Osnabrück, 20 February 1795.
111 NAM: 1985-12-15-5: GO, Ghent, 7 and 17 February 1794; TNA: AO 16/53/2: GO, Tournay, 25 May 1794 and AO 16/53/3: GO, Tournay, 17 June 1794.

On 17 January 1794, units were instructed to send returns of bedding and all other articles they had received for their barracks to brigade majors for forwarding to the adjutant-general's office, together with lists of their officers' quarters. No doubt in preparation for the forthcoming campaign, further returns were requested on 20 January, this time of each regiment's camp equipage, accounting for any deficiencies and stating the condition of each item. Both of these returns were still being asked for one month later, on 17 February.[112] The department also assisted units in obtaining equipment they needed. All except heavy cavalry regiments had a tumbrel for their small arms ammunition, which was usually obtained on application to the artillery park, though a general order dated 9 December 1794 offered to obtain these for units without one if they could submit a requisition. Regimental surgeons were also invited on 20 February 1795 to send returns of medicines they required so the adjutant-general's office could obtain them.[113]

Supervision of Hospitals

The adjutant-general's department was also responsible for the supervision of army hospitals. A general order dated 17 June 1794 directed a captain and subaltern immediately to attend the hospitals at Ghent and St Ghislain, reporting their state and condition on arrival. This was established as a monthly duty henceforth, involving roll calling and ensuring cleanliness, regular messing and general good conduct. Any directions or orders from the physicians and surgeons were also to be enforced. A subsequent general order of 13 November stated that men sent to the hospitals must be accompanied by officers or non-commissioned officers in proportion to their numbers and to ensure that they did not discard their necessaries en route as had frequently been done. Anything found to be missing would be charged to each regiment using lists to be prepared by the hospital purveyor.[114]

It may be inferred from the oft repeated orders from headquarters that the greater volume of paperwork required in 1794 placed a burden on already hard-pressed regimental staff, especially since operations increasingly dictated a war of movement. Without it, however, the ability of the headquarters staff to manage troops and equipment was significantly compromised.

The Quartermaster-General's Department

Personnel

The contingent first ordered to Flanders was made up of a detachment from the Brigade of Foot Guards. One of their number, Colonel Robert Johnstone of the 3rd Foot Guards, was appointed as its quartermaster-general on 11 March 1793 and two days later to the expeditionary force as a whole. Johnstone had been commissioned into the 3rd Foot Guards on 5 April 1773 and on 18 November 1790 was promoted to colonel in the Army. According to the anonymous 'Officer of the Guards', he had seen service with the Scotch Brigade, a

---

112 NAM: 1985-12-15-5: GO, Ghent, 17 and 20 January and 17 February 1794.
113 NAM: 1985-12-15-5: GO, Courtray, 16 March 1794; TNA: AO 16/53/7: GO, Arnhem, 9 December 1794 and AO 16/53/7: GO, Osnabrück, 20 February 1795.
114 TNA: AO 16/53/3: GO, Tournai, 17 June 1794 and AO 16/53/6: GO, Arnhem, 13 November 1794.

formation consisting of several battalions in the Dutch Army, so was able to speak Dutch.[115] He was presumably familiar with the country, but no evidence of previous staff experience has been found.

Johnstone only held the position until 18 May, when he was succeeded by Colonel James Moncrieff of the Royal Engineers, at which point Johnstone became his deputy.[116] Herbert Taylor described him as: 'a good-hearted but irritable little man, very vain, and very empty, who owed his appointment to his knowledge of the French and German languages and to the ready use of his pencil.'[117] Despite this rather unflattering description, the 'Officer of the Guards' was kinder to Johnstone: 'Great minds must at times unbend; a Prime Minister has been known to chase a butterfly; and it was a favourite amusement at head-quarters to open batteries with cherry-stones, or pellets of bread upon the D.Q.M.G. whose good nature was proverbial.'[118]

James Moncrieff was selected as quartermaster-general by the Government and interviewed by the Prime Minister on the morning of 7 March when he was offered the position. He arrived at headquarters at Dordrecht on 24 March, though his commission was backdated to 25 February and for some unknown reason the appointment was not announced in general orders until 12 May.[119] It was highly unusual for a technical officer to occupy the position, but one reason behind it lay in Moncrieff's considerable active service experience. He was born in 1744, so aged 48 or 49 at the time he proceeded to Flanders, thus being by some years the oldest man on the staff. He had trained at the Royal Academy, Woolwich, between 1759–1762 and was commissioned as an ensign in the 100th Regiment, with which he served at the taking of Havana in June 1762. He transferred to the Royal Engineers on the disbandment of his regiment in November 1763, remaining in either the West Indies or North America until the outbreak of the American War of Independence. He served at the Battle of Brandywine (11 September 1777), but it was in the southern theatre that he distinguished himself most, serving at Stono Ferry (20 June 1779) and Savannah (9 October 1779), where he was responsible for constructing fortifications enabling the British to hold the town. He participated in the capture of Charleston (April–May 1780) and was placed in charge of its defences thereafter. Back in Britain, Moncrieff was appointed deputy quartermaster-general on 14 July 1790 and served as quartermaster-general to the troops encamped at Bagshot during the summer of 1792, so owed the same appointment three years later to extensive active service combined with staff experience. The numerous fortified towns in Flanders made it highly desirable to have an officer of proven experience and distinction as the senior Royal Engineer with the army – another example of dual roles held by members of the staff.[120]

---

115 NAM: 1985-12-15-4: GO, 11 March 1793; TNA: AO 16/52 p44: Watson to Rose, 7 May 1793 and Anon., *Officer of the Guards*, vol.1, pp.100–101.
116 TNA: HO 51/147: p.97 and WO 25/1: p.147: Commission appointing Colonel Robert Johnstone Deputy Quartermaster-general, 18 May 1793.
117 Taylor (ed.), *Taylor Papers*, p.28.
118 Anon., *Officer of the Guards*, vol.1, p.88.
119 TNA: WO 25/41: p.76, Commission appointing Colonel James Moncrieff Quartermaster-general, 25 February 1793; NAM: 1985-12-15-4: GO, 12 May 1793; Pitt to George III, 7 March 1793 and York to George III, 25 March 1793, in Aspinall (ed.), *Later Correspondence*, vol.2, pp.18 and 24.
120 R.N.W. Thomas, 'Moncrieff, James (1744–1793), army officer and military engineer', *ODNB*, <https://doi.org/10.1093/ref:odnb/18950>, accessed 5 June 2020 and WLCL: JM, Yonge to Moncrieff 4 June 1792.

Herbert Taylor regarded Moncrieff as: '... an able and very gallant man (indeed, he exposed his person uselessly). He had distinguished himself in America. He spoke only English, or rather Scotch'.[121] According to First Lieutenant Thomas Fenwick of the Royal Artillery, Moncrieff: '... has very much got the ear of the Duke of York'.[122] General Sir Henry Clinton also had a very high opinion of him: 'I have a great opinion of Moncrief & ... I know no one among the whole list of Genie I should prefer but he exposes his person too much, which considering the consequence he is of is unpardonable.'[123] Moncrieff was killed at the abortive siege of Dunkirk, as reported by the Duke of York to King George: 'I have however greatly to lament poor Colonel Moncrief who was shot through the head with a grape-shot towards the end of the action, and who, though not yet dead, cannot possibly, according to the surgeon's account, recover.'[124]

Johnstone apparently thought he would succeed Moncrieff as quartermaster-general and was therefore disappointed by the arrival at headquarters of Colonel the Hon Henry Edward Fox on 8 October. He supposedly decided to continue as deputy on account of the relative comfort enjoyed by officers at headquarters, compared to those: '...rous'd by the four o'clock fife'.[125] But this was not to last for long, as Johnstone became commanding officer of the 3rd Foot Guards when Colonel John Watson was promoted to major general on 20 December 1793.

Fox was appointed quartermaster-general on 26 September 1793 and was the third individual to hold the position in approximately seven months, though he remained in post until after February 1795 when active operations ceased.[126] He was born on 4 March 1755, so aged 38 when he proceeded to Flanders. He was commissioned in the 1st Dragoon Guards on 16 September 1770 but transferred to the 38th Regiment in 1773 and, apart from just over one year with the 49th Regiment in 1777–1778, he spent the rest of his regimental career with the 38th. Like Moncrieff, Fox had been on active service during the American War, being present at the battles of Concord (19 April 1775), Bunker Hill (17 June 1775), Long Island (27 August 1776), White Plains (28 October 1776) and Brandywine (11 September 1777). Fox also had Royal connections, for he was appointed aide-de-camp to the King on 12 March 1783 and it is assumed that he consequently knew the Duke of York.[127]

Fox's arrival at headquarters coincided with the severe indisposition of Major General Gerard Lake, who had fallen ill in September before going home the following month. He was not to return to Flanders until March 1794 but once again his health gave way and he departed the army in late May, never to return. Fox was therefore drawn into a significant operational role, probably not envisaged when he was first appointed quartermaster-general

---

121 Taylor (ed.), *Taylor Papers*, p.27.
122 Leslie (ed.), 'Campaigning in 1793–Flanders', p.26
123 WLCL: Henry Clinton Papers: vol.235, Sir Henry Clinton to Henry Clinton, 28 June 1793. Genie means 'engineer' (French).
124 York to George III, 7 September 1793, in Aspinall (ed.), *Later Correspondence*, vol.2, p.88.
125 Anon., *Officer of the Guards*, vol.1, pp.100–101.
126 TNA: HO 51/147: pp.113–114 and WO 25/41: p.188: Commission appointing Colonel Henry Edward Fox Quartermaster-general, 26 September 1793.
127 R.N.W. Thomas, 'Fox, Henry Edward (1755–1811), army officer', *ODNB*, <https://doi.org/10.1093/ref:odnb/10034>, accessed 5 June 2020.

– not that he would have resisted such a thing, given his wide military experience. It appears that before writing to his father on 23 May 1794 York had also consulted Erskine about the matter:

> Should your Majesty not wish particularly to send another Major-General to command the brigade of the line, General Fox, who has now distinguished himself so much with this brigade, will very willingly continue in the command of it, and I understand there is nothing new in it, as Sir William Erskine when Quarter Master General in America constantly commanded a brigade.[128]

Lieutenant General the Honourable Henry Edward Fox, by Charles Turner after Thomas Phillips. (Anne S.K. Brown Military Collection)

We have seen that Fox's dual role of quartermaster-general and formation commander has been criticised by both Ward and Glover, despite this being eighteenth century practice.[129] By the end of 1794, however, Harry Calvert was to remark that: '… General Fox is too much occupied in his staff employment to be reckoned as a major general, though his zeal induces him to come forward as such whenever he can'.[130]

The appointment of Robert Johnstone's replacement, Lieutenant Colonel Robert Brownrigg of the 88th Regiment, on 27 November 1793 has already been noted and, as with Fox, he remained in post until after operations ceased in early 1795. There were several other members of the department in 1793, the chief of whom was Captain John Sontag who served as deputy assistant quartermaster-general between 17 May and 2 July 1793 when he was appointed captain of guides.[131] Sontag was first commissioned in the 12th Light Dragoons on 8 September 1780 and held a variety of posts on the staff of the army in Flanders. The 'Officer of the Guards' supplied a pen portrait of him:

---

128 York to George III, 23 May 1794, in Aspinall (ed.), *Later Correspondence*, vol.2, p.211.
129 Glover, *Peninsular Preparation*, p.197 and Ward, *Wellington's Headquarters*, pp.20–21.
130 Calvert to Dalrymple, 9 November 1794, in Verney (ed.), *Calvert*, p.385.
131 NAM: 1985-12-15-4: GO, Tournay, 17 May 1793 and Estreux, 2 July 1793; TNA: AO 16/52: p.98, enclosure in Murray to Watson, 16 July 1793 and WO 25/41: p.148: Commission appointing Sontag Captain of Guides, 2 July 1793.

This gentleman, in various capacities, exerted himself with the most persevering activity in the service of his royal highness's *family*, ... He was, at the time these letters were first written, in the *Quarter Master General's* department, and his method of *chalking up* on the doors, the names of those officers who were to take possession of the best houses in the villages, through which the army passed, deserves to be recorded. The particular flourish too with which he formed the *talismanic SAR* (son altesse royale) was frequently admired. He was afterwards *captain of guides*, then of the waggoners; in short, it would have been impossible to have carried on the war without his friendly aid.[132]

He rejoined the quartermaster-general's department on 28 April 1794 and remained with it until being appointed military commandant of hospitals on 23 January 1795.[133]

Two other men also held the title of deputy assistant quartermaster-general. The first of these was Louis de Lindenthal, appointed on 15 April 1794 and a Monsieur de Vibraye, appointed on 23 October 1794. They were given the ranks of major and captain respectively in the 'Foreign Corps in the pay of Great Britain' but nothing more is known of their backgrounds, though Lindenthal was appointed captain of guides on 19 March 1795.[134]

A total of 18 assistants to the quartermaster-general served between May 1793 and January 1795. One of these, Captain George Gordon, has already been mentioned in connection with his appointment as deputy assistant adjutant-general on 11 March 1794, so only served in the quartermaster-general's department during the 1793 campaign. Another officer, Lieutenant John Rutherford of the Royal Engineers, was captured on 17 September 1794. A total of four men were appointed in 1793, nine in 1794 and one in 1795. It was not possible to trace the dates of appointment for a further four officers.

Transport – Wagons

By far the most time consuming and significant issue engaging the department concerned transportation. Without regulation, the army would have been paralysed by the number of wheeled vehicles and horses accumulated by officers and regiments alike. Accordingly, the quartermaster-general was responsible for enforcing the proper allocation of transport, how vehicles and horses could first be obtained (or later disposed of) and arranging for their inspection. The department was also responsible for organising them on the line of march (see Appendix IV) and for the payment of bat and forage money.

The first general order mentioning the regulation of wheeled transport was given on 5 August 1793 as the Duke of York's force was preparing to leave Valenciennes and commence its approach march to Dunkirk.[135] This stated that no wagons were allowed to follow the army except those belonging to the artillery or commissariat. Units were only permitted to keep two carts, for the surgeon and quartermaster respectively. One officer

---

132 Anon., *Officer of the Guards*, vol.1, pp.79–80.
133 TNA: AO 16/53/1: GO, Cateau, 28 April 1794 and AO 16/53/7: GO, Deventer, 23 January 1795.
134 TNA: AO 16/53/1: GO, Cateau, 28 April 1794; AO 16/53/6: GO, Arnheim, 23 October 1794 and AO 16/53/8: GO, Osnabruck, 19 March 1795.
135 NAM: 1985-12-15-4: GO, Estreux, 5 August 1793.

and 30 men per brigade were to serve as a baggage guard, and all baggage wagons were to be delivered to headquarters at 4:00 a.m. on 6 August to be placed under the direction of Captain Sontag.

The arrival of additional regiments from Britain and Ireland in 1794 made the regulation of transport of greater priority. Prior to the commencement of the 1794 campaign orders were issued that only one two-wheeled cart was to be allowed for the officers of each troop or company, with the quartermaster-general being ordered to turn out of the line any second cart discovered '& direct the Guard to pillage it'.[136] Carts for private use were only permitted for unit commanding officers, the adjutant-general and quartermaster-general and their deputies, the aides-de-camp and secretary to the Duke, the deputy judge advocate, the captain of guides and the baggage master. Brigade staff (brigade majors and aides-de-camp) were permitted to share one cart between every two officers. Officers were also warned that operational considerations could result in carts being ordered away from the army, so all were encouraged to retain bât horses (horses used to carry baggage) carrying items that might be required urgently. Further orders were issued eight days later, on 23 March, stating that commissariat and bread wagons attached to units were to be used only for carrying bread – presumably as some had tried to circumvent the regulations.

One of the keys to controlling the number of wagons was to restrict the volume of personal baggage. Prior to the 1794 campaign, officers and their units were ordered to hand in all surplus gear at a closed store in a barrack at Ghent designated by the quartermaster-general for that purpose. Each regiment was to send a careful non-commissioned officer and soldier as a guard. It was prohibited to use any wheeled transport for other ranks' camp equipage as tents and camp kettles would always be required on the line of march, so these items had to be carried by bât horses.[137]

As the 1794 campaign got underway, orders were given for other categories of wheeled transport. This resulted from the formation of the Corps of Royal Waggoners in an attempt to reduce the dependency on civilian contractors. Each brigade was to have one officer attached from the Corps, with one non-commissioned officer attached to each regiment to superintend the drivers in the care of horses and wagons. All wagons secured under contract were to be immediately returned and the drivers replaced with enlisted men, whilst all impressed wagons and drivers were to be discharged as soon as the transport scale was achieved. Cavalry units were to be permitted two bread and eight forage wagons, whilst infantry units had three bread and four forage wagons, all with four horses and two drivers each. Providing horses to draw these wagons was another of the quartermaster-general's responsibilities. A farrier and forge cart were to be attached to each brigade to shoe the commissariat horses and repair damage to the wagons under the direction of the attached Corps of Royal Waggoners officer, who reported to the brigade commander. The Royal Artillery and Royal Military Artificers were to have one officer, two NCOs, one wheelwright and one farrier with a forge cart attached to them. This scale was slightly amended in June 1794 when the wagonmaster-general was ordered to provide each unit with two wagons for

---

136 NAM: 1985-12-15-5: GO, Courtrai, 15 March 1794.
137 NAM: 1985-12-15-5: GO, Courtrai, 20 and 23 March 1794.

the convalescents, spare arms, accoutrements and regimental appointments, though this may have been a temporary measure.[138]

The department also provided wagons for sick soldiers unable to march. The Corps of Royal Waggoners operated spring wagons, a crude form of suspension, which the army was reminded were solely under the control of the quartermaster-general and only to be used for transporting wounded men, though they could be used to carry non-emergency cases. There were no formal medical units as such, so a reminder was given that a number of spring wagons must be held in the vicinity of troops likely to be going into action.[139]

So much for controlling the convoy of wagons accompanying the field army. Managing their procurement and eventual disposal was equally important for maintaining discipline and ensuring favourable civil-military relations. Repeated orders were issued that no wagons were to be impressed by unit commanding officers, except in cases of the most pressing necessity and then only after obtaining approval from the general officer commanding the district, the quartermaster-general or the commissary-general. The regular channel for obtaining such approval was through a signed order given by the quartermaster-general, but this appears to have been more disregarded than observed on the basis of the number of general orders issued on this topic. Wagons were to be acquired by the quartermaster-general's department, as indicated in an order dated 30 April 1794 directing one sergeant and 10 mounted light dragoons to attend at the office at Le Cateau to assist Sontag in impressing wagons for six or seven days.[140]

Continuous monitoring of transportation was required, with the personnel from the quartermaster-general's department conducting inspections and requiring returns of all the commissariat wagons and horses attached to units. In May 1794, general officers, departments and brigade majors were ordered to submit returns of all wagons, horses and drivers attached to each regiment. Bread and forage wagons had to be identified separately, together with an indication of how many were hired, impressed or belonged to the commissariat. An equivalent list had to be compiled for drivers, giving their names and showing which were enlisted, hired or came with impressed wagons. As the army departed the Austrian Netherlands, the returns requested focused as much on whose territory they had been acquired in, be it the Austrian Netherlands or the United Provinces, as on their state of repair.[141]

Having acquired wagons and horses and issued them to units according to the approved scale, the work of the department then turned to ensuring that these resources were properly managed. A general order of 2 March 1794 stated that wagons had been overloaded and

---

138 TNA: AO 16/53/2: GO, Tournay, 20 May 1794; AO 16/53/3 GO, Tournay, 13 June 1794 and AO16/53/7: GO, Deventer, 20 January 1795. Horses – AO16/53/1: GO, St Amand, 9 April 1794 and Veaux, 18 April 1794.
139 TNA: AO 16/53/3: GO, Tournay, 23 June 1794 and AO 16/53/6: GO, Wicken, 20 September 1794.
140 NAM: 1985-12-15-4: GO, Orchies, 14 August 1793; 1985-12-15-5: GO, Courtrai, 15 March 1794; TNA: AO16/53/1: GO, St Amand, 14 April 1794; AO16/53/1: GO, Cateau, 30 April 1794; AO 16/53/6: GO, Groesweek, 28 September 1794 and AO16/53/7: GO, Osnabruck, 3 March 1795.
141 NAM: 1985-12-15-4: GO, Camp before Dunkirk, 28 August 1793; TNA: AO16/53/1: GO, Cateau, 24 April 1794; AO 16/53/2: GO, Tournay, 13 and 15 May 1794 and AO 16/53/7 GO, Arnhem, 10 December 1794.

the horses beaten when they proved incapable of pulling the excessive weight, so officers of all units were urged to investigate any complaints and take the necessary action.[142]

Another responsibility was to control wagons on the line of march. This had been a problem in 1793, for John Charles Kerr was appointed baggage master on 20 February 1794 and subsequently given the rank of 'Major in the foreign troops in the pay of Great Britain'. He was assisted by John Orde who on 2 March 1794 was given the local rank of 'Captain in the Army on the Continent only'. These two men were subsequently provided with three assistant baggage masters-general – Ensign David on 18 June, Lieutenants Charles Samson on 26 July and Anthony L'Estrange on 8 September. Little is known of their background. Both David and Samson belonged to independent companies, whereas L'Estrange had been a half-pay lieutenant in the 104th Regiment since 1783, until transferred at full pay to the 88th on 25 September 1793. These men formed a section within the quartermaster-general's department, tasked with reporting the arrival of the baggage to him after each day's march.[143]

Establishing their authority took time. A general order of 8 May stated that officers' servants and batmen were inattentive and disobedient to the orders of the baggage master, with some being guilty of great insolence (see Appendix IV). Several measures were enacted to improve matters. First, the regulations were ordered to be read to all connected with the baggage, and carefully explained to increase understanding of the baggage master's role and what in turn was required of them. Second, the baggage master was empowered to inflict immediate punishment on any transgressors, and third, each regiment was ordered to appoint a non-commissioned officer to regulate their batmen on the line of march. Lastly, each regiment was ordered to appoint a careful sergeant as the unit's permanent baggage master, who was to be answerable to the baggage master-general for the proper behaviour of the drivers. These measures took time to take effect, as a general order of 6 June stated of the baggage master-general: 'This officer has the sole direction of the Baggage and of all officers noncommiss'd officers or Guards appoint'd to the charge of it.' He 'has H.R.H.s express orders to put under an arrest any officer or to confine any noncommiss'd officer who may at any time dispute his authority or neglect his orders.'[144]

Aside from establishing discipline in the baggage train, the quartermaster-general was also responsible for controlling the movements of wheeled transport. A general order of 28 July stipulated that bread and forage wagons were to be positioned immediately in the rear of the units to which they belonged when advancing, and immediately in front when retiring. By early October, when the army had crossed the River Waal, it was ordered that all wheeled transport was to join the park of heavy baggage and that no wagons or carts were to leave it or to pass from the north side of the river over the pontoon or swing bridges unless they had a written order from the quartermaster-general or his deputy.[145]

---

142 NAM: 1985-12-15-5: GO, Harlebeke, 2 March 1794.
143 TNA: HO 51/147: p.209 and WO 25/42: p.19: Commission appointing Charles Kerr Baggage Master, 20 February 1794; NAM: 1985-12-15-5: GO, Harlebeke, 2 March 1794 and St Amand, 31 March 1794; TNA: AO 16/53/1: GO, Cateau, 28 April 1794 and AO 16/53/3: GO, Tournay, 18 June 1794.
144 TNA: AO 16/53/2: GO, 8 May 1794 and AO 16/53/3: GO, Tournay, 6 June 1794.
145 TNA: AO 16/53/4: GO, Rosendale, 28 July 1794 and AO 16/53/6: GO, Nymeguen, 8 October 1794.

Transport – Bât Horses

Bât horses were a means of retaining key items of camp equipment with regiments during a campaign. They were used for carrying the men's tents on a scale of three horses per troop or company for the line and four per company for the Foot Guards. The scale was increased in March 1794 by the addition of one bât horse per company to carry camp kettles, and one per regiment was allowed for the carriage of the sergeant major's, quartermaster's, quarter-guard and main-guard tents. Also in 1794, a horse was allocated to every regiment to carry the surgeon's medicine chest. There were strict instructions that bât horses were not to be used for any other purpose unless ordered by a general officer or the commander-in-chief. The responsibility for acquiring troop or company bât horses lay with the captain commanding, who was granted an allowance of £10 per horse, raised to 18 guineas on 13 March 1794. The horses used to carry the surgeon's equipment and guard tents were bought by the unit commanding officer, with an allowance of £2,10 for the purchase of pack saddles for them. Regiments were permitted to allocate a maximum of five bât men per company in the Foot Guards regiments and four per company for regiments of the line. It is clear that not all units were able to equip themselves, leading to a request at the end of August 1794 for any surplus pack saddles to be returned to the quartermaster-general for distribution to regiments which had none until new items could be provided. Many of the horses witnessed hard service and these were shot or otherwise disposed of following an inspection by the department in December 1794.[146] Bât and forage money was claimed via the quartermaster-general and returns were requested every 200 days.[147]

Troop Movements

A key aspect of the quartermaster-general's work was associated with the movement of troops. The department's own people conducted each column or paid for civilian guides if these were needed.[148] If the troops were to encamp at their next location, columns were preceded by staff from the department, regimental quartermasters and camp colour men in order to lay out each regiment's designated area prior to its arrival and to guide the soldiers to it. The camp colour men generally comprised a non-commissioned officer and man from each troop or company of a regiment acting as assistants to the regimental quartermaster. These small teams from the units designated to move would generally parade the evening before the march was to take place, or else early in the morning prior to its commencement, in order to receive orders from the quartermaster-general. As well as organising camps, the quartermaster-general's department also allocated quartering in towns after holding discussions with the magistrates, and none were authorised to occupy a billet without a signed order from the quartermaster-general or his deputy. A balance had to be struck

---

146 NAM: 1985-12-15-5: GO, Ghent, 5 and 11 January and 2 March 1794 and Courtrai, 15, 20, 21, and 23 March 1794; TNA AO 16/53/5: GO, Oosterhout, 24 August 1794 and AO 16/53/7: GO, Arnhem, 1 December 1794.
147 NAM: 1985-12-15-5: GO, Courtrai, 21 March 1794; TNA: AO 16/53/2: GO, Tournai, 4 and 7 May 1794 and AO 16/53/6: GO, Arnhem, 8 November 1794.
148 TNA: AO 16/53/4: GO, 2 July 1794 and Rosendale, 28 July 1794; AO 16/53/6: GO, Wicken, 20 September 1794 and Groesweek, 28 September 1794 and AO 16/53/7: GO, Deventer, 26 January 1795.

between finding suitable accommodation, on the one hand, and causing distress or hardship to the local population on the other.[149]

Having organised transportation, provided guides and arranged camps or quarters, the next task of the quartermaster-general's department was to issue a wide variety of equipment and supplies for the use of the army in camp or quarters.

Camp Equipment

Soldiers were accommodated in tents during the campaigning season. They came in two official patterns. The first, referred in the general orders to the 'old' or 'square' pattern was used by some units in 1793 before being replaced by the 'new' or 'bell' tent. The issue scale was one tent for 15 men with the sergeants of each troop or company sharing another, whilst the sergeant major and quartermaster had their own. Each tent was also issued with two camp kettles. The department maintained stores at Ghent, Valenciennes and Tournai from which the whole army was re-equipped prior to the 1794 campaigning season. The situation changed in late June 1794 when units under the command of Lord Moira arrived at Ostend without the requisite camp equipment, leading to a general order of 3 July 1794 stipulating that each troop or company had to send one tent, one tent pole, pegs, a mallet and one camp kettle to the quartermaster-general. Five weeks later on 10 August 1794, another general order required each regiment equipped with bell tents to send one to the department whilst units having the old pattern of square tents were to send two. These tents were intended as a temporary relief to the 28th and 57th Regiments which had none, so an appeal was made to any unit able to supply more, which would be returned once the 28th and 57th had been issued their own equipment. An order of 27 September required each regiment to send a tent and camp kettle to the artillery park for the men acting as drivers, but on 10 December all units were required to return their tents to the quartermaster-general's store at Arnhem since they were required by the Secretary-at-War to be sent back to England. Ten days later, all units were ordered to send returns of their camp equipment with the number of each item required and how or why anything became unserviceable. Apart from camp equipment, the department was also responsible for issuing fuel and candles, for which brigade majors were to submit returns at 10:00 a.m. every Sunday.[150]

Connected with transportation were the returns for forage that the quartermaster-general's department collected before forwarding to the Commissariat. These had to be submitted by units one day in advance and no regiment was permitted to forage for itself without authorisation from the department. Similar returns had to be submitted to the quartermaster-general for wood and straw, which were for either two or four days supply at

---

149 Camps – NAM: 1985-12-15-4: GO, Baseele, 19 May 1793, Estreux, 6 and 8 June 1793; TNA: AO 16/53/2: GO, St Amand, 2 May 1794 evening orders; AO 16/53/4: GO, Contick, 21 July 1794 and Rosendale, 25 July 1794. Quartering – NAM: 1985-12-15-5: GO, Ghent, 15 February 1794; TNA: AO 16/53/1: Craig to Officer Commanding Royal Artillery, St Amand, 9 April 1794; AO 16/53/6: GO, Grossbeek, 21 September 1794 and AO 16/53/7: GO, Arnhem, 23 November 1794.
150 NAM: 1985-12-15-5: GO, Ghent, 13 January 1794 and Courtray, 20 and 23 March 1794; TNA: AO 16/53/1: GO (After Orders), St Amand, 14 April 1794; AO 16/53/2: GO, Tournai, 4 May 1794; AO 16/53/4: GO, 2 July 1794 and Grammont, 3 July 1794; AO 16/53/5: GO, Oosterhout, 10 August 1794 and Berlikom, 7 September 1794; AO 16/53/6: GO, Groesbeek, 27 September 1794 and AO 16/53/7: GO, Arnhem, 10 and 20 December 1794.

a time, and in January 1795 the department requested returns for beef at the rate of 1 lb per man effective and doing duty.[151]

Miscellaneous Responsibilities

The department was not only engaged in supplying equipment for the camp and quarters. It also issued entrenching tools, for which regiments were ordered on 21 March 1794 to send returns of what was in their possession, as well as any missing items, which were charged to the unit concerned. Tools were issued on the scale of one spade and shovel for each troop or company. Materials for sinking wells, such as buckets, ropes and boards, could be supplied by the department or else paid for in the event that units had procured their own.[152]

As we have seen, one of the adjutant-general's roles was associated with the supply of arms, clothing and equipment. The quartermaster-general also maintained some responsibility for this, by preparing returns of items required. Clothes had been donated by the public in Britain during the winter of 1793–1794 and a general order dated 12 February asked regiments to submit returns of women and children in need to the department as soon as possible; this was still being requested on 17 February. In a general order of 11 March 1794, the Brigades of Guards and the line regiments were required to give the quartermaster-general returns of the greatcoats needed to complete the present establishment and in July, commanding officers were requested to send returns of all appointments and other articles required to the quartermaster-general's department at Antwerp.[153]

The clothing situation had deteriorated by September 1794 when commanding officers met at the adjutant-general's office to discuss a solution. The meeting concluded with the quartermaster-general undertaking to put the optimum measures in place, with officers being directed to proceed to the stores at Helvoetsluys to select what was required. Items still needed tailoring to fit, so the department undertook to arrange transport to the various villages roundabout for this to be done.[154] After the retreat from the Austrian Netherlands, many men were without shoes, so regiments were instructed to submit returns for the number needed. The small quantities donated from Britain would be issued from the store in proportion to the number available, but units already in receipt had to contribute 5/– per pair, with the money used to buy more. Shoes remained a problem three months later, and regiments were ordered on 18 January 1795 to apply to the department for them, as well as for blankets. In addition to clothes, shoes and blankets, in a general order dated 5 February 1795 regiments were asked to submit returns to headquarters of arms and accoutrements required for men returning from the hospital for onward transmission to the department.[155]

---

151 Forage – NAM: 1985-12-15-4: GO, Bergen op Zoom, 6 April 1793; TNA: AO 16/53/2: GO, Tournay, 6 and 31 May 1794 and AO 16/53/4: GO, Oosterhout, 5 August 1794. Wood and straw: AO 16/53/3: GO, 25 June 1794; AO 16/53/4: GO, Roosendale, 25 July 1794 and AO 16/53/5: GO, Oosterhout, 22 August 1794. Beef: AO 16/53/7: GO, 19 January 1795.
152 NAM: 1985-12-15-5: GO, Courtrai, 21 March 1794; TNA: AO 16/53/4: GO, 26 July 1794 and AO 16/53/5: GO, 9 August 1794.
153 NAM: 1985-12-15-5: GO, Ghent, 12 and 17 February 1794 and Courtrai, 11 March 1794 and TNA: AO 16/53/4: GO, Conteig, 14 July 1794.
154 TNA: AO 16/53/5: GO, Berlikom, 6 September 1794.
155 TNA: AO 16/53/6: GO, Arnheim, 28 October 1794; AO 16/53/7: GO, Deventer, 18 January 1795 and AO 16/53/7: GO, Rhené 5 February 1795.

Another area of co-operation with the adjutant-general's department concerned personal losses of property and equipment sustained during the 1793 and 1794 campaigns. The returns of losses requested by the adjutant-general during the first half of 1794 have already been mentioned. Once these were received, they were passed to a board of claims consisting of Lieutenant General Harcourt, the quartermaster-general and his deputy to assess officers' submissions. The board appears to have had a variable number of additional members including general officers and personnel from the adjutant-general's department.[156]

The two departments also co-operated on the distribution of soldiers' pay. A general order of 12 September 1794 requested regiments to prepare their muster rolls for the period 25 December 1793 to 24 June 1794 and submit them via brigade majors to the adjutant-general's office. One week later, regiments were ordered to copy them to the quartermaster-general by 1 October so that a general return for payment could be submitted to London.[157] Another matter to be resolved concerned the gratuity of 4d per day in lieu of spirits given to soldiers erecting field works in August 1794. The officer commanding at each work site had to produce a roll of men from each regiment from which these payments were made.[158]

The final responsibility assumed by the quartermaster-general concerned the conveyance of regimental women and children wishing to return to Britain, which was an adjunct to the department's transport role. Requests to commanding officers for lists of women whose husbands had been killed or taken prisoner and wished to return home were sent in May, August and October 1794, though it is unknown how many took advantage of the offer. Rather than returning destitute to Britain, the alternative would presumably have been to remarry or else to seek employment in one of the hospitals where soldiers' wives worked as nurses.[159]

The Barrack Master-General's Department

The barrack master-general's department in Britain did not officially exist until 30 May 1794, when the King appointed Colonel Oliver De Lancey as the first incumbent.[160] For an army in the field, barracks were only required during winter quarters, when active campaigning was normally expected to cease, so the first requirement for them came at the close of the 1793 campaign.

As we have already seen, Colonel John Hayes St Leger served as deputy adjutant-general in 1793 before being appointed barrack master-general on 22 January 1794, to be joined by his deputy Captain Thomas Carteret Hardy transferring from deputy assistant adjutant-general on 5 February 1794. Two other men also received the same appointment at a similar

---
156 NAM: 1985-12-15-5: GO, Ghent, 26 January 1794; TNA: AO 16/53/3: GO, Tournay, 16 June 1794; AO 16/53/5: GO, Oosterhout, 12 August 1794 and AO 16/53/7: GO, Arnhem, 26 November 1794.
157 TNA: AO 16/53/5: GO, Berlikom, 12 September 1794 and AO 16/53/6: GO, Wichen, 19 September 1794.
158 TNA: AO 16/53/5: GO, Oosterhout, 18, 19 and 29 August 1794.
159 TNA: AO 16/53/2: GO, Tournay, 27 May 1794; AO 16/53/5: GO, Oosterhout, 10 and 18 August 1794 and AO 16/53/6: GO, Arnheim, 23 October 1794.
160 Anon., *The First Report of the Commissioners of Military Enquiry. Office of the Barrack Master General* (London: House of Commons, 1806), pp.5–6.

time, these being Robert Bulfill Carre on 27 January and Lieutenant James Watson of the 14th Regiment on 5 February.[161] Little is known of Carre, though an individual of the same name married a Catherine Hunt in New York on 21 August 1783.[162] His name does not appear in the *Army List* so it must be assumed that he was a civilian. Watson was born in 1772 and commissioned an ensign in the Army in 1783 at the age of 11, so his actual service commenced when he transferred to the 14th Regiment on 25 September 1787. A fourth deputy assistant was appointed on 23 August 1794 listed in general orders as 'Ensign Charles Pitt of the 44th Regiment' but no such officer existed in that unit, or indeed in the Army, so it is assumed that Lieutenant Charles Phillips of the 44th Regiment is the individual meant. The final person to join the department was Major William Burnett of the 14th Regiment on 2 December 1794 as deputy barrack master-general. St Leger appears to have gone home by this time, so Burnett may have assumed responsibility for the department during the final weeks of the campaign.[163]

St Leger was in post some time before his appointment was actually announced, since a general order dated 1 January 1794 stated that units were to send returns for wood and straw to the department while in barracks but to the quartermaster-general when in the field or cantonments. Correspondence from Brook Watson, the commissary-general, to the Treasury regarding money provided for the barrack master-general stated that St Leger had been preparing barracks and stables as early as November 1793 when presumably he was still a member of the adjutant-general's department. A general order of 26 February stated that troops forming the garrison of Kortrijk were deemed to be in barracks, so the quarters were to be regulated by the barrack master-general, who would send an officer to whom all applications for quarters must be made. As far as officers were concerned, claims for lodging money in Ghent had to be signed by the unit commanding officer stating the dates they were occupied from and to, together with the name of the person owning the property. It is assumed that similar regulations pertained in other places.[164]

The department was responsible not only for the provision of suitable buildings for use as barracks, but also for their contents including stores, fuel, candles, bedsteads, bedding and stoves. Barrack supplies were mostly sourced via the commissary-general's department. St Leger placed an order for blankets on 2 December 1793 with the Treasury promising to ship 11,000 at the end of the month. Coals for barrack heating were also sourced from Britain, with 4,500 chauldrons (5,424 tons) expected at the end of December. These were calculated on the basis of one chauldron (2,700 lb) per room per week for 12 men. Candles, on the other hand, could be sourced locally at one week's notice for a cheaper price than at home.[165] It is assumed that items such as bedsteads, sheets and stoves were procured locally.

---

161 NAM: 1985-12-15-4: GO, Ghent, 27 January and 5 February 1794.
162 Anon., *New York Marriages Previous to 1784* (Baltimore: Clearfield Company, 1999), p.67.
163 TNA: AO 16/53/5: GO, Oosterhout, 25 August 1794 and AO 16/53/7: GO, Arnhem, 2 December 1794.
164 NAM: 1985-12-15-5: GO, 1 January 1794 and Harlebeke, 26 February 1794 and Courtrai, 15 March 1794.
165 TNA: AO 16/52: St Leger to Watson, Ghent 2 December 1793 and Motz to Rose, Ghent 27 and 30 December 1793. TNA: AO 16/53/6: GO, Arnheim, 26 October 1794 states 'A Chauldron of Coals 36 Bushells each weighing 75 Pounds'.

Financial accountability remained in force for Government property, and a general order of 27 January 1794, repeated on 10 March, stated that commanding officers were to remain responsible for all items issued by the department when in barracks during winter quarters. Regiments were also requested at the beginning of February to send a return to the department of the augmentation they expected before the start of the campaigning season, presumably so that provision could be made for barrack space and fittings. Clean sheets were issued every four weeks and 'field blankets' were only to be used on duty and not intermixed with the blankets issued by the barrack master-general, which would be returned once the army took the field.[166]

The Provost Marshal

The principal role of the provost marshal was the maintenance of order in quarters, camps and in the field. This also encompassed civilian followers such as drivers, sutlers and wives of the soldiers.

John Phillips was appointed provost marshal by the Duke of York 'until His Majesty's pleasure is known,' which was announced in general orders on 2 May 1793. The official appointment, a Royal Warrant dated 31 March 1793, granted Phillips the rank of 'Captain in the Army on the Continent of Europe only' was therefore backdated, suggesting that he had been working on an unofficial basis for some time already.[167] Nothing is known of his background and the only officer of this name in the *Army List* was on the English half-pay and formerly in Donkin's Regiment, a garrison battalion disbanded in 1783.

Phillips spent the whole of the 1793 campaign working only with a designated number of cavalry troopers, as mentioned in a general order dated 9 August 1793:

> The irregularities Committed last night are such, as disgrace the Country & the service they Belong to.
>
> A Corporal & 4 Dragoons to attend the provost every day, till further orders, & the Commander in Chief Expressly orders that any soldier or follower of a Camp Committing any Excesses may be executed immediately.[168]

The enforcement of camp discipline was raised on 28 August during the siege of Dunkirk when one sergeant and eight dragoons were ordered to attend the Austrian provost marshal who had positive orders to inflict immediate punishment on any person committing a depredation. Soldiers discovered any distance from the camp were to be regarded as deserters.[169] The size of the detachment allocated to the provost marshal was variable, since a general order dated 1 April 1794 stipulated that one non-commissioned officer and six men of the

---

166 NAM: 1985-12-15-5: GO, Ghent, 11 and 27 January, 3 February and Courtrai, 10 March 1794.
167 NAM: 1985-12-15-4: GO, Tournay, 2 May 1793; TNA: HO 51/147 p.82 and WO 25/41 p.79: Commission appointing John Phillips as Provost Martial, 31 March 1793.
168 NAM: 1985-12-15-4: GO, Burlon, 9 August 1793.
169 NAM: 1985-12-15-4: GO, Camp before Dunkirk, 28 August 1793.

dragoons were always to be on duty with him. These men were relieved at the same time and in the same manner as the orderly dragoons, with regiments to be on duty in rotation.[170]

As well as enforcing discipline, the provost marshal was also responsible for securing suspects prior to the administration of justice in the form of a court martial or, in exceptional circumstances, summary justice. The only known occasion when these men may have had cause to celebrate was on 12 August 1793 when general orders announced that all prisoners held by the provost were to be pardoned in commemoration of the Prince of Wales' birthday.[171]

One final responsibility held by the provost concerned the regulation of trade undertaken by sutlers. He had to provide the English standard weights used by them in the course of their business and to ensure that all those used by the British Army, including those in the magazines, were suitably stamped.[172]

The Deputy Judge Advocate

The deputy judge advocate was tasked with the execution of the Crown's powers under the Mutiny Act, including the organisation of courts martial.

Gerald Fitzgerald was appointed deputy judge advocate on 12 May 1793.[173] As with so many of the staff, he was commissioned into the 1st Foot Guards on 29 October 1777 and by the time of his appointment was a lieutenant and captain, receiving promotion to captain and lieutenant colonel on 25 September 1793. Probably as a result of this promotion, he was replaced by Lieutenant and Captain William Wynyard on 15 November 1793 as has already been mentioned. Fitzgerald, who was married, had a rather colourful life subsequent to the campaign as in September 1797 he eloped with his first cousin, aged 16, who was subsequently discovered hidden in his London house. The affair being a matter of honour, a duel was fought with her brother in Hyde Park on the morning of 1 October, without result. Ammunition being expended, the pair agreed to resume the next day. Both were arrested before this could happen and Fitzgerald was dismissed from the Army. Nothing daunted, he pursued the girl to Ireland but was shot dead by her grandfather, who was subsequently cleared of murder.[174]

Returning to the staff appointment, Fitzgerald, and subsequently Wynyard, was responsible for organising the date, location and personnel involved with courts martial. This was done by issuing an appropriate general order:

> A Gen'l Court Martial to sit tomorrow at Tournay at ten o'clock in the morning for the trial of all Prisoners brought before it. The members are desired to send in the dates of their rank in the army immediately to the Judge Advocate also the

---

170 NAM: 1985-12-15-5: GO, St Amand, 1 April 1794.
171 NAM: 1985-12-15-4: GO, Orchies, 12 August 1793.
172 NAM: 1985-12-15-5: GO, Ghent, 3 January 1794.
173 TNA: HO 51/147: p.98 and WO 25/41: p.147: Commission appointing Captain Gerald Fitzgerald Deputy Judge Advocate, 12 May 1793.
174 See Aspinall (ed.), *Later Correspondence*, vol.2, p.629, footnote 1.

Prisoners Names & crimes to be given in to the Judge Advocate immediately with the list of the Evidences, who must be properly warned by the Prosecutor.[175]

The President of this particular court martial was Major General Ralph Dundas and the members comprised Lieutenant Colonels Gordon Drummond (8th Regiment), Henry Pigot (3rd Foot Guards), the Hon Fitzroy Stanhope and Alexander Dury (both 1st Foot Guards), Majors William Ramsay (14th Regiment) and John Vandaleur (5th Dragoon Guards), together with one captain drawn from each of the Blues, 2nd and 6th Dragoons, Royal Artillery, 37th and 53rd Regiments, with four from the Brigade of Guards.

The composition of the court is interesting, consisting of a general officer as president, six field officers (four lieutenant colonels and two majors) and 10 captains, making 17 officers in total. The work undertaken by the deputy judge advocate is apparent, starting with arranging the date, place and time the court would sit, together with nominating the individuals comprising it. The identity of the prisoners, their alleged offences and a list of the witnesses were also collected. This particular court martial was delayed for one day until Thursday 22 May and heard seven cases, some with multiple accused.

The judge advocate then had to collect the court documents and seek approval for the recommended sentences from the Duke of York. This took some time, and the first result was not announced in general orders until 29 May, seven days later, which related to Captain George Williams of the Royal Artillery who had been accused of frequently going beyond the advanced videttes and holding a correspondence with the enemy. It was established that he had actually gone too far forward only once, most likely to check the field of fire from his battery, and all charges were dismissed. The next sentence to be finalised, on 4 June, was on Quartermaster Thomas Jephcoate of the 16th Light Dragoons, who had been placed under arrest for allegedly disobeying the orders of the baggage master-general, a charge of which he was acquitted. The other ranks' sentences were not announced until 5 June, 14 days after the court sat. These included five soldiers and two followers sentenced to 1,000 lashes each for offences including aggravated plundering, desertion and theft, and one soldier awarded 500 lashes for assaulting three Austrian officers in the streets of Tournai. This example shows a clear sentencing hierarchy, with officers first followed by warrant officers and then other ranks.[176]

Some idea of the judge advocate's workload is shown by the frequency with which courts martial were held. There were between one and three per month between June and December 1794, making a total of 16 during the second half of the year. Much obviously depended on the operational situation of the army, though the heaviest workload occurred in October and November 1794 when three were held in each month. No other personnel have been traced in this department, so it appears that the entire responsibility fell to one man.

---

175 TNA: AO 16/53/2: GO, Tournay, 20 May 1794.
176 TNA: AO 16/53/2: After orders, Tournay, 29 May 1794 and TNA: AO 16/53/3: GO, Tournay, 4 and 5 June 1794.

Towards a Professional Staff?

From the allied perspective, the Flanders campaign represented coalition warfare similar to that practised during the wars of the Spanish and Austrian Successions and the Seven Years' War in Europe. Nations committed military assets to a varying degree, sometimes commanded in person by a head of state, but notionally under the overall command of a senior figure agreed by all participants; each nation had war aims that either agreed or diverged from those of their allies. Strategy was decided at councils of war, at which participants had to be of an equal rank or social status in order to obtain decisions favourable to them. Against this background, it is no surprise that the Duke of York was tasked with commanding the British expeditionary force, since he was a senior member of the Royal Family and had been trained for military service.

The review of his staff has shown that a number of men in key positions were appointed in part due to their linguistic abilities, including the Duke's aides-de-camp Charles Craufurd and Henry Clinton, his secretaries, Edwin Hewgill and Herbert Taylor, and the initial quartermaster-general, Colonel Robert Johnstone. Another of the Duke's aides-de-camp, Harry Calvert, was familiar with French but offered the following advice to a young man seeking a military career: 'Languages are the *sine quâ non* to an officer who wishes to rise above the common routine of regimental duty; and I have myself felt very severely the misfortune of not understanding German.'[177]

Another staff member with linguistic abilities was John Murray, who was extracted from the 3rd Foot Guards by the Duke of York in April 1793 and appointed aide-de-camp to *Feldmarschall* Wilhelm von Freytag, commanding the Hanoverian contingent:

> As it will be absolutely necessary for Marechal Freytag to have an English Aide-de-Camp attached to him I have taken the liberty to recommend to him Sir James Murray's brother who was page to your Majesty and is now in the Third Regiment. As he talks German and French perfectly well he will be of great use to the Marechal.[178]

The mastery of foreign languages was a valuable skill in the eighteenth century, both for keeping up with the latest military thinking (principally in French or German) and for practical use on campaign.[179] It is probable that other British staff officers also had a command of French and German, though at this distance of time it is not possible to know for sure. Some individuals, on the basis of their names, were probably either French émigrés or seconded from allied forces, including five of the 18 assistants to the quartermaster-general (Offany, Vischer, Vibraye, Visselier and Chasspot) and two of the five assistant provost marshals (Krugg and Baumeister). These men were always in a minority, but their presence suggests a willingness and ability to adapt to local conditions and the demands of a multi-national force.

---

177 Calvert to John Calvert, 26 April 1793, in Verney (ed.), *Calvert*, pp.69–70.
178 York to George III, 17 April 1793 in Aspinall (ed.), *Later Correspondence*, vol.2, p.29.
179 Conway, *The British Army*, pp.71–72.

Several staff members had acquired extensive campaign experience in the American War, including the quartermaster-generals, James Moncrieff and Henry Fox, the adjutant-generals, Sir James Murray and Sir James Craig and two of the Duke's aides-de-camp, Harry Calvert and William Wynyard. Most staff members were either too young to have fought in America, or else served in regiments that did not participate, such as the Foot Guards or heavy cavalry.

The subsequent careers of staff members have barely been discussed so far due to reasons of space, but these are also indicative of their abilities in 1793–1795. Of the Duke's eight aides-de-camp or secretaries, only Bentinck and Childers did not hold a staff position at Horse Guards or in a military district in England after 1794. Calvert, for example, served as adjutant-general between 1799–1820 as did Taylor from 1828, and Clinton held the same position in India, 1802–1805, Portugal in 1808 and in Ireland in 1809. Robert Brownrigg, who it will be remembered served as deputy quartermaster-general in 1793–1795, held the same position at the Horse Guards between 1803–1811. Robert Anstruther, who also served in the same department in 1794–1795 was selected by Sir Ralph Abercromby as his quartermaster-general in the Mediterranean in 1800 and was subsequently deputy quartermaster-general in England and adjutant-general in Ireland. Hewgill served as deputy barrack master between 1798–1803. If the net is widened to include officers who served in operational roles, David Dundas was appointed quartermaster-general at the Horse Guards in 1796 and subsequently served as commander-in-chief between 1809–1811.

The valiant attempt by staff officers of all grades to impose order on chaos by means of paperwork could broadly be considered as a typical Enlightenment project; a way-station on the road to today's micro-managed information state. And so indeed it might have been, were it not also the long-established method of providing a commanding general with an estimate (as exact as possible) of the effective men in his army, and the condition of their weapons and equipment – by the month, the week and ultimately the day – and then bringing them into action. Such were the size and complexity of the professional armies of the time – recognisably 'modern' armies as they had become – that without this flow of information a general could neither formulate, nor carry out his plans, and in the Duke of York's case, co-ordinate his actions with those of his allies – upon whom, moreover, he depended for many key services. Closely linked with these historic military requirements was a public obligation to seek value for money and combat fraud. These latter issues had perplexed European armies and their civilian paymasters from the turn of the Middle Ages – yet were somehow never resolved, as the protracted and sleazy winding-down of the American War had only recently shown. Even so, if that conflict had gone better, the British public and their political masters might have been more forgiving, just as they had at the triumphant conclusion of the Seven Years' War in 1763. Instead, military defeat and pervasive corruption (for such it appeared to be) were equated with deep moral failings. Next time, public servants, including the officers of the British Army, would be expected to try harder. Taking as our starting point the detail set out in this chapter (most of it for the first time) it must surely be conceded that they did, and that they were as 'professional' as circumstances allowed them to be. The contribution of the staff was by no means the most disappointing characteristic of York's army – as will appear in the following chapters. But as always, however well-conceived in peacetime, and however diligently pursued, an empire of paper did not survive intact after first contact with the enemy, and hardly at all once the army was fighting on the back foot, as it was so often during 1794–1795. Querulous demands from headquarters for repeat returns speak powerfully to that. On such occasions, as indeed at many times in the Army's history, these enquiries were likely to be ignored, and staff officers as a breed brought into ill-merited disrepute. Yet, once we take into account the ad hoc process of bringing the expeditionary force together in the first place, it is remarkable how its staff arrangements worked at all. It remained to be seen what improvements could be brought about in later phases of Britain's involvement in the Revolutionary and Napoleonic Wars.

3

The Commissariat

In most military histories, the question of army supply frequently takes second place behind the more glamorous subjects of strategy, tactics and personality. Commissariat activities are usually ignored, unless they had a decisive impact on the campaign.[1] This tendency has led to the, perhaps subconscious, belief that armies glided across the landscape with scant regard for the provision of food, clothing, forage, equipment or cash with which to pay the troops. The work of a limited number of authors has highlighted the importance of supply as a major factor in the conduct of military operations, but relatively little campaign specific work has been done to examine how these general themes actually worked in practice.[2] It may be argued, as Jeremy Black has done, that: 'Logistics were a factor at the tactical, operational and strategic levels of war'. Armies with an adequacy of finance were capable of maintaining goodwill with the host nation, supplying themselves from fixed magazines whilst remaining concentrated and avoiding dispersal to engage in '… the strategy of pillage'.[3] Toby Redgrave has also discussed the link between armies and the sources of their provisions in connection with the Peninsular War (1808–1814), stating that a reliance on depots dictated operational distances and required greater transport resources, whereas sourcing locally meant less transport, hence greater manoeuvrability but with a heavier reliance on cash.[4] As far as British land forces during the French Wars are concerned, only the Peninsular War has attracted some limited attention from writers on logistical matters, but most of this unfortunately remains unpublished.[5] This chapter therefore aims to establish how logistics

---

1 For example, Burgoyne's Saratoga campaign (1777) or Massena's halt before the lines of Torres Vedras (1810–1811).
2 Bowler, *Logistics*; J.A. Lynn (ed.), *Feeding Mars: Logistics in Western Warfare from the Middle Ages to the Present* (Colorado: Westview Press, 1993); M.L. Van Creveld, *Supplying War: Logistics from Wallenstein to Patton* (Cambridge: Cambridge University Press, 1977) and M. Howard, 'The Forgotten Dimensions of Strategy', *Foreign Affairs*, vol.57:5, 1979, pp.975–976.
3 J. Black, 'Logistics and the Path to Military Modernity. Britain and the Crucial Advantage of Naval Strength, 1793–1815', *Nuova Antologia Militare*, vol.1:3, June 2020, p.10.
4 T.M.O. Redgrave, *Wellington's Logistical Arrangements in the Peninsular War, 1809–1814* (Unpublished PhD thesis. University of London, 1979), p.8.
5 G. Espírito Santo and P. de Brito, *A logística do exército Anglo–Luso na guerra Peninsular* (Parede: Principia Editora, 2012); C. Chilcott, *Maintaining the British Army, 1793 to 1820* (Unpublished PhD thesis. Bath Spa University, 2006); T. Kirby, *The Duke of Wellington and the Supply System during the Peninsula War* (Unpublished Master's thesis. Fort Leavenworth, 2011); Redgrave, *Wellington's*

were structured, resourced and operated in the field, and how this compared with earlier eighteenth century conflicts.

Before proceeding further, it would be as well to define some terminology. Using Antoine Henri Jomini's *The Art of War* as his reference point, Martin Van Creveld defined logistics as: '… the practical art of moving armies and keeping them supplied'.[6] According to this definition, logistics may therefore include the provision of arms, clothing, medical facilities, engineering and other services, as well as the actual movement of armies. As a result of the separation of powers in the British military, these functions largely fell outside the remit of the Commissariat department in Flanders, which was concerned more with 'supply'. For the purposes of this chapter, 'supply' is taken to comprise the principle duties of the commissary in providing food, forage and cash, together with the acquisition and distribution thereof.[7]

The Eighteenth Century Commissariat

The commissariat arrangements of British armies on campaign underwent a considerable degree of evolution during the eighteenth century as the state gradually assumed control of what had previously been held in the hands of a limited number of individuals serving with the army in the field.

In the War of the Spanish Succession, the Duke of Marlborough's army in Flanders had no dedicated commissariat service attached to it. As a result, the field commander became personally involved in supply issues on an almost daily basis, and although he had an exceptional grasp of what needed to be done, he lacked a specialised hierarchy to look after the details. This provided unscrupulous people, officers and civilians alike, with opportunities to profit from the army supply-chain, including manipulating exchange-rates when cash and credit were shuffled between Britain, the United Provinces, the Austrian Netherlands and Germany. Yet ensuring a reliable transfer of coin to the army was seen as a vital supplement to the rough-and-ready procurement methods of old, such as foraging for victuals and fodder by force of arms, or levying 'contributions' in cash from towns and villages in the army's path. An army which paid its way was more likely to be tolerated by the civilian population, who now had a chance to make money during its passage through their lands. This was especially important when the army was operating in friendly territory, as it was for so much of the time in the Low Countries. The same principle would apply in 1793–1795. But it must be noted early on that for the system to work well, operations needed to proceed at a relatively sedate pace.

As long as local banking centres continued to function, credit-notes were honoured and ready money obtained, profiteering was inevitable, and in truth, it was tolerated to a high degree during the War of the Spanish Succession. Without it there would have been little incentive to the money-men at home and abroad to assist in the first place, for such was

---

    Logistical Arrangements and T. McLauchlan, *Wellington's Supply System during the Peninsular War, 1809–1814* (Unpublished Master's thesis, McGill University, 1997).
6   Van Creveld, *Supplying War*, p.5.
7   The separation of powers in the organisation of the British Army (including the division of responsibilities for supply) has been fully discussed in Ward, *Wellington's Headquarters*, pp.5–34 and Glover, *Peninsular Preparation*, pp.14–45.

the distressed state of public finances in that era that their expertise was not risk free. As usual in British war-making, as long as things went well, contrivances which at other times would have been regarded as underhand were winked at. Marlborough's famous 'March to the Danube' in 1704 could hardly have taken place without them. But once it seemed that the war would last forever, and that it was only kept going by the cupidity of the Dutch, and the lust of Marlborough and his cronies for power and riches, the tide of opinion turned. At audit-time, arrangements accepted until then as necessary and expedient came to look like extremely sharp practice. Marlborough's reputation slumped, as did that of his quartermaster-general in Flanders, Lieutenant General William Cadogan, who among other financial dodges had succeeded in cornering the army's bread and forage contracts and wagering on the outcome of operations.[8]

By the Seven Years' War, the Treasury had undertaken the responsibility for supply arrangements, so the principal control exercised over the Commissariat was cost. The commissariat function with the field army could therefore be regarded as sitting between the Treasury on the one hand and the Army on the other, being responsible for organising and inspecting the local distribution of supplies; the result was that it became subject to criticism by both – if supplies ran short or if the costs seemed excessive. At the start of the war, contracts with suppliers were prepared by the Treasury for specific numbers of troops, but sometimes long before the actual numbers were known, causing a tendency towards overspending. The contractors would assemble provisions and make arrangements with sub-contractors, a process that could take time due to negotiations between supplier networks often crossing national borders. The result was a supply system that was very rigid and unresponsive to changes in local conditions or sudden demands, since troops could be dispatched to a new location at a faster rate than the supplies needed to subsist them were acquired. The Commissariat did not supply all commodities, since contracts for meat, for example, were made by individual regiments:

> In *Germany* every Regiment of the *British* Troops contracted with a Butcher, who was obliged to carry along with them, at all times, a certain Number of live Sheep and Oxen to kill when wanted, and to sell the Meat at a fixed Price. Every Soldier was obliged to take a certain Quantity, which was paid for by Stoppages made in his Pay; and this Meat was boiled in the Camp Kettles, with such Roots and Greens as could be got.[9]

This practice continued in Flanders, with a general order of 21 May 1793 directing commanding officers of regiments to arrange their entire meat supply through a reliable contractor.[10]

---

8 I.P. Phelan, 'Marlborough as Logistician', *Journal of the Society for Army Historical Research*, Vol.67, 1989, pp.253–257 and Vol.68, 1990, pp.36–48 and 103–119; Stansfield, *Early Modern Systems*, pp.84–115 and Van Creveld, *Supplying War*, p.7.
9 D. Monro, *An Account of the Diseases Which Were Most Frequent in the British Military Hospitals in Germany, from January 1761 to the Return of the Troops to England in March 1763* (London: A. Miller, D. Wilson and T. Durham, 1764), pp.346–347.
10 NAM: 1985-12-15-4: GO, Baiseaux, 21 May 1793.

One other issue that reappeared in 1793–1795 was the scarcity of trained men to undertake commissariat duties, since knowledge of business was required together with a taste for military life. Language skills were also important, so personnel were enlisted locally. Various other issues also affected the management of the commissariat in the field. Possibly the most important of these were restrictions imposed on the commissary-general himself, since the several men to hold this position were not authorised to draw on a sufficient quantity of Treasury funds from continental money-markets until late in the war.

The lack of a formal commissariat structure headed by an individual with sufficient powers perpetuated the opportunities for massive corruption and negligence on the part of subordinate officials and contractors. Not only did the Government and the British taxpayer suffer from this, but so did the welfare of the troops, who were likely to desert the army to hunt for subsistence or alienate the local population by pillaging. This was only remedied by the gradual evolution of a more structured commissariat after the first two years of the war, with the appointment of men armed with sufficient authority from Government and the consequent reduction in opportunities for profiteering. During the Seven Years' War, both the structure of the commissariat, and the responsibilities given to individuals administering it, were in a process of continuous development and there was marked progress in achieving a more commercial approach to the business of supply. A significant increase in the number of commissaries was made after 1759, as well as extra magazine-keepers, clerks, craftsmen and general labourers. Rates of pay for senior officials were addressed in 1762, due to the inability to attract suitably qualified men in sufficient numbers. From 1760 there were also the beginnings of specialisation within the Commissariat, with individuals being assigned to specific roles such as the planning and organisation of supply, the control and execution of contracts, or the processes involved with accounting and settlement. By this time, the Treasury allowed men on the spot greater freedom in arranging supply contracts that had previously required approval in London, with deputy paymasters accompanying detachments of troops having the authority to issue money on the warrants of a commissary.[11]

Although the commissariat structure at the close of the Seven Years' War was still imperfect and contained a number of inefficiencies, it was significantly more effective in 1762 than it had been in 1758. It is unfortunate that it was dismantled almost as soon as peace returned, with the result that many of the lessons learned had mostly been forgotten by the outbreak of the American War in 1775. This was partly inevitable, for staff locally recruited in Germany could not be kept on after the end of campaigning, but the want of such assistance in America invited waste and corruption. Daniel Chamier, the first commissary-general appointed there, failed to assert himself (his malleable personality might have accounted for that) and as a result he was ill-equipped to resist the encroachments of other departments. The theatre-commander, General Thomas Gage, did little to help him. The result was that each department sourced what it required, often forcing prices up through competition. The

---

11   R. Browning, 'The Duke of Newcastle and the Financial Management of the Seven Years War in Germany', *Journal of the Society for Army Historical Research*, vol.49, 1971, pp.20–35; H.M. Little, 'The Emergence of a Commissariat During the Seven Years War in Germany', *Journal of the Society for Army Historical Research*, vol.61, 1983, pp.201–214 and H.M. Little, 'Thomas Pownall and Army Supply, 1761–1766', *Journal of the Society for Army Historical Research*, vol.65, 1987, pp.92–104.

situation continued after Daniel Weir was appointed commissary-general in 1777, caused again by a lack of support from Generals William Howe and Henry Clinton as successive commanders-in-chief. Although Weir was an experienced man, the chaos with which he was surrounded caused a complete breakdown in the procedures for controlling costs.

This situation was only rectified in early 1782 when the Government appointed Brook Watson as head of the Commissariat Department. Unlike any of his predecessors, Watson received the full backing of the latest (and final) commander-in-chief in America, Lieutenant General Sir Guy Carleton, so was able to end many of the abuses and to establish a formal structure for the commissariat with written instructions for each of his principal subordinates. However, a basic flaw existed in the system, which was the commissary-general remained personally liable for any discrepancies in all issues, receipts and expenditures, meaning that he was compelled to spend far more time on his accounts than concentrating on the broader problems of departmental efficiency and army supply.[12]

Thus, by 1793, there existed much accumulated experience of how to supply a field army. As early as 1782, Watson had submitted a plan for the complete reorganisation of the commissariat. This was never acted upon and, given the end of the war within one year of Watson's appointment, there was little incentive for the Government to pursue the matter further. However, in June 1789 Pitt had sought his views concerning the duties of a commissary-general. Watson strongly recommended that the post should exist in peace as well as in war, so that expenditure could be accurately monitored, costs reduced and efficiencies made in the dispatch of supplies overseas.[13] Despite this interest from the Prime Minister, Watson's suggestions were not adopted and the Army remained without a commissariat function until after the outbreak of war with France.

The Role of the Treasury

A fully functioning commissariat was an essential part of a field army, but the British Commissariat was a civilian organisation under Treasury control, and it sparked to life only in time of war. It is therefore worth examining the role of the Treasury in some detail, since it was this institution which shaped the Commissariat and provided the directing force behind its operations.

Personnel
On the outbreak of war with France in February 1793, the initial priority for the Treasury was to appoint a commissary-general with experience of supply issues, and who was capable of forming a department to the standard required by the expeditionary force. Unsurprisingly, the man chosen for this task was Brook Watson.

---

12   R.A. Bowler, 'Sir Henry Clinton and Army Profiteering: a Neglected Aspect of the Clinton-Cornwallis Controversy', *William and Mary Quarterly*, third series, vol.31, 1974, pp.111–122 and R.A. Bowler, 'The American Revolution and British Army Administrative Reform', *Journal of the Society for Army Historical Research*, vol.58, 1980, pp.66–77.
13   TNA: PRO 30/8/187: Watson to Pitt, 4 June 1789, Chatham Papers.

Watson was born in 1735, so aged 58 when he proceeded to Flanders. He was orphaned at the age of six and sent to live with a relative in Boston, Massachusetts, until going to sea. This career was short lived as he lost a leg to a shark whilst swimming off Havana, by which time his relative had become bankrupt, and he recuperated in Nova Scotia with a new guardian. It was here that he gained his first experience as a commissary, first at the siege of Beauséjour in 1755 and then under Major General James Wolfe at Louisbourg in 1758. He proceeded to London the following year and spent the best part of the next two decades as a merchant trading mainly to America. He achieved some standing during this period, becoming a member of the first committee at Lloyds in 1772 and helping form a body of light horse volunteers in 1779. Thus, Watson already had some 27 years of business and military experience behind him before his appointment as commissary-general to the forces in North America in March 1782. This appointment lasted for one year before he returned to Britain. It was during the 10 years between the end of the American War and the outbreak of war with France in 1793 that his position as a public figure took off. He was elected a Member of Parliament in 1784 as a Government candidate and remained as such until resigning his seat on proceeding to Flanders in 1793. He also served as chairman of the Commons select committee on the Regency in 1788. Watson was active in the Corporation of London, being elected a city alderman in 1784, Sheriff in 1785–1786 and Lord Mayor in 1796–1797. Other appointments included service as a director of the Bank of England for several terms between 1784 and 1806, before being deputy governor in 1806–1807; his close association with Lloyds led to him being appointed chairman between 1796 and 1806.[14] The decades spent in business, together with his service as a commissary in North America, made Watson an experienced member of the Duke of York's staff, and it is clear that his ability to organise and control his department was largely responsible for the adequacy of supplies in 1793–1795.[15] His experience was clearly recognised in the army, and on at least one occasion he was asked to negotiate on behalf of the Ordnance Department commissaries, even though they had their own autonomous structure.[16] He was also regarded as a useful man to know, and General Sir Henry Clinton advised his son Henry, one of the Duke of York's aides-de-camp: 'Pray be civil to Mr Watson the Com'ry that he may be so to you some how'. Clinton followed his father's advice, dining with Watson on 10 July 1793.[17] Watson remained a strong supporter of Pitt after resigning his seat in Parliament and maintained a correspondence with the Prime Minister. Watson's letters to Pitt, although few in number, are valuable in assessing the

---

14   E. Lloyd, and J. Shields, 'Watson, Sir Brook, first baronet (1735–1807), merchant and army official', *ODNB*, <https://doi.org/10.1093/ref:odnb/28829>, accessed 5 June 2020 and 'WATSON, Brook (1735–1807), of East Sheen, Surr', *The History of Parliament Online*, <https://www.historyofparliamentonline.org/volume/1790-1820/member/watson-brook-1735-1807>, accessed 11 July 2021. The National Gallery of Art in Washington D.C. holds the painting 'Watson and the Shark' by John Singleton Copley (1738–1815), accession number 1963.6.1. See colour illustration in this volume.
15   TNA: AO 16/52: pp.73–76, Watson to De Diemar, 16 June 1793 and H. Le Mesurier, (1801) *The British Commissary, in Two Parts*, (London: T. Egerton, 1801), pp.78–84.
16   TNA: AO 16/52: pp.67–69, Watson to Rose, 14 June 1793.
17   WLCL: Henry Clinton Papers: vol.235, Sir Henry Clinton to Henry Clinton, 2 June 1793; UML: The Clinton Papers (uncatalogued): Henry Clinton to Sir Henry Clinton, 10 July 1793.

mood at headquarters and the attitude of the army towards its leaders – matters in which Pitt undoubtedly had an interest.[18]

Watson was appointed 'Commissary General' on 27 February 1793 and subsequently received a warrant as 'Superintendent and Director of Forage, Provisions necessaries and Extraordinaries of our Army now serving or to serve on the Continent of Europe' on 1 March 1793 with a salary of £4 per day.[19] The three specific tasks given to him in his commission were '… inspecting the Rates and Goodness …', '… viewing and taking an Account of …' and '… to settle and adjust all accounts relating…' to the stores, in other words quality control, stock taking and auditing. The warrant was more specific:

> We do hereby authorize and empower the said Brook Watson to procure and provide Forage, provisions, Bread and Waggons, and Waggon Horses, Wood, Straw and all other necessaries, and Conveniences commonly called Contingencies for the use of our said Army consulting the Commander in Chief of our said Army as to the places where Magazines of Forage should be laid up & the quantities to be provided at each place and as to the removal and delivery thereof to such place or places as the necessity of the service may require.

It will be noticed that no mention was made of money in either the commission or warrant, despite the fact that none of the listed duties could be performed without it, nor could the troops be paid. This requirement, fundamental to every task undertaken by a commissary, is examined in greater detail below.

When Watson proceeded to the United Provinces he was accompanied by Henry Motz, appointed as deputy commissary-general, and Robert Gould as assistant commissary-general. All three had received commissions from both the Treasury and the War Office which gave them the necessary authority to act as guardians of the public money with which they were entrusted and to fulfil their role in supplying the army.[20] Little is known regarding the background of either Motz or Gould. The former was described by Herbert Taylor as, '… a Hessian by birth, was a man of superior resource …' whilst the latter served for only about six months before he fell ill and died at Menen in October 1793.[21] All three men joined the army over two weeks after the troops, embarking on the ship *Cleopatra* at Sheerness and disembarking at Helvoetsluys on 17 March. Watson arrived at army headquarters in Dordrecht two days later.[22]

Aside from Motz and Gould, the Treasury recruited John Bessell as assistant commissary with a salary of 20/– per day, though with a Treasury commission only, ranking him below

---

18 These are in TNA: PRO 30/8/187: Chatham Papers.
19 TNA: HO 51/147: pp.54–55, Commission appointing Brook Watson as Commissary General, 27 February 1793 and T 52/80: pp.273–275, King's Warrant appointing Brook Watson as Superintendent and Director of Forage, Provisions, necessaries and Extraordinaries, 1 March 1793.
20 TNA: HO 51/147: pp.56–57, Commission appointing Henry Motz as Deputy Commissary General, 27 February 1793; HO 51/147: p.58, Commission appointing Robert Gould as Assistant Commissary General, 27 February 1793.
21 TNA: AO 16/52: pp.156–157, Watson to Rose, 10 October 1793 and Taylor (ed.), *Taylor Papers*, p.29.
22 TNA: AO 16/52: pp.3–4, Watson to Rose, 17 and 19 March 1793.

Watson, Motz and Gould.[23] He was a German who also spoke English and French, being described by Watson as a man of business, so ideally suited to the work required; he was immediately sent to Nijmegen and Emmerich to establish magazines for the Hanoverian troops en route to the army. Not all personnel were found by the Treasury, and a key issue during Watson's first weeks in Flanders was to recruit suitably qualified staff. By the middle of April, he had hired Gideon Duncan as assistant commissary on a salary of 10/6 per day, Theodor Thriemann as interpreter and messenger at 5/– per day and Frederick Bussenius as wagonmaster at 4/6 per day. He also had three clerks who joined the department between 6 and 16 April, each being paid 10/6 per day. One of these, Charles Lutyens, took leave to England for the recovery of his health in December 1793, so may have been appointed by the authorities at home; the other two (Francis Coffin and Thomas Greet) were recruited locally by Watson, but it is not known how they came to his notice. By 17 April the department numbered 10 men including Watson.[24]

The difficulties of procuring suitably qualified commissaries were significant and Watson was concerned that the pay of 20/– per day for assistant commissaries, who formed the backbone of the department, provided little incentive to men possessing suitable qualifications, and was insufficient recompense for undergoing the hardships and dangers of active service. The problem was only alleviated in February 1794 when the Treasury obtained War Office agreement to allow assistant commissaries half pay of 7/6 per day, this being a significant incentive to well qualified individuals since it was a retainer for possible future services and provided a small income. An additional 5/– per day was paid them by the Treasury. These new arrangements were agreed only on the basis that no-one employed in the Commissariat would receive any perquisite or remuneration on top of their official pay.[25] Returning to the situation in 1793, the Treasury wrote to the commissary-general during the first week in April asking for a list of all the staff he required.[26] Watson's request for more assistance on 17 April met with an assurance six days later that two appointments would be made as soon as possible. This was done just over a fortnight after Watson's original request, when the Treasury appointed Benjamin Mee as assistant commissary together with Captain Frederick De Diemar (of whom more below) later in the month.[27] Mee's appointment appears to have been the result of family influence with the diplomat, Lord Malmesbury, though he was also the brother-in-law of the second Lord Palmerston.[28] The Treasury was equally rapid in meeting Watson's subsequent requests for additional commissaries in 1793 and in 1794, with appointments generally being made within one month.[29]

---

23 TNA: T 52/81: p.194, King's Warrant appointing John Bessell as Assistant Commissary, 1 March 1793.
24 TNA: AO 16/52: pp.19–21, Watson to Rose, 15 April 1793 and AO 16/52: pp.21–23 and pp.204–207: Watson to Long, 17 April 1793 and 1 January 1794.
25 TNA: WO 58/167: pp.78–79, Rose to Watson, 28 February 1794.
26 TNA: WO 58/167: pp.2–3, Rose to Watson, 3 April 1793.
27 TNA: WO 58/167: pp.11–12, Rose to Watson, 17 May 1793; AO 16/52: pp.52–55, Watson to Rose, 23 May 1793 and T 52/80: p.322, King's Warrants appointing Benjamin Mee and Frederick De Diemar as assistant commissaries.
28 B. Connell, *Portrait of a Whig Peer: Compiled from the Papers of the Second Viscount Palmerston, 1739–1802* (London: Andre Deutsch, 1957), p.285.
29 For example, James Newland and John Brawn were appointed on 10 July following a letter from Watson dated 14 June. TNA: AO 16/52: pp.67–69, Watson to Rose, 14 June 1793; WO 58/167: p.27:

Recruitment continued throughout the remainder of 1793 as magazines were established at various locations and required management (see Appendix III). Watson outlined where the 26 members of the Commissariat were based in a return dated 24 December 1793. He and his deputy, Henry Motz, were located at headquarters with two clerks and the wagonmaster whilst magazines were located at Tournai, Oudenaarde, Kortrijk, Ypres and Nieuwpoort. The six assistant commissaries were based at Bruges, Tournai, Ostend, Nieuwpoort and Diksmuide, and two at Ghent, whilst Havilland Le Mesurier, who had by then replaced the deceased Robert Gould as assistant commissary-general, was at Bruges. The 10 clerks were distributed between these locations, with the exception of Robert Hugh Kennedy (who subsequently served as Wellington's commissary-general for much of the Peninsular War) based at Dendermonde.[30]

The recruitment of assistant commissaries lasted until the army retreated into Germany at the end of January 1795, with nine men joining in 1794 and a further two in January 1795. Nearly all these appointees were civilians, meaning that details of their background and experience are sometimes difficult to confirm. Some were recruited locally, whereas others were sent from Britain and a minority were military personnel. One of these was Captain Frederick De Diemar of the 60th Regiment whose Army rank dated from 20 June 1778 and his rank in the regiment from 24 September 1787; he was appointed assistant commissary on 24 May 1793 and was described by Watson as: '… a Gentleman very conversant with business and well acquainted with the language of the Continent'.[31] Captain George Munro received the same appointment one year later, on 28 May 1794. The only individual in the 1794 *Army List* with the correct name and rank was Captain Lieutenant and Captain George Munro of what in the 1795 *Army List* became the 95th Regiment, whose regimental rank dated from 30 October 1793. Lieutenant Digby Hamilton of the 2nd Dragoons was appointed '… inspecting Com'y for superintending the Receipt of Forage for the Cav'y, Inf'y & departments of the Army (the Artillery excepted)' on 31 January 1794. He was subsequently promoted to major in the foreign corps raising for the service of Great Britain and succeeded Captain James Poole when the latter returned to Britain for the recovery of his health in December 1794.[32]

One key appointment lacking was that of deputy paymaster, which caused Watson considerable inconvenience. It was unfortunate that this was not rectified by the Treasury for over four months, and when the appointee, Captain Edward Williams, did eventually arrive on 11 July he had to spend several days in learning his business.[33] Watson was also inconvenienced by the lack of a commissary of accounts until Charles Mason, who had previously served in Germany during the Seven Years' War, was appointed on 21 June with a salary

---

Rose to Watson, 9 July 1793 and T 52/80: p.322, King's Warrants appointing James Newland and John Brawn as assistant commissaries.
30 TNA: AO 16/52: pp.204–207, Watson to Long, 1 January 1794. This is the first written evidence of Kennedy's presence in the commissariat structure.
31 TNA: WO 58/167: pp.11–12, Rose to Watson, 17 May 1793.
32 NAM: 1985-12-15-5: GO, Gent, 31 January 1794 and TNA: AO 16/53/7: GO, Arnhem, 2 December 1794.
33 TNA: AO 16/52: pp.3–4, Watson to Rose, 19 March 1793; T 52/80: p.370, King's Warrant appointing Edward Williams as Deputy Paymaster, 6 July 1793; T 1/719: Paymaster-general to Treasury, 25 June 1793 and AO 16/52: pp.89–90, Watson to Rose, 12 July 1793.

of £2 per day.³⁴ As commissary of accounts, Mason was: 'To examine, audit and certify all accounts whatsoever of money due for forage, provisions, necessaries and extraordinaries.' This was of the greatest use to the Commissariat Department in monitoring the supplies issued, since the receipts signed by regimental officers were checked against the contents of the magazines concerned, which in theory provided an accurate account of the stores in hand. The point should be made, however, that Mason's certification of the accounts did not remove Watson's personal liability for any expenses that the Treasury might later deem unnecessary. Rather, his principal duty from the Treasury's viewpoint was to ensure that the arithmetic contained in the accounts was correct, before submitting them to the Treasury for auditing.³⁵ The lack of specialist financial personnel for the first four months of the campaign was highly detrimental, since the deputy commissary, Henry Motz, had to perform the duties of deputy paymaster and commissary of accounts in addition to his normal function. The initial shortage of staff also meant that the over worked commissaries were so taken up with their duties that when Mason reached headquarters he discovered that there were no accounts to check, since Watson and his colleagues had found no time to prepare them. This situation continued throughout the remainder of the year, and Mason quickly discovered that what accounts he was given were rarely accompanied by the necessary certificates of purchase and other supporting documentation.³⁶

The type of abuse these individuals were appointed to check concerned the issuing of rations. The Commissariat Department was aware that some units were drawing more rations than they were entitled to, but the extent to which this happened could not be checked without an official to monitor it. This abuse was especially prevalent amongst the Hanoverian contingent, which, as Watson later discovered, had been drawing rations according to their theoretical strength and not for the number of men and horses actually present.³⁷ The problem was alleviated to some extent by the activities of the commissary of musters, Major William Gunn, but the number of units in the army meant that a single official could not provide a regular statement of strengths without the cooperation of the adjutant-general.

Aside from these inconveniences, there was an additional problem arising from the late appointment of a commissary of accounts and the consequent backlog of work following his arrival with the army. This concerned the late payment of invoices submitted by contractors who had provided supplies or transportation during the 1793 campaign. None could be paid until Mason had examined the accounts provided by the commissaries, together with their associated vouchers, and his decision was final. These delays caused many suppliers to cease doing business with the army because they were unable to wait the length of time it took for their bills to be paid. The result was that only one major supplier remained for the

---

34 TNA: T 52/80: p.379, King's Warrant appointing Charles Mason as Commissary of Accounts, 21 June 1793; HO 51/147: p.93, Commission appointing Charles Mason as Commissary of Accounts, 21 June 1793; WO 58/167: pp.17–18, Rose to Watson, 31 May 1793 and T 27/43: pp.331–332, Rose to Mason, 9 July 1793.
35 TNA: AO 16/52: pp.107–108, Watson to Mason, 21 July 1793 and AO 16/52: pp.116–117, Watson to Rose, 2 August 1793.
36 TNA: T 1/724: Mason to Rose, 5 November 1793 and T 1/739: Mason to Rose, 16 December 1794.
37 TNA: AO 16/52: pp.83–85, Watson to Rose, 2 July 1793 and AO 16/52: pp.104–106, Watson to Rose, 23 July 1793.

1794 campaign, since the scale of his operations enabled him to absorb a longer wait than his smaller competitors.[38] As is discussed further below, this was Ernst Jacob Eckhardt who, being effectively the sole supplier, could charge higher prices. This was a fact noted by the Treasury, which also advised Watson to avoid relying so heavily on Eckhardt, and to establish magazines in case he failed in his contractual obligations.[39]

One further appointment, the absence of which was keenly felt during 1793, was that of wagonmaster-general. The Dutchman, Frederick Bussenius was appointed on 1 April 1793 and placed in charge of the selection of horses and drivers for a consideration of 10/- per day. He was a horse breeder by trade but was only hired on a four-month contract, which expired at the end of July. Bussenius worked alongside another Dutchman, Alexander Robays, who was placed in charge of the 'Waggon Department' at the commencement of the 1793 campaign, also at 10/- per day.[40]

The arrival of Lord Moira's force in mid-1794 caused Watson some disquiet, since the head of his commissariat, Alexander Davison, also held the title of 'Commissary General.' The problem had arisen because Davison was appointed in November 1793, at a time when Moira's troops were intended to be sent to aid French royalist insurgents in La Vendée, rather than to Flanders. The Treasury initially attempted to solve the difficulty by informing Watson that Davison would be under his orders but, as Watson replied on 27 June: 'The moment Mr. Davison shall sign himself Commissary General the people of this Country and all Bankers will look on my authority as superseded and the Credit of the Public Bills experience a wound.' The difficulty was eventually solved by 1 July when the Treasury informed Watson that Davison was not to proceed with Moira's force.[41] Although many of the appointments necessary for the efficient operation of the Commissariat Department were not made until the beginning of the 1794 campaign, the above examples demonstrate that the Treasury was both receptive to Brook Watson's recommendations, he being the person best placed to make them, and effective in response to his requests. Accordingly, a high priority was given to the demands of the expeditionary force, and the cost of fulfilling them set aside.

A final point has to do with the unknown number of locally-recruited personnel, who were an integral part of commissariat operations. These comprised wagon drivers, boatmen, labourers employed at the different magazines and for such tasks as loading or unloading various forms of transport. These individuals were not recorded in the official documentation, so the true extent to which they were used remains unclear. Some of them would have been employed directly by civilian contractors, others may have been soldiers sent 'on command' to assist, and yet more, local 'casuals', recruited according to need.[42] The employment of foreigners at middle and senior management levels within the commissariat

---

38 Le Mesurier, *The British Commissary*, pp.43–46.
39 TNA: WO 58/167: pp.101–102, Rose to Watson, 10 October 1794. See also AO 1/209/606: E.J. Eckhardt, victuals for the continent, 1793–1795.
40 TNA: AO 16/52: pp.25–29 and 277–278, Watson to Rose, 20 April 1793 and 22 May 1794.
41 TNA: WO 58/167: pp.96–97, Rose to Watson, 20 June 1794; PRO 30/8/187: Watson to Rose, 27 June 1794, Chatham Papers and WO 58/167: p.98: Rose to Watson, 1 July 1794.
42 This issue is discussed in the context of the Peninsular War by Redgrave, *Wellington's Logistical Arrangements*, pp.30–33.

structure (such as Henry Motz and John Bessell) demonstrated the ability to compensate for shortages in personnel or skills by utilising the financial power of the state.[43]

Issuing Instructions

The second function of the Treasury was to issue instructions on procedural matters, especially around the procurement and paying-out of hard cash, as mentioned above in connection with the commissariat during the Seven Years' War. When Watson sailed to America in 1782 he had done so without any clear idea of the real nature of his job, as the Treasury replied to his request for instructions by informing him that there were none and never had been for any of his predecessors. This was remedied in 1793 when the Treasury issued him with a set of instructions dated 9 March authorising him to draw and negotiate bills of exchange for the pay and subsistence of the army. Significantly, Watson was entrusted to do this himself, without direct Treasury involvement, and was merely enjoined to negotiate at the most favourable exchange rate and with the least commission. Once procured, cash was deposited with the deputy paymaster and Watson had to obtain vouchers from two merchants stating the prices were in line with the market. The vouchers, together with a witnessed receipt from the vendor, were to be authorised by the Duke of York in person. Watson was also instructed to submit his accounts every two months, to keep a strict record of all the provisions and stores purchased or issued and to obtain certificates for any stores lost, damaged or destroyed.[44] Taken as a whole, these Treasury regulations provided Watson with perhaps the greatest powers ever given to a British commissary-general during the eighteenth century. It is possible that he had made it quite clear to the Prime Minister what was required prior to setting out for the army. Whatever, the Treasury had placed great personal trust in Brook Watson.

Despite being adequately informed as to his overall powers and responsibilities, Watson did not receive guidance on several matters of detail before his departure. One of these concerned the payment of bât and forage money, which is illustrative of the difficulties experienced by the commissariat in supplying an army in the field. As was mentioned in Chapter 2, bât money was paid approximately every 200 days to officers responsible for the upkeep of the regimental transport, such as company commanders, surgeons and paymasters, whereas forage money was paid to all officers officially authorised to keep horses. At his first meeting with the Duke of York on 19 March 1793, Watson was ordered to issue bât and forage money, for which he was given authority to draw a bill for £50,000. He was understandably reticent to make payments according to the unofficial scale set by headquarters when the army first disembarked, due to his personal liability for any over-payments. The problem was not so much one of raising the necessary cash, but rather that he had received no instructions as to the different rates payable to officers according to their rank. The Treasury decided in early April to transmit this money to the regimental agents in England, and received a list of all officers eligible for such payments one month later, but it was unfortunate that the matter was not settled until the beginning of September when the money was actually paid out. This tardiness may not be wholly ascribed to the Treasury, since delays had been

---

43 Chilcott, *Maintaining the British Army*, pp.61 and 63.
44 Bowler, 'Administrative Reform', pp.73–74 and Le Mesurier, *The British Commissary*, pp.64–67.

experienced in obtaining the requisite scale of allowances from the adjutant-general and the commander-in-chief.[45] Despite this, it is clear that Watson was under considerable pressure to have the matter settled, since many officers had expended large sums of their own money and had been led by the Duke of York to expect relatively swift repayment.

A further matter which generated significant correspondence between Watson and the Treasury during 1793 concerned the arrangements for supplying and paying the Hanoverian and Hessian contingents. The sums involved were significant, and this affected Watson's responsibilities for providing money in local currency (which will be discussed below). Watson had sought instructions in early April concerning the payment of the Hanoverians and the matter was settled six weeks later when the Treasury arranged for their pay to be transmitted to Baron Alvensleben, the Hanoverian minister in London, every two months.[46] Watson was also well served regarding information on the ration scales used by the Hanoverians, receiving a reply from the Treasury only 10 days after his initial request.[47]

Details for operating the contracts for the Hessian troops were not so easily settled, however. The Treasury initially arranged for the payment of the Hesse Cassel troops to be made to the minister of the Landgrave in London. However, this decision was overturned three months later when he was instructed to pay £30,000 in September and to assume responsibility for paying the Hesse Darmstadt and Baden Durlach soldiers.[48] As with pay, the difficulties over arranging other supplies to the Hessians took somewhat longer to resolve than for the Hanoverians. After waiting from July to December for any instructions from London, Watson settled the matter himself by applying the ration scales set for Dutch troops.[49] These were all matters that could have been settled when the contracts were originally signed, and the reason they were not may have been due to the involvement of several Government departments, which shows how much quicker business went when the Treasury alone had responsibility. It is also likely that affairs concerning the Hanoverians were more easily settled since their government was responsible to King George III, in his capacity as Elector of Hanover, whereas this was not the case with the Hessians.

One area in which the Treasury had not been involved was in issuing instructions to the assistant commissaries serving in Flanders. Havilland Le Mesurier received his appointment on 31 July 1793 and subsequently wrote: '... the Assistant Commissaries sent out to the Continent during the late Campaigns, received no other information from the Treasury, than notice of their appointment, and verbal orders to join at head quarters'.[50] Those without

---

45 TNA: AO 16/52: pp.3–4, 15, 43, 59, 65–66, 93–95 and 140–142: Watson to Rose, 19 March, 4 April, 7 May, 1 and 11 June, 16 July and 4 September 1793; T 1/713: Watson to Treasury, 11 June 1793 and T 1/721: De Lancey to Long, 14 August 1793.
46 TNA: WO 58/167: pp.4 and 12, Rose to Watson, 9 April and 24 May 1793 and AO 16/52: pp.79–80, Watson to Rose, 25 June 1793.
47 TNA: AO 16/52: pp.83–85, Watson to Rose, 2 July 1793 and WO 58/167: p.31, Rose to Watson, 12 July 1793.
48 TNA: WO 58/167: pp.21–22, Rose to Watson, 21 June 1793; WO 58/167: p.61, Long to Watson, 13 September 1793; AO 16/52: pp.176–177, Watson to Rose, 15 November 1793 and AO 16/52: pp.178–180, Watson to Rose, 19 November 1793.
49 TNA: AO 16/52: pp.89–90, Watson to Rose, 12 July 1793 and AO 16/52: pp.186–188, Watson to Rose, 3 December 1793.
50 Le Mesurier, *The British Commissary*, p.2.

previous commissariat experience had to learn on the job. The situation was only rectified in late May 1794 after Brook Watson had the time to prepare a comprehensive set of instructions that were issued to all assistant commissaries appointed after that date, when precise duties and responsibilities were set out in writing for the first time. The foremost of these was to ensure that suitable storage facilities were provided for the supplies entrusted to them and that accounts were completed on the 15th and last day of every month, to be submitted to the commissary-general together with all supporting vouchers. The business of checking the flow of supplies in and out of magazines, which was done by completing weigh bills, formed the next part of the instructions, followed by the order that receipts should be returned by the receiving party for any supplies issued. Needless to state, any stores the assistant commissary purchased had to be verified by a written receipt, whilst he had to order an official survey on supplies which were found to be damaged. Weighing equipment had to be used to minimise the possibility of future complaints regarding short weights being issued. Aside from the actual management of the magazine, assistant commissaries were informed that: 'Commissariat Articles are Meal, Bread, Forage, Fuel and Straw…' and were urged to make themselves aware of the availability of these items in the surrounding district together with details of any contractors who might be able to supply them. The instructions closed with sample copies of standardised forms for reporting flows of receipts, issues and cash.[51]

Provision of Supplies

A third matter in which the Treasury was closely involved concerned the dispatch of supplies to the army from England in cases where similar articles could not be obtained locally. The first test of the Treasury's organisational skills came soon after Watson and his colleagues arrived in the United Provinces, when the fledgling Commissariat Department was faced with the immediate task of finding food and forage for the army. Without any prior network of merchants and bankers from whom supplies could be obtained, Watson discovered that he was unable to furnish enough provisions, so was forced to write to the Treasury requesting 250 tons of flour and 1,000 tons of hay to be sent out from England, since seasonal factors meant both commodities were difficult to obtain locally. Having received Watson's requests during the second week in April, the Treasury wrote to assure him that the requisite supplies would be sent to Ostend as ordered.[52] The mechanisms for fulfilling a request such as this were already in place, since in peacetime it was the responsibility of the Treasury to obtain provisions (especially bread, wood, straw and forage) for the troops at home and abroad, and this was done through public advertisement. The offers submitted were passed to the Comptrollers of Army Accounts who selected the lowest bidder and arranged the contract. The Comptrollers were sent a record of the deliveries made by the governor of the relevant garrison who checked them and then paid the contractor; a final check on the transaction was made retrospectively by the Commissioners for Auditing the Public Accounts. For troops on foreign service, supplies dispatched from England were purchased

---

51 Le Mesurier, *The British Commissary*, pp.78–84.
52 TNA: AO 16/52: pp.16 and 17–18, Watson to Rose, 5 and 8 April 1793; WO 58/167: pp.5–6, Rose to Watson, 12 and 16 April 1793; AO 16/52: pp.21–23 and 33, Watson to Long, 17 April 1793 and Watson to Rose, 26 April 1793.

by the Navy Victualling Board, which routinely performed this function for the ships of His Majesty's fleet and was accustomed to the process of negotiating with contractors. The task of delivering supplies to overseas garrisons was undertaken by the Commissioners for Transports.[53]

Despite this well-defined procedure, the mechanisms for obtaining supplies during peacetime were initially inadequate for provisioning an army on active service, and Watson grew increasingly desperate as he saw the countryside being denuded of forage. George Rose, the Treasury Secretary, wrote to Watson on 7 May that: 'My Lords [Commissioners of the Treasury] … direct me to repeat to you that the utmost Exertions are making to forward the sending to Ostend the Flour and Hay you have written for,' but it was not until a month after Watson's original request that the ships actually arrived.[54] Watson continually stressed the general difficulty of procuring hay and oats due to the season of the year, and this led the Treasury to approach the deputy adjutant-general, Colonel Oliver De Lancey, in the middle of May.[55] De Lancey duly procured 1,000 tons each of oats and hay, dispatching the whole to Ostend by the end of the month at a cost of £15,000.[56] This second consignment was conveyed to the army in approximately half the time the first had taken, but it is not clear whether this was due to the intervention of De Lancey in the matter. These supplies alleviated Watson's difficulties in providing for the cavalry until July, when he requested a further 125 tons of oats which were received the following month.[57] After these initial difficulties during the first four months of the 1793 campaign, the effectiveness of Watson's own arrangements meant that he was able to find almost all supplies himself, with the exception of such items as coal, rugs, blankets and entrenching tools which were more difficult or expensive to obtain on the continent than in England. As will be discussed below, it was only when the army retreated first to the River Meuse and then to the Waal during the autumn of 1794 that he once again assumed a greater dependence on supplies from home.[58] Far from being obstructive in the matter of meeting Watson's requests for supplies, there were at least two instances when the Treasury acted on its own initiative. The first occurred in May 1793 when the continued shortage of forage in Flanders led them to purchase 450 tons of hay to be stored at several ports in England to be ready for shipping as soon as it was

---

53 Anon., *Nineteenth Report from the Select Committee on Finance &c. Secretary at War, Comptrollers of Army Accounts, and Paymaster General* (London: House of Commons, 1797), pp.78–79 and Anon., *The Eighteenth Report of the Commissioners of Military Enquiry Appointed by Act of 45 Geo. III. Cap. 47. Office of the Commissariat* (London: House of Commons, 1812), p.251.
54 TNA: WO 58/167: pp.6–7 and 9–10, Rose to Watson, 19 April and 7 May 1793 and AO 16/52: p.49, Watson to Rose, 14 May 1793.
55 TNA: T 1/718: De Lancey to Rose, 27 May 1793; T 52/80: p.332, Treasury to De Lancey, 30 May 1793, King's Warrants and WO 58/167: pp.22–23, Rose to Watson, 28 June 1793.
56 TNA: T 1/718: De Lancey to Rose, 27 May and 1 June 1793 and T 1/719: Navy Office to Rose, 2 July 1793.
57 TNA: AO 16/52: pp.93–95, Watson to Rose, 16 July 1793 and WO 58/167: pp.53–54, Long to Watson, 2 August 1793.
58 Watson requested 50,000 lb of biscuit in September 1794, 2,000 tons of wheat meal in November and 32,000 lb of salted pork in December. TNA: WO 58/167: p.100, Long to Watson, 19 September 1794; WO 58/167: p.105: Rose to Watson, 11 November 1794 and T 27/44: p.151, Rose to Commissioners of Victualling, 12 February 1794.

needed.[59] The second concerned a similar quantity of bread, sufficient for 40,000 men for one month, which the Treasury ordered at the end of June 1794.[60]

The role of the Treasury was thus of crucial importance to the success of the commissariat. It now remains to examine how the Commissariat Department in Flanders actually went about fulfilling its principal functions of providing the army with food, forage and cash.

The Commissariat on Campaign

Cash

The first essential requisite for the commissariat was to obtain a secure financial base so that cash in local currencies could be used to pay contractors. The procedure was first to secure permission from the Duke of York to draw on the Treasury, after which the necessary documents were prepared. When the money was actually required, bills were given to an agent to negotiate at the best available exchange rate before the product was either held on account or passed to Watson or another appointed person. Bills could also be submitted to mercantile houses in payment for goods and services, but in both cases the Treasury required receipts for the items purchased together with the agent's accounts every two months. Once the deputy paymaster arrived in July 1793, specie was passed to him for paying the troops.[61]

Soon after his arrival in Flanders, Brook Watson visited the firm of Crawfurd & Co. in Rotterdam to discuss contractual terms. These were confirmed in a letter dated 25 March, which stated that a commission of a half of one percent was payable for negotiating bills of exchange with the Treasury whilst supplies could be procured with a two percent commission with payment by bills of exchange on which no commission would be payable. Watson also obtained terms from the firm of Melville & Wolff in Amsterdam, which were for a one percent commission for negotiating bills of exchange and a two percent commission for obtaining ready money. As both these firms were located in the United Provinces, Watson also visited Messrs Werbrouck & Co. of Antwerp, from whom he obtained £682,0,3 in gold, and Jean-Baptiste de Loose of Ghent, who charged one percent commission on negotiating bills with the Treasury.[62] Bills were the easiest method to obtain money, but Watson's use of them was limited by the rates of exchange. When these fell in August 1793, the Treasury was unable to send cash or allow Watson the continued use of bills, and instead had to approach private merchants in order to keep the army solvent.[63] Obtaining sufficient quantities of money with which to support the army assumed some importance from April 1794 when Watson calculated that a monthly sum of £200,000 was required to supply bread for

---

59   TNA: WO 58/167: pp.11–12, Rose to Watson, 17 May 1793.
60   TNA: WO 58/167: pp.97–98, Rose to Watson, 30 June 1794.
61   TNA: WO 58/167: pp.49–50, Rose to Watson, 23 July 1793 and AO 16/52: p.213, Motz to Rose, 4 January 1794.
62   TNA: AO 16/52: pp.6–7, Melville & Wolff to Watson, 25 March 1793; AO 16/52: pp.8–9, Crawfurd & Co. to Watson, 26 March 1793 and AO 16/52: pp.34–35: Watson to Rose, 3 May 1793.
63   TNA: AO 16/52: p.120, Watson to Rose, 4 August 1793; T 27/43: p.390, Rose to the Governor and Deputy Governor of the Bank of England, 14 August 1793 and WO 58/167: pp.57–59, Rose to Watson, 16 August 1793.

60,000 men and forage for 35,000 horses, as well as providing for the French prisoners. Only half of the requisite amount could be found in the Austrian Netherlands. The balance had to be obtained from the United Provinces and elsewhere, meaning the banking arrangements necessary to support the army assumed greater complexity as it grew in size. By early 1795 Watson was experiencing difficulties in obtaining cash. Bankers and merchants had little prospect of redeeming bills on the Treasury in London at a time when the British army was retreating, meaning there would be little recourse should payment fail to arrive. The Treasury appears to have been prompt in its response to this problem, sending Watson £100,000 in Spanish dollars in March 1795, but this circumstance underlines the correlation between operational success and the ability to sustain an army in the field.[64]

Food and Forage

Having secured ready access to money, the second function of the commissariat was to procure food and forage. When they first landed, the troops were provided with bread money, but this practice was soon discontinued by the Duke of York, and replaced by an issue of 1½ lb of bread per man from 25 March 1793. Officers' ration scales are rarely mentioned in the records but appear to have been 20 percent greater than the other ranks' issue, while five percent was allowed for wastage in the quantities purchased. In the majority of cases, bread was supplied ready-made, the principal ingredient being either flour, rye meal or a combination of the two. When this was unavailable, the troops were given ship's biscuit, but this was usually held in reserve for use in emergencies. At the end of 1793 the daily field ration consisted of 1 lb of bread or flour together with 12 ounces of pork, to be substituted with beef if unavailable, with the meat being procured by the regiment. Horses had a standard daily ration of 10 lb each of oats and hay, though the former could be substituted with beans and wagon horses received an additional 2 lb of oats per day. These ration scales were subject to adjustment according to the local supply situation so, for example, a general order of 17 December 1794 stated that heavy cavalry and draft horses were entitled to 14 lb of oats and 7 lb of hay, whereas light cavalry, bât and saddle horses received 2 lb less of oats. Just over one month later, on 21 January 1795, this was altered to 5 lb oats and 15 lb of hay. Another important commodity was 36 lb of straw issued per week per tent when encamped, with an additional 12 lb in the first week. Each soldier was also issued with 3 lb of wood per day for fuel (or 2 lb of coals in lieu) and each officer 6 lb, out of which the regimental sutler was to be supplied.[65] The commissariat also provided more limited quantities of other items, such as pease (dried peas) and bran, though these were mostly the responsibility of the individual unit to procure.[66]

---

64 TNA: AO 16/52: pp.265–266, Watson to Rose, 15 April 1794; AO 16/52: pp.269–270, Watson to Rose, 28 April 1794 and WO 58/167: pp.116–119, Rose to Watson, 10 March 1795.
65 NAM: 1985-12-15-4: GO, Tournay, 6 May 1793.
66 TNA: AO 16/52: pp.5–6, Watson to Rose, 29 March 1793; NAM: 1985-12-15-4: GO, Bergen-op-Zoom, 7 April 1793; TNA: AO 16/53/7: GO, Arnhem, 17 December 1794 and Deventer 21 January 1795. Information on ration scales may also be calculated from the details of Watson's contracts: AO 16/52: pp.34–35, Watson to Rose, 3 May 1793; T 27/44: p.108, Long to Commissioners of Victualling, 17 December 1793; NAM: 1985-12-15-5: GO, Courtray, 13 March 1794; TNA: WO 1/172: pp.327–380, Motz to Harcourt, 5 February 1795 and NAM: 1965-06-54-1: Regimental Orders of the 5th Dragoon Guards, 2 and 10 April 1794.

The quantities required of all these commodities could be very large. Watson contracted on 14 June 1793 with Pierre Martens of Ghent to supply all the British troops' bread requirements for delivery at Tournai. This involved 1,000,000 lb of meal consisting of two thirds rye and one third wheat at 6 Brabant Florins per 100 lb Brabant weight, which would supply 23,000 men for 40 days, the whole to be transported in designated weekly quantities over a five-week period. The contract also provided for the same quantity of oats to supply 20,000 horses for five days.[67] In July 1793, Watson contracted with the firm of S. Dhani for 30 days of supplies to be delivered to Ghent or Bruges commencing on 21 August, amounting to 6,000,000 lb of hay, 4,000,000 lb of oats, 735,000 lb of wheat meal, 840,000 lb of rye meal and 540,000 lb of straw; these quantities were calculated to supply the army for one month.[68] It should be stressed, however, that although these provisions provided the basis of the troops' diet, they were additional to those the soldiers procured themselves. The pressure on resources was greatest during the winter months or in areas with high concentrations of troops, though for those on outpost duty, such as Cornet Taylor White of the 7th Light Dragoons, foraging could be considerably easier: 'We live at no expence here as we have only to go into the Houses and look about for what we want & into the Fields for cows Pigs &c and vegetables of all kinds so that we live extremely well as we have plenty of every thing without paying a Farthing.'[69]

Assistant Surgeon James Dickson of the 1st Dragoons reported a similar happy situation in May 1794, but only when the local population did not consider themselves threatened:

> The country people from the village [Marquain] and several from Tournay bring every morning to the camp plenty of bread, butter, cheese, eggs, milk and coffee ready made. When we make an attack however we are very badly off, the peasants fly away from us as far as they can, and take away everything they can carry with them; in this case every man seizes what he can get, and it is then allowable (especially if in an enemy's country) to enter the deserted homes and take anything we can find.[70]

The great majority of supplies were obtained from contractors, with only a very small proportion being sent from England. By early May 1793, Watson had built up enough stocks to supply the bread ration for 42 days, with oats and hay for 60, a not inconsiderable achievement in the six weeks since he landed in the United Provinces.[71] One matter which required constant attention was the manner in which contracts were let, since over reliance on a single contractor could be problematic should that individual fail to perform. One example of this concerned a contract that Watson signed in early September 1793 with Ernst Jacob Eckhardt for 5,400 tons of oats to be delivered weekly to Ostend, Bruges and Nieuwpoort. Over three months later only 2,200 tons had been received and Watson feared that the remainder would

---

67 TNA: AO 16/52: pp.67–69, Watson to Rose, 14 June 1793 and T 27/45: pp.118–119, Rose to Comptrollers of Army Accounts, 23 December 1794.
68 TNA: AO 16/52: pp.113–115, Watson to Rose, 27 July 1793.
69 NAM: 1976-12-100: White to his father, 2 September 1793.
70 A.A. Cormack (ed.), *James Dickson, M.A., 1769–1795, Army Surgeon* (Aberdeen: Privately published, 1968), pp.60–61.
71 TNA: AO 16/52: pp.34–35, Watson to Rose, 3 May 1793.

not be forthcoming.⁷² Details of those contracts which can be traced reveal that Watson used at least six different suppliers during his first six months in Flanders. Although some of this diversification would have been due to concerns over performance, other factors were the nature of the supplies or services contracted for and where they were to be delivered. For example, in July 1793 when Watson wished to establish a magazine in Ghent, it made sense to use the contractor Pierre Martens, since he was based in the town.⁷³ Despite these considerations, Watson obtained the majority of his supplies from Eckhardt during the latter part of 1794 and 1795, with one contract made on 19 August 1794 being for 3,000,000 lb of wheat meal, 20,000,000 lb of oats, 16,000,000 lb of hay and 2,000,000 lb of straw. Although the lack of competition between suppliers meant the contractor could charge more for the provisions he sold, this was outweighed by the convenience of having one large counterparty at a time when the army was on an extended line of operations in a country with few resources.⁷⁴ Contractors were only paid when they produced proof of delivery, usually in the form of a receipt signed by a storekeeper or commissary, and consignments were phased on a weekly basis over the term of the contract. In cases where a service was provided, such as wagons or horses, payment would be at a fixed rate, either according to the volume of goods transported from one named location to another or as a flat fee by the week or month.

Magazines

A crucial aspect of the Commissariat Department's duties was the administration of magazines, the means by which supplies were collected, stored and distributed to the army. Watson was ordered at the end of March 1793 to establish magazines, and he therefore dispatched commissaries to Emmerich and Nijmegen to provision the Hanoverians during their march to join the army, to create a larger magazine at Antwerp for them, and others at Ostend and Bruges for the British.⁷⁵ When the army marched south at the end of April further magazines had to be established at Tournai and Ghent, but the commissaries encountered difficulties in stocking the former since important supplies could only be obtained at great cost, and the location of the army was primarily dictated by operational requirements rather than the supply situation.⁷⁶

Although the provisions collected at most of these places supplied the Duke of York's army for over a year, some magazines had a relatively short lifespan once the reason for establishing them had passed. Nijmegen, for example, was used for only two months, with the contents ordered to be sold at the end of May 1793, the distance and cost of moving them elsewhere being too great. Veurne was another temporary magazine where provisions were collected for troops engaged in the abortive siege of Dunkirk in August and September 1793 and several others at Nieuwpoort, Diksmuide, Kortrijk, Ypres and Oudenaarde were used whilst the troops were in winter quarters in 1793–1794.⁷⁷

---

72 TNA: AO 16/52: pp.140–142 and 193–195, Watson to Rose, 4 September and 13 December 1793.
73 TNA: AO 16/52: pp.109–112, Watson to Rose, 26 July 1793.
74 TNA: T 27/45: pp.118–119, Rose to Comptrollers of Army Accounts, 23 December 1794 and Anon., *Eighteenth Report*, pp.280 and 349.
75 TNA: AO 16/52: pp.5–6, 16 and 19–21, Watson to Rose, 29 March, 5 and 15 April 1793.
76 TNA: AO 16/52: pp.30–31 and 47–48, Watson to Rose, 26 April and 12 May 1793.
77 TNA: AO 16/52: pp.52–55, Watson to Rose, 23 May 1793 and AO 16/52: pp.204–207, Watson to Long, 1 January 1794.

The mechanisms for ensuring continued supplies to the magazines could be complex and troublesome, due to the basic conflict between subsisting an army from static magazines during a war of movement, and the fine line which the commissaries had to draw between locating magazines well to the rear, and thus relatively secure from enemy attack, and having them nearer the troops, in order to ease the distribution of supplies, but which increased the risk of enemy interference. From a commissariat perspective, the most challenging phase of the campaign began in mid-1794, when the army's retreat through the Austrian Netherlands led to the draw-down of magazines in Bruges, Tournai, Ypres, Kortrijk and Ostend to minimum levels, and their contents distributed elsewhere. Once any available river transport had been commandeered for artillery and regimental gear, most of the supplies (at Ghent and Dendermonde especially) had to be abandoned. This resulted in the loss of 1,000,000 lb of rye meal, 3,000,000 lb each of oats and hay and 56,000 lb of biscuit, costing an estimated £100,000.[78] This was the equivalent of enough bread for 35,000 men for 24 days and 20,000 horses for 15 days.[79]

Transportation
Transportation assets were acquired by contract in 1793, in the same manner as food and forage. The troops were located at Dordrecht during March, so supplies were located at or close to the ports at which they had been discharged. This changed when the army marched south to Tournai during the first three weeks of April. Watson therefore made a contract with a Mr. Saiys to provide 9,000 lb of bread and 10,000 lb each of oats and flour between 16 April and 17 May. These supplies were to be divided into rations at fixed prices:

 10 lb of oats and 10 lb of hay at 12 sols
 12 lb of oats and 10 lb of hay at 13 sols
 8 lb of oats, 10 lb of hay and 5 lb of straw at 12½ sols
 3 lb of bread at 3¼ sols[80]

Watson was responsible for transporting the whole, so he finalised a contract with Pierre Martens of Ghent on 26 April for 70 wagons – 40 bread wagons at 23 Louis d'Or each and 30 forage wagons at 21 Louis d'Or. The first cavalry to arrive at Ostend in early May brought supplies of forage with them, but Watson had to procure the means to transport it. He therefore contracted with Jean-Baptiste de Loose of Ghent on 3 May for 60 wagons with four horses each to be paid at the rate of 24 sols per 100 lb of supplies delivered. Watson calculated that this arrangement would deliver 240,000 lb of forage per day, but the contract had to be cancelled because the distance between Ostend and Tournai was too great and the wagons

---

78 TNA: AO 16/52: p.303, Watson to Rose, 7 July 1794; AO 16/52: pp.303–304, Newland to Watson, 6 July 1794 and PRO 30/8/187: Mee to Watson, 2 November 1794, Chatham Papers.
79 1,000,000 lb of rye minus five percent for wastage equals 950,000 lb. With a baking ratio of 3:4 this would produce 1,266.666 lb of bread or 844,444 rations of 1½ lb each. 35,000 men would consume this in 24 days. The baking ratio is taken from Le Mesurier, *The British Commissary*, p.21. Daily horse rations have been taken as 10 lb of oats plus 10 lb of hay. The small volume of biscuit has not been included in these calculations.
80 TNA: AO 16/52: pp.25–29, Watson to Rose, 20 April 1793. Sols were copper coins and were a unit of currency in the Austrian Netherlands.

employed frequently broke down. He therefore made a new contract with de Loose on 23 May for 100 wagons of four horses each at 8 florins per day with 10 lb of oats to be provided for each horse. De Loose would also provide four conductors charged at 6 Austrian schillings per day.[81] Until this movement could be completed, the 7th, 11th, 15th and 16th Light Dragoons were unable to leave Ostend, their port of disembarkation, since the supplies they had brought with them could not immediately be transported to Tournai.[82]

Watson recognised that water transport was not only cheaper than road, but also more efficient, since losses were minimised, but he was greatly hampered by the shortage of river craft, or bilanders,[83] since the Dutch Commissariat also used the same method of transport. A lack of wagons was also experienced at various times. Once the army came near to Valenciennes, it was supplied from the Austrian magazine at Quiverain for a period of three weeks from 22 May, but only two days of bread and forage were obtainable at each issue and Watson advised the Treasury that the frequent unavailability of wagons to transport these supplies 10 miles to where the men were located: '… has caused murmurs and discontents extremely painful to my mind'.[84]

A bilander, by Pearson Scott Foresman. (Public Domain)

---

81 A schilling was a unit of currency in the Austrian Netherlands, equivalent to approximately 7 pence sterling in 1793. C. Este, *A Journey in the Year 1793, through Flanders, Brabant, and Germany, to Switzerland* (London: Debrett, 1795) p.83.
82 TNA: AO 16/52: pp.30–31 and 34–35 and 52–55, Watson to Rose, 26 April, 3 and 23 May 1793; PRO 30/8/187: Watson to Pitt, 5 May 1793, Chatham Papers; T 27/45: pp.118–119, Rose to Comptrollers of Army Accounts, 23 December 1794 and York to George III, 31 May 1793, in Aspinall, *Later Correspondence*, vol.2, p.45.
83 Bilander – a small two-masted cargo vessel mostly used on canals.
84 TNA: AO 16/52: pp.57–58 and 60–63, Watson to Rose, 29 May and 6 June 1793.

By 24 December 1793, transport controlled by the Commissariat comprised 102 covered and 16 open wagons together with 41 covered wagons for the sick and wounded and 300 horses. However, the majority of the transport was contracted, and consisted of 220 wagons with four horses each; the establishment for the field bakery was additional to this.[85] Leaving the field bakery aside, these figures show that 42 percent of the wagons and 25 percent of the horses were contracted.

The experience of contracting transport services during the 1793 campaign led to an overhaul of the arrangements in early 1794. Despite the presence of Bussenius and Robays, Watson had discovered during the first campaign that the time spent in contracting for, purchasing and administering the hundreds of wagons, horses and drivers required by the army was considerable. He also calculated that hiring wagons and teams involved an additional annual expenditure of nearly £19,000 with nothing else to show, since the transport was returned to its owners. He presented his case for the formation of a wagon corps in purely financial terms as a cost saving measure, but it is almost certain that he wished to reduce the considerable burden on himself through the appointment of a wagonmaster-general who would undertake the responsibility for administering transport arrangements, while also eliminating the uncertainties of using civilian drivers.[86]

Watson's proposal led to the creation of the Corps of Royal Waggoners under the command of Captain James Poole, who arrived at headquarters on 14 May 1794, some four months after the Treasury had received Watson's initial request for assistance.[87] Poole's duties concerned the haulage of supplies, which was a commissariat function, and of baggage, the responsibility of the quartermaster-general via the newly created position of baggage master following the appointment of John Kerr on 20 February 1794. Poole's reporting lines were therefore to the commissary-general, except when hauling baggage when he followed the directions of the quartermaster-general. This division of responsibilities for essentially similar tasks accounted for inefficiency, when the friction of operational pressures was in conflict with the smooth functioning of the army's haulage requirements. Meanwhile, the first company of Royal Waggoners embarked at Blackwall on 14 March, the second on 1 April and the third two weeks later, but they appear to have been sent with no harnesses for the horses or uniforms for themselves.[88] The officers commanding them were either already serving on the staff in Flanders or mostly senior non-commissioned officers from a variety of cavalry and infantry regiments. Alexander Robays was transferred from his position as wagonmaster and appointed a captain commanding one of the two Dutch companies, whereas John Sargent had been deputy assistant quartermaster-general, also received a commission as captain. The newly-promoted lieutenants included quartermasters from the 2nd Dragoons, Coldstream

---

85   TNA: AO 16/52: pp.204–207, Watson to Long, 1 January 1794.
86   TNA: AO 16/52: pp.207–209, Watson to Rose, 14 January 1794.
87   TNA: AO 16/52: pp.207–209, 272–273 and 274–276, Watson to Rose, 14 January, 6 and 16 May 1794 and R.N.W. Thomas, 'The Corps of Royal Waggoners and Army Transport During the Campaign in the Low Countries, 1794–1795', *Journal of the Society for Army Historical Research*, vol.76, 1998, pp.157–162.
88   TNA: AO 16/52: pp.255–258 and 288, Watson to Rose, 24 March and 30 May 1794; AO 16/52: p.90, Rose to Watson, 11 April 1794; WO 4/291: pp.244–248, Rose to Yonge, 17 March 1794 and WO 58/167: pp.86 and 88–89: Rose to Watson, 28 March and 4 April 1794.

Guards and 53rd Regiment, whilst ensigns included a quartermaster from the Chatham staff and sergeants from the 16th Light Dragoons and 37th Regiment. Although the non-commissioned officers were intended to have been raised from amongst the cavalry pensioners at the Royal Hospital, Watson was dissatisfied to discover that: 'The Drivers sent from England are most of them ignorant in their Duty, and none of them capable of Driving four Horses'.[89] This, together with the future bad reputation of the corps, was almost certainly due to the haste with which it was raised and the inability to secure the services of qualified individuals who would have carried out their duties more effectively. As far as unit organisation was concerned, the original four companies raised in Britain were amalgamated into the three that were sent over to Flanders. Watson raised a further two companies from locally recruited Dutch. The original establishment was for four sergeants, four corporals, four farriers, four collar makers, four wheelwrights and one hundred men per company, with the whole commanded by a captain assisted by two subalterns. Two further companies accompanied Lord Moira's force, which arrived at Ostend in late June 1794.[90]

The reform of the transport system in early 1794 also included watercraft, the most efficient and cheapest method of transporting goods. However, the canals were often in poor repair and it was sometimes difficult to obtain canal boats (or bilanders) due to the needs of other allied contingents in the combined army. This led Watson in March 1794 to place orders for 80 bilanders to carry supplies on the Rivers Scheldt and Lys, plus the canals connecting them, but these had first to be built and were not delivered until the middle of May. He also ordered 40 barges, the last of which was scheduled for delivery by the end of May, when Watson was able to report that he then had 61 bilanders with three more shortly to be delivered.[91]

In addition to the procurement of wagons, the Commissariat was also responsible for buying horses. The recruitment of Frederick Bussenius on a four-month contract from 1 April 1793 has already been mentioned and he no doubt played a key role in the acquisition in March 1793 of 180 horses at 180 Florins each for the use of the artillery. A total of 385 horses were purchased up to the end of April, but this number was insufficient and the Duke of York ordered Watson to procure an additional 600, mainly for the artillery, of which 168 had been delivered to them by 24 December; he therefore made a contract on 14 June for this number at a cost of £20 per horse delivered to Ostend as the ordnance commissaries were inexperienced in such matters. When Watson proceeded to England in December 1793, he left a raft of instructions for his deputy, Henry Motz. Amongst these was an order to purchase up to 1,000 horses for the forthcoming campaign, with 250 to be delivered per week commencing from 8 February and all to be complete by 1 March. The animals were to be aged between five and seven years old, 'perfectly sound' and all must pass survey.[92]

---

89   TNA: AO 16/52: pp.277–278, Watson to Rose, 22 May 1794.
90   TNA: WO 26/35: p.274, Commission ordering James Poole to raise the Corps of Royal Waggoners, 7 March 1794.
91   TNA: AO 16/52: pp.52–55, 159–160, 248–252 and 265–266: Watson to Rose, 23 May and 21 October 1793, 14 March and 15 April 1794.
92   TNA: AO 16/52: pp.5–6 and 34–35: Watson to Rose, 29 March and 3 May 1793; AO 16/52: pp.200–203: Motz to Rose, 27 December 1793 and AO 16/52: p.207, A General Return of Waggons, Carts,

Field Bakery

An important factor in the administration of the Commissariat was the acquisition of the Hanoverian Field Bakery. This was a unit of His Majesty's Electoral Forces and was hired at the insistence of the Duke of York for the significant cost in the 1793 campaign of £4,500.[93] The bakery fulfilled a crucial role, since the ration issue of 1½ lb of bread formed the basis of the troops' daily diet. This had been provided by contractors during the first three months of the campaign, but Watson triumphantly reported on 6 June: 'I have the satisfaction to inform their Lordships that the Field Bakery from Hanover is complete in all its parts. [It is] most perfectly well appointed under the direction of a Commissary conversant in his business and is now at work'.[94] The bakery consisted of 10 ovens and when fully operational was able to provide bread for 30,000 men, but when it first arrived only six ovens could be utilised due to insufficient manpower, so only the Hanoverian contingent could be supplied initially. Bread was baked either in loaves weighing 6 lb each or in 'portions' of 2 lb, with the ingredients including wheat meal, rye meal and salt. According to Le Mesurier, the ovens required heating for 10 or 12 hours and were then capable of baking five batches every 24 hours, or six in an emergency, in which case the quality of the bread deteriorated.[95]

The bakery was initially established just inside the French border at Sebourg during the siege of Valenciennes, but it subsequently moved to Ypres, becoming operational there on 14 August. This was not to last long as another move was made to Veurne at the end of the month to support the force besieging Dunkirk. Proximity to water was a key factor in determining a suitable location for the bakery. Unfortunately, this important resource was too far distant for the bakers' convenience at their new location and they became mutinous. Watson had to arrest the ringleaders at the head of a file of dragoons before persuading them back to work; being civilians, they could not be disciplined in the same way as troops.[96] The incident was potentially serious, since Watson greatly feared the army would be forced to abandon the siege of Dunkirk for lack of bread. When the mutiny first erupted, he requested the Treasury send out 200 tons of ship's biscuit to Nieuwpoort, but this was only sanctioned on 7 September and would not have arrived in time to alleviate any shortage had the bakers not returned to work.[97]

The field bakery was successfully extricated from the failure at Dunkirk and moved to Nieuwpoort on 10 September where it halted until ordered to Bruges two days later. It appears to have remained there throughout the winter and on 6 December Watson was able to inform the Treasury that: 'I think it will be more than able to supply the whole Army within distance to be furnished by it'. The Hanoverian assistant commissary in charge, G.S. Wöltge, asked to be discharged in March 1794, though Watson was keen to retain his services and asked if he could be transferred to the Commissariat Department instead, which was done.[98]

    Horses and Harness of the Commissary General's Department, Ghent 24 December 1793.
93 TNA: AO 16/52: pp.15–16, Watson to Rose, 4 April 1793 and AO 16/52: p.50, Watson to Rose, 17 May 1793.
94 TNA: AO 16/52: pp.60–63, Watson to Rose, 6 June 1793.
95 TNA: AO 16/52: pp.67–69 and 91–92, Watson to Rose, 14 June and 12 July 1793.
96 TNA: AO 16/52: pp.135–136, Watson to Rose, 31 August 1793.
97 TNA: AO 16/52: p.134, Watson to Rose, 29 August 1793.
98 TNA: AO 16/52: pp.189–192 and 248–252, Watson to Rose, 6 December 1793 and 14 March 1794 and WO 58/167: pp.82–83, Rose to Watson, 18 March 1794.

The field bakery moved to within the French border at Vieux-Condé by the start of the 1794 campaign, but the loss of Ypres forced its withdrawal first to Dendermonde on 24 June, and then to Antwerp two days later on the orders of the Duke of York. Once set up there, Watson was able to report on 7 July that it had the capacity to supply bread for 40,000 men.[99] Unfortunately, the further proceedings of the bakery are unknown, as Watson's letter book extends no further than early July 1794.

Allied Cooperation
The army was also well subsisted on various occasions during 1793 as a result of excellent working relations with the Austrians, but their magazines were not always complete enough to supply all of Watson's needs. This was very evident during the Duke of York's march from Tournai to Quiverain at the end of May, when the Austrians agreed to provide their allies with rations for 21 days from the magazine located in the latter town. It transpired that the Hanoverian contingent received insufficient bread during this march, the consequences of which Watson was only too well aware, as he wrote to the Treasury that: 'My feelings on these occasions are not to be described for hunger cannot be satisfied by reasonings'.[100] The Austrian Emperor assisted directly by attaching his civil commissary, Ortz de Bulloy, to the Commissariat Department so that York's troops could more easily obtain provisions when in the Austrian Netherlands. In return for Austrian support, Watson was able to alleviate the Imperial shortage of cash by providing £6,000 for the pay of their troops at the end of August. He subsequently lent the Austrians 1,800 tons of oats from magazines at Ostend and Bruges, and in February 1794 dispatched 360 tons of rye meal to them. Help was also received from the Dutch Commissariat, which supplied Watson with money to purchase bread and forage in August 1794 when the troops were acutely short of supplies. The allies also exchanged magazines occasionally, in order that the troops of each army could be provisioned more conveniently.[101] This happy situation was not to last, however. By late December 1794 the Duke of York noted that:

> The general disposition of the Dutch nation is certainly exceedingly inimical to His Majesty's Troops, and has shewn itself upon every occasion in the strongest manner, but particularly of late in the difficulties which have been made in some instances, and the absolute refusal in others of furnishing the necessary means for the conveyance of the provisions and Forage to the Army.[102]

The army benefited from further allied cooperation in respect of duties on imported goods. After a request from Watson in late October 1793, the Dutch Government was approached early the following month by Lord Grenville and the necessary passport for free passage up the River Scheldt was provided within 10 days, but import duties on at least some items

---

99   TNA: AO 16/52, pp.298–299, 300–301, 303, Watson to Rose, 24 and 26 June and 7 July 1794.
100 TNA: AO 16/52: pp.60–63, Watson to Rose, 6 June 1793.
101 TNA: AO 16/52: pp.120–122, 135–136, 159–160 and 212–217, Watson to Rose, 8 and 31 August, 21 October 1793 and 7 February 1794 and NAM: 1978-04-73: p.225, Mr. Watson's correspondence with the Auditors of the Public Accounts, February 1796–June 1803.
102 TNA: WO 1/170: p.597, Observations of His Royal Highness the Duke of York, 23 December 1793.

delivered to ports in the United Provinces were still being paid in July 1794.[103] This was not the case in the Austrian Netherlands, when in February 1794 the Emperor granted an exemption on import duties for all military supplies.[104]

Prisoners of War

Aside from the principal role of the Commissariat Department in providing and distributing food, forage and cash to the army, Brook Watson was also placed in charge of the accommodation and subsistence of prisoners. This developed into a significant problem during the course of 1794 and undoubtedly added considerably to his workload. The principal difficulty was to find appropriate ships in which to house the prisoners, a task that Watson was given in March. The Navy Board was unable to provide any vessels, but they did authorise the Commissioner for Transports at Ostend, Lieutenant Home Popham RN, to supervise the purchase and fitting out of any that could be found locally.[105] Two vessels were bought in May and named *Famars* and *Lincelles* after allied victories in the 1793 campaign, but they would only accommodate some 1,300 men which was about half of the total. The immediate problem was solved the following month when the *Glatton*, with a capacity for 2,000 prisoners, was purchased. The effort expended in these duties led Watson to press for the responsibility to be transferred elsewhere, but despite assurances of every assistance from the Treasury, he was never relieved of it.[106] The problem resurfaced in November, when it was found that most of the prisoners were almost naked. The Treasury ordered 2,600 sets of clothing from the Royal Navy's Sick and Hurt Board for their use.[107] Incidents such as these greatly increased the commissariat workload, and undoubtedly got in the way of its main task of supplying the troops. That the responsibility was allocated to Watson at all is perhaps indicative of the lack of interest or understanding at headquarters of non-operational matters, a factor which could seriously affect the working of the Commissariat Department, as will be discussed further below.

How Effective were the Army's Supply Methods?

Having discussed the means by which the Treasury and the commissariat provided a flow of supplies to the army in the field, it now remains to examine their effectiveness in doing so. The initial problem faced by both the Treasury and Brook Watson resulted from the absence of a commissariat department at home from which to appoint personnel for overseas expeditions. The appointment of commissary-general in the home commissariat was made only

---

103 TNA: AO 16/52: pp.160–161, Watson to Rose, 25 October 1793; WO 58/167: pp.63–64, Rose to Watson, 1 November 1793; AO 16/52: p.172, Watson to Rose, 10 November 1793; WO 58/167: pp.82 and 98–99, Rose to Watson, 7 March and 25 July 1794.
104 TNA: AO 16/52: pp.218–220, Watson to Rose, 7 February 1794.
105 TNA: AO 16/52: pp.248–252, Watson to Rose, 14 March 1794; WO 58/167: pp.85–86, Rose to Watson, 25 March 1794 and AO 16/52: p.273, Watson to Rose, 13 May 1794.
106 TNA: AO 16/52: pp.277–278, Watson to Rose, 22 May 1794; WO 58/167: pp.91–92 and 95–96, Rose to Watson, 27 May and 20 June 1794 and AO 16/52: pp.298–299, Watson to Rose, 24 June 1794.
107 TNA: AO 16/52: pp.184–186, Watson to Long, 25 November 1794 and WO 58/167: pp.67–68, Rose to Watson, 3 December 1794.

after the troops had departed for the United Provinces and the incumbent, Captain Robert Bisset, was only empowered to make contracts for the supply of troops in camp. Contracts for other purposes were made by the Treasury, meaning that much of Bisset's role was spent in administering them. Given that Watson reached the United Provinces nearly three weeks after the first troops arrived, he was unable to establish a network of merchants, contractors and bankers who could be used to obtain the supplies required in advance. The need for large volumes of food and forage, coupled with the total absence of any existing magazines, does much to explain the initial difficulties experienced by the Commissariat Department, and induced local suppliers to raise prices for articles which were in demand by the army.[108] For these reasons, Brook Watson struggled to supply the troops for the first two months after his arrival, though perhaps not for the cause that the Duke of York explained to the King on 17 May: 'I am affraid that having been accustomed to the American War, where the provision came almost wholly from England, he does not know now in what manner to begin the business, and from an over anxiety to do well he proceeds with such a degree of caution in making his contracts that the business is considerably impeded.'[109]

The main cause of the problem was the rapid retreat of the French through the Austrian Netherlands and the swift advance of the allies in their wake. This war of movement was at odds with the intention to provision the army from static magazines. The supply difficulties associated with the army's move from Ostend to Tournai in April 1793 were responsible for the only recorded instance of troop movements being constrained by shortcomings in the Commissariat. The problem is illustrative of the good inter-allied cooperation which existed at this period, since it was alleviated somewhat when Coburg gave his consent to the British troops being provisioned from Austrian magazines, and a strong reciprocal arrangement developed between the two armies.[110] Once the 1793 campaign began, the Treasury went far to assist Watson by providing personnel, supplies and instructions on points of detail, but with only a few exceptions its policy regarding commissariat matters remained essentially reactive.

By October 1793, the bulk of supplies available to the army were located at Bruges and Ghent, both of them connected to inland waterways for onward transportation to troops based further south (Appendix III, Table III.1). A total of 1,732 tons of wheat and rye meal for making bread were stocked of which 634 tons (37 percent) was held at Bruges and 902 tons (52 percent) at Ghent. With a bread ration of 1½ lb per man per day, this would be sufficient to feed an army of 35,000 men for three months.[111] A reserve supply of 444 tons of biscuit was held at Ostend which would provide the equivalent of 28 days rations for the same number of men consuming 1 lb per day. As far as horses were concerned, the principal magazines for oats were at Bruges, with 1,804 tons (34 percent) and Ostend with 2,650 tons or 50 percent. The total stock of 5,351 tons at all five magazines would be sufficient for

---

108 Anon., *Eighteenth Report*, pp.251, 310 and 347.
109 York to George III, 17 May 1793, in Aspinall, *Later Correspondence*, vol.2, p.39.
110 TNA: AO 16/52: pp.30–31, Watson to Rose, 26 April 1793 and AO 16/52: pp.51–52, Watson to Rose, 19 May 1793.
111 1,732 tons minus five percent for wastage and a baking ratio of 3:4 would produce 2,194 tons of bread, or sufficient for 35,000 men for 94 days at 1½ lb per day. See Le Mesurier, *The British Commissary*, p.21.

40,000 horses for 30 days on the basis of a ration of 10 lb per day. Supplies of hay were more evenly distributed, with 2,241 tons at Bruges (31 percent), 2,812 at Ghent (39 percent), 622 tons at Tournai (eight and half percent), 1,090 tons at Ostend (15 percent) and 536 tons at Antwerp (seven percent). The 7,301 tons of hay stocked would provide for the same number of horses for 41 days with a 10 lb ration. Although these comprised the majority of commodities assembled, the magazines also contained smaller quantities of beef, beans, pease, bran and straw.[112]

Undoubtedly the toughest supply problem with which the Commissariat Department had to deal was caused by the allies' retreat during the winter of 1794–1795. Fortunately, Watson had foreseen this in October and partially alleviated it by stocking three weeks of meal and oats on board ships: '… out of immediate danger from the Enemy'.[113] Many supplies were lost due to the rapid French advance, and when Watson was ordered in November to establish magazines sufficient for 60,000 men and 35,000 horses the task must have been considerable, particularly at a season when frost and snow prevented canal transportation and greatly hindered the same by road. Despite this, Lieutenant Lewis Jones of the 57th Regiment was able to state in mid-November: '… but the want of provisions, which had been stated in the public prints, was a vague report, for at this time they had never been without bread, meat, and forage.'[114]

This was not to last, however, and Lieutenant General Harcourt was led to complain to the Duke of York on 1 January 1795: 'It is mortifying in the extreme to be again under the necessity of representing that very precarious as I have found the supplies of the Army, the state of our magazines, if they ever deserved the name, proves to be still worse than I ever imagined'.[115]

The question of finding adequate supplies assumed greater importance as regards the movements of the army during the retreat than at any time since the troops had first disembarked in March 1793. By the end of January 1795 Watson found that no more bread or forage could be procured in the United Provinces and urged that a movement should be made as soon as possible to the River Ems, where he could arrange for supplies to be stocked prior to the arrival of the troops. When he was subsequently ordered to establish a magazine for 2,400 men and 600 horses for 90 days at Coevorden, Watson calculated that he would require 1,728 wagon loads carrying 1,000 lbs each to move the 181 tons of meal, 60 tons of salt meat and 265 tons each of oats and hay required. The whole operation was estimated to take four or five weeks to complete, even if the necessary wagons could be procured and the roads were still open, which demonstrates the relatively long timescales requisite for provisioning even small forces adequately.[116] In fact, the reliance upon magazines had reduced somewhat from the second half of 1794 when operational circumstances greatly increased the difficulties of supplying the troops from semi-permanent depots. Instead, it became

---

112 Appendix III, Table III.1. For brevity, pounds avoirdupois have been converted into imperial tons at 2,240 pounds per ton.
113 TNA: PRO 30/8/187: Watson to Pitt, 4 October 1794, Chatham Papers.
114 Jones, *Historical Journal*, p.143.
115 TNA: WO 1/172: p.36, Harcourt to York, 1 January 1795.
116 TNA: WO 1/172: pp.291–294, Watson to Wallmoden, 17 January 1795 and WO 1/172: pp.377–380, Motz to Harcourt, 5 February 1795.

increasingly common for units to procure their own provisions and issue bons, or commissaries orders, to their suppliers. This practice resulted in a growing loss of central control over the purchase and distribution of food and forage, meaning the Commissariat Department was either faced with paying suppliers on the strength of the bons they produced, or else refusing to do so and thus compromising regimental arrangements.[117]

The weather was not the only challenge facing Watson. Another developed in February 1795, when many of the north German states prohibited the movement of meal and forage between parishes, meaning the troops could only obtain supplies from the parish in which they happened to be at the time. The Regency of Osnaburg, however, went one stage further by issuing an ordinance against furnishing the troops with any supplies at all. This accentuated Watson's difficulties in carrying out Wallmoden's orders for magazines containing three months supplies to be established on the River Weser.[118] It is highly probable that the north German states were heavily influenced by the parlous appearance of the army, which made payment uncertain, and being in retreat it was in any case unlikely to remain in their territory for very long. There was also a reduced chance of the soldiers exacting revenge against the authorities who were denying them provisions, due to the overriding importance of more pressing operational concerns. There was clearly a strong correlation between military success and the ease by which an army could be subsisted.

Although most of these difficulties were caused by purely operational matters, the ability of the Commissariat to supply the army was sometimes seriously affected by the lack of timely information of intended troop movements. When Watson first joined the army in March 1793, he was impressed with what he had seen and wrote to Pitt that he had gained the Duke of York's confidence and understanding on commissariat matters. This meeting of minds was not long lasting, it would seem, for Watson was soon telling his Treasury masters that he could supply the army if: '…timely information shall be given me of intended movements, otherwise their Lordships will not hold me responsible'.[119] The cooperation which existed between the British and Austrian commissaries helped to alleviate the difficulties arising from occasional poor communications between the Commissariat and other departments at headquarters. Despite this, the problem of insufficient information persisted. At the time of the abortive siege of Dunkirk in August–September 1793, the Duke's staff neglected to inform Watson of a change in the approach-march to the town. This was bad enough, but things got worse when the retreat began. A small magazine had been set up at Veurne, where the men could be issued with supplies en route, but to Watson's dismay they pushed on to Dixmude, where nothing was in place at all. As Watson told Pitt, the situation was only saved by a reserve of two days' supply of biscuit: '… which I have kept as the apple of my Eye since April last.' Although such rapid troop movements were unrepresentative of most operations carried out by the army, Watson was quick to remind the Treasury that they could result in irregular issues of provisions and heavy wastage. The adverse effects of the

---

117 NAM: 1978-04-73: pp.108–109 and 143–145, Watson to Deare, 23 March 1797 and 15 December 1798.
118 TNA: WO 1/828: pp.255–293, Rose to Huskisson, 10 March 1795, enclosing the correspondence between Wallmoden and Brook Watson between 14–26 February 1795.
119 TNA: PRO 30/8/187: Watson to Pitt, 20 March 1793, Chatham Papers and AO 16/52: pp.47–48, Watson to Rose, 12 May 1793.

situation were accentuated when Watson discovered that he was unable to move the supplies so carefully stockpiled at Veurne, the commissariat horses having been requisitioned to haul siege guns away from Dunkirk, leaving his wagons stranded.[120] Many other wagons had been removed altogether, and Watson complained of:

> ... the irregular proceedings of the Troops, who seized Waggons and Horses of every description to carry Baggage Women & Children, to the general Panick spread over the Country which prevents the Inhabitants from giving their assistance; out of 200 Waggons engaged by Contract I know not where to find ten and those belonging to the Crown have been seized on and are dispersed.[121]

The concern over poor communications between the army and commissariat diminished during the remainder of the campaign, and the evidence suggests that the Duke of York tried to give Watson ample warning of forthcoming troop movements, also seeking his advice on provisioning issues. The single exception was during the Duke's absence in England in February 1794 when Freytag and Erskine moved the whole army forward to the French frontier, where Watson had not established any magazines. The difficulty appears to have been temporary, however, as the commissary-general wrote three months later that he had made ample provision for the army and had heard no complaints over shortages.[122]

The Commissariat Department was also constrained by seasonality, particularly since the campaign was fought in an area with no existing British military presence, or reserves of food and other supplies. This meant that some items were extremely difficult to procure at the time they were needed, such as oats and hay, the lack of which affected the cavalry in particular. Watson was able to find his own sources for these two articles after local crops had been harvested in the late summer of 1793 but had been more heavily dependent on receiving shipments from England for the first months of that year.

Many of these difficulties could have assumed greater proportions had not the individuals appointed by the Treasury been of a generally high calibre. It is unfair to state, as one author has done, that commissariat officers: '... were not overscrupulous, and in fact tended to come from the very worst elements of the commercial world'.[123] Indeed, Watson was very quick to prevent any possibility of conduct that might be perceived as untoward. Gideon Duncan, an assistant commissary based at Ostend to superintend the unloading of vessels arriving there with supplies, had purchased four wagons and their horses to help with unloading nine ship-loads of oats. Duncan claimed a pressing need, but the problem was that he had not received authorisation to use public funds, so the vehicles effectively belonged to him. He received a severe reprimand from Watson on account of this being just the kind of transaction which, during the American War, had blended so readily with corruption – until,

---

120 TNA: AO 16/52: pp.124–126, Watson to Long, 19 August 1793; PRO 30/8/187: Watson to Pitt, 14 September 1793, Chatham Papers and AO 16/52: pp.144–147, Watson to Rose, 16 September 1793.
121 TNA: AO 16/52: pp.144–147, Watson to Rose, 16 September 1793.
122 TNA: PRO 30/8/187: Watson to Murray, 6 October 1793, Chatham Papers; AO 16/52: pp.228–242, Watson to Rose, 24 February 1794; AO 16/52: pp.272–273, Watson to Rose, 6 May 1794 and AO 16/52: pp.277–278, Watson to Rose, 22 May 1794.
123 Ward, *Wellington's Headquarters*, p.71.

that is, officers were forbidden to own any transport vehicles.[124] There was only one proven instance of fraud amongst all the personnel appointed, which concerned John Bessell, an assistant commissary since March 1793. Bessell was found guilty at a court martial held in September 1795 of signing false receipts for the delivery of supplies and sentenced: '… to be cashiered with every mark of Infamy and disgrace'.[125] It was perhaps fortunate for Bessell that he died later that year and so presumably avoided refunding the money he had stolen. That fraud was not a problem probably resulted from Watson's experience of its effects in America, added to the warnings issued from time to time by the Treasury:

> It should be distinctly understood by every Person in your Department that if any of them shall be found to have profitted in any manner directly or indirectly beyond the Allowances stated in their Commissions, immediate Dismissal and Forfeiture of the intended Half Pay will be the Consequence, without a possibility of the offending Party being ever afterwards employed in any public Situation.[126]

George Don, who as a lieutenant colonel served as acting adjutant-general to the Duke of York's army from late 1794, informed the Commissioners of Military Enquiry in 1806 that he had no reason to believe that any frauds had been perpetrated by commissariat officers serving in the Low Countries. There had been difficulties, however, in verifying the charges made by contractors since their accounts could only rarely be checked at the same time provisions were delivered. This was due to several reasons, the foremost of which was the commissary of accounts had only been appointed some months after the campaign began, which imposed an immediate gap between the first accounts he audited and the period to which they related. Once George Mason commenced work, he discovered that many of the assistant commissaries compiled their accounts defectively and, in most cases, only dispatched them after the magazines had been closed and the Austrian Netherlands abandoned, meaning that accounts could be doctored by falsely inflating the quantity of items issued. Problems such as this were due to the piecemeal nature in which the Commissariat Department was assembled, the lack of instructions on matters of detail and the absence of an existing reservoir of trained personnel familiar with commissariat duties.[127]

To sum up: the 1793–1795 campaign highlights the challenges experienced in supplying a British expeditionary force overseas. In the first instance, the commissariat was only brought into existence in time of war. Precious time was needed to develop an efficient structure, populated by individuals familiar with their business. This problem was compounded when the first commissariat staff only arrived some weeks after the troops landed, having been dispatched with no food or forage with which to provision them before local supplier networks could be developed.

At a tactical level, the magazine system developed in the late seventeenth century as a solution to the problem of feeding larger armies in areas with insufficient resources, was the

---

124 TNA: T 1/721: Duncan to Mitford, 7 August 1793, Treasury Board Papers.
125 Le Mesurier, *The British Commissary*, pp.113–117.
126 TNA: WO 58/167: pp.78–79, Rose to Watson, 28 February 1794.
127 Anon., *Eighteenth Report*, pp.284–286, 300 and 347.

methodology used by the allies in 1793–1795.[128] Whereas in 1793 the expeditionary force primarily used hired transport, especially for deliveries between magazines and the points of consumption, the defects of this system led to assets being partly taken under the direct control of the consumer in a manner familiar to students of warfare from the nineteenth century onwards. Full use was made of the apparatus developed during the Seven Years' War and American War, including detailed ration scales for both men and horses, commercial contracts for the provision of both supplies (food and fodder) and transport, together with fixed magazines, the entire edifice being underpinned by an administrative and financial system of sufficient maturity to provide the cash and other resources required to ensure the mechanism worked.

What the campaign demonstrated was that having once set up supply contracts and magazines (the latter often static) ongoing support for the army was critically dependent on good operational outcomes. The allies' prospects began to fade from mid-1794 to be followed by a punishing winter retreat, the inevitable consequences of which caused mounting difficulties in the procurement of specie, food and forage. Local bankers or contractors were reluctant to step forward to help when there seemed little chance they would ever be repaid. As for the magazines themselves – so conscientiously brought together – these were often made up of perishables, cumbersome and hard to move without a large transport capability, which often did not exist. In any case, a huge quantity of fodder would have been needed for the very animals assigned to haul the carts, and this, we know, was not forthcoming at the worst time of the year. Moreover, a supply convoy was a significant military asset in itself, and the fact that troops would have to be assigned to protect it (or at best to remain in its vicinity to be supplied) was a drain on fighting resources. In 1793, when the army was operating in friendly territory, the issue of convoy escorts had not arisen, but from the onset of the 1794 campaigning season, the Duke of York allocated 200 men for that important duty.[129]

In short, there were problems every which way. If the magazines were located too close to the front line, they were vulnerable to attack. If posted too far to the rear, excessive transport resources were required to bring them forward. Any failure to coordinate troop movements with the movement of supplies resulted in confusion and waste. To confound matters, seasonal weather fluctuations, disappointing performance on the part of contractors, and the fickle loyalties of the local population made the life of a commissary even harder. Often these were occurrences beyond their control, or even that of the army staff. And there is something else, never to be forgotten. If difficulties had accumulated for the commissariat, an active and determined enemy had much to do with them.

For all that, the expeditionary force, and indeed the Treasury, were very fortunate to have Brook Watson on hand. Not only did he bring great experience to the role of commissary-general, but he was also responsible for putting sound methodology in place, and training up a group of men, predominantly civilian, who were to provide outstanding service to the British Army until the victorious conclusion of the Revolutionary and Napoleonic Wars. Among them were Henry Motz who served as commissary-general during the Helder expedition (1799) and the Egyptian campaign (1801), Havilland Le Mesurier, who wrote

---

128 The development of the magazine system is discussed by Van Creveld, *Supplying War*, pp.17–26.
129 TNA: AO 16/52: p.268, Watson to Rose, 25 April 1794.

The British Commissary first published in 1796 and the following year was commissary-general of the southern district of England, and Robert Kennedy, who acted as Wellington's commissary-general in the Peninsula. For all its many frustrations and disappointments, the Flanders Campaign of 1793–1795 had been an undeniable proving-ground in the formation of the British Army's professional commissariat service.

> # 4

The Medical Services

The ability of an army to fight – its very existence even – is dependent to a large degree on the physical fitness of the rank and file. There is consequently a strong correlation between the efficiency of an army in providing food, equipment (such as clothing or tents), and medical care, and its success in maximising the numbers of men available for operations. However, the quality of military medicine during the eighteenth century could be highly variable both between armies, within the same army in different theatres of operations, and in all armies over time.

Recent studies of eighteenth century military medicine have focused on specific campaigns, the status of medical men serving with the British Army, the increasing acceptance of military medicine as a discipline, the ailments commonly affecting soldiers and the gradual professionalisation of military medicine, with practitioners making the army their chosen career, rather than drifting between military and civilian practice.

Medical Services in the Eighteenth Century

Medical personnel had accompanied British armies in the field throughout the eighteenth century, but the status accorded to them was low. Surgeons were the most junior staff officers in a regiment, ranking below the most recently commissioned ensign, despite the years of study and financial outlay they incurred. An indication of the low status accorded to medicine by officers of the British Army can be found in an analysis of 42 personal military libraries by Ira D. Gruber, which revealed that out of the 650 titles listed, only two were medical texts. The figure rises very slightly to six books from 1,265 titles catalogued in all the officers' libraries combined, but this only represented one percent of the whole. There was nearly five times more interest in naval topics.[1]

When war appeared likely in Flanders in 1701, one of the first things the ailing King William III did was to commence reorganising the Army, part of which was to seek advice on medical provision. The result was an arrangement with the contractor John Hudson, whereby he was paid a fixed sum per patient in return for providing medical care, bread, bedding and clothing. A medical staff of two physicians, an apothecary-general, three

---

1   Gruber, *Books and the British Army*, Appendices A and A4.

surgeons and a surgeon's mate was recruited, whilst a general hospital was established adjacent to a similar Dutch facility at 'sHertogenbosch. A reciprocal arrangement was established between the allies, with the Dutch accepting British patients and vice versa. A network of 'flying' hospitals was also established for both British and allied troops during the first campaign in 1702.[2]

Medical facilities expanded during the war, with a second hospital established at Breda in 1703, again adjacent to a Dutch facility, and an additional physician and surgeon were dispatched from England. The practice at this time was to close hospitals when the army retired to winter quarters and the sick were sent to Britain. The highly mobile nature of the 1704 campaign necessitated the hospital being transported down the rivers Rhine and Main by boat, with transit facilities established at Cassel, Heidenheim and Nordlingen. The transit was directed by the Duke of Marlborough in person, as was the location of the hospitals. A further innovation was the hiring of local medical practitioners to provide additional cover. As the strategic situation developed during the remainder of the war, hospitals were opened in a variety of locations including Maastricht, Liège, Ghent, Menen, Kortrijk and Brussels, though not all at the same time.[3] The relative success of the medical arrangements with Marlborough's army were in stark contrast to contemporaneous campaigns in Spain and Portugal, which were characterised by muddle, incompetence and self-interest. As usual with military administration, much depended on the breadth of view, personality and drive of the theatre commander and his quartermaster-general – qualities evidently lacking in Spain.[4]

A hospital accompanied the army sent to Flanders in 1742 at the start of the War of the Austrian Succession consisting of a director, physician, chief surgeon, master-apothecary and two mates, four hospital mates and a matron. This staffing level was significantly augmented during the war. The key difference compared to 1702–1712 was that no contractor was appointed to administer it and matters were instead handled by Charles Peters and John Pawlett, respectively Physician General and Surgeon General, in London. A report written in 1785 by Robert Adair, Inspector of Regimental Infirmaries, summarised medical arrangements in eighteenth century campaigns and suggested that matters went well for the entire war because the general hospitals were adequately resourced and the army remained concentrated, thus facilitating care of the sick. The director was provided with authority to recruit the staff required, subject to the agreement of the physician and surgeon, and to acquire the necessary provisions. Adair also stated that the staff were contented in their positions and were not distracted from patient care by thoughts of promotion and career development. A noted cost-cutter, Adair was of the opinion that the only significant improvement would have been in the purchase of medicines, which was done annually without regard to stock management and related costs.

As during the War of the Spanish Succession, hospitals tended to operate during the period of a campaign only. Care for the sick was provided either in regimental hospitals

---

2   E.E. Gruber von Arni, *Hospital Care and the British Standing Army, 1660–1714* (Aldershot: Ashgate, 2006), pp.112–115.
3   Gruber von Arni, *Hospital Care*, pp.119–120, 122, 124–125, 128 and N. Cantlie, *A History of the Army Medical Department* (London: Churchill Livingstone, 1974), vol.1, p.66.
4   Gruber von Arni, *Hospital Care*, pp.178 and 187 and Cantlie, *Army Medical Department*, vol.1, p.67.

when the troops were in winter quarters or more exceptionally at a base hospital, such as one established at Ghent in September 1741 until its capture by the French in August 1745. Due to the temporary nature of most hospitals, the sick tended to be accommodated in huts erected for the purpose, or in existing buildings that had been rented or appropriated. So called base hospitals could actually be relatively small, sometimes insufficient for the number of patients. The mortality rate for the entire war was a respectable 7.9 percent despite four regiments having been stationed in Walcheren and Zealand, which had increased the overall sickness rate for the army to 20 percent in 1747.[5]

A hospital was sent to America in 1753 under Sir James Napier as Director, of which Adair remarked: 'I am justified in saying it was the only Hospital we ever had that was free from Censure'.[6] This hospital was a mobile version of a general hospital, seeking to combine the organisation of a more sedentary establishment with that of a 'flying' hospital following experiences gained during the War of the Austrian Succession. To achieve this goal, women accompanying the army were recruited, especially from the higher number of spouses permitted to accompany the 44th and 48th Regiments. As things turned out, not all the women were keen to volunteer, and had to be coerced.[7] General Thomas Gage, the post-war commander-in-chief in the colonies, lobbied to have the hospital retained, but without success.

This generally positive experience was not to be replicated during the Seven Years' War in Europe, where the hospital attached to the army in Germany was properly equipped but weakly managed. A general hospital was opened at Coesfeld in August 1758, with each regiment ordered to send one soldier's wife for nursing duties under the threat of being dismissed from the army if she refused. A 'flying' hospital also operated in closer proximity to the troops and was likewise staffed by female nurses sent by each regiment. Unlike in previous wars, hospitals remained open during winter quarters with one at Munster and a base hospital at Bremen. These facilities were inadequate to cope with the significant increase in sickness following the Battle of Warburg (21 July 1760), a consequence of the troops camping on the battlefield and contracting dysentery, followed by an outbreak of typhus when the sick and wounded were crowded together in hospital. This resulted in a sickness rate of about 29 percent in December 1760 and 18 percent in April 1761 with reports of a far higher incidence of mortality.[8] A key contributor to failure was that the civilian staff

---

5   BL: IOR H/84: pp.551–559, Observations on the Hospital by R. Adair Esq Inspector General, enclosure no.7, in Correspondence &c with General Sloper regarding the health of the troops 1784, 10 June 1785; Cantlie, *Army Medical Department*, vol.1, pp.89–90 and 93 and P.E. Kopperman, 'Medical Services in the British Army, 1742–1783', *Journal of the History of Medicine and Allied Sciences*, vol.34:4, 1979, pp.428–430.
6   BL: IOR H/84: p.552, Observations on the Hospital.
7   S. Fatherly, 'Tending the Army: Women and the British General Hospital in North America, 1754–1763', *Early American Studies*, vol.10:3, 2012, pp.569–578 and P.E. Kopperman, 'The British Army in North America and the West Indies, 1755–83: A Medical Perspective', in G.L. Hudson (ed.) *British Military and Naval Medicine, 1600–1830* (Amsterdam: Editions Rodopi, 2007), pp.53–54.
8   Cantlie, *Army Medical Department*, vol.1, pp.123–126 and E. Charters, *Disease, War, and the Imperial State. The Welfare of the British Armed Forces during the Seven Years War* (London: The University of Chicago Press, 2014), p.103. Charters calculates a 29 percent sick rate on the basis of a total strength of 19,609 men but without providing the source. Data for the sick were taken from Barrington to Newcastle, February 1761, in Hayter, (ed.), *Secretary-at-War*, pp.62–63.

provided in 1757 were only adequate for the force of six infantry and six cavalry regiments initially dispatched, but were unequal to handling the number of patients from 17 infantry and 15 cavalry units serving in theatre by late 1760. Many of the staff had no experience of military medicine and little assistance could be obtained from the soldiers detailed to work in the hospitals.[9]

Similar outcomes were experienced during the American War, when the small hospital sent to Boston in 1775 had to be expanded rapidly to cater for a large increase in troop numbers. Adair attributed some of the failings to hospital staff putting more effort into advancing their careers than looking after the sick. By 1777 the base hospital was located at New York and staffed by five physicians, three purveyors, eight surgeons, eight apothecaries and 60 hospital mates. The remaining personnel consisted of locally enlisted clerks, storekeepers, stewards and cooks, together with soldiers' wives serving as nurses. The increased size of the establishment led to Jonathan Mallet being appointed chief surgeon in January 1776. Lord Howe recommended him to the Secretary-at-War as director of the New York hospitals, but this was turned down and Dr John Nooth, a physician already serving there, was instead confirmed as Superintendent General of Hospitals for the British Forces in April 1779. Dr Michael Morris was appointed Inspector of Hospitals in January 1777 to perform a similar function for the regimental hospitals.[10] The appointment of Nooth is illustrative of the precedence given to physicians over surgeons, since his MD (awarded by Edinburgh University in 1766) gave him a higher status than Mallet's 22 years' service as a surgeon in North America.

In the final analysis, the success or failure of the medical contribution to an expeditionary force must lie in the prevailing mortality rate. Deaths amongst the British troops during the entire war have been estimated at 1.8 percent in battle and 10 percent from disease, compared to two percent and 18 percent respectively for the Americans.[11] The mortality rate for the British was therefore marginally higher than the 7.9 percent experienced in Flanders during the War of the Austrian Succession.

Several common themes regarding military medical care emerged during the middle years of the eighteenth century. General hospitals could be plagued by indiscipline, with personnel at all levels sometimes ignoring their duties. Theft of the patients' equipment or belongings was widespread, as was alcoholism. Although nurses and orderlies could be dismissed by a physician or surgeon for these offences, it was not so easy to discipline members of the medical staff (purveyors, apothecaries, physicians and surgeons), who could only be removed by the hospital board. Any holding a more senior appointment than that of mate could also appeal to the local commander-in-chief. Discipline was in theory handled by military officers seconded to the hospitals for varying lengths of time, but the fact that transgressions occurred, possibly on a widespread basis, suggests that it was not enforced as intended. Hospitals could also be places of tension between individuals, in addition to factionalism caused by grievances, competition for promotion, dislike of colleagues or conflicts over authority or precedence. All or any of these circumstances could result in poor morale and neglect of duty, with the result that medical care suffered. Many disputes were

---

9   Cantlie, *Army Medical Department*, vol.1, p.131 and BL: IOR H/84: pp.551–559, Adair, Observations.
10 Cantlie, *Army Medical Department*, vol.1, p.142 and BL: IOR H/84: pp.551–559, Adair, Observations.
11 L.C. Duncan, *Medical Men in the American Revolution* (New York: Kelley, 1970), pp.374–375.

attributed to the deep and ongoing jealousies between physicians and surgeons, with the former usually being placed in charge of hospitals on overseas expeditions despite having scant knowledge of military medicine. Physicians often refused interference or advice from surgeons, who generally possessed exactly this type of experience.[12] This led to the creation of a Medical Board in order to regulate the management of hospitals on campaign and the provision of medicines and other stores. The other major initiative was the appointment of a Director of Hospitals based at army headquarters, with the aim of improving communications between the force commander and the medical branch. All hospitals could now, at least in theory, be administered centrally.[13]

Unfortunately, the risks attendant on sending men to a general hospital were not confined to neglectful medical attendants. Transportation to or between facilities often required long journeys, causing many patients to die before reaching their destination. The specially designed spring wagons recommended for this service were often not used, and this was an additional cause of suffering and death. This issue was one of the features of hospital mismanagement witnessed in Germany by Dr Richard Brocklesby when serving as a physician during the Seven Years' War:

> … the humane Officers complained and lamented the losses, our troops from time to time sustained by ill-timed removals, and by injudiciously harassing of soldiers, sick in fevers, from one hospital to another, sometimes distant 100 or 150 miles; on which occasions, the sick were conveyed in open boats, sometimes in open wagons, and (too often) sometimes without any requisite provision made for transporting them at all: no wonder if one third of the numbers, so hurried about, were liable to perish between one hospital and another.[14]

Having arrived, the transmission of infectious diseases caused by overcrowding could be an additional hazard. This was noted by Sir John Pringle during the War of the Austrian Succession, leading him to recommend that as many men as possible should be treated in regimental hospitals where patients were likely to receive a greater level of attention, since the costs associated with general hospitals meant these usually had insufficient personnel. He also argued that regimental hospitals were less likely to suffer from crowded conditions and the spread of contagion. Brocklesby was justifiably outraged about the same issue when writing in connection with the Seven Years' War, remarking that 'fevers of various kinds'

---

12   Eighteenth-century medicine had a tripartite structure, with university-trained physicians, responsible for treating diseases, at the top of the hierarchy, apprentice-trained surgeons (conducting physical procedures) in the middle and apothecaries (responsible for drugs and having some medical knowledge) at the bottom. This was less applicable in the military context, since regimental surgeons were responsible for treating all medical issues, whether surgical or disease related, and the distinction commonly made by contemporaries was between regimental practice and the general hospitals. Charters, *Disease, War, and the Imperial State*, pp.36–37.
13   Cantlie, *Army Medical Department*, vol.1, pp.120–121, 131 and 143.
14   R. Brocklesby, *Œconomical and Medical Observations, in two parts. From the Year 1758 to the Year 1763 inclusive. Tending to the Improvement of Military Hospitals, and to the Cure of Camp Diseases, Incident to Soldiers* (London: T. Becket and P.A. De Hondt, 1764), pp.34–35 and Cantlie, *Army Medical Department*, vol.1, p.128.

accounted for eight times more deaths than battle casualties. A reduction in the transportation of patients between regimental and general hospitals had been made during the War of the Austrian Succession through the introduction of a 'flying' hospital.[15]

On a brighter note, the practical competence of the physicians and surgeons was generally good. Each were appointed by the physician general and surgeon general respectively, with the former generally being graduates of a major British or European university, such as Oxford or Cambridge, and a member of the College of Physicians. Surgeons, on the other hand, were more likely to have worked their way through the various grades and thus have knowledge of military medicine. Their expertise was witnessed at Albany in October 1777 by James Thacher, an American army surgeon, following the surrender of Lieutenant General John Burgoyne's army at Saratoga:

> The foreigners are under the care and management of their own surgeons. I have been present at some of their capital operations, and remarked that the English surgeons performed with skill and dexterity, but the Germans, with few exceptions, do no credit to their profession; some of them are the most uncouth and clumsy operators I ever witnessed, and appear to be destitute of all sympathy and tenderness towards the suffering patient.[16]

High technical standards were made possible by ensuring that appointments at general hospitals were almost never sold, meaning that men were assigned first and foremost on account of their ability. Unfortunately, this was not so in the case of lower-ranking apothecaries and mates, as many of them were regimental appointees, where the selection criteria were neither reliable nor consistent.

It was generally felt that regimental surgeons lacked the necessary skills for the positions of physician or surgeon in a general hospital, but their level of experience would be sufficient for the post of apothecary. For this reason, the War Office deemed it unsuitable for regimental surgeons to fill vacancies at the general hospital in New York in 1781. This was partly because the post of regimental surgeon was purchased in the same manner as any other officers' commission and without any stipulation regarding professional competence. Many regimental surgeons had previously served as assistant surgeons, having been appointed by proprietary colonels of regiments for reasons other than their formal qualifications, or even proven competence. The best that can be said is that they may have penetrated the military-medical environment via a non-academic, or non-technical route. But Dr Robert Hamilton, surgeon's mate of the 10th Regiment between 1780–1785 had a more benevolent view of these people. For it seemed to him that some of the men who had attended university gained little from the experience: 'Many there spend whole seasons without ever applying to anything serious, or scientific, till not only the time allotted for their stay has elapsed, but

---

15 BL: IOR H/84: pp.551–559, Adair, Observations; Kopperman, 'Medical services', pp.432–433; J. Pringle, *Observations on the Diseases of the Army* (London: Miller, Wilson, Durham & Payne, 1761), pp.viii and 104–107; Brocklesby, *Œconomical and Medical Observations*, p.200, Cantlie, *Army Medical Department*, vol.1, p.121 and S.R. Frey, *The British Soldier in America. A Social History of Military Life in America during the Revolutionary Period* (Austin: University of Texas Press, 1981), pp.48–50.
16 J. Thacher, *Military Journal of the American Revolution* (New York: Arno Press, 1969), p.112.

their money has been exhausted'.[17] Some such men obtained positions in the army, especially in time of war, as did others who had never received training at any medical school. Even if they had, the examinations conducted at Surgeons Hall lasted only about 15 minutes and the questions asked were easy and standard.[18] The remedy often suggested to improve regimental hospitals was to offer higher pay and thus make the profession more attractive, as suggested by Robert Adair in his 1785 report:

> What Education can a Man be expected to have who is to look for no more than Four Shillings a day? If the Pay was augmented to Six Shillings a more perfect Education might be required and a more strict Examination made into their Proficiency in Physic & Surgery than is the case at present. This augmentation would be a Trifle, & the Army would reap unspeakable Advantages from it.[19]

This unfortunately did not tell the entire story, for 1/– per day was deducted from the surgeons pay for 'stoppages' meaning that his remuneration was precisely the same as for his assistant, who was paid 3/6 with 6d deducted for stoppages. The same issue also applied to hospital mates, as the Army Medical Board wrote to Lord Amherst, Commander-in-Chief at Horse Guards, on 8 March 1794 that the low pay and inferior situation of these men was not 'a sufficient compensation for the services of any person of proper Education, or even a subsistence, at a time when better Emoluments are held forth in other services'.[20] Once again the problem was one of long standing, with the consequences noted by Dr Richard Brocklesby in 1764: '… an absolute neglect of a liberal education in the generality of Surgeons are all together apt amongst them to induce Quackery, or, at best, a narrowness in thinking about medical subjects'.[21] The War Office was under constant pressure to reduce costs, so chose not to increase pay and instead placed a greater reliance on the general hospital system. On campaign, commanders-in-chief tended also to have a higher regard for the medical staff and the general hospital, so during both the Seven Years' War and the American War regimental hospitals were subject to inspections. The increasing importance with which the general hospital was regarded on campaign was also shown by the greater number of staff appointed to it by the War Office in each successive conflict during the eighteenth century.[22]

There was another consequence of the inadequate pay awarded to regimental surgeons, and this concerned the provision of medicines. For regiments numbering up to 500 men,

---

17 R. Hamilton, *The Duties of a Regimental Surgeon Considered: With Observations on the General Qualifications; and Hints Relative to a More Respectable Practice, and Better Regulation of that Department* (London: T.N. Longman, 1794), vol.1, pp.78–79.
18 Kopperman, 'The British Army in North America', pp.55–58 and M.H. Kaufmann, *Surgeons at War: Medical Arrangements for the Treatment of the Sick and Wounded in the British Army during the Late 18th and 19th centuries* (Westport: Greenwood Press, 2000), p.3.
19 BL: IOR H/84: pp.551–559, Adair, Observations.
20 TNA: WO 7/101: p.18, Medical Board to Amherst, 8 March 1794.
21 Brocklesby, *Œconomical and Medical Observations*, p.37.
22 TNA: WO 7/101: pp.18–20, Medical Board to Amherst, 8 March 1794; Hamilton, *Regimental Surgeon*, vol.1, pp.3 and 121–122; Kopperman, 'Medical services', pp.434–435 and 443–447 and Frey, *British Soldier*, p.49.

surgeons were provided with £70 per annum for medicines, the hire of hospitals and the medical expenses attending detachments and recruiting parties; a larger sum was provided in proportion to the size of the unit above this number. During the American War, some regimental surgeons either appropriated all of the money to supplement their meagre pay, or else purchased the cheapest and worst medicines they could and pocketed what was left, with the result that either the health of the soldiers was compromised or else they sought treatment from civilian practitioners instead. Such doings led to the creation of the post of Inspector of Regimental Infirmaries in 1756. The first incumbent was Robert Adair.[23]

Accounts of the Flanders campaign of 1793–1795 are negative regarding the standard of medical care provided to the troops. Sir John Fortescue, in typically pithy style, went so far as to state that: 'But the very worst department of all was that of the hospitals, wherein the abuses were so terrible that men hardly dared to speak of them'.[24] This was in marked contrast to developments in the Royal Navy during the second half of the eighteenth century, where the focus on cleanliness and diet had greatly reduced the incidence of sickness. Not only the work of medical professionals such as Dr James Lind were responsible for this, as most naval officers had the job of implementing basic medical precautions on a daily basis whilst in command at sea and were also aware of the importance of retaining their crews' health.[25] That this was generally not the case in the Army may be ascribed to differences in attitude and in the organisational structure of medical provisioning between the services.

The Administration of Military Medicine

Prior to December 1796, each regiment had a surgeon and a mate appointed to supervise the health of the soldiers.[26] In addition to regimental medical personnel, the Army also had physicians, purveyors, staff surgeons, apothecaries and hospital mates based at general hospitals at home and abroad. These facilities could be considerably larger than regimental hospitals and were places where more complex operations were performed or where patients were sent if their recovery was likely to be lengthy. It is this category of medical personnel which is referred to below as 'medical staff' in order to distinguish them from those employed regimentally.[27]

Prior to 1793, the Army Medical Department had in theory been jointly superintended by Sir Clifton Wintringham (the Physician General) and John Hunter (the Surgeon General and Inspector General of Regimental Infirmaries). Wintringham, however, was too

---

23 Hamilton, *Regimental Surgeon*, vol.1, pp.6–7 and 148; Frey, *British Soldier*, p.50 and Cantlie, *Army Medical Department*, vol.1, pp.102–103.
24 H. Bunbury, *Narratives of Some Passages in the Great War with France (1799–1810)* (London: Peter Davies, 1927), p.xxi and Fortescue, *History of the British Army*, vol.4, p.299.
25 N.A.M. Rodger, *The Wooden World: An Anatomy of the Georgian Navy* (London: Collins, 1986), pp.98–112.
26 Anon., *Fifth Report of the Commissioners of Military Enquiry, Army, Medical Department* (London: House of Commons, 1808), p.28.
27 Hospital mates were not members of the medical staff, but they have been included for the purposes of this chapter in order to distinguish between the medical personnel at general hospitals and those employed regimentally.

incapacitated to attend to his duties, so the full responsibility for organising general hospitals, selecting medical personnel, and providing supplies and equipment fell on his colleague. When Hunter died on 16 October 1793 his offices were split between John Gunning, who assumed the role of Surgeon General, and Thomas Keate, who became Inspector General of Regimental Infirmaries.[28] These three men – Wintringham, Gunning and Keate – comprised the newly-revived Army Medical Board, first established by the Duke of Cumberland in 1756, but which had since fallen into abeyance. It was only to last for three months in this form, however, since Wintringham died on 10 January 1794 and was replaced by Sir Lucas Pepys as Physician General.[29]

John Gunning, Surgeon General. (From the Witt Library, Courtauld Institute. Wellcome Collection)

The Board was theoretically the directing force behind the affairs of the Army Medical Department since it was authorised to appoint personnel in addition to supplying medical stores to the troops stationed at home and overseas. For the sake of clarity, this chapter makes reference to the Army Medical Department prior to the death of John Hunter in October 1793 and to the Army Medical Board thereafter.

The responsibilities of the Board regarding appointments were initially poorly defined, but in theory they were as ordered in a letter from the Commander-in-Chief, Lord Amherst, to Gunning and Keate on 17 October 1793:

> It is the King's Command that the Surgeon General, and the Inspector to the Regimental Hospitals, shall <u>on all occasions consult together on the appointments</u> proposed by them of Physicians and Surgeons for the Hospitals and for the medical staffs abroad and at home, and also of the Surgeons to be appointed to regiments, and <u>shall jointly sign the said Recommendations</u>.[30]

---

28 TNA: WO 1/1072: p.389, Yonge to Gunning, 17 October 1793; WO 1/1072: p.387, Dundas to Gunning, 17 October 1793 and HO 51/147: p.149, Commission appointing Thomas Keate as Inspector of Regimental Hospitals, 17 October 1793.

29 TNA: HO 51/147: p.183, Commission appointing Sir Lucas Pepys as Physician General, 15 January 1794; Cantlie, *Army Medical Department*, vol.1, p.211; T.H.A. Chaplin, *Medicine in England during the Reign of George III: The Fitzpatrick Lectures Delivered at the Royal College of Physicians 1917–1918* (London: Henry Kimpton, 1919), pp.77–78 and Anon., *Fifth Report*, pp.3–4.

30 TNA: WO 1/1072: p.388, Amherst to Gunning and Keate, 17 October 1793.

That these responsibilities of the Board did not work in practice is abundantly clear in the friction which prevailed between almost all those who had an interest in medical affairs. As far as the Board was concerned, this was largely due to the absence of any clear instructions from the War Office regarding the division of work between Board members. This was a legacy of the role once played by John Hunter, who held the posts of Surgeon General and Inspector General jointly. When these appointments were split on his death, Gunning found that: '... they are so blended together as to create confusion,' which resulted in conflict between Gunning and Keate, with the latter seeking to conduct the entire business of the department himself.[31] This took several months to resolve by mutual agreement, with Pepys and Gunning assuming responsibility for some of the correspondence formerly handled by Keate.[32]

Sir Lucas Pepys, Physician General, by J. Godby after H. Edridge. (Wellcome Collection)

As the appointment of medical personnel comprised the main function of the Army Medical Board, it is worth considering how this was done and, in particular, the role of the various interest groups in the appointment process before examining the Board's other functions and the well-being of the soldiers comprising the Army.

The Role of the Army Medical Board

Although the reformed Army Medical Board only dated from after the death of John Hunter in October 1793, the functions undertaken by the Army Medical Department prior to this date have been included here for the sake of preserving a continuous narrative.

Personnel

During John Hunter's tenure between 1790–1793, medical appointments and promotions had been conducted according to a strict system of seniority. A young gentleman would first be appointed mate to a regiment in order to gain practical experience until he was

---

31 TNA: WO 1/1072: pp.403–406, Gunning to the Secretary at War, 31 July 1794.
32 TNA: WO 1/1072: pp.390–401, Gunning to the Secretary at War, 28 May 1794.

appointed mate at a general hospital. The next step was regimental surgeon, where he had overall supervision of a unit of cavalry or infantry before progressing to staff surgeon or apothecary at a general hospital. The highest appointments were those of physician and purveyor.[33] This system ensured that all medical personnel were treated equally and were reasonably assured of progressing to a senior appointment so long as they continued to serve in the army. However, the principal drawback was that by the time men reached the medical staff they were too old to perform their duties adequately and were often unaware of new developments in medical practice. Gunning and Keate recognised this and instituted their own system of promotion so that men were only placed on half-pay in recognition of their former good services and not as a retainer for the future. This meant that younger men were appointed to the medical staff in preference to those with greater service but whom the Army Medical Board felt were inadequate for vacant positions.[34]

It took some time for the authorities in London to appoint medical staff to serve with the army in Flanders, meaning that soldiers were cared for by regimental surgeons for approximately the first two months of the 1793 campaign. The work of appointing medical staff only commenced on 10 April 1793 when John Hunter buttonholed the Secretary-at-War, Sir George Yonge. In the course of a fortnight's correspondence, it was settled that Drs Gregory West and Robert Smith would be appointed physicians at £1 per day, Vincent Wood as purveyor with the same salary, Thomas Young and Andrew Grieves as surgeons at 10/- per day and John Offrell and Rudolph Rhodes apothecaries also at 10/-; all of these men received appointments dated 25 April 1793. In addition, the purveyor was allotted one clerk at 5/- per day and 10 hospital mates were appointed, the first six on 26 April and the remaining four not until 23 May.[35]

Something should be mentioned of their previous experience. West and Smith had been on half-pay when they received their appointments in 1793. West had been appointed an apothecary in America on 23 October 1782 before being placed on half-pay on 11 February 1784. He had used his time wisely, being awarded a Doctor of Medicine (MD) degree from King's College, Aberdeen, in 1786 and it is assumed he worked in private practice thereafter. It should be noted that both St Andrews and Aberdeen granted the MD on the basis of an oral examination and certificates of competence only, and Paul Kopperman notes: 'Contemporaries roundly denounced the practice, and there appears to have been abuse'.[36] West's only other brief period of official employment prior to 1793 was between 20 October and 11 November 1790 when he was appointed physician to the forces destined for the planned expedition to South America. A return made by the adjutant-general's department

---

33 TNA: WO 7/97: pp.101–102, Hunter to Amherst, 28 February 1793 and L.G. Stevenson, 'John Hunter, Surgeon-General 1790–1793' in *Journal of the History of Medicine*, vol.19, 1964, pp.239–266.
34 TNA: WO 7/99: Keate to Gunning, 2 November 1793 and WO 7/98: pp.146–147: Hospital Board to Amherst, 23 November 1793.
35 TNA: WO 4/291: pp.37–39, Hunter to Yonge, 10 and 17 April 1793; WO 4/291: pp.44–46, 49–50 and 67, Yonge to York, 25 and 26 April and 23 May 1793; HO 51/147: p.78, Commissions appointing Gregory West as Physician, Thomas Young as Surgeon, Vincent Wood as Purveyor and John Offrell as Apothecary, 25 April 1793 and WO 25/41: pp.69–70 and 87–88, Commissions appointing the Hospital Staff, 25 April 1793.
36 Kopperman, 'The British Army in North America', in Hudson (ed.) *British Military*, p.57.

dated 16 July 1793 gives him the title of 'Physician General and Chief' of the General Hospital.[37]

Robert Smith had achieved his position of physician through what may be termed a professional, rather than an academic, route. He was born in 1745, so was aged 47 or 48 in 1793. He had been appointed surgeon to the 63rd Regiment on 2 October 1765 before promotion to staff surgeon in North America on 1 April 1779, serving as such until 25 December 1783 when he was placed on half-pay.[38] It is immediately apparent from the careers of West and Smith that the Army Medical Department placed a higher value on academic qualifications than on regimental service. Smith served for 18 years as a regimental and staff surgeon during a major war, whereas the grand total of West's military experience was 16 months as an apothecary. The critical difference between them was West being an MD, which catapulted him over the head of the older man with longer service and led to his appointment as chief of the general hospital. This situation could not endure for long.

The third senior appointment was of Vincent Wood as purveyor. He was born in 1750 and had been a surgeon in the Royal Artillery prior to his exchange into the 15th Dragoons on 12 June 1767. He had been appointed apothecary in North America on 1 January 1776 and promoted to staff surgeon on 7 May 1782. It is not known what he did thereafter, since his name does not appear in either the full or half-pay sections of the 1793 *Army List*. He was probably older than Gregory West, and had at least 15 years of military experience in comparison to West's 16 months.[39]

Of the surgeons, Thomas Young was the most senior and held the title of 'Surgeon General & Deputy Purveyor'.[40] He was appointed hospital mate in 1776, before transferring to the 1/1st Regiment as surgeon on 22 November 1780 and then Surgeon of Hospitals on Grenada on 1 August 1792 from which position he was posted to Flanders. By this time, Young had over 16 years' experience of military medicine and was subsequently to serve in senior positions in the West Indies in 1795, the Helder in 1799 and Egypt in 1801.[41] The remaining staff appointed in April 1793 were all serving as regimental surgeons. Andrew Grieves had served 12 years with the 53rd Regiment, having been appointed on 31 January 1781; given that the regiment was already in Flanders, it appears likely that Hunter perused the list of medical personnel there and sought to promote some of the longest serving men. For an unknown reason, Grieves' promotion to staff surgeon lasted only until 22 April 1794 when he exchanged with William Tudor, taking his position as regimental surgeon to the 2nd Dragoon Guards, which was also serving in Flanders. This demotion and significant loss of pay was not to harm Grieves' career, as he was appointed Assistant Inspector of Hospitals on 16 September 1795 and Inspector of Hospitals in North Britain on 19 July 1798.[42]

---

37 TNA: AO 16/52: p.98, Return of General and Staff Officers entitled to Bât and Forage Money, 16 July 1793 and A. Peterkin and W. Johnston, *Commissioned Officers in the Medical Services of the British Army 1660–1960* (London: The Wellcome Historical Medical Library, 1968), vol.1, entry 1020.
38 Peterkin and Johnston, *Commissioned Officers*, entry 733.
39 Peterkin and Johnston, *Commissioned Officers*, entry 746.
40 TNA: AO 16/52: p.98, enclosure in Murray to Watson 16 July 1793.
41 Peterkin and Johnston, *Commissioned Officers*, entry 972.
42 Peterkin and Johnston, *Commissioned Officers*, entry 979.

The senior of the two apothecaries was John Offrell, who was described as 'Apothecary General' in the bât and forage money list already mentioned. He was born in 1745 and had 16 years' service with the 29th Regiment, to which he had been appointed regimental surgeon on 28 February 1776, serving with them during the American War.[43] The other apothecary was Rudolph Rhodes, who was appointed surgeon to the 25th Regiment on 18 November 1768, remaining for over 10 years before transferring to the 1st Dragoon Guards on 28 July 1779. Rhodes therefore had 24 years' experience of military medicine prior to 1793 and appears to have been willing to improve his knowledge as he also gained an MD from King's College, Aberdeen, that year.[44]

Whilst the hospital staff was responsible for the direction of the department, the actual care of patients was undertaken primarily by the mates. Of the men appointed in April and May 1793, one had been a surgeon's mate since 1785, two more since 1787, one since 1788 and another since 1790; the careers of the remainder are unknown, though at least one of them was awarded a diploma from the College of Surgeons in London prior to his appointment. As regards their subsequent careers, 10 achieved the rank of regimental surgeon – four within six months, five between April and December 1794 and one in June 1795.[45] Hunter appointed another five hospital mates in June and early July 1793, but all of these men departed in 1794, either on promotion (to regimental surgeon, staff surgeon and surgeon to the garrison of Martinique respectively), or they died.[46]

The careers of the medical staff and hospital mates appointed up to July 1793 have been outlined in some detail, because after this date the business of selection became more problematic due to a developing conflict between London and Dr Hugh Kennedy, appointed as Inspector General of Hospitals with the army in Flanders on 29 July 1793. Before looking in more detail at the men serving in the general hospital after this date it would be as well to discuss why Kennedy was sent to Flanders in the first place.

When the original hospital staff had been sent out, a set of 'Instructions for the Conduct of the Medical Staff' had been prepared by Hunter and sent to the Duke of York by Sir George Yonge on 8 May 1793.[47] These placed the hospital staff under the orders of the Commander-in-Chief and aimed to prevent conflict between the different medical departments by clearly defining the responsibilities of each. The overall management of both the general and regimental hospitals was to be in the hands of physicians, except in purely surgical cases when staff surgeons had authority. Apothecaries were to be in charge of storing and issuing medicines and to act as surgeons should they be required to do so, whilst mates were to be assigned as directed by physicians and surgeons. Physicians were to decide which staff were deployed on detached duty and were urged to take no account of seniority when doing

---

43   Peterkin and Johnston, *Commissioned Officers*, entry 859.
44   Peterkin and Johnston, *Commissioned Officers*, entry 761.
45   Peterkin and Johnston, *Commissioned Officers*, entries 1179, 1180, 1186, 1191, 1246, 1262, 1327, 1352, 1353 and 1403.
46   Peterkin and Johnston, *Commissioned Officers*, entries 1226, 1273 and 1328. The two men who died were not commissioned.
47   TNA: WO 4/291: pp.55–59, Yonge to York and enclosure 'Instructions for the conduct of the Medical Staff serving with the British Forces under the Command of His R.H. the Duke of York', 8 May 1793.

so. The reasoning behind placing physicians in charge was clearly outlined by Dr Richard Brocklesby, himself a physician during the Seven Years' War:

> Every person who knows that Surgery is but a small part of the study of Physick, that it only teaches the cure of external diseases, such as properly require the knife, or plaister, and a manual neatness in bandages, &c. will easily grant, that a mere Surgeon ought not, with any justice to the patient, to attempt the practice of physick.[48]

The majority of instructions were directed at the purveyor, indicating that the principal concern of the War Office was to control costs. The purveyor was to take charge of all the hospital stores, medicines excepted, and to issue them as requested in writing by physicians and surgeons. These could include items such as fuel, candles, wine, vinegar, and fresh provisions. He was also responsible for recruiting hospital servants (clerks, the storekeeper, the steward, the cook, nurses and others as required), whilst always minimising costs. The steward kept an account of the provisions issued, communicating this to the purveyor daily, whilst maintaining a separate account of any extra expenditure on soldiers' wives and children.

Evidence for women working in hospitals is sparse, as they were rarely part of the official establishment, but clearly they were employed as nurses, laundresses, cooks and in other support roles. The widows of soldiers killed at the Schellenburg in 1704 were ordered to work in the hospital in return for food and accommodation whilst arrangements were made to return them to England.[49] Gruber von Arni has noted that 20 nurses were employed during the winter of 1704–1705 in the Nordlingen hospital and between 38 and 50 between 1706–1712 at the Bijloke hospital in Ghent, concluding that: '… nurses were regarded as a common and essential component of patient care'.[50] Until the mid-eighteenth century, the hospital staff included a female matron, though this position had been replaced by that of head nurse, who was not a member of the staff, by the time of the American War.[51] Dr Donald Monro described the illness and cure of a young mother named Andrews who was serving as a nurse at the military hospital at Osnabrück in January–February 1763 and it is assumed that she was the wife of a soldier. He also wrote extensively regarding the duties of nurses working at general hospitals, stating that: '… the Sick are attended by Nurses, who are commonly Soldiers Wives'.[52] The fact that separate accounts were kept for them in the 1793 instructions strongly suggests that this was generally acknowledged at the time, even if it was not officially recognised by having women included in the official personnel establishment. That this was handled on an unofficial basis is evident from a general order dated 18 May 1793, instructing: 'The Battalions to leave 12 Men & 12 Women, to assist in the

---

48 Brocklesby, *Œconomical and Medical Observations*, pp.37–38.
49 Gruber von Arni, *Hospital Care*, p.127.
50 Gruber von Arni, *Hospital Care*, pp.135 and 184.
51 Kopperman, 'The British Army in North America', in Hudson (ed.), *British Military*, p.53 and footnote 5.
52 Monro, *An Account of the Diseases*, pp.27–30, 384–387 and 405 footnote l.

Hospital also Two Cooks' when the army departed Tournai for Valenciennes.[53] Assuming three Foot Guards, two line and two flank battalions (the 37th Regiment being in garrison in Ostend), this meant detaching 84 soldiers, 84 women and 14 cooks, possibly also soldiers, to the general hospital.

Soldiers 'not in the British Service' could be admitted to the hospital only so long as the purveyor obtained a written order from the commander-in-chief; whether this was always possible under active service conditions is unknown. As with the Commissariat, accounts had to be shown periodically (in this case, every three months) to the commander-in-chief, together with all the supporting vouchers, in order to obtain approval for the accrued expenditure of funds. The stoppage of 4d per day was made in respect of every patient in order to pay for medicines and subsistence whilst in the general hospital, which was paid to the purveyor quarterly. Finally, the purveyor had to prepare returns of sick and wounded men for the commander-in-chief and liaise with individual units regarding the return of recovered men to them.

It was mentioned above that the appointments made by Hunter had the potential for causing discord, and it did not take long for rivalries to surface over personal zones of responsibility and management protocols. It was for these reasons that the Army Medical Department appointed an Inspector of Hospitals to take charge of the establishment and ensure efficient running. The man chosen for this job was Dr Hugh Kennedy, who was: '… vested with the superintendence & controul of all matters regarding the medical department, subject of course, to the orders of H.R.H. but he is not to interfere with the regulations for conducting the Purveyor's branch of business'. Kennedy's commission was dated 17 July 1793.[54]

Kennedy was born in 1735. He was awarded an MD at Edinburgh University in 1754 and admitted a Licentiate of the College of Physicians in 1765. He was elected physician at the Middlesex Hospital on 1 February 1759, holding this position for over 23 years. He also served in a military capacity, being appointed physician on 7 January 1762 in Lord Albermarle's expedition to Havana. After a period of half-pay, he was re-employed on 1 January 1776 and subsequently became Inspector of Regimental Infirmaries in North America in July 1777. Kennedy was physician to the Prince of Wales and maintained a correspondence with him during the campaign.[55] Despite his undoubted technical abilities and movements in the highest echelons of society, Herbert Taylor's judgment of his organisational skills was damning: 'The hospital was not well established or regulated, although there were many good physicians and surgeons on the staff, but the Director-General was incompetent to the situation.'[56]

---

53 NAM: 1985-12-15-4: GO, Tournay, 18 May 1793.
54 TNA: WO 4/291: pp.95–96, Yonge to Murray, 29 July 1793 and HO 51/147: pp.100–101, Commission appointing Dr Hugh Kennedy as Inspector of the Hospitals for the Service of our Forces serving on the Continent, 17 July 1793.
55 Peterkin and Johnston, *Commissioned Officers*, entry 656 and Kennedy to the Prince of Wales, 13 September 1793, in A. Aspinall (ed.), *The Correspondence of George Prince of Wales* (London: Cassell, 1964), vol.2, pp.386–387.
56 Taylor (ed.), *Taylor Papers*, p.29.

The Army Medical Department appointed Kennedy to address the want of unity amongst the hospital staff in Flanders. They were soon to discover that they had created an additional problem for themselves when, within one month of his appointment, Hunter wrote to Lord Amherst complaining that Kennedy had obtained the Duke of York's agreement for George Hollings to be appointed staff surgeon despite the fact that he had never seen a gunshot wound or served in the Army. Kennedy continued to put his own men forward to fill vacancies and clearly stated his intention to do so without reference to London though, he conceded, he would take their wishes into consideration. The conflict was only resolved in January 1794, when Gunning and Keate sought clarification from Lord Amherst, who replied that all recommendations should be made by the Army Medical Board and forwarded by them to him for appointment by the King.[57]

Having established the correct procedure, the Board now required regular lists of all medical personnel with the army in Flanders to identify vacancies and make recommendations. Kennedy, however, felt aggrieved at losing his prerogative over appointments and simply ignored the repeated requests of Gunning and Keate for these returns. Despite an appeal to the Secretary-at-War, who was requested to order Kennedy to transmit quarterly lists, the Board never managed to achieve their wishes.[58] Keate vented his frustration in a letter to Dr Gregory West, one of the original physicians appointed to the hospital staff in Flanders in April 1793: 'I have 20 times requested a Return, & if he refuses much longer he will have a different kind of request made him by others of which I have given him a hint, but it avails nothing.'[59]

Although not openly stated in his correspondence with Hunter, or subsequently with the Army Medical Board, Kennedy informed Sir Everard Home, who called on him at the general hospital at Bruges in September 1793, that he considered: '… himself as acting under the Duke of Y. without any reference to the Surgeon Gen'l or any one in England but the Command'r in C.'[60]

As well as contending with the Inspector General of Hospitals, there were also gratings between the Army Medical Board and officers in Flanders. One example concerned John Joberns who the Board recommended for promotion from hospital mate to staff surgeon in February 1794. The appointment was rejected by Colonel James Craig, the Duke of York's adjutant-general, so the Board members sought the advice of Lord Amherst who even consulted the King on the matter. The issue was regarded by the Board as a matter of principle but was in truth the consequence of War Office neglect in not issuing comprehensive instructions on

---

57   TNA: WO 7/98: pp.34–35, Hunter to Amherst, 29 August 1793; WO 7/99, pp.34–35 and 57–58, Keate to St Leger, 8 November 1793 and Gunning and Keate to Amherst, 28 November 1793; WO 7/100: pp.37–38, 42 and 50 and 44–47, Gunning and Keate to Amherst, 1 January 1794, Amherst to Gunning and Keate, 4 and 12 January 1794 and Gunning to Kennedy, 6 January 1794 and James Dickson to Catherine Dickson, 5 August 1794, in Cormack (ed.), *James Dickson*, p.68.
58   TNA: WO 7/100: pp.53–56, Keate to St Leger, 13 January 1794; WO 7/100: pp.60–61, Keate to Kennedy, 22 January 1794; WO 7/100: p.65, Keate to the Secretary at War, 22 January 1794 and WO 7/101: pp.79–80, 86–87 and 133, Keate to Kennedy, 19 and 23 April and 23 May 1794.
59   TNA: WO 7/101: pp.148–150, Keate to West, 2 June 1794.
60   TNA: WO 4/291: p.121, The report of Sir [Everard] Home sent with the powers of the Surgeon and Inspector Gen'l. of Hospitals to examine into the Surgical Departments of the Military Hospitals under the command of H.R.H. The Duke of York, 30 September 1793.

the procedure for appointing medical personnel. In the event, the matter was settled quickly when the King decided that all appointments of medical personnel to regiments should be made by proprietary colonels, and that the Army Medical Board should make recommendations to them.[61] This did not address the central problem, which was that the Board had to confirm medical appointments and satisfy itself that each individual was suitably qualified. It did not take long for the issue of prerogative to raise itself a second time, when in May the commanding officer of the 14th Regiment refused to accept the appointment of David Shea as mate to his regiment. This resulted in considerable inconvenience to the rejected individual, who had travelled from home to take up his appointment, but also undermined the Board's aim to supply the army with suitably qualified personnel.[62] The entire issue of recommendation and appointment was eventually settled in June when Amherst wrote to the Board: 'That the King does not intend to exclude the Colonels who raise Regiments from recommending their Staff, as has been usual, but that no Surgeon or Mate can be appointed, if the Medical Board do not think his Abilities, and Professional Knowledge equal to the intended appointment'.[63]

Given such goings-on, it was a little hard on the Board to be criticised for the failings of people they had not actually appointed. One hospital mate was singled out for censure by Captain and Lieutenant Colonel Charles Barnett of the 3rd Foot Guards. In reply, the Board stated that the individual concerned was a known drunkard, but had nevertheless been appointed by no less a person than Lieutenant General Harcourt: '... which clearly shews the incompetency and impropriety of military officers interfering in the appointment of Medical Men'.[64] Just as members of the Army Medical Board were peeved when their appointments were rejected by army officers, the reverse was also the case. A state of conflict therefore existed throughout the campaign in Flanders as each side sought to secure the right of patronage.[65]

To recapitulate: appointments of medical personnel had been made solely by the Army Medical Department (effectively, John Hunter) between April and July 1793, when Hugh Kennedy was appointed Inspector. From July 1793 until January 1794 both the Board and Kennedy were appointing their own men with varying levels of reference to the other, though it is almost impossible at this distance of time to know with certainty exactly which appointments originated from either side. The primacy of the Army Medical Board was re-established in January 1794, when recommendations for staff appointments were to be made to the King, though it is not clear how effective this might have been given the lack of information on vacancies from Kennedy. In the following month it was decided that the Board should make recommendations for regimental appointments to proprietary colonels who, confusingly, could not sanction anything without it being agreed by the Board. Despite all of this, there is evidence that men were appointed without any reference to the

---

61 TNA: WO 7/100: p.78, Pepys, Gunning and Keate to Amherst, 11 February 1794 and WO 7/100: p.86, Memorandum of a meeting between Amherst and George III, 18 February 1794.
62 TNA: WO 7/101: pp.117–118, Keate to Kennedy, 13 May 1794 and WO 7/101: pp.123–124, Medical Board to Amherst, 14 May 1794.
63 TNA: WO 1/896: p.223, Amherst to Medical Board, 7 June 1794.
64 TNA: WO 7/102: pp.10–11, Medical Board to York, undated but written in the first week of July 1795.
65 For example, the Board refused to appoint an individual recommended by Harry Calvert, aide-de-camp to the Duke of York. Calvert to Dalrymple, 28 September 1794, in Verney (ed.), *Calvert*, p.338.

Army Medical Board. We may conclude that strong opinions existed in different parts of the medical profession, with interested parties including the King, Lord Amherst, the Duke of York and proprietary colonels, resulting in a lack of common criteria and agreed standards.

A considerable number of hospital staff were appointed between August 1793 and the end of January 1795 when the army crossed into Germany. No complete list of these men exists but a compilation of names mentioned in the available correspondence comprises six physicians, six deputy purveyors, 10 staff surgeons, seven apothecaries and 70 hospital mates. Of the physicians, one is unidentified but the remaining six had all been awarded MD degrees between 1786 and 1791; none had any previous military experience. Three of the six deputy purveyors appointed in 1793 and 1794 had experience as surgeons or hospital mates dating as far back as 1780 in one case, 1784 in another and 1787 in a third. Two men had no previous military experience and the remaining man had been a hospital mate, but it is unknown for how long. Nine of the 10 surgeons were men with previous military experience. Four had been regimental surgeons with commissions dating from 1787, 1788, 1791 and 1794 respectively; five of the remainder had either been regimental or hospital mates. As already mentioned, George Hollings had been appointed surgeon by the Duke of York in August 1793 without reference to the Army Medical Board, thus the debate over who had the authority to make such decisions. The last group of hospital staff appointed between July 1793 to January 1795 were the seven apothecaries, only one of whom had no previous medical experience. The remaining six had all served as regimental surgeons with their dates of appointment being 1764, 1780, 1782, 1787, 1788 and 1790. Some mention should be made of the large number of hospital mates. Of the 70, 15 (21 percent) were promoted to staff positions, three returned to Britain, possibly accompanying the sick, one transferred to Jamaica in the same capacity, and one appears to have died. As far as can be ascertained, eight men were appointed without reference to the Army Medical Board.

If we take the deputy purveyors, surgeons and apothecaries as a single group of men, 19 of the 23 had previous military experience (83 percent). Of these 19, 10 (43 percent) already had commissioned rank as regimental surgeons, whilst a further nine (39 percent) worked as either regimental or hospital mates prior to receiving a staff appointment. It is also apparent that vacancies for deputy purveyors were filled by men receiving their first commissioned post, staff surgeons were almost equally divided between regimental surgeons and mates, and apothecaries were almost all drawn from regimental surgeons. These positions were mostly filled by men who had come through what may be termed the professional route.

What of the hospital mates who, not strictly being members of the hospital staff, nevertheless comprised the majority of personnel working in the general hospitals? Service records survive for 17 of the 87 men appointed (19 percent) and show that 10 (59 percent) served as a regimental mate prior to their appointment, five had not (17 percent) and the previous careers of two are unknown, though these last two men had each obtained a diploma from the College of Surgeons in 1791 and 1792 respectively. A total of 13 men possessed this diploma prior to their appointment as hospital mate, and the remaining four had served as a regimental mate.[66] These results suggest that hospital mates were all qualified in some way

---

66 TNA: WO 25/3904: pp.62, 85, 122, Records and particulars of Professional Education-Surgeons, also: WO 25/3905: pp.28, 144; WO 25/3907: pp.91, 123; WO 25/3909: pp.17, 51, 73, 169, 200 and WO 25/3910: pp.36, 39, 59, 78,150, 157.

prior to their appointment, either through experience, or as a holder of a diploma, or both. The only remaining question is whether the sample is representative of the entire cohort of hospital mates but, for the purposes of this study, the evidence suggests that unrest over promotions amongst clinicians in 1794 was not likely to have been caused by appointments at the lower end of the general hospital hierarchy.[67]

The appointment of physicians represented a sharp contrast, since all owed their appointments to academic qualifications, none having previously served in a military capacity. This is attributable to the Physician General, Sir Lucas Pepys, whose own experience was limited to civil practice and who sought to raise the standard of military medicine by appointing physicians with the highest academic qualifications. This effectively ended the promotion prospects of existing medical personnel, many of whom had spent years in military service, in favour of more recently qualified individuals with no practical understanding of an army or the ailments of soldiers. Worse still, these men from civil life were paid more and placed in charge of their older and more experienced colleagues. It is perhaps unsurprising that this sharp contrast between 'academics' and 'professionals' made for a situation ripe with discord.

Supplies

A second function of the Army Medical Board was to oversee the shipment of medicines and medical supplies to the hospital staff (regimental surgeons, on the other hand, were responsible for providing their own instruments and, until 1796, their own medicines using the aforementioned allowance). The first difficulty had cropped up during summer 1793, when it was found that many surgical instruments were of poor manufacture, though an immediate investigation was made by contacting 'Mr Evans the instrument maker' and the matter settled. The War Office was responsible for ordering supplies other than medicines and, on the evidence available, acted with alacrity. This particularly concerned the provision in March 1794 of 50 spring wagons for transporting sick soldiers, the first of which reached Ostend within a month of the request being received in London.[68] This immediacy was also evident in the business conducted by the Board, which sent out the equipment for a 'flying hospital' in March 1794 consisting of 1,500 sets of bedding (including sheets, blankets and palliasses), five hospital tents, 100 cots and 50 stretchers. In June, Keate dispatched a consignment of bedding and palliasses as soon as the items had been requested by Francis McDonnell, staff surgeon in charge of the detached hospital at Ostend, ending his letter: 'You will be so good as to inform me of your further wants & necessities & I shall lose no time in endeavouring to relieve them'.[69]

---

67 The social and professional background of men entering the field of military medicine from 1790 is discussed in detail by M. Ackroyd, L. Brockliss, M. Moss, K. Retford and J. Stevenson, *Advancing with the Army. Medicine, the Professions, and Social Mobility in the British Isles, 1790–1850* (Oxford: Oxford University Press, 2006), pp.60–151.
68 TNA: WO 4/291: p.126, 'The report of Sir [Everard] Home'; WO 4/291: pp.81–82, Lewis to Murray, 26 June 1793; WO 4/291: pp.227–228, Lewis to Messrs Trotters, 8 March 1794; WO 58/167: pp.74–77, 79–80 and 86, Rose to Watson, 21 February, 4 and 28 March 1794; Anon., *Fifth Report*, pp.28 and 40 and Anon., *Officer of the Guards*, vol.2, p.14–15.
69 TNA: WO 7/101: p.165, Keate to McDonnell, 18 June 1794 and Cantlie, *Army Medical Department*, vol.1, p.218.

Despite these efforts by the authorities at home, the shortage of medicines and other medical sundries was disturbing. This was particularly so during 1794, when six senior members of the hospital staff accused Kennedy of causing unnecessary suffering by failing to ensure that adequate supplies were available. A court of enquiry to investigate these charges was held at Tournai on 9 June by order of the Duke of York and found that the accusations were indeed justified. That said, blame was attributed to foul weather and adverse winds, which held up the dispatch of necessary items from England. The episode was symptomatic of the continuing disagreements between various members of the medical staff and of which the Army Medical Board appear to have been largely unaware. They were contacted by Lord Amherst in August 1794, as a result of which Gunning visited the army in Flanders. But despite this special mission by the Surgeon General the subsequent delivery of medicines did not always match demand.[70]

Casualty Evacuation
A third activity undertaken by the Army Medical Board was the evacuation of sick and wounded soldiers to Britain. This was first recommended by Sir Everard Home, who inspected the military hospitals in September 1793, leading the War Office to make preparations to receive sick soldiers at Deal Naval Hospital, and surgical cases at the York Hospital, Chelsea.[71] The supervision of these activities was undertaken by Thomas Keate who took a close interest in the evacuation of casualties and issued a stream of instructions regarding the two hospitals. The two surgeons in charge of the naval hospital at Deal were each paid 10/- per day for their services in addition to an allowance of 6/8 per patient for which they were: '... to provide all kinds of medicines of the very best quality as well as surgical applications'.[72] The hospital at Deal had a capacity for 200 patients. But when Keate made his inspection on 27 October 1793 he discovered many defects, such as poor ventilation, a lack of wine for refreshment, and even a want of beds, for until now the patients lay in hammocks. Francis McDonnell, staff surgeon in charge of the hospital at Ostend, was ordered to supervise the embarkation of patients and Kennedy was given instructions to send any surgical cases up the Thames to Chelsea. Ships bringing patients from Flanders were ordered to disembark the sick at Deal before proceeding to Deptford, since it had proved impossible to find vessels willing to sail from Deal directly to Chelsea. Onward transportation was either by land or barge and, pleasant to report amid such gloom, great care was exercised by all concerned.[73]

---

70 T. Keate, *Observations on the Fifth Report of the Commissioners for Military Enquiry. And More Particularly of those Parts of it which Relate to the Surgeon General* (London: Hatchard, 1808), p.19 and Dickson to Catherine Dickson, 28 October 1794, in Cormack (ed.), *James Dickson*, p.92.
71 TNA: WO 4/291: pp.121–122, 'Home's report', 30 September 1793 and WO 4/291: pp.118 and 141–142, Yonge to Murray, 7 October and 5 November 1793.
72 TNA: WO 7/99: pp.11–12, Keate to Boys, 4 November 1793; WO 7/99: pp.14–19, Report of ye State of Soldiers from Flanders placed in the Naval Hospital at Deal, every one of whom I saw & examined on Sunday Oct 27 1793 accompanied with some observations & proposals for improving the same [by Thomas Keate]; WO 7/99: pp.68–71, Keate to Kennedy, 3 December 1793; WO 7/100: pp.23–24, Keate to Boys, 18 December 1793; WO 7/100: p.30, Keate to Boys and Willoughby, 24 December 1793.
73 TNA: WO 4/291: p.118, Yonge to Murray, 7 October 1793; WO 7/99: p.14–19, 'Report of ye State of Soldiers'; WO 7/99: pp.22–23, Keate to Yonge, 5 November 1793; WO 7/99: pp.68–71, Keate to

The first batch of patients, 156 men, embarked at Ostend on about 21 December 1793, to be followed by 364 more at the end of February. Conditions at Deal took a turn for the worse in January, when the two staff surgeons in charge wrote to Major General Edward Smith, commanding the Coastal District:

> We think it proper to inform you that a fever of a putrid tendency is spreading through the hospital which we trace to a want of Cloathing in the Military; some of whom came in without shirts; and many with only one, which have been some weeks without a change. All the nurses are infested, and one is dead. It becomes therefore a very serious matter to every body in the Hospital; and we beg you will have the goodness to order necessary clothing as soon as possible.[74]

Smith responded the same day, instructing the surgeons to indent straight away for whatever clothing was needed, and not to hesitate in calling on him for assistance.[75]

During the first half of 1794, the traffic of sick and wounded repatriated from Flanders was modest enough to be handled at Deal and Chelsea. It appears that Keate may have tempted fate by informing both Kennedy and West on 10 June that both hospitals were nearly empty and suggesting that the overcrowding then experienced in the Flanders hospitals could be relieved by repatriating more patients. By August, a total of 1,900 sick and wounded had accumulated on board transports at the mouth of the Scheldt, of whom 226 men, 32 women and 18 children arrived at Deal on 24 August. These numbers were far greater than could be accommodated in existing hospitals, meaning that Keate had to scour southern England for additional space to house the growing number of men being sent home. The conditions in which patients were dispatched from the United Provinces caused the authorities at home much concern. One convoy of 14 ships had 844 men, 64 women and 25 children on board of whom 107 men, 4 women and 1 child had died, due to the '… very foul and filthy state…' of the conditions on board and the fact that only 12 medical personnel were in attendance, meaning that some ships must have had none at all.[76] An additional problem for the authorities was their need to screen the true number of sick and wounded from public knowledge, especially the more distressing cases, which would be seen by the public as another indicator the war was going badly. The large volume of sick and wounded also imposed a heavy strain on the army in Flanders. This, alas, caused fatal outcomes for many patients. In November, one assistant surgeon reported that of 190 men detailed to be sent to England, 60 had died in six weeks. However, once in England the chances of recovery were reasonably good. The naval hospital at Deal, for example, admitted a total of 737 patients between September 1793 and December 1794 of whom only 62 (eight percent) died, most as a result of a dysentery epidemic during August 1794.[77]

Kennedy, 3 December 1793; WO 1/896: pp.307–308 and 323, Smith to Yonge, 14 and 17 January 1794.
74   TNA: WO 1/896: p.333, Boys and Willoughby to Smith, 23 January 1794.
75   TNA: WO 7/100: p.26, Keate to Boys, 21 December 1793; WO 7/101: p.1, Keate to Boys, 20 February 1794 and WO 1/896: p.335, Smith to Boys and Willoughby, 23 January 1794.
76   WO 1/896: pp.651–653, Keate to Windham, 27 December 1794.
77   TNA: WO 7/101: pp.157–158, Keate to Kennedy, 10 June 1794; WO 7/101: p.159, Keate to West, 10 June 1794; WO 1/896: pp.609–618, Report of Mr. Keate, Inspector of Hospitals, relative to the

The facilities at Deal, Chelsea, and subsequently at Colchester, were an important part of the medical plan to cater for the large number of sick and wounded arriving from Flanders. They were expanded as the need arose, with four temporary wards being added at Chelsea, raising capacity there to 700 patients at any one time. A total of 1,180 patients from Flanders were treated there, including 150 women and children. Buildings in the vicinity of the hospital at Deal were also appropriated for the sick, giving a capacity of 300, but the largest facility was at Colchester where the barracks were converted into a general hospital for 1,500 patients; smaller facilities were provided at Harwich and elsewhere.[78]

The Medical Department during the Flanders Campaign

Some assessment needs to be made of the scale of the demands placed on the Medical Department before discussing the resources provided to meet them and whether the strategy adopted met with success.

Sickness
The magnitude of the task facing medical personnel in Flanders may only be assessed through a quantitative analysis of the number of soldiers sick and wounded during the campaign. Although the surviving data can only be described as partial, since few of the monthly army returns and none of the weekly hospital states survive, enough remains for such an analysis to be undertaken. Information on sickness-rates has been amplified by consulting the regimental muster books for four infantry regiments: the 14th, 37th and 53rd, which were among the first to arrive in Flanders in 1793, and the 33rd which joined in July 1794. Information on the number of wounded has been taken from casualty returns sent to the War Office after every action, though these did not include men wounded on outpost duty or in minor skirmishes, so represent the minimum number of wounded. In the following discussion the word 'sick' is used to include all soldiers receiving medical attention, whether they were sick or wounded, reflecting the terminology used in the documents on which this study is based.[79]

Of the units chosen for more detailed analysis, musters rolls survive only for the 14th Regiment for the first three months of 1793. The regiment was garrisoned at Chatham Barracks in January and February when four percent and five percent respectively of the rank-and-file were sick. The 14th moved to Dover Castle the following month and the muster of 1 March indicated this had increased to nine percent. During the intervening period, the net strength of the regiment increased by 38 men, all of whom were recruits.

---

    temporary provision at Chelsea &c for the reception of sick & wounded, 2 August 1794; WO 1/896: pp.431–432, Smith to Lewis, 24 August 1794; Dickson to Charles Dickson, 29 November 1794, in Cormack (ed.) *James Dickson*, p.98; WO 1/896: pp.531–532, Smith to Lewis, 24 December 1794 and WO 1/896: pp.553–554, Boys to Smith, 25 December 1794.

78 Keate, *Observations on the Fifth Report*, pp.47–48.
79 See Appendices I and II.

This, and the change in barracks, were the only obvious factors to explain the number of rank-and-file sick – a matter which will be discussed further below.[80]

In 1793, the number of British troops in the Duke of York's army was small, numbering just under 8,000 of all ranks, meaning that the number of soldiers requiring medical attention was manageable. The muster books for the 14th, 37th and 53rd regiments all provide data for the six months ending on 24 June 1793. At that date, each unit had 22 percent, 23 percent and 28 percent of the rank-and-file sick respectively, having been in Flanders for exactly three months.[81] The similarity in the number of sick in these regiments suggests that the three Foot Guards battalions present in Flanders had comparable sickness rates, though the absence of muster books for them (other than for the battalions in garrison at home) precludes analysis. That this was probably the case is substantiated by the army states of 15 October and 1 December 1793, which have been extracted from Appendix I, Tables I.1 and I.2.

Table 1: Rank-and-file sick, 1793

Date	Infantry	Cavalry	Royal Artillery	Royal Military Artificers	Total
15 October	935 (23%)	404 (19%)	98 (13%)	37 (21%)	1,474 (21%)
1 December	879 (19%)	455 (16%)	105 (19%)	N/A	1,439 (18%)

Sources: TNA: WO 1/167: pp.334–335 and 785–787.

Table 1 indicates that sickness levels in the infantry were slightly higher than for the cavalry. Cavalry regiments in Flanders were approximately half the strength of infantry battalions, yet had the same medical establishment, so the surgeon and mate could devote more time to individual cases. Cavalry units also had a greater proportion of trained soldiers, since nearly all consisted of only four troops of men chosen from regiments located at home. Cavalry recruits were generally of better character and intelligence than those from the infantry and, by implication, more able to look after themselves. Sir John Pringle, writing at the time of the War of the Austrian Succession, noted that cavalry troopers experienced a lower incidence of sickness on account of their uniform cloaks, which helped keep them dry by day and warm by night.[82] The slight fall in the numbers of sick for the army as a whole between October and December was probably due to the troops returning to winter quarters and the reinforcement of two regiments of Dragoon Guards with lower than average sickness rates. Although Table 1 does not present data by individual unit, it is significant that the 53rd Regiment had only 14 percent sick on 15 October (the lowest for any infantry unit) which was almost certainly due to it being in the relative comfort of the Nieuwpoort garrison, rather than in the field (Appendix I, Table I.1). Another factor affecting sickness rates was the extent to which regiments repatriated men to England. The few surviving musters

---

80 Anon., *Fifth Report*, Appendix No.23 (A) and TNA: WO 17/115: 14th Regiment monthly returns 1759–1805.
81 TNA: WO 12/3118: Muster books and pay lists, 14th Regiment; WO 12/5102: Muster books and pay lists, 37th Regiment and WO 12/6317: Muster books and pay lists, 53rd Regiment.
82 TNA: WO 3/11: pp.77–78: Fawcett to York, 27 March 1793; WO 3/11: p.79, adjutant-general's order, 2 April 1793; Houlding, *Fit for Service*, p.264 and Pringle, *Observations*, p.19.

prevent a detailed analysis, but one for the 14th Regiment for the six months ending on 24 December 1793 shows that the unit dispatched home 75 sick during December, lowering the incidence of sickness amongst the rank-and-file from 26 percent on the first day of that month to 16 percent just over three weeks later.[83]

Although the hospital returns have not survived, it is known from evidence presented by Dr James Borland to the Commissioners for Military Enquiry in 1807 that most of the sick were tended in regimental, rather than general, hospitals in 1793. By December of that year, the British element of the Duke of York's army comprised 13 cavalry and seven infantry units. Assuming that each had a surgeon and a mate, there were approximately 42 regimental medical staff with the army including two attached to ordnance units (see Chapter 6). Of the appointments made by the Army Medical Board in 1793, approximately 24 staff surgeons and hospital mates were serving at the end of the year, with a further eight hospital mates appointed independently by the Duke of York. This meant that approximately 1,450 men sick in December would have had at least 74 medical personnel to care for them (not including physicians, purveyors or apothecaries), or 1 to every 20 men. This approximation would have varied enormously between units, and between the regimental and general hospitals, but it does suggest that the total number of medical personnel was sufficient for the army's needs.[84] This compares with the ratio of 43 patients to one surgeon or assistant surgeon which '… cannot be supposed to be an oppressive duty to active and capable men…' according to Dr Robert Jackson.[85]

There are unfortunately no strength returns for the Duke of York's army for the first six months of 1794, for most of which period the troops were in winter quarters. Data are also incomplete from those units selected for closer analysis, with the exception of the 53rd Regiment which on 24 June had 793 rank-and-file of whom 237 were sick (29 percent). This high percentage may have been due to the arrival at the beginning of April of recruits for Abercromby's brigade, of which the 53rd Regiment formed a part. These men were sent out from England with insufficient clothing, and it would appear from one eyewitness account that they were physically incapable of enduring the rigours of a campaign.[86] Table 2 (extracted from Appendix I, Tables I.4 to I.9) indicates the high percentage of sick in the 53rd at the end of June appears unrepresentative of the army, and indeed of the unit itself only a week later when its sickness rate fell to 19 percent.

---

83 TNA: WO 12/3118: Muster books & pay lists, 14th Regiment and NAM: 1976-07-44-2: Muster Roll of the 14th Regiment, 25 June–24 December 1793.
84 Anon., *Fifth Report*, Appendix No.23 (A) and Appendix No.30 p.22. Appointments made by the Army Medical Board are principally in TNA: WO 7/97–102: Medical Department out-letters and WO 1/896–897: Army Medical Board correspondence with the War Office. See also Peterkin and Johnston, *Commissioned Officers*.
85 R. Jackson, *A System of Arrangement and Discipline for the Medical Department of Armies* (London: John Murray, 1805), pp.15–16.
86 TNA: WO 12/6317: Muster books & pay lists, 53rd Regiment and Calvert to Dalrymple, 8 April 1794, in Verney (ed.), *Calvert*, p.187.

Table 2: Rank-and-file sick, 1794

Date	Infantry	Cavalry	Royal Artillery	Royal Military Artificers	Total
1 July	1,330 (17%)	455 (12%)	38 (8%)	9 (13%)	1,832 (15%)
1 August	2,540 (13%)	397 (10%)	51 (7%)	12 (12%)	3,000 (12%)
5 August	2,553 (13%)	392 (10%)	51 (7%)	10 (10%)	3,006 (12%)
1 September	3,151 (16%)	391 (10%)	58 (7%)	9 (9%)	3,609 (14%)
27 November	6,452 (33%)	N/A	57 (29%)	18 (23%)	N/A
24 December	7,360 (39%)	205 (7%)	44 (24%)	14 (18%)	7,623 (34%)

Sources: TNA: WO 1/170: pp.131–137, 373, 387–404, 551–563 and WO 1/171: pp.309 and 621.

As in 1793, the highest percentage of sick soldiers was in the infantry, as shown in Table 2. Some infantry units were particularly prone to sickness. One of these was the 80th Regiment, whose commanding officer wrote home on 16 October that it had 355 men sick (40 percent). Indeed, the brigade commander stated in the following month that the 80th had: '… deposited sick all over Holland'.[87] By early February 1795, the Regiment had 396 of its men (48 percent of the rank-and-file) on the sick list. A total of 228 men were either killed in action or died of wounds or sickness during the campaign, and a further 210 were mustered out of the unit as medically unfit.[88] The very high sickness rates in the 80th Regiment were probably due to it being newly raised and containing a significant proportion of recruits. The evidence from eyewitnesses substantiates that similarly placed regiments had up to one half of their strength sick during the last months of 1794.[89]

In contrast to the infantry, sickness levels in cavalry regiments remained stable throughout 1794 and even declined. All but two of the 15 cavalry regiments serving in Flanders by December 1794 had been there since at least November 1793 and thus were seasoned to field service. Of the other two, the 8th Light Dragoons arrived at the end of April 1794 and one squadron of the 14th Light Dragoons two months later; although sickness rates in the 14th were average for the cavalry, it was no coincidence that those for the 8th were consistently the highest for any mounted unit (21 percent on both 1 July and 1 August, and 19 percent on 1 September). Differing percentages of sick between the infantry and cavalry were also a reflection of their duties, with the former bearing the brunt of outpost work in the bitterly cold winter of 1794–1795, whilst a higher proportion of the latter were in quarters. Higher levels of sickness amongst the Royal Artillery and Royal Military Artificers at the end of 1794 reflected the harassing service which fell to them whilst supporting the infantry at the outposts in highly inclement conditions.

---

87 C.T. Atkinson (ed.), 'Gleanings from the Cathcart MSS', *Journal of the Society for Army Historical Research*, vol.29, 1951, p.147.
88 Marquis of Anglesey (ed.), 'Two brothers in the Netherlands, 1794–1795', *Journal of the Society for Army Historical Research*, vol.34, 1956, p.99; C.M. Duncan-Jones, (ed.), *Trusty and Well Beloved. The Letters Home of William Harness an Officer of George III* (London: SPCK, 1957), p.57; H.C.B. Cook (ed.), 'The St George diary. A Junior Regimental Officer in the Low Countries, 1794–95', *Journal of the Society for Army Historical Research*, vol.47, 1969, p.242 footnote 41 and TNA: WO 1/617: pp.529–561, York to Dundas, 29 July 1795.
89 For example, Brown, *Impartial Journal*, pp.209–215 and James Dickson to Catherine Dickson, 5 November 1794, in Cormack (ed.), *James Dickson*, p.93.

Very few data are available for 1795 and there are no returns for the Duke of York's army as a whole. At the beginning of February, however, total infantry strength was 19,857, of whom 6,015 rank-and-file (some 30 percent) were reported sick. This indicates a reduction when compared to the last available return at the end of December 1794, possibly because men were unable to report sick during the retreat to Bremen or they died; unfortunately, the December 1794 return only enumerates men 'present' and 'sick', thus preventing an analysis of those missing (see Appendix I, Table I.9). The regimental returns for those units analysed in greater detail show the 53rd Regiment had 43 percent sick on 30 April, which reduced to 36 percent by 24 June, and the 33rd Regiment had 42 percent sick on 1 May, which reduced to a more manageable 29 percent also by 24 June. Similar reductions were achieved by the 37th Regiment, which had 39 percent sick in early February and 23 percent on 1 June. These figures clearly show that the legacy of the Flanders campaign remained with the units serving there for many months afterwards.[90]

The rapid increase in sickness rates during 1794 and 1795 placed exceptional strain on the medical establishment. The problem was addressed through the appointment of extra medical staff, so by the end of 1794 (allowing for promotions and returns to England) the establishment in Flanders had increased by two physicians, one deputy purveyor, five staff surgeons, three apothecaries and 47 hospital mates. Of the latter, 21 were appointed in April 1794 as the campaign recommenced after winter quarters, and a further 13 were appointed in October followed by seven in November to cope with the marked incidence of sickness.[91] The number of medical staff at the end of December 1794 numbered approximately 58 hospital mates and nine staff surgeons, to which must be added approximately 86 regimental medical personnel.[92] These men were responsible for 7,965 sick of all ranks (Appendix I, Table I.9) making a staff/patient ratio of 1:55, though this does not include purveyors and apothecaries, or those with no extant records of appointment. Nevertheless, this ratio is dramatically higher than the 1:20 which pertained one year earlier, suggesting the appointment of new medical staff failed to keep up with the growing numbers of sick. It is impossible to be certain of the situation in the first months of 1795, due to the absence of adequate strength returns, but it is highly likely on the basis of available evidence that the staff/patient ratio increased even further.

Some attempt should be made to situate these sickness patterns into the context of earlier eighteenth century wars. Repeated campaigns in Europe uncovered a correlation between sickness and seasonality. Troops generally remained in winter quarters until at least April or May when green forage could be used as animal fodder. Sir John Pringle noted that sickness levels during the campaigns of 1745–1747 were slightly higher when troops took the field in April compared to the following month. The rate of increase in men reporting sick declined after the first two or three weeks of a campaign as they became hardened to

---

90 TNA: WO 1/617: pp.529–561, York to Dundas, 29 July 1795; WO 17/168: 53rd Regiment monthly returns, 1789–1812; WO 17/142: 33rd Regiment monthly returns, 1759–1812; WO 17/147: 37th Regiment monthly returns, 1769–1812 and WO 12/6317: Muster books and pay lists, 53rd Regiment.
91 TNA: WO 7/97–102: Medical Department out–letters and WO 1/896–897: Army Medical Board correspondence with the War Office.
92 This is based on 15 cavalry, 27 infantry and the Royal Artillery/Royal Military Artificers all having two surgeons each.

conditions and the days grew warmer. By mid or late August, however, what Pringle had termed 'the great sickness', or dysentery, commenced, which he ascribed to colder nights and increasing damp, with the prevalence depending on varying summer temperatures. Dysentery persisted until early October, only to be replaced by 'remitting fever' until after the men returned to winter quarters.[93] Monro recorded a very similar trend in 1778 during the great training encampment at Coxheath, near Maidstone in Kent. The highest number of sick prior to October was 656, but this rose to 721 on 1 October and 777 on 1 November. He discovered that:

> After the 26th of October, the troops did not enjoy that particular share of good health they had through the summer, for several, after the heavy rains, were taken with violent colds, and pleuritic and other inflammatory disorders, and pains of the breast, and with fevers, which they carried (as I before observed) with them into quarters.[94]

In the following year at the same location, sickness levels peaked on 1 November and then fell until the encampment broke up three weeks later. Pringle encountered higher levels of sickness when an army kept the field into November, leading him to conclude that it was wiser to launch the campaign season in April and end no later than October.[95]

Despite the often vague descriptions of ailments at this period it is possible to be more specific about the diseases to which soldiers fell victim. Several case studies examined by Padraig Lenihan have indicated that morbidity amongst soldiers on campaign peaked during the late summer and autumn as a result of dysentery and typhoid caused by a lack of sanitation. Once removed to a general hospital, soldiers were subject to overcrowding, thus providing ideal conditions for the spread of 'hospital fever' or typhus. This was one of the principal illnesses experienced by armies on campaign and was caused by insanitary conditions, overcrowding and inadequate diet, all of which encouraged the presence of disease spread by lice.[96] Aside from dysentery, typhoid and typhus, the harsh conditions endured by the soldiers during the winter of 1794–1795 are likely to have induced pneumonia and meningitis in addition to frostbite. Horrific though the effects of these undoubtedly were, they were unfortunately not unusual. Soldiers accommodated in tents on the Hudson River had their hair and bodies frozen to the ground in November 1759 whilst 153 men from the garrison of Quebec suffered frostbite the following month when out on firewood parties.[97] The level of medical knowledge during the late eighteenth century meant that little distinction could be made between these ailments, let alone providing the specific cause and cure for each.

---

93 Lenihan, *Fluxes, Fevers*, pp.14–15 and 17–18; Pringle, *Observations*, pp.118–120 and D. Monro, *Observations on the Means of Preserving the Health of Soldiers; and of Conducting Military Hospitals* (London: J. Murray, 1780), vol.1, pp.171 and 314–316.
94 Monro, *Observations on the Means of Preserving the Health of Soldiers*, vol.1, pp.177 and 201–202.
95 Pringle, *Observations*, p.121.
96 Lenihan, *Fluxes, Fevers*, pp.58–59.
97 S. Brumwell, *Redcoats: The British Soldier and War in the Americas, 1755–1763* (Cambridge: Cambridge University Press, 2002), p.149.

Battle Casualties

Battle casualties were a tiny minority of those needing medical attention. The general hospital at Bruges, for example, housed 500 sick and wounded in September 1793, yet the extant casualty returns show the number of wounded men recorded for the entire year was only 542 all ranks (see Appendix II, Tables II.1 to II.9).[98] The returns for all ranks wounded in battle during 1794 was 763 (see Appendix II, Tables II.10 to II.19), though, as Table 2 has shown, the number of sick was some 10 times higher by the end of December.[99] Things deteriorated in January 1795, when Lieutenant General Harcourt informed the Duke of York that some infantry battalions were reduced to only 150 men fit for duty; the number of wounded listed in casualty returns for that month was 229 (see Appendix II, Tables II.20 to II.23).

The Care of Sick and Wounded Soldiers

Medical personnel with the Duke of York's army faced significant challenges in caring for the sick, whose numbers increased greatly as the campaign progressed. It is now time to investigate how Dr Kennedy and his colleagues tackled the problem.

The first attention a sick or wounded soldier received was from his regimental surgeon or mate. Some units also employed a nurse to work in the regimental hospital, if a building could be procured for one, but it is not known whether these individuals also accompanied units on active service. Regiments rarely possessed the facilities to treat long-term or difficult cases, so these were sent to a general hospital along with any patients for whom there were no beds available in the regimental hospital. Regimental hospitals were staffed only by surgeons, so it is likely that soldiers contracting infections were sent to general hospitals under the care of more qualified physicians. Regimental hospitals of Foot Guards regiments were much better equipped than those of line units, with each being equipped for 40 patients with cots available for one man in every 50, together with paillasses, sheets, pillow cases and ward equipment including close-stools, urinals, bed pans, cooking and feeding utensils. On campaign, however, even the Foot Guards had no transport provided to move this equipment, let alone their sick, which reinforced the tendency for all sick men to be treated in general hospitals. Indeed, a general order dated 23 March 1794 ordered regiments to send all men rendered unfit for duty through sickness to the general hospital at Ghent, and those who fell ill after taking the field to the flying hospital located nearer the army, so that: '… regiments will not be incumbered with them, and not under the necessity of Carrying about Hospital Stores with them'. This order was issued after the benefit of experience during the 1793 campaign, as it was in direct contrast to one issued on 18 May 1793 which instructed regimental surgeons only to send their worst cases to the general hospital.[100] It was also the case that some of the regimental practitioners simply lacked the skill and knowledge necessary to treat their patients to the same standard as their civilian counterparts. Unfortunately,

---

98 Grenville to George III, 15 September 1793, in Aspinall (ed.), *Later Correspondence*, vol.2, pp.93–95.
99 BL: Add Ms 46,710: General return of Kill'd, Wounded, Missing & Prisoners of War of the British Troops under the Command of His Royal Highness the Duke of York from 17th April 1794 to 14th January 1795, Don Papers vol.9. There were 382 other ranks killed, 1,170 wounded, 384 missing and 1,351 prisoners.
100 NAM: 1985-12-15-4: GO, Tournay, 18 May 1793 and 1985-12-15-5: GO, Courtray, 23 March 1794.

the Army Medical Board's work in addressing how regimental appointments were made came too late to have a material bearing on the Flanders campaign.[101]

The lack of transport for the sick during the retreat to Bremen in early 1795 led to a general order stating they should be sent to general hospitals. However, one observer noted that all units on the line of the River Waal in December 1794 kept their sick in regimental hospitals since they had no means of transporting them elsewhere and in any case considered there was little chance of their patients' surviving if they were sent to general hospitals. In retrospect, regimental hospitals were to be preferred, not least for their relatively low cost. Articles were purchased for them only when needed and nursing services could be supplied from unit fatigue parties, whereas the staff at general hospitals had to be hired and additional wages paid.[102]

Prior to the introduction in March 1794 of field, or 'flying', hospitals, general hospitals were the only other type of establishment caring for the sick and wounded. A general hospital was established at Bruges during the 1793 campaign, but the increased numbers of sick in the latter half of the year quickly filled it, and a second hospital was set up at Menen. Both were shifted to Ghent after the French advance, but another hospital at Ostend, where sick men were looked after on their arrival or departure from Flanders, was fortunately able to remain in place.[103] The Ghent hospital was finally closed as the French continued their advance, and was relocated to Antwerp between 5–19 July, before moving once again to Rhenen on the Nederrijn; a second hospital was opened at Gorcum on the Meuse.[104]

In the opening phase of the war in 1793, it had been possible to send far fewer men to general hospitals than in the following year. At that time, the smaller number of patients reduced the risk of overcrowding and onward infection. But now things were much different. Dr Robert Jackson of the 3rd Regiment remarked that mortality in the general hospitals accounted for 60 per cent of the men sent there. These were mainly infantry, as the cavalry had greater means at their disposal to transport the sick and wounded. It is reasonable to assume that many men sent to general hospitals with minor ailments fell victim to the infectious diseases which raged there. Nathaniel Sinnott, who served as a mate at a general hospital (most likely Rhenen or Gorcum) recorded this as one of the greatest causes of mortality. As he witnessed: 'Men in fluxes, fevers, and rheumatism, were placed in the same ward, and all made use of the same vessels indiscriminately. The consequences must be obvious; those who were recovering from one disease caught another'.[105] There were also several other disadvantages with the general, as opposed to regimental, hospitals. Shortages of medical staff meant the use of convalescents for nursing duties, which often resulted in their relapse, meaning that few men ever returned to their units. Whether convalescent or

---

101 Keate, *Observations*, p.18 and Hamilton, *Regimental Surgeon*, vol.1, pp.6 and 22–23.
102 R. Jackson, *An Outline of the History and Cure of Fever, Endemic and Contagious* (London: Longman, Murray & Highley, 1798), p.11; TNA: WO 1/897: pp.83–90, 'Advantages obtained for the British Army in Holland Decem[be]r 1794' [by Dr Jeremiah FitzPatrick]; Anon., *Fifth Report*, p.64 and Keate, *Observations on the Fifth Report*, pp.54–55.
103 TNA: WO 4/291: p.120, 'Home's report', 30 September 1793; WO 7/98: p.139, Hunter to Amherst, 3 July 1793 and Cantlie, *Army Medical Department*, vol.1, pp.214–215.
104 Cantlie, *Army Medical Department*, vol.1, p.219.
105 N. Sinnott, *Observations, Tending to Show the Mismanagement of the Medical Department in the Army* (London: J. Murray and S. Highley, 1796), p.6.

not, many orderlies were soldiers who, in the absence of discipline, took little care of the patients, and routinely stole from them.[106] It may have been because of this that many men were sent to hospital without their necessaries, lest these should fall into the wrong hands, or become a charge on the regiment if they were not returned – as seemed highly likely, such was the prevailing mortality. A general order of 13 November 1794 blamed the men themselves, insisting that from now on all patients must be accompanied to the hospital by an officer or non-commissioned officer to prevent them discarding their necessaries. Any equipment found wanting would be charged by the purveyor to the regiment concerned. This practice hardly helped the recovery of sick soldiers, who were consequently unprepared for the winter when their resistance to infection was already low.[107]

When the number of patients began to increase significantly during September 1794, it was decided to place them on board hospital ships at Gravendeel near Dordrecht, since suitable buildings for general hospitals were not made available by the Dutch. It was recognised at the time that this solution was regrettable, as the Duke of York informed Henry Dundas:

> I have ever been thoroughly sensible of the many objections which there are to employing Transports as Hospital Ships, besides the great expense which the hire of these vessels is to Government. It is therefore from necessity alone that I have been induced to make use of any of them in this way; for, in spite of every remonstrance and entreaty on my part, as well as that of Lord St Helens it has hitherto been totally impossible for us to obtain from the Dutch Government sufficient Buildings to place the sick under cover.[108]

Hospital Mate James Dickson was ordered to Dordrecht with a colleague on 15 September 1794 after being placed in charge of four bilanders containing 300 sick, with orders to place them on board the hospital ships there. On arrival he discovered there were 12 ships in total, each with 60 or 70 patients. He was ordered to the *Hewson*, with a staff consisting of a steward, cook, barber, nurse, six orderly men and two washer-women – a rare insight into the types of support personnel assigned to a hospital ship. By the end of the month, as Dickson told his sister, the number of hospital ships had risen to 15, with not less than 70 patients aboard each one, plus 300 convalescents. Dickson thought his ship one of the most healthy, since only an average of four patients died every week, but: 'In this however I can claim no merit, as for weeks together I have not had a single article of medicine to give them'.[109] Things deteriorated in December when, in defiance of the established customs of war, the French kept up their advance into the United Provinces – where the hospital ships lay frozen in the ice. Dickson was ordered to send all his patients to Helvoetsluys by land, but in the meantime found 150 of them fit to carry arms and mustered them to defend the ships.[110]

---

106 Sinnott, *Observations*, pp.7–8.
107 TNA: AO 16/53/6: GO, Arnhem, 13 November 1794; Anon., *Fifth Report*, Appendix No.23 (A); Jackson, *Fever*, p.26; Atkinson, 'Cathcart MSS', p.148; Brown, *Impartial Journal*, p.207.
108 TNA: WO 1/171: pp.329–330: York to Dundas, 27 November 1794.
109 James Dickson to Catherine Dickson, 28 October in Cormack (ed.), *James Dickson*, p.92.
110 James Dickson to his father, 22 September, to Catherine Dickson, 28 October and to Charles Dickson, 30 December 1794 in Cormack (ed.), *James Dickson*, pp.85–86, 91–92 and 99.

The third category of hospital was the field or 'flying' hospital. These were located at Nijmegen and Arnhem on the River Rhine. A third facility was set up, being the second at Arnhem, at the end of December 1794 to take the sick from regimental hospitals along the line of the River Waal. Given the components for a 'flying' hospital that the Army Medical Board dispatched in March 1794, it is likely that these facilities were tented. They were supplemented by bilanders or barges in which patients were transported through the canal system from one hospital to another.[111]

Discipline

As far as patients were concerned, discipline in regimental hospitals was generally maintained by corporals or sergeants who were themselves patients. Dr Richard Brocklesby noted that regimental hospitals were sometimes located up to five miles away from the unit when in camp, meaning that patients lacked proper supervision, so: 'If no guard is placed there, as soon as ever a soldier is able to crawl out, you will be sure to find him all day long lounging about, if not drunk in some alehouse where he can get gin'.[112] This caused yet another problem affecting general hospitals, meaning that officers and men had to be detached 'on command' from fighting units to supervise patients – the convalescents especially. As troop numbers increased from mid-1794 onwards, things got worse. A general order dated 17 June stated that a captain and subaltern were immediately to attend the hospitals at Ghent and St Ghislain to assist the staff: '… in preserving regularity amongst the patients, particularly amongst the Convalescents'. Countermeasures included repeated calling of the roll, keeping quarters clean and tidy, ensuring regularity in messing arrangements and general conduct, and enforcing instructions from the physicians and surgeons. The officers detailed for this duty were to inspect the premises on arrival and report direct to the adjutant-general, being replaced every four weeks. With hindsight, however: 'The short duration of the Term of the duty precludes a possibility of their acquiring a sufficient knowledge of the management and superintendence of an Hospital'.[113] No mention has been found of measures to impose discipline in either regimental or general hospitals in Flanders prior to 17 June 1794, but the fact these orders had to be issued in the first place suggests they were either partly, or wholly, lacking hitherto. Brocklesby had published a set of regulations for the management of a 'camp hospital' 30 years before, as had Monro for a 'convalescent hospital', so presumably some of the hospital staff knew what was expected of them.[114] Despite this, the fact that troops had to be sent to keep order implies that civilian control of the hospitals was ineffective.

---

111 Jackson, *Fever*, p.26; TNA: WO 1/897: pp.115–118, FitzPatrick to Nepean, 29 December 1794 and BL: Add Ms 46,702: pp.118–119, FitzPatrick to Don, 19 December 1794, Don Papers, vol.1.
112 Brocklesby, *Œconomical and Medical Observations*, p.53.
113 Hamilton, *Regimental Surgeon*, vol.1, pp.94–95; TNA: AO 16/53/3: GO, Tournay, 17 June 1794 and WO 1/171: pp.479–487, Considerations on the necessity of establishing a Corps for the interior Duty of the Hospitals of the British Army.
114 Brocklesby, *Œconomical and Medical Observations*, pp.81–85 and Monro, *An Account of the Diseases*, pp.390–408.

His Royal Highness the Duke of York, by John Hoppner. (Anne S.K. Brown Military Collection)

Sir James Henry Craig, by Thomas Lawrence. (McCord Museum, M999.24.1)

Jeffery Amherst, 1st Baron Amherst, 1784, by Robert Edge Pine. (Yale Center for British Art, Paul Mellon Fund)

Friederich Josias, Prinz von Sachsen Coburg. (Anne S.K. Brown Military Collection)

Marquis Cornwallis landing at Ostend in June 1794. (Anne S.K. Brown Military Collection)

'Watson and the Shark', by John Singleton Copley, see p.102.
(National Gallery of Art, Ferdinand Lammot Belin Fund, Washington DC, 1963.6.1)

John Hunter (1728-1793), surgeon and anatomist. Oil painting after Sir Joshua Reynolds. (Wellcome Library no. 45669i)

William Pitt, Studio of Thomas Gainsborough RA, 1727–1788. (Yale Center for British Art, Paul Mellon Collection, B1981.25.300)

'The Grand Attack on Valenciennes, by the Combined Armies under the command of His Royal Highness the

Duke of York, on the Twenty-Fifth of July 1793', Philip James de Loutherbourg. (Anne S.K. Brown Military Collection)

'Flannel coats of mail against the cold or the British ladies patriotic presents to the Army', by Isaac Cruikshank. (Anne S.K. Brown Military Collection)

'An early lesson of marching', by George Moutard Woodward, and Thomas Rowlandson. (Anne S.K. Brown Military Collection)

British Army baggage wagon and escort, by Thomas Rowlandson. (Anne S.K. Brown Military Collection)

'Recruits', by Henry William Bunbury. (Anne S.K. Brown Military Collection)

The Duke of Richmond portrayed two weeks after the failure at Dunkirk, captioned: 'Thou hast done those things thou ought not to have done and hast left undone those things thou ought to have done'. By Isaac Cruikshank. (Anne S.K. Brown Military Collection)

'Royal British Artillery', unknown artist, 1795. (Anne S.K. Brown Military Collection)

'The Artillery Driver', by Robert Dighton Snr. and Carington Bowles. (Anne S.K. Brown Military Collection)

Abuses

Aside from these purely logistical and administrative considerations, there was a catalogue of abuses in the general hospitals. Foremost was the neglect of patients, much of it the result of sheer ignorance. Men suffering from a variety of ailments were often put in the same bed which, together with a general lack of hygiene, accounted for most infections there.[115] Instances of neglect reached a height in 1795, and Dr Robert Jackson of the 3rd Regiment graphically described one scene he witnessed in the village of Dorum, north of Bremen, in April of that year:

> ... the half of whom [the patients], at least, were covered with rags, incrusted with dirt, and over-run with vermin, emaciated, to the last degree of emaciation, by dysentery, or rather by fever in dysenteric form; the degree of weakness in many was extreme, some were speechless and insensible, others delirious, and two or three maniacal, but advancing as is commonly observed to be the case, in the recovery of health; the misery was great, and the means of relief were inadequate; – such as existed were diligently employed.[116]

One abuse for which the general hospitals were particularly noted concerned the embezzlement of wine and spirits. This was first spotted by Brook Watson, the commissary-general, who communicated his unease to the Treasury. The problem was indeed significant, for alcohol consumption had more than doubled during the six months to November 1794 during which a total of 20 pipes were received from England compared to only 18 for the 12 months to May 1794. It was commonly believed in the army that these supplies were consumed by medical personnel in the general hospitals instead of being given to the patients. The Army Medical Board suggested that in future the physician or surgeon in charge of a hospital should sign for the quantity of wine and spirits issued, and that a purveyor or one of his staff should ensure that they were properly administered to the sick.[117]

Although the abuses outlined above were common and excited extreme indignation in the army, it would certainly not be true to state that all medical staff were equally guilty. Mrs Mary Harcourt saw a convoy of wounded British soldiers passing through Brussels in May 1794 and noted that she was: '... happy to see them so well taken care of; so many surgeons, such excellent carriages, every comfort their situation could admit of'.[118] James Dickson, serving as a hospital mate at the field hospital at 's-Gravenmoer in August 1794 appears from his letters home to have been diligent, spending six hours every day with the patients.

---

115 Anon., *Officer of the Guards*, vol.1, p.116 and vol.2, pp.89–91 and 99–100; J. McGrigor, *The Autobiography and Services of Sir James McGrigor, Bart.* (London: Longman, Green, Longman and Roberts, 1861), p.32; Jackson, *Fever*, p.20 and TNA: WO 40/22: Memorandum relative to the Organisation of the Medical Staff of the Army, 13 November 1805, [by James Borland].
116 Jackson, *Fever*, p.23 and Brown, *Impartial Journal*, pp.225–226.
117 TNA: T 1/736: Windham to Rose, 3 November 1794; T 27/45: p.40, Rose to Secretary at War, 6 November 1794; WO 1/896: pp.263–265, Army Medical Board to Windham, 10 November 1794; T 1/736: Windham to Rose, 12 November 1794, enclosing Army Medical Board to Windham, 10 November 1794; Cantlie, *Army Medical Department*, vol.1, p.222 and Anon., *Officer of the Guards*, vol.2, pp.89–91.
118 E.W. Harcourt (ed.), *The Harcourt Papers*, (Oxford: Privately published, 1880), vol.4, part 2, p.436.

When he was later given medical charge of a hospital ship at Gravendeel he had no difficulty in providing for the sick: '... any article of diet I can name by sending a note to the Purveyor, who is obligded [sic] to provide whatever I order for the use of the ship or my patients, cost what it will and charge it to Government'.[119]

In their defence, it should be stated that the circumstances under which medical staff operated were often very challenging. One of the chief complaints against them was associated with overcrowding, which was not helped by the Dutch refusal to make additional buildings available, so this matter was beyond the control of the medical staff.[120] Operational requirements also had a major bearing on sickness rates and the standard of medical care available. The continuation of the 1794 campaign through the winter undoubtedly resulted in increased numbers of sick, and insufficient means of transporting them during the retreat of 1795 meant that 250 were abandoned to the enemy at Rhenen. We have seen that James Dickson was even forced to use sick men in his charge to defend the hospital ships from an anticipated French attack in January 1795. Their subsequent march to rejoin the army killed many of his patients who became frostbitten or else did not survive being transported in wagons.[121]

Despite these factors, the overwhelming weight of evidence indicates that the general hospitals were ill-managed, the patients neglected and any experience that had been learned in former wars forgotten. As one eyewitness wrote: '... I verily believe no army ever exhibited in its hospitals a more lamentable spectacle of indiscipline and abuse'.[122] By the end of 1794, the situation regarding medical care had deteriorated to such an extent that at least one brigade commander established his own hospital to avoid sending men either to Rhenen or Gorcum. Senior officers of the army were powerless to remedy the situation, since medical matters did not fall within their jurisdiction, but they frequently appealed for action from the authorities at home. As Lieutenant General Harcourt wrote to the Duke of York in December 1794: 'If something is not decided upon, and very speedily too, the sending of the sick to the General Hospital under the present administration of it is doing little better than devolving them to destruction'.[123]

Factors Contributing to Sickness in the Army

Recruits
One of the main causes of sickness was typhus, from which the 88th Regiment suffered greatly when in garrison at Bergen-op-Zoom. James McGrigor, the unit surgeon, noted that

---

119　James Dickson to his father, 23 August and 22 September 1794, in Cormack (ed.), *James Dickson*, pp.73 and 86.
120　TNA: WO 1/171: pp.329–330, York to Dundas, 27 November 1794.
121　Brown, *Impartial Journal*, p.219; TNA: WO 1/171, pp.293–294, York to Dundas, 24 November 1794; WO 1/171: p.636, Harcourt to York, 25 December 1794; WO 1/172: p.166, Harcourt to York, 21 January 1795; James Dickson to Christian Dickson, 28 January 1795, in Cormack (ed.), *James Dickson*, p.101 and Harcourt (ed.), *Harcourt Papers*, vol.4, part 2, p.560.
122　W. Fergusson, *Notes and Recollections of a Professional Life* (London: Longman, 1846), p.57.
123　Atkinson, 'Cathcart MSS', p.148; TNA: WO 1/170: p.177, Craig to Amherst, 12 August 1794; WO 1/171: p.611, Observations of His Royal Highness the Duke of York, 23 December 1794 and WO 1/171: pp.482–484, Harcourt to York, 15 December 1794.

it: '… may be said to have been a prevalent disease in the army, more especially in all the new levies' which suggests that recruits were unable to maintain sufficiently high standards of hygiene and were increasingly prone to sickness. This view was strongly supported by Dr Robert Jackson, surgeon of the 3rd Regiment, who noted that units which had firm discipline or had been well recruited suffered little from sickness. In contrast, those which contained a higher proportion of recruits were very prone to sickness and it was noted by an officer on the Duke of York's staff that the majority of men returned to Britain during the campaign were recruits '… whose constitutions were at that time scarcely formed' whereas the older soldiers had survived. The same occurred to French troops encamped near the Rhine in 1734–1735, when new recruits perished in such numbers that further reinforcements were withheld. We have already seen that infantry units had higher sickness rates than cavalry in 1793–1795, and their greater proportion of raw recruits will be considered in Chapter 5.[124] Putting this to one side, typhus was a chronic problem in the general hospitals due to overcrowding, and as the organism is carried by parasites this is entirely consistent with accounts of hospitals in 1794. The cause of the sickness prevailing in the 80th and 85th Regiments is unknown for certain, but both units had been transported to the United Provinces on board transports containing infected bedding used in the West Indies. A lack of hygiene and overcrowding appear likely, with the most probable cause being typhus.[125]

Clothing Shortages

Aside from the physical shortcomings of many recruits, all soldiers could be prone to sickness as a consequence of missing or defective clothing. The importance of warm clothing to prevent illness was discussed by Drs Richard Brocklesby and Duncan Monro following the Seven Years' War, and had it not been for the efforts of those at home in England in sending more warm clothing to the army, many more soldiers would have fallen sick and died. The gentlemen of Sunderland, for example, sent a total of 382 flannel waistcoats and 894 pairs of stockings to Ostend in November and December 1793.[126] Donated clothing was also issued to the women and children accompanying the army.[127] The clothing situation had not improved at the end of August 1794 when Colonel James Craig was forced to admit: 'I am confident this is the worst provided British Army with respect to Cloathing that ever was in

---

124 TNA: WO 1/172: p.89, Harcourt to York, 9 January 1795; McGrigor, *Sir James McGrigor*, pp.19, 24–25 and 31–32; Jackson, *Fever*, pp.5, 25 and 46; Lenihan, *Fluxes, Fevers*, p.103; Atkinson, 'Cathcart MSS', p.148; Anon., *Officer of the Guards*, vol.2, pp.110–111 and Calvert's diary, 9 April 1793, Calvert to John Calvert, 26 April 1793 and Calvert to Dalrymple, 8 April 1794, in Verney (ed.), *Calvert*, pp.52–53, 67–68 and 187.
125 Atkinson, 'Cathcart MSS', p.147 and Anglesey, 'Two brothers in the Netherlands', p.99. A similar situation resulted in 17 of the 23 journeymen employed by a tradesman in Ghent dying of fever from refitting 'A parcel of old tents…' used as bedding by sick soldiers proceeding to the city from Germany in 1743. Pringle, *Observations*, p.27.
126 Brocklesby, *Œconomical and Medical Observations*, pp.94–95; Monro, *An Account of the diseases*, pp.315–317; BL: Add Ms 40,633: pp.88, 98 and 114, James Graham to the officer commanding British troops, 28 November, 6 and 17 December 1793, Stewart of Afton Papers, vol.1.
127 NAM: 1985-12-15-5: GO, Ghent, 12 and 17 February 1794. Public donation of clothing to soldiers was a recognised form of charitable giving; Sir John Pringle mentioned the distribution of flannel waistcoats donated by the Quakers to the King's troops serving during the 'Forty-Five'. Pringle, *Observations*, p.41.

the Field'.[128] The role of the adjutant-general's department in administering the distribution of clothing and shoes donated from Britain was discussed in Chapter 2, but the problem lasted until the end of the campaign, as Craig informed Evan Nepean on 3 November 1794:

> Our sick increase very fast and we are naked & bare footed – I don't suppose there are ten good pair of shoes in any Company in the Army – I wish to God you would send us – but it must be immediately – 20,000 pair of good shoes. We will pay for them but let us have them over without a moments delay.[129]

Despite supplies sent from home, Colonel Craig saw battalions with between 40 and 50 men marching barefoot.[130]

Tents

An additional factor contributing to sickness was a lack of adequate tentage, forcing many soldiers to lie in the open. The Duke of York wrote to Henry Dundas on 1 August 1794 requesting new tents be sent for all the units lately arrived, apart from the 8th, 12th, 33rd and 44th Regiments, which, it is inferred, must have been better equipped. Two that were not were the 28th and 57th Regiments, neither of which had any tents at all, so all units were ordered on 10 August to send either one round tent or two of the old square pattern for issuing to these units.[131] Craig foresaw the consequences on the soldiers' health, informing Evan Nepean at the War Office: 'Most if not all these Regiments have old rotten tents totally unfit for the latter season of a campaign. From these causes we have a great number of men now laying in the open air and I own I deride the consequences.'[132]

Weather

A major factor influencing sickness rates was the weather. The close of 1793 had not been particularly cold, but was excessively wet, so the troops could rarely dry themselves, their bedding or equipment. The 'Officer of the Guards' noted: 'Such was the wetness of the season, while they were encamped near Camphain, that the soldiers every morning might be seen *lading* the water from their tents by *hat-fulls*; they were but scantily provided with *straw*, and consequently fell rapidly sick.'[133] In contrast, the summer of 1794 was hot, with temperatures as high as 80°F (26.7°C) on 24 April and between 80° and 87°F (30.6°C) during the week of 10–17 July. The troops were unprepared for the extremely cold weather they experienced during the winter of 1794–1795, when temperatures fell to as low as 8°F (-13.3°C) from Christmas Day through most of January.[134] Although the temperature alone

---

128 TNA: WO 1/170: p.285, Craig to Nepean, 31 August 1794.
129 TNA: WO 1/171: p.11, Craig to Nepean, 3 November 1794.
130 TNA: AO 16/53/6: GO, 28 October 1794 and WO 1/171: p.617, Observations of Major Genl. Craig on the subject of clothing, 23 December 1794.
131 TNA: WO 1/170: p.9, York to Dundas, 1 August 1794 and AO 16/53/5: GO, Oosterhoot, 10 August 1794.
132 TNA: WO 1/170: p141, Craig to Nepean, 5 August 1794.
133 Anon., *Officer of the Guards*, vol.1, p.116.
134 Harcourt (ed.), *Harcourt Papers*, vol.4, part 2, pp.399, 405, 427, 481, 571, 577, 581 and 591.

was not sufficient to increase sickness levels significantly, its effects were accentuated by the lack of warm clothing and the fact that many were camped in the open. There is no doubt, however, that freezing weather in January 1795 was responsible for the demise of many individuals exhausted by their exertions during the retreat.[135]

Remedies

Everard Home

Sir John Hunter sent his brother-in-law, Everard Home, on a tour of inspection of the hospital department in September 1793. His instructions were to confer with the Duke of York and Dr Kennedy regarding the surgical department and to make whatever arrangements as he (Home) thought necessary.

Home was born in 1756 and had studied at St George's Hospital as a pupil of John Hunter. He was appointed assistant surgeon at the naval hospital at Plymouth in 1778 before serving in Jamaica as a staff surgeon with the Army between 1779–1784. He continued his career at St George's after his return, being appointed assistant surgeon in 1787 and a lecturer in anatomy in 1792.[136]

After landing in Flanders, Home went directly to the Duke of York's headquarters at Torhout, where he arrived on 14 September, shortly after the retreat from Dunkirk, and explained the purpose of his mission. He then visited Dr Hugh Kennedy at the general hospital at Bruges and was soon told that only he had the authority to superintend matters relating to the provision of health care, which Home reported, 'shewed me that my stay on the Continent could not materially promote the service'.[137] Nevertheless, Home visited the different hospitals to observe the treatment of the surgical cases, following which he prepared a set of regulations that were approved by Kennedy before they were passed to one of the staff surgeons, Andrew Grieves.

Home stated in his report: 'I have the pleasure to say that the Hosp'ls are in as good a state as it is possible to expect, when all the disadvantages under which they were formed are considered' but noted that the recent rapid movements of the army (following the retreat from Dunkirk) resulted in a large number of sick.[138] These men had been sent to the hospitals without any prior warning, meaning that insufficient accommodation had been prepared to receive them. Kennedy therefore established a general hospital at Menen, which was managed by regimental surgeons, in order to prevent any additional influx of patients to the main hospital at Bruges.

One of the issues identified by Home was the distance that sick and wounded men were forced to travel before they reached a hospital and: 'That a report hav'g been very generally circulated, that the wounded men in the diff't Engagem'ts have not been properly taken

---

135 TNA: WO 1/171: p.281, Craig to Nepean, 24 November 1794 and Anon., *Officer of the Guards*, vol.2, pp.99–101.
136 N. Coley, 'Home, Sir Everard, first baronet (1756–1832), surgeon', ODNB, <https://doi.org/10.1093/ref:odnb/13639>, accessed 21 June 2020.
137 TNA: WO 4/291: p.122, 'The report of Sir [Everard] Home'.
138 TNA: WO 4/291: p.125, 'The report of Sir [Everard] Home'.

care of'. He therefore recommended the establishment of a 'flying' hospital staffed by two surgeons, a deputy purveyor, a clerk and two wagons loaded with stores in order to take care of wounded men (though later in his report he suggested that six covered wagons were the minimum necessary, implying three separate units of two wagons with associated personnel). These stores were to include bedding, cooking utensils, various food items (including sago, portable soup, sugar and barley) and medical equipment such as bandages, lint, thread, pins, tape and old linen for bandages. Home also suggested that a general hospital should be established at Ostend for men unable to take the field after disembarkation in Flanders in order to prevent them being transported to Bruges or wherever the general hospital happened to be located.[139]

Home remained in Flanders for approximately two weeks and returned home by 30 September, completing his report four days later. This was only 12 days before the death of Sir John Hunter but, despite this, his recommendations were acted upon, with the equipment for the 'flying' hospital being sent out in March 1794 and the hospital at Ostend established in November 1793.

Improvements at the Start of the 1794 Campaign

Aside from a 'flying' hospital, a further improvement in response to experiences gained in 1793 were 50 spring wagons for the use of sick and wounded men. These had been requested by the Commissariat Department in consultation with the Treasury, and attracted attention at the highest levels as Brook Watson was informed on 21 February 1794:

> The Construction of the Waggons for the Sick, and wounded Soldiers has been particularly attended to by His Royal Highness the Commander in Chief as well as by General Fox, and Col. Craig, and fifty are provided with the utmost Expedition on the plan approved of, which will be shipped for Ostend as soon as possible.[140]

The Treasury intended to send these wagons in batches of 10, together with a workman tasked with setting them up on arrival, with the first consignment being shipped from Blackwall on 14 March. The provision of the wagons was very well received by the troops, as noted by the 'Officer of the Guards':

> There were many valuable improvements made upon the last Campaign; the first and most essential was, the Spring Waggon, for the conveyance of the sick and wounded. How many poor wretches in 1793, were dragged for miles in miserable Flemish carts, constructed upon the most awkward principles; in one of which, a man, even in high health, would feel every joint nearly dislocated, as he was jolted over the paved roads. What must have been the sufferings of our fellow creatures, smarting under the most excruciating torments of gun-shot wounds![141]

---

139 TNA: WO 4/291: pp.129–33, 'The report of Sir [Everard] Home'.
140 TNA: WO 58/167: pp.74–77, Rose to Watson, 21 February 1794.
141 Anon., *Officer of the Guards*, vol.2, pp.14–15.

Jeremiah FitzPatrick

Although the War Office had received several complaints about the medical arrangements and personnel serving with the Duke of York's army during the first half of 1794, they felt no sense of urgency to investigate the problem. After all, Sir Everard Home had reported back favourably from his tour of inspection in September 1793. It was only in August 1794, when John Gunning was asked by the Duke of York to look specifically into the matter, that any real notice was taken. The immediate response was to appoint Dr Jeremiah FitzPatrick to the newly created post of 'Inspector of Health for the Land Forces' reporting to the War Office. FitzPatrick's duties were principally confined to the troops at home, such as advising on the erection of new barracks and hospitals, or the inspection of existing facilities. He was particularly requested to investigate transport vessels and the wellbeing of the troops both before and after embarkation, a favourite subject of his and one on which he had campaigned for some time. His other duties were to inspect the medical facilities with the army in Flanders, including such matters as the troops' accommodation and casualty evacuation.[142]

FitzPatrick's background is obscure, but it is thought he was born in about 1740 to well-off Catholic parents in County Westmeath. He received his medical training overseas, possibly in Paris, becoming involved in prison reform from the late 1770s, for which he was knighted in 1782. He became concerned with military medicine in 1790, having witnessed conditions on board transports taking soldiers from Cork to Plymouth, and his forthright opinions, together with his energy and no-nonsense approach, led to his War Office appointment in 1794.[143]

Given the number of sick in Flanders, and the reports received from the army, FitzPatrick prioritised a visit to the Duke of York's headquarters during the first half of December. What he discovered shocked him, as he reported back to the War Office, 'Such Misery and wretchedness as I found can scarcely be described; an apparent want of every thing, and a real want of many necessary articles'.[144] The three hospitals he inspected at Arnhem on 19 December (the field hospital, Gast House church and Verka church) were all inadequate in one way or another, mainly through a lack of ventilation or fuel for the stoves, which meant that everything was permanently damp. The worst was the Verka church which was 'uncommonly filthy',[145] and housed men with no proper covering for warmth. Perhaps the worst hospital he visited was for the Hanoverian troops located at Leiden. The patients had no more than one blanket each and were often lying on mattresses covered in excrement. The food was wholly inadequate and but for the help of a local Dutch doctor the fate of the patients would have been even worse. Reverting to his primary task of inspecting transport ships, FitzPatrick visited a convoy of 12 vessels at Helvoetsluys which were bound for

---

142 TNA: WO 1/897: pp.1–6, Nepean to FitzPatrick, 8 September 1794; R.L. Blanco, 'The Soldier's Friend – Sir Jeremiah Fitzpatrick, Inspector of Health for Land Forces' in *Medical History*, vol.20, 1976, pp.402–421 and O. MacDonagh, *The Inspector General. Sir Jeremiah Fitzpatrick and the Politics of Social Reform, 1783–1802* (London: Croom Helm, 1981), pp.171–177.
143 J. Kelly, 'Fitzpatrick, Sir Jeremiah (c. 1740–1810), physician and campaigner for prison reform', ODNB, <https://doi.org/10.1093/ref:odnb/61603>, accessed 21 June 2020.
144 TNA: WO 1/897: pp.107–110, FitzPatrick to Nepean, 25 December 1794.
145 BL: Add Ms 46,702: pp.118–119, FitzPatrick to Don, 19 December 1794, Don Papers, vol.1.

England with 1,200 sick on board. The conditions which he found rivalled anything on land: '… that in so inconsiderate, and I may say in so cruel a mode, poor wretches were never sent on Board; In Ships ill suited and filthy'.[146] FitzPatrick found the same methods of treatment pertained in all the hospitals he visited, regardless of the ailment, and the medical staff only visited the patients at set times and never during the night, even if some were close to death. If a soldier became convalescent, the allowance for his diet was reduced from 16d per day when sick to only 4d, which caused a relapse in many.[147]

Having inspected the hospitals, FitzPatrick busied himself in attempting to improve the common soldier's living conditions by focusing his attention on a wide variety of issues including improving their huts, beds, kitchens and diet.[148] The improvements initiated by FitzPatrick at the end of 1794 were undoubtedly of great value, but did nothing to remedy the underlying causes of the failed medical system in Flanders.

An Assessment of the Medical Department in Flanders

The primary cause of the problem lay in the administration of the Army Medical Board itself. The deaths of Adair in 1790, his successor Hunter in 1793 and Wintringham in 1794 meant the reconstituted Army Medical Board comprised men who had little opportunity to become accustomed to their roles at a time when the country was already at war. The lack of comprehensive instructions from the War Office regarding the division of responsibility amongst the Board's members, and their collective relationship with Dr Kennedy in Flanders, meant much time and energy was wasted in matters such as patronage, which had little directly to do with the care of the sick and wounded. At the same time, the Board was faced with finding medical personnel for expeditions to Toulon, Corsica, Portugal and the West Indies, as well as making arrangements for the reception of large numbers of sick soldiers from the Duke of York's army.[149]

The inexperience of the individuals comprising the Board was responsible for alienating many of the medical men serving in Flanders. Their decision to appoint physicians from civilian life meant that men placed in charge of the hospitals had little experience of military medicine, battle injuries and ailments commonly affecting soldiers. This chapter has shown that approximately 83 percent of the hospital staff (excluding physicians) already had previous military medical experience while 59 percent of the mates, for whom service records survive, had experience as a regimental mate. This criticism can therefore apply only to the physicians directing the hospitals.[150]

---

146 TNA: WO 1/897: pp.91–94, FitzPatrick to Nepean, 10 December 1794.
147 TNA: WO 1/897: pp.111–113, FitzPatrick to Major Lowe, 21 December 1794 and WO 1/897: pp.83–90, Advantages obtained for the British Army in Holland Decem[be]r 1794.
148 TNA: WO 1/897, pp.83–90, Advantages obtained for the British Army in Holland Decem[be]r 1794 and BL: Add Ms 46,702: pp.156–157, FitzPatrick to Don, 24 December 1794, Don Papers, vol.1.
149 Keate, *Observations on the Fifth Report*, pp.4–5; Chaplin, *Medicine in England*, p.78 and TNA: WO 7/100: pp.21–22, Keate to Kennedy, 17 December 1793.
150 C. Kelly, *War and the Militarization of British Army Medicine, 1793–1830* (London: Routledge, 2011), p.13; Keate, *Observations on the Fifth Report*, pp.13–15 and 17; Anon., *Fifth Report*, p.22, Appendix No.23 (A) and Appendix No.30; TNA: WO 1/172: pp.245–252, Harcourt to York, 11 February 1795;

Whether or not regimental staff were justified in their grievances over blocked promotions, the perception that they had been deserted by those in London to whom they had formerly looked for support did nothing for their morale. A linked complaint developed in 1794, when the widespread practice of sending sick men to general hospitals became prevalent. It appeared to many regimental medical personnel that they were now no longer permitted to care for the sick of their own units, in addition to having their traditional promotion routes blocked by those whom they considered less competent. The result was recorded a decade later by James Borland, who served as surgeon's mate to the 42nd Regiment and subsequently as a hospital mate in Flanders:

> In this ill humour many Regimental Surgeons feeling themselves deserted were led to desert their sick and wounded, who were sent without ceremony promiscuously to the different General Hospitals; where they came under the care of Medical Officers who had never before seen a Military Hospital or a sick Soldier, who confined their exertions to the formal prescriptions of Medicines and diet, and who trusted the application and approbation to Hospital Mates and Stewards and Ward Masters and Nurses and orderlies equally ignorant and inexperienced in the discipline of a Military Hospital with themselves.[151]

Although many and loud were the complaints regarding orders to send the sick to general hospitals in 1794, there were in fact sound reasons for doing so. Dr Robert Jackson, surgeon to the 3rd Regiment, highlighted the cause when he described landing with his unit at Bergen-op-Zoom at the end of July 1794 and almost immediately participating in the army's retreat to successive defence lines along the Rivers Meuse, Waal and Lek. Conditions in the regimental hospitals were often grim, and Jackson described his facility as being an open barn where it was not permitted to light fires despite the intense cold, with the men poorly clothed and lacking blankets. Only when units remained in static positions could large numbers of sick be cared for regimentally. The 3rd Regiment were encamped with other units in a ploughed field at Lent on the right bank of the River Waal in November and December 1794 when a total of 150 men became sick with fever, but only one man died.[152] No unit had sufficient transport for the sick or wounded in a war of movement and, had they done so, the consequent congestion on the road system would have made military operations problematic. It therefore made sense to separate fighting units from hospital patients and administer them centrally, though from a purely medical standpoint this aggravated all the causes from which they had died: overcrowding, lack of proper sanitation and cleanliness, and the consequent transmission of disease from patient to patient.

Plenty of standard texts on military medicine were available to those who chose to study them. Sir John Pringle, for example, had produced a medical history of the campaigns of 1742–1748 which ran to three editions by 1761. He had drawn attention to many of the issues

---

Sinnott, *Observations*, pp.12–15; Kaufman, *Surgeons at War*, pp.29–30 and Peterkin & Johnston, *Commissioned Officers*, vol.1, p.65.
151 TNA: WO 40/22: Memorandum relative to the organisation of the Medical Staff of the Army, 13 November 1805, [by James Borland].
152 Jackson, *Fever*, pp.11–14.

that affected the welfare of soldiers half a century later, such as overcrowding and infection in hospitals, the consequences of an inadequate diet and the lack of hygiene. These factors were repeated by Dr Richard Brocklesby following the Seven Years' War.[153] Ignorance of past practice amongst medical practitioners and regimental officers must therefore be ascribed as a contributory factor. Despite this, morbidity was little different to the levels experienced in campaigns earlier in the century, when the incidence of dysentery peaked at between 20–30 percent of the troops engaged. This could rise as high as 50 percent in the case of the three battalions of Foot Guards encamped at Warburg in 1760.[154]

The effectiveness of the medical department was severely compromised by friction between senior personnel in Flanders. The specific cause is unknown, though it is highly likely that differences in the respective status of physicians and surgeons, resulting from the academic entry route of the former and the professional career paths pursued by the purveyors, staff surgeons and apothecaries was a major source of conflict; this may have encouraged personal friction and animosity.[155] Indiscipline in military hospitals was also not new to the Flanders campaign. Dr Richard Brocklesby, who was appointed Physician General to the Ordnance in March 1794, had written 30 years earlier: 'It is well known, that numbers of brave men are annually lost in the hospitals, for want of order and proper subordination among the Physical Officers'.[156] The friction was bad enough for the Duke of York to order a board of enquiry under Lieutenant General Harcourt to examine the army's hospital management. At the same time, the Duke had been all too well aware of '… the shameful acrimony and hatred of some of the Gentlemen in the Medical department against Dr Kennedy', also leading him gratefully to accept the Secretary at War's offer to send the Surgeon General, John Gunning on a tour of inspection. It is clear that Dr Kennedy and his senior colleagues lacked the ability or the energy to administer the medical department effectively, thus compromising the care offered to patients. All of this occurred despite the instructions issued by the War Office in 1793, which outlined the duties and responsibilities of each member of the medical staff, and the well documented precedents from former campaigns.[157] Ultimately, it was left to senior army officers in Flanders to resolve the problem, but their intervention came only in December 1794 when the situation had already become too difficult. Their plan was to recruit qualified ward-masters and orderly men, upon whom much of the immediate nursing tasks would fall, thus allowing convalescents, who had been performing these duties despite having no medical experience, to rejoin their units. Although this fully costed plan was laudable in its intentions, the fact that it had first to be approved by the Duke of York and the authorities in England meant that it was impossible to implement before the close of the campaign.[158]

---

153 Pringle, *Observations*, pp.95–117 and Brocklesby, *Œconomical and medical observations*, pp.58–59.
154 Lenihan, *Fluxes, Fevers*, pp.172–173.
155 L.S. King, *The Medical World of the Eighteenth Century* (New York: Krieger, 1958), pp.1–29 and Kopperman, 'Medical services', p.433.
156 Brocklesby, *Œconomical and Medical Observations*, p.27.
157 TNA: WO 1/172: pp.245–252, Harcourt to York, 11 February 1795; WO 4/291: pp.55–59, 'Instructions for the conduct of the Medical Staff'; BL: IOR H/84: pp.551–559, 'Observations on the Hospital by R. Adair' and BL: Add Ms 37,842: p.69, York to Windham, 23 August 1794, Windham Papers, vol.1. Harcourt's report was sent to Windham with this letter, but it is no longer with it.
158 TNA: WO 1/171: pp.479–487, Considerations on the necessity of establishing a Corps for the interior Duty of the Hospitals of the British Army and Harcourt (ed.), *Harcourt Papers*, vol.4, part 2, pp.573–574.

The calculated negligence of Dr Kennedy in failing to inform the Army Medical Board of the state of affairs in Flanders was undoubtedly another factor that compromised the medical department's effectiveness. This was almost certainly caused by sensitivity over patronage, and his perception that any information he provided might be used to his disadvantage. Although medical personnel in Flanders were responsible to the Duke of York as Commander-in-Chief, he was professionally unqualified to oversee a specialised department and the time of greatest mismanagement coincided with pressing operational difficulties which required his more immediate attention. The problem was referred to the War Office on a number of occasions during the second half of 1794, but the speed with which medical affairs deteriorated prevented any quick remedy.

The fundamental problem, however, was that Britain lacked an established military medical service at the beginning of the French Wars, and the effects of improvisation during active operations became all too painfully obvious. This chapter has shown that the situation in Flanders was little different from previous eighteenth century campaigns, especially at the beginning of the conflict. Reforms in the regimental medical establishment of the Army would gather pace from 1796, when surgeons received increased pay, their assistants were granted commissioned status and the procurement of medicines was made the responsibility of the Apothecary General. The Army Medical Board was itself disbanded by Royal Warrant in March 1798, one month after the death of John Gunning, with each of the members being made individually, rather than jointly, answerable for their respective areas of responsibility. Further reforms in the management of the Army's medical services were made thereafter, but these failed to eliminate further mismanagement, such as the treatment of sick or wounded men evacuated from La Coruña in 1808 or Walcheren in 1809.[159]

Yet for now we are left with a nasty feeling that in 1793 mediocre performance had somehow been expected, and was to a degree tolerated, despite the efforts and genuine concern of many of those closely involved – right up to the Duke of York himself. The term 'expendable' had yet to be applied to soldiers in war, but in the medical context of 1793–1795 it is hard to avoid. We shall hear more of it in Chapter 5.

---

159 The Battle of Corunna took place on 16 January 1809. The British rearguard embarked on the 18th. Troops began arriving home four days later. The sick-list was already shockingly high. British troops withdrew from Walcheren on 9 December 1809. During the campaign 4,000 of them had died, only 106 in combat. Nearly 12,000 veterans of the campaign were still reported sick in February 1810, and the 'Walcheren Fever' was transmitted to Wellington's army in the Peninsula.

5

The Regiments

The actual business of fighting the enemy was the role of the cavalry and infantry regiments of the British Army, which are the subject of this chapter. The Royal Artillery, Royal Engineers and Royal Military Artificers were controlled by the Board of Ordnance and had a separate organisational structure, which is the subject of Chapter 6.

The British Army fought a series of major wars during the eighteenth century, all of which involved a rapid expansion in manpower that was to be equally quickly demobilised following the peace. A total of 33,000 men were discharged from the Army in 1712–1713, immediately following the end of hostilities. As a result, the Army establishment had to rise from 18,000 men in 1739 to 62,000 in 1742 at the start of the War of the Austrian Succession, only for the British establishment to be cut to 30,000 men in 1748 before rising again to 85,000 in 1759.[1] Such sudden and drastic changes with the onset of peace were bound to have a telling effect. Soldiers reverted to their mundane duties of keeping public order (there was no functioning civil police force), sending out anti-smuggling patrols and (in Ireland) raiding illegal distilleries. None of these roles was conducive to military effectiveness in a combat situation. Worse, they often resulted in the wide dispersal of units in outposts either at home or overseas, much reduced in numbers as they already were. Many officers departed on long periods of leave, taking it in turns to stay with their scattered companies, or at a distant regimental headquarters. Subalterns were often left in day-to-day command of the men. Unit training suffered. Overall military effectiveness declined. Then, at the outbreak of war, there was a paroxysm of activity as the process went into reverse. New officer appointments were made, these unduly influenced, it was often said, by favouritism and the practice of buying and selling commissions. The ranks were bolstered with new recruits needing basic training, for this was a volunteer army lacking a cadre of trained reserves. Experienced non-commissioned officers and picked men were drafted from other units to help out. Expeditionary forces needed in a hurry were assembled by drafting men from other units, even as these too attempted to make themselves 'Fit for Service'. Unless the officers of the drafted units could find a crafty way around it, the best and fittest men were those most often taken. Such was the British way of making war.

---

1   Fortescue, *History of the British Army*, vol.2, pp.3, 82–83, 267 and 364 and Barnett, *Britain and Her Army*, pp.165 and 190.

The aim of this chapter is to examine the state and condition of the regiments that served in Flanders in order to assess their preparedness for war together with their performance during the conflict. This also involves a discussion of military administration in the nine years following the disappointing conclusion of the American War. There is also a new appreciation of the role of women in the day-to-day life of a regiment. They are a shadowy presence in the records, but large numbers accompanied the army on campaign and provided the regiments with a variety of support services hard to find elsewhere. Their presence impacted on the field army through transport, accommodation, child-care, subsistence, discipline and relations with the civil population.

The Army's Experience During the Years of Peace, 1783–1793

The Restructuring of 1783

The American War lasted for over seven years, and by the time preliminary articles of peace were signed in January 1783 the British Army consisted of 35 regiments of cavalry, three regiments comprising seven battalions of Foot Guards, and 113 battalions of regular infantry. The great majority of these units were held on the British establishment, at a cost declared to Parliament of over £2,000,000 per annum. Retrenchment was inevitable and necessary – but how could it be done? The initial plan developed by the Commander-in-Chief, General Henry Seymour Conway, and agreed by the Earl of Shelburne's cabinet, was to retain 30 regiments of cavalry, three regiments of Foot Guards and 67 battalions of regular infantry. The 28,000 men on the British establishment would have an estimated cost of £830,000 per annum, with an additional body of troops (15,000 strong) based in Ireland and financed from Irish revenues; the Irish Establishment.[2]

This plan did not long survive the fall of the Shelburne ministry and no sooner had the Fox-North coalition government come to power in April 1783 than Conway was instructed to cut the estimates for the British Establishment to a mere £700,000. The distribution of the Army for the defence of the home islands and the empire concerns us less here, but the key issue of internal unit composition does since, in order to make such savings, Conway argued that regiments would be so much reduced as to make future augmentations at the beginning of a conflict extremely difficult. These cuts fell primarily on the cavalry and infantry of the line, since the Foot Guards' functions of protecting the sovereign and maintaining public order in the capital meant they could not be reduced in numbers much beyond their present establishments. Instead, each battalion of line infantry, which Conway had originally envisaged as numbering 507 all ranks, was now further reduced to 471 all ranks in eight companies compared to a wartime establishment of about 700 men. Curiously, although the number of rank-and-file was reduced, the officers belonging to the two companies per battalion disbanded in June 1783 were not, leading to stagnated promotion prospects until this matter was addressed in 1787.

By the time the coalition government fell in December 1783, the Army had undergone a massive reduction in the number of units and in their internal structure. Recruiting

---

2   Pimlott, *Administration of the British Army*, pp.6–8.

difficulties meant that many regiments were under strength, since most of the men enlisted for three years' service during the American War departed. Morale tottered.[3]

The Administration of the Army, 1783–1793

During the nine years between the resignation of General Conway at the end of 1783 and the appointment of General Lord Amherst in January 1793 strategic decisions regarding the Army were primarily taken by William Pitt, the Prime Minister. Divisions in Cabinet made collective discussion difficult, a situation that was only improved from June 1789 when Pitt's ally, William, Lord Grenville, was transferred from Paymaster of the Forces to become Home Secretary.[4] Grenville subsequently became Foreign Secretary in June 1791 and was replaced by Henry Dundas at the Home Office. Dundas was a key ally of Pitt, having originally urged his appointment as Prime Minister.[5] The importance of the Home Secretary in military matters was considerable, because since the department's reorganisation in 1782 he controlled both the internal affairs of Britain and Ireland and those of the colonies. These included, for example, arrangements for troops at home and overseas, often involving the requisition of resources from the Admiralty and Board of Ordnance, and extensive correspondence with military authorities. The Foreign Secretary also had a potentially strong interest in military affairs overseas, the colonies excepted.[6]

It was primarily Pitt, his close political ally Dundas and Lord Grenville who decided on the strategic role of the British Army, in peacetime as much as in war. Their recommendations were forwarded to the King for his approval, which was usually given. What the politicians could not do, however, was to advise on military details such as drill, tactics, clothing, and the official tariff for officers' commissions. Though the King often decided on officer promotions in person, he might also consult the Board of General Officers. The Lord Lieutenant of Ireland had much to say concerning units stationed there, and the War Office, headed by the Secretary-at-War, who could access the monarch directly if needed, presided over many points of detail, including public order issues, officer absenteeism, recruitment and desertion.[7]

As noted earlier, officer absenteeism was a nagging peacetime concern. The reduction in troop numbers seemingly gave them less work to do and many had been overseas for long periods during the American War, so when the chance came they took leave. There was little incentive to do anything about this in peacetime but, as might be expected, problems bubbled to the surface.[8] Private James Aytoun, serving with the 58th Regiment at Drogheda in 1786, noted all eight captains of companies were continually absent on leave. The regiment was reviewed in June, shortly after the arrival of a new commanding officer, and:

---

3 Pimlott, *Administration of the British Army*, pp.9–16.
4 J. Ehrman, *The Younger Pitt. The Years of Acclaim* (London: Constable, 1969), pp.183–186.
5 C. Matheson, *The Life of Henry Dundas First Viscount Melville 1742–1811* (London: Constable, 1933), pp.93–94.
6 Pimlott. *Administration of the British Army*, pp.46 and 52.
7 Pimlott, *Administration of the British Army*, pp.41–46.
8 Pimlott, *Administration of the British Army*, pp.211–216.

... had the men known as little of their exercises as Major Horsfall, the regiment would have been drilled by the general's orders. But the soldiers led the officers, who depended implicitly on the right or left hand man of the company for direction and manoeuvres were so much in rotation that the men in the ranks knew, when one manoeuvre took place, what was the next.[9]

When war broke out again in 1793, the problem of officer absence had still not been resolved.

The besetting crime of desertion among the rank-and-file also remained, caused principally by the soldier's poverty, as the purchase of necessaries, routine stoppages and inflation left him badly short of cash.[10] Since unemployment, or under-employment, lay at the root of many enlistments, there was little incentive to remain in the ranks if the economic situation improved. Methods of tackling desertion included arrest and court martial, stoppages of pay, physical punishment, overseas postings, or service in a penal battalion.[11] But this piecemeal approach, often differing between regiments, did not penetrate the heart of the matter.

It may rightly be inferred from the above that recruiting was also a severe challenge. Low pay, better opportunities in the civilian work-place, the modest size of the Army and its reputation as a career of last resort all served as deterrents.[12] The administrative structures in place for recruiting men in Ireland had been suspended as part of the post-1783 cuts, and it was not until 1790 that opposition from the Lord Lieutenant was overcome and the country was again opened to regiments based elsewhere. Most recruits came from Britain, but the lack of central control meant the process was largely left up to regiments themselves, especially in the case of units stationed overseas, since the War Office possessed no means of knowing which were operating recruiting parties at home. This was eventually remedied at the end of 1789 when Colonel Henry Fox, subsequently the Duke of York's quartermaster-general in Flanders, was appointed to superintend all recruiting parties sent from regiments serving abroad. A second inspector-general fulfilled the same function for parties sent out by regiments stationed in Britain, and to these senior officers were added subalterns and non-commissioned officers to train the recruits as they arrived at the Chatham Depot.[13]

Peacetime Training and Service

The analysis of unit movements during the eighteenth century undertaken by John Houlding has shown that approximately one third of the infantry was serving overseas in the period

---

9   J. Aytoun, *Redcoats in the Caribbean* (Blackburn: Blackburn Recreation Services, 1984), p.4.
10 Necessaries comprised a large number of items included clothing (forage cap, shirts, stockings, gaiters, shoes), the means to clean it (brushes, pipe clay, blacking), required personal items (powder, pomatum, soap, razors) and services (washing, tailoring). Stoppages were made for the surgeon (medicines), paymaster (loss of exchange) and off-reckonings (Chelsea Hospital, Exchequer fees, Paymaster General, regimental agent). G.A. Steppler, *The Common Soldier in the Reign of George III, 1760–1793* (Unpublished PhD thesis. University of Oxford, 1984), pp.42–45.
11 Captain Joseph Wall's independent company stationed in West Africa was used as a penal unit until being withdrawn in 1783–1784. After that, persistent deserters were either executed or sentenced to serve overseas for life. The Irish establishment sent them to the 3/ or 4/60th Regiment stationed permanently in the West Indies. Pimlott, *Administration of the British Army*, pp.225–229.
12 Pimlott, *Administration of the British Army*, pp.223–227.
13 Pimlott, *Administration of the British Army*, pp.238–257.

1783–1793. A key consequence was that units so deployed often suffered major difficulties with recruitment, since suitable men were unavailable in places such as Gibraltar, Canada, India or the West Indies. Recruitment at home was expensive and slow to deliver results, which induced many commanding officers to retain men with the colours who should have been given their discharge on account of age or infirmity. Aside from recruitment problems when stationed overseas, units were often widely dispersed meaning that few opportunities existed to bring men together for training purposes. Furthermore, the climate in many overseas stations ranged from the debilitating heat of the West Indies to the freezing latitudes of Canada and was not conducive to maintaining the men's health.[14] The issue of units spending many years in overseas garrisons was alleviated to some extent through an increasingly systematised annual rotation. This had originally been introduced in 1764 but went into abeyance on the outbreak of the American War; it was resurrected in 1787, covering Britain, Ireland and Gibraltar, the West Indies and Canada to a lesser extent, and India not at all. Despite this, the practice of drafting men between units about to go on service or proceed overseas, or from units about to proceed home to those remaining, also resulted in a certain proportion of regiments remaining chronically under strength.[15]

The adverse effects of overseas postings mostly affected the infantry. Cavalry regiments almost always remained either in Britain or Ireland, yet they, together with the infantry also stationed there, encountered many of the same ill effects already noted for units based overseas. Perhaps the foremost of these was dispersal, which made training difficult and acted against unit cohesion. The principal cause of this, in Britain at least, was inadequate barrack accommodation, which was expensive to construct and maintain but was also a time-honoured, though increasingly out-moded, expression of hostility to standing armies. Other than in hot-spots like the Scottish Highlands, or Ireland in general, it was thought that soldiers, however humble or degraded they might be in the popular imagination, were also citizens, and should not be isolated from their fellow countrymen. The consequence was that men were accommodated when in quarters or on the march in a variety of livery stables, houses of public entertainment, victualling and ale houses. The construction of barracks in Ireland was less of a political issue, and indeed was actively encouraged, by which means many of the larger towns were adequately provided by the 1740s. By 1792 there was provision for the accommodation of some 20,000 men, including ordnance troops and invalids, in all the forts and barracks in Britain and the Channel Islands, but it was only from the following year that a systematic attempt was made to construct a permanent barrack network.[16]

A second reason for dispersal was the nature of the Army's role in peacetime. The limited number of regiments available had to counter civil unrest, aid to the civil power and

---

14 Houlding, *Fit for Service*, pp.13, 15–16.
15 TNA: WO 379/1: 'Disposition of His Majesty's Land Forces, 1737–91'; TNA: WO 379/2: 'A Table of the Reliefs of the Several Regiments of Infantry from the Year 1763, shewing at what time each Regiment entered upon its present Station, from what Station it was moved, and by what Regiment Relieved'; Houlding, *Fit for Service*, pp.14 and 22 and J. Shy, *Toward Lexington. The Role of the British Army in the Coming of the American Revolution* (Princeton: Princeton University Press, 1965), pp.274–277.
16 Houlding, *Fit for Service*, pp.38–41 and Rogers, *British Army*, pp.38–39.

smuggling activities, quite apart from any function associated with actual defence. These roles existed both in Ireland and Britain, so that despite the provision of public accommodation in the former to include a considerable network of small posts for detachments performing exactly the same duties as their colleagues housed in billets in Britain, the adverse effects of dispersal from the perspective of unit training and cohesion remained the same.[17]

Many soldiers were employed either officially on Government works projects, in specialist regimental duties or unofficially to supplement their pay. For example, the construction or repair of fortifications, roads or canals, the haulage of provisions or fuel, and guarding military installations. Those with skilled trades prior to enlistment could be employed as craftsmen and individual soldiers received work regimentally as tailors, cobblers, barbers, or to look after the arms of absent colleagues; others were officers' servants or in charge of the unit's bât horses. Additionally, men stationed in many locations were often permitted, and sometimes even encouraged, to seek outside employment, since this fostered integration with the local community and thus helped to mitigate the perceived danger of separating the Army from civil society. The types of employment sought by men of the Foot Guards included labouring in the London docks, portering, farm work (haymaking or assisting with the harvest), and providing opera and playhouse guards during the season from November to July. These represented daily or weekly employment, but other soldiers worked as 'outliers' and were excused duty in return for which they received no pay but were required to attend a weekly foot-drill on Sunday mornings after which they would be marched off to church.[18] Such opportunities varied according to unit location, the season of the year, the attitude of the officers and the skills or motivation of the individual soldier. In summary, few regiments were physically concentrated and engaged in warlike training during times of peace.

Aside from dispersal, there also existed the issue of recruitment for units based in the British Isles. Through an extensive examination of inspection returns and other records, Houlding discovered that the average infantry regiment during peacetime existed at 90 percent of its establishment of which 16 percent were recruits. In wartime, strengths fell to 83 percent of establishment whereas the proportion of recruits increased to 27 percent. The situation in the cavalry was slightly better, with regiments averaging 95 percent of their establishments during peacetime, of which nine percent were recruits. During wartime, strengths fell to 94 percent of establishments but the proportion of recruits rose to 19 percent.[19]

A further issue affecting cavalry was that their horses were put to grass for up to four months a year, typically between May and September, so were unavailable for training. During this time, the men were restricted to foot-drill only and, even when the horses did return to their regiments, several weeks were required for them to achieve full fitness.[20]

---

17 Houlding, *Fit for Service*, pp.3 and 52–57.
18 Houlding, *Fit for Service*, p.15; Rogers, *British Army*, p.38. D.N. Hagist, *Noble Volunteers. The British Soldiers who Fought the American Revolution* (Yardley, Pennsylvania: Westholme, 2020), pp.30–36 and Steppler, *The Common Soldier in the Reign of George III*, pp.85–88.
19 Houlding, *Fit for Service*, pp.390–391.
20 Houlding, *Fit for Service*, pp.292–293.

In summary, the 10 years prior to the outbreak of war with Revolutionary France in 1793 were characterised by a dramatic downsizing of the Army as a whole, by changes in the structure of individual units of cavalry and infantry, by the resumption of normal peacetime activities including aid to the civil power, by recruitment problems leaving regiments below establishment, by the dispersal of individual units, and by the switch from administration by a commander-in-chief to that of the King and politicians in 1783. What Houlding has termed 'the friction of peace' meant that most regiments went to war only knowing basic arms-drill (the 'manual exercise') and the 'platoon exercise', by which they were taught to manoeuvre in penny packets. The regiment was normally concentrated once a year for review by a senior officer, which usually saw frantic efforts to put things in order. But unless the men attended a large-scale camp of exercise, they had little experience of how to march in extended column, or deploy into line – perhaps in close contact with the enemy – until they reached an actual theatre of operations. This was partly an outward sign of desperation, for it was the only way under the British system that the framework of an army could be kept in being. As a consequence, armies for active service had to be hurried into existence and even improvised on a hand-to-mouth basis, as was plainly the case in 1793.[21]

Trial Run: The Peacetime Mobilisations of 1787 and 1790

The Dutch crisis of 1787, when the prospect of war with France seemed imminent, led the War Office to order an augmentation of infantry regiments on the British establishment serving outside India. These consisted of eight companies each of 49 non-commissioned officers and men. Regiments were ordered on 22 September 1787 to increase each of the existing companies by one sergeant, one drummer and 14 privates. The ninth and tenth companies, disbanded in 1783, were also ordered to be re-raised, with each to consist of one captain, one lieutenant, one ensign, three sergeants, three corporals, two drummers and 56 men. An eleventh, or recruiting, company was also ordered, this to have one captain, one lieutenant, one ensign, eight sergeants, eight corporals, four drummers and 30 men. The crisis over, on 2 November the War Office ordered a return to the previous establishment.

In truth, the mobilisation had proved a failure. Many regiments stationed overseas had insufficient recruiting parties at home, so were unable to augment at such short notice. In any case, few recruits could be persuaded to enlist and there were insufficient commissioned officers, since the number of supernumeraries retained in 1783 had largely vanished through natural wastage. The result was that not one of the 47 battalions ordered to augment came close to their war establishment. The experiment to raise the two additional companies had proved unworkable. The lesson was quickly absorbed, however, and at the end of November the War Office instructed that all regiments of foot should henceforth consist of 10 companies, each of 40 rank-and-file.[22] Another key outcome of the Dutch crisis was that the British and Irish establishments were synchronised in terms of their financial administration and, more importantly as far as we are concerned here, in the actual composition of both cavalry and infantry units, with effect from 1 April 1788. This meant that regiments

---

21 Houlding, *Fit for Service*, pp.348–358. Houlding examined Dettingen (27 June 1743), Prestonpans (20 September 1745) and the Monongahela (9 July 1755).
22 Pimlott, *Administration of the British Army*, pp.268–273.

became interchangeable between the British and Irish establishments without having either to recruit or shed manpower as they moved between the two.[23]

It was not long before these new arrangements were put to the test. Spanish authorities had seized several British merchant vessels at Nootka Sound on the west coast of Vancouver Island in July 1789. The British Government did not learn of this incident until January 1790, but no action was envisaged at that stage. This changed when the principal owner of the seized ships arrived in London three months later, stating that the crews had been imprisoned and maltreated by the Spanish. In May 1790 Parliament voted the necessary funds to augment the Army in the probability of war with Spain. The War Office was quick to act, ordering line regiments to increase each company by one sergeant, one drummer (or two fifers in grenadier companies) and 19 privates, while the Foot Guards companies were ordered to have one additional corporal and 10 privates. In contrast to the experience of only three years before, the recruitment drive of May to November 1790 resulted in some 13,000 men joining the Army, which filled the existing vacancies in the units concerned and went significantly towards raising their establishments to the level ordered.[24]

Until September 1790, the mobilisation was for a defensive war intended to protect the home islands, outposts in the Caribbean, and the fortress of Gibraltar from Spanish attack. After some 2,300 men from eight regiments had boarded the fleet as marines and the colonies had been reinforced, Britain was left dangerously bare of troops, highlighting the absence of a central reserve. Orders were therefore issued for an augmentation of existing invalid companies (out-pensioners from Chelsea Hospital) and for raising 12 more for garrison duties. Two companies of the New South Wales Corps were also landed from a convict ship in Portsmouth Harbour to take over defensive duties. It was only later in the year, after all these measures had been enacted, that ministers could consider an offensive operation against Spanish colonies on the east coast of South America. To this end, two battalions were sent to the Caribbean in October 1790, but this simply highlighted once again the lack of any reserve, as their departure left only six effective line battalions in the whole of Britain. Under the circumstances it was just as well that the crisis petered out by the end of the month.[25]

The solution found to address the lack of a reserve was to raise independent companies of infantry commanded by captains and subalterns, a cost-cutting device which did not require the appointment of expensive field officers. By the end of October 1790, a total of 184 half-pay captains or full-pay lieutenants had been issued with beating orders, with each company to consist of one captain, one lieutenant, one ensign, four sergeants, five corporals, two drummers and 95 men. Recruits had to be sent to the Chatham Depot for inspection, with captains receiving five guineas for each recruit approved and lieutenants three. In practice, officers could offer recruits whatever bounty they could afford to pay, often recouping their outlay by selling commissions to the highest bidder, unless they wished to bestow them on family and friends. The Secretary-at-War had oversight of the newly appointed captains, not least as this required the King's approval, but not the subaltern officers. It was now possible to bring the established regiments up to strength by taking in recruits from the

---

23   Pimlott, *Administration of the British Army*, pp.286–289.
24   Black, *British Foreign Policy*, pp.233–256 and Pimlott, *Administration of the British Army*, pp.292–299.
25   Pimlott, *Administration of the British Army*, pp.309, 312, 317–320 and 324.

independent companies, and as far as Government was concerned, roughly 5,700 men were raised by these means. But for the time being the men were ineffective in practical terms, as they needed to be assimilated and trained.[26]

Mobilisation in 1793

The Appointment of a Commander-in-Chief

The Army had no commander-in-chief after General Conway resigned in November 1783 until Lord Amherst was appointed at the end of January 1793. Amherst was a distinguished soldier, having served during the War of the Austrian Succession and the Seven Years' War. Louisbourg was captured in 1758, during his tenure as Commander-in-Chief in North America, but his crowning achievement was the conquest of Canada between 1760–1763. He later served as Commander-in-Chief of the Army between 1778–1782 and thus had experience of the role during a major continental war, though he was not known for his ability to work with politicians and often failed to argue his case when they took decisions with which he disagreed. Moreover, he was no longer in his prime.[27]

Amherst was interviewed by Pitt on 20 January 1793, a few days before his seventy-sixth birthday. He agreed to have his name placed before the King, to whom Pitt reported: '… but at the same time desired that it might be represented to your Majesty that he was apprehensive his age might render him less equal than he had been to the fatigues of an active situation'.[28] What was required at this time was a vigorous and active commander-in-chief. Despite all his past achievements, which were considerable, it is highly questionable whether Amherst possessed the capacity to fulfil that role, as Henry Dundas reflected several years later to Lord Grenville: 'Lord Amherst was a worthy and respectable old man, and nobody shall ever hear me say a disrespectful thing of him; but the mischief he did in a few years will not be repaired but by the unremitting attention of many.'[29]

Amherst held office for two years until being replaced as Commander-in-Chief by the Duke of York in February 1795. Amherst's duties included the nomination of officers to the King for promotions and appointments, the planning of troop movements, and all matters relating to training and discipline.[30] He has been heavily censured for his recruiting policy, the despatch of untrained units to Flanders, and for the manner in which many officers

---

26 Pimlott, *Administration of the British Army*, pp.326–330 and 347.
27 W.C. Lowe, 'Amherst, Jeffrey, first Baron Amherst (1717–1797)', *ODNB*, <https://doi.org/10.1093/ref:odnb/443>, accessed 5 March 2021. Amherst's role during the Seven Years' War is discussed by Rogers, *British Army*, pp.129–152 and selected correspondence from 1758–1760 is in R. Middleton (ed.), *Amherst and the Conquest of Canada* (Stroud: Sutton Publishing, 2003). His journals for the years 1758–1763 were edited by J.C. Webster (ed.), *The Journal of Jeffery Amherst. Recording the Military Career of Jeffery Amherst in America from 1758 to 1763* (Chicago: University of Chicago Press, 1931).
28 Pitt to George III, 21 January 1793, in Aspinall (ed.), *Later Correspondence*, vol.1, p.647.
29 Dundas to Grenville, 21 July 1798, in Historical Manuscripts Commission (ed.), *Dropmore*, vol.4, p.264.
30 Houlding, *Fit for Service*, p.155.

achieved brevet rank in 1794.[31] It may have been closer to the truth that he was simply out-manoeuvred by the vigour of Pitt, Dundas and Grenville, and his shortcoming was more that he did not push the professional interests of the Army strongly enough.

Recruitment on the Outbreak of War

Mobilisation of Britain's land forces commenced even before war was declared. The militia, the primary military reserve in England, commenced mobilisation in December 1792. These men were nominated by ballot according to set criteria, but the available evidence indicates that the majority of men were in fact paid substitutes; under no circumstances were militia units permitted to recruit by beat of drum as the regulars were. The equivalent in Scotland were the Fencibles, of which nine battalions were raised. Volunteer units of all arms were formed by order of Lord Amherst in 1793, but their numbers were small. Further measures, including the Supplementary Militia and Provisional Cavalry, lay in the future and do not concern us here.[32] The available evidence suggests that competition for recruits for regular units was not significantly compromised by home defence forces, since their augmentation in mid-1794 came too late for recruits to be sent to Flanders.

On 1 November 1793, line regiments were ordered to increase their establishments from 600 men to 1,050 within three months. The incentive was that one additional lieutenant colonel and one major would be added to each regiment. The senior major was to become the junior lieutenant colonel, thus allowing the two senior captains to receive promotion, the two senior subalterns to receive their companies and, at the far end of the scale, two ensigns to be recruited. The scheme was also pursued in regiments of cavalry along equivalent lines. The attraction from the Government's viewpoint was the cost of recruiting lay with the officer doing the work and, if he succeeded in achieving his target for promotion, the commission he vacated reverted to the Crown and could be sold to offset official expenses. This system changed in 1794 when officers gaining rank from achieving their recruiting targets were allowed to receive a part of the proceeds from all the commissions sold by men lower down the promotion chain. In some units, money from the sale of commissions was paid into a regimental fund. As with the independent companies raised in 1790, it was left to the authorised officers to choose their own subalterns from the half pay list, but as this supply became exhausted they were permitted to sell commissions. Despite these potentially attractive terms, no unit succeeded in raising sufficient men and in June 1794, 31 regiments were permitted to cease the attempt, though 15 more were settled at an establishment of 850 men.[33]

A more circuitous method of finding men for existing regiments was to use officers of proven recruiting ability to raise independent companies of varying sizes, and three attempts were made to do this, the first in January–February 1793. By late February 1794 it was apparent that the augmentation of line regiments was not going to plan and it can have been no coincidence that further independent companies were authorised in March

---

31 Glover, *Peninsular Preparation*, pp.149–151.
32 J.R. Western, *The Recruitment of the Land Forces of Great Britain, 1793–1799* (Unpublished PhD thesis, University of Edinburgh, 1953), pp.3, 145–146, 148–149, 154 and 237 and C. Emsley, *British Society and the French Wars 1793–1815* (London: Macmillan, 1979), pp.36–39.
33 Western, *The Recruitment of the Land Forces*, pp.40–42 and 63–66.

and October 1794, though Henry Dundas thought it best to restrict their number following opposition from the King, possibly a result of lobbying by the colonels of 'old' regiments. In January 1793, the bait for officers authorised to raise these companies was set at full pay for the half pay captains or promotion for the full pay lieutenants, which they received after raising 50 men. In 1794, captains had to raise 100 men and lieutenants 50 before they gained promotion.[34]

New units of line cavalry and infantry were also raised during this first wartime recruiting drive commencing on the outbreak of war. The cavalry regiments do not concern us, since none served in Flanders, though it is possible that some of the recruits did find their way there as reinforcements. A number of the new infantry units did serve under the Duke of York, including the 79th, 84th, 85th, 87th, 88th and 89th Regiments, all of which had letters of service dating from between August 1793 and February 1794, being placed on the establishment between 17 August 1793 and 27 November 1794.[35] Eyewitnesses in Flanders thought little of them, due to their obvious lack of training, dearth of equipment and inadequate clothing.

Why were established regiments relatively unsuccessful in the augmentation of 1793? The foremost reason was the shortage of officers who could be spared for recruiting duties, meaning that young and inexperienced men were used, rather than those who would have been more ideally suited. Existing regiments also had their normal duties to fulfil, of which recruiting was but one, so they did not have the resources to compete in the market with newly raised units or independent companies, whose sole business was to find men. The success of the new units may also have owed much to the connections and wealth of officers holding letters of service, who had, after all, been authorised to proceed in the first place due to these very factors. As we shall see, many officers complained bitterly at seeing men with wealth but limited experience being promoted over their heads, though measures were taken to mitigate this, such as the requirement to nominate half pay officers. From 1794, officers given letters of service were required to have a certain degree of seniority amounting to three or four years for a captain. Those of longer standing received levy money at a higher rate, with captains of six years standing receiving 18 guineas while officers with less had 12. The Government also tried to level the field by providing additional financial support to those having letters of service but lacking abundant financial resources. All was not quite so comfortable for those with money, however. Without the necessary experience, it was relatively easy for them to be fleeced by those who had more knowledge of the minutiae of military detail, and this group of men was more likely to comprise established military officers.[36]

In the final analysis, the results told their own story. A total of 17,033 rank-and-file (corporals and privates) were recruited during 1793 and a further 38,563 in 1794, far exceeding what had been achieved in previous wars and the complete opposite of what had occurred in 1787.[37] The existing model of recruiting by independent companies had been a success at the end of 1790 and was used again with effect in 1793–1794. However, the method-

---

34 Western, *The Recruitment of the Land Forces*, pp.43, 46 and 63 and Ferguson, *The Army in Ireland*, pp.138–139.
35 TNA: WO 379/2: 'A Table of the Reliefs' and Fortescue, *History of the British Army*, vol.4, pp.931–932.
36 Western, *The Recruitment of the Land Forces*, pp.40–42, 68–69 and 77–79.
37 Fortescue, *History of the British Army*, vol.4, p.940.

ology was extended at the end of 1793 to include completely new regiments, which involved some men achieving senior ranks without having the concomitant experience. Whilst many serving officers took exception to this measure, the fact remained that many regiments in the existing order of battle had failed to achieve their quota of recruits by the end of 1793, despite being offered the same incentive.

Regimental Organisation

When war was declared in 1793, the Army consisted of 30 regiments of cavalry (three of Household Cavalry, seven of Dragoon Guards, six of Dragoons and 14 of Light Dragoons), seven battalions in three regiments of Foot Guards and 81 battalions in 77 regiments of line infantry. In addition, there were the New South Wales Corps, The Queen's Rangers stationed in Upper Canada, and 36 independent companies of invalids in England, Scotland and the Channel Islands.[38] At the end of 1792, 16 cavalry regiments were stationed in Britain and a further 12 in Ireland, with only two overseas. The situation was very different with the infantry, of which 45 battalions were at home (24 in Ireland and 21 in Britain including the Foot Guards), with the remaining 43 overseas.[39] In March 1793, just under six weeks after war was declared, the Army in Britain (excluding Ireland) consisted of 14 regiments each of cavalry and infantry, excluding the four remaining battalions of Foot Guards after three had already proceeded to Flanders. Companies of invalids, 38 in number, manned various fortifications, and nine companies belonging to regiments serving in India were based at Chatham and Purfleet. While the majority of infantry regiments were concentrated, this only applied to five of the cavalry units. The Royal Horse Guards (known as the 'Blues'), which proceeded to Flanders in June 1793, had five troops in Manchester and four troops located 100 miles to the south, with two in Birmingham and one each in Leicester and Coventry. Another regiment also posted to Flanders in June was the 1st Dragoons, which had two troops each in Blandford, Salisbury and Dorchester, thus being dispersed across a 40-mile sector.[40] With regiments constantly on the move, and the high rates of dispersal to be expected when engaged on internal security duties, unit cohesion was compromised and the opportunities for combined arms training strictly limited.

Cavalry
The basic sub-unit of a regiment of cavalry was the troop. The officers comprised one captain, one lieutenant and one cornet, who were assisted by one quartermaster, two sergeants and two corporals. Prior to January 1793, the peacetime establishment consisted of 28 troopers and one trumpeter. Cavalry regiments all consisted of six troops apart from the Royal Horse Guards and the 1st Dragoon Guards which each had nine. This changed shortly after the outbreak of war when all regiments having six troops were ordered to raise

---

38 Anon., *A List of the Officers, 1793*.
39 Pimlott, *Administration of the British Army*, pp.381–385 and Ferguson, *The Army in Ireland*, p.139.
40 TNA: WO 5/68: Quarters of the Regular Forces in Great Britain, 11 March 1793.

three more.[41] Apparently due to recruitment problems in 1793, some regiments of heavy cavalry serving in Flanders, including both the 5th and 6th Dragoon Guards, formed two light troops from smaller men and horses. These were trained as light dragoons, though it is not certain whether they served overseas.[42] When on service, two troops would typically form one squadron, with the senior of the two troop leaders commanding both.

The original intention of the Horse Guards was to send over regiments complete, but this was altered in late March 1793 when the Adjutant-General, Lieutenant General Sir William Fawcett, wrote to the Duke of York that three quarters of the 11th and 16th Light Dragoons were raw recruits, so it was decided to despatch only four troops per regiment, thus keeping the recruits at home for further training. According to the 'Officer of the Guards', it was Major General Ralph Dundas (the designated brigade commander) who made this proposal, with the idea that the troops at home could then be used as a reserve to replace casualties.[43] This meant that all the cavalry units serving in Flanders consisted of four troops, except for the 1st Dragoon Guards with six, due to its higher establishment.[44]

The composition of the cavalry troop varied according to the type of regiment concerned. On the outbreak of war, a troop of the Royal Horse Guards consisted of one captain, one lieutenant, one cornet, one quartermaster, three corporals, one trumpeter and 40 men. An additional corporal and 10 troopers were subsequently added to this establishment on 25 May 1793. Regiments of Dragoon Guards, Dragoons and Light Dragoons had the same number of officers, but had three sergeants, three corporals, one trumpeter and 47 troopers per troop.[45] Each of the 46 troops belonging to the 11 regiments of cavalry sent to Flanders during 1793 was to consist of 50 rank-and-file.[46] This was not to last long, however, since the establishment for Light Dragoon regiments was increased on 24 September 1793 by the addition of one sergeant, one corporal and 24 troopers per troop, leading to each troop having four sergeants, four corporals and 71 troopers, an order that was subsequently applied to three regiments of Dragoon Guards and four of Dragoons on 24 January 1794.[47] All the cavalry units serving in Flanders at that time, apart from the 5th and 6th Dragoon Guards (which had come from the Irish establishment), were now on this higher establishment.

---

41 Houlding, *Fit for Service*, p.420 and TNA: WO 3/11: p.38, Circular to Colonels and Commanding Officers, 12 February 1793.
42 R. Cannon, *Historical Record of The Sixth Regiment of Dragoon Guards or The Carbineers* (London: Longman, Orme and Co, 1839), p.75; L.B. Oatts, *I Serve. Regimental History of the 3rd Carabineers (Prince of Wales's Dragoon Guards)* (Privately published, 1966), p.72 and NAM: 1985-12-15-5: GO, Ghent, 17 January 1794.
43 TNA: WO 3/11: pp.77-78, Fawcett to York, 27 March 1793 and Anon., *Officer of the Guards*, vol.1, p.36.
44 TNA: WO 3/11: p.95, Adjutant-General's Order, 1 May 1793.
45 Royal Horse Guards: TNA: WO 24/579: p.15 and WO 24/580: p.6, Dragoon Guards, Dragoons and Light Dragoons: WO 24/579: pp.16-17.
46 TNA: WO 3/11: pp.108-110 and 79: Fawcett to Sir Robert Abercromby, 24 May 1793 and Fawcett to York, 2 April 1793.
47 TNA: WO 24/579: p.18, A further augmentation to five regiments of Light Dragoons and WO 24/585: p.2.

Infantry

The basic sub-unit in a regiment of line infantry, the company, was also commanded by a captain and assisted by one lieutenant and one ensign. According to the peacetime establishment, the non-commissioned officers consisted of two sergeants and three corporals with one drummer per battalion company, replaced by a fifer in the grenadier company and a bugler in the light company; there were 40 privates per company. Regiments consisted of eight battalion companies together with two flank companies,[48] one of grenadiers and the other of light infantry. The establishments of 48 line battalions were increased by one sergeant, one drummer and 17 privates per company on 24 January 1793. This resulted in each battalion company consisting of one captain, one lieutenant, one ensign, three sergeants, three corporals, two drummers and 57 privates, with flank companies having two lieutenants and no ensigns. A further 10 battalions were ordered to the same establishment between February and September 1793.[49] The establishment was raised again on 25 December 1793 to 81 privates per company for 13 regiments, including 11 that were either serving in Flanders or would do so in 1794, though other units which served in the campaign, such as the 89th, remained at the lower level. Others still, such as the 87th and 88th had their establishments raised from 57 to 100 privates per company on 8 May and 15 August 1794 respectively.[50]

We have already seen that regiments seldom achieved their designated peacetime strength and fared even less well during wartime when establishments were higher, coupled with the constant drain of manpower from casualties and sickness. It was not unusual that the three line infantry units serving in Flanders during the 1793 campaign (the 14th, 37th and 53rd Regiments) were all under strength at the commencement of the war and were thus forced to augment their numbers by absorbing recruits from newly raised independent companies. The main body of the 37th Regiment embarked at Leith on 19 March 1793 with a smaller detachment following on 9 April and an even smaller one from Chatham on an unknown date. Taken together, the regiment comprised 30 officers, 34 sergeants, 35 corporals, 23 drummers and 470 privates; when the five sergeants, two corporals, three drummers and six privates recruiting are added, together with a further 10 privates sick or recruits not joined, the unit was deficient of 84 privates, though had a surplus of nine sergeants, seven corporals and six drummers. The 53rd Regiment was also under-strength, embarking at Leith on 20 March with a second detachment on 9 April and a third from Chatham. The unit numbered 27 officers, 27 sergeants, 26 corporals, 19 drummers and 463 privates, though 12 sergeants, eight corporals, seven drummers and 34 privates were recruiting, six privates were on furlough and 21 were recruits not yet joined; this made the unit 46 privates short, but there was a surplus of nine sergeants, four corporals and six drummers. The third line infantry unit to embark for the United Provinces was the 14th Regiment at Deal on 22 March to be followed by a small detachment from Chatham under Ensign James Greaves. Altogether, the regiment comprised 30 officers, 33 sergeants, 23 drummers and 646 corporals and privates;

---
48   So called because the grenadier company took station on the right when the battalion was drawn up in line and the light company occupied the left.
49   TNA: WO 24/579: pp.7–9 and 22.
50   TNA: WO 24/580: pp.1 and 14 and WO 24/585: pp.26–28 and 44–45. The regiments with 81 privates per company were the 3rd, 14th, 19th, 27th, 28th, 37th, 42nd, 53rd, 54th, 57th and 59th.

the regiment therefore had three sergeants, three drummers and 46 rank-and-file (corporals and privates) more than its official establishment by its embarkation date.[51]

The establishment for line regiments was increased by a War Office circular of 1 November 1793 (taking effect on 25 December) to four sergeants, four corporals, two drummers and 81 privates per company.[52] The addition of one sergeant, one corporal, one drummer and 44 privates per company, if achieved, resulted in 91 non-commissioned officers, drummers and privates per company in November 1793 compared to 46 prior to January 1793 (an increase of 98 percent). This could only be achieved by a marked influx of untrained men and a corresponding decline in unit efficiency until the recruits could be absorbed and become trained soldiers.

Foot Guards regiments had a slightly different establishment than those of the line. The three Foot Guards regiments were ordered to augment each of their companies by one sergeant, one corporal and 17 privates on 24 January 1793. This brought the composition of each battalion company up to one captain, one lieutenant, one ensign, four sergeants, four corporals, two drummers and 71 privates. Corporal Brown of the Coldstream Guards stated that the number of privates was subsequently reduced to 56 per company three days later, though this was certainly not the official establishment.[53] A return of the three battalions of Foot Guards ordered on foreign service dated 22 February 1793 showed the 1st Foot Guards with 40 sergeants, 24 drummers and 670 rank-and-file (corporals and privates) compared to the Coldstream Guards and 3rd Foot Guards each with 36 sergeants, 20 drummers and 603 rank-and-file. This suggests that the 1st Foot Guards embarked with 10 companies, whereas the other two regiments had nine, which is supported by Sir William Fawcett transmitting an order, on 27 June 1793, to increase the establishment of each of the 28 Foot Guards companies already in Flanders by 10 men. These reinforcements embarked on 9 July and joined their regiments on 27 July.[54] Shortly after this, on 7 August 1793, the official establishment for the Foot Guards regiments was raised by one sergeant, one corporal and 24 privates, bringing each company up to five sergeants, five corporals and 95 privates.[55]

The Foot Guards regiments also differed in composition compared to the line, with the 1st Foot Guards consisting of 24 battalion companies and four grenadier companies in three battalions, whereas the Coldstream Guards and 3rd Foot Guards each had 16 battalion companies and two grenadier companies in two battalions each. Light companies therefore only existed in line regiments at the outbreak of war in 1793. The higher establishment of the Foot Guards compared to the line meant they had a significant reserve of trained men at

---

51 C.T. Atkinson, *Regimental History. The Royal Hampshire Regiment* (Published by the regiment: 1950), p.134; TNA: WO 25/1146: pp.86–89 Embarkation Returns and HO 50/384: Yonge to Dundas, 7 March 1793. Yonge requested shipping sufficient for 689 officers and men, 60 women and 12 servants per regiment, which was the full establishment rather than the actual strength.
52 TNA: HO 50/384: War Office circular, 1 November 1793 and TNA: WO 24/580: p.14,
53 TNA: WO 24/579: p.19, Augmentation to the Three Regiments of Foot Guards, from 24th January 1793, inclusive; Brown, *Impartial Journal*, p.2 and Houlding, *Fit for Service*, p.420.
54 BL: Add Ms 34,448: p.284, Enclosure in Grenville to Auckland, 22 February 1793, Auckland papers vol.37; WO 3/11: p.128: Fawcett to the Field Officers in Waiting, 27 June 1793; WO 3/11: pp.137–138, Fawcett to Murray, 5 July 1793 and Brown, *Impartial Journal*, pp.56–57.
55 TNA: WO 24/579: p.21, A further Augmentation to the Three Regiments of Foot Guards, from 7th August 1793, inclusive.

home that could be utilised to ensure the battalions in Flanders remained at their establishment level. This was similar to the cavalry regiments with their depot troops left in Britain or Ireland, and in stark contrast to line infantry regiments, which went overseas with no such reserve and could therefore only be reinforced by recruits or trained men drafted from elsewhere to replace casualties or the sick.

As far as the micro-organisation of an infantry regiment was concerned, each company was divided into squads of about 10 men commanded by a corporal or sergeant. The squad ate together and received much of their instruction from the non-commissioned officer in charge, who was also responsible for their discipline, turnout and inspecting the mens' necessaries. When in the field, the squad shared a tent, the men lying on straw, and all sleeping inside the same two blankets sewn together into a tube to prevent anyone taking more than his share. The men crawled into the tube to sleep with head and feet alternately. Convention dictated that the oldest soldier slept at the far end of the tent and the youngest at the entrance, meaning that he often received the results of men getting up in the night and not going beyond the tent door when answering calls of nature.[56] Corporal Brown of the Coldstream Guards remarked that 12 tents were allowed per company in August 1793, suggesting that these were the old square model designed for one squad each. Twelve would therefore provide for between 72 and 96 men per company, depending on the number in each squad. An order for 1,200 tents was placed with Messrs Trotter in January 1794 after a pattern approved by Lieutenant General Harcourt and these were issued in Flanders from April 1794. Each tent had room for 16 men, and two camp kettles were issued per tent, which suggests they were each designed to accommodate two squads.[57]

It is also important to note that the stereotype of ignorant and disobedient soldiers kept in check by the threatened or actual use of the lash was often very far from the truth. Dr Robert Hamilton, Assistant Surgeon of the 10th Regiment between 1780–1785 observed:

> We do not always find the lowest orders of mankind in the ranks. If we enquire, we shall often discover youths who have been tenderly bred up; and men long accustomed to better days. The son, perhaps, of some worthy clergyman, that the giddiness of youth hurried thoughtless into this way of life. The once flourishing farmer; or the reputable tradesman. I knew instances of all these; of many whom misfortunes drove into the service. Some indeed entered it through folly.[58]

Flank Battalions

It had been the practice since 1742 for grenadier companies to be detached from their regiments and formed into élite provisional units when on campaign. The same practice was also followed when light companies were formed by units stationed in North America

---

56 Brumwell, *Redcoats*, p.120; B. Cuthbertson, *Cuthbertson's System for the Complete Interior Management and Œconomy of a Battalion of Infantry. A new edition, with corrections* (Bristol: Rouths and Nelson, 1776), pp.14–15 and Steppler, *The Common Soldier in the Reign of George III*, pp.137–138.
57 TNA: HO 50/385: Lewis to unknown, 24 January 1794 and Brown, *Impartial Journal*, pp.61 and 98–99.
58 R. Hamilton, *Regimental Surgeon*, vol.1, p.214.

during the Seven Years' War and then from 1771–1772 when they became a permanent part of line regiments.[59]

Exactly the same practice was followed when Major General Gerard Lake issued an order on 23 February 1793, before the troops had embarked for Flanders, that the grenadier companies of the Brigade of Guards were to comprise a separate unit under the command of Colonel Charles Leigh of the 3rd Foot Guards, with Lieutenant and Captain Hugh Campbell of the same regiment appointed adjutant, and Sergeant Duncan McFarlane as the quartermaster. This new unit consisted of two companies from the 1st Foot Guards and one each from the other two regiments.[60] Five weeks later, another general order was issued for each battalion in the Guards Brigade in Flanders to contribute 27 men towards the formation of a new light company. The whole was to consist of one captain, three lieutenants, four sergeants, five corporals and 81 privates, with the company to be commanded by Captain and Lieutenant Colonel James Perryn of the 1st Foot Guards.[61]

The need for light troops remained, leading Horse Guards on 15 April 1793 to order the raising of eight light companies by the Foot Guards regiments at home, four by the 1st Foot Guards and two each by the other regiments. Some rapid training must have ensued, since the men were ordered to be recruited rather than transferred from the existing battalion companies of each regiment. These companies were placed on the establishment on 25 June 1793 each consisting of one captain, two lieutenants, four sergeants, four corporals, one drummer and 71 privates. They were soon after increased to five sergeants, five corporals and 95 privates on 7 August 1793, at the same time as the battalion companies already discussed.[62] Three of the new light companies, one from each regiment, were swiftly despatched to Flanders the following month, reaching the Guards Flank Battalion 27 July 1793 thus increasing the unit to eight companies, four each of grenadiers and light infantry.[63]

A similar process was undertaken in 1794, when four light companies (two from the 1st Foot Guards and one each from the other regiments) embarked on 5 July 1794, reaching the Guards Flank Battalion on 17 July. The Guards Flank Battalion now consisted of 12 companies, four of grenadiers and eight of light infantry, making it difficult to manage in the field, so it was split on 20 July, with the grenadiers forming one battalion commanded by Captain and Lieutenant Colonel the Hon Fitzroy Stanhope, and the light infantry another, commanded by Colonel Sir James Duff, both of the 1st Foot Guards.[64]

Unlike the Foot Guards, the three line regiments in Flanders during the 1793 campaign already had one grenadier and one light company each. These battalions reached the vicinity

---

59 Houlding, *Fit for Service*, pp.91–92.
60 NAM: 1985-12-15-4: Brigade Orders by Major General Lake, Orderly Room, 1st Gds, 23 February 1793 and Brown, *Impartial Journal*, p.3.
61 NAM: 1985-12-15-4: GO, Dordt, 30 March 1793.
62 TNA: WO 4/147: pp.153–158, Yonge to Colonels of the Guards, 15 April 1793; WO 24/580: p.20, Augmentation of Eight Companies of Light Infantry, to the Three Regiments of Foot Guards, from 25th of June 1793 inclusive; Brown, *Impartial Journal*, pp.79–80; F.W. Hamilton, *The Origin and History of the First or Grenadier Guards* (London: Murray, 1874), vol.2, p.311 and D. Mackinnon, *Origin and Services of the Coldstream Guards* (London: Bentley, 1833), vol.2, pp.59 and 363–364.
63 Brown, *Impartial Journal*, pp.56–57.
64 TNA: WO 25/1146: p.135, Emb'n Ret'n of Foot Guards for Flanders, 5th July 1794 and Brown, *Impartial Journal*, p.181.

of Antwerp by 9 April and a general order dated 13 April directed the six flank companies to be detached from their parent units and formed into a composite battalion under Major Robert Mathews of the 53rd Regiment. The staff of the Line Flank Battalion were subsequently appointed by a general order dated 17 April. The battalion was not to last long, however, since heavy losses sustained during the siege of Dunkirk in early September meant that it was broken up and the flank companies returned to their regiments.[65]

The problem of insufficient light infantry was highlighted during the 1793 campaign, leading the Duke of York to despatch his adjutant-general, Colonel James Craig, to the King of Prussia in late March 1794. Craig was tasked with conveying the Duke's request for 4,000 light infantry as a personal favour, but this was refused.[66]

Regiments on Campaign

Unit Effectiveness

We have already discussed the effects on training of the 'friction of peace' and the difficulties regiments experienced in achieving their establishment numbers, even in peacetime. We have also seen the significant differences between peacetime and wartime establishments and that augmentations could only be achieved at the cost of unit effectiveness until such time as recruits had been fully trained. It now remains to examine what this meant in practical terms once the regiments reached Flanders, whether they were defective in terms of their equipment and training and, if so, the impact this may have had on their performance in the field.

Difficulties were anticipated even before some units left England. Sir William Fawcett, the Adjutant-General at the Horse Guards, wrote to the Duke of York on 5 March 1793 regarding the brigade of line infantry comprising the 14th, 37th and 53rd Regiments soon to be sent to Flanders: 'They will be completed to 600 Rank & File, from the Independent Companies, before they embark; I wish we could give them disciplined Soldiers instead of such raw Recruits; but, that, in the present State of Affairs here, your R.H. knows is in a manner impracticable.'[67]

Fawcett was even more apologetic to Major General Ralph Abercromby, the designated brigade commander:

> What you will do with the raw undisciplined Stuff you carried with you, & of which, one half at least of your Brigade, must be composed, I am at a loss to know; & you may assure yourself, that if I had been consulted upon the occasion, I should have fallen upon some mode, more likely to answer the purpose, than that which was adopted with so much Precipitation.[68]

---

65 NAM: 1985-12-15-4: GO, Lokeren, 13 April 1793 and Bruges, 17 April 1793 and H. O'Donnell, *Historical Records of the 14th Regiment, now the Prince of Wales's Own (West Yorkshire Regiment), from its Formation in 1685, to 1892* (Devonport: Swiss, 1893), pp.54 and 61.
66 Earl of Malmesbury, *Diaries and Correspondence*, vol.3, p.83. Craig's interview with the King of Prussia took place on Saturday 22 March 1794.
67 TNA: WO 3/11: p.45, Fawcett to York, 5 March 1793.
68 TNA: WO 3/11: p.88–89, Fawcett to Abercromby, 19 April 1793.

The scale of the problem was exposed in the monthly returns. The 14th Regiment was inspected at Chatham Barracks on 1 June 1792, by which time it had a strength of 23 officers, three staff, 19 sergeants, 12 drummers and 326 rank-and-file.[69] The unit recruited heavily at the beginning of 1793, with 12 officers, 10 sergeants, six drummers and 74 rank-and-file so engaged on 1 January, when it had a strength of 30 officers, 22 sergeants, 12 drummers and 340 rank-and-file. Two months later, when the regiment moved from Chatham to Dover Castle, the total strength had risen to 27 officers (two having departed to independent companies), 24 sergeants, 18 drummers and 426 rank-and-file. During these two months, the regiment increased from 374 all ranks (officers excepted) to 468, suggesting that 94 individuals (25 percent) were either recruits or had been drafted from other regiments. Despite this, the regiment was still six sergeants, two drummers and 174 rank-and-file below its establishment strength.[70] As we have seen, when embarking at the end of March, the regiment numbered 669 rank-and-file, indicating a rapid influx of 225 recruits or draftees, representing a 47 percent increase in numbers since 1 January. Unfortunately, there are no extant monthly returns for the 37th Regiment between November 1791 and June 1795 or for the 53rd Regiment until April 1795.[71]

The reality was that both the 37th and 53rd Regiments were 'totally unfit for service' when they landed in Flanders in early April 1793, or so thought Lieutenant and Captain Harry Calvert of the Coldstream Guards, who continued in a letter to his father: 'The recruits that were sent to complete them, immediately before their embarkation, are worse than any I ever saw, even at the close of the American War'.[72] The 37th, aside from its flank companies which, as we have seen, formed a part of the Line Flank Battalion, was sent to garrison Ostend and did not participate in active operations until the commencement of the siege of Dunkirk in late August.[73] It is assumed that this interval of over four months was spent in intensive training which was resumed after the Dunkirk operation. The regiment met with disaster on 20 October 1794 when it was attacked by up to 60 French hussars while in the process of withdrawing along a dyke at Druten in good order with its battalion guns. The cavalry were first thought to be from the émigré Rohan Hussars serving with the allies and were allowed to get too close before the mistake was realised. The result was the 37th lost 13 officers, one sergeant and 420 rank-and-file killed, wounded and missing, with only two officers and 80 other ranks managing to escape.[74] Although this was an unfortunate tactical error, the suspicion remains that a unit having greater experience might have spotted the danger earlier and thus avoided disaster.

The 53rd Regiment was in slightly better condition and although initially sent to garrison Bruges it rejoined the 14th Regiment in Abercromby's brigade in time to participate at the battle of Famars on 23 May 1793. As with many other regiments, the military effectiveness

---

69 TNA: WO 27/72: Return of His Majesty's 14th (or Bedfordshire) Regiment of Foot Commanded by Major General Hotham, as reviewed at Chatham Barracks 1st June 1792 by Major General Ainslie.
70 TNA: WO 17/115: 14th Regiment monthly returns, 1759–1805.
71 TNA: WO 17/147: 37th Regiment monthly returns, 1769–1812 and WO 17/168: 53rd Regiment monthly returns, 1789–1812. There are also no inspection returns for these regiments in WO 27/72.
72 Calvert to John Calvert, 26 April 1793, in Verney (ed.), *Calvert*, pp.67–68.
73 Atkinson, *The Royal Hampshire Regiment*, pp.135–136.
74 Jones, *An Historical Journal*, pp.132–133 and Calvert to his sister, 21 October 1794 and Calvert to Dalrymple, 22 October 1794, in Verney (ed.), *Calvert*, pp.364–366.

of the 53rd greatly suffered as a result of its experiences in the years preceding the outbreak of war. It returned home in August 1789 after 13 years in Canada and by June 1790 recruited up to 78 percent of its establishment strength. During the next 12 months 100 worn out men were discharged and 150 were recruited, but could not be trained when the regiment served as marines on board the fleet between July and November as part of the Spanish Armament. The regiment commenced marching from Plymouth to new quarters at Glasgow in late February 1791, again making any training of the recruits impossible. It was unsurprising that the reviewing officer classified the 53rd Regiment as unfit for service when he inspected it at Glasgow in June 1791, since 50 percent of the men had been recruited to meet the establishment strength.[75] Despite all three regiments of this brigade being barely serviceable, the reinforcements embarked at Sheerness and Gravesend on 1 November 1793 consisted of recruits, not trained men.[76]

The problems resulting from sending recruits to Flanders continued in 1794. Three hundred were assembled at Chatham Barracks for the 14th, 37th and 53rd Regiments in March before being shipped to Ostend. Harry Calvert saw them on their arrival and wrote to Colonel Sir Hew Dalrymple: 'The recruits for General Abercromby's brigade arrived a few days ago; they much resembled Falstaff's men, and were as lightly clad as any Carmagnole battalion'.[77] A second batch of 500 recruits for the same units was sent to Flanders in April followed by 220 more in July.[78] Abercromby's brigade was not the only formation to suffer, as Major General Richard Whyte's brigade comprising the 12th, 38th and 55th Regiments landed at Ostend in April 1794, joining the allied army the following month: '… they are said to be in a shocking state, badly clothed, and some without firelocks'.[79] The Duke of York wrote:

> Indeed the Brigade which arrived from England in the Spring, and was employed at first in Flanders, had so many new recruits that Major General White [sic] was under the necessity of sending back two hundred men of the 38th Reg't the very day before the Troops were engaged, as being so unfit for any service that they were an incumbrance to Him.[80]

The disembarkation return for the 38th Regiment suggests it consisted of only five companies, since the officers comprised one lieutenant colonel, one major, five captains and 10 subalterns in addition to the adjutant, quartermaster and surgeon. A total of 165 rank-and-file were absent sick in Ireland, on command or recruiting and a further 21 rank-and-file were reported sick, though still with the regiment, leaving only 467 rank-and-file present and fit for duty. The embarkation return dated 1 April 1794 stated the regiment had 548

---

75   Houlding, *Fit for Service*, p.133.
76   TNA: HO 50/384: Lewis to Nepean, 26 October 1793 and WO 3/11: p.204–206, Fawcett to York, 31 October 1793. The numbers were: 14th Regiment – one sergeant, one corporal and 42 privates, 37th and 53rd Regiments – 33 privates each. WO 25/1146: p.113, Embark'n Ret'n of the 14th, 37th & 53d for the Continent. Chatham B's 3d Nov'r 1793.
77   Calvert to Dalrymple, 8 April 1794, in Verney (ed.), *Calvert*, p.187.
78   TNA: HO 50/385: pp.285, 413 and 613, Lewis to Nepean, 12 March, 16 April and 4 July 1794.
79   Calvert to Dalrymple, 11 May 1794, in Verney (ed.), *Calvert*, pp.205–206.
80   TNA: WO 1/171: p.609, Observations of His Royal Highness the Duke of York, 23 December 1794.

privates 'wanting to complete'.[81] The 12th, 38th and 55th Regiments had been stationed in Ireland and, together with all the other infantry there, were without their flank companies, which had been hived off to the West Indies as part of Lieutenant General Sir Charles Grey's expedition. In order to compensate, these regiments consisted of 10 battalion companies, each having an establishment of one captain, one lieutenant, one ensign, four sergeants, four corporals, two drummers and 81 privates.[82]

Sad to tell, these were not isolated incidents. The 54th, which joined the army in July 1794 as a part of Lord Moira's force, returned from Canada in October 1791 only to discharge 102 of its 200 rank-and-file the following year as being unfit for further duty. These men were replaced through the incorporation of two independent companies in March 1793 and a third in May, allowing the regiment to reach its establishment strength by July. By January 1794 only two subalterns had more than five years' service, since the remainder had departed, having been attracted by the promotions available from raising independent companies.[83] Another unit in Lord Moira's force, the 87th Regiment, was seen at Bergen-op-Zoom on 28 July 1794 by James McGrigor, regimental surgeon to the 88th, who noted:

> ... although the majority of them had muskets, they were without accoutrements, and the usual kit of soldiers ... this unformed corps was hurried from Dublin, where they were raised, to the scene of action; and their irregularities rendered them more formidable to their friends than to their enemies. They were sent from the army into garrison.[84]

Regiments such as the 54th and 87th clearly had no business being in Flanders. The 87th had only been raised on 18 September 1793 and was not to survive long on campaign, being taken prisoner *en bloc* at Bergen-op-Zoom when the Dutch surrendered the fortress to the French.[85] Sir James Craig referred to regiments such as these in a letter to Evan Nepean, Under Secretary of State for War, on 5 August as containing: '... many Recruits who do not know one end of their firelocks from the other, & many who will never know it'.[86]

Perhaps the worst instance of sending untrained recruits to Flanders concerned the five infantry units landed at Flushing on 26 August 1794 under the command of Colonel Henry, Lord Mulgrave. Two of them (the 31st and 34th Regiments) were without their flank companies, which had been sent to the West Indies. They were in woeful condition. The 31st required 'at least' 240 stands of arms and had 400 men sick. The 34th had 20 cartridges per man while the 79th had only eight, and one officer per company. The 84th '... have hardly had any opportunity of forming the soldiers' since the regiment was constantly moving since

---

81 BL: Add Ms 40,634: p.46, Disembarkation return of His Majesty's 38th Regt of Foot, Ostend, 29th April 1794, Stewart of Afton Papers vol.2 and TNA: WO 25/1146: p.123: Embarkation Return of 38th Foot. Monkstown, near Cork 1st April 1794.
82 TNA: WO 24/585: pp.12–14.
83 C.T. Atkinson, *The Dorsetshire Regiment* (Oxford: Oxford University Press, 1947), vol.2, pp.45–46.
84 McGrigor, *Sir James McGrigor*, p.24.
85 J.B.M. Frederick, *Lineage Book of British Land Forces 1660–1978* (Wakefield: Microform Academic Publishers, 1984), vol.1, p.263 and M. Cunliffe, *The Royal Irish Fusiliers 1793–1950* (Oxford, Oxford University Press, 1952), pp.8–9.
86 TNA: WO 1/170: p.141, Craig to Nepean, 5 August 1794.

being raised, while the 85th had 30 cartridges per man but they '… never have had arms in their hands'.[87] It was unsurprising that Harry Calvert remarked: 'Five more regiments are on their road to join, without field-pieces, without ammunition, and many without arms!'[88] Given that several of these Regiments had only recently been raised it is indeed surprising that sending them on service so soon could have been contemplated. The 84th Regiment, for example, was raised on 2 November 1793, the 85th on 18 November the same year, both being placed on the establishment on 1 March 1794, and the 79th was only expanded into a full regiment on 19 February 1794.[89]

Lest it be thought that only the infantry suffered from such high proportions of recruits, similar circumstances also affected the cavalry, since 562 recruits with 596 horses embarked on 15 March 1794 to be closely followed by 629 more with 649 horses.[90]

What, then, was the effect of sending semi-trained units on campaign? The 37th Regiment required more than one year in quiet garrison duties in order to become fit for service. The unit spent until late August 1793 at Ostend, Bruges and Menen before briefly participating in the siege of Dunkirk and then entering winter quarters at Oudenaarde. It rejoined the army for the 1794 campaign and fought as part of the line brigade at the Battle of Tourcoing on 17–18 May 1794 where it acquitted itself satisfactorily, but suffered 200 all ranks killed, wounded and missing (see Appendix II, Table II.13).

It is unfortunately not possible to trace patterns in the effectiveness of other line infantry regiments in Flanders since only the 14th, 37th and 53rd served in the theatre of operations between April 1793 and May 1794 with the exception of two months spent by the 19th, 42nd and 57th Regiments in late 1793.[91] The next units to arrive were the three regiments comprising Major General Whyte's brigade in late April and early May 1794, but they served under Austrian command until mid-June when they were sent to form the garrison of Ostend. Information regarding their training, condition or effectiveness in the field is therefore absent for the first few months of their service in Flanders, since they do not feature in general orders issued by the Duke of York's headquarters, in casualty returns or in eyewitness accounts of participants. The fact that they only reached Flanders some seven months before the campaign was effectively over means that any analysis of their performance remains problematic. What was the case for Whyte's brigade must also apply to the numerous units that joined the Duke of York's army in July 1794, most notably the 12 infantry regiments disembarking at Ostend with Lord Moira in late June (compare Appendix I, Tables I.4 and I.5).

No mention has been made so far of the effectiveness of either the cavalry or Foot Guards regiments in Flanders. The reason for this is that no material has been discovered, either from official sources or the accounts of participants, indicating deficiencies in equipment or training having an impact on their performance. The likely reason is

---

87 TNA: WO 1/170: pp.259 and 266, Mulgrave to Dundas, 26 and 28 August 1794.
88 Calvert to Dalrymple, 7 October 1794, in Verney (ed.), *Calvert*, pp.351–352.
89 TNA: WO 379/2: 'A Table of the Reliefs' and Frederick, *Lineage Book*, vol.1, pp.141, 194 and 323.
90 TNA: HO 50/385: pp.327–331, Lewis to Nepean, 20 March 1794.
91 These regiments landed at Ostend on 12 September 1793. The 19th, 57th and three companies of the 42nd joined the army two days later. They re-embarked at Ostend on 12 November. Brown, *Impartial Journal*, p.76, Calvert's diary, 16 September 1793, in Verney (ed.), *Calvert*, p.133 and Duckers (ed.), *A Diary of the Flanders Campaign*, pp.31 and 35.

Embarkation of Lord Moira's Troops at Southampton, 20 June 1794 (Preliminary Study). (Yale Center for British Art, Paul Mellon Fund, B1977.14.5718)

because all cavalry regiments had a minimum of two troops remaining at home from which to draw replacements. Much the same applied to the Foot Guards, since only the first battalions of each regiment proceeded on service, meaning that half the strength of each regiment (or two thirds in the case of the 1st Foot Guards) was at home and could fulfil a similar function. We have seen that the cavalry and Foot Guards expanded rapidly after the outbreak of war, but recruits could be adequately trained at the depots so there was little need to send them to Flanders in overwhelming numbers. This was not the case with the line infantry, almost all of which consisted of single battalion regiments sent to Flanders and other theatres in their entirety, so that training had to be undertaken on campaign as best it could. Operational factors from mid-1794, when the great majority of line infantry regiments arrived in Flanders, did not provide training opportunities given the situation of the army at that time.

Officers
A key aspect determining the success or otherwise of regiments on campaign was, as ever, the leadership and experience of the officers. Some mention should therefore be made of the status of the officer corps immediately prior to the outbreak of war before looking in more detail at some of the units that fought in Flanders. The analysis below aims to compare the

officers serving in Flanders with the wider study of the British Army's officer corps during the eighteenth century undertaken by John Houlding.[92]

By 1793 the Army contained approximately 2,900 officers. Leaving the exigencies of wartime aside, it has been estimated that some two thirds of the commissions held at any one time were purchased. Of the remainder, a number secured commissions through being sons of deserving officers or impecunious widows, or else being of good family and having served for a period of time in the ranks as a volunteer. Detailed research by John Houlding has revealed that by 1792, the average cavalry lieutenant colonel had served 21 years in the Army before attaining their present rank, or 23 years if in the infantry. Majors had served an average of 19 years in the cavalry or 24 years in the infantry, captains in both arms had served 10 years as subalterns before their promotion and lieutenants had served five years as a cornet or four years as an ensign. By 1793, cavalry lieutenant colonels had spent an average of 10.5 years at this rank, or nine years if in the infantry, cavalry majors had an average of five years in their present rank (six years in the infantry). Cavalry captains also had five years (eight in the infantry), lieutenants had 3.5 years and 5.5 years respectively and, lastly cornets had served for an average of 2.5 years compared to three years for ensigns. Houlding concluded that the officer corps was characterised by men who entered the service for life and amassed a considerable amount of experience. Long years of slow promotion, although not in itself an absolute guarantee of military merit, led most officers to be thoroughly proficient in their business.[93]

How did the regiments in Flanders compare to these statistics? It will be remembered that the brigade of the 14th, 37th and 53rd Regiments represented the only British line infantry serving there until Major General Whyte's brigade landed some 13 months later. Taking each of these units in turn, the 14th was commanded by Lieutenant Colonel Welbore Ellis Doyle from 23 March 1793 but he was appointed quartermaster-general to Lord Moira's expedition to La Vendée on 24 November.[94] Doyle had already served for four years as commanding officer, having received his rank in the regiment on 13 March 1789, though he held the same rank in the Army since 21 March 1782 when he was appointed lieutenant colonel of the 105th Regiment, subsequently disbanded. He saw extensive active service in America from 1775 until the end of the war. Doyle was supported by a trio of long-serving senior officers comprising Alexander Ross, William Browne and William Ramsay. Ross received the rank of major in the regiment on 13 March 1789 whereas the other two both received theirs in the Army on 18 November 1790 and would soon both be promoted to lieutenant colonel in the Army on 1 March 1794. Despite Ross being senior to Browne, it was the latter who commanded the 14th Regiment after the departure of Lieutenant Colonel Doyle since Ross was unwell and departed for home on 4 December but returned on 12 July 1794.[95] Browne was reported wounded and missing at Tourcoing on 17–18 May, so it was

---

92 Houlding, *Fit for Service*, pp.99–116.
93 Houlding, *Fit for Service*, pp.99–116.
94 TNA: AO 16/52: p.100, Return of General and Staff Officers entitled to Bât and Forage Money, Head Quarters Etreux 16 July 1793 and NAM: 1985-12-9: GO, Portsmouth, 24 November 1793. All promotion dates here and below are taken from the *Army List* unless otherwise specified.
95 NAM: 1976-07-45: pp.15, 17, 21: Diary of Captain Thomas Powell, 14th Foot, March 1793–March 1796.

Ramsay who commanded the 14th Regiment at the Battle of Tournai on 22 May 1794 and appears to have remained until Ross returned two months later.[96] These three men were promoted captains in the regiment as long ago as 1775, and Ross had been appointed lieutenant in the 14th on 18 September 1765; both Browne and Ramsay previously served in the 35th Regiment, being promoted to lieutenant in 1758 and 1764 respectively. The correlation between experienced officers and unit discipline was noted by the Duke of York in a letter to the King on 11 April 1794: 'I am sorry to say that the 14th regiment, from being the best disciplined regiment under my command, has now since Colonel Doyle left them become exceedingly relaxed, and frequent complaints have been brought to me against them for robberies and various other crimes.'[97]

In this case, the exigencies of war, whereby the stability of a single commanding officer was replaced by three different individuals commanding the regiment at various times, must be held responsible for the deterioration in discipline, even though the officers themselves may have been individually competent.

The 37th Regiment was in a different situation. It was commanded by Lieutenant Colonel Sir Charles Ross since 16 March 1791. Ross was first commissioned cornet in the 7th Dragoons in 1780 and had remained a cavalryman until receiving his promotion to major in the 37th Regiment on 13 June 1787. He was aged 30 in 1793, had seen no active service and, of his 13 years in the Army, less than six were in the infantry. Despite this, he was designated temporary commander of the line brigade in general orders dated 22 April 1794.[98] Ross' second in command was Major the Hon Charles Hope, who received his rank on 12 April 1793, a matter of days after the 14th Regiment landed in Flanders. Hope was another former cavalryman, having been commissioned cornet in the 3rd Dragoon Guards on 11 May 1785, and his infantry experience only commenced on 9 March 1791 when he transferred as a lieutenant to the 37th Regiment. He was subsequently to command the regiment in Flanders and, as we have already seen, was so placed when it met with disaster at Druten on 20 October 1794.[99] Of the six captains who served in Flanders in 1793, one received his commission the previous year and three more in 1793.[100] Only John Wilbar Cook, who had been a captain in the 37th since 7 March 1783, and Stafford Lightburne, who was promoted captain lieutenant in the regiment on 18 October 1787, could be described as having some experience. Lightburne faced a court martial on 31 July 1794 for alleged misbehaviour before

---

96 *London Gazette*, 13,660, 23 May 1794, p.467; TNA: AO 16/53/2: GO, Tournay, 24 May 1794 and NAM: 1976-07-45: pp.23–24, Diary of Captain Thomas Powell.
97 York to George III, 11 April 1794, in Aspinall (ed.), *Later Correspondence*, vol.2, p.194.
98 TNA: AO 16/52: pp.232–242, Abstract of Forage Money to the Generals and Staff of the British Army serving in Flanders for the Year 1793; 'LOCKHART ROSS, Sir Charles, 7th Bt. (1763–1814), of Balnagown, Ross', *History of Parliament Online*, <https://www.historyofparliamentonline.org/volume/1754-1790/member/ross-charles-1763-1814>, accessed 23 February 2021 and TNA: AO 16/53/1: GO, Cateau, 22 April 1794.
99 'HOPE, Hon. Charles (1768–1828), of Waughton, Haddington', *History of Parliament Online*, <https://www.historyofparliamentonline.org/volume/1790-1820/member/hope-hon-charles-1768-1828m>, accessed 10 March 2021.
100 Joseph Baird, captain, 37th, 20 July 1792; Robert Hedley, captain, 37th, 12 April 1793; Hugh Robert Duff, captain, 37th, 26 October 1793; William Spread, lieutenant, 37th, 8 August 1792, captain, independent company, 1 November 1793.

the enemy during the Battle of Tournai on 22 May, being placed under arrest by Major Hope following charges brought by his brother officers. He was cleared, but:

> In approving of the above sentence HRH the Commander in Chief feels himself Called upon in Justice to the discipline of His Majesty's Army, to express in strong terms his displeasure at the Conduct of Subordinate Officers proffering an accusation of this nature against their immediate Commander for which there Seems to have been so little foundation.[101]

This incident suggests that the spirit of harmony and trust between members of the officer corps was lacking at this time. Whatever the exact causes, having served in the regiment since 1775 Lightburne transferred out less than three weeks after the date of his exoneration and was promoted major in the 119th Regiment on 22 August 1794 and lieutenant colonel in the 53rd Regiment on 1 September 1795. The court martial, coupled with the collective inexperience of the commanding officer, second-in-command and company commanders may not be seen in a positive light.

The last of the line infantry units in this brigade was the 53rd Regiment. It was initially commanded by Lieutenant Colonel Richard Symes, who received his regimental commission just under one year previously on 26 April 1792 but his Army rank dated from 31 December 1782; he was recalled to England in August before receiving promotion to colonel in the Army on 12 October 1793. Symes was commissioned in the 14th Regiment on 23 June 1762, so had served in the Army for nearly 31 years by 1793. He saw active service when a company commander in the 52nd Regiment at Bunker Hill, Long Island, Harlem Heights and elsewhere. His second-in-command, and subsequently the commanding officer of the 53rd, was Robert Mathews, who received a major's commission in the regiment on 22 September 1783 before promotion to lieutenant colonel in the Army on 13 November 1793. He served as a captain with the 8th Regiment during the American War, having been commissioned ensign in that regiment on 28 February 1761. Mathews had therefore been an infantry officer for 32 years by 1793 and a field officer for over nine; he was a man of considerable experience and had seen active service. The next most senior of the company commanders was James Wiseman, who was commissioned in the 30th Regiment on 16 April 1764. On the outbreak of war his regimental commission as a captain dated from 2 August 1775 but he had to wait until 15 July 1794 before receiving a regimental commission as major in the 55th Regiment. In the meantime, he was promoted successively to major and lieutenant colonel in the Army on 18 November 1790 and 1 March 1794 respectively. Wiseman therefore had 29 years of Army service by 1793 and also experienced active service in America where the 53rd Regiment was sent late in 1775. Of the remaining company commanders serving in Flanders, three received captain's commissions between 1775 and 1778 in addition to Wiseman, one in 1788 and one was appointed captain lieutenant in 1787.[102] The junior company commander was Captain Francis Garden, who received his commission on 23 May 1792.

---

101 TNA: AO 16/53/4: Pass Order, 2 August 1794 and UNL: Pw Ja 448: Captain Lightburn's court martial, Bentinck Papers.
102 TNA: AO 16/52: pp.232–242: Abstract of Forage Money, identifies the Company commanders; WO 6/7: p.190, Dundas to Murray, 16 August 1793. The dates of promotion in the 53rd Regiment were:

Table 3 summarises the number of years that officers in each regiment had held their rank up to the outbreak of war on 1 February 1793. The individuals included in the analysis were all serving on the outbreak of war and are known to have been with their regiments in Flanders during 1793 as they received forage money for that year. Officers who also served in Flanders, but received their first commissions after the outbreak of war, have not been included. The commencement of service in each rank is taken as the earlier of the regimental appointment or the Army rank; brevet rank has been ignored for the purposes of this analysis. The number of years in each case has been rounded up to the nearest year.

Table 3: Average Number of Years Spent by Officers in their Present Commissions as at 1 February 1793

Rank	14th Regiment	37th Regiment	53rd Regiment
Lieutenant Colonel	4	2	10
Major	4	N/A	5
Captain	14	3	8
Captain Lieutenant	1	5	5
Lieutenant	6	6	8
Ensign	2	1	3
Number of Officers	18	20	24

Sources: *Army List*, various dates.

Table 3 clearly shows the relative inexperience of the 37th Regiment, especially amongst the company commanders or captains, who averaged three years in their rank compared to eight years in the 53rd and 14 years in the 14th. The same applies to the commanding officers or lieutenant colonels, where once again the 14th and 53rd had men with a greater number of years' service in their rank. This lack of experience at commanding officer level was accentuated by the 37th also having a new second-in-command, or major, shortly after the outbreak of war. David Douglas Wemys was the major on the outbreak of war, but received promotion to lieutenant colonel in the 18th Regiment on 12 April 1793 and did not serve in Flanders, hence no officer of this rank is included in the analysis for the 37th Regiment. The average number of years the subalterns held their respective ranks, on the other hand, is remarkably similar between all units.

Table 4 examines the average number of years' service the officers of each rank had in the Army between being first commissioned as cornets or ensigns and the outbreak of war. The relative lack of experience of the 37th Regiment's commanding officer and company commanders in comparison to the other two units is again marked, as it is for the lieutenants.

John Baird, 1 December 1775, Thomas Scott 8 October 1777, George Mure 25 February 1778, John Bellaers 22 August 1788. William Houghton had been appointed captain lieutenant on 24 September 1787. Promotions have been taken from *Army Lists* of various dates.

Table 4: Average Number of Years Between First Commission and 1 February 1793

Rank	14th Regiment	37th Regiment	53rd Regiment
Lieutenant Colonel	22	13	31
Major	31	N/A	28
Captain	28	13	20
Captain Lieutenant	15	17	22
Lieutenant	11	8	14
Ensign	2	4	4
Number of Officers	18	20	24

Sources: *Army List*, various dates.

This analysis of 62 officers in the line infantry brigade during 1793 indicates that the 37th had issues with inexperience and, on the basis of the Lightburne court martial, possibly poor discipline (which could also be ascribed to the officer corps' collective inexperience). Aside from a brief appearance during the siege of Dunkirk, the regiment spent 1793 in garrison, as we have seen. Although it fought well at Tourcoing on 17–18 May 1794 and again during the Battle of Tournai four days later, its performance was marred due to internal dissensions amongst the officers, leading to one of its longest-serving members seeking promotion opportunities elsewhere.

The analysis also indicates a correlation between the number of years served by the officers in each rank and in the Army on the one hand, and the discipline and effectiveness of the regiment on the other. Many of the senior officers in the 14th and 53rd Regiments had served in the Army for well over 20 years, some for over 30, and had seen active service during the American War. These findings, at least as far as the 14th and 53rd Regiments are concerned, match the previously discussed analysis carried out by John Houlding, that the officer corps primarily comprised long-service professionals. Unfortunately, no returns appear to have survived for 1794 listing the names of officers actually serving in Flanders, especially during the second half of that year when significant numbers of line infantry units reached the theatre of operations. The hazards of simply analysing the names in the *Army List* are illustrated by the aforementioned note that the 79th Regiment proceeded to Flushing with only one officer per company. The 1795 *Army List*, published on 1 January that year, lists two lieutenant colonels, seven captains, one captain lieutenant, 10 lieutenants and eight ensigns, or 28 officers compared to the 10 supposedly landed on 26 August. Any further analysis remains problematic without complete disembarkation returns, or a list of officers entitled to payment of bât and forage money, thus resolving who saw service and who did not.[103]

A second issue affecting the officer corps resulted from the sharp increase in infantry units posted to Flanders from mid-1794, as participants reported that regimental officers were called upon to command brigades without having the necessary experience, due to the scarcity of general officers. Although this could be regarded as strictly a command issue,

---

103 Fortescue, *History of the British Army*, vol.4, pp.302–303 and Anon., *A List of the Officers, 1795*, p.181.

and not a regimental one, the fact that regimental officers were involved in providing the solution is the reason for discussing the matter here.

In early August 1794, Colonel James Craig, the Duke of York's adjutant-general, alerted the War Office that the army's poor state of discipline made it necessary to send out more general officers.[104] Not enough was done to remedy the situation, and matters deteriorated even further.[105] Harry Calvert summed it up in early November: 'The want of general officers to command brigades has, in this army, been an evil of the most serious nature, and has been attended with the very worst consequences'. Writing of the period between July and September 1794 he continued: 'In this time, the command of brigades devolved on young men newly come into the service, whose years and inexperience totally disqualified them for the situation. I could mention lads of one-and-twenty who had never been on service before.'[106]

Calvert was not alone in thinking this. His fellow aide-de-camp, Major Henry Clinton, told his father of the bad consequences resulting from the too rapid expansion of the army:

> The want of discipline arises from the army's having been [for a] great part of the war without Major Gen'ls and brigades commanded by boys not 2 or 3 years in the army, and from this new method of getting rank which has been the cause of whole Reg'ts being left with not above 3 or 4 subalterns, and most of the Cap'ts entirely without experience.[107]

At a more senior level, Major General Lord Cathcart remarked in a letter home of boys '... not fit to find their way home from school...' being allowed to purchase their way to senior ranks in the Army.[108] This issue only affected the infantry, since the cavalry units in Flanders arrived during the first half of 1793 accompanied by a sufficient number of general officers to command them.[109] These formations therefore achieved a high degree of stability that lasted for the duration of the war. This was also the case with the infantry in 1793, which consisted only of two brigades – one of Foot Guards and the other of line regiments. A second line infantry brigade, commanded by Major General Alexander Stewart, joined the Duke of York during the first week of July 1794, consisting of the 12th, 38th and 55th Regiments.[110] As we have seen, these three regiments initially served under Austrian command before forming the garrison of Ostend; none were accompanied by their flank

---

104 TNA: WO 1/170: pp.139–142, Craig to Nepean, 5 August 1794.
105 BL: Add Ms 37,874: pp.105–108 and 119–120, Calvert to Windham, 20 and 30 October 1794 and to Pelham, 22 October 1794, Windham Papers vol.33.
106 Calvert to Dalrymple, 9 November 1794, in Verney (ed.), *Calvert*, pp.384–385.
107 WLCL: Henry Clinton Papers: vol.235, Henry Clinton to Sir Henry Clinton, Arnhem, 17 November 1794.
108 Atkinson, (ed.), *Cathcart MSS*, p.153.
109 TNA: WO 3/11: p.95, Adjutant-General's order. This provides the cavalry order of battle for the 11 regiments that saw service in Flanders, together with which general officers were to command each of the three brigades and their overall commander, Lieutenant General Sir William Erskine.
110 Stewart had been ordered to 'have everything in readiness to evacuate Ostend at the shortest notice' on 24 May 1794, see BL: Add Ms 40,634: p.88, Craufurd to Stewart, 23 May 1794. Stewart's brigade first appeared in general orders on 8 July 1794, see TNA: AO 16/53/4: GO, Sempf, 8 July 1794.

companies, which were in the West Indies. Finally, a third line brigade commanded by Colonel Richard Vyse joined the Duke of York a few days later, consisting of the 8th, 33rd and 44th Regiments, all of which disembarked at Ostend on 21 and 25 June, also without their flank companies. As with the 12th, 38th and 55th Regiments already mentioned, these units consisted of 10 battalion companies, all having 81 privates per company, apart from the 33rd which had 95.[111] Vyse's brigade was evacuated from Ostend by sea on 29–30 June to Antwerp where they disembarked on 11 July and from thence proceeded overland to join the army.[112]

All the line infantry with the army thus far was in brigades commanded by senior officers, but this was to change from late August 1794. The largest influx of infantry units arrived in Flanders under the command of Lord Moira, disembarking at Ostend on 27 June (See Appendix I, Table I.3). After a skilful march across the axis of the French advance, this force joined the Duke of York's army on 9 July. The 12 infantry regiments were divided into three brigades each under the command respectively of Lord Cathcart, Charles Graham and Peter Hunter, all of whom were substantive colonels holding the rank of local brigadier general. Lord Moira's force was kept as a separate entity for several days after it joined the Duke of York due to sensibilities regarding his local rank. This resulted in Moira returning to England on 20 July since his rank as local lieutenant general on the continent of Europe was dated 26 November 1793 effectively leap-frogging him over the heads of seven more senior officers already serving in Flanders: Ralph Abercromby, David and Ralph Dundas, Alexander Stewart, Samuel Hulse, Robert Laurie and Nesbit Balfour.[113] His three brigadiers remained with the army until mid-August before departing for home, leaving their brigades with no general officer in command.[114] General orders of 29 August 1794 stated, 'In all cases during the absence of a Major General, or where none is appointed to a Brigade, the senior officer commands it'.[115] An analysis of unit commanding officers may therefore reveal who the brigade commanders actually were between 29 August and the next reorganisation on 13 November and whether they included 'boys not 2 or 3 years in the army'.[116]

As a preliminary to this analysis, it would be helpful to provide the line infantry brigade structure as specified in the general order of 29 August:

---

111 TNA: WO 24/585: pp.12 and 14–15.
112 TNA: WO 1/169: pp.657–659, Vyse to Dundas, 29 June 1794; WO 1/170: p.467, Vyse to Dundas, 2 July 1794; Anon., *Officer of the Guards*, vol.2, p.65 and NAM: 1976-07-45: p.29, Diary of Captain Thomas Powell. This brigade first appeared in general orders of 12 July 1794, see AO 16/53/4: GO, Head Quarters, 12 July 1794.
113 Graham, *Memoir of General Graham*, pp.141–142; *London Gazette*, 13,596, 23–26 November 1793, p.1052.
114 Brigadier Generals Lord Cathcart, Charles Graham and Peter Hunter were last mentioned by name in the general orders of 12 August 1793 after which the line infantry brigades were simply referred to by their numbers. TNA: AO 16/53/5: GO, Oosterhoot, 12 August 1794. Harry Calvert stated 'From the time Lord Cathcart left us – which, if I recollect right, was about the 23rd of July'. Calvert to Dalrymple, 9 November 1794, in Verney (ed.), *Calvert*, pp.384–385. Lord Cathcart returned to Flanders in mid-November 1794, see Atkinson, (ed.), *Cathcart MSS*, p.147.
115 TNA: AO 16/53/5: GO, Helvoet, 29 August 1794.
116 WLCL: Henry Clinton Papers: vol.235, Henry Clinton to Sir Henry Clinton, Arnhem, 17 November 1794.

1st Brigade
3rd, 40th, 55th, 59th and 89th Regiments

2nd Brigade
8th, 27th, 28th and 57th Regiments

3rd Brigade
12th, 33rd, 42nd and 44th Regiments

4th Brigade
14th, 37th, 38th and 63rd Regiments

5th Brigade
19th, 53rd, 54th and 88th Regiments[117]

The Brigade of Guards is omitted from this analysis, as is the 6th Brigade, which was formed by general order on 13 November 1794. According to Corporal Robert Brown, though not mentioned in the general order of 29 August, the 1st Brigade was commanded by Major General Stewart and the 4th Brigade by Major General Fox. This coincides with a general order issued on 13 November 1794, so it is reasonable to assume that these officers also commanded their brigades prior to this date.[118]

Commencing in numerical sequence with the 1st Brigade, many of the commanding officers were relatively new in post. These included Lieutenant Colonels John, Lord Newark, of the 3rd Regiment, who received his regimental rank on 20 November 1793, Charles Handfield of the 89th, whose regimental commission dated from 8 December 1793 and Donald McDonald of the 55th whose commission dated from six days later ('a most excellent officer' according to Harry Calvert)[119] but who had first entered the Army as an ensign in the 60th Regiment on 14 February 1760. George Don of the 59th had been promoted lieutenant colonel in his regiment on 9 April 1789 but he was soon to be appointed deputy adjutant-general on 21 November 1794. Stephen Bromfield of the 40th Regiment had regimental rank dating from 12 October 1787 and a colonel in the Army from 1 March 1794. At the opposite extreme was Lieutenant Colonel William, Lord Craven, who assumed command of the 3rd Regiment on 25 September 1794 following the retirement of Lord Newark. He had been commissioned ensign in the 45th Regiment only the previous year and after promotion through the 80th was on 7 March 1794 a lieutenant colonel in the 84th before transferring to the 3rd six months later. Lord Craven was born on 1 September 1770, so aged just 24 at this time.[120] Given these details, Lord Craven must

---

117 TNA: AO 16/53/5: GO, Helvoet, 29 August 1794.
118 TNA: AO 16/53/6: GO, Arnhem, 13 November 1794 and Brown, *Impartial Journal*, p.191. Major-General Alexander Stewart had previously commanded the Ostend garrison and Major General Henry Fox doubled as the quartermaster-general.
119 Calvert to Dalrymple, 7 November 1794, in Verney (ed.), *Calvert*, p.380.
120 'General William Craven, 1st Earl of Craven', <https://www.thepeerage.com/p2053.htm#i20527>, accessed 24 February 2021.

surely be one of those officers referred to so disapprovingly by Harry Calvert and Henry Clinton in their letters home in November, though it is highly unlikely that he actually commanded the 1st Brigade.[121] As an aside, it is worth noting that every officer of the 3rd Regiment in the 1795 *Army List* had received a regimental commission since October 1790, with one exception.[122] The brigade commander, Major General Alexander Stewart, was not a well man and proceeded home where he died on 16 December 1794.[123] Although there is no specific evidence for this, it is possible that one of the regimental commanders did assume temporary command of the 1st Brigade at some point between August and late November 1794, when Major General James Coates arrived to assume command.[124] Given his relative seniority, the most likely candidate as a temporary brigade commander was Colonel Stephen Bromfield of the 40th Regiment, though his presence in Flanders is unconfirmed.

The 2nd Brigade, unlike the 1st, had no general officer until Major General the Hon John Thomas De Burgh arrived on 20 September according to the journal of Lieutenant and Captain John Atherley of the Coldstream Guards.[125] This left approximately two to four weeks when the brigade was commanded by one of the regimental commanding officers. Similar to the 3rd Regiment, no officer of the 8th listed in the 1795 *Army List*, had received his commission prior to February 1790. Lieutenant Colonel Gordon Drummond had a regimental commission dating from 22 April 1794 and had not accumulated much experience, having been commissioned ensign in the 1st Regiment as recently as 21 September 1789. He had not quite reached his 22nd birthday when he landed in Flanders and had less than five years' service in the Army.[126] The 27th Regiment was in hardly a better position, since Lieutenant Colonel John Thomas Buller received his regimental commission on 20 November 1793 having been first commissioned as a cornet in the 1st Dragoons on 3 June 1783. He had been in command for only nine months when the regiment landed at Ostend, and in the Army for 11 years. Another youthful lieutenant colonel was the Hon Edward Paget, who received his regimental commission in the 28th Regiment on 30 April 1794 having first entered the Army as a cornet in the 1st Life Guards as recently as March 1792. Paget was born on 3 November 1775, so aged only 19 at this time and therefore

---

121 Calvert to Dalrymple, 9 November 1794, in Verney (ed.), *Calvert*, pp.384–385 and WLCL: Henry Clinton Papers: vol.235, Henry Clinton to Sir Henry Clinton, Arnhem, 17 November 1794.
122 The exception was Captain Charles McMurdo, whose regimental commission dated from 9 December 1780, though he had received promotion to major in the Army on 1 March 1794. Anon., *A List of the Officers, 1795*, p.101.
123 'STEWART, Alexander I (c.1739–94), of Afton, Ayr and Cairne, Wigtown', *History of Parliament Online*, <https://www.historyofparliamentonline.org/volume/1754-1790/member/stewart-alexander-1739-94>, accessed 25 February 2021.
124 NAM: 1997–10–31: Manuscript journal of Captain John Carter Atherley, Coldstream Guards. Atherly's entry for 30 November 1794 mentioned: … 'MGen'ls Coates, Gordon & L'd Cathcart arrived a few Days ago'; The first official mention of Coates in command of the 1st Brigade is in TNA: WO 1/171: pp.579–582: Cantonments of the Army under the Command of His Roy'l High's the Duke of York: 19th Dec'r 1794.
125 NAM: 1997–10–31: Manuscript journal of Captain John Carter Atherley.
126 H.M. Stephens, 'Drummond, Sir Gordon (1772–1854)', *ODNB*, <https://doi.org/10.1093/ref:odnb/8066>, accessed 26 February 2021.

another prime candidate for the irritation expressed by Calvert and Clinton.[127] Finally, the 57th Regiment was commanded by Lieutenant Colonel Hay Macdowall since 6 April 1791. He was by a significant margin the most experienced commanding officer in the brigade, having served in the Army for over 18 years. It is probable that Macdowell served as the interim commander of the 2nd Brigade in August and September 1794, which was probably just as well given the lack of experience evident amongst the other three senior officers.

Two of the regiments in the 3rd Brigade, the 33rd and 44th, were based in Antwerp in July with the 8th Regiment, the whole under the command of Major General Nisbet Balfour.[128] Antwerp was evacuated at the end of the month, so it is assumed that Balfour continued in command of these units, but this is not certain. Captain Atherley remarked that Balfour assumed command of the 3rd Brigade on 20 September.[129]

The senior unit in the brigade was the 12th Regiment, whose lieutenant colonel, Thomas Trigge, was promoted major general on 12 October 1793, so did not serve with the regiment. The commanding officer was Lieutenant Colonel Frederick Bowes, whose regimental commission dated to 1 March 1794.[130] He had served for nearly 30 years in the 64th Regiment, having been commissioned ensign on 11 November 1761, and had seen extensive service in North America where the regiment had been posted in 1768. Bowes transferred to the 1/82nd Regiment as lieutenant colonel with regimental rank of 22 October 1794 and was succeeded in the 12th Regiment by Henry Harvey Aston on the same date.[131] Both of the two senior brigades contained a youthful commanding officer, and the 3rd Brigade was no exception. In this case it was Lieutenant Colonel the Hon Arthur Wesley of the 33rd, the future Duke of Wellington. Wesley was first commissioned in the 73rd Regiment on 7 March 1787 and, following the swift promotion possible for the scions of families possessing money or influence, he had secured a lieutenant colonel's commission dated 30 September 1793. He therefore had just over seven years Army service and was aged 25 when he landed in Flanders.[132] The 42nd Regiment was commanded during the campaign by Major George Dalrymple whose commission dated from 16 March 1791, since the lieutenant colonel, Charles Graham, was a colonel in the Army and serving as a brigadier general under Lord Moira. Dalrymple was promoted captain on 25 August 1778, and saw considerable service with the 42nd during the American War as a company commander. The most junior unit in the 3rd Brigade was the 44th Regiment commanded by Lieutenant Colonel Robert Riddell, who received his regimental commission on 26 November 1793. Riddell had served in the Army, both in cavalry and infantry regiments, since first being commissioned cornet in the 9th Dragoons on 16 December 1775. Despite his 18 years Army service prior to arriving in Flanders, he had only been promoted to major in the 18th Light Dragoons on 31 March

---

127 Anglesey, Marquis of, (ed.), 'Two brothers in the Netherlands, 1794–95', *Journal of the Society for Army Historical Research*, vol.34, 1956, p.75 and C.A. Harris, 'Paget, Sir Edward (1775–1849)', *ODNB*, <https://doi.org/10.1093/ref:odnb/21106>, accessed 26 February 2021.
128 Harrington (ed.), *With the Guards in Flanders*, p.89 and H.M. Stephens, 'Balfour, Nisbet (1743–1823)', *ODNB*, <https://doi.org/10.1093/ref:odnb/1193>, accessed 26 February 2021.
129 NAM: 1997-10-31: Manuscript journal of Captain John Carter Atherley.
130 TNA: WO 25/42: p.363, Commission Book, 1793–1794.
131 TNA: WO 25/42: pp.393 and 396, Commission Book, 1793–1794.
132 For Wesley's service in 1794–1795, see: R.N.W. Thomas, 'Wellington in the Low Countries 1794–1795'. In *The International History Review*, vol.11, 1989, pp.14–30.

1793, so the greater part of his leadership experience had been as a company commander in the 32nd Regiment between 1780 and 1792 and then as a troop commander in the 12th Light Dragoons in 1792–1793. There is no evidence that Major General Balfour was absent for any reason but, had this been the case, the senior lieutenant colonel in the 3rd Brigade was Arthur Wesley of the 33rd Regiment.

The 4th Brigade contained the 14th and 37th Regiments, which have already been discussed above, and it will be remembered that they were commanded by Lieutenant Colonels Alexander Ross (from 12 July 1794) and Charles Hope respectively. The 38th Regiment was commanded by Lieutenant Colonel Thomas Pitcairn, whose commission dated from 14 December 1793. He received a lieutenant's commission in the 14th Regiment on 13 January 1776 but two years later was promoted to captain in the newly raised 82nd, the same unit in which James Henry Craig, the adjutant-general in Flanders in 1794–1795, was serving as a major. Pitcairn had already commanded a brigade consisting of the 8th Light Dragoons, his own unit and the 55th Regiment at Ghitz on 13 June when they had been under Austrian command.[133] The final unit in the 4th Brigade was the 63rd Regiment, which had two lieutenant colonels. Stephens Howe received his commission on 31 July 1789 whereas his more junior colleague, the Hon John Leveson Gower, was promoted lieutenant colonel on 2 July 1794. No evidence has been found to suggest that Howe served in Flanders, whereas the 20-year-old Leveson Gower was definitely there in January 1795 so it is assumed that he was also commanding the regiment during the second half of 1794.[134] As we have seen, Major General Henry Fox was appointed quartermaster-general on 26 September 1793 though was also the designated general officer commanding the 4th Brigade at this time. There must have been occasions when Fox was occupied by his staff duties and the command of the brigade devolved upon one of the battalion commanders. The most senior of these by date of commission was Lieutenant Colonel Thomas Pitcairn of the 38th Regiment, who could by no means be described as either youthful or inexperienced.

The 5th Brigade was another with no designated general officer to command it, though the 13 November reorganisation took place at about the same time as Lord Cathcart returned to the army, having been appointed major general on 3 October 1794. It is assumed that this brigade was therefore commanded by one of the lieutenant colonels from late August for a period of about 10 weeks. The senior unit in the 5th Brigade was the 19th Regiment. Its lieutenant colonel was James Coates, whose commission dated from 26 October 1775, but he was promoted major general on 28 April 1790 so did not serve in a regimental capacity in Flanders. The next senior officer was Major William Houston, whose commission dated from 30 May 1794. He was first commissioned ensign in the 31st Regiment on 31 July 1781,

---

133 BL: Add Ms 46,710: p.116, Return of Officers, Non Commissioned Officers & Privates Killed, Wounded & Missing in the 8th Regt Light Dragoons & Brigade of Infantry under the Command of Lt Colonel Pitcairn in the Army under Major General Hammerstein at Ghitz on the 13th June 1794. Don Papers, vol.9.

134 BL: Add Ms 46,703: p.14, Leveson Gower to Harcourt, 11 January 1795. Don Papers, vol.2. The following erroneously states that Leveson Gower was serving in the West Indies between 1793–1796: 'LEVESON GOWER, John (1774–1816), of Bill Hill, nr. Wokingham, Berks', *History of Parliament Online*, <https://www.historyofparliamentonline.org/volume/1790-1820/member/leveson-gower-john-1774-1816>, accessed 25 February 2021.

so had 13 years Army service by the time he landed in Flanders and was aged 28.[135] The 53rd Regiment has already been discussed above and was commanded by Major Robert Mathews, who received his commission on 22 September 1783. The commander of the 54th Regiment was Lieutenant Colonel William Goodday Strutt, whose regimental commission dated from 4 April 1792, and who was first commissioned ensign in the 61st Regiment on 23 May 1778; he was aged about 32 in 1794.[136] The junior unit in the brigade was the 88th Regiment, which had two lieutenant colonels. The senior was Robert Brownrigg who served in Flanders as deputy quartermaster-general from November 1793, so the regiment was commanded by Lieutenant Colonel Frederick Keppel, who received his commission on 28 March 1794. He was commissioned ensign in the 1/1st Regiment on 30 May 1780, so had 14 years experience in the Army by the time he arrived in Flanders. The senior regimental officer serving in the 5th Brigade was Lieutenant Colonel William Strutt, so it is assumed that he commanded the formation from the end of August 1794 until the next reorganisation of the line infantry in mid-November.

The following table provides a snapshot of the average number of years Army service the line infantry commanding officers had as at the brigade reorganisation of 29 August 1793, together with the number of years they had in their current rank. The analysis aims to capture the situation in Flanders between the 29 August and 13 November reorganisations. The sample size of 23 individuals is two higher than the number of units because both the 3rd and 12th Regiments had two commanding officers in this period.

Table 5: Line Infantry Commanding Officers' Army Service as at 29 August 1794

Formation	Years in Commission	Years in Army
1st Brigade	4	26
2nd Brigade	1	10
3rd Brigade	1	19
4th Brigade	0	16
5th Brigade	3	19
Average Number of Years	2	18
Number of Officers	23	23

Sources: *Army List*, various dates.

Table 5 shows the majority of commanding officers were of very recent appointment. Indeed, 10 of the 23 were promoted in 1794 and a further six were promoted to command their units in 1793. To these may be added a further three (Majors William Houston of the 19th, George Dalrymple of the 42nd and Robert Mathews of the 53rd) who became *de facto* commanding officers due to the absence of their seniors. This left four officers who had held their appointments for more than one year, of which one (Lieutenant Colonel Lord Newark,

---

135 H.M. Chichester, 'Houston, Sir William, first baronet (1766–1842)', *ODNB*, <https://doi.org/10.1093/ref:odnb/13877>, accessed 26 February 2020.
136 M. Christy, 'Strutt, William Goodday (bap. 1762, d. 1848)', *ODNB*, <https://doi.org/10.1093/ref:odnb/26688>, accessed 26 February 2020.

of the 3rd Regiment) retired during the period under examination. The experience of unit command amongst this group was therefore low.

Table 5 also shows that the cohort had served an average of 18 years in the Army since first commissioning, but this figure must be taken with caution as it hides a very wide variation between individuals. Seven officers had between 30 and 39 years Army service and a further four had between 20 and 29 years; these 11 men could therefore be regarded as having accumulated a high or very high level of experience. Of the remaining 10 officers, six men had served in the Army for less than 10 years, with the extremes being Lieutenant Colonels Lord Craven of the 3rd Regiment, the Hon Edward Paget of the 28th and the Hon John Leveson Gower of the 63rd who had been first commissioned in 1793, 1792 and 1791 respectively. The remaining commanding officers had between 10 and 19 years Army service.

Rank alone had placed a high proportion of inexperienced men in command of units, and indeed of formations, during a major war, and this did not bode well for the discipline and fighting performance of the Duke of York's army. This, together with the absence of a sufficient number of general officers during a critical phase of the 1794 campaign, goes far to explain the tactical reverses and disciplinary failings that characterised the second half of that year.

Women and Servants

Women

The attitude of the Army towards women was equivocal. On the one hand, regimental officers regarded them as a nuisance, a threat to discipline and an encumbrance on active service but, on the other, they fulfilled many useful functions that were integral to the interior economy of the regiment. The participation of women in the medical context was discussed in Chapter 4, but further detail of their role is required to obtain a more complete picture of the regiment on campaign.

The greatest concern the Army had was of soldiers marrying women who were considered unsuitable in some way. This was primarily due to the already low pay soldiers received after various stoppages were deducted, meaning that unless a wife worked hard and was prepared to earn enough to pay for food and other necessaries, their husbands might be reduced to relying on charity or tempted to sell parts of their equipment to compensate. The second fear was that women of loose morals might compromise the health of the men. For this reason, Major General Edward Braddock ordered all women accompanying the troops on their march to the Monongahela river in 1755 to submit to a medical examination, this also occurred during the siege of Gibraltar in 1779–1783. A further concern was the perception that they engaged in the sale of alcohol to the men, a major underlying threat to good discipline. This trade could have been performed by men as well as women, or by sutlers who were not soldiers' wives, but the latter tended to be blamed.[137] The wives and children

---

137 B. Cuthbertson, *Cuthbertson's System for the Complete Interior Management of a Battalion of Infantry. A new edition, with corrections* (Bristol: Rouths and Nelson, 1776), pp.156–158; Brumwell, *Redcoats*, p.122; Kopperman, 'The British High Command', pp.17–18 and Steppler, *The Common Soldier in the Reign of George III*, pp.105–108.

of soldiers accompanying their menfolk on campaign also represented a public liability, as the cost of their accommodation and subsistence, however small, had to be accounted for.

In theory at least, the ability to control unsuitable marriages lay with company commanders, whose approval had to be sought. This regulation was instituted in 1685, providing for strong penalties to be taken against men who transgressed while discouraging officers from granting permission except in exceptional circumstances.[138] For this reason, ministers of religion were warned not to marry soldiers without first having obtained a certificate that the union had received official sanction. The number of women accompanying the army on various overseas campaigns during the eighteenth century suggests the official position was not rigidly adhered to, probably because units could not function without them. Food had to be cooked, uniforms needed washing and mending, and the sick had to be cared for in the regimental hospital – all of these were important roles that would otherwise have meant either taking men from the ranks or else hiring labour at a cost to regimental funds.[139] Consequently, there existed a form of social contract by which women offered their labour and in return were paid and received a ration even though they were not officially held on the strength of the regiment. Attempts to over-charge for the jobs they were doing or to withdraw their labour disturbed the equilibrium and invited official sanction, such as the cancellation of rations, being ordered to leave the army or no longer having a free passage back to England.[140]

The surgeon Dr. Robert Hamilton was greatly in favour of having women attached to regiments for another reason. He favoured promoting 'marriage with modest women' since male children commonly joined the ranks and became the best soldiers. He was keen to suggest that regimental surgeons should equip themselves with reference books dealing with female medical issues, such as childbirth.[141] Having served with the 10th Regiment between 1780–1785, Hamilton was clearly familiar with the various issues affecting women in a regimental context. Foremost among these was poverty, which frequently prevented women from seeking medical aid when they were sick. His solution was to establish a fund of £30 through contributions from the officers and those of the rank-and-file with paid employment outside the regiment, together with fines levied for drunkenness or syphilis; he calculated this would be sufficient to provide for 20 families over two weeks.[142]

It was common practice during the eighteenth and early nineteenth centuries for a designated number of women to accompany regiments when they were posted overseas.

---

138 J. Hurl-Eamon, *Marriage and the British Army in the Long Eighteenth Century* (Oxford: Oxford University Press, 2014), pp.8, 28, 32–33.
139 P.E. Kopperman, 'The British High Command and Soldiers' Wives in America, 1755–1783,' *Journal of the Society for Army Historical Research*, vol.60, 1982, p.15 and D.N. Hagist, 'The Women of the British Army in America', RevWar'75, <http://www.revwar75.com/library/hagist/britwomen.htm#46>, accessed 1 September 2021.
140 Fatherly, 'Tending the Army', pp.575, 584 and 589; Hurl-Eamon, *Marriage and the British Army*, pp.193–195 and Brumwell, *Redcoats*, p.125.
141 Hamilton, *Regimental Surgeon*, vol.1, pp.63 and 294–295. See also: Hurl-Eamon, *Marriage and the British Army*, pp.64–69.
142 R. Hamilton, *Thoughts Submitted to the Consideration of the Officers in the Army, Respecting the Establishment of a Regimental Fund, for the Relief of the Sick and Necessitous Wives of the Private Soldiers* (London: S. Simmons, 1783), pp.6, 9–10, 24–36.

However, the total number of married men in the regiment could be considerably greater, meaning that many women were forced to remain at home after parting with their husbands for an indefinite period. The philanthropist Jonas Hanway stated that about one man in six was married, which would add up to eight or nine women accompanying a cavalry troop of 50 men, or 11 per infantry company of 60 men, including non-commissioned officers.[143] The unofficial scale approximated to six women per troop or company allowed to follow their husbands overseas, all of whom must be married to soldiers of the regiment and receive official sanction to do so. This scale agrees fairly closely with the 50–60 women accompanying selected infantry regiments in the New York area in 1779–1780, but was subject to change according to the exigencies of the service. Corporal William Todd of the 30th Regiment stated that general orders required all women and sick to remain in camp when the unit embarked for the Rochefort expedition in August 1757, with 'Only two Women per Company to be Allow'd on Board to wash for the Men, & to have provisions the same as the Men'.[144]

Shipping capacity for 248 men was ordered for each of 10 cavalry regiments embarking for Flanders in April 1793, so one might expect just over 40 men to have been married, yet only 25 women were authorised to embark. The 1st Dragoon Guards were permitted 38 women to accompany them on the basis that the regiment had six troops instead of four. Unfortunately, few embarkation returns survive for cavalry units and, of those, some make no mention of women and children. Returns with this information are extant for the 5th and 6th Dragoon Guards and the 1st and 6th Dragoons, which show that 56 women accompanied each of the first two regiments, while 19 and 17 respectively accompanied the second two. One explanation is that both Dragoon Guards units came from the Irish establishment where different regulations could have applied.[145]

Using the embarkation return for the Guards Brigade dated 22 February 1793 as an example, the 1st Foot Guards had 734 non-commissioned officers and men, which would suggest that if Hanway's estimate is correct, approximately 120 men were married. However, only 60 women actually accompanied the regiment to Flanders, indicating that about half the wives had to remain at home. Both the Coldstream and 3rd Foot Guards landed in Flanders with 659 non-commissioned officers and men each, and the number of women permitted to accompany them was 54 per regiment, making 168 for the brigade as a whole.[146]

Embarkation returns survive for all the line infantry units serving in Flanders, but the one for the 14th Regiment makes no mention of women and children. Given that regiments proceeded to Flanders at different times from March 1793 onwards, not all of the women would have been present at the same time, though it is assumed that those returning home for whatever reason would have been replaced by arrivals accompanying reinforcements.

---

143 J. Hanway, *The Soldier's Faithful Friend: Being Moral and Religious Advice to Soldiers* (London: Dodley and Sewel and Brew, 1776), p.47.
144 Hagist, 'The Women of the British Army' and A. Cormack and A. Jones (eds), *The Journal of Corporal William Todd 1745–1762* (Stroud: Sutton Publishing Limited, 2001), p.20.
145 TNA: HO 50/384: Yonge to Dundas, 25 March and 5 April 1793 and WO 25/1146: Embarkation Returns.
146 BL: Add Ms 34,447: p.284, Enclosure in Grenville to Auckland, 22 February 1793. Auckland Papers vol.36; TNA: HO 50/385: pp.293–297, Lewis to Nepean, 15 March 1794.

The number of women with each regiment varied from 47 with the 54th to 111 with the 63rd, but the most common number was 60, which was the total accompanying eight units. If it is assumed that 60 women accompanied the 14th Regiment, the total with the line infantry would have reached 1,442 by the end of 1794. Women were almost always accompanied by children, and 742 were listed with the line infantry, though the embarkation returns for the 14th, 87th and 88th Regiments provide no data so this must be regarded as a minimum number. The 44th had the fewest with 15 while the 63rd Regiment had 95. A breakdown of women and children by regiment is shown in Appendix I, Table I.3 for the units comprising Lord Moira's force.[147]

Putting the above figures together, and assuming that 25 women accompanied all of the cavalry regiments apart from the 1st Dragoon Guards with 38, the 5th and 6th Dragoon Guards with 56 each, the 1st Dragoons with 19 and the 6th Dragoons with 17, this would mean that 436 women accompanied the cavalry by the end of 1793. We have already noted that 168 women were authorised to embark with the Guards Brigade, and 174 with the line brigade, assuming 60 to have been with the 14th Regiment. This provides a total for the army of 778 women in 1793 not including those embarked with ordnance troops. By the end of 1794, the army in Flanders had expanded to 15 cavalry and 27 infantry units. Using known data for the infantry and the above assumptions for the cavalry, over 2,100 women must have accompanied the army at this stage in the campaign, which does not include women attached to the Royal Artillery and Royal Military Artificers. The embarkation returns for line regiments suggest that children numbered approximately 50 percent of the number of women, though the returns for three regiments make no mention of children, so this figure must be regarded as a minimum. By the end of 1794 it would be reasonable to assume that about 1,000 children also accompanied the army.

In addition to the officially married spouses of sergeants and the rank-and-file, there were likely to have been an indeterminate number of unofficial marriages or casual relationships that could have raised the proportion of women left at home considerably, though the numbers are not possible to quantify, at least through military records.[148] Some officers may also have been accompanied by their wives, but only one instance of this has been found in Flanders. In these cases, women would have been paid for and subsisted by their husbands, rather than the state, and therefore left no official trace.

What, then, was the experience of women once they reached Flanders? Aside from their role working as nurses in the hospitals, the records make little mention of them during the 1793 campaign, which suggests that matters proceeded relatively smoothly. This was not the case in 1794, however, when numbers of women seriously impeded the troops' withdrawal following the defeat at Tourcoing on 18 May. The resulting general order is worth quoting in full as it clearly lays out exactly what the problems were and how they would be managed,

> It is HRH the Commander in Chief's order, that whenever the Troops or any particular Corps march without their Camp equipage, no woman is under any pretence whatever to be permitted to accompany or follow the Column. HRH

---

147 TNA: HO 50/384: Yonge to Dundas, 7 March 1793 and WO 25/1146: Embarkation Returns.
148 Hurl-Eamon, *Marriage and the British Army*, pp.42–43.

desires this may be considered as a standing order, and expects that Commanding officers of Reg'ts will take care that it is most strictly complied with. It is necessary at the same time to warn the women & followers of the army, that the Provost Martial is hereby directed to inflict on every offender the most exemplary Punishment, and if the offence deserves it, even to execute on the spot any woman, or follower of the army of any description whatever who by cruelty or plundering and marauding may bring disgrace on the Troops under HRH command.

This order to be read at this Evening's Roll Call, at the head of every Troop & Company throughout the army, on which occasion all the women & followers of the army are to be ordered to attend, that none may plead ignorance of the awfull punishment, to which they will subject themselves to this crime, & HRH relies with confidence, on the assistance of every officer, to prevent the glory so justly acquired by this army in the field, being sullied by acts of inhumanity & depredation.[149]

The prospect of the punishments mentioned in this general order should have induced the women to conduct themselves with greater discretion, but unfortunately this was not so. The Duke of York observed women accompanying the troops on the march between Pottes and Tournai on 19 June in direct contradiction to the general order of 23 May. The sanction announced on this occasion was that any woman found to have disobeyed orders again would have her bread ration immediately withdrawn.[150]

As their conduct during the retreat from Tourcoing suggests, the principal complaint against women was their propensity for plundering. In their defence, this must partly have arisen because the army provided them with only one half of a ration (without rum), and children with one quarter.[151] As we already discussed in connection with the duties of the judge advocate (Chapter 2), women were in trouble soon after the army landed in Flanders in 1793 when Rose Archer and Sarah Cotton, attached to the Guards Flank Battalion, were found guilty of theft but pardoned following strong representations from the inhabitants of Pittem; their punishment was that they were removed from the army.[152] A similar punishment was directed against women guilty of improper conduct in the hospitals, who were threatened with removal and losing their free passage home, but how rigorously these punishments were enforced may be open to question.[153] Herbert Taylor's personal view was:

> But nothing could be worse than the women who followed the English and Irish regiments. There was little regulation as to number; they were seldom under contract, and would often remain behind to plunder houses and villages after the march of the troops whose depredations they had escaped … Some of them would also prowl about the field of a recent action, and would not spare the wounded – friend or foe – in their search for plunder.[154]

---

149 TNA: AO 16/53/2: GO, Tournay, 23 May 1794.
150 TNA: AO 16/53/3: GO, Head Quarters, 20 June 1794.
151 NAM: 1985-12-15-9: GO, Head Quarters, 1 March 1794.
152 NAM: 1985-12-15-4: GO, Courtrai, 21 April 1793.
153 NAM: 1985-12-15-4: GO, Estreux, 16 July 1793 and Kopperman, 'British High Command', p.25.
154 Taylor (ed.), *The Taylor Papers*, p.30.

Despite this, the army appears to have taken reasonable care of the women accompanying it. In February 1794, regiments were asked to submit returns to the quartermaster-general of their women and children so that issues of clothes donated from the general public in England could be issued to them.[155] Similarly, returns of women whose husbands had been killed or taken prisoner, and who wished to return home, were requested in May, August and October 1794 so that transportation could be provided.[156] At the beginning of 1794, blankets were made available on application to regiments 'for the use of the Lying in and sick soldiers Wives'.[157]

One aspect of the female experience on campaign concerned their involvement in actual fighting. Although women serving in action must be considered as a rarity, they did occasionally become casualties from enemy action either from accompanying troops encountering the enemy unexpectedly or from venturing too close to the front line.[158] This occurred during the fighting withdrawal from Tourcoing on 18 May 1794, as related by Corporal Robert Brown of the Coldstream Guards: 'The women also, who inadvertently had been permitted to follow us, caused no small disorder; some were killed, others wounded, and some loaded with plunder, so as to be unable to keep up with the men.'[159]

That women had been allowed to accompany the troops on this day was also witnessed by the 16-year-old Cornet Robert Wilson of the 15th Light Dragoons. Whilst attempting to form a rear-guard during the withdrawal from Roubaix he came across 'pretty Sally, the pride of the British fair' who offered him 'one of her best kisses for my exertions'. Sally was attached to the 14th Regiment and first came to Wilson's attention when she 'arrested the career of the Court and Staff, and fixed their gaze for several minutes' during the review of the allied army at Le Cateau-Cambrésis on 16 April 1794.[160] Wilson's memoirs were written many years later and the doubtful tone of his remarks may reflect attitudes at that time, since there were no accounts of Sally by other participants.

There was also one reported case of a woman serving in action with a British cavalry regiment as witnessed by an unknown individual accompanying Lord Moira's force:

> Here I ought not to omit mentioning the courageous and intrepid conduct of a female, who was wife to one of our dragoons; she singly mounted, and on going to meet the enemy, rode alongside of her husband with her drawn sabre, and with the greatest glee singing 'Ah non, non, non, pauvre Madelon, will never quit her lover.'
>
> This intrepid girl was very handsome, and was in several engagements with her husband during the course of the campaign; in all of which she acquitted herself with great gallantry; she was dressed in a kind of blue uniform habit, nearly

---

155 NAM: 1985-12-15-5: GO, Ghent, 12 and 17 February 1794.
156 TNA: AO 16/53/2: GO, Tournay, 27 May 1794; AO 16/53/5: GO, Oosterhout, 10 and 18 August 1794 and AO 16/53/6: GO, Arnheim, 23 October 1794.
157 NAM: 1985-12-15-5: GO, Ghent, 13 January 1794.
158 Brumwell, *Redcoats*, p.124.
159 Brown, *Impartial Journal*, pp.144-145.
160 H. Randolph (ed.), *Life of General Sir Robert Wilson* (London: John Murray, 1862), vol.1, pp.61 and 91.

resembling the dress of the light dragoons, and wore also a hat full of black beaver feathers, which at a distance had the appearance of a helmet.[161]

Which regiment she was with is unknown, but on the assumption that her jacket was an imitation of a light cavalry uniform, it could have been one of the six light dragoon regiments that were serving with the army by the second half of 1794. Her name suggests that she was French, quite possibly an émigré, which perhaps explained her undoubted zeal in action.

The only attested case of an officer's wife accompanying her husband was Mrs Mary Harcourt, the wife of Lieutenant General the Hon William Harcourt, who embarked at Deal on 15 October 1793 for Ostend and endured the full rigours of the retreat in January 1795. Her experience would have been far from ordinary, as she took her own carriage and horses from England and on arrival was provided with an escort of two troopers from the 16th Light Dragoons.[162] Her considerable relief on reaching Brussels also revealed her motivation for joining her husband:

> I cannot describe the joy I feel to be again so near him; anxious I must be, but here I have opportunities of having my anxiety relieved, and I would not take millions to be again in England. I shudder when I look back to the misery I used to feel; listening to every creaking door that opened; expecting letters, and afraid to read them when they came; fancying my own shadow that of some one come to tell me bad news; and, if good arrived, knowing that time enough had elapsed since its date to have it followed by bad. Thank God, I know now that he is safe and well.[163]

Mary Harcourt joined her husband at Tournai on 15 October, writing early the following month that: 'It is very odd that I am the only *wife* here; there are, I believe, two or three ladies of another description'.[164]

Official records regarding women are sparse, even though wives accompanying other ranks overseas were subsisted by the army. Their presence is scarcely mentioned except in cases when their behaviour elicited official disapproval, which thus provides an unbalanced view of their relationship with the army. The records which do mention women are not always reliable as regards their numbers, or in differentiating between women and children.[165] Part of this can be explained by the status of soldiers' wives. They were neither on the strength of the regiment as they received no regular pay, nor were they civilians, since they received a ration, accommodation and remained subject to military law. In other words, they were *of* the army, but not *in* it.

---

161 Anon., *A Journal Kept in the British Army, from the Landing of the Troops Under the Command of Earl Moira, at Ostend, in June 1794, to their Return to England the Following Year* (Liverpool: privately published, 1796), pp.30–31.
162 Harcourt (ed.), *The Harcourt Papers*, vol.4, part 2, pp.381–382.
163 Harcourt (ed.), *The Harcourt Papers*, vol.4, part 2, p.384.
164 Harcourt (ed.), *The Harcourt Papers*, vol.4, part 2, p.407.
165 Hurl-Eamon, *Marriage and the British Army*, pp.22–23.

The presence of soldiers' wives with the army was accepted, albeit reluctantly, by most senior officers. They recognised the tasks women performed were necessary, that they may have assisted the recruitment of married men and their presence may have helped to stem desertion. Suspicions regarding their supposed promiscuity, propensity for plunder and as suppliers of alcohol arose partly from a lack of distinction between soldiers' wives on the one hand and casual followers of the army on the other.[166] Whatever the justice of the case, senior officers were usually determined to keep women under strict control through the use of threats and sanctions. They were tolerated, but only so long as they provided essential support services and remained within the behavioural norms of the regimental society in which they lived.

Servants

A brief mention should be made of servants. These were trained soldiers taken from the ranks with one assigned to each of the officers to whose company he belonged. In a well managed regiment they still had to mount guard when their officer did so and remained subject to inspections of arms and equipment. They received additional pay and their officer had to supply them with suitable working clothes to avoid undue wear and tear to their uniforms.[167]

As was the case with the regiment's women, an allowance for servants was also made when the War Office requested shipping capacity to transport units overseas. When elements from 11 cavalry regiments went to Flanders in April 1793, the number of servants embarked was equal to the number of officers from each regiment.[168] The Foot Guards had a higher allowance of servants, since the three regiments embarking at the end of February 1793 had 90 officers but were accompanied by 108 'servants and soldiers'. A similar pattern was evident one year later when reinforcements for all three regiments were sent to Flanders consisting, *inter alia*, of 15 officers and 22 servants.[169] One possible explanation is that the additional men were not actually servants but in charge of the bât horses carrying officers' baggage, tents for all ranks and other heavier items.

The Price of Experience

Structures existing at the start of any conflict usually reflect the changes that were made to solve the problems of the last. Organisations evolve and adapt to circumstances by undergoing change. It is clear from this discussion of British regiments sent to Flanders in 1793–1794 that they had neither changed nor adapted, and thus were unprepared to fight the armies of revolutionary France.

The hard lessons of 1793–1794 were learned by the Government, as Henry Dundas wrote to Lord Grenville in 1798: '… we must not run wild with economy on the return of peace,

---

166 Kopperman, 'The British High Command', pp.16–17.
167 Cuthbertson, *Cuthbertson's System*, pp.154–156.
168 TNA: HO 50/384: Yonge to Dundas, 25 March and 5 April 1793.
169 BL: Add Ms 34,447: p.284, Enclosure in Grenville to Auckland, 22 February 1793. Auckland Papers vol.36 and TNA: HO 50/385, pp.293–297, Lewis to Nepean, 15 March 1794.

for upon the application of that principle indiscreetly at the conclusion of the last war, our regiments were frittered down to a state of perfect inefficiency.'[170]

The civilian administration of the Army between each of the wars in the eighteenth century was geared primarily towards maintaining social order and protecting Britain's interests at home and abroad. The transfer from a peace to a war footing therefore caused a significant hiatus, just at a time when this was least desirable, and it was hard to avoid confusion. After 1794, the roles of the Commander-in-Chief and the Secretary for War became permanent and the dual administration of the Army – civil in peacetime and military in war time – ceased.[171]

The Flanders experience also highlighted that although raising men for rank was a quick and relatively productive short-term expedient, it was also accompanied by significant problems. The temptations it offered denuded the Army of experienced officers in existing regiments as the lure of promotion drew them away to form new units. Existing regiments thus came to be officered by men with significantly less service, while new units had men promoted beyond the level of their experience. By the second half of 1794 the Duke of York's army contained infantry regiments commanded by lieutenant colonels aged 25 (the Hon Arthur Wesley, 33rd), 24 (Lord Craven, 3rd), 22 (Gordon Drummond, 8th), 20 (the Hon John Leveson Gower, 63rd) and 19 (the Hon Edward Paget, 28th). No matter what their future achievements may have been, the only way such men could function effectively would have been through strong support from senior regimental officers and non-commissioned officers. When this was not forthcoming, disasters such as at Druten on 20 October 1794, which befell the 37th Regiment under the 26-year-old the Hon Charles Hope, could occur. Raising for rank also caused deep unrest and a fracturing of morale amongst more senior officers with longer service. Witnessing younger or inexperienced individuals receiving promotion to senior positions has never been perceived with favour in any organisation, at any time. In short, this time-honoured methodology resulted in levels of desperation and cynicism which tainted everyone it touched, not to mention the callous neglect often inflicted on the luckless recruits. That this seems to have been regarded as almost a natural phenomenon does not speak well of the politicians and soldiers involved. Anachronistic as it may be, the term 'expendable' is again hard to avoid.

To make things even worse, newly raised units, and many recruits for those already serving in Flanders, were hustled overseas before they were trained or even equipped. The loss of life this occasioned must surely be offset against the otherwise numerically successful recruitment campaigns of 1793 and 1794. The cause must in part lie in the number of men required for the projects devised by Pitt, Dundas and Grenville, including the West Indies, La Vendée and Toulon, quite apart from Flanders. It was clear that ministers were not prepared to wait for recruits to be trained before launching them into these theatres of operations. The Foot Guards and cavalry regiments were largely protected due to having depots at home, but the same was not the case for the line infantry, which suffered accordingly. One may suspect that this was the principal failing of Lord Amherst as Commander-in-Chief. His unease at working with politicians and unwillingness to put forward his own arguments, if and

---

170 Dundas to Grenville, 21 July 1798, in Historical Manuscripts Commission (ed.), *Dropmore*, vol.4, p.264.
171 Pimlott, *Administration of the British Army*, p.367.

when he disagreed with his political masters, may well be the key as to why this tragedy was allowed to unfold. The Duke of Richmond, the only other professional soldier in the Cabinet, had told William Pitt as early as 5 April 1793:

> That there is besides a circumstance that makes it perfectly unadvisable for England to send British forces to act immediately on the Continent, which is that our army, cavalry and infantry, consists almost wholly of recruits, no part of which, men or horses, have been raised two months, and the greater part of which are at this moment only raising.[172]

Richmond also urged Pitt to try and understand: 'That men just raised upon paper were not soldiers…', a truth that failed to receive recognition given the number of such recruits despatched to Flanders in 1793–1794.[173] Had Amherst joined his voice to that of Richmond, the outcome might have been different.

---

172 J. Holland Rose, 'The Duke of Richmond on the conduct of the war in 1793', in *English Historical Review*, vol.25, 1910, p.555.
173 TNA: WO 30/81: Minutes of [a] Conversation with Mr. Pitt, 10 April 1793.

6

The Ordnance

The role and responsibilities of the Board of Ordnance at home were described in Chapter 1. As we have seen, it was not part of the British Army, but an ancient department of state, quite different in its structure and organisation to the chain of command for the cavalry and infantry. Its uniforms were blue instead of the red predominantly worn by the Army, there was no purchase or sale of commissions, and the Board operated a different system of pay and rations. All ordnance officers attended the Royal Military Academy, Woolwich, established in 1741, prior to receiving a commission. Here, they were taught subjects including fortification, mathematics, drawing and French, this being the only formal school of instruction provided for officers until the formation of the staff college at High Wycombe in May 1799, catering for men from other branches of the military.

Ordnance Services

This chapter covers ordnance services in the field; their composition, organisation and effectiveness on campaign. In research terms, much still remains to be done to improve our understanding of the many ways in which the Board of Ordnance conducted its business, but the campaign of 1793–1795 is compact enough for a new insight into its practical tasks in time of war.

The Ordnance Train
A principal responsibility of the Board towards field armies was the provision of a train, consisting of artillery, engineers and stores. This represented an entirely self-contained entity throughout the eighteenth century, even having its own commissaries and paymaster. For example, the Royal Artillery was responsible for sourcing its own forage during the American War, often in competition with the commissary-general's department. It also had its own military chest, its financial accounts were not subject to the approval of the commander-in-chief, and it was partly civilian in nature.[1]

During the War of the Spanish Succession, the manhandling of guns in the field was to a large extent a civilian concern, under the Controller of the Train, his wagon-masters,

---
1 Bowler, *Logistics*, pp.35–37.

commissaries and conductors. In action the guns were served by detachments from the Royal Regiment of Artillery – a uniformed Board of Ordnance formation. Rather similarly, military engineers were uniformed Board of Ordnance officers, but the artisans were civilian, likewise the staff responsible for receiving, issuing, and accounting for stores. Although the size and composition of the train depended on the nature of the expedition for which it was formed, the significant number of personnel, the volume of equipment and the scale of the transportation required made it an expensive item. A train in 1703 consisting of 14 sakers,[2] ten 3-pounders, four 10-inch and six 8-inch guns cost over £45,000 including wages, as did the train in Flanders in 1708. At this period, officers were not as specialised in their roles as they were to become later. Many were drawn from the infantry and could fulfil both engineering and artillery functions in the field, additionally serving with their regiments, and some armies could be accompanied by pontoon and pioneer companies each commanded by captains serving respectively as bridge master and captain of pioneers.[3]

The transportation resources required were considerable.[4] The autonomous nature of the Board meant that it arranged shipping to deliver the train to a theatre of operations prior to 1793, but land transportation would generally be contracted on arrival, since the cost of moving the required number of horses and wagons direct to the theatre was prohibitive. The Royal Artillery had its own wagon and local shipping services from 1778 in America, with horses being procured either through a levy on the countryside, or via contractors for a given number of animals over a designated period. The numbers required were large, with 470 horses being used to haul twenty-five 24-pounder guns and 200 for 10 guns of the same calibre in Flanders in 1706. In the campaign of 1747 in Germany, four horses were used to pull a heavy 3-pounder, seven for each heavy 6-pounder, 11 for a heavy 9-pounder and 15 for a heavy 12-pounder.[5] The artillery in Lieutenant General John Burgoyne's army in North America employed four horses to pull a 6-pounder and three horses for a 3-pounder in 1777.[6] Horses for wagons carrying the associated tools, ammunition and equipment used to operate the artillery were additional.[7] As might be expected with such bulky equipment, mobility was not a term often associated with the train. Its slow pace of movement often delayed the swifter marching infantry, a case in point being the late arrival of Cornwallis' division at Brandywine (11 September 1777) due to delays caused by the terrain. Topographical features such as the extensive woods and plentiful rail fences found in North America also restricted movement and provided cover for enemy sharpshooters, who singled out gunners for special attention. Transportation issues could seriously affect

---

2   Prior to the standardisation of English cannon types by Albert Borgard in 1716, canon were categorised according to their calibre, weight and length. After 1716, they were categorised according to the weight of projectile fired. A saker had a bore of between 3¼ and 3¾ inches and fired a ball of between 4 and 6 lb.
3   Scouller, *Queen Anne*, pp.173–176, 182 and 186.
4   Duffy, *Fire and Stone*, pp.90–91.
5   Artillery of the same calibre was classified according to the length and weight of the barrel, which also dictated the size of the powder charge.
6   Scouller, *Queen Anne*, pp.181–182; J. Muller, *A Treatise of Artillery* (London: John Millan, 1768), p.179 and J. Burgoyne, *A State of the Expedition from Canada, as Laid Before the House of Commons, by Lieutenant-General Burgoyne* (London: J. Almon, 1780), p.70.
7   Bowler, *Logistics*, p.36.

ammunition supply, especially in campaigns where the army moved in areas distant from the fleet or a depot, with potential shortages limiting fire support, as at Freeman's Farm (19 September 1777) during the Saratoga campaign.[8]

The engineers developed later as a distinct service. Commissions were not given to engineer officers until 1757 and the Corps of Engineers was not formed until 1759. The service was reorganised in 1789 when the 'royal' title was added and most of the civilian artificers employed by the Board were gathered together and enlisted into the Royal Military Artificers. The officers of the Royal Engineers comprised a professional corps which in peacetime was employed in the construction of permanent facilities at home and abroad. On campaign, they planned and built fieldworks and advised the commander-in-chief on the best way to lay siege to fortifications. Both before and after 1789, they employed civilian tradesmen and labourers who came directly under the commander-in-chief, as did their transportation requirements, and they were paid by the army. Much of the labour was provided by soldiers seconded for the purpose, for which they received 6d additional daily pay and a double ration of rum. Although officers of the Royal Engineers served during the American War (we discussed the extensive service of Sir James Moncrieff in Chapter 2) the artificers working for the Board at this time were civilians and did not serve there.[9]

The Board of Ordnance as a Supplier of Arms, Ammunition and Equipment

Apart from providing the train, a key role of the Board was as a supplier of small arms and ammunition to the Army, in addition to other equipment. The mechanism for doing this had developed during the eighteenth century, by which firearm components were manufactured in London and Birmingham according to patterns laid down by the Board. Once these were sent to the Tower of London, they were inspected for their quality of workmanship and materials before being sent to selected contractors for assembly, or 'setting up'. The system resulted in the 'King's Pattern for Land Service' (known as the 'Land Pattern') long-arms issued to the Army from 1722 after which the only changes needed in wartime were in the number of contractors needed for setting up. After the Peace of Aix-la-Chapelle in 1748 much of the work was taken in-house to the Small Gun Office in the Tower of London, including the introduction of new metal ramrods. The requirement for contractors greatly reduced during the years of peace but erupted again in 1755 on the outbreak of the Seven Years' War, when it was found that many of the London gun makers refused to work without significantly increased remuneration. This led to the Board engaging with a single contractor for setting up firearms, which worked well, due in part to the large existing stock of relatively new weapons already held in the Tower. The smoothness of the operation received a jolt during the American War when the Board over anticipated the number of muskets required, with the result that standards fell, since the checks on workmanship and components formerly undertaken at each stage of the manufacturing process could no longer be performed.

---

8   M.H. Spring, *With Zeal and Bayonets Only. The British Army on Campaign in North America, 1775–1783* (Norman: University of Oklahoma Press, 2008), pp.196–197.
9   Bowler, *Logistics*, pp.36–37; Curtis, *The Organization of the British Army*, pp.8–9 and Rogers, *British Army*, pp.36–37.

The 10 years prior to 1793 were therefore characterised by stocks of often not very well-made arms. Procedures ensuring quality control that worked so well prior to 1775 had been significantly loosened, and after the peace of 1783 there was little opportunity to re-establish them since no new components were required. Matters were not helped by the decision in 1790 to introduce a new infantry musket, but by 1793 insufficient tooling-up had been undertaken, and the workmen were unfamiliar with the new requirements. These factors were greatly accentuated by the rapid expansion of the Army, the mobilisation of the militia and volunteers, and the requirement to arm large numbers of French *émigré* units, all of which overwhelmed the Board. By 5 October 1793, there were 5,356 'Short Land' pattern muskets remaining in store in the Tower of London, whereas requisitions had been received for 5,730. The scale of this demand led to standards being relaxed in order to utilise less skilled parts of the workforce, this becoming official policy from 1797. The Board had to purchase two consignments of 10,000 muskets at Liège in late 1793, and it was a part of these shipments which the Duke of York ordered to be intercepted before they were loaded for export at Ostend in order that his army could be supplied with the 'one Thousand Stand of new arms' it required. These were used to arm the recruits of the 12th, 38th and 55th Regiments.[10] Despite these measures, the Board also turned to the East India Company, from whom they purchased 7,440 muskets in early 1794, the majority for troops in Ireland.[11] These factors in part explain why the Board struggled to supply sufficient firearms to units sent to Flanders in 1794, as discussed in Chapter 5.

An integral component of the ammunition used by both the Royal Navy and the Army, of course, was gunpowder, a resource managed by the Board since Mediaeval times. As with small arms, the principal feature of gunpowder manufacturing was massive demand during wartime dwindling to almost nothing after peace was declared. Manufacturers could not therefore rely on the Board for a constant volume of business, which led them to develop markets with private buyers on whom they depended during times of peace. Requirements increased sharply in wartime and the manufacturers' attempts to supply all their buyers simultaneously meant that production failed to meet the Board's targets. This was compounded by insufficient technical knowledge of gunpowder production and testing (proofing), which led to a high percentage of powder delivered to the Board failing proof.[12]

All this had not mattered overmuch during the War of the Austrian Succession, since some 22 percent of the gunpowder delivered to the Board comprised damaged stock that had been reprocessed by the powder-mills under contract. This powder was taken from Royal Navy ships returning to port or had been in lengthy storage; what could be used

---

10 TNA: HO 50/370: pp.59–61, Richmond to Dundas, 11 October 1793; HO 50/371: Richmond to Dundas, 17 March 1794; WO 1/168: pp.505–506, York to Dundas, 19 March 1794; and BL: Add Ms 40,634: p.94, Craufurd to Stewart, 25 May 1794, Stewart of Afton Papers, vol.2.

11 D.W. Bailey, *The Board of Ordnance and Small Arms Supply* (Unpublished PhD thesis, King's College London, 1988), pp.247–254; TNA: HO 50/370: p.63, 'State of the Receipts, Issues & Demands from the Tower between the 29th September and 5th October 1793 inclusive, together with what remain'd in Store on that Day', enclosed in Richmond to Dundas, 11 October 1793; HO 51/371: Richmond to Dundas, 11 February 1794 and D.F. Harding, *Smallarms of the East India Company 1600–1856. Volume 1: Procurement and Design* (London: Foresight Books, 1997), pp.30–31 and 373.

12 J. West, *Gunpowder, Government and War in the Mid-Eighteenth Century* (London: Boydell Press, 1991), pp.16–17 and 58–74.

for military exercises or royal salutes was returned to store, but the remainder was subject to reprocessing.[13] The unprecedented demands created by the global scale of the Seven Years' War left the Board little choice but to contract for some 28,000 barrels of Dutch powder between 1756–1758. Only about half of the powder contracted from suppliers at home between 1755–1757 was actually delivered, and this was one of the reasons why the Board decided to purchase its own mill at Faversham in 1759, though this failed to provide solutions to the production issues experienced by private suppliers or to the percentage of powder failing proof. The Board faced local shortages at some magazines during the war, but stocks were balanced by transferring gunpowder from alternative locations.[14] Various administrative improvements were made after the American War, including transferring the Board's gunpowder manufacturing and proofing activities from the surveyor-general to the Royal Laboratory in 1783, thus increasing efficiency. As is discussed further below, technical advances from the 1770s onwards by William Congreve and others led to improvements in both the manufacture and proofing of gunpowder.[15]

The great assemblage of *matériel* required for a European war, not to speak of the various other overseas expeditions planned by the Government, led to the introduction of legislation prohibiting the export or coastwise shipping of gunpowder, arms and ammunition, legislation last used in 1755 at the start of the Seven Years' War.[16] The Government's motivation was to ensure that sufficient stock remained at the mills should it be required, but the legislation had proved less than effective in 1755 since curtailing exports also meant loss of business and tax revenue.

The scale of the Board's task in supplying arms and equipment is illustrated by a return dated 13 September 1793, prepared for the regiments allocated to Lord Moira. On the basis of 600 rank-and-file, the supplies provided for one regiment were:

400 Ball Cartridges per Man
Field Pieces 2 Guns
Ammunition, Tumbrels & Waggons in proportion
Flints a proper proportion
1 Wagon for Musquet Cartridges
10 spades – 1 per Company
10 Pick Axes – one Ditto[17]

When the Foot Guards and line brigades initially went to Flanders in early 1793, the Duke of Richmond calculated the quantity of reserve ammunition on the basis of 300 rounds

---

13 West, *Gunpowder, Government and War*, pp.23–24.
14 West, *Gunpowder, Government and War*, pp.50–52, 57–60, 166 and 194.
15 West, *Gunpowder, Government and War*, pp.178–185.
16 An Act to enable His Majesty to restrain the Exportation of Naval Stores; and more effectually to prevent the Exportation of Salt Petre, Arms and Ammunition, when prohibited by Proclamation or Order in Council, 33 Geo.3, c.2, in Anon., *The Statutes at Large of England and of Great-Britain: from Magna Carta to the Union of the Kingdoms of Great Britain and Ireland* (London: Eyre and Strahan, 1811), vol.18, pp.4–6.
17 BM: Add Ms 40,633: p.15, Articles to be provided by the Ordnance for Two Brigades of Infantry going on Foreign Service, 13 September 1793. Stewart of Afton Papers, vol.1.

per man or 180,000 rounds weighing 21,120 lb per battalion of 600 men. He reckoned that each wagon had a carrying capacity of 12 hundredweight (1,344 lb) and would require three horses to pull it, with one driver. This equated to 16 ammunition wagons and drivers, with 51 horses per battalion of 600 men, which serves to quantify the 'ammunition, tumbrels and wagons in proportion' mentioned above. The Duke of Richmond performed an equivalent calculation for the light cavalry, presumably the four troops each from the 7th, 11th, 15th and 16th Light Dragoons sent to Flanders in late April and early May 1793. He despatched three wagons, 12 horses and six drivers with one conductor to carry 67 rounds of carbine ammunition and 33 of pistol per man for this brigade.[18]

On campaign, each infantryman was supposed to carry 60 rounds of ammunition and each cavalryman 24 rounds, though Adye remarked 'the cartouche boxes of the infantry are made of so many shapes and sizes, that it is impossible to say exactly what ammunition they will contain'.[19] Musket cartridges were packed in boxes of 770 each, though in *The Bombardier and Pocket Gunner* Ralph Adye remarked at a slightly later period that they were packed in half barrels containing 1,000 rounds of musket or 1,200 carbine cartridges; musket flints were packed in kegs of approximately 2,300 each.[20] For the army in Flanders, first-line reserves for each light cavalry regiment and battalion of infantry were carried in a tumbrel under the charge of the unit quartermaster, but a general order of 2 September 1794 transferred the responsibility for the infantry tumbrels to the artillery detachment accompanying the regiment; in cases where a regiment had no battalion guns, the unit quartermaster remained in charge. When the tumbrels themselves needed replenishing, commanding officers had to requisition the artillery park, which held the army's reserve ammunition. A note from Lord Howe, the Lieutenant General of the Ordnance, stated that this was carried in 'common artillery waggons' drawn by three horses and with a capacity of 13,000 musket ball cartridges for the infantry or 19,500 carbine ball cartridges for the cavalry.[21] The artillery park's responsibilities did not end with just issuing ammunition, however, since units had to return any damaged cartridges to them for disposal, a process which appears to have been conducted monthly.[22] It is also possible that the components to make cartridges were assembled by personnel from the artillery park, though this could also be undertaken at the regimental level as Corporal William Todd of the 12th Regiment noted that the camp colour men were assigned this task when on campaign in Germany in 1761.[23]

---

18 TNA: WO 6/7: Part B pp.29 and 38, A list of the Horses, Waggons and Drivers that would be wanting to move the Fourteen Light Six Pounder Guns that are attached to the Seven Battalions of British Infantry, now in the Low Countries and to carry the Ammunition for the Guns and for the Troops, enclosure 5 in Richmond to Dundas, 19 April 1793 and A List of Horses, Waggons and Drivers embarked with the Detachment of Light Dragoons to carry the Ammunition ordered by Lord Amherst to attend them on Service in the Low Countries, enclosure in Richmond to Dundas, 26 April 1793.
19 R.W. Adye, *The Bombardier and Pocket Gunner* (London: T. Egerton, 2nd edition, 1802), p.7.
20 TNA: WO 6/7: Part B p.180, Enclosure 1, Ordnance Office, 3 August 1793 in Dundas to Murray, 6 August 1793.
21 NAM: 1985-12-15-5: GO, Courtray, 16 March 1794; TNA: AO 16/53/5: GO, Berlicom, 2 September 1794; AO 16/53/7: GO, Amerongen, 5 January 1795 and WO 1/779: pp.1–5: Sir William Howe's rough notes, 20 May 1794.
22 NAM: 1985-12-15-4: GO, Tournay, 2 May 1793 and Estreux, 1 June 1793.
23 Cormack and Jones (eds), *The Journal of Corporal William Todd*, p.141.

Aside from arming the troops, the Board of Ordnance was also responsible for supplying some items of camp equipment, such as tents. Mention has already been made of the new pattern of tent issued to the troops in Flanders from April 1794. These were made by Trotter & Co., under a contract with the War Office let by the Secretary-at-War. This was symptomatic of a process that became increasingly widespread throughout the period of the French Wars, by which the War Office gradually encroached on the preserves of the Board of Ordnance by contracting for camp and other equipment and storing it in depots that were not controlled by the Board. This was a clear duplication of resources and risked abandoning the checks and balances so carefully preserved in the structure of the Board, whose head and principal members were accountable to Parliament, and which had long-established procedures for accepting and issuing stores.[24]

The Duke of Richmond as Master General of the Ordnance, 1793–1795

The performance of the Board of Ordnance in 1793–1795 must be seen against a background of strong political differences on matters of war policy between the Duke of Richmond, appointed Master General in 1782, and other Cabinet members. Despite his undoubted intellect and energy, Richmond has been termed 'Tactless, irritable, unsociable…'[25], meaning that he never developed a close working relationship with either the Prime Minister or other Cabinet colleagues. His high-handed management of the committee on defence expenditure, which he chaired (including his suppression of unwelcome evidence) generated political opposition, leading to the proposed legislation being defeated in Parliament in February 1786 – an outcome that was predominantly ascribed to Richmond.[26]

Despite being the Cabinet's *de facto* military advisor, Richmond was not one of the inner circle of ministers formulating war policy – in fact, the reverse was true. He strongly objected to the dispersal of Britain's military force between the various projects masterminded by Pitt, Dundas and Grenville, and to the prosecution of a major campaign on the continent for which Britain was not equipped either militarily or in terms of public support. He advised the Prime Minister two days before the allied strategy meeting scheduled for 7 April 1793 at Antwerp: 'It strikes me that if your ideas are quite clear that we must make expeditions on the coast of France and to the West Indies our principal object as soon as we are able, it would be far better, indeed fairer, immediately to apprise the meeting at Antwerp of such being our resolution…'[27]

The differences of opinion were brought into sharper focus when Richmond wrote to Henry Dundas on 1 July 1793 in which he derided operations in Flanders and the various expeditions planned to the West Indies, Mauritius, the Mediterranean and Brittany, as they

---

24 Clode, *The Military Forces of the Crown*, vol.1, pp.210–212.
25 Ehrman, *The Younger Pitt*, p.186.
26 Ehrman, *The Younger Pitt*, pp.516–519.
27 J. Holland Rose, 'The Duke of Richmond on the Conduct of the War in 1793', in *English Historical Review*, vol.25, 1910, p.554. Background regarding Richmond's status in the Cabinet is discussed in: A.G. Olson, *The Radical Duke. The Career and Correspondence of Charles Lennox, Third Duke of Richmond* (Oxford: Oxford University Press, 1961), pp.91–94.

collectively served to: '… fritter away the small force that Great Britain can ever supply and make it respectable no where'. This he termed '… some foolish game…', a label that must have been calculated to antagonise Dundas.[28] Dundas forwarded this letter to the King, who: '…cannot see that his having been called upon to communicate any plans he may possess of St. Maloes was a reason to renew a formel protest against every measure as yet addopted for carrying on the war'.[29] Relations deteriorated during the summer, to the extent that further correspondence from Richmond forwarded to the King at the end of September led the monarch to declare: 'There is so much chicanery in the correspondence of the Duke of Richmond that I scarcely can suppose any real reconciliation is possible'.[30] The result was that Richmond stopped attending the Cabinet or taking part in discussions with fellow ministers, which led to a further cooling in relations between himself and the Prime Minister. As the months went by, the situation became intolerable, to the extent that when Richmond did seek a reconciliation in December 1794, Pitt took six weeks to reply and then informed him on 26 January 1795: '… that the execution of the important duties of your department is incompatible with a state which precludes confidential intercourse on all the points of public business'.[31] In other words, Richmond was sacked from his position as Master General and Cabinet member.

Quite apart from disagreements with his Cabinet colleagues, Richmond's relations with the Duke of York were not good, for two reasons. First, Richmond felt himself aggrieved at the chief field command in the war being given to a general junior to him in seniority (Richmond's commission as general was dated 20 November 1782 and the Duke of York's 12 April 1793), as he wrote to the Prime Minister on 17 September 1793:

> I know that my objections to the Flanders War are supposed to have arisen from the Duke of York's having had that command which I might have hoped to have been entrusted with, and that therefore, all my opinions on this subject being supposed to be biased and not very acceptable, I have never been consulted on the means of conducting it.

Warming to his theme, Richmond criticised the King for not '… letting the Duke of York begin by learning his Profession in a subordinate Rank, before so young a man was trusted in supreme command with the Lives of Thousands'. He continued by attacking Pitt, Dundas and Grenville, declaring '… some errors might have been avoided, if the Direction of operations had not been so much confined as it has been to the Civil Departments'.[32] The second cause of antagonism lay in the duel that the Duke of York fought in May 1789 with the Duke of Richmond's nephew, Captain and Lieutenant Colonel Charles Lennox of the Coldstream Guards.[33]

---

28 BL: Loan MS 57/107: Richmond to Dundas, 1 July 1793. Melville Papers.
29 George III to Dundas, 8 July 1793, in Aspinall (ed.), *Later Correspondence*, vol.2, p.58.
30 George III to Dundas, 25 September 1793, in Aspinall (ed.), *Later Correspondence*, vol.2, p.103.
31 Pitt to Richmond, 26 January 1795, in Historical Manuscripts Commission (ed.), *Report of the Manuscripts of Earl Bathurst Preserved at Cirencester Park* (London: HMSO, 1923), pp.710–711 and Pitt to George III, 28 January 1795, in Aspinall (ed.), *Later Correspondence*, vol.2, p.298.
32 BL: Loan MS 57/107: Richmond to Pitt, 17 September 1793. Melville Papers.
33 J. Ehrman, *The Younger Pitt. The Years of Acclaim* (London: Constable, 1969), pp.287–288; Olson, *Radical Duke*, pp.95–96 and Burne, *The Noble Duke of York*, pp.28–32.

Artillery

The Royal Artillery comprised four battalions, each of 10 companies, until a fifth of five companies was raised on 14 August 1794. Artillerymen furnished detachments for the pair of battalion guns used by regular infantry, militia and fencible regiments. The peacetime allocation per regiment was four men, but this rose in wartime to 15, thus placing a significant strain on human resources and explaining the large number of infantrymen performing this role on campaign, as discussed further below. A second duty was to man fixed defences, consisting of various fortifications around the coast of Britain, including Plymouth, Portsmouth, the Tower of London, in batteries on the Medway estuary and Crown territories overseas.[34]

Personnel

We discussed the establishments for cavalry and infantry regiments in Chapter 5. The equivalent for a company of Royal Artillery in April 1793 was one captain, one captain lieutenant, three lieutenants, three sergeants, four corporals, four bombardiers, two drummers and 80 gunners making 98 all ranks. In practice, every company was significantly under strength, and the number 'wanting to complete' ranged between 13 and 39 as at 1 April 1793. The establishment was raised by the addition of one sergeant, two bombardiers and 10 gunners in line with a Royal Warrant dated 11 September 1793, giving a strength of 111 all ranks.[35] One year later, the war establishment of an artillery company, together with their pay, was:

1 Captain, 10s per day
1 Captain Lieutenant, 6s per day
2 First Lieutenants, 5s per day each
1 Second Lieutenant, 4s per day
4 Sergeants, 2s per day each
4 Corporals, 1/10 per day each
6 Bombardiers, 1/8 per day each
100 Gunners, 1s per day each
2 Drummers, 1s per day each[36]

The rapid expansion of the Army discussed in Chapter 5 thus also affected the Royal Artillery, with each company increasing its establishment strength by 23 percent between April 1793 and November 1794.

---

34 TNA: WO 1/779: pp.133–142, Richmond to Dundas, 1 September 1794 and Duncan, *History of the Royal Regiment of Artillery*, vol.1, p.405 and vol.2, p.2.
35 TNA: WO 17/2557: Monthly returns of the Royal Regiment of Artillery, 1 April and 1 November 1793; HO 50/370: pp.75–82: 'Warrant for sundry augmentations in the Royal Regiment of Artillery', enclosed in Rogers to Pollock, 14 October 1793 and HO 50/370: p.343, Haddock to Nepean, 28 November 1793.
36 TNA: WO 1/779: p.205, 'Strength of a Company of the Royal Regiment of Artillery on the War Establishment of 1794', enclosed in Crew to Huskisson, 3 November 1794.

The official establishment did not always reflect the actual strength of an artillery company on service, but nevertheless agreed fairly closely with the breakdown of Major Jesse Wright's Company of the 1st Battalion, the main body of which reached Helvoetsluys on 18 March 1793. Here, they had to lighten their ship's draft by disembarking their powder and most of their equipment into two bilanders before proceeding to Dordrecht. The remainder of this company, under Captain Lieutenant William Borthwick, landed at Helvoetsluys on 24 March, having occupied one ship of a small convoy including three transports with the 14th Regiment, the whole escorted by the frigate *Syren*. Aside from the officer commanding and his second in command, the remainder of the company comprised six subalterns, three sergeants, seven corporals, four bombardiers, five first gunners, 94 second gunners and two drummers. This company was employed manning the 14 light 6-pounder battalion guns of the Foot Guards and line brigades; the Foot Guards provided one sergeant, one corporal and 56 guardsmen as additional gunners and it is assumed that the line brigade did something similar.[37]

Major Wright was the senior Royal Artillery officer in Flanders for some six weeks. His many additional responsibilities gave him considerable worry, as he wrote to his wife on 30 April:

> I had no instructions from the Board about any one thing, left entirely in the dark, and it would almost appear a trap laid for me to be sacrificed. I am at present so involved in difficulties about the said command that I know not what to do, and no one I have with me is fit to give advice.[38]

There were two main points of contention: accounting for money as it was being spent and the making of appointments – either or both of which could be repudiated by the Master General or the Board as a whole, thus dumping the liability on Wright. For his part, Wright estimated that he needed an allowance of 15/- or 20/- per day to cover these costs but was shortly afterwards allotted only 10/-, which, he informed his wife '… won't keep me in dinners'.[39] Perhaps his largest outlay was for bât and forage money which he paid at the rate of 20/- per day for himself and 5/- for each of the four subalterns, being the same rate as in the American War. The money was lent to Wright by Captain and Lieutenant Colonel Richard, Lord Cavan of the Coldstream Guards, who supplied several instalments of £100 each. Wright had also made various appointments, since he had no staff or specialist workmen.[40]

Wright's burden was eased by the arrival of two more companies, which embarked at Woolwich on 10 May 1793, since this reinforcement was commanded by Major William

---

37   NAM: 1985-12-15-4: Brigade Order, 26 March 1793; George III to Dundas, 20 April 1793, in Aspinall (ed.), *Later Correspondence*, vol.2, p.29; Leslie (ed.), 'Campaigning in 1793–Flanders', pp.10, 17, 20 and 22; BL: Add Ms 34,449: p.328, Captain Manley, R.N. to Auckland, Helvoetsluys 26 March 1793. Auckland papers vol.38; TNA: WO 17/2557: Monthly return of the Royal Regiment of Artillery, 1 April 1793 and Duncan, *History of the Royal Regiment of Artillery*, vol.1 p.173 and vol.2 p.56–57.
38   Leslie (ed.), 'Campaigning in 1793–Flanders', p.21.
39   Leslie (ed.), 'Campaigning in 1793–Flanders', p.15.
40   Leslie (ed.), 'Campaigning in 1793–Flanders', pp.11, 13 and 24.

Congreve, who was selected by the Duke of Richmond as the expeditionary force's artillery commander. It included the artillery staff consisting of an adjutant (First Lieutenant Archibald Robertson), a surgeon, a surgeon's mate, a commissary and paymaster, a commissary of horse, a clerk of the stores and a conductor of stores. The craftsmen comprised a cooper, a carpenter, three smiths, two collar makers and a farrier and there were also 114 drivers with 84 horses. Aside from the staff and support personnel, there were, of course, the two companies – Captain George Wilson's of the 1st Battalion and Captain Thomas Trotter's of the 4th Battalion. Taken together, these numbered two captain lieutenants, five first lieutenants, four second lieutenants, four sergeants, five corporals, nine bombardiers, six first gunners, 192 second gunners and three drummers. These numbers differ slightly from those proposed by Richmond on 26 April (Appendix VI), but the two companies manned the guns comprising the artillery park.[41] Captain James Winter's Company, from the 1st Battalion, also proceeded to Flanders in May 1793. A third detachment left Woolwich on 26 August 1793 commanded by Major William Huddleston with Captain Francis Laye's Company of the 4th Battalion. It included Captain Lieutenant James Boag, First Lieutenants Henry Shrapnell, Charles Waller, Robert Beevor and Robert Lawson, Second Lieutenants Henry Geary, Thomas Lacy and Gother Mann, 11 non-commissioned officers, 232 gunners, three drummers and four drivers, together with 18 women and three children. This detachment accompanied the siege train sent for the reduction of Dunkirk, together with two companies of the Royal Irish Artillery commanded by Captains John Pratt and Joseph Shewbridge; these were subsequently withdrawn in early November for service in the West Indies under Sir Charles Grey.[42]

Given his important status in the Duke of York's army, it would be worth pausing to consider William Congreve's career prior to 1793. He was a highly experienced officer and aged 50 at the time he arrived in Flanders. He had been commissioned lieutenant fireworker in the Royal Artillery on 4 February 1757 at the age of 14, so had already seen 36 years' service, part of which included the siege of Louisbourg in 1758, the captures of Havana and Martinique in 1762 and during the American War between 1776–1779. His career for the nine years after 1783 was primarily devoted to technical improvements, especially in raising the quality of gunpowder manufactured for the Navy and the Army. Poor quality control and inadequate production volumes had caused serious complaints during both the Seven Years' War and American War, leading the Government to consider closing its mill at Faversham. This was averted when Congreve suggested a number of reforms, the success of which led to

---

41 TNA: WO 55/1401: p.90, 'Return of the Detachment of the R[oyal] R[egiment] of Artillery at present in the Low Countries and of the Detachment embarked this day to join the army there, Woolwich, 10 May 1793', enclosed in Drummond to the Board of Ordnance, 10 May 1793. A return dated 14 July 1793 stated that 29 non-commissioned officers and 239 gunners from the 1st Battalion, six non-commissioned officers and 66 gunners from the 4th Battalion and one solitary gunner from the Horse Brigade were serving in the Low Countries on that date. WO 6/7: Part B p.97, 'State of the Non Commissioned Officers & Gunners in Great Britain & the Low Countries, 14th July 1793'.

42 TNA: WO 6/7: Part B p.201, Rogers to Nepean, 28 August 1793, enclosed in Dundas to Murray, 29 August 1793; HO 50/369: p.307, Enclosure in Richmond to Dundas, 21 August 1793; HO 50/370: p.241, Dundas to Richmond, 9 November 1793; Duncan, *History of the Royal Regiment of Artillery*, vol.1, pp.176, 179, 254 and 257 and vol.2, p.57 and J.J. Crooks, *History of the Royal Irish Regiment of Artillery* (Dublin: Browne and Nolan, 1914), p.278.

the subsequent acquisition of the Waltham Abbey mill in 1787 after which both were used as the standard for private manufacturers. Congreve was promoted to major in the Army in 1783, when he was appointed deputy comptroller of the Royal Laboratory at Woolwich with responsibility for the manufacture and proofing of gunpowder; he was made comptroller in 1789.[43] He remained the Duke of York's artillery commander until July 1794 when he returned home as his '… Health is in such a State as to render Him unfit for Service at present'.[44] Congreve was promoted to lieutenant colonel in August 1793. He was replaced by Lieutenant Colonel John Stewart, commanding the artillery in Lord Moira's expedition.

Table 6: Return of the Royal British Artillery Serving in the Low Countries Commanded by Lieut. Col. Wm Congreve. Camp at Menin, 6 October 1793

	Officers	Sergeants	Corporals	Bombardiers	Gunners	Drummers	Total
Effective with the park	15	7	7	11	162	7	209
On command at Ostend		1			7		8
Sick at Ostend	2	1	2		11	1	17
Sick at Bruges					26		26
Sick in Menin		1		2	60		63
Employed				1	7		8
Officers' servants					32		32
Artillerymen as drivers					69		69
Artillerymen with park wagons					38		38
With Battalion guns	10	2	4	6	113		135
TOTAL	27	12	13	20	525	8	605

Table 6 shows the number of Royal Artillery personnel serving in Flanders by 6 October 1793.[45] Two points should be noted. First, the table relates only to the Royal Artillery and not the Royal Irish Artillery, a separate unit. It does not include drivers (other than any

---

43 W.Y. Carman, 'Sir William Congreve, 1741–1814', in *Journal of the Society for Army Historical Research*, vol.51, 1973, pp.63–68; W.D. Cockroft, *Dangerous Energy. The Archaeology of Gunpowder and Military Explosives Manufacture* (London: English Heritage, 2000), pp.32–48; S.H. Mauskopf, 'Chemistry in the Arsenal: State Regulation and Scientific Methodology of Gunpowder in Eighteenth-Century England and France, in B.D. Steele and T. Dorland (eds), *The Heirs of Archimedes. Science and the Art of War Through the Age of Enlightenment* (Cambridge, Massachusetts: The MIT Press, 2005), pp.307–308 and S.H. Mauskopf, 'The Crisis of English Gunpowder in the Eighteenth Century', in U. Klein and E.C. Spary (eds), *Materials and Expertise in Early Modern Europe* (Chicago: University of Chicago Press, 2009) pp.309–315.
44 TNA: WO 1/169: p.447, York to Dundas, 17 June 1794.
45 TNA: WO 1/167: p.227, Return of the Royal British Artillery Serving in the Low Countries Commanded by Lieut. Col. Wm Congreve. Camp at Menin, 6 October 1793, enclosed in Murray to Dundas, 6 October 1793.

who might have been seconded from the Regiment) since these were civilians. The table indicates that a relatively high proportion of the Royal Artillery personnel in Flanders were sent to assist with the battalion guns, amounting to 37 percent of the officers, 27 percent of the non-commissioned officers and 23 percent of the other ranks (if one assumes each of the 10 officers was accompanied by a servant). It is possible that the percentage of other ranks is a minimum, since some of the 69 drivers may also have been assigned to battalion guns. Should these assumptions prove correct, one may surmise that approximately 24 percent of Royal Artillery personnel were deployed with the battalion guns and 35 percent with the artillery park, with most of the remainder sick.

The return dated 15 October 1793 (see Appendix I, Table I.1) shows an increase in personnel to 39 officers (i.e., officers and staff), 24 non-commissioned officers and 743 other ranks. This is accounted for by the inclusion of the two Royal Irish Artillery companies sent to assist with the battering train landed for the siege of Dunkirk which were not included on the 6 October roll. The two Irish companies had departed Flanders approximately one month before the date of the 1 December return (Appendix I, Table I.2), which therefore shows a sharp drop in Royal Artillery numbers to 17 officers (including staff), seven sergeants and 553 rank-and-file. The Royal Artillery numbered as follows some six weeks later:

Table 7: Return of the Royal British Artillery commanded by Lieutenant Colonel William Congreve serving in the Low Countries, 17 January 1794.

	Officers	Surgeons	NCOs	Gunners	Drummers	Servants	Total
Effective at Ghent	15	2	38	255	7	24	341
Employed as conductors			8	2			10
Employed as drivers				24			24
Absent for health	2						2
Absent private business	4		1	5			10
Absent without leave	1						1
On command	7		10	73			90
Sick			5	107			112
TOTAL	29	2	62	466	7	24	590

The reduction in numbers is also apparent, with 31 officers (including surgeons), 62 non-commissioned officers and 497 other ranks (gunners, drummers and officers' servants) representing a drop of 21 percent in the number of officers and 27 percent in the number of remaining personnel, though exact comparisons are difficult given the lack of consistency in classifying staff and non-commissioned officers.[46] The significant increase in non-commissioned officers from 45 on 6 October 1793 to 62 on 17 January 1794 (a 38 percent increase) was the result of the number of corporals rising from 34 to 47 in October.[47] It may

---

46 TNA: WO 1/168: Return of the Royal British Artillery commanded by Lieutenant Colonel William Congreve serving in the Low Countries, 17 January 1794, enclosed in York to Richmond, 25 January 1794.
47 TNA: WO 17/2557: Monthly returns of the Royal Regiment of Artillery, 1 October and 1 November 1793.

be because these men needed the authority to command infantrymen seconded to work the battalion guns.

The return dated 1 July 1794 (see Appendix I, Table I.4) shows that 470 other ranks were serving in Flanders at that time, a very similar total to 17 January. The Royal Artillery was strengthened shortly after the 1 July return by the arrival of Lord Moira's force, which contained Captain Ashton Shuttleworth's Company of the 4th Battalion and two companies of Royal Irish Artillery, the whole commanded by Lieutenant Colonel John Stewart.[48] This explains the increase to 762 other ranks on 1 August (Appendix I, Tables I.5 and I.6). The return of 1 September (Appendix I, Table I.7) shows 845 Royal Artillery other ranks in Flanders, indicating the arrival of a third company of Royal Irish Artillery. It also shows that 38 percent of the men were 'on command', which is similar to the projected number manning the battalion guns, as previously mentioned. The sharp fall in numbers evident on 27 November 1794 (Appendix I, Table I.8), represented a reduction of 77 percent, due to the withdrawal of the companies commanded by Captains Thomas Trotter, Francis Laye and Ashton Shuttleworth, all of whom were required in the West Indies.[49] A few words are necessary regarding the three companies of Royal Irish Artillery that landed in Flanders with Lord Moira's force. One of these, No.5 Company, was remarkably badly equipped and its commander, Captain Lieutenant William Buchanan, described the personnel as consisting '… wholly of Recruits who have nothing but their Jackets and are in want of Clothing and many other Articles',[50] an assessment with which the Duke of Richmond concurred when he gave orders for camp equipage to be supplied to it. No.5 Company was destined to form part of the defences of Bergen-op-Zoom, while the two companies of Royal Irish Artillery commanded by Captains William Wright and John Daniel Arabin accompanied Lord Moira.[51]

The serious shortage of officers and men for the Royal Artillery had been an issue from the very outset of the campaign, when Major Jesse Wright told his wife that he had: '… only 12 guns with me, and what with sickness and other casualties I can only man 10 of them' (2 May 1793).[52] Sir James Murray pleaded with Dundas for a reinforcement of sailors from the fleet, but was told on 1 August 1793 that this would not be forthcoming, as the Navy had other things to do.[53] In 1794, the issue became even more pressing, though confined initially to a want of sheer muscle-power required to manhandle guns across the terrain, as noted in a general order of 11 May when the army was defending Tournai: 'Whenever the Guns in the redoubt in front of any Brigade are to be moved for the purpose of action the Brigade must assist the Officer Com'g them with such men as may be necessary. The number allotted to them not being sufficient for moving tho' it is for working them while in the redoubts.'[54]

---

48 Shuttleworth's company joined Lord Moira's force from December 1793. TNA: WO 17/2557: Monthly return of the Royal Regiment of Artillery, 1 December 1793.
49 For example, TNA: WO 1/779: pp.133–137, 353–356 and 409–416, Richmond to Dundas, 1 September, 17 and 20 December 1794.
50 TNA: WO 46/23: p.77, Richmond to Buchanan, 27 July 1794.
51 TNA: WO 46/23: pp.76–77, Richmond to Buchanan, 27 July 1794 and Richmond to Crew, 27 July 1794; Duncan, *History of the Royal Regiment of Artillery*, vol.1, p.259 and Crooks, *Royal Irish Regiment of Artillery*, p.274.
52 Leslie (ed.), 'Campaigning in 1793–Flanders', p.22.
53 TNA: WO 6/7: Part B p.141, Dundas to Murray, 1 August 1793.
54 TNA: AO 16/53/2: GO, Tournay, 11 May 1794.

Later in the year, the manpower shortage also affected the more skilled work of operating the guns, possibly because the large influx of infantry units in mid-1794 was not matched by a corresponding rise in trained gunners to crew the additional pieces. Increasing numbers of infantrymen were put to work on the battalion guns, as stated in a general order of 1 August, directing that the regiments affected must remedy the deficiency, ensuring that the soldiers assigned: '… must be stout able men, and in every respect fit, for the service for which they are destined'.[55]

The shortage of trained gunners became a feature of the army during the second half of 1794 and was a source of frequent complaint by Harry Calvert in his correspondence with William Windham, the recently appointed Secretary-at-War, and the Hon Thomas Pelham.[56] The increased need for soldiers for the battalion pieces led to a general order of 28 October directing one soldier to replace one Royal Artilleryman on each battalion gun in the army.[57] Assuming that every unit had two battalion guns, this meant 54 gunners returning to the artillery park to be replaced by the same number of infantry soldiers from the ranks. Personnel shortages not only concerned the number of trained gunners, but also included a lack of officers and non-commissioned officers, as Sir William Erskine informed Colonel James Craig on 28 October: 'I have had great Complaints from the different Regts. about their artillery men. They have scarcely any officers, and few non commissioned officers to keep their men, and drivers, in order. Their Horses are in bad order, and many of them require to be changed. We have Batterys and no Cannon.'[58]

There was also a shortage of specialists, and an appeal was made for any men familiar with tin-working to report to the Royal Artillery. As with all units, not all men were sufficiently fit to endure the rigours of a campaign. A series of medical boards were held during early February 1794 to identify such men, and 27 from the Royal Artillery and Royal Military Artificers were returned to England.[59]

The subsistence of gunners attached to infantry units also caused concern. A general order of 10 August 1794 stated that these men must be included in the returns of bread and forage for the regiment as a whole, in order that they could receive their subsistence.[60] The implication is that they had not been fed regularly up to this point. If so, the regiments guilty of this neglect are likely to have been the ones that arrived in Flanders in mid-1794, many of which had young and inexperienced officers (as discussed in Chapter 5) who may not have fully understood their duty.

Organisation

The Royal Artillery had several roles in Flanders, each of which required different equipment. The most numerous type of guns were the two light 6-pounders attached to each infantry battalion. As this was usually only done on the declaration of war, most units

---

55   TNA: AO 16/53/4: GO, Rosindael, 1 August 1794.
56   BL: Add Ms 37,874: pp.105–106,107–108 and 119–120, Calvert to Windham, 20 and 30 October 1794 and Calvert to Pelham, 22 October 1794. Windham Papers vol.33.
57   TNA: AO 16/53/6: GO, Arnheim, 28 October 1794.
58   BL: Add Ms 46,702: pp.60–61, Erskine to Craig, Osterhout, 28 October 1794. Don Papers, vol.1.
59   NAM: 1985-12-15-5: GO, Ghent, 13 January and 15 February 1794.
60   TNA: AO 16/53/5: GO, Oosterhoot, 10 August 1794.

would not have had the opportunity to train with them unless the regiment had attended a camp of exercise.[61] The regimental allocation of battalion guns was well described in late-June 1794 by one of Lord Moira's contingent:

> It may be necessary to observe, that to every Regiment of Foot, are attached two light Brass Six-pounders, to each of which belong twelve Artillery-Men, and three Horses with their drivers; besides an Ammunition Waggon and Tumbril, to each Regiment, which were very heavily laden; the Horses were brought over from England, and were of the most spirited kind, and in the highest keep, otherwise they would not have been able to have gone through the hardships and fatigues which they continually underwent.[62]

The actual breakdown of the detachment seconded to each battalion was one subaltern, two non-commissioned officers, eight gunners and three drivers. The relatively light weight of the guns enabled them to keep up with the infantry and clear obstacles such as ditches or hedges more easily.[63] When the expeditionary force landed in the United Provinces, the intention had been only to defend that territory, not to pursue the retreating French. Consequently, the battalion guns were supposed to travel via the waterways, and no means were provided for them to move otherwise. Once the objective changed, the Board had to find three horses and one driver per gun, with an extra nine horses, three drivers, and three wagons for the 396 rounds of ammunition required. The 14 battalion guns accompanying the infantry sent to Flanders in early 1793 therefore needed 168 horses, 56 drivers and 42 wagons. But even this took no account of spares, which were calculated at the rate of one additional wagon for every 20, one spare horse for every 10 and one spare driver for every three spare horses, which would bring the totals up to 44 wagons, 62 drivers and 185 horses.[64] The Guards Flank Battalion was also armed with battalion guns, with the Royal Artillery detachment being commanded by First Lieutenant Thomas Fenwick.[65] It is not certain whether this also applied to the Line Flank Battalion, as surviving correspondence refers only to seven battalions being so equipped. It is possible that the battalion guns of the 37th Regiment, in the Ostend garrison for most of 1793, were utilised by the Line Flank Battalion but no mention of this has been found in the available records. All battalion guns were withdrawn to the artillery park on 15 June 1793 during the siege of Valenciennes, rejoining their respective battalions on 5 August, one day before the army departed after the capture of the town. The same procedure was followed at Dunkirk on 28 August 1793.[66]

---

61 Houlding, *Fit for Service*, p.335.
62 Anon., *A Journal Kept in the British Army*, p.11.
63 Duncan, *History of the Royal Regiment of Artillery*, vol.2, p.55. Richmond informed Dundas that the Royal Artillery crew for a pair of battalion guns was 15 men. TNA: HO 50/371: Richmond to Dundas, 27 March 1794.
64 TNA: WO 6/7: Part B, pp.27 and 29, Richmond to Dundas, 19 April 1793 and 'A list of the Horses, Waggons and Drivers'.
65 NAM: 1985-12-15-4: GO, Courtray, 22 April 1793 and Leslie (ed.), 'Campaigning in 1793–Flanders', p.25.
66 NAM: 1985-12-15-4: GO, Estreux, 15 June and 5 August 1793 and GO, Camp before Dunkirk, 28 August 1793.

Adye notes the absence of any standard procedure for the deployment of battalion guns in action, but they generally took station on the right of the battalion when it was drawn up in line. When in combat, they would be positioned nearest the enemy and had to be mindful not to obstruct the manoeuvres of the unit to which they were attached.[67]

Not all infantry units had battalion guns. The general order of 1 August 1794 stated 'The Regiments which have Field Pieces attached to them'.[68] Given the date, this is most likely to have applied to some of the units reaching Flanders during the late summer of 1794, so it may be no surprise that another general order, dated 26 September, refers to: 'A Great increase of artillery being on its way to the army'.[69] Presumably, the additional artillery had arrived by early November, when the 78th, 79th, 80th, 84th, 85th and 88th Regiments were ordered to the artillery park at Arnhem immediately, for employment: '... as Drivers to the Guns and Waggons which are to be attached to the Regiments'.[70] All except the 88th Regiment had been part of Lord Mulgrave's force which landed at Flushing in August and September, at least some regiments of which were known to have been without field pieces, according to Harry Calvert.[71] Only 16 light 6-pounder battalion guns accompanied the 10 infantry regiments comprising Lord Moira's force, suggesting that two of these units were not so equipped.[72]

Another eyewitness, Herbert Taylor, stated that the distribution of guns to battalions: '... was changed after the first campaign, when brigades and half-brigades were formed and employed with corps as required'.[73] This does not appear to have been the case, since the only guns with battalions were light brass 6-pounder pieces that would not have been very effective when formed in a battery, other than at close range. Lieutenant Lewis Jones of the 57th Regiment referred to '... the field pieces belonging to the twelfth, thirty-eighth, and forty-fourth regiments...' deployed against the French at Walheim bridge near Malines on 16 July 1794.[74] Numerous general orders throughout 1794 also refer to battalion guns, as discussed shortly. What Taylor may be referring to are the heavier calibre guns from the artillery park being more frequently used in field operations in 1794 (see Appendix VI for the composition of the park in 1793). For example, Captain and Lieutenant Colonel Andrew Drummond of the 1st Foot Guards was ordered to march from Ghent to Kortrijk on 16 February 1794 with a force including 'A field piece with the proper ammunition' from each Foot Guards battalion, accompanied by four 12-pounder guns and two howitzers from the reserve artillery.[75] The detachment would therefore have included 10 guns, of which six were of a considerably heavier calibre than the standard battalion pieces. The reserve artillery was

---

67 Adye, *The Bombardier and Pocket Gunner*, pp.21–24.
68 TNA: AO 16/53/4: GO, Rosindael, 1 August 1794.
69 TNA: AO 16/53/6: GO, Grosbeck, 26 September 1794.
70 TNA: AO 16/53/6: GO, Arnhem, 9 November 1794.
71 Calvert to Dalrymple, 7 October 1794, in Verney (ed.), *Calvert*, pp.351–352.
72 TNA: WO 1/779: p.101, 'An account of Ordnance sent with the Expedition under the Command of Earl Moira', enclosed in Crew to Nepean, 7 August 1794.
73 Taylor (ed.), *Taylor Papers*, pp.26–27.
74 Jones, *An Historical Journal*, p.93.
75 NAM: 1985-12-15-5: GO, Ghent, 15 February 1794 and Brown, *Impartial Journal*, pp.90–91. The warning order for this move was given on 10 February, in which the Corps of Artificers were also ordered to hold themselves in readiness to accompany the artillery.

ordered to detach two 12-pounders, four heavy 6-pounders and two howitzers on 9 April 1794 to join 'the Hessian Corps' though it is not clear how these guns were to be deployed or how long they remained with the Hessians.[76] Harry Calvert also noted the arrival from Ostend of a Royal Artillery detachment at Valenciennes on 22 July 1793, stating in his diary that they were chiefly equipped with 'long 6-pounders'.[77] The artillery park was significantly augmented after the arrival of Lord Moira's force, which was equipped with:[78]

8 iron 24-pounders
4 brass medium 12-pounders
6 brass heavy 6-pounders
10 brass 4-pounders (of French manufacture)
2 brass 3-pounders
1 brass 8-inch howitzer
6 brass 5½-inch howitzers
1 brass 8-inch mortar
6 brass 5½-inch mortars

That the artillery was formed into batteries in 1794 is beyond dispute. A general order of 19 April specifically mentioned this in connection with the action at Vaux, fought two days earlier: 'His Royal Highness desires Captain Boag and Lieutenant Page of the Royal Artillery will accept his thanks for the very spirited and able manner in which they conducted the Battery committed to their care.'[79]

The choice of whether to form batteries or not appears to have been left with the force commander. Lieutenant General John Burgoyne, for example, formed three batteries each of four 6-pounder guns during the Saratoga expedition in 1777 in addition to 10 pieces of heavier ordnance utilised for demolishing earthworks.[80] The issue is more that batteries or 'brigades' at this period were not standardised in terms of either the number or calibre of guns so it is difficult to know exactly what types of piece were used in each case. A return of British reserve artillery at Klingelbeek and Tuil on 8 December 1794 listed 27 pieces classified as heavy 3-pounders, heavy 6-pounders, medium 12-pounders, and both light and heavy 5½-inch howitzers.[81] Adye stated that guns of the artillery park were generally formed in brigades of four or six pieces, with one sixth of the total comprising a reserve.[82]

Aside from guns assigned to battalions and the reserve park, artillery was also used for defending walled towns. As far as is known, all these pieces were either found in situ, or else supplied by the Austrians for locations in the Austrian Netherlands and by the Dutch for fortresses in the United Provinces. The gunners and support services were most likely

---

76   NAM: 1985–12–15–5: GO, St Amand, 8 April 1794.
77   Calvert's diary, 22 July 1793, in Verney (ed.), *Calvert*, p.91.
78   TNA: WO 1/779: p.101, 'An account of Ordnance sent with the Expedition under the Command of Earl Moira', enclosed in Crew to Nepean, 7 August 1794.
79   NAM: 1985–12–15–5: GO, Cateau, 19 April 1794.
80   Burgoyne, *A State of the Expedition from Canada*, p.10.
81   BL: Add Ms 46,711: Return of Ordnance & Ammunition in the Park of Artillery at this place, under the command of Lieut Col. John Stewart, Klingerbeck 8th Decem'r 1794. Don Papers, vol.10.
82   Adye, *The Bombardier and Pocket Gunner*, p.24.

provided from the same source. Limited ordnance resources, due to the small numbers of men available, were therefore likely to have been confined to the repair of fortifications, though records implying the presence of working parties from the infantry are sparse.

It is worth noting that although the first units of horse artillery were formed in England in 1793, none of these served in Flanders.

Mobility and Transportation
The two officers with responsibility for artillery transportation were Mr Eastaff (Commissary of Horses) and Captain George Williamson (Commissary of Artillery).[83] As will become apparent, the scale of their task was considerable, both in the acquisition and organisation of drivers and horses.

The lack of artillery mobility was a routine complaint in Flanders. The main obstacle was a shortage of drivers. Those sent out from England in 1793 were civilians who were not originally contracted to serve overseas as the Duke of Richmond informed Henry Dundas: 'If they are to be engaged in this service fresh bargains must be made with the Drivers, but probably a small bounty will induce them to serve abroad instead of at home'.[84] Henry Dundas informed Sir James Murray on 6 August 1793 that '… it is now become extremely difficult to get persons to engage in that service',[85] which prompted headquarters to appeal for suitably qualified men from infantry regiments. That same month, the Foot Guards Brigade was ordered to supply 20 men and the line brigade 15 men to the artillery park for this purpose, while in 1794 newly joined regiments were combed for men who were accustomed to horse care.[86] The seriousness of the deficiency from September 1794 onwards resulted in appeals to commanding officers turning into direct orders, which suggests that numbers were seen as more important than men experienced in the role. A general order of 26 September told every infantry unit, with the sole exception of the Guards Flank Battalion, to send six men to the artillery park immediately. They were to be paid 9d per day for the extra duty and commanding officers were promised the men would be returned to their regiments once they could be replaced by drivers obtained for the purpose.[87] There were 25 infantry battalions in the army at this time (see Appendix I, Table I.7), so this order resulted in 150 soldiers being removed from front line units. A further requisition of soldiers was made on 9 November, when 10 men were demanded from each of six named infantry regiments, thus raising the number of soldiers employed as drivers to at least 210.[88] The ongoing shortage of drivers led the artillery commander, Lieutenant Colonel John Stewart, to warn Harcourt on 27 December that in the likelihood of any sudden movement the guns and

---

83 Possibly Thomas George William Eastaff (c.1772–1854) who graduated from the Royal Military Academy in 1793 and spent most of his career from 1795 employed by the Board of Ordnance as a surveyor and draftsman in Newfoundland and Quebec. EASTSTAFF (Eastaff), THOMAS GEORGE WILLIAM, army officer, surveyor, and draftsman, *Dictionary of Canadian Biography*, <http://www.biographi.ca/en/bio/eaststaff_thomas_george_william_8E.html>, accessed 8 September 2021.
84 TNA: WO 6/7: Part B, p.28, Richmond to Dundas, 19 April 1793.
85 TNA: WO 6/7: Part B, p.178, Dundas to Murray, 6 August 1793.
86 NAM: 1985-12-15-4: GO, Estreux 20 August 1793; TNA: AO 16/53/4: GO, 17 July 1794.
87 TNA: AO 16/53/6: GO, Grosbeck, 26 September 1794.
88 TNA: AO 16/53/6: GO, Arnhem, 9 November 1794.

wagons would all have to be abandoned for want of drivers.[89] This indeed occurred only a few days later on 4 January 1795, when Corporal Brown noted: 'This morning the artillery began to destroy the limbers and carriages of the guns on the several batteries; as all guns, ammunition, &c. that cannot be taken away, are ordered to be destroyed.'[90]

A second and equally important issue affecting artillery mobility was the lack of horses. The role of the Commissariat in procuring horses for the artillery in 1793 was discussed in Chapter 3. The Board of Ordnance at home had only 300 artillery horses with a further 200 under contract, which were simply not enough for the Flanders army.[91] By 21 February 1794, the artillery had 647 horses, of which 32 were for officers, and the Royal Military Artificers had 46, with 10 for officers and the remainder for wagons. Despite these numbers, the artillery still had 456 horses 'Wanting to Complete' meaning that it was 41 percent short of establishment, which goes a long way to explain its mobility issues. A memorandum prepared by Lieutenant Colonel William Congreve the following month stated that the artillery then had 158 wagons, 754 horses and 229 drivers for the 24 guns of the park and the battalion guns, but that a further 133 wagons, 1,635 horses and 1,107 drivers were needed to supply existing deficiencies and cater for the four additional 5½-inch howitzers and four medium 12-pounder guns intended to be sent to Flanders.[92] This had an adverse impact on the army's other operations, since the artillery proved unable to move itself from winter quarters to the borders of France in February 1794 without commandeering 260 horses from the Commissariat. As Brook Watson told his bosses in the Treasury: 'Undoubtedly the service required this aid yet I cannot but lament the injury which will ensue to my Train [which] would I hoped have been found in perfect Condition to commence the Campaign'.[93]

The mobility problem was not confined only to the quantity of horses, but also the purposes to which they were put. The adjutant-general informed the War Office on 8 September 1794 that having three horses allowed for the tumbrels and ammunition wagons was insufficient given the state of the roads, since the rolling stock was 'so cumbersome and heavy'.[94] The Duke of York ordered that an extra horse should be added to each team. On consultation with the commander of the Hanoverian artillery, Colonel Craig learned that horses in their service were never allowed to pull more than 400 lb in weight. In contrast, the British tumbrels and ammunition wagons carried between 15.5 cwt up to 17 cwt (1,736 lb to 1,904 lb). This resulted in each of the three horses pulling between 579 lb and 635 lb or between 45–59 percent more than was permitted in the Hanoverian artillery.[95]

The poor quality of the roads was a third factor inhibiting mobility. To help overcome this, all artillery guns and wagons, together with all commissariat wagons accompanying the army, were ordered on 14 May 1794 to be equipped with a large fascine to be used for filling

---

89 BL: Add Ms 46,702: p.162, John Stewart to Harcourt, Renkum, 27 December 1794. Don Papers, vol.1.
90 Brown, *Impartial Journal*, pp.213–214.
91 TNA: WO 6/7: Part B, p.28, Richmond to Dundas, 19 April 1793.
92 TNA: WO 1/168: p.525, Return of Ammunition Waggons, Horses & Drivers wanted for the British Royal Artillery, Courtray, 19 March 1794.
93 TNA: AO 16/52: p.227, General Return of the number of Horses in each Corps and Department of the army under the Command of His Royal Highness the Duke of York, Head Quarters, Ghent, 21st Feb'y 1794 and AO 16/52: pp.228–229: Watson to Rose, 24 February 1794.
94 TNA: WO 1/168: p.64, York to Dundas, 7 January 1794.
95 TNA: WO 1/170: pp.369–371, Craig to Nepean, 8 September 1794.

potholes and other obstructions. This order was neglected, and the continuing absence of fascines led to it being repeated on 1 September.[96]

Some idea may be gained of the number of wagons, horses and drivers involved by looking into the rate of ammunition expenditure. Most ammunition was held by the artillery park meaning that the pair of light 6-pounder pieces used as battalion guns were accompanied by a wagon containing only 138 rounds of ammunition pulled by three horses until late 1794, as noted above. First-line ammunition would therefore have been 69 rounds per gun. The action at the Forest of Raismes on 8 May 1793 involved four battalion guns shooting for two hours. Assuming each gun fired one round-shot every two minutes, this would have resulted in the expenditure of 240 rounds in total. The first-line supply comprised 276 rounds on the basis of two full ammunition wagons for the four guns, meaning that the day's work would have used up almost one full wagon-load of ammunition. Battalion guns could fire much faster in exceptional circumstances, with the consequent expenditure of ammunition significantly greater, as volunteer James Wood noted a British gun crew firing a light 6-pounder 10 times in one minute on 31 May 1747 as part of a demonstration for the Duke of Cumberland and the Prince of Hesse.[97] Heavier pieces of ordnance held in the artillery park used the same type of wagon with less ammunition, comprising 120 rounds for a heavy 6-pounder, falling to 66 for a medium 12-pounder and 60 for a 5½-inch howitzer. If we take the siege of Valenciennes as an example (discussed further below) with guns firing once every 22 minutes, a medium 12-pounder or 5½-inch howitzer would shoot through one wagon load of ammunition every day, thus placing a significant strain on the numbers of wagons, horses and drivers available.[98]

Aside from artillery ammunition, the park needed the equivalent of between 14–18 wagons just to carry the 180,000–240,000 rounds of ammunition required for one battalion of 600 infantrymen mentioned at the start of this chapter, on the basis of about 13,000 rounds per wagon, not including the barrels of spare flints. The scale of the transportation task becomes apparent when one considers that the three line and four Foot Guards battalions with the army in 1793 required between 98–126 wagons just for musket ammunition, and some 400 horses to pull them. According to the scale of 100 wagons per mile of road suggested by Adye, the infantry small arms ammunition convoy would have taken up between 1.0–1.3 miles if proceeding in line ahead.[99] In practice, the reserve ammunition carried with the army in 1793 amounted to 240 rounds per man, or the equivalent of 78 wagon loads at 13,000 rounds per wagon. Whatever the case, the volume of transport required led the Duke of York to propose taking the field in 1794 with 176 rounds of reserve ammunition per man, which would have meant only 57 ammunition wagons being required for a force of seven infantry battalions each of 600 men, or a reduction of 27 percent in the transport requirement.[100] Colonel Craig commented on the scale of transport needed for

---

96 TNA: AO 16/53/2: GO, Tournai, 14 May 1794 and AO 16/53/5: GO, Berlicom, 1 September 1794.
97 R. Whitworth (ed.), *Gunner at Large. The Diary of James Wood R.A.1746–1765* (London: Leo Cooper, 1988), p.40.
98 Adye, *The Bombardier and Pocket Gunner*, pp.17–19 and Leslie (ed.), 'Campaigning in 1793–Flanders', p.46.
99 Adye, *The Bombardier and Pocket Gunner*, p.84.
100 TNA: WO 1/168: pp.505–507, York to Dundas, 19 March 1794.

the artillery: 'How the Artillery horses are in the Order which they are, I wonder, for they are allowed but two Captain commissaries to take care of all the immense train of Horses & Drivers which belong to them. It is ridiculous to suppose that they can execute the fortieth part of what is necessary.'[101]

An improvement in the transportation system was introduced at the commencement of the 1794 campaign, when each artillery company in Flanders had one sergeant conductor and 15 'gunners and drivers' added to its establishment, with the three companies belonging to the 4th Battalion (commanded by Captains Thomas Trotter, Francis Laye and Ashton Shuttleworth) having an increased number of between 22 and 26 from August 1793 onwards. These men had been raised according to the Royal Warrant of 11 September 1793, with each company having a theoretical establishment of one sergeant conductor and 40 drivers, meaning that the units in Flanders were significantly under strength. The great majority of these additional personnel were not directly attached to artillery companies, however, and presumably doing duty with the park or battalion guns. They numbered 224 men in March 1794 rising to 344 by August.[102] This development represented increased professionalism, through an assumption of greater control over transportation and a reducing dependence on hired civilian labour. Just as the shortcomings of the Commissariat transport system led to the formation of the Corps of Royal Waggoners in early 1794, failings in the artillery train resulted in the formation of the Corps of Captains, Commissaries and Drivers in September of the same year. Under this reorganisation, a Captain Commissary of Horse was appointed to every park of artillery overseas with several military or civilian Conductors of Horse and labourers to act as drivers. Horses were purchased centrally by the agent G.C. Hopkinson & Son.[103] Unfortunately, these reforms came too late and the Corps did not participate in the campaign in Flanders.

Many of the issues regarding dislocations between the stores and personnel discussed in Chapter 3 also affected the ordnance troops. When the army withdrew from Tournai, Captain Commissary George Williamson wrote to the Duke of Richmond on 4 July 1794 stating that the Duke of York had ordered the field ammunition and stores to be removed from magazines there and sent by water to Condé, where the remainder of the stores were kept on eight bilanders. It now transpired that Condé was itself compromised by the French advance, putting at risk the ordnance *matériel* stored there. It was still not possible to remove the bilanders six days later, when Williamson also had to report the disagreeable intelligence that the French had captured an ordnance ship at Ostend, laden with guns, stores and ammunition.[104]

The delivery of gunpowder to the United Provinces became yet another problem for Williamson. In December 1794 the Burgomasters of Rotterdam and surrounding districts objected to Board of Ordnance transports loaded with gunpowder entering the port. They

---

101 TNA: WO 1/170: pp.369–372: Craig to Nepean, 8 September 1794.
102 TNA: WO 17/2557: Monthly returns of the Royal Regiment of Artillery, 1 March to 1 November 1794.
103 C.H. Massé, *The Predecessors of the Royal Army Service Corps* (Aldershot: Gale & Polden, 1948), p.3; C.E. Franklin, *British Napoleonic Field Artillery* (Stroud: Spellmount, 2008), p.26 and Anon., *The Seventeenth Report of the Commissioners for Military Enquiry: appointed by Act of 45th Geo.III. Chap.47th. Ordnance* (London: House of Commons, 1812), pp.151 and 258.
104 TNA: WO 46/23: pp.17 and 18–19, Williamson to Richmond, 4 and 10 July 1794.

insisted the dangerous commodity be trans-shipped in smaller, locally hired craft for storage in remote creeks. Whether these demands arose from a fear of explosion, a wish to create out-of-season job opportunities for local boatmen, or from a growing antipathy to the allies, is not clear. What is clear is that the cost of hiring these vessels in winter was not cheap.[105]

Effectiveness

The primary round fired by artillery was solid shot, effectively an iron ball weighing up to 12 pounds, the largest calibre generally used by field artillery. While solid shot could inflict casualties up to about 900 yards, canister (a thin metal case filled with many small shot that burst on firing, acting like a shotgun) was more effective at shorter distances of up to about 400 yards. Howitzers were also used extensively by the Royal Artillery in Flanders, being designed to launch their projectiles in a high arc towards the target. The shell they fired, filled with a powder charge ignited by a fuse, was most effective against buildings, which they regularly set on fire, and against cavalry, since exploding shells terrified the horses.[106]

A list of stores and equipment prepared by the Board for 12 light 6-pounder battalion guns included 4,500 'Round Shot fixd to wood bottoms' and 1,500 'Tin case shot'. This was the equivalent of 375 round shot and 125 case shot per gun in a ratio of 3:1.[107] Lists of ammunition for guns of the artillery park were prepared by William Congreve in March 1794. Each medium 12-pounder required 450 'Round shot fixed to bottoms of wood', 50 'Empty shells of 4 2/5 inches diameter fixed to junk wads', 50 case shot 'containing 12 one pound shot in each' and 50 case shot containing '96 two oz. shot in each'. Finally, the 5½-inch howitzers required 475 'Empty shells of 5½ inches Diameter', 25 carcasses, 50 case shot containing '144 two ounce shot in each case' and 50 case shot containing 'nine 2lb shot in each'.[108] These lists indicate that 75 percent of the munitions for the light 6-pounder battalion guns and 12-pounders of the artillery park comprised round shot, whereas 80 percent of howitzer ammunition consisted of common shell, 16 percent case shot and 4 percent carcass, which were incendiary devices.

The morale effect of artillery was considerable; it killed at a distance, and its effects could be devastating. Corporal George Robertson described a hit by French artillery on one of his gun crew during the siege of Valenciennes: 'I commanded one of those Guns one day on the Battry, when a 24 pound shot went thro' one of my men's shoulders & brock my Gun wheel. The blood & flesh of the man was all over my Cloas.'[109]

Even spent rounds could do considerable damage. At the Battle of Vaux (17 April 1794), the Guards Brigade formed up in line of battle in a hollow way 'a considerable distance' from the French artillery when two spent balls: '… which sloping down the bank, went directly through the ranks, killed two men, broke the colour staff of the 3d regiment in the ensign's

---

105 TNA: WO 1/779: pp.361–362, Williamson to Richmond, 8 December 1794.
106 C. Duffy, *The Military Experience in the Age of Reason* (London: Routledge & Kegan Paul, 1987), pp.160–162.
107 TNA: HO 50/317: 'Proportion of Stores necessary to accompany the undermentioned ordnance', enclosed in Hadden to Nepean, 31 March 1794. This document also notes that the 12 guns with their associated ammunition and equipment weighed 80 tons and cost £2779,5,10½.
108 TNA: WO 1/168: pp.505–522, York to Dundas, 19 March 1794 with enclosures.
109 J.W. Fortescue, 'A Conqueror of France – The Corporal of Valenciennes', in *The Times*, 27 July 1928, pp.15–16.

hand, and wounded five more'.¹¹⁰ Despite being of small calibre, the battalion guns could also be highly effective. On 24 August 1793, Corporal Robert Brown witnessed: 'The two guns attached to the flank battalion did infinite execution among the French infantry as they retreated; having got the command of a certain spot over which the enemy must pass, they cut them down by platoons at a time'.¹¹¹

Artillery used in sieges comprised much larger calibres than was practical to use in the field. The Austrian train deployed against Valenciennes consisted of 12, 18 and 24-pounder guns and '… a great many Very large Mortars'.¹¹² The effects of a bombardment could be considerable and the Duke of York wrote to his father that about one third of Valenciennes was destroyed during the siege, with the ruins: '…more shocking than can be described'.¹¹³ Corporal Brown described the scene in more detail when he viewed Valenciennes on 2 August 1793, the day after the garrison marched out:

> To view it from the ramparts on the east side of the town, which was most exposed to our cannon, nothing could appear more distressed and ruinous; not a house could be seen that was not either burnt or partly thrown down; the streets filled with rubbish, mixed with cannon balls and pieces of shells. The miserable inhabitants who now durst crawl out of their hiding places, looked blank and doubtful; they were released from the terrors of death, but all was destroyed, and the uncertainty of their future condition impressed the marks of dejection deeply on every countenance.¹¹⁴

It is perhaps unsurprising that the devastation included a considerable number of casualties amongst the defenders. The garrison of Valenciennes was said to have been about 11,000 men at the start of the siege, but only 5,000 marched out when the city capitulated, since 4,000 had been killed and 1,500 wounded.¹¹⁵ These figures were additional to the unknown number of civilians killed and wounded.

Captured Artillery

The allies captured a significant amount of French artillery, both in battle and from sieges of fortified places. There is little information on how this equipment was put to use, though it is assumed that the artillery captured in sieges was retained for defensive purposes after the damaged fortifications were repaired. The allies traded captured artillery amongst themselves, though whether this was to supplement existing stocks or for some other reason is not known. An example was the notification Commissary-General Brook Watson received from the Duke of York on 2 November 1793 that a total of £420 had been paid to the Austrian *Generalmajor* Kray for 12 cannon and two howitzers at £20 each and 14 tumbrels at £10 each acquired following his capture of Marchiennes on 29 October 1793. The 'Officer of the

---

110 Brown, *Impartial Journal*, p.111.
111 Brown, *Impartial Journal*, p.71.
112 Harrington (ed.), *With the Guards in Flanders*, p.26.
113 York to George III, 2 August 1793, in Aspinall (ed.), *Later Correspondence*, vol.2, p.69.
114 Brown, *Impartial Journal*, pp.59–60.
115 Harrington (ed.), *With the Guards in Flanders*, p.34.

Guards' stated that the cannon, howitzers and 22 tumbrels were brought to the British camp at Camphin-en-Pévèle the following day.[116]

Orders given on 12 May 1794 stated that all captured cannon, tumbrels and colours must be delivered to the artillery park, after which an application must be made within three days to the Commissariat by the commanding officer of the unit performing the capture. The reward money was at the same rate as paid to *Generalmajor* Kray, with the addition that £12 was due for each captured horse and £10 for a colour. In the event of disputes, the reward money would be paid to whichever unit actually deposited the items in the artillery park and unit commanding officers were then left to resolve the division of the money. The general order implies that no payments had then been made for items captured on 17, 24 and 26 April. These captures were considerable, for 'near 50 pieces of Cannon' were taken on 26 April at Beaumont alone.[117] These guns were difficult to use due to differences of calibre and the inferior casting techniques used in their production, making them 'liable to accident'. Nevertheless, at least 26 were shipped to Britain at the end of 1793.[118]

Engineers

The Corps of Royal Engineers consisted only of officers, who were attached as required to companies of non-commissioned officers, artisans and workmen of the Royal Military Artificers. At the start of 1793 there were 11 companies of Royal Engineers until a warrant was issued at the end of January for the raising of two more, making 13 in total.[119] According to the 1793 *Army List*, the officers serving in the Royal Engineers on the outbreak of war numbered five colonels, five lieutenant colonels, 13 captains, 14 captain lieutenants, 27 first lieutenants, 10 second lieutenants and one quartermaster. The Corps of Royal Engineers in Ireland added a few more to these numbers, but only one director, one lieutenant colonel (both of whom ranked as colonels in the Army), two majors, one captain lieutenant and two first lieutenants, making 82 officers in all. The Royal Military Artificers was intended for service in Britain and more civilian than military in composition. Recruits were enlisted as labourers on the same pay and allowances as men joining the artillery. If it was subsequently found they were of good character and skilled as a carpenter, wheelwright, smith, stonemason, bricklayer or painter they were given two guineas bounty and promoted to the rank of artificer, which also meant their subsistence money was raised from 6d to 9d per day.[120] The number of personnel engaged in engineering services in Flanders was extremely small, as Herbert Taylor remarked: 'Our engineers were few, and the officers in very small propor-

---

116 TNA: AO 16/52: p.183, York to Watson, 2 November 1793 and Anon., *Officer of the Guards*, vol.1, p.115.
117 TNA: AO 16/53/1: GO, Cateau, 28 April 1794 and AO 16/53/2: GO, Tournay, 12 May 1794.
118 TNA: WO 1/169: p.141, Memorandum, endorsed 'R[eceived] from Col. Craig 27th May 1794' and HO 50/370: pp.218 and 465: Richmond to Dundas, 5 November 1793 and 'An account of French Guns received from Ostend by the *Triumph* transport embarked by Order of Major General Ainslie'.
119 W. Porter, *History of the Corps of Royal Engineers* (Chatham: The Institution of Royal Engineers, 1889), vol.1, p.217.
120 TNA: WO 55/1402: p.283, Circular to the Battalion offices. This is undated but between correspondence of 17 and 19 May 1793.

tion – no sappers and miners; no pontoniers. The Hanoverians had a train of pontoons which was brought up in the following campaign [1794], and for the use of which we paid largely.'[121] This was to change on 11 September 1793, when the King ordered four companies to be raised specifically for foreign service, two of which were intended for Flanders.[122]

Personnel

The first detachment of Royal Military Artificers landed at Helvoetsluys on 24 March 1793 from the same vessel as Captain Lieutenant William Borthwick and the remainder of Major Jesse Wright's company of Royal Artillery. This consisted of five non-commissioned officers, 30 artificers, one drummer and 50 labourers, the whole commanded by Captain Alexander Sutherland and Second Lieutenant William Stewart of the Royal Engineers. Several more Royal Engineer officers joined the army on 19–20 June 1793 including Captain Gother Mann, First Lieutenant William Gordon and Second Lieutenants Thomas l'Ans and William Rudyerd. The chief engineer in Flanders was Colonel James Moncrieff, who arrived in the United Provinces a few days in advance of the engineer detachment, reaching headquarters at Dordrecht on 24 March. He also held the appointment of quartermaster-general of the expeditionary force (see Chapter 2). The first section of the Duke of Richmond's instructions for Moncrieff, covering operational matters, made no mention of his dual role and instead were framed in the expectation that his presence in the United Provinces would be temporary; Captain Sutherland was therefore made responsible for paying the detachment of Royal Military Artificers. Moncrieff was enjoined to serve with the British forces only, unless his advice was sought by the Dutch Government, in which case this would be conveyed to him through Lord Auckland, the British ambassador at The Hague. These operational instructions concluded: 'As soon as it may appear to you that your assistance can be dispensed with in Holland you are to apply to the Commanding Officer of the British Troops for leave to return to England, as your service is much wanted here.'[123] Richmond then set out to Moncrieff what form of supply-orders, receipts and delivery certificates would be acceptable to the Board of Ordnance.

To return to the Royal Engineer detachment; Alexander Sutherland was first commissioned as a practitioner engineer and ensign on 4 December 1770, so had served in the Army for over 22 years by the time he landed in Flanders. He was appointed bridge master on 12 May 1793, so it is assumed that he continued in command of the artificer company until the arrival of Gother Mann six weeks later. Mann was commissioned as a practitioner engineer and ensign on 27 February 1763 at the age of 16, so had served in the Army for 30 years by the time he went to Flanders. He had been taken prisoner by the French at Dominica in September 1778 and subsequently served in New Brunswick. He was dispatched to report

---

121 Taylor (ed.), *Taylor Papers*, p.27.
122 TNA: HO 50/370: pp.95–97, 'Warrant for establishing a Corps of Royal Military Artificers and Labourers for Foreign Service' and T.W.J. Connolly, *History of the Royal Sappers and Miners, from the Formation of the Corps in March 1772, to the Date when its Designation was Changed to that of Royal Engineers, in October 1856* (London: Longman, Brown, Green, Longman, and Roberts, 1857), vol.1, p.88.
123 TNA: HO 50/368: pp.257–261, Instructions for Colonel Moncrieff Royal Engineers, 13 March 1793, enclosure in Richmond to Dundas, 15 March 1793 and Connolly, *History of the Royal Sappers and Miners*, vol.1, p.83.

on the defences of Ostend in July 1793 to satisfy the fears of Henry Dundas that it was insufficiently defended and produced a report suggesting limited repairs. This was accepted by the Duke of York on the basis of the low cost involved, but the work was stopped when Dundas declared that he did not wish the British Government to assume any expense that could potentially be borne by others.[124] The three senior Royal Engineer officers were therefore not short of experience, at least in terms of their years of service.

The artificer company in Flanders received a significant reinforcement as part of the ordnance train for the siege of Dunkirk when First Lieutenant Ralph Henry Bruyeres and Second Lieutenant Robert Cooper embarked on board the *William and Mary* transport on 26 August with two non-commissioned officers, 66 men, 14 women and six children. They brought the strength of the company up to seven non-commissioned officers, 41 artificers, one drummer and 104 labourers, though three of the artificers were killed during the siege of Dunkirk.[125] The great majority of engineering personnel served with the main army under the Duke of York, but reinforcements under Sir Charles Grey arrived in late October 1793 for the defence of Nieuwpoort included two non-commissioned officers and 28 artificers commanded by Lieutenant Colonel Elias Durnford; these troops were withdrawn at the same time as the infantry they accompanied.[126] A further reinforcement was received when Lord Moira's force joined the army in early July 1794, with Captain Lieutenant William Johnston and Lieutenants John Rowley and William Ford of the Royal Engineers, with two non-commissioned officers and 22 men from the Royal Military Artificers. As the then senior engineer officer in Flanders, Johnston was placed in command by the Duke of Richmond.[127]

The shortage of Royal Engineer officers was not helped by casualties suffered in action. Often at the forefront of any siege-work, theirs was a dangerous job. The death of Colonel James Moncrieff, killed by a wound to the head at Dunkirk in September 1793, was mentioned in Chapter 2. Captain Alexander Sutherland was in the act of crossing a road at Lannoy when he was hit in the thigh by a French cannon ball on 28 October 1793, dying a few moments later. Henry Calvert praised his: '… ability in his profession and worth in private life will make him long and sincerely regretted by all who knew him'.[128] Similar sentiments were expressed by the Duke of York in a letter to the King: 'I have very much to regret poor Captain Sutherland of the Royal Engineers who was killed by a cannon shot. He was a most excellent officer and whose zeal for the service made him volunteer going on this expedition.'[129]

---

124 TNA: AO 16/52: pp.98–101, Return of General and Staff Officers entitled to Bât and Forage Money, enclosure in Murray to Watson, 16 July 1793; WO 1/166: pp.565–566, Murray to Dundas, 16 July 1793 and Porter, *History of the Corps of Royal Engineers*, vol.1, pp.205, 215.
125 TNA: WO 6/7: Part B, p.201, Rogers to Nepean, 28 August 1793, enclosed in Dundas to Murray, 29 August 1793 and Connolly, *History of the Royal Sappers and Miners*, pp.83–86 and 94–95.
126 BL: Add Ms 40,633: p.55, H. Dundas to Grey, 8 November 1793. Stewart of Afton Papers vol.1, and Connolly, *History of the Royal Sappers and Miners*, p.86.
127 TNA: WO 1/779: pp.145–146, Richmond to Dundas, 5 September 1794; WO 25/1146: p.139, Embarkation Return of the Army under Lord Moira (for the Continent), Southampton 19th June 1794 and WO 46/23: p.93, Haddon to Johnson, 30 July 1794.
128 Brown, *Impartial Journal*, p.83 and Calvert's diary, 28 October 1793, in Verney (ed.), *Calvert*, p.162.
129 York to George III, 29 October 1793, in Aspinall (ed.), *Later Correspondence*, vol.2, p.115.

Despite his appointment as bridge master, Sutherland was one of the few Royal Engineer officers in Flanders and was thus employed in other engineering services, such as when he accompanied Sir James Murray on an inspection of the defences of Ostend in June 1793.[130] He was one of the senior Royal Engineer officers with the Army, having been first commissioned on 4 December 1770, and his death had a notable impact. Lieutenant John Rutherford was also wounded at Lannoy due to a case of mistaken identity when a trooper of the 15th Light Dragoons failed to recognise his uniform and cut him in the head.[131] He had been appointed assistant quartermaster-general in 1793 and was captured by the French while reconnoitring their position at Boxtel prior to the British counter-attack on 17 September 1794.[132] Five men from the Royal Military Artificers were also captured in 1794, but no engineering personnel were either killed or wounded that year.[133]

The few surviving strength returns for the army indicate a fall in the number of Royal Military Artificers during 1794. The Army State dated 15 October 1793 (Appendix I, Table I.1) shows a total of 173 rank-and-file present, but this fell to only 69 on 1 July 1794 (Appendix I, Table I.4). There was an increase to 97 one month later (Appendix I, Table I.5) which can be accounted for by the addition of 31 men accompanying Lord Moira. There was a slight drop in November and December (Appendix I, Tables I.8 and I.9) since the number of Royal Military Artificers in the Army was small, meaning they were much in demand for employment beyond Flanders. On 5 September, the Duke of Richmond asked Dundas for the engineer detachment accompanying Lord Moira's force to be returned. They had been working on fortifications in the Channel Islands, and work had been 'much impeded' by their absence. Their services were also required in the West Indies. Once again in the story of British war-making, the available jam was spread very thin.[134]

Differences between the Foot Guards and the line have already been discussed in terms of their unit structures, and the provision of artificer services was no different. A brigade order of 7 March 1793 stated that each Foot Guards regiment left at home was to send nine artificers to their respective battalions in Flanders to act as pioneers.[135] The Guards Brigade in Flanders therefore possessed its own artificer capability that may have performed similar functions to the Royal Military Artificers; no evidence has been found of the line regiments possessing artificer sections, though they would have had one man per company detailed as a pioneer.

Aside from personnel, the Royal Military Artificers also required equipment and transportation, as with other branches of the army. Table 8 shows what the initial detachment commanded by Captain Alexander Sutherland that landed in Flanders in March 1793 was equipped with.[136]

---

130 NAM: 1985-12-15-4: GO, Tournay, 12 May 1793; York to George III, 7 June 1793, in Aspinall (ed.), *Later Correspondence*, vol.2, p.49.
131 Brown, *Impartial Journal*, p.83 and Calvert's diary, 28 October 1793, in Verney (ed.), *Calvert*, p.162.
132 Anon., *Officer of the Guards*, vol.2, p.73.
133 BL: Add Ms 46,710: General Return of the Killed, Wounded Missing & Prisoners of War of the British Troops under the Command of His Royal Highness the Duke of York from 17th April 1794 to 14th January 1795. Don Papers, vol.9.
134 TNA: WO 1/779: pp.145–146: Richmond to Dundas, 5 September 1794.
135 NAM: 1985-12-15-4: Brigade orders, 23 February and 7 March 1793.
136 TNA: WO 6/7: Part B, p.38, The Number of Waggons, Horses and Drivers required to carry the Ammunition, Artificers Tools and Baggage of the Detachment of Royal Military Artificers and

Table 8: The Number of Waggons, Horses and Drivers required to carry the Ammunition, Artificers Tools and Baggage of the Detachment of Royal Military Artificers and Labourers at present on Service in the Low Countries, 26 April 1793

	Waggons	Horses	Drivers
For the Ammunition of the Detachment	1	3	1
For Artificers Tools	3	9	3
For Intrenching Tools	3	9	3
For One Forge Cart		2	1
To attend ditto	1	3	1
For the Commanding Officer's Tent & Baggage	1	3	1
For one Captain & one Subaltern ditto	1	3	1
For four Non Commissioned Officers eighty Privates and One Drummer ditto	1	3	1
	11	35	12

Duties in the Field

The principal duty of the engineers was to design and supervise the construction of field works at times when the allied armies were in static positions. This activity was mainly confined to 1794 since the campaigning season of 1793 was taken up by the sieges of Valenciennes and Dunkirk.

The Duke of York's army provided part of the covering force for the siege of Landrécies, which was undertaken by the Dutch. Their investment commenced on 20 April 1794 while the Duke's headquarters were established to the south-west, at Le Cateau-Cambrésis, between 19 April and 2 May. Soon after the troops arrived in position, large working parties were provided to construct field works, as Corporal Brown of the Coldstream Guards noted on 21 April 1794:

> A working party, consisting of three subalterns, four serjeants, four corporals, and 300 men, was furnished by our brigade this day, for the purpose of throwing up redoubts and strengthening our position.
>
> The working parties continued; they are generally relieved twice in twenty-four hours, and work as long as they can see; they are paid at the rate of four pence per diem.[137]

This work was completed by 24 April, consisting of 'five Redoubts constructed in front of the Camp'.[138] The Guards Brigade built No.1 Redoubt on the right and the Hessians constructed No.5 on the left. It is not known specifically which formations were responsible for the remaining three, though Austrian battalions provided their garrisons suggesting they may also have been responsible for the construction. No.1 Redoubt had a picquet of

---

Labourers at present on Service in the Low Countries, enclosure in Richmond to Dundas, 26 April 1793.
137 Brown, *Impartial Journal*, p.119.
138 TNA: AO 16/53/1: GO, Cateau, 24 April 1794.

two officers and 100 men from the 3rd Foot Guards, with the 53rd Regiment allocated to No.5: '... mounting in it a constant piquet of a Captain two Subalterns & 70 men, with non Comd officers in proportion'.[139] The redoubts also contained artillery, though the number of pieces or their calibre is not known. It was from an observation point on the top of No.1 Redoubt that the Duke of York ordered the cavalry charge at Beaumont on 26 April, when the combined British and Austrian troops defeated the French, who lost their commanding general and some 3,000 men.[140] This action spelled the demise of French attempts to relieve Landrécies, and the town fell to the Dutch after a siege of only 10 days.

The defeat of the Austrian *Feldzeugmeister* Clerfayt at Mouscron on 29 April led him to withdraw to Tournai. The Duke of York was ordered to join him, and his headquarters were at Tournai from 3 May to 24 June when extensive field works were constructed west of the town as described by Corporal Brown on 26 May 1794:

> Ever since we have taken this position we have had a great number of men employed at work.
>
> A chain of redoubts runs all along the front and flanks of this extensive encampment from the Scheldt on the right to the Orchies road on the left, and so well calculated for defence, that we are under no apprehension of being taken by storm.[141]

No mention was made of this work in general orders until 27 May, so it is possible that much of it was conducted by troops other than the British, which is supported by an order for a working party of 100 men from the Guards Brigade to report to *Oberst* Zack of the Austrian Engineers. This party was increased to 250 men on 28 May.[142]

Although the soldiers, principally from the infantry, endured plenty of digging duties in April and May, there was to be no respite when the army reached the vicinity of Oosterhoot, where the Duke of York's headquarters were established between 4–29 August 1794. Lieutenant Charles Stewart of the 28th Regiment remarked that the chief occupation of the army during this period was: '... in throwing up fleshes [flèches] in the sand hills in front of the camp'.[143] Work began soon after their arrival, as Corporal Brown noted on 8 August: 'This day the engineers and others pointed out places for throwing up redoubts, batteries, &c. in front of the encampment and working parties were ordered accordingly.'[144]

A 'pass order'[145] of 8 August ordered a strong working party of two captains, five subalterns, eight sergeants, 16 corporals, two drummers and 400 men to commence work the following day; a quota was drawn from each infantry brigade. An identical working party was ordered for the next five days, augmented to 500 men on 15 August. A separate party, 250 strong, began work on a daily basis from 9 August. It is unlikely this work was popular, as a general order of 15 August stated: 'It having been remarked that several of the Corps

---

139 TNA: AO 16/53/1: GO, Cateau, 30 April 1794.
140 Brown, *Impartial Journal*, p.123.
141 Brown, *Impartial Journal*, p.155.
142 TNA: AO 16/53/2: GO, Tournay, 27 and 28 May 1794.
143 Grazebrook (ed.), 'The campaign in Flanders of 1793–1795', p.11.
144 Brown, *Impartial Journal*, pp.188–189.
145 An additional order issued some time after the main orders of the day.

work extremely ill at the Field works upon which the army is now employed for our own defence…' that any repetition would lead to the withdrawal of the daily spirit ration.[146] Matters seem to have improved as general orders of 18 August stated that an officer of the quartermaster-general's department was to pay 4d each afternoon in lieu of spirits to the men employed. The officer commanding at each work was to have a list of soldiers' names and the regiments to which they belonged for this purpose. The importance of the additional pay was such that the men were not to be marched back to camp until the gratuity had been paid. When this could not be done for some reason, such as on 19 August when a violent rainstorm prevented the distribution of the allowance, brigade majors were ordered to transmit to headquarters the lists of men employed the next day at 8:00 a.m. so they could be paid.[147] Working parties only ceased when the army departed Oosterhout on 29 August.

Engineering works were also an important aspect of the defence line along the Waal, as described by Corporal Brown on 24 October 1794:

> The whole of the river is commanded by our guns, and batteries erected all along the dyke at convenient distances, besides which, a road is made behind the dyke for guns, carriages, &c. to pass and repass; and the river Waal rolls down in such a torrent that to construct any thing like a bridge over it, would require much time and trouble.[148]

The defences also included eight warning beacons along the river line, and elevated signal positions on two churches nearby. The extent to which signalling was conducted during the campaign is unknown, though Congreve did utilise a primitive system when the army was encamped near Menen in 1793, by making signals with the adapted sails of a windmill.[149] A working party of 400 men commenced '… on the Left of the Line, between the Town [Nijmegen] & the Windmills on the heights on the Left' on 17 October 1794, reporting to *Oberst* Schneider of the Hanoverian Engineers; these works continued for the next two days.[150] Separately, commanding officers of all units located on the north bank of the Waal between Bommel and Nijmegen were ordered to ensure that the way behind the dyke was wide enough for guns and infantry to pass. They were also urged to contact the burgomasters of local villages to obtain labour and bridging materials; each regiment was ordered to have 100 fascines made.[151] Captain Lieutenant William Johnstone of the Royal Engineers was responsible for the construction of artillery batteries at Lent, where the carpenters from a significant number of infantry regiments were ordered to proceed on 10 November for a

---

146 TNA: AO 16/53/4: GO, Oosterhoot, 8 August 1794 and AO 16/53/5: GO, Oosterhoot, 9–29 August 1794
147 TNA: AO 16/53/5: GO, Oosterhoot, 18 August 1794.
148 Brown, *Impartial Journal*, p.203.
149 BL: Add Ms 46,702: p.106, Memorandum by Captain John Johnson, nd [November 1794]. Don Papers, vol.1, and C. ffoulkes, 'Notes on the Development of Signals used for Military Purposes', in *Journal of the Society for Army Historical Research*, vol.22, 1943, p.24.
150 TNA: AO 16/53/6: GO, Nymeguen, 16, 17 and 18 October 1794.
151 TNA: AO 16/53/6: GO, Arnheim, 24 October 1794.

period of 10 days, though it appears they were actually on this duty until 24 November.[152] Prior to this, the British established artillery support on the left, or south, bank of the River Waal consisting of a mortar battery commanded by First Lieutenant George Adam Wood.[153] These new batteries on the opposite bank commanded the bridge over the River Waal and the road to Nijmegen, located on the south bank.

Leaving field works aside, a second duty performed by the Royal Military Artificers was to head the columns of march in order to clear aside any obstacles in advance of the troops, and particularly to assist the artillery.[154] Possibly due to the shortage of artificers, similar duties were also performed by villagers co-opted for the purpose: 'Each Batt'n & each Reg't of Cavalry is to carry with them 12 Peasants of the Village at which it is quartered to act as Pioneers, they must have spades with them. They shall be paid and shall have Rations of Bread.'[155]

For most movements of the army, the artificers formed a section of the advance party. They often departed one day prior to the remainder of the troops and consisted of 'The Artificers, Camp Colourmen & pioneers' under the command of Colonel James Moncrieff, whose duty it was to identify and mark out camps for the units following behind.[156] When the army departed Tournai for Valenciennes on 18 May 1793, for example, the advance party was ordered to parade at 10:00 a.m. whereas the main body did not depart until 6:00 a.m. the following morning.[157]

Siege Operations

Valenciennes (2 June–28 July 1793)
The siege of Valenciennes had been agreed by the allies as an early objective of the 1793 campaign, and on 26 May Prince Cobourg appointed the Duke of York to command the operations while the Austrians provided the covering force.[158] There then followed some disagreement as to who would perform the role of chief engineer. Lord William Bentinck's journal entry for 2 June stated that Colonel James Moncrieff, '… was first intended would have the management of the siege', but five days later he noted: 'Owing to some difference of opinion between the Austrian & English engineers, Col Moncrieff he [sic] does not proceed with the works first proposed'. The situation became clear on 9 June when: 'The Austrian engineers are to have the direction of the works against the town'.[159] Henry Clinton outlined

---

152 TNA: AO 16/53/6: GO, Arnheim, 10 November 1794 and AO 16/53/7: GO, Arnheim, 24 November 1794.
153 Grazebrook (ed.), 'The campaign in Flanders of 1793–1795', p.14.
154 TNA: AO 16/53/2: GO, 16 May 1794 and A.V. Papacino d'Antoni, *A Treatise on Gun-Powder; a Treatise on Fire-Arms; and a Treatise on the Service of Artillery in Time of War. Translated from the Italian…by Captain Thomson of the Royal Regiment of Artillery* (London: T & J Egerton, 1789), p.341.
155 TNA: AO 16/53/1: GO, St Amand, 14 April 1794.
156 NAM: 1985-12-15-4: GO, Tournay, 17 May 1793.
157 NAM: 1985-12-15-4: GO, Tournay, 17 and 18 May 1793.
158 Bentinck to Auckland, 10 April 1793, in Auckland (ed.), *William, Lord Auckland*, vol.3, p.15 and York to George III, 27 May 1793, in Aspinall (ed.), *Later Correspondence*, vol.2, p.43.
159 UNL: Pw Ja 610: Bentinck's Journal, entries for 2, 7 and 9 June 1793.

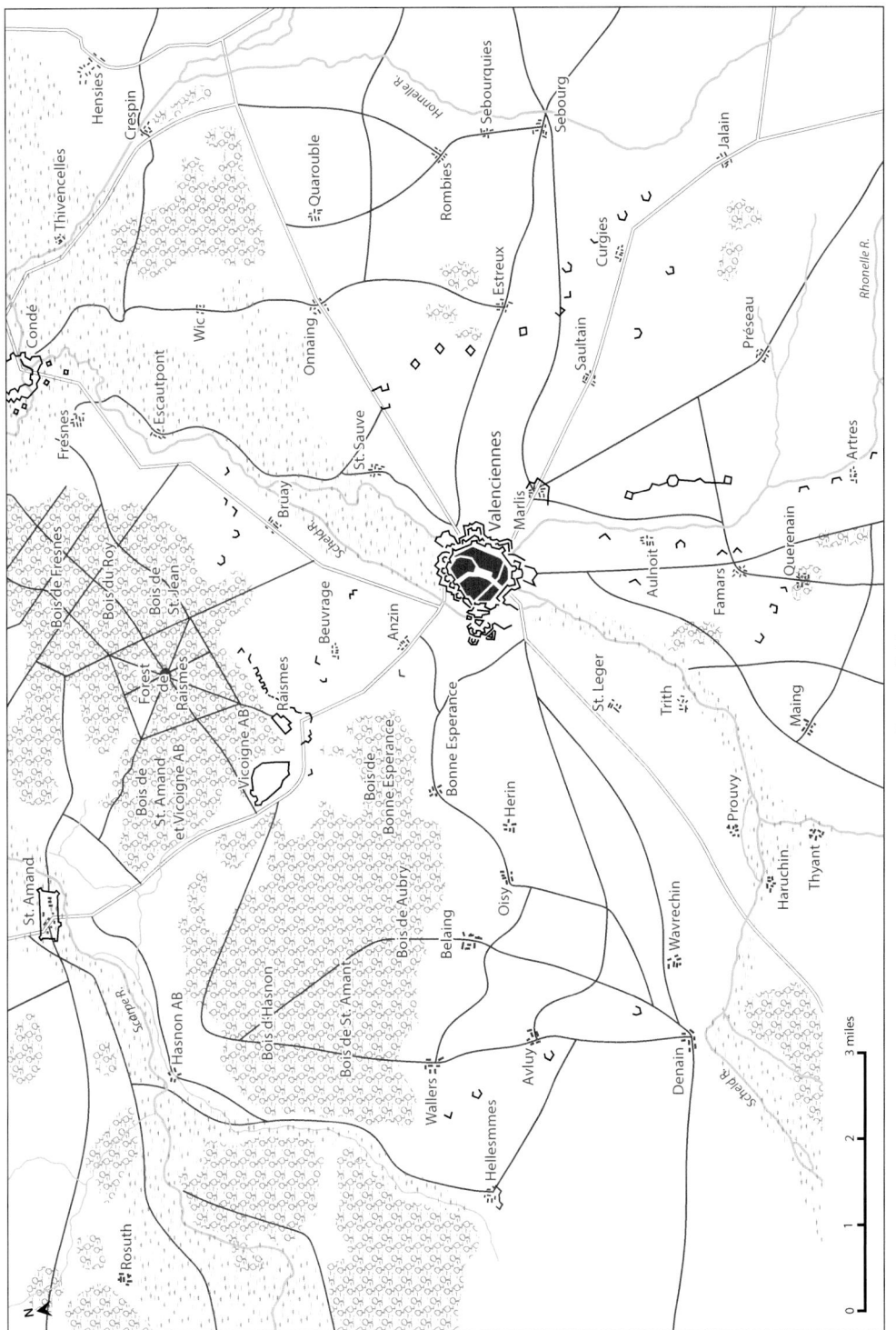

Map 3 Siege of Valenciennes.

the situation in a letter to his father of 7 June: 'The fact is although the D[uke] has the Command they [the Austrians] are to do every thing. Moncrief after beginning to work is put out of the question. He very wisely says they have the means & will of course make use of them, the only difference is they proceed according to rule. Moncrief might have done otherwise.'[160]

Herbert Taylor went even further, stating that the Austrian *Feldzeugmeister* Joseph de Ferraris had direction of the siege, but the 'Officer of the Guards' noted that Ferraris '… superintended the formation of the trenches'. Certain it was, though, that the Austrian *Oberst* Froman replaced Moncrieff as chief engineer after Ferraris objected to Moncrieff's plan of proceeding at a much faster pace than was comfortable for the Austrians.[161]

What initiated the debate was an operation conducted on 2 June, when a working party assembled at 8:00 p.m. consisting of one captain, three subalterns, four sergeants, four corporals and 166 men from the Foot Guards Brigade joined by one captain, two subalterns, four sergeants, four corporals and 100 men from the line infantry brigade.[162] These men were placed under the direction of Colonel Moncrieff and broke ground during the night, aiming to approach a hollow way running 200 yards between the villages of Saint-Saulve and Marly on the town's eastern side, which was intended to become the second parallel. Unfortunately, this work could not be completed in time, so the men were withdrawn at 2:00 a.m. on 3 June. The French were observed bringing artillery to bear on the unfinished work the following day, which persuaded Moncrieff to abandon this project. He therefore employed two working parties each of 250 men to construct a square redoubt opposite the large hornwork which was the principle feature of Valenciennes' eastern defences.[163]

The first 10 days of the siege were occupied in constructing communications to the intended line of the first parallel. The army was then ready to start digging the parallel on the night of 13–14 June, for which a total of 4,500 men were employed, divided into six brigades (see Appendix V). Each brigade was under the direction of an engineer officer and was allocated a designated sector, varying in strength from 400 to 1,200 men according to the task allotted. Only the first three brigades (No.1 British and Nos.2 and 3 Austrian), numbering 2,700 men, were to be employed on the first night. The men were strictly ordered not to make fires or smoke and to keep the strictest silence:

> It is necessary that the officers commanding the working parties, should make their men understand, that the preservation of their Lives, depends upon their working with their utmost diligence during the Night, so that by day Break they may be Covered, against the Heavy fire which will then take place, from the Enemy's works.[164]

The workmen remained undetected, and by morning had managed to dig deep enough to cover themselves from hostile fire. They were relieved at 8:00 a.m. on 13 June by the

---

160 WLCL: Henry Clinton Papers: vol.235, Henry Clinton to Sir Henry Clinton, Estreux, 7 June 1793.
161 Taylor (ed.), *Taylor Papers*, p.36; Verney (ed.), *Calvert*, pp.96–97 and Anon., *Officer of the Guards*, vol.1, p.46.
162 NAM: 1985-12-15-4: GO, Estreux, 2 June 1793.
163 UNL: Pw Ja 610: Bentinck's Journal, entry for 3 June 1793.
164 NAM: 1985-12-15-4: GO, Estreux, 12 June 1793.

other three brigades of workmen. A further five battalions, or 3,000 men, and 300 cavalry provided the covering force. As far as the Royal Military Artificers were concerned, the non-commissioned officers and most of the more skilled men acted as foremen in charge of 300–400 men each.[165] Having constructed the first parallel, it now remained to build the batteries, so a working party of 750 men (of which four captains, 10 subalterns and 612 men were British) under a field officer assembled at 6:00 p.m. on 13 June. These were to be covered by a party of 485 men, with both detachments conducted to their positions by officers of the engineers. The working parties for the batteries continued each morning and evening until 16 June.[166]

The complete contrast between the Austrian resources and those of the British was reinforced when the battering train of 180 cannon and mortars arrived. 'Major Congreve says he never saw such fine artillery' wrote the Duke of York to the King.[167] Colonel Sir Hew Dalrymple of the 1st Foot Guards wrote in wonderment to his wife on 22 June that:

> The Austrians have a profusion of every kind of Workman & Tool … for War is carried on here in a Stile that no idea can reach … Think of 200 pieces of Heavy Cannon with every thing belonging to them coming from Vienna in Waggons; drawn by remarkable good Horses, even the Carriages of the Guns, Wheels and all came in Waggons.[168]

The Austrians also provided significantly greater manpower for the siege. The besieging army numbered 18,335 men, of which the Austrians comprised 8,186 (45 percent), the Hanoverians 6,956 (38 percent) and the British (including the Hanoverian 2nd Grenadier Battalion) 3,213 or 17 percent.[169] Due to the dangers inherent in siege warfare, these statistics were used to ensure a fair allocation of men from each nation to the working parties and covering force.

The Duke of York summoned the town when the batteries were completed on 14 June 1793. This was predictably refused, on which a mortar battery was ordered to open fire. All 14 batteries in the first parallel were in action by the afternoon of 18 June, amounting to forty-eight 24-pounder guns, 24 mortars and fourteen 12-pounders in two batteries set up to fire red-hot shot. These were worked continuously, aimed at the fortifications during the day and the town at night.[170] Although the Austrians supplied the heavy guns, the officers and men of the Royal Artillery were allocated certain batteries to operate them, as First Lieutenant Thomas Fenwick wrote to his wife on 21 June: 'The first night the English opened

---

165 York to George III, 14 June 1793, in Aspinall (ed.), *Later Correspondence*, vol.2, pp.50–51; UNL: Pw Ja 610: Bentinck's Journal, entry for 12 June 1793; WLCL: Henry Clinton Papers: vol.235, Henry Clinton to Sir Henry Clinton, Estreux, 14 June 1793 and Connolly, *History of the Royal Sappers and Miners*, p.83.
166 NAM: 1985-12-15-4: GO, Estreux, 13, 14, 15 and 16 June 1793.
167 York to George III, 11 and 18 June 1793, in Aspinall (ed.), *Later Correspondence*, vol.2, p.50.
168 NAM: 1994-03-129: Papers and correspondence associated with Gen. Sir Hew Dalrymple.
169 NAM: 1985-12-15-4: GO, Estreux, 12 June 1793.
170 York to George III, 14 and 18 June 1793, in Aspinall (ed.), *Later Correspondence*, vol.2, p.50.

their Battery of Mortars (borrowed from the Austrians) we surprised the whole army by the fire we kept up … from seven in the evening till one o'clock the next afternoon.'[171]

Meanwhile, Corporal George Robertson commanded one of the eight 12-pounder guns forming another battery manned by the Royal Artillery during the siege. The work would have been hard, as the men operated shifts of 24 hours in common with workmen digging the trenches. The only battery of this description was at the extreme left (southern) end of the line of attack, operating initially against the village of Marly before being moved to the second parallel and firing at the southern angle of the horn-work when advanced to the third. It would have been one of the two 12-pounder batteries firing heated shot.[172]

Communications to the intended line of the second parallel were commenced on 16 June and the parallel itself, which comprised the hollow way that Moncrieff had attempted to reach on 2–3 June, was completed during the night of 20–21 June. The batteries were moved forward and commenced fire on the town four days later. Most British observers commented that the Austrian engineers were very slow and methodical, and what some may have regarded as 18 lost days is illustrative of the difference between the respective views of the Austrian and British engineers. In the meantime, Colonel Moncrieff was busy during the night of 21–22 June in constructing a new battery at Briquet for six cannon and the same number of 8-inch howitzers. This battery enfiladed the ramparts of Valenciennes to such a degree that it was reported the defenders lost 500 men on the first day it was opened. The sap to the third parallel was commenced during the night of 28–29 June and the parallel itself had been equipped with 19 mortars and eight guns by 9 July. These were subsequently augmented by some of the 32-pounder guns taken from the walls of Condé when that town surrendered on 10 July. The artillery had been due to open fire the same day, but it was subsequently decided to wait until three mines, or 'globes of compression', were ready, which was not until 23 July. Miners had been at work since 6 July, directing their efforts against the horn-work. The first mine was detonated at 9:00 p.m. on 25 July with the remaining two at eight-minute intervals. Three columns then rushed forward, the right and centre formed by Austrian troops and the left by British, Hanoverians and Hessians under the command of Major General Ralph Abercromby. The British component comprised 150 men from the Guards Brigade under Colonel Charles Leigh of the 3rd Foot Guards and the same number of men from the line infantry brigade commanded by Lieutenant Colonel Welbore Ellis Doyle of the 14th Regiment. This column also included Captain Alexander Sutherland leading 30 men from the artificer company, whose job it was to cut down the palisades.[173]

The ammunition expended during the bombardment of the town was considerable, and represented a very significant logistical undertaking for the Austrian field train. According

---

171 Leslie (ed.), 'Campaigning in 1793–Flanders', p.27.
172 J.W. Fortescue, 'A conqueror of France – The Corporal of Valenciennes', in *The Times*, 27July 1928, pp.15–16 and Jones, *An Historical Journal*, map 'Plan of the Siege of Valenciennes'.
173 WLCL: Henry Clinton Papers: vol.235, Henry Clinton to Sir Henry Clinton, Estreux, 21, 25 June and 9 July 1793; UNL: Pw Ja 610: Bentinck's Journal, entry for 29 June 1793; NAM: 1985-12-15-4: GO, Estreux, 25 July 1793; York to George III, 9, 23 and 26 July 1793, in Aspinall (ed.), *Later Correspondence*, vol.2, pp.58–59, 63 and 65; Taylor (ed.), *Taylor Papers*, p.36; Anon., *Officer of the Guards*, vol.1, pp.51 and 56 and Connolly, *History of the Royal Sappers and Miners*, p.83.

'Vue de l'Assaut du chemin couvert de Valenciennes 25/26 Juli 1793', by J. Petrich.
(Anne S.K. Brown Military Collection)

to Lieutenant and Captain Roger Morris of the Coldstream Guards: 'We fired during the Siege 433800 Shot & Shell', which calculates to over 11,724 rounds per day between 18 June, when the batteries first opened, to 25 July, when the town was taken by storm.[174] Although this seems an extremely high number, we know that the Austrian siege train contained 180 guns, which would have meant firing 65 rounds per gun per day, or one round every 22 minutes. This rate of fire is similar to the number of rounds per gun '… demanded by a very able officer, for the intended siege of Lille in 1794…' which was based on 50 rounds per gun for each of the 24-pounders, 10-inch and 5½-inch mortars, and 30 rounds per gun for the 8-inch howitzers.[175]

The Austrians supplied the ordnance required for the siege, the covering army, a significant number of the workmen and much of the engineering expertise. Their methods were undoubtedly successful in ensuring the minimum of allied casualties and ultimate success, but this came at a considerable cost in terms of time. It had taken 26 days from work commencing on the saps to the first parallel to starting the third, and a further 27 days to construct the third parallel and storm the city, principally because the mines took 17 days to prepare. What may be regarded as the undue time taken to prosecute the siege

---

174 Harrington (ed.), *With the Guards in Flanders*, p.34. William Windham stated that 146,000 shot and shells were fired between 18 June and 26 July, not counting the batteries at Briquet and Mount Augin. Baring (ed.) *William Windham*, p.281.
175 Adye, *The Bombardier and Pocket Gunner*, pp.31–32.

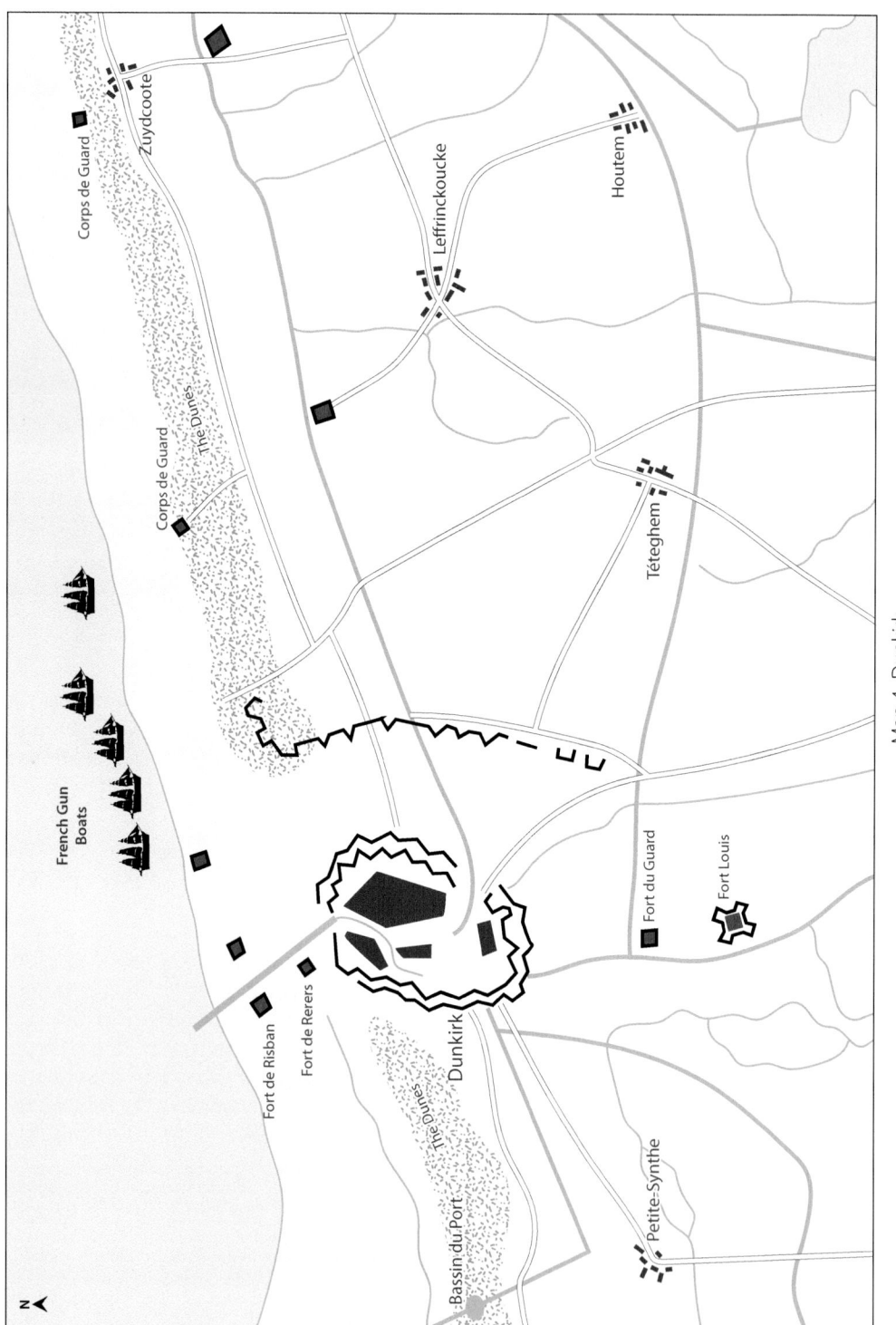

Map 4 Dunkirk.

of Valenciennes was to have consequences for the second siege undertaken by the Duke of York's army, that of Dunkirk.

Dunkirk (23 August–7 September 1793)
The failure to take Dunkirk by siege marked a turning point in the British campaign in Flanders. The town was identified by both the King and the Government as a key objective from the very start of the war, leaving the Duke no choice on whether to conduct this operation. What follows will focus only on ordnance issues during the army's preparations for the siege and the siege itself.[176]

We have already seen that almost all of the ordnance deployed against Valenciennes was supplied by the Austrians or, during the latter part of the siege, taken from the walls of Condé after its capture on 10 July 1793. This meant the Duke of York was entirely dependent on receiving a battering train from Britain before he could commence operations against Dunkirk. Sir James Murray provided William Pitt with a monumental list of the ordnance required in early July 1793 and the Board of Ordnance ordered the equipment to be prepared on 11 July. Murray was assured by Henry Dundas on 19 July that all would be prepared and shipped to Nieuwpoort ready for operations to start. Difficulties began to appear at this stage, principally caused by the lack of artillerymen, which could only be alleviated by the arrival of two companies from Ireland. Various promises followed that the battering train would arrive on time, but it was not until the first week in August that part of it was despatched. The remainder only sailed during the second half of the month, including detachments of Royal Artillery gunners and Royal Military Artificers.[177]

Eleven transports finally reached Nieuwpoort on the morning of 27 August but only two of them had a shallow enough draft to enter the port, so the other nine sailed to Ostend, where they arrived the next day, with a further convoy arriving on 31 August.[178] These vessels carried 24 mortars, thirty-six 24-pounder guns and Major William Huddlestone with the two companies of Royal Irish Artillery already mentioned.[179] Working parties were sent from the army to unload the ordnance, with one of 50 men under Lieutenant and Captain Roger Morris of the Coldstream Guards hauling ten 24-pounder iron guns from the boats and widening the roadways over various ditches on 28 August. A working party of one subaltern and 150 men was ordered the following day to assist in unloading artillery stores. It was not for another three days that the artillery was in a position to move to Dunkirk in barges from Ostend, arriving '… slowly *one* by *one*…' according to the 'Officer

---

176 The Dunkirk operation has been examined in depth by M. Duffy, '"A Particular Service": the British Government and the Dunkirk Expedition of 1793', in *The English Historical Review*, 1976, pp.529–554.
177 TNA: WO 6/7: Part B, pp.82–97, 98–102, 135–142, 144–5, 176–178, 183–186, 191–192 and 199–200, Dundas to Murray, 19 and 30 July and 1, 2, 6, 16, 23 and 29 August 1793.
178 WLCL: Henry Clinton Papers: vol.235, Henry Clinton to Sir Henry Clinton, 28 August 1793.
179 There is some confusion regarding the exact number of artillery pieces on the transports, since Murray gave 24 mortars and thirty-six 24-pounders, whereas a report prepared by Commissary of Artillery George Williamson stated that three 5½-inch brass and one iron mortar, and forty-nine 24-pounders were received by the park of artillery. TNA: WO 1/166: pp.815–818 and 823–826: Murray to Dundas, 28 and 31 August 1793 and HO 50/370: p.37, 'Return of Ordnance and Stores arrived at the Park of Royal Artillery at Zoutcoote near Dunkirk between the 28th of August and 5th of September 1793' enclosed in Williamson to Richmond, 27 September 1793.

of the Guards'.[180] As far as the reinforcements were concerned, First Lieutenant Thomas Fenwick wrote to his wife on 30 August: 'I wish there had been more men and Officers, for the duty will come extremely hard'. These men did not march until 1 September and joined the army the next day.[181]

Aside from the lack of an artillery train, the other key difference between Dunkirk and the siege of Valenciennes was the nature of the ground which, being on the coast, was predominantly sand with a high water table.[182] This was accentuated by the ability of the French to open the sluices of the Nieuwpoort-Dunkirk canal, thus flooding the many irrigation ditches that were a feature of the area, so digging trenches to form parallels was not an option for Colonel Moncrieff. It is possible that this was only fully realised on arrival, since Harry Calvert stated that a trench was commenced during the night of 24–25 August, running from the coastal dunes to beyond the left flank of the army. Instead, the engineers supervised the building of a chain of redoubts with gabions and fascines, which were connected with a roadway to the rear. The redoubts themselves were furnished with field artillery accompanying the army, but which was not of a sufficiently large calibre to damage the fortifications. Work proceeded apace, with a working party of 60 men being attached to the chief engineer from 30 August with orders to make 20 gabions each, while Roger Morris saw '… in the woods numbers of Country Peasants employed in making fascines & Gabions' on 5 September.[183] Sand was also an unsuitable material on which to place the heavy artillery, so Moncrieff used the same method he had utilised at Charleston (April–May 1780), as described by the 'Officer of the Guards':

> Huge frames made of wood, but as light as a feather,
> That take all to pieces, and then put together.
> To be *knock'd up* in England and sent to us here.[184]

The frames reportedly took one night to erect and were then filled with sand before the guns were placed on top. All this effort was to prove of no avail, since the French assembled an overwhelming force of 45,800 men to defeat the covering army of 14,500 men commanded by the Hanoverian *Feldmarschall* Wilhelm von Freytag at Hondschoote on 6–7 September. This forced the Duke of York to abandon the siege and the army commenced its withdrawal at midnight on 7 September, leaving behind 32 pieces of 24-pounder ordnance from the siege train together with 300 barrels of powder and various other stores for which there was

---

180 Anon., *Officer of the Guards*, vol.1, p.86.
181 WLCL: Henry Clinton Papers: vol.235, Henry Clinton to Sir Henry Clinton, 28 August 1793; NAM: 1985-12-15-4: GO, Camp before Dunkirk, 28 and 29 August 1793; Duckers (ed.), *A Diary of the Flanders Campaign*, p.30; Harrington (ed.), *With the Guards in Flanders*, p.39; Leslie (ed.), 'Campaigning in 1793-Flanders', p.28 and Calvert's diary, 2 September 1793, in Verney (ed.), *Calvert*, p.118.
182 Colonel Sir Hew Dalrymple noted: '… a Trench very suddenly indeed fills with water if it exceeds a foot & a half in Depth'. NAM: 1994-03-129-1-4: Campaign diary.
183 NAM: 1985-12-15-4: GO, Camp before Dunkirk, 30 August 1793; Brown, *Impartial Journal*, p.72; Harrington (ed.), *With the Guards in Flanders*, p.39 and Calvert's diary, 24 August 1793, in Verney (ed.), *Calvert*, p.110.
184 Anon., *Officer of the Guards*, vol.1, p.84.

neither sufficient transport nor water in the canal to evacuate them by barge. Four of the 24-pounder guns were subsequently recaptured from the French on 30 November outside Nieuwpoort.[185]

Until now, no British army had conducted a siege of a first-class European fortress solely from its own resources. The Board of Ordnance struggled to meet the demands placed on them by Moncrieff and Congreve, especially for 10-inch mortars, travelling carriages and timber for the frames supporting the artillery. General Sir Henry Clinton, who had served as Commander-in-Chief in North America in 1778–1782, wondered why artillery captured at Valenciennes and Condé could not have been used against Dunkirk instead. There is no definitive answer to this conundrum, except that by the time both towns had fallen, arrangements to supply a siege train had been put in hand in England. The shortage of trained artillerymen also meant that gunners from the Irish establishment were deployed, whom the Duke of Richmond considered to be trained to a lower standard.[186]

Aside from the loss of so much ordnance and engineers' stores, the death of Colonel James Moncrieff was a major blow to the army. He was severely wounded on 7 September by a grape-shot that hit the back of his head and was found unconscious in the hands of Austrian soldiers by Captain and Lieutenant Colonel John St Leger and some Foot Guards officers. The Austrians had removed anything of value from his body and may have mistaken him for a Frenchman given his blue uniform coat and the absence of the designated allied identification symbol of a white handkerchief on his left arm.[187]

An Assessment of the Ordnance Troops in Flanders

As with most aspects of Britain's military capability in 1793, the Board of Ordnance was unprepared for the start of a protracted European war. We discussed in Chapter 5 how the men of some regiments were sent to Flanders with no muskets (Major General Richard Whyte's brigade) or incomplete ammunition (Lord Mulgrave's brigade). The regiments with Lord Mulgrave were also without battalion guns from the time of their landing at Flushing on 26 August 1794 until early November. All of this equipment was the responsibility of the Board of Ordnance to supply, and it is clear that the rapid expansion of the Army, and the multitude of expeditions planned by the Government, had stretched its capabilities beyond what was then possible.

The Duke of York regarded the shortage of Royal Artillery officers and men a 'serious disadvantage'.[188] The consequence was that some battalions had up to 60 of their men

---

185 Calvert's diary, 8 September 1793, in Verney (ed.), *Calvert*, p.121; Duffy, "A Particular Service", pp.548–549 and Anon., *Officer of the Guards*, vol.1, p.113. Henry Clinton wrote to his father, 'The great misfortune is we have lost 35 pieces of heavy artillery 300 barrels of powder 20000 shot with a great quantity of Engineers stores' in WLCL: Henry Clinton Papers: vol.235, Henry Clinton to Sir Henry Clinton, 9 September 1793. Hew Dalrymple thought that thirty-four 24-pounder guns and at least four mortars were lost. NAM: 1994-03-129-1-4: Campaign diary.
186 WLCL: Henry Clinton Papers: vol.235, Sir Henry Clinton to William Henry and Henry Clinton, 30 July 1793 and Duffy, "A Particular Service", pp.539–541.
187 Porter, *History of the Corps of Royal Engineers*, vol.1, p.219.
188 TNA: WO 1/171: p.609: Observations of His Royal Highness the Duke of York, 23 December 1794.

working the guns, which not only weakened their fighting strength but was bad for discipline as they were beyond the reach of their officers. The number of infantrymen doing duty with the artillery gradually rose during 1794. A breakdown of the 'other' category in the army returns comprising Appendix I has not been provided for reasons of space, but the return of 1 July 1794 included 165 soldiers attached to the Royal Artillery, with between 17 and 32 men from each infantry unit with the exception of the Guards Flank Battalion and the 38th and 55th Regiments. This rose to 228 men in the return one month later, 262 in the return of 1 September, 885 on 27 November and 900 on 24 December.[189] The issue of personnel shortage existed from the very start of the 1793 campaign, when in May 1793 Major Jesse Wright had crews for only 10 of the battalion guns, but it became acute following the rapid influx of units to the army from mid-1794 onwards. Herbert Taylor thought the Royal Artillery officers and men were 'well instructed' but the service was let down by the guns being of too light a calibre to match the French pieces, which had greater range. He also considered their poor mobility was caused by inferior, locally purchased, horses and hastily recruited drivers.[190]

Despite these difficulties, the Royal Artillery performed well in Flanders. The Duke of York personally thanked Major Jesse Wright and two of his section commanders, First Lieutenants Thomas Fenwick and Alexander Watson, for their work in supporting the Coldstream Guards and Guards Grenadier Battalion in the Forest of Raismes on 8 May 1793. During the action, a shot from one of Fenwick's guns mortally wounded the Marquis de Dampierre, commanding the *Armée du Nord*.[191] The praise given to Captain James Boag's battery at Vaux on 17 April 1794 has already been mentioned. The following month, First Lieutenant Robert Lawson was also mentioned in general orders for 'his conduct & activity' on 10 May, possibly during the Austrian attack on Kortrijk.[192]

Royal Artillery casualties were high, despite their relatively low numbers. First Lieutenant James de Peyster, commanding the battalion guns attached to the 3rd Foot Guards, was killed by a cannon ball at Linselles on 18 August 1793. The 'Officer of the Guards' stated that: 'He had seen much active service in America, was an officer of great professional merit, and fell deservedly regretted'.[193] First Lieutenant Charles Thornton, attached to the Guards Flank Battalion when First Lieutenant Thomas Fenwick was appointed quartermaster in May, lost an arm on 28 October 1793 at Lannoy.[194] In 1794, Major Jesse Wright and five men were killed and First Lieutenants Turtliff Boger and Thomas Downman with 45 men were wounded at Tourcoing on 18 May when their battery was charged by French cavalry. Total casualties during 1794 comprised one officer, two sergeants and seven other ranks killed, two officers, one sergeant and 72 other ranks wounded and two officers two sergeants and 74

---

189 TNA: WO 1/171: pp.609–610, Observations of His Royal Highness the Duke of York, 23 December 1794 and Appendix I, Tables I.4–I.5 and I.7–I.9.
190 Taylor (ed.), *Taylor Papers*, p.27.
191 Leslie (ed.), 'Campaigning in 1793–Flanders', pp.23–25.
192 TNA: AO 16/53/2: GO, Tournay, 16 May 1794.
193 Anon., *Officer of the Guards*, vol.1, p.72.
194 Brown, *Impartial Journal*, p.83; Calvert's diary, 28 October 1793, in Verney (ed.), *Calvert*, p.162.

other ranks taken prisoner, losses which only accentuated the ongoing shortage of trained men.[195]

The Royal Engineers and Royal Military Artificers only numbered approximately 100 men and are scarcely mentioned in any accounts of the Flanders campaign. Colonel James Moncrieff's personal contribution was more as the army's quartermaster-general than as chief engineer, since the Austrians assumed control of siege operations at Valenciennes while his only independent command at Dunkirk ended unfinished and in failure through causes that were not attributable to him. His death deprived the Duke of York of a highly experienced engineer. He was not replaced, meaning the army was dependent on lower-ranking Royal Engineer officers or on more senior men from allied contingents after September 1793. The role of the artisans and workmen of the Royal Military Artificers was to supervise working parties of soldiers engaged in digging trenches at Valenciennes or field works at Le Cateau-Cambrésis, Tournai, Oosterhout and along the River Waal.

The picture that emerges of the Board of Ordnance troops is that they were dedicated, brave and highly trained, but as an arm of the service they were chronically under-resourced. The provision of skilled technical troops and their equipment in sufficient quantities took considerable resources, which was not something that could be resolved within the timescale pertaining in 1793–1795.

---

195 BL: Add Ms 46,710: General Return of the Kill'd, Wounded Missing & Prisoners of War of the British Troops under the Command of His Royal Highness the Duke of York from 17th April 1794 to 14th January 1795. Don Papers, vol.9; Duncan, *History of the Royal Regiment of Artillery*, vol.2, p.63, and Brown, *Impartial Journal*, p.138.

7

Conclusion

Britain's first military campaign in Europe against the armies of the French Revolution lingers in the collective memory as a humiliating defeat. Blame is attached primarily to Frederick, Duke of York, the British field commander in the Low Countries. It is sealed for all time with a popular song; 'The Grand Old Duke of York' who, with his 'ten thousand men', manoeuvres to no purpose up and down a hill, which might (or might not) be the hill on which stands the town of Cassel, rising high above the Flanders plain. The tune itself is of great antiquity. Many satirical verses have been set to it. The words, in strikingly similar form, have been applied to Richard, Duke of York (later King Richard III of England); to Prince Maurice of Orange (1567–1625) in a version still familiar to the Dutch scouting movement; to a hapless king of France in a version sung by a Tudor stage clown; to King James II of England, and even Napoleon Bonaparte. The variant familiar to us today was not set down in print until 1913, when it was included by Arthur Rackham in his nursery rhyme collection *Mother Goose*.[1]

This is all very amusing, but it should also be taken as a stern warning when we approach the Campaign of 1793–1795 – especially when it comes to the apportionment of blame. What at first seems straightforward, especially when contrasted, as it usually is, with the victorious career of Arthur Wellesley, First Duke of Wellington (plain Lieutenant Colonel Arthur Wesley of the 33rd in 1794), becomes less so as we probe into the military resources at the Duke of York's disposal, and the precarious strategic position in which he was placed from the outset of hostilities. With that in view, the preceding chapters have looked in depth (and mostly for the first time) at the components gathered in haste to form the British expeditionary force to the Low Countries, their day-to-day workings in the field and, resulting from that, the army's ability (or otherwise) to surmount the obstacles in its way – some of them self-imposed. For as we have seen, enemy activity, however decisive in the long term (the allied campaign was at first expected to be a walkover) was only one of those phenomena.

The relatively narrow compass of the action in space and time (as compared, say, to the Peninsular War of 1808–1814) also makes it possible to offer some more general reflections on the waging of war by a professional (volunteer) army at the waning of the *Ancien Régime* and the barely perceived dawn of a new age. Faced by the same unprecedented challenge, the Prussian general and military theorist Karl von Clausewitz focused on making

---

1   A. Rackham, *Mother Goose. The Old nursery Rhymes. Illustrated by Arthur Rackham* (London: Heinemann, 1913).

sense philosophically of what he had experienced in the course of the Revolutionary and Napoleonic Wars, and expressing it in the form of a guide to thinking for army officers and others involved in formulating state policy. Hence, in his famous chapter 7 on 'Friction' in Book One of *On War*, whilst the minutiae of staff-work, the complexities of supply, or the wastage of men and equipment on campaign are inherent in every paragraph, Clausewitz did not find it helpful to describe them. But in the case of the 1793–1795 Campaign – at least as far as the British contingent of the allied army is concerned – it is possible to see in detail how 'friction' kicked in and subsequently gathered pace. Furthermore, it is instructive (not to say ironic) to observe how, in a cruel paradox, it was compounded by the piling-up of the very paperwork necessary to set the army in motion and keep it there. The volume of bureaucracy, in the form of orders, requisitions, requests, returns, reports and official correspondence – not to speak of private letters and papers passing to and from the army – is itself a signifier of the advent of 'modern' armed forces; likewise the abundance of officers, civil and military, whose task it was to process it. No longer an assemblage of a few thousand quasi-freebooters, unleashed on the countryside with unpredictable results, armies now comprised many thousands of men, who must be raised, disciplined, fed, armed, clothed, moved from place to place and kept in good health – all to fight in the right place at the right time. During the nineteenth and twentieth centuries, as armies soared in number, with ever more complex technical and logistical needs, the mass of paperwork expanded to a point where fighting men generally scorned it. The German portmanteau term for this parallel form of war-making, '*Papierkrieg*', embodies their mixed sense of resentment, disdain and comedy. In the Duke of York's little army, exactly contemporary to those Clausewitz would have known, we see these doings at a formative stage, and as a result can go a short distance beyond what he has to tell us.

Eighteenth Century Warfare – but Running Hot

The preceding chapters have recounted how participants in Flanders complained loudly about a multitude of failings in the military administration of the expeditionary force. These encompassed, *inter alia*, the Duke of York's leadership, an inept commissariat, maladministration in the general hospitals, coupled with unacceptable sickness rates, indiscipline, a failed recruiting strategy, the over-promotion of unqualified officers and a shortage of technical specialists. Such issues have come to characterise the experience of Flanders in 1793–1795, though fail to acknowledge that similar experiences were encountered by British armies in wars conducted in Europe and elsewhere during the eighteenth century.

The ad hoc nature in which the Duke of York's staff was assembled was shared by Lieutenant General Sir Charles Grey, who was offered command of the West Indies expedition as late as 18 August 1793 when the troops were intended to sail on 20 September (which was subsequently deferred). He had little time to find specialist officers, especially since his desired commanders for the Royal Artillery, Royal Engineers and medical department were either unavailable or unwilling to go.[2] Grey seems to have enjoyed a much greater role in

---

2   Duffy, *Soldiers, Sugar and Seapower*, pp.41–45.

choosing the individuals to occupy staff positions, whereas the Duke of York was largely presented with men chosen for him (such as Sir James Murray, Colonels Robert Johnstone and James Moncrieff, Brook Watson and Dr Hugh Kennedy), only initially having the freedom to select his aides-de-camp; even the Duke's personal surgeon was appointed by the Army Medical Department. The Duke also suffered from key headquarters personnel arriving well after the troops, including the commissariat staff on 17 March 1793 and the medical staff not until April and May, with the Inspector of Hospitals not appointed until 17 July. All this displayed an absence of planning and preparation on the part of the authorities at home.

Given the absence of any formal officer training apart from of a technical nature by the Board of Ordnance, the ad hoc formation of the staff is unsurprising. There was no pool of suitable officers and, in any case, eighteenth century army staffs tended to be formed on the basis of patronage and connections with training being 'on the job'. Secondly, the mission given to the expeditionary force changed dramatically from the defence of the United Provinces to that of a small component in a large allied army engaged primarily in a succession of sieges on the northern border of France. The amended objective implied considerably more resources than initially provided, while the number of fighting troops significantly increased with the addition of cavalry units in 1793 and infantry in 1794. Both developments necessitated a steady increase in the number of staff officers. The dual role performed by several members of the headquarters staff (Moncrieff as quartermaster-general and chief engineer or Fox as quartermaster-general and infantry brigade commander) had precedents during the American War of 1775–1782 and earlier conflicts.

Despite these challenges, the men assembled to form the Duke of York's staff were generally capable and talented. Many occupied key staff positions in the Army for several decades after the Flanders campaign ended and to them must be given some credit for structural changes in the British Army and the increased professionalism that resulted in a greater measure of operational success as the French Wars progressed. Despite the lack of organised training offered by the service, many staff officers possessed linguistic skills that were vital when the expeditionary force formed a small component of the allied combined army and had taken it upon themselves either to study their profession in Europe or to seek experience with the armies of other European states. The only senior officer to lose his position was Sir James Murray, who was sacked as adjutant-general in December 1793 following his underperformance during the first campaign. The need for a change was recognised and managed swiftly by the King, senior politicians (including the Prime Minister) and the Duke of York in such a way that the latter continued to work with Murray during the 1799 Helder expedition.

The relatively smooth operation of the commissariat is perhaps in contrast to some other features of the Duke of York's army. The reasons for this were, firstly, that it was placed in the hands of business professionals familiar with making contractual arrangements and, secondly, that the working relationship these men enjoyed with the Treasury was excellent. The financial mismanagement and profiteering that had characterised the commissariat during the American War were almost absent in Flanders, and there was only one recorded case of a commissary being charged with misdemeanours. Criticisms of the department resulted from factors over which the commissaries could exercise little personal control, such as swift and often unannounced movements of the army (some for unavoidable operational reasons) and the seasonal shortage of key commodities. Effective provisioning depended on reliable communications between headquarters staff and the commissaries. The system generally worked well when the army was poised on the borders of France and could rely on a network of depots and transportation contracts, but unsurprisingly it started to creak as the army withdrew under pressure into the United Provinces. The continuation of operations during the winter of 1794–1795, and the unplanned retreat of the army into Germany at a season when commodities were scarce, proved the undoing of the depot system, which was by its nature less able to cope with a war of movement.

The Medical Department attracted by far the greatest volume of criticism both during and after the Flanders campaign. It is noteworthy that this criticism was limited to the administrative level in 1793, being focused on relationships amongst the hospital staff in Flanders and between them and the Army Medical Department in London, rather than on the actual provision of medical care to the sick and wounded. This changed as 1794 progressed, reaching a crescendo by the winter of that year. There were two principal causes for this. First, the system of promotions pursued by London placed academically qualified but inexperienced physicians in charge of the hospitals, thus initiating conflict with all the other members of the hospital staff who saw their route to promotion effectively blocked. Secondly, the large influx of recruits from mid-1794 onwards greatly increased the proportion of men unacclimatised to war, which coupled with the widespread shortage of clothing and the harshest winter in 30 years, massively increased the sick list. Evidence of this is provided by the extant returns, which show that the infantry suffered a morbidity of 19–23 percent during the winter of 1793, whereas a year later the figure had climbed to 33–39 percent. Cavalrymen, on the other hand, displayed much lower levels of sickness, with 16–19 percent and 7 percent respectively. While these rates appear high, they were actually little different to those from earlier eighteenth century conflicts in which British troops had been engaged in Europe. Sickness rates were 20 percent in Walcheren in 1747, 29 percent in Germany during the winter of 1760 or 50 percent in the Guards Brigade encamped at Warburg in the same year. From this perspective, the Flanders experience was not unprecedented. The question should really be whether it was acceptable or preventable, and as we have seen, the response was very equivocal.

As an instrument of state power the British Army was tiny in comparison to the land forces of many European nations; 38,945 rank-and-file in 1793, excluding Royal Artillery.[3] Troop shortages were nothing new in Britain at the start of other eighteenth century wars, and often resulted in the adoption of expedients, only to be terminated unceremoniously once the crisis had passed. These included Special Recruiting Acts offering high bounties and short-term enlistments used in 1708, 1756–1757 and 1778–1779 and Press Acts operating between 1704–1712, 1745–1746, 1755–1757 and 1778–1779. These targeted vagrants, debtors and the socially undesirable. Another method was to form companies specifically tasked with recruiting, as was done in 1727–1729, 1744–1748, 1755–1756 and from 1775. A method used in 1760–1761 was to raise independent companies, or augment existing ones, which were either brigaded to form new regiments or attached to existing units.[4] Given the

---
3   TNA: WO 1/903: Return of the Effective Men in the British Army 1793–1806, p.33.
4   G.W. Morgan, *The Impact of War on the Administration of the Army, Navy and Ordnance in Britain, 1739–1754* (Unpublished PhD thesis. Leicester University, 1977), pp.132–142; Clode, *The Military*

time required to obtain trained soldiers under all of these measures, significant military assets from overseas were also utilised. For example, large numbers of Dutch were brought over in 1715–1716, 1719 and 1744, while in January 1746 substantial numbers of Dutch and Hessian troops were serving in Britain. Similarly, 12 Hanoverian and eight Hessian battalions were encamped at Coxheath and Winchester respectively in 1756.[5]

In 1793 Britain did not call on foreign troops to defend the home islands, yet in manpower terms the Army was ill-prepared for a European war. This was accentuated by the multitude of expeditions and other projects planned by Pitt, Dundas and Grenville (which also led to many flank companies of regiments in Flanders being diverted to the West Indies), and the fact that additional manpower was also required by the Royal Navy. Amherst responded to the manpower problem in the same way his predecessors had done: recruiting through independent companies and raising new regiments – admittedly on a more ambitious scale than anything attempted to date. The established regiments sent out their recruiting parties in parallel with this effort. The demand for available men was intense – but it is noteworthy that there was no resort to coercive recruitment, even though it had been tried as recently as the American War. In short, matters proceeded via a 'business as usual' method, yet somewhat akin to putting a jet engine in a rickshaw.

A by-product of this bustling phase of recruitment – at least as far as the officer corps was concerned – was that the average commander of a line infantry regiment serving in Flanders at the end of August 1794 had previously served only zero to four years in post as a lieutenant colonel. Ten of these officers had been promoted that year, hard on the heels of six promoted only the year before. Three of the infantry commanding officers had obtained their *first* commission in the Army within the previous three years, and five of them were aged between 19 and 25. Though it may be unwise to equate age and seniority with competence, it is unsurprising that operational effectiveness could on occasion be compromised by a lack of wisdom and experience at unit command level. Indeed, some infantry regiments were considered so defective on their arrival in theatre that it was felt they could not be relied on in action. Instead, they were sent direct to a garrison. Examples included the 37th Regiment, sent to Ostend for most of 1793, and the 87th sent to Bergen-op-Zoom in July 1794 for similar reasons, while 200 recruits from the 38th were returned to Ostend in June 1794 shortly after their arrival.

A further reason behind the erosion of operational capability was that some infantry regiments were sent to Flanders in 1794 without essential equipment, including firearms and ammunition. Among them were three regiments comprising Major General Whyte's brigade that landed at Ostend in April 1794 and five regiments landed at Flushing in August 1794 under the command of Lord Mulgrave. Many of these regiments were also devoid of battalion guns, which were only supplied the following November. The responsibility for all of these shortcomings lay with the Board of Ordnance, which clearly failed to meet the needs of a rapidly expanding army. Blame for ordering these benighted regiments to Flanders in the first place lay elsewhere, of course. The Board also failed to provide in a timely manner the siege train required to besiege Dunkirk, though in mitigation it should be stated that the

---

Forces of the Crown, vol.2, pp.25–26; Whitworth, *Field Marshal Lord Ligonier*, p.346 and Houlding, *Fit for Service*, pp.117–120.

5   Houlding, *Fit for Service*, p.323, footnote 1.

initial correspondence from the expeditionary force on this subject was directed to William Pitt rather than the Duke of Richmond. The fact that no less a personage than the Master General, Charles Lennox, 3rd Duke of Richmond thought that the Flanders enterprise was a bad idea in the first place and, moreover, had a strained personal relationship with the Duke of York, can hardly have smoothed the way to good working practices. Just as with the travails of the medical department, here was another example of poor working relations becoming a drag on the conduct of operations. However, the behaviour of the Board of Ordnance troops on service was exemplary. Their officers in particular were experienced, well-respected in the army, and the losses they sustained in combat were much regretted. It was a pity that there were simply too few of them in the first place.

As discussed below, while it is far from the intention here to excuse or negate these failures, the fact that many issues kept recurring during wars fought by Britain in the eighteenth century strongly suggests that military administration was constrained by systemic weakness. A fundamental shift in approach was required by Government agencies in Britain for any material uplift in operational effectiveness to result.

Transitioning to War

Successive eighteenth century governments had adhered to a model which perceived the Army as a glorified police force, useful only in its role of maintaining public order and for guarding the King's territories overseas. Numbers were primarily minimised to achieve cost savings, but in part to mitigate the deep mistrust in which the institution was held by some politicians and the general public. Administrative structures reflected the uses for which the Army was seen to exist and represented the default position after each conflict.[6] This model was no longer sustainable by 1793, since the sheer scale of the forces unleashed by the French Revolution, the multiple theatres of operation and the long drawn-out nature of the conflict forced ensuing governments to change their perception of the Crown's land forces, together with the framework required to administer the Army.

Although the Government recognised the Army required a re-energised administrative structure on the outbreak of war, and hence the appointment of a commander-in-chief, the initiative suffered from Lord Amherst's advanced age and incapacity, together with the time required to integrate his office into the Government's operations. One of his duties was to review proposals for raising new regiments.[7] While it is argued here that his policies successfully achieved the recruitment goal, what proved immensely detrimental to the army in Flanders was sending these units to an operational theatre before the men were adequately trained or armed and the officers knew their business. Recruiting for rank on the scale in which it was undertaken also caused significant dissatisfaction and a faltering of morale amongst serving officers, who saw men better placed on the patronage ladder gaining preferment over the heads of veterans.

---

6   Morgan, *The Impact of War*, pp.160 and 380–381 and Steppler, G.A., 'The British Army on the Eve of War', in Guy, A.J. (ed.), *The Road to Waterloo. The British Army and the Struggle against Revolutionary and Napoleonic France, 1793–1815* (London: National Army Museum, 1990), pp.4–6.
7   Pimlott, *Administration of the British Army*, p.362 and footnote 2.

The demands placed on Britain's resources by various expeditions during the first 18 months of the war resulted in a very severe strain on the Army. By late 1794, Harry Calvert was writing to his friend Sir Hew Dalrymple:

> We want artillerymen, we want a general officer at the head of the artillery, we want drivers and smiths; we want three major-generals of infantry; we want a commanding engineer of rank and experience; we want a total reform in our hospital; we want, at least, two out of the four brigades of mounted artillery with which his Grace of Richmond is amusing himself in England; we want a total stop put to that most pernicious mode of bestowing rank on officers without even the form of recommendation, merely for raising (by means of crimps) a certain number of men, to restore to the army those independent and disinterested feelings, and those high principles which should actuate a soldier, and form the basis of military discipline of a free country, and to relieve deserving officers from the intolerable grievance of seeing men without merit, without family, or the smallest pretension to any military ability, pass over their heads, and arrive at a very high, and till now a very respectable rank in the army, solely through the medium of a rascally crimp.[8]

Despite the various shortcomings that Flanders exposed in the structural composition of the British Army, the experience of the campaign was certainly not lost on politicians and administrators at home, or indeed on the participants themselves.

To a great extent, the severe lessons learned during the American War were already incorporated into the commissariat structure as the staff proceeded to Flanders. The services of Brook Watson were critical to this end, since he alone of anyone in the Duke of York's headquarters had personal experience of what had been done during the previous conflict. As Commissary-General, he was responsible for the acquisition of all commissariat supplies while the Commissary of Accounts examined the financial expenditure, and the Deputy Paymaster paid the invoices. Gone were the practices common in America whereby some officers maintained a personal stake in the commodities being supplied and the wheels to carry them, and where separate accounts were maintained by various headquarters departments. One area that did require an overhaul concerned transportation, since the purchase or hire of wagons and horses proved unmanageable in 1793. The unreliability of some contractors and local shortages led the Commissariat to adopt the policy of taking transportation 'in-house', by having bilanders constructed locally and through the formation of the Royal Waggoners. While these initiatives achieved some measure of success, disciplinary problems undermined the effectiveness of the Waggoners and the unit was disbanded in August 1795. It did, however, establish a precedent for the future management of transportation services.

A reform of the medical services had to wait until a Royal Warrant of 30 November 1796. This re-titled regimental mates as assistant surgeons and provided them with commissions instead of the warrants they previously held. They thereby achieved officer status which helped to alleviate the deep dissatisfaction that had characterised this group of professionals

---

8   Calvert to Dalrymple, 12 October 1794, in Verney (ed.), *Calvert*, pp.359–360.

in 1794. The Royal Warrant also increased the daily pay of regimental surgeons from 6/– to 12/– in the cavalry and 4/– to 10/– in the infantry, while that of their assistants increased from 3/6 to 5/– per day.[9] The provision of medical services for future expeditions also benefitted greatly from the involvement of men such as James McGrigor, William Fergusson and Robert Jackson, all of whom had served in Flanders and witnessed the failings there first-hand. A trend towards the increased professionalism in the higher direction of military medical services was apparent, as was the abandonment of an ad hoc administrative structure staffed by part-time civilians.[10]

The key issue of officer promotions that so adversely affected the performance of the army in Flanders, especially during the second half of 1794, came from the policy pursued by the Secretary-at-War, Sir George Yonge, who held the position for most of the 12 years from July 1782, and of Lord Amherst following his appointment as Commander-in-Chief in January 1793. Having experienced at first hand the consequences of over-promotion and officers ignorant of their business, this was one of the first tasks addressed by the Duke of York when he was appointed Commander-in-Chief of the British Army in February 1795. A minimum age of 16 was required for a first commission, subalterns had to serve for two years before promotion to captain, and officers had to serve at least six years before promotion to major. The Duke was also instrumental in supporting the establishment of the staff college at High Wycombe in 1799.[11]

The onset of a major European war, together with the experience of campaigning in Flanders, also initiated a number of changes in the way in which Board of Ordnance services were handled, much of which centred on the provision of additional transport for the field train. This included the formation of the Field Train Department in October 1793 and the Corps of Captain Commissaries and Drivers in September 1794. As a result, a Captain Commissary of Horse, several Conductors of Horse and labourers acting as drivers were appointed to artillery parks serving overseas replacing the hired civilian drivers (or seconded infantrymen) who performed these duties in Flanders. The Board's responsibility for shipping materials overseas was also streamlined in early 1793 when it was passed to the Navy Board and then to the Transport Office in July 1794, placing much of the acquisition of shipping services under central control.[12] Aside from transportation, Board initiatives included the formation of horse artillery units for the first time, when two troops were raised on 1 January 1793 and a further four on 1 November. Although these units did not serve in Flanders, it at least showed that the Board was prepared to change and adapt to the requirements of armies in the field.[13]

---

9   Ackroyd et al, *Advancing with the Army*, pp.47 and 50 and Cantlie, *Army Medical Department*, vol.1, p.198.
10   Kelly, *War and the Militarization of British Army Medicine*, p.12 and Ackroyd et al, *Advancing with the Army*, p.25.
11   Burne, *The Noble Duke of York*, pp.227–230 and Glover, *Peninsular Preparation*, pp.147–154 and 198–199.
12   Anon., *The Fifteenth Report of the Commissioners of Military Enquiry Appointed by act of 45 G.III C.47. Ordnance* (London: House of Commons, 1811), p.335.
13   Frederick, *Lineage Book*, vol.1, p.430.

Last Thoughts

After nine years of peace, neither the British Army nor the Board of Ordnance were prepared for war in 1793. This should not be taken as unusual since, as we have seen, similar circumstances prevailed earlier in the century.

This work has sought to analyse the machinery required for operating the British expeditionary force in Flanders, but what of its commander, the Duke of York? Did, or indeed, could, he have influenced any of the structures discussed here? The answer is, no, he could not. The Duke's only official military position prior to February 1793 was as proprietary colonel of the Coldstream Guards. He had no position with any of the state agencies directing aspects of the Army's management or the allocation of its resources – the War Office, the Horse Guards, the Treasury, and the Board of Ordnance. As the commander of an expeditionary force, he was not consulted on the management of the Army at home where the bulk of his military resources originated. Once in Flanders, his time was fully taken up by Britain's allies in the combined army, operational matters, official reports to the King and Government ministers (Henry Dundas and, from July 1794, William Windham), and the maintenance of discipline. Matters of military detail were, by and large, delegated to his subordinates. The Duke therefore had little choice but to accept the resources he was given, managing them as best he could; thus we have ineffective regiments sent into garrison for training, an extra horse allocated to cumbersome ammunition wagons, or the appropriation from Ostend of 1,000 muskets for his ill-equipped infantry. He did, however, make his views known to the King and senior ministers, but these were rarely committed to paper, instead being delivered face-to-face, during his brief sojourn in London in early 1794.[14] We can only guess at what they may have been and the forcefulness with which they were conveyed.

The Duke's opportunity to effect change in the British Army came only after his appointment as its Commander-in-Chief in February 1795. He was undoubtedly young and inexperienced during his time in Flanders (neither of which were the cause of operational failure), yet he was also subordinate to the Austrian high command and dependent on them for key resources until a late stage in the campaign. This made the consequences of the Austrian withdrawal in early July 1794 all the harder, and the anticipated perception of this in Britain was forcefully expressed by the Duke to Coburg:

> I own I am at length driven to the necessity of openly stating to Your Serene Highness, that the opinion which the British nation must have on the subject cannot be any other than that we are betrayed and sold to the Enemy. And Your Serene Highness knows that in a country such as Great Britain popular opinion is not to be despised.[15]

---

14 York to George III, 15 November 1793 and 11 January 1794, in Aspinall (ed.), *Later Correspondence*, vol.2, pp.120 and 145. The Duke departed Ghent on 5 February and returned to Kortrijk on 5 March 1794.
15 TNA: WO 1/169: p.826, York to Coburg, 7 July 1794.

Apart from expressing his view, there was little else the Duke could do. He was a personable man with a strong sense of duty, but he lacked the dominant personality of a Marlborough or Cumberland and, despite being a Royal Prince, he had no power base at home. This may indeed explain why his reputation could be impugned so readily following the campaign's failures.

From the strictly operational point of view, it is reasonable to ask whether the Army's lack of preparedness had a decisive impact on the outcome of the campaign. The answer is surely, no. In the first place, the double belt of fortified towns stretching across the northern border of France had resisted every attacking army during the entire eighteenth century. The allied combined army battered itself against this obstacle for 15 months, failing only against Maubeuge and Dunkirk, yet was unable to penetrate the barrier. The *'pré carré'* fulfilled its intended function admirably, allowing the French to regroup, train and re-equip until the revolutionaries were able to beat the allies in the field at Hondschoote and Wattignies in September and October 1793. From the allied perspective, the game was up by the end of that year. The fortress towns against which they expended so much labour had bought the required time for French armies to emerge in numbers so large that the allies had no chance of beating them in the field. Secondly, the British expeditionary force was simply too small and too under-resourced to make a difference. Only the big battalions fielded by Austria and Prussia could have swung the war in the allies' favour, and co-operation between the two was most unlikely when seen against a backdrop of mutual suspicion generated by rivalry in Eastern Europe – partitioned Poland especially. Both powers regarded these factors of greater importance than the loss of the Austrian Netherlands, or family connections with the Bourbons and Dutch Stadtholder. Unexpected and unpalatable losses in Flanders, coupled with a lack of finance, led both Austria and Prussia to abandon any attempt to restore the *status quo ante*. We may therefore regard the inability to defeat France, especially in 1793, as a diplomatic failure, not as a military one. The collective attention of the allied powers was not focused sufficiently on a single object, whereas that of the French was. With the majority of the allied forces withdrawing eastwards from mid-1794, the much smaller armies fielded by Britain and the United Provinces could only seek to delay the French advance as long as possible, but they were numerically too insignificant to have any chance of defeating them in battle. Both Lord Cornwallis and the Duke of Brunswick refused the allied command when offered, as both rightly saw the appointment as nothing other than a poisoned chalice. The Duke of York was not in this enviable position.

For the British, the structures discussed in this book evolved into those of more familiar campaigns less than one generation later. This is unsurprising, for the successors of the men who fought in Flanders reaped the benefits of evolutionary change in the administrative organisations necessary for armies to operate in the field. As events showed, especially in 1794, the dramatically larger citizen armies and increased tempo of campaigning changed the nature of warfare as it had existed prior to the French Revolution. Systems and structures take time to evolve in response to changed circumstances and it was an open question in Britain how far these changes ought to go. The evolutionary nature of change ensured that considerable developments took place in every structure discussed in this book during the eighteenth century, a process that accelerated during its final decade and continued for the remainder of the French Wars. From the British perspective, the Flanders Campaign of 1793–1795 therefore represented just one brief point, though an important one, on this evolutionary path.

Notes on the Appendices

Abbreviations

The following apply to Appendices I and II:

Att   Attached
Dr   Infantry drummers and fifers
Gun   Gunners
NCO   Non-commissioned officers
Off   Officers
QM   Quarter Masters
R & F   Rank & File (i.e. corporals and privates)
Sgt   Sergeants
Tr   Cavalry trumpeters

Explanations

On Command   Men extra-regimentally employed (e.g. drivers, guards, hospital orderlies)
Staff
    Appendix I: Regimental staff – chaplain, adjutant, quartermaster, surgeon
    Appendix II: Army staff – officers non-regimentally employed

For reasons of space, the following categories in the original manuscript returns have been omitted:
    Horses
    Changes since the last return
    German auxiliaries and émigré units
    Names of officer casualties

Arithmetical errors in the original documents have been corrected.

Appendix I

Strength Returns

Table I.1: State of the British Troops in Flanders under the command of His Royal Highness the Duke of York. Head Quarters, Tournay 15th October 1793

	Present					Rank & File				Wanting to Complete		
	Officers	Staff	QM	Sgt	Tr/Dr	Present	Sick	On Command	Other*	TOTAL	Sgt	Tr/Dr	R & F
Royal Horse Guards	6	2	2	8		151	39			190			2
1st Dragoon Guards	10	4	4	12	14	138	61			199			1
2nd Dragoon Guards	9	2	4	9	3	158	35	1		194			6
3rd Dragoon Guards	10	3	3	11	3	168	22	11		201			11
1st Dragoons	11	2	4	11	3	174	27	11		212		1	
2nd Dragoons	9	1	3	11	4	154	30	17		201			11
6th Dragoons	9	2	4	12	4	121	52	21		194			7
7th Light Dragoons	8	3	4	9	3	135	50	23		208			4
11th Light Dragoons	7	1	3	8	2	158	22	18		198			2
15th Light Dragoons	9	2	3	9	4	164	27			191			9
16th Light Dragoons	7	1	4	12	4	143	39		6	188			13
[Guards] Flank Battalion	22	3		32	19	405	142	40		587	3		213
1st Foot Guards	17	5		23	12	357	106	89		552	2		248
Coldstream Guards	22	5		26	8	352	134	63	1	550	8		250
3rd Foot Guards	20	4		33	7	354	138	71		563		1	237
14th Regiment	17	3		18	18	359	141	87	15	602			
37th Regiment	26	4		24	15	350	190	34	1	575			15
53rd Regiment	27	4		26	18	433	84	52	18	587			13
Royal Artillery	35	4		13	11	638	98	7		743			
Royal Military Artificers	13			4	1	106	37	30		173			
TOTAL	294	55	38	311	153	5,018	1,474	575	41	7,108	13	2	1,042

* Other: Missing, On Command, On Furlough.
TNA: WO 1/167: pp.334–335: Enclosure in Murray to Dundas, 15 October 1793.

Table I.2: Return of the British Troops on Service in Flanders under the Command of His Royal Highness the Duke of York. Head Quarters, Tournay, 1st December 1793.

	Present						Rank & File				Wanting to Complete		
	Officers	Staff	QM	Sgt	Tr/Dr	Present	Sick	On Command	Other*	TOTAL	Sgt	Tr/Dr	R&F
Royal Horse Guards	8	2	3	12	4	131	30	19		180			12
1st Dragoon Guards	14	4	6	16	6	203	83	3		289			11
2nd Dragoon Guards	7	2	3	10	4	126	41	35		202			10
3rd Dragoon Guards	8	1	4	12	4	135	44		6	185			15
5th Dragoon Guards	11	1	5	17	6	282	31	19		332			4
6th Dragoon Guards	14	3	6	18	6	307	24		2	333			3
1st Dragoons	11	3	3	11	2	146	26	19		191			21
2nd Dragoons	8	2	4	10	3	162	21	26		209		1	3
6th Dragoons	9	2	2	10	4	117	50	29		196			15
7th Light Dragoons	10	2	3	9	4	122	33	39		194	4		110
11th Light Dragoons	7	3	4	9	3	123	33	43		199	4		105
15th Light Dragoons	7	2	3	13	3	152	21	15		188			116
16th Light Dragoons	11	2	4	11	4	156	18	10		184	4		119
Royal Artillery	15	2		7	7	318	105	123		546			
[Guards] Flank Battalion	24	3		33	20	556	102	46		704			96
1st Foot Guards	16	4		27	16	539	111	88		738			62
Coldstream Guards	21	4		43	12	629	96	68	1	794		1	6
3rd Foot Guards	14	4		34	5	492	101	71		664			136
14th Regiment	13	1		22	15	389	163	29	37	618			232
37th Regiment	21	3		28	14	400	159	27	24	610			260
53rd Regiment	23	3		36	18	409	147	25	10	591			259
TOTAL	272	53	50	388	160	5,894	1,439	734	80	8,147	12	2	1,595

The Royal Military Artificers were not listed separately and may have been included with the Royal Artillery.
* Other: Missing, On Command, On Furlough.
TNA: WO 1/167: pp.785–787.

APPENDIX I   273

Table I.3: Embarkation Return of the Army under Lord Moira (for the Continent), Southampton 19th June 1794

Regiment	Officers	Staff	Sergeants	Drummers	Rank & File	Women	Children
19th Regiment	14	4	33	19	537	60	31
27th Regiment	22	3	35	17	540	60	45
28th Regiment	18	2	36	20	589	60	63
40th Regiment	18	4	22	17	615	48	24
42nd Regiment	18	4	34	21	498	60	27
54th Regiment	16	4	33	19	532	47	37
57th Regiment	18	3	39	19	572	56	33
59th Regiment	20	4	36	18	605	61	27
87th Regiment	16	2	42	22	739	90	0
89th Regiment	16	3	28	22	465	60	43
Royal Artillery	7	0	5	0	100	0	0
Royal Irish Artillery	10	0	15	0	153	0	0
Royal Military Artificers	3	0	2	0	22	3	0
TOTAL	196	33	360	194	5,967	605	330

TNA: WO 25/1146: p.139.

Table 1.4: Monthly return of the British Troops under the Command of His Royal Highness the Duke of York, 1st July 1794

	Present					Rank & File				Wanting to Complete		
	Officers	Staff	QM	Sgt	Tr/Dr	Present	Sick	On Command	Other*	TOTAL	Sgt	Tr/Dr	R&F
Royal Horse Guards	12	3	1	13	4	132	23	21	16	192			16
1st Dragoon Guards	15	4	6	15	5	263	64		24	351			
2nd Dragoon Guards	5	2	3	13	4	181	12	15	23	231			
3rd Dragoon Guards	9	2	3	10	3	137	38	36	23	234			
5th Dragoon Guards	8	3	6	18	6	162	28	96	24	310			14
6th Dragoon Guards	8	2	5	14	6	189	35	61	25	310			14
1st Dragoons	7	4	4	8	3	152	21	30	16	219			
2nd Dragoons	6	2	2	10	4	159	25	5	16	205			11
6th Dragoons	9	2	3	9	4	161	16	15	31	223			8
7th Light Dragoons	12	1	4	15	4	173	33	71	17	294			7
8th Light Dragoons	7	3	8	26	6	207	61	26	3	297			96
11th Light Dragoons	7	1	3	16	4	245	29	28	19	321			
15th Light Dragoons	8	2	2	14	3	219	55	35	16	325	1		
16th Light Dragoons	6	2	4	16	3	251	15	23	17	306		1	
Royal Artillery	22	5		13	6	185	38	184	63	470			
Royal Military Artificers	5			1	1	33	9	13	14	69			
[Guards] Flank Battalion	17	3		38	18	597	130	2	66	795			
1st Foot Guards	20	7		38	16	615	94	25	103	837			
Coldstream Guards	19	3		33	15	572	91	8	84	755			
3rd Foot Guards	19	3		34	8	520	147	8	100	775			
12th Regiment	18	4		29	15	619	89	29	115	852			
14th Regiment	15	2		25	14	417	189	29	165	800			
37th Regiment	11	3		21	16	384	156	44	225	809			
38th Regiment	19	3		26	16	301	61	74	78	514			
53rd Regiment	15	2		21	16	336	162	20	315	833			
55th Regiment	14	3		24	19	354	211	48	96	709			
TOTAL	313	71	54	500	219	7,564	1,832	946	1,694	12,036	1	1	166

* Other: For cavalry: On Furlough, Prisoners of War, Bât Men; For infantry: Recruiting, On Furlough, Prisoners of War, With Artillery, Bât Men & Pioneers, Sick in England.

TNA: WO 1/170: p.373, Enclosed in Craig to Nepean, 8 September 1794.

Table I.5: Monthly return of the British Troops under the Command of His Royal Highness the Duke of York, 1st August 1794

(a) Cavalry

	Present					Rank & File					Wanting to Complete		
	Officers	Staff	QM	Sgt	Tr	Present	Sick	On Command	Other*	TOTAL	Sgt	Tr	R & F
Royal Horse Guards	8	3	1	5	2	116	20	80	16	232			
1st Dragoon Guards	10	3	5	18	5	263	47	17	24	351			
2nd Dragoon Guards	5	2	3	13	4	192	12	23	23	250			
3rd Dragoon Guards	7	2	3	10	3	163	23	22	23	231			
5th Dragoon Guards	10	2	6	17	6	201	26	56	24	307			17
6th Dragoon Guards	9	2	6	12	6	216	25	43	26	310	1		14
1st Dragoons	10	4	4	12	3	168	28	7	16	219			
2nd Dragoons	8	2	3	11	4	178	18	2	16	214			2
6th Dragoons	10	2	3	10	4	178	12	10	31	231			
7th Light Dragoons	14	1	4	15	4	266	32	32	18	348			
8th Light Dragoons	9	2	6	16	6	207	61	26	3	297			96
11th Light Dragoons	7	1	4	14	4	262	17	21	19	319			
14th Light Dragoons	4	1	2	6	2	87	12			99			1
15th Light Dragoons	8	3	2	14	4	217	49	31	16	313			
16th Light Dragoons	8	2	4	16	3	265	15	19	17	316			
TOTAL	127	32	56	189	60	2,979	397	389	272	4,037	1		130

* Other: On Furlough, Prisoners of War, Bât Men.

(b) Infantry

	Present					Rank & File				Wanting to Complete		
	Officers	Staff	QM	Sgt	Dr	Present	Sick	On Command	Other*	TOTAL	Sgt	Dr	R & F
Royal Artillery	34	9		19	9	459	51	178	74	762			
Royal Military Artificers	8			2	1	67	12	1	17	97			
Guards Grenadier Battalion	10	3		19	11	315	66		26	407			
Guards Light Infantry Battalion	20	1		40	12	669	96		57	822			
1st Foot Guards	21	6		38	15	588	100	42	98	828		1	
Coldstream Guards	18	3		36	15	598	109	3	84	794			6
3rd Foot Guards	18	3		34	8	565	124	4	103	796			5
3rd Regiment	21	4		36	20	512	15	32		559			291
8th Regiment	15	3		34	20	643	57	13	90	803			47
12th Regiment	13	4		30	17	654	69	4	124	851			
14th Regiment	13	2		23	15	619	205	23	159	1,006			
19th Regiment	16	4		30	19	490	80	28	7	605			245
27th Regiment	20	2		33	14	482	73	11	9	575			275
28th Regiment	18	2		29	17	531	69	23	18	641			209
33rd Regiment	17	4		32	13	718	113	61	120	1,012			
37th Regiment	12	4		21	17	572	183	54	220	1,029			
38th Regiment	19	4		25	16	306	72	49	89	516			334
40th Regiment	17	3		21	14	590	91		18	699			
42nd Regiment	19	4		30	21	452	50	45	22	569			281
44th Regiment	14	3		34	16	540	33	54	83	710	1	1	140
53rd Regiment	19	4		24	20	509	207	13	297	1,026			
54th Regiment	16	4		26	15	462	93	50	6	611			239
55th Regiment	16	4		27	16	465	171	41	93	770			80
57th Regiment	21	4		40	19	514	99	13	3	629			221
59th Regiment	20	3		33	17	554	106	14	9	683		1	167
63rd Regiment	19	3		30	10	832	22	55	34	943			57
87th Regiment	16	4		40	23	678	86	256	2	1,022			28
88th Regiment	13	2		23	18	618	78	64	18	778			
89th Regiment	14	3		23	21	393	73	36	23	525			75
TOTAL	497	99		832	449	15,395	2,603	1,167	1,903	21,068	1	3	2,700

* Other: Recruiting, On Furlough, Prisoners of War, Attached to Artillery, Bât Men, Sick in England.
TNA: WO 1/170: pp. 387–404, Enclosed in Craig to Nepean, 8 September 1794.

Table I.6: State of the British Troops under the Command of His Royal Highness, the Duke of York. Camp at Oosterhoute 5th August 1794

Brigade	Regiments	Present					Rank & File		
		Officers	QM	Sergeants	Tr/Dr	Present	Sick	Total
Maj-Gen. D. Dundas	2DG, 6DG, 2D, 6D	32	15	46	18	918	67	985
Maj-Gen. R. Dundas	Blues, 3DG, 5DG, 1D	35	14	44	14	885	97	982
Maj-Gen. Sir R. Laurie	7LD, 11LD, 15LD, 16LD	36	14	59	15	1,179	115	1,294
Col. Vyse	1DG, 8LD, 14LD	21	11	39	13	632	113	745
Royal Artillery		34		19	9	711	51	762
Royal Military Artificers		4		2	1	87	10	97
Brigade of Guards		87		167	73	3,217	429	3,646
1st Brigade	3rd, 63rd, 88th	53		89	48	2,165	115	2,280
2nd Brigade	8th, 44th, 33rd	51		100	49	2,290	235	2,525
3rd Brigade	12th, 55th, 38th	62		82	49	1,806	311	2,117
4th Brigade	14th, 53rd, 37th	43		66	53	1,924	626	2,550
5th Brigade	19th, 54th, 42nd	51		86	55	1,562	223	1,785
6th Brigade	27th, 89th, 28th	52		85	52	1,519	222	1,741
7th Brigade	40th, 59th, 57th	56		91	50	1,703	306	2,009
87th Regiment		17		40	28	936	86	1,022
TOTAL		634	54	1,015	527	21,534	3,006	24,540

TNA: WO 1/170: pp.131–137, Enclosed in York to Dundas, 5 August 1794.

Table I.7: Monthly return of the British Troops under the Command of His Royal Highness the Duke of York, 1st September 1794

(a) Cavalry

	Present						Rank & File					Wanting to Complete	
	Officers	Staff	QM	Sgt	Tr	Present	Sick	On Command	Other*	TOTAL	Sgt	Tr	R & F
Royal Horse Guards	10	3	1	13	3	180	13	18	16	227			
1st Dragoon Guards	14	4	4	19	6	261	45	5	24	335			
2nd Dragoon Guards	5	2	4	12	4	203	18	3	23	247			
3rd Dragoon Guards	8	2	3	12	3	157	26	10	23	216		1	7
5th Dragoon Guards	11	2	6	17	6	239	26	15	24	304			20
6th Dragoon Guards	12	3	6	13	6	245	28	12	25	310			12
1st Dragoons	8	4	4	11	3	171	26	6	16	219			
2nd Dragoons	5	2	3	11	4	180	15	1	16	212			4
6th Dragoons	10	2	3	12	4	175	16	9	31	231			
7th Light Dragoons	12	1	4	14	3	239	30	41	18	328	1		
8th Light Dragoons	9	3	5	16	6	224	54	3		281			151
11th Light Dragoons	8	1	4	15	4	265	16	14	22	317			
14th Light Dragoons	2	1	2	5	1	88	7			95			
15th Light Dragoons	9	2	2	14	4	211	62	20	16	309		1	5
16th Light Dragoons	8	2	4	16	3	267	9	21	16	313			
TOTAL	131	34	55	200	60	3,105	391	178	270	3,944	1	2	199

* Other: On Furlough, Prisoners of War, Bât Men.

APPENDIX I 279

(b) Infantry

	Present							Rank & File			Wanting to Complete		
	Officers	Staff	QM	Sgt	Dr	Present	Sick	On Command	Other*	TOTAL	Sgt	Dr	R & F
Royal Artillery	36	9		21	12	390	58	322	75	845			
Royal Military Artificers	6			2	1	65	9	7	16	97			
Guards Grenadier Battalion	12	3		19	11	310	69		26	405			
Guards Light Infantry Battalion	20	1		39	11	637	116	3	65	821			
1st Foot Guards	17	6		38	15	593	102	22	109	826		1	
Coldstream Guards	17	4		37	15	592	110	5	84	791		1	9
3rd Foot Guards	25	2		36	8	558	127	5	103	793		1	7
3rd Regiment	21	4		38	19	471	61	27		559			291
8th Regiment	20	3		27	17	529	188		83	800			50
12th Regiment	17	4		27	17	653	103	3	112	871			
14th Regiment	26	2		24	17	595	196	20	202	1,013			
19th Regiment	14	3		28	19	445	85	75	5	610			240
27th Regiment	20	2		35	16	472	87	7	9	575			275
28th Regiment	20	3		31	16	549	58	30	15	652			198
33rd Regiment	18	4		32	13	703	174		133	1,010			
37th Regiment	10	3		22	18	535	257	44	208	1,044			
38th Regiment	21	4		24	16	323	89		110	522			328
40th Regiment	15	3		28	17	577	90		19	686			164
42nd Regiment	17	4		27	17	412	64	72	22	570			280
44th Regiment	16	3		34	19	591	60	3	76	730			120
53rd Regiment	20	4		25	21	526	159	9	342	1,036			
54th Regiment	16	4		30	21	459	90	54	6	609			241
55th Regiment	17	4		25	19	469	211	3	104	787			63
57th Regiment	20	4		39	19	494	92	36	2	624			236
59th Regiment	19	4		38	18	564	86	14	9	673			177
63rd Regiment	21	4		29	10	757	117	29	33	936			64
87th Regiment	16	4		38	18	486	168	280	76	1,010			40
88th Regiment	14	3		24	18	567	115	64	18	764			
89th Regiment	15	3		20	21	405	77	25	17	524			76
TOTAL	526	101	0	837	459	14,727	3,218	1,159	2,079	21,183	0	3	2,859

* Other: Recruiting, On Furlough, Prisoners of War, With Artillery, Bat Men, Sick in England.
TNA: WO 1/170: pp. 551–563 and 689: Enclosed in Craig to Nepean, 26 September and 'Monthly Return of His Majesty's 87th Regt Foot, 1st September 1794' enclosed in Craig to Nepean, 9 October 1794.

Table I.8: State of British Infantry under the Command of His Royal Highness the Duke of York. 27th November 1794

Brigade	Present					Artillery				Sick		
	Officers	Sgt	Dr	R & F	Canon	Officers	NCO	Men	Attached*	Officers	Sgt	R & F
Royal Artillery	13	9	13	139	27				206		1	57
Royal Military Artificers	3	2	1	60					1			18
Brigade of Guards	77	142	48	2,345	10	5	10	60	96	6	12	919
1st Brigade	82	136	86	2,027	8	4	8	52	125	13	20	891
2nd Brigade	87	121	65	1,983	8	3	8	56	129	8	36	807
3rd Brigade	78	106	61	2,056	6	3	7	42	81	7	29	946
4th Brigade	64	86	54	1,482	8	3	7	40	145	8	34	1,212
5th Brigade	72	90	65	1,493	6	3	6	42	60	19	11	750
6th Brigade	75	104	57	1,501	4	1	4	28	42	8	32	927
TOTAL	551	796	450	13,086	77	22	50	320	885	69	175	6,527

* Attached: Infantry serving with the Royal Artillery.
TNA: WO 1/171: p.309: Enclosure in York to Dundas, 27 November 1794.

Table I.9: Morning State of the British Troops. 24th December 1794

Cavalry

Brigades	Present				Sick		
	Officers	Sergeants	Trumpeters	Rank & File	Officers	Sergeants	Rank & File
Maj-Gen. D. Dundas	14	22	10	333	1	1	26
Maj-Gen. R. Dundas	37	47	15	823		2	79
Col. Vyse	24	37	20	842	11	14	96
Light Cavalry	40	47	13	846		3	4
TOTAL	115	153	58	2,844	12	20	205

Infantry

Brigades	Present				Sick			Artillery				
	Off	Sgt	Dr	R & F	Off	Sgt	R & F	Cannon	Off	NCO	Gun	Att*
Royal Artillery	14	9	11	143	4	1	44	29				195
Royal Military Artificers	3	2	1	63			14					1
Brigade of Guards	70	127	50	2,081	10	20	1,161	10	5	10	60	93
1st Brigade	79	138	82	1,712	5	36	988	8	4	8	32	132
2nd Brigade	89	113	63	1,838	5	48	948	8	4	8	53	127
3rd Brigade	70	100	57	1,837	6	35	1,033	6	4	19	60	82
4th Brigade	67	90	52	1,299	12	33	1,318	8	3	8	40	145
5th Brigade	65	72	54	1,097	4	57	892	6	3	6	40	84
6th Brigade	73	102	58	1,634	4	34	1,020	4	2	4	26	41
TOTAL	530	753	428	11,704	46	264	7,418	79	25	63	311	900

* Attached: Infantry serving with the Royal Artillery.
TNA: WO 1/171: p.621.

Appendix II

Casualty Returns

Table II.1: Return of the Killed Wounded, Missing of the Second Brigade of British Infantry commanded by Major General Abercromby in the action of the 23rd May 1793

	Killed			Wounded				Missing			
	Officers	Sgt	Dr	R & F	Officers	Sgt	Dr	R & F	Officers	Sgt	Dr	R & F
Line Flank Battalion:												
– 14th Regiment								2				
– 37th Regiment			1					2				
– 53rd Regiment				1				2				
14th Regiment						2		5				
53rd Regiment								1				
TOTAL			1	1		2		12				

Source: TNA: WO 1/166: p.299, Enclosure in Murray to Dundas, 24 May 1793.

APPENDIX II 283

Table II.2: A return of the Killed, Wounded and Missing of the British troops in the attack of the 25th of July 1793

	Killed				Wounded				Missing			
	Officers	Sgt	Dr	R & F	Officers	Sgt	Dr	R & F	Officers	Sgt	Dr	R & F
Guards Flank Battalion						1		1				
1st Foot Guards	1				1	1		3				
Coldstream Guards								1				
3rd Foot Guards								2				
Line Flank Battalion					1			3				
14th Regiment								1				
53rd Regiment								2				1
TOTAL	1				2	2		13				1

Source: TNA: WO 1/166: p.623, Enclosure in Murray to Dundas, 26 July 1793.

Table II.3: Return of Killed and Wounded of the British Troops under the Command of His Royal Highness the Duke of York at the Siege of Valenciennes. Head Quarters Estreux, 27th July 1793

	Killed				Wounded				Missing			
	Officers	Sgt	Dr	R & F*	Officers	Sgt	Dr	R & F	Officers	Sgt	Dr	R & F
Guards Flank Battalion				7		2		18				
1st Foot Guards	1			9	1	1		18				
Coldstream Guards				3	1	1		13				
3rd Foot Guards				8				21				
Line Flank Battalion					1	1		12				
14th Regiment		1		4	1			14				
53rd Regiment				4				17				
Royal Artillery				3				4				
Royal Military Artificers				1								
TOTAL	1	1		39	4	6		117				

* Includes died of wounds.
Source: TNA: WO 1/166: pp.643, Enclosure in Murray to Dundas, 28 July 1793.

Table II.4: Return of the Killed, Wounded & Missing of the Brigade of Light Dragoons Commanded by Major General Dundas on the 8th Instant. Camp Bourlon, 9th August 1793

	Killed			Wounded				Missing			
	Officers	Sgt	Tr	R & F	Officers	Sgt	Tr	R & F	Officers	Sgt	Tr	R & F
11th Light Dragoons				1				1				
15th Light Dragoons												
16th Light Dragoons				2								6
TOTAL				3				1				6

Source: TNA: WO 1/166: p.727, Enclosure in Murray to Dundas, 9 August 1793.

Table II.5: Return of the number of Rank and File of the three Battalions of Foot Guards under the Command of Major General Lake who engaged the French on the 18th of August 1793

	Killed				Wounded				Missing			
	Officers	Sgt	Dr	R & F	Officers	Sgt	Dr	R & F	Officers	Sgt	Dr	R & F
Royal Artillery	1			1				3				
1st Foot Guards		2		19	5	2		42				
Coldstream Guards	1			8	3	2		40				
3rd Foot Guards			1	7	1	2		43				
TOTAL	2	2	1	35	9	6		128				

Source: TNA: WO 1/166: p.765, Enclosure in Murray to Dundas, 19 August 1793.

Table II.6: Return of the Killed, Wounded and Missing of the British and Hessian Troops in the action of the 24th of August 1793

	Killed				Wounded				Missing			
	Officers	Sgt	Dr	R & F	Officers	Sgt	Dr	R & F	Officers	Sgt	Dr	R & F
Royal Artillery				3	1			7				
Guards Flank Battalion	1	1		8	1			25				
Line Flank Battalion				5				25				1
Hessians	3			13	3			36				
TOTAL	4	1		29	5			93				1

Source: TNA: WO 1/166: p.807, Enclosure in Murray to Dundas, 26 August 1793.

Table II.7: Return of the Killed, Wounded & Missing of the 2nd Brigade of British Infantry, September 6th 1793

	Killed				Wounded				Missing			
	Officers	Sgt	Dr	R & F	Officers	Sgt	Dr	R & F	Officers	Sgt	Dr	R & F
14th Regiment		1		9	5	1	1	36				
37th Regiment	1							3				
53rd Regiment								4				
TOTAL	1	1		9	5	1	1	43				

Source: TNA: WO 1/167: p.49, Enclosure in Murray to Dundas, 7 September 1793.

Table II.8: Return of the Killed, Wounded and missing of the British Detachment at the attack of Lannoi, under the Command of Major General Abercromby, 28th October 1793

	Killed				Wounded				Missing			
	Officers	Sgt	Tr/Dr	R & F	Officers	Sgt	Tr/Dr	R & F	Officers	Sgt	Tr/Dr	R & F
7th Light Dragoons (1 squadron)								2				
15th Light Dragoons (1 squadron)				1	1			3				
Royal Artillery					1							
Royal Military Artificers	1											
Guards Flank Battalion												
3rd Foot Guards								2				
TOTAL	1			1	2			7				

Source: TNA: WO 1/167: p.463, Enclosure in Murray to Dundas, 29 October 1793.

Table II.9: Return of the killed & Wounded, of the British & Hessians, at the Siege of Nieuport. Ostend, November the 1st 1793.

	Killed				Wounded				Missing			
	Officers	Sgt	Dr	R & F	Officers	Sgt	Dr	R & F	Officers	Sgt	Dr	R & F
Royal Artillery								4				
42nd Regiment						1		5				
53rd Regiment	1			12	1	1		32				
Hessians				4	5	5		29				
TOTAL	1			16	6	7		70				

Source: TNA: WO 1/167: pp.577, Enclosure in Murray to Dundas, 1 November 1793.

Table II.10: Return of the Killed & Wounded &c in the action, 24th April 1794

	Killed					Wounded					Missing				
	Off	QM	Sgt	Tr	R & F	Off	QM	Sgt	Tr	R & F	Off	QM	Sgt	Tr	R & F
Royal Horse Guards															
3rd Dragoon Guards		1	1		36					2					7
1st Dragoons					1					2					
11th Light Dragoons					1										
15th Light Dragoons					16	1		1		11					
TOTAL		1	1		54	1		1		15					7

Source: TNA: WO 1/168: pp.745, Enclosure in York to Dundas, 25 April 1794.

APPENDIX II

Table II.11: Return of Killed Wounded &c on the 26th April 1794

	Killed					Wounded					Missing				
	Off	QM	Sgt	Tr	R&F	Off	QM	Sgt	Tr	R&F	Off	QM	Sgt	Tr	R&F
Royal Horse Guards		1			15			4		16					
1st Dragoon Guards					6					13					1
3rd Dragoon Guards	2		1		14	2		2		6	1				
5th Dragoon Guards					9	1	1			8					4
1st Dragoons					6	1		2		11					
7th Light Dragoons					1					19					
11th Light Dragoons															
16th Light Dragoons					1					14					
TOTAL	2	1	1		52	4	1	8		87	1				5

Source: TNA: WO 1/168: p.797, Enclosure in York to Dundas, 28 April 1794.

Table II.12: Return of Killed & Wounded on 10th May 1794

	Killed					Wounded					Missing				
	Off	QM	Sgt	Tr/Dr	R&F	Off	QM	Sgt	Tr/Dr	R&F	Off	QM	Sgt	Tr/Dr	R&F
Staff						1									
Royal Horse Guards					2	1				8					1
2nd Dragoon Guards					2										2
6th Dragoon Guards			1		6	1				3					6
1st Dragoons										19					
2nd Dragoons					6	1		2		9					2
6th Dragoons					3					7					
7th Light Dragoons										4					
11th Light Dragoons					7					3					
15th Light Dragoons										14					
16th Light Dragoons					3	2		2		5					1
14th Regiment					1										
TOTAL			1		30	6		4		73					12

Source: TNA: WO 1/169: p.53, Enclosure in York to Dundas, 11 May 1794.

Table II.13: Return of Kill'd & Wounded on the 17th & 18th of May 1794

	Killed					Wounded					Missing				
	Off	QM	Sgt	Tr/Dr	R&F	Off	QM	Sgt	Tr/Dr	R&F	Off	QM	Sgt	Tr/Dr	R&F
7th Light Dragoons										6					15
11th Light Dragoons	1*						1			1					
15th Light Dragoons					5	1†				14					2
16th Light Dragoons					1					2					5
Royal Artillery			1		4	2		1		17	1			1	26
Royal Military Artificers															5
Guards Flank Battalion			1		17	3		1		54			2	3	25
1st Foot Guards					5					7					20
Coldstream Guards									1	6					9
3rd Foot Guards					1			1		8					32
14th Regiment					8					22	1		3	2	68
37th Regiment			2		11	2		4		34	2		4	1	140
53rd Regiment						3		1		14	1		8	2	191
TOTAL	1		4		53	11	1	8	1	185	5		17	9	538

* Surgeon.
† Surgeon's Mate. A warrant officer but included as an officer for ease of presentation.
Source: TNA: WO 1/169: p.101, Enclosure in Craig to Nepean, 19 May 1794.

Table II.14: Return of Killed Wounded & Missing on the 22nd May 1794

	Killed					Wounded					Missing				
	Off	QM	Sgt	Tr/Dr	R&F	Off	QM	Sgt	Tr/Dr	R&F	Off	QM	Sgt	Tr/Dr	R&F
7th Light Dragoons															5
Royal Artillery			1							2					
14th Regiment			1		4	1		1		28					
37th Regiment					1	3		5		24					2
53rd Regiment					6	3		1		23					12
TOTAL			2		11	7		7		77					19

Source: TNA: WO 1/169: p.121, Enclosure in York to Dundas, 23 May 1794.

Table II.15: Return of the killed wounded and missing of the British Troops on the 13th June 1794 at Ghitz

	Killed					Wounded					Missing			
	Off	QM	Sgt	Tr/Dr	R&F	Off	QM	Sgt	Tr/Dr	R&F	Off	QM	Sgt	Tr/Dr	R&F
38th Regiment					1			1		2					4
55th Regiment			1		4	2		2		29					9
TOTAL			1		5	2		3		31					13

Source: TNA: WO 1/169: p.445, Enclosure in Stewart to Dundas, 15 June 1794.

Table II.16: Return of Killed, Wounded & Missing of the Corps under the Command of Lieutenant General The Earl of Moira at Alost 6th July 1794

	Killed					Wounded					Missing				
	Off	QM	Sgt	Tr/Dr	R&F	Off	QM	Sgt	Tr/Dr	R&F	Off	QM	Sgt	Tr/Dr	R&F
8th Light Dragoons	1				2	1	2			9	1				4
14th Light Dragoons					1					2					
27th Regiment								1		1					
42nd Regiment										1					
54th Regiment								1		4					3
57th Regiment															1
59th Regiment										1					
87th Regiment					1					1					
TOTAL	1				3	2	2	2		19	1				8

Source: TNA: WO 1/169: pp.865, Enclosure in York to Dundas, 10 July 1794.

Table II.17: Return of the killed, wounded, and missing of the army under the Command of HRH the Duke of York the 15th September 1794

	Killed					Wounded					Missing				
	Off	QM	Sgt	Tr/Dr	R&F	Off	QM	Sgt	Tr/Dr	R&F	Off	QM	Sgt	Tr/Dr	R&F
1st Dragoon Guards										1					
8th Light Dragoons															1
14th Light Dragoons										2					
Guards Grenadier Battalion								2		5					
Guards Light Infantry Battalion										2					
1st Foot Guards					5	1				1					14
12th Regiment					1	1				1			3	1	44
33rd Regiment													1		1
44th Regiment															4
TOTAL					6	2		2		12			4	1	64

Source: TNA: WO 1/170: p.445, Enclosure in York to Dundas, 17 September 1794.

Table II.18: Return of Killed, Wounded and Missing, in the Sortie from Nymeguen under the Command of the Hon. Major General De Burgh on the 4th November 1794

	Killed					Wounded					Missing				
	Off	QM	Sgt	Tr/Dr	R&F	Off	QM	Sgt	Tr/Dr	R&F	Off	QM	Sgt	Tr/Dr	R&F
15th Light Dragoons					1					5					1
8th Regiment					2	1				9					
27th Regiment					1	1				10					1
28th Regiment										5					3
55th Regiment						2		1		11			1		7
63rd Regiment						3		2		63					7
78th Regiment					8	5		7		46					
TOTAL					12	12		10		149			1		19

Source: TNA: WO 1/171: p.93, Enclosure in York to Dundas, 7 November 1794.

Table II.19: Return of Killed, Wounded & Missing of the British Troops, under the Command of Major General David Dundas, at the attack of Tuyl 30th December 1794

	Killed				Wounded				Missing			
	Off	QM	Sgt	Tr/Dr	R&F	Off	QM	Sgt	Tr/Dr	R&F	Off	QM	Sgt	Tr/Dr	R&F
19th Regiment					1					4					
33rd Regiment					2										
42nd Regiment									1	6					
78th Regiment	1				1	1				4			1		
80th Regiment					1					3					
Loyal Emigrants										1					
TOTAL	1				5	1			1	18			1		

Source: TNA: WO 1/172: p.31, Enclosure in Dundas to Walmoden, 31 December 1794.

Table II.20: Return of Killed, Wounded, and Missing of the Troops under the Command of Major General David Dundas at Geldermalsen. 5th January 1795

	Killed					Wounded					Missing			
	Off	QM	Sgts	Tr/Dr	R&F	Off	QM	Sgts	Tr/Dr	R&F	Off	QM	Sgts	Tr/Dr	R&F
Staff						1									
11th Light Dragoons					1					6					2
Royal Artillery										11					4
33rd Regiment					1	1				6			1		
42nd Regiment					1	1				7					
78th Regiment						1				24					
TOTAL					3	4				54			1		6

Source: TNA: WO 1/172: p.101, Enclosure in Dundas to Harcourt, 6 January 1795.

Table II.21: Return of the Killed, Wounded, & Missing of the Troops under the Command of Major General Lord Cathcart the 8th January 1795

	Killed				Wounded					Missing				
	Off	QM	Sgts	Tr/Dr	R&F	Off	QM	Sgts	Tr/Dr	R&F	Off	QM	Sgts	Tr/Dr	R&F
Royal Artillery										6					
14th Regiment					6	2		1		20					6
27th Regiment	3				3	3				16					1
28th Regiment								2		65					
British Hulans					1					2					
Piquet of the 3d Brigade					1	1				2					
TOTAL	3				11	6		3		111					7

Source: TNA: WO 1/172: p.119, Enclosure in Dundas to Harcourt, 9 January 1795.

Table II.22: Return of the Killed, Wounded and Missing of Major General Coates's Brigade in the action 10th January 1795*

	Killed					Wounded					Missing				
	Off	QM	Sgts	Tr/Dr	R&F	Off	QM	Sgts	Tr/Dr	R&F	Off	QM	Sgts	Tr/Dr	R&F
Royal Artillery						2				2					1
40th Regiment					3	3		3	1	27					2
59th Regiment								1							8
79th Regiment															
TOTAL					3	5		4	1	29					11

* Slightly higher figures are given in TNA: WO 1/172: p.509, Enclosure in Walmoden to York, 23 February 1795.
Source: TNA: WO 1/172: p.139, Enclosure in Harcourt to York, 13 January 1795.

Table II.23: Return of Killed, Wounded, and Missing in the Attack near Rhenen on the 14th January 1795

	Killed					Wounded						Missing				
	Off	QM	Sgts	Tr/Dr	R&F	Off	QM	Sgts	Tr/Dr	R&F	Off	QM	Sgts	Tr/Dr	R&F
Guards Grenadier Bn										1					
Guards L.I. Bn						1				4					1
1st Foot Guards						1				3					
Coldstream Guards															1
3rd Foot Guards										1					5
54th Regiment										1					3
85th Regiment															3
89th Regiment					1										9
TOTAL					1	2				10					22

Source: TNA: WO 1/172: pp.175, Enclosure in Harcourt to York, 16 January 1795.

Appendix III

Magazine States

Table III.1: General return of meal, oats, straw &c in the King's magazines in Flanders & Brabant, Tournay, 15 October 1793

Magazine*	Wheat Meal (lb)	Rye Meal (lb)	Biscuit (lb)	Beef (barrels)	Oats (lb)	Beans (lb)	Pease (barrels)	Bran (sacks)	Hay (lb)	Straw (lb)	Coals (lb)†
Bruges	826,400	177,800			4,041,407				5,021,799	138,472	
Ghent	542,400	1,478,850			593,120				6,297,800	53,426	
Tournay	193,200	112,500			217,015	475,000	11	62½	1,393,382	213,284	
Ostend	100,000		994,000	9	5,935,115			119	2,441,650		2,617,650
Antwerp	226,000	222,000			1,200,000				1,200,000	500,000	
TOTAL	1,888,000	1,991,150	994,000	9	11,986,657	475,000	11	181½	16,354,631	905,182	2,617,650

* The dates of returns for each magazine were: Bruges, 11 October; Ghent, 12 October; Tournay, no date; Ostend, 9 October; Antwerp, 1 October.

† Coals totalled 969½ chauldrons. A GO dated 26 October 1794 defined 'A Chaldron of Coals [as] 36 Bushells each weighing 75 Pounds'.

Source: TNA: AO 16/52: pp.163–164, Enclosure in Watson to Rose, 1 November 1793 and AO 16/53/6: GO, 26 October 1794.

APPENDIX III   295

Table III.2: General return of meal, oats, hay, straw &c in the King's magazines in Flanders and Brabant on the 22nd December 1793

Magazine	Wheat Meal (lb)	Rye Meal (lb)	Biscuit (lb)	Beef (barrels)	Oats (lb)	Beans (lb)	Bran (sacks)	Hay (lb)	Straw (lb)	Candles (lb)	Coals (lb)
Ghent	512,200	711,400			5,606,600			10,030,340	796,200	12,049	2,272,718
Bruges	399,750	584,020			2,355,123			9,037,269	450,549	7,867	470,439
Ostend	51,800		964,400		700,000		100	1,134,000	2,800	1,312	
Ypres	58,200										
Courtray					410,150			740,996		1,000	
Tournay	193,200	112,500	33,600	8	380,308	11,650	51½	352,540	155,654		
Oudenarde					150,000			160,000			
Antwerp	226,000	222,000			1,200,000			1,200,000	500,000		
TOTAL	1,441,150	1,629,920	998,000	8	10,802,181	11,650	151½	22,655,145	1,905,203	22,228	2,743,157

Source: TNA: AO 16/52: pp.204–207, Enclosure in Watson to Long, 1 December 1793.

Table III.3: General return of meal, oats, hay, straw &c in the King's magazines in Flanders and Brabant, [dated] Ghent 21st February 1794

Magazine	Wheat Meal (lb)	Rye Meal (lb)	Biscuit (lb)	Beef (barrels)	Pease (barrels)	Bran (sacks)	Oats (lb)	Hay (lb)	Straw (lb)	Candles (lb)	Coals (lb)
Ghent	800,600	502,750					6,827,618	11,519,094	3,654,663	10,174	3,861,402
Bruges	527,200	382,770					2,274,822	8,897,459	712,458	3,013	2,612,149
Ostend	26,600		964,400			99	2,820,000	1,550,000			600,000
Nieuport	80,000	160,000					360,000	360,000	200,000		1,174,500
Ypres	344,800	279,200					146,440				
Courtray							60,551				
Tournay	193,200	112,500	33,600	8	11	51½	670,166	438,236	257,650		
Oudenarde								1,203,181			
Antwerp	226,000	222,000					1,200,000	1,200,000	500,000		
TOTAL	2,198,400	1,659,220	998,000	8	11	150½	14,359,597	25,167,970	5,324,771	13,187	8,248,051

Source: TNA: AO 16/52: pp.228–230, Enclosure in Watson to Long, 24 February 1794.

Table III.4: General Return of Meal, Oats, Hay, Straw &c in the King's magazines in Flanders and Brabant, on the 31st May 1794

Magazine	Wheat Meal (lb)	Rye Meal (lb)	Biscuit (lb)	Beef (barrels)	Pease (barrels)	Bran (sacks)	Oats (lb)	Hay (lb)	Straw (lb)	Candles (lb)	Coals (lb)
Ghent	210,400	1,894,800	45,168				9,221,537	9,167,500	3,783,180	6,181	1,707,811
Bruges	101,484	714,484	6,136				152,937	6,492,419	965,554	3,126	920,595
Ostend	78,600	172,000	18,000			97	1,207,960	998,727	30,000		1,342,500
Nieuport			327,376	154	80		332,600	233,981	244,200		
Ypres	94,400	157,600					360,000	461,470	32,910		
Courtray											
Tournay	501,104	533,300	168,200	8	11	43	1,132,551	1,416,510	650,609		
Oudenarde											
Antwerp	2,635,400	3,189,400					10,337,168	21,562,019	3,361,942		
Valenciennes							516,400	125,400			
TOTAL	3,621,388	6,661,584	564,880	162	91	140	23,261,153	40,458,026	9,068,395	9,307	3,970,906

Source: TNA: AO 16/52: p.297, Enclosure in Watson to Long, 17 June 1794.

Appendix IV

March Discipline

Head Quarters Tournay
8 May 1794
Parole Quirinus
C.S. Copenhagen

His Royal Highness the Commander in Chief understanding that Great irregularities prevail in the march of the Baggage of the army, and that officers Servants & Batmen not only are inattentive & disobedient to the directions of the Baggage Master General but that many of them have even been guilty of great insolence to him in the Execution of his duty, He desires that the officers Servants and Batmen of every Regiment may be assembled and that the following Standing Regulations for the movement of the Baggage of the army may be read to them, and that it may be at the same time explained to them fully.

The Baggage Master has His Royal Highness's positive orders to enforce his authority by inflicting immediate Punishment on any Batman or Servant who may be guilty of any disobedience or Insolence.

The carts and Baggage Waggons are always to have their Portion of Forage with them, and as it must frequently happen that the Baggage may be absent from the army for a few days, the Baggage Guard and Batmen must be provided with four days Subsistence.

Each Regiment to appoint a Non Commissioned Officer to regulate the Batmen on a march.

The Bat Horses march upon that Flank of their Regiment which is not the Point Flank, and whenever there are Defilies – that is – whenever they cannot march on the Flank of the Regiment, they must follow it close in the Rear, but they must in this case keep well up, and as many as possible a Breast. Otherwise they create too great a distance between the Battalions.

When they march upon a Flank, they must absolutely keep upon the Flank of their own Troop or Company, and not be straggling to that of another. No carriage whatever is to be allowed in the Column of Troops excepting the Ammunition Carriages.

Baggage
A Careful Serjeant in each Regiment who is not to be changed, is to be appointed Baggage Master to the Regiment, whose Duty will be to assemble the Baggage at the Hour appointed,

attend it and arrange it in the Line of March and to be answerable to the Baggage Master General for the proper behaviour of the Drivers & Servants with the Baggage.

No Baggage Waggon or Cart whatsoever is to be permitted to change its place or Rank appointed to it, or break the Line, or stop when they think proper, but are to follow as close as possible, and whoever disobeys this order to be severely punished on the spot.

The Baggage either forms a separate Column or Marches in the Rear of the Column to which it respectively belongs according to circumstances at the time of the march.

The greatest order must be preserved in the movement and arrangement.

The Baggage Master and his officers assisted by His Guard and the different Regimental Baggage Guards must keep up the strictest discipline amongst the Drivers.

If the Baggage follows the Column to which it belongs, it moves in the following order viz.

The Generals Commanding the Column, then that of the Brigades as they follow in the Column, with the Officers Commanding Brigades at the Head of that of their respective Brigades.

Wherever the Commander in Chief's Baggage is, of course it goes first, and it is immediately followed by the Military Chest, which must be attended by a proper Guard.

If the Baggage of the army forms a separate Column, the Commander in Chief's with His Staff, marches first.

Then the Military Chest.

Then that of the Generals and Lt. Generals of the army in seniority and then that of the Brigades, the Baggage of each Commanding officer if in Brigade, marches at the Head of that of his Brigade.

Such reserve ammunition as does not march in the Column of Troops always preceeds all Baggage whatever.

The Forage Waggons follow the Baggage of their respective Brigades.

The Baggage Master General is solely responsible for the orders of the Baggage, and he must always have a proper number of his officers with that of each Column.

If there is a Gen'l Escorte ordered for the baggage, the Baggage Master takes his directions as to the hour of march, Route &c, from the officer Commanding the Escorte, but he himself is solely charged with the interior management of the Baggage.

The Waggons must always be kept close up, and no one upon any account, must be suffered to loiter behind. If a Waggon breaks down in a narrow Road, it must instantly be put on one side, and the Bagg'e must be taken up by the next waggon of the same Brigade.

The Baggage Master General must report the safe arrival of the Baggage to the Quarter Master Gen'l.

Upon marches the Baggage Master must have a Guard of a non commissioned officer & 4 Dragoons and all the Baggage Guards of the Brigades and Regiments are under his immediate direction.

At the hour fixed for the army to move off the Ground it will be expected the Tents are struck, the Baggage Loaded, and the Troops formed at the Head of their Incampments.

The Bat Horses are to be drawn up a Hundred Paces in the Rear of their Respective Regiments Ranked by Troops or Companies from Right to Left, as the Troops or Companies stand in the Regiments or Battalions.

The Carriages of the Regiment are to be drawn together behind the centre of it, a Hundred Paces in the rear of the Bat Horses under the proper Baggage Guard, and arranged in a Rank as nearly as possible.

The officers Commanding Brigades are to be responsible for this and are on each day's march to send a Subal'n officer from their Brigades with the Baggage to see the orders relating to it complied with, and those that the Baggage Mas'r Gen'l may give on the march enforced.

If there is no order to the Contrary the Bat Horses move off with their Regiment, but the Wheel Carriages do not stir upon any account till directed to do so, by some person of the Bag'e Masr's Department whose orders they must instantly comply with.

When the army is to move or detailed order of march is given, and the Baggage Master receives from the Qua'r M'r General or His Deputy the orders respecting the march of the Baggage, for which it is his business to give the proper directions to the Baggage of the Regiments.

In this there can be no difficulty if the Baggage of each Regiment is drawn up with its proper Guard in the manner here described.

The Cattle of course follow the Columns in which the Baggage of the Brigade to which they belong marches, and the Drivers are to be equally under the orders of the Baggage Master.

The Commander in Chief is convinced that all officers will see the necessity of the utmost regularity being observed in the movement of Baggage, and that they will consequently take care that these regulations are strictly adhered to, and it is to be understood that officers are to be responsible that their Carriages punctually attend at the hours directed, and that their servants conform implicitly to the orders here given.

When the heavy baggage is ordered not to move with the army, the Reg'ts forage waggons are not to be considered of this discription, but are to attend their Corps with the Bat Horses and whenever the Bat horses are ordered not to proceed, those carrying the men's Camp Kettles and officers Canteens not to be included.

It being indispensably necessary that the Commander in Chief should be assured that there are at all times a sufficient number of officers with every Reg't in Camp ready to turn out in case of the Line being suddenly ordered under arms H.R.H. therefore orders that no officers leave the Camp without the knowledge of the officer Commanding the Regiment to which he belongs who is to be answerable to the General or other officer Commanding the Brigade that there are never less than half the officers of their respective Regiment present.

The Com'r in Chief desires to remind the General Officers that he looks up to them for the due execution of this as well as of all orders whatever each in his respective Brigade.

No soldier is on any account to pass the Piquets of the Army; nor is any one to come to Town but on particular business when he is to have a written pass.

Officers Servants and Batmen tho' not included in the above are however not to be absent from camp unless upon their Master's business, and officers are expressly desired to prevent their Servants absenting themselves more than is indispensible for that purpose.

The above are to be considered as standing orders for the army.[1]

---

1   TNA: AO 16/53/2: GO, Tournay, 8 May 1794.

Appendix V

Dispositions for Opening the First Parallel at Valenciennes

Estreux 12th June 1793[1]

Parole Silvester
C.S. Landaus

Major General of the Day tomorrow C'l Oyenhausen
Field Off'r British Lt Colo'l Gascoigne
Field Off'r Hanovn Lt Colo'l Thun
Additional Field officer for the Post at Briquet this Evening Lieutenant Colonel Finch.

Disposition
Number of Troops Wanted for opening ye Trenches & forming the 1st Parallel.

In Beginning the Siege the utmost Exertion is required to Expedite the work as much as possible for which reason the Regiments must furnish as many Workmen as their strength will permit. Every precaution must be taken as well to Cover the Workmen, as to prevent successful Sallies from the Garrison.

To this end will be required to make the necessary communications, and forming the first parallel, on the 1st night of opening the Trenches, 4,500 Workmen divided into Six Brigades.

To Cover the Workmen, & to secure them against Sallies, will be required five Battalions & 300 Cavalry.

The Workmen must be Divided by the Officers commanding Brigades & Regiments from which they are furnished into Six Brigades which must be regularly Numbered off from one to Six. The officers Commanding these Brigades must pay particular attention to their own Numbers & to the Strength of their Brigades, in order that they may answer at once to both these points when Called upon by the Engineers.

The 1st 3 Brigades to work at the first parallel, want as follows

---

1 The source actually has a date of 1794, indicating that the document must represent a near contemporary copy of an original, since the siege of Valenciennes took place in 1793.

Brigade No.1 on the Left by Marle to the 1st Break of the Parallel. This will be Led to the place of assembly in the Hollow between Saltain & Marle	)) 750)
Brigade No.2 in the Center of the Parallel, Extending across the Road From Stone Quarry This will be Led to the place of assembly in the Hollow of the Left of the Road from Estreux to St Sauve	)) 750))
Brigade No.3 is to Work from the Right of the Road that Leads to the Stone Quarry across the St Sauve Road towards the Scheld, also at Boseau for a Battery of Eight Twenty four pounders	)) 1200)
Brigade No.4 Works at the communication on the Left, behind the village of Marles. This will lead to the same place of assembly as the Brigade No.1	)) 600)
Brigade No.5 Works at the communication in the Cautie. This will be led to the same place of assembly as the Brig'de No.2	)) 800
Brigade No.6 Works at the Communication on the Right of St Sauve. This will be led to the same place of assembly as the Brig'e No.3	)) 400
The Total of the Whole	4,500

Each of these Brigades must be Conducted from the Camp to the appointed place of assembly by an officer of Engineers, in doing which care must be taken to Conceal the Troops & the destination of their march, and also the direction as much as possible. The same officers conduct them from the places of assembly to the Depots in front of them, where they receive their Tools. In these Depots the Brigades of Workmen deposit their arms & pouches in the most regular order, take the Tools in their hands & wait the arrival of the officer of Engineers, who is to place them to work.

The time of the march of each Brigade from the Camp must be Exactly ascertained as their distances from the places of assembly are unequal, and as they must all be at their appointed Depots at half an Hour past 7 o'clock at the Latest.

Upon the March to the Trenches no man must be allowed to Strike fires or to Smoke. The greatest silence must be observed and care must be taken that this silence is not interrupted by the Clashing of the Tools. No workman is to Begin till every thing is in proper order and till orders are Given for that purpose, either by word of mouth or by a Signal. It is necessary that the officers commanding the working parties, should make their men understand, that the preservation of their Lives, depends upon their working with their utmost diligence during the Night, so that by day Break they may be Covered, against the Heavy fire which will then take place, from the Enemy's works.

These Working parties must be Relieved at 8 o'Clock in the Morning, therefore the relieving Brigades must be formed & Numbered before hand.

These must be conducted to the same Depots that the first Brigades went to according to their respective Numbers by officers belonging to those Troops that are already at work in the Trenches (because the Engineers must not quit the Workmen) from whence they will be Conducted by Engineers to the Relief of Workmen in the Trenches.

All these circumstances relative to the workmen must be made known to the Regiments employed on this service.

The following distribution will be made of the covering party & the Reserve.

Upon the Left Exclusive of the usual post at Marlis – One Battalion of Infantry, 2 Canon & 150 Cavalry will be posted in the Rear of that Village. These will be Conducted from their Camp to the post assigned to them by an officer of Engineers.

In the Centre behind the Trenches, near the Depot No.2 One Battalion of Infantry which will also be Conducted to its post by an officer of the Engineers.

Upon the right of the village of St Sauve, exclusive of the Post that is normally there, One Battalion of Infantry with Five Canon & 150 Cavalry which will also be Conducted from the Camp & posted by an officer of Engineers. Epaulments will be ready for the Cavalry, behind which the men may dismount, but they must keep together & be in readiness to mount when required.

Lastly, one Battalion with 2 Canon in reserve at the Depot No.4, which is destined to Support either straight to the Front, or to the Right Flank, as occasion may require, and it will also be Conducted to the Depot & posted by an officer of the Engineers.

The Chain of Light Troops that run along the Hollow way from St Sauve to Marlis must be doubled & Beyond the Hollow way some men that are to be depended upon must lay down & Watch the Enemy.

These men must not fire and the Troops who Compose this Chain must on no account be allowed to fire untill the officers shall perceive the Enemy is actually making a Sally. In course the officers will pay great attention to this.

In this last mentioned Case, that is if the enemy actually makes a Sally in force, which is easily ascertained, the officers posted in the Hollow way retire with their Troops on the left towards Marlis, and those on the right towards St Sauve.

The Workmen are not to Leave off work on this account, & much less are they to disperse untill they are ordered to Leave off Work.

When this order is Given, they retire regularly along the Communications to the Right & Left from the Centre to the Depots where they assembled which the officers Commanding them must pay the Greatest attention to, & the Covering Battalions advance & take post along the parallel.

The reserve Battalions advance to a Moderate distance in the Rear of these and the Battalions that are in front await the Enemy at the parallel. As soon as the Enemy Crosses [the] Hollow Way to advance against the parallel and Begins a fire of small arms with our Troops posted in the Trenches the Cavalry on both Flanks advances & attacks these in the Flanks & in the Rear.

The Workmen that have retreated to their Depots take up their arms & put on their Belts, formed in regular order close to the Reserve Battalion that is nearer to them & is not with it.

In order that the Covering parties may not get into Confusion and fire upon each other in a Dark night, each officer Commanding a post & the officers under his Command must be accurately informed where the yagers, the Free Corps & covering posts on his Right & Left & in his Rear are placed.

In this manner each Commanding officer will know whether he is to expect support, or whether he is to depend alone upon the troops under his particular Command.

These troops of the Chain which Compose that part of it not formed in the Hollow Way retire at day to the Right & Left towards Marlis & St Sauve, likewise that Battalion which is posted behind the Centre of the Trenches must retire at Day Break to the Depot No.3.

The other Battalions as they are well covered will keep their posts & when the Cannonade is extremely heavy they may Ly down.

Of the Division Posting & of the Number of Troops which [blank] day of opening the Trenches.

The Number of Troops req'd on this.

Effective Strength of the Besieging Army in Infantry of the Line is as follows.

[Key]	Imperial	English including 2nd Hanv'n Grend'r Batt'n	Hanv'n	Total
[Total strength]	8,166	3,213	6,956	18,335
[A. Workmen]	1,970	800	1,730	4,500
[B. Men for covering battalions]	1,340	485	1,175	3,000
[A + B]	3,310	1,285	2,905	7,500
[Duty men remaining in camp]	4,876*	1,928	4,051	10,855†

* The number of Imperial duty men remaining in camp should read (8,166 minus 3,310 =) 4,856.
† The total number of duty men remaining in camp should read (18,335 minus 7,500 =) 10,835.

The 1st Column is the Total Strength of each Nation.
2nd Column is the No. of workmen that each Gives in proportion to their strength.
3rd Column is the 5 Covering Battalions to 600 men each.
4th Column total of Duty Men of each Nation.

Strength of the Besieging Army
Austrians	8,186
English Include'g the 2nd Grend'r Battalion	3,213
Hannoverians	6,956
Total	18,335
No. of workmen each day	4,500
Covering party 3000 Infantry & 300 Cavalry	7,500
Remained in Camp	10,855[2]

The above mentioned No. of workmen will be divided into 6 Brigades.

---

2   This should read (18,335 minus 7,500 =) 10,835.

Brigade No.1 – Consists of 750 Workmen and they are given by the English who is to assemble near Soultain on the Right of the English Camp.

Brigade No.2 – 750 Austrians in the rear of the Regim't of Brechainville in the Bottom between Estreux & Saltain.

Brigade No.3, Austrians, 1200 in the Bottom near the rear of the Reg't of Wartensleben by the Windmill of St Sauve on ye left of the Chaussée of Valenciennes.

No.4, Hannoverians, 600, near Soultain on the Right of the English Camp with the Brigade No.1

No.5, Hannoverians, 800, in the rear of the Regiment of Brechainville in the Bottom between Estreux & Saltain with the Brigade No.2.

No.6, Hannoverians, 400, in the Bottom near the Regiment of Wartensleben by the windmill of St Sauve on the Left of the Chaussée of Valenciennes with the Brigade No.3.

Distribution of the Covering Party
One Batt'n of 600 men, with 2 Canon, assembles on the Right of the English Camp near Soultain with the Brigade No.1 & 4, and 100 English Cav^y & 50 Austrians.

2 Battalions each 600 men, one of them Austrians, the oy'r [other] Hannoverians, both without Cannon, assemble behind the Regiment Brechainville, in the Bottom between Estreux & Saltain with the Brigades No.2 & 5.

2 Battalions each 600, one Hannoverian & the other Austrian, with a Company of 140 Austrians added to it in order to make out the 600 men, each Battalion bring 2 field pieces and they assemble in the Bottom near the Regim't of Wartensleben, by the windmill of St Sauve on the Left of the Chaussée of Valenciennes with the Brigades No.2 & 6.

150 Austrian Cav'y assemble w't ye last mentiond Batt'n.[3]

---

3 NAM: 1985-12-15-4: GO, Estreux, 12 June 1793.

Appendix VI

Field Train of Artillery Ordered to attend the British Troops in the Low Countries, exclusive of the Battalion Guns now there

(a) Ordnance, Wagons, Horses and Drivers

Ordnance Number and Nature	For Ordnance		For Ammunition &c			Total Number of		
	Horses	Drivers	Wagons*	Horses	Drivers	Horses	Drivers	Conductors
4 medium 12-pounders	28	8	24	72	24	100	32	
8 heavy 6-pounders	48	24	24	72	24	120	48	
2 New Pattern 5½ Inch Howitzers	8	4	8	24	8	32	12	
2 Old Pattern 5½ Inch Howitzers	6	2	8	24	8	30	10	
4 Royal Mortars in a Waggon			1	3	1	3	1	
3 Forge Carts and 3 Waggons	6	3	3	9	3	15	6	
1 Gyn &ca			1	3	1	3	1	
For Artificers Tools and Baggage			4	12	4	12	4	
For Park Rope, Pickets for all Horses, Grease &c			4	12	4	12	4	
Officers' Horses						21		
TOTAL	96	41	77	231	77	348	118	

* The above Ammunition Wagons will carry for each Medium 12-pounder and Heavy 6-pounder 396 rounds, with one quarter to be case shot. For each 5½ inch howitzer 200 shells, 10 carcases and 30 rounds of case shot. The shells and carcases may be used either for the Howitzers or Mortars.

(b) Wagons, Horses and Drivers for Tents and Baggage

Field Officers' Waggon for Tent & Baggage			1	3	1	3	1	
4 Captains ditto			2	6	2	6	2	
8 Subalterns ditto			4	12	4	12	4	
1 Adjutant and 1 Quarter M'r ditto			1	3	1	3	1	
Surgeon and Mate ditto			1	3	1	3	1	
Paymaster & Commy of Stores ditto			1	3	1	3	1	
Comm'y of Horse & Clerk of Stores ditto			1	3	1	3	1	
Mess Man			1	3	1	3	1	
Non Comm'd Officers & Privates ditto			3	9	3	9	3	
Conductors and Drivers ditto			3	9	3	9	3	9
TOTAL			18	54	18	54	18	9

(c) Wagons for Artisans

2 Collar Makers				1				
1 Farrier				1				
3 Smiths				1				
TOTAL				3				

(d) Spares

1 Medium 12-pounder carriage	3	1				3	1	
1 Heavy 6-pounder carriage	3	1				3	1	
1 Royal Howitzer carriage	2	1				2	1	
Waggons 1 to every 20			5	15	5	15	5	
Horses 1 to every 10						42	14	
TOTAL	8	3	5	15	5	65	22	

(e) Civil Establishment

Paymaster and Commissary of Stores
Commissary of Horse
Clerk of Stores
Conductor of Stores
1 Cooper
2 Collar Makers
1 Carpenter
3 Wheelers
1 Farrier
3 Smiths

(f) Detachment of Royal Artillery

	Field Officer	Captains	Subalterns	Surgeon	Mate	Adjutant & Quarter M'r	Non Comm'd Officers	Gunners
4 medium 12-pounders		1	1				4	40
8 heavy 6-pounders	1	2	2			2	8	80
2 New Pattern 5½ Inch Howitzers		1					2	20
2 Old Pattern 5½ Inch Howitzers			1				2	20
Surgeon & Mate				1	1			
Officers' Servants								16
For Casualties			4				1	
TOTAL	1	4	8	1	1	2	17	176

Source: TNA: WO 6/7: pp.36–37, Enclosure in Richmond to Dundas, 26 April 1793.

Bibliography

Manuscript Sources

British Library (BL)
Western Manuscripts
Add Ms 34,447 to 34,451 Auckland Papers
Add Ms 37,842 to 37,935 Windham Papers
Add MS 40,633 to 40,635 Stewart of Afton Papers
Add MS 46,702 to 46,711 Don Papers
Loan MS 57/107 Melville Papers

India Office Records and Private Papers
IOR/H/84 Military Papers, 1760–1787

The National Archives (TNA)
AO 1 Auditors of the Imprest and Commissioners of Audit: Declared Accounts, 1500–1849
AO 16 Auditors of the Imprest and Successors, 1568–1910
HO 50 Military Correspondence, 1782–1840
HO 51 Military Entry Books, 1758–1855
PRO 30/8 Chatham Papers, 1708–1806
T 1 Treasury Board Papers, 1557–1946
T 27 Treasury Out-Letters, 1668–1920
T 52 Entry Books of Royal Warrants, 1667–1857
WO 1 War Office In-Letters, 1756–1868
WO 3 Commander-in-Chief Out-Letters, 1765–1868
WO 4 Secretary-at-War Out-Letters, 1684–1861
WO 5 Secretary-at-War Marching and Militia Orders, 1683–1852
WO 6 Secretary of State for War Out-Letters, 1793–1859
WO 7 War Office Out-Letters, 1715–1862
WO 12 General Muster Books and Pay Lists, 1732–1878
WO 17 Office of the Commander-in-Chief: Monthly Returns to the Adjutant General, 1754–1866
WO 24 Papers concerning establishments, 1661–1975
WO 25 Returns of Officers' Services, 1660–1938
WO 26 Entry Books of Warrants, Regulations and Precedents, 1670–1817
WO 27 Inspection Returns, 1750–1914
WO 30 Miscellaneous Papers, 1776–1870
WO 40 Secretary-at-War In-Letters, 1753–1815
WO 46 Ordnance Office Out-Letters, 1660–1861
WO 55 Ordnance Office and War Office: Miscellaneous Entry Books and Papers, 1568–1923
WO 58 Commissariat Department Out-Letters, 1793–1888
WO 379 Disposition and Movement of Regiments, Returns and Papers, 1737–1967

National Army Museum (NAM)
1965-06-54-1	Orderly Book of the 5th Dragoon Guards, February to April 1794
1976-07-44-2	Muster Roll of the 14th Foot, 25 June to 24 December 1793
1976-07-45	Diary of Captain Thomas Powell, 14th Foot, March 1793–March 1796
1978-04-73	Mr. Watson's correspondence with the Auditors of the Public Accounts, February 1796 to June 1803
1985-12-9	Order book, 24 November 1793-7 July 1794
1985-12-15	Papers of Major General Charles Barnett, 3rd Foot Guards, 1786-1803
1994-03-129	Papers and correspondence associated with General Sir Hew Dalrymple
1997-10-31	Manuscript journal of Captain John Carter Atherley, Coldstream Guards

The University of Manchester Library (UML)
The Clinton Papers (uncatalogued).

University of Nottingham Libraries, Manuscripts and Special Collections (UNL)
Pw Ja	Papers of Lord William H. Cavendish Bentinck (1774–1839).

William L. Clements Library, University of Michigan (WLCL)
Henry Clinton Papers, Volumes 235 and 288.
James Moncrieff Papers.

Printed Primary Sources

Adye, R.W., *The Bombardier and Pocket Gunner* (London: T. Egerton, 2nd edition, 1802)
Anglesey, Marquis of (ed.), 'Two brothers in the Netherlands, 1794–95', *Journal of the Society for Army Historical Research*, vol.34, 1956, pp.74–106
Anon., *An Accurate and Impartial Narrative of the War by an Officer of the Guards* (London: Cadell & Davies, nd)
Anon., *The Proceedings of a General Court Martial Held at the Horse Guards ... Upon the Trial of Lord George Sackville* (Cork: Bagnell and Swiney, 1760)
Anon., *A List of the Officers of the Army and Marines with an Index*, (London: War Office, 1793, 1794 and 1795)
Anon., *A Collection of State Papers Relative to the War against France* (London: Debrett, 1795)
Anon., *A Journal Kept in the British Army, from the Landing of the Troops under the Command of Earl Moira, at Ostend, in June 1794, to their Return to England the Following Year* (Liverpool: privately published, 1796)
Anon., *A Collection of Orders, Regulations, and Instructions for the Army; on Matters of Finance and Points of Discipline*, (London: T. Egerton, 1807)
Anon., *The Statutes at Large of England and of Great-Britain: from Magna Carta to the Union of the Kingdoms of Great Britain and Ireland* (London: Eyre and Strahan, 1811)
Aspinall, A., (ed.), *The Correspondence of George Prince of Wales* (London: Cassell, 1963-71)
Aspinall, A., (ed.), *The Later Correspondence of George III* (London: Cambridge University Press, 1966–70)
Atkinson, C.T. (ed.), 'Gleanings from the Cathcart MSS', *Journal of the Society for Army Historical Research*, vol.29, 1951, pp.144–157
Auckland, W. (ed.), *The Journal and Correspondence of William, Lord Auckland* (London: Richard Bentley, 1861–1862)
Aytoun, J., *Redcoats in the Caribbean* (Blackburn: Blackburn Recreation Services, 1984)
Baring, H. (ed.), *The Diary of the Right Hon. William Windham, 1784–1910* (London: Longmans Green and Co, 1866)
Bland, H., *A Treatise on Military Discipline: in Which is Laid Down and Explained the Duty of the Officer and Soldier, through the Several Branches of the Service* (London: Johnston, 8th ed. 1759)
Brocklesby, R., *Œconomical and Medical Observations, in two parts. From the Year 1758 to the Year 1763 inclusive. Tending to the Improvement of Military Hospitals, and to the Cure of Camp Diseases, Incident to Soldiers* (London: T. Becket and P.A. De Hondt, 1764)
Brown, R., *An Impartial Journal of a Detachment from the Brigade of Foot Guards, commencing 25th February, 1793, and ending 9th May, 1795* (London: Stockdale, 1795)
Bunbury, H., *Narratives of Some Passages in the Great War with France (1799-1810)* (London: Peter Davies, 1927)

Burgoyne, J., *A State of the Expedition from Canada, as Laid Before the House of Commons, by Lieutenant-General Burgoyne* (London: J. Almon, 1780)

Connell, B., *Portrait of a Whig Peer: Compiled from the Papers of the Second Viscount Palmerston, 1739-1802* (London: Andre Deutsch, 1957)

Cormack, A.A., (ed.) *James Dickson, M.A., 1769-1795, Army Surgeon* (Aberdeen: Privately published, 1968)

Cormack, A. and Jones, A. (eds), *The Journal of Corporal William Todd 1745-1762* (Stroud: Sutton Publishing Limited, 2001)

Cook, H.C.B. (ed.), 'The St. George diary. A Junior Regimental Officer in the Low Countries, 1794-95', *Journal of the Society for Army Historical Research*, vol.47, 1969, pp.233-250

Cuthbertson, B., *Cuthbertson's System for the Complete Interior Management and Œconomy of a Battalion of Infantry. A new edition, with corrections* (Bristol: Rouths and Nelson, 1776)

Duckers, P. (ed.), *A Diary of the Flanders Campaign 1793-1796. Lt. Col. James Russell 1st (King's) Dragoon Guards* (Shrewsbury: Spink & Son, 2013)

Duncan-Jones, C.M. (ed.), *Trusty and Well Beloved. The Letters Home of William Harness an Officer of George III* (London: SPCK, 1957).

Este, C., *A Journey in the year 1793, through Flanders, Brabant, and Germany, to Switzerland* (London: Debrett, 1795)

Fergusson, W., (1846) *Notes and Recollections of a Professional Life* (London: Longman, 1846)

Fortescue, J.W., 'A Conqueror of France – The Corporal of Valenciennes', in *The Times*, 27 July 1928, pp.15-16

Granville, C. (ed.), *Lord Granville Leveson Gower (First Earl Granville). Private correspondence 1781 to 1821* (London: John Murray, 1916)

Grazebrook, R.M. (ed.), 'The Campaign in Flanders of 1793-1795. Journal of Lieutenant Charles Stewart, 28th Foot', *Journal of the Society for Army Historical Research*, vol.29, 1951, pp.2-17

Hamilton, R., *Thoughts Submitted to the Consideration of the Officers in the Army, Respecting the Establishment of a Regimental Fund, for the Relief of the Sick and Necessitous Wives of the Private Soldiers* (London: S. Simmons, 1783)

Hamilton, R., *The Duties of a Regimental Surgeon Considered: with Observations on the General Qualifications; and Hints Relative to a More Respectable Practice, and Better Regulation of that Department* (London: T.N. Longman, 1794)

Hanway, J., *The Soldier's Faithful Friend: Being Moral and Religious Advice to Soldiers* (London: Dodley and Sewel and Brew, 1776)

Harcourt, E.W. (ed.), *The Harcourt Papers*, (Oxford: Privately published, 1880)

Harrington, P. (ed.), *With the Guards in Flanders. The Diary of Roger Morris 1793-1795* (Warwick: Helion, 2018)

Hayter, T. (ed.), *An Eighteenth Century Secretary-at-War. The papers of William, Viscount Barrington* (London: The Bodley Head, 1988)

Historical Manuscripts Commission (ed.), *Report on the Manuscripts of J.B. Fortescue Esq., preserved at Dropmore* (London: HMSO, 1905)

Historical Manuscripts Commission (ed.), *Report of the Manuscripts of Earl Bathurst preserved at Cirencester Park* (London: HMSO, 1923)

Holland Rose, J. (ed.), *Pitt and Napoleon: Essays and Letters* (London: G. Bell & Sons, 1912)

Jackson, R., *An Outline of the History and Cure of Fever, Endemic and Contagious*, (London: Longman, Murray & Highley, 1798)

Jackson, R., *A System of Arrangement and Discipline for the Medical Department of Armies* (London: John Murray, 1805)

James, C., *An Universal Military Dictionary, in English and French; in Which are Explained the Terms of the Principal Sciences that are Necessary for the Information of an Officer* (London: T. Egerton, 1816)

Jones, L.T., *An Historical Journal of the British Campaign on the Continent, in the year 1794; with the Retreat through Holland, in the year 1795* (Birmingham: Swinney & Hawkins, 1797)

Keate, T., *Observations on the Fifth Report of the Commissioners for Military Enquiry. And more Particularly of those Parts of it which Relate to the Surgeon General* (London: Hatchard, 1808)

Le Marchant, D. (ed.), *Memoirs of the late Major-General Le Marchant* (London: Samuel Bentley, 1841)

Le Mesurier, H., (1801) *The British Commissary, in two parts* (London: T. Egerton, 1801)

Leslie, J.H., (ed.), 'Campaigning in 1793-Flanders', *Journal of the Society for Army Historical Research*, vol.8, 1929, pp.2-32

McGrigor, J., *The Autobiography and Services of Sir James McGrigor, Bart.* (London: Longman, Green, Longman and Roberts, 1861)

Malmesbury, Earl of, *Diaries and Correspondence of James Harris, First Earl of Malmesbury* (London: Richard Bentley, 1844-1845)

Minto, Countess of (ed.), *Life and Letters of Sir Gilbert Elliot, First Earl of Minto from 1751 to 1806* (London: Longmans Green & Co, 1874)
Molesworth, R., *A Short Course of Standing Rules, for the Government and Conduct of an Army, Designed for, or in the Field* (London: Dodsley, 1744)
Monro, D., *An account of the Diseases Which Were Most Frequent in the British Military Hospitals in Germany, from January 1761 to the Return of the Troops to England in March 1763* (London: A. Miller, D. Wilson and T. Durham, 1764)
Monro, D., *Observations on the Means of Preserving the Health of Soldiers; and of Conducting Military Hospitals* (London: J. Murray, 1780)
Muller, J., *A Treatise of Artillery* (London: John Millan, 1768)
Papacino d'Antoni, A.V., *A Treatise on Gun-Powder; a Treatise on Fire-Arms; and a Treatise on the Service of Artillery in Time of War. Translated from the Italian...by Captain Thomson of the Royal Regiment of Artillery* (London: T. & J. Egerton, 1789)
Pringle, J., *Observations on the Diseases of the Army* (London: Miller, Wilson, Durham & Payne, 3rd edition, 1761)
Randolph, H. (ed.), *Life of General Sir Robert Wilson* (London: John Murray, 1862)
Sinnott, N., *Observations, Tending to Show the Mmismanagement of the Medical Department in the Army* (London: J. Murray and S. Highley, 1796)
Taylor, E. (ed.), *The Taylor Papers, being a Record of Certain Reminiscences, Letters, and Journals in the Life of Lieut.-Gen. Sir Herbert Taylor* (London: Longmans, Green, & Co., 1913)
Thacher, J., *Military Journal of the American Revolution* (New York: Arno Press, 1969)
Verney, H., (ed.), *The Journals and Correspondence of General Sir Harry Calvert* (London: Hurst & Blackett, 1853)
Webster, J.C. (ed.), *The Journal of Jeffery Amherst. Recording the Military Career of Jeffery Amherst in America from 1758 to 1763* (Chicago: University of Chicago Press, 1931)
Whitworth, R. (ed.), *Gunner at Large. The Diary of James Wood R.A.1746–1765* (London: Leo Cooper, 1988)
Windham, W., *The Windham Papers* (London: Herbert Jenkins, 1913)

Parliamentary papers

Anon., *Journal of the House of Commons*, vol.43 (London: House of Commons, 1795)
Anon., *Nineteenth Report from the Select Committee on Finance &c. Secretary at War, Comptrollers of Army Accounts, and Paymaster General*, (London: House of Commons, 1797)
Anon., *The First Report of the Commissioners of Military Enquiry. Office of the Barrack Master General* (London: House of Commons, 1806)
Anon., *Fifth Report of the Commissioners of Military Enquiry, Army, Medical Department* (London: House of Commons, 1808)
Anon., *The Eleventh Report of the Commissioners of Military Enquiry. Departments of the Adjutant-General and Quarter-Master General*, (London: House of Commons, 1810)
Anon., *The Thirteenth Report of the Commissioners of Military Enquiry. The Master General and Board of Ordnance* (London: House of Commons, 1811)
Anon., *The Fifteenth Report of the Commissioners of Military Enquiry Appointed by act of 45 G.III C.47. Ordnance* (London: House of Commons, 1811)
Anon., *The Seventeenth Report of the Commissioners for Military Enquiry: appointed by Act of 45th Geo.III. Chap.47th. Ordnance* (London: House of Commons, 1812)
Anon., *The Eighteenth report of the Commissioners of Military Enquiry appointed by Act of 45 Geo. III. Cap. 47. Office of the Commissariat* (London: House of Commons, 1812)

Secondary Sources

Ackroyd, M., Brockliss, L., Moss, M., Retford, K. and Stevenson, J., *Advancing with the Army. Medicine, the Professions, and Social Mobility in the British Isles, 1790–1850* (Oxford: Oxford University Press, 2006)
Anon., *New York Marriages Previous to 1784* (Baltimore: Clearfield Company, 1999)

Atkinson, C.T., *The Dorsetshire Regiment* (Oxford: Oxford University Press, 1947)
Atkinson, C.T., *Regimental History. The Royal Hampshire Regiment* (Glasgow: Privately published: 1950)
Baker, N., *Government and Contractors. The British Treasury and War Supplies 1775-1783* (London: The Athlone Press, 1971)
Ball, P., *Neither Up nor Down. The British Army and the Flanders Campaign 1793-1795* (Warwick: Helion, 2020)
Barnett, C., *Britain and Her Army* (London: Cassell, 2000)
Belloc, H., *Tourcoing* (London: Stephen Swift, 1912)
Black, J., *British Foreign Policy in an Age of Revolutions 1783-1793* (Cambridge: Cambridge University Press, 1994)
Black, J., 'Logistics and the Path to Military Modernity. Britain and the Crucial Advantage of Naval Strength, 1793-1815', *Nuova Antologia Militare*, vol.1:3, June 2020, pp.3-15
Blanco, R.L., 'The Soldier's Friend-Sir Jeremiah Fitzpatrick, Inspector of Health for Land Forces', *Medical History*, vol.20, 1976, pp.402-421
Blanning, T.C.W., *The French Revolutionary Wars 1787-1802* (London: Hodder Headline, 1996)
Boatner, M.M., *Cassell's Biographical Dictionary of the War of American Independence 1763-1783* (London: Cassell, 1963)
Bowler, R.A., 'Sir Henry Clinton and Army Profiteering: A Neglected Aspect of the Clinton-Cornwallis Controversy', *William and Mary Quarterly*, third series, vol.31, 1974, pp.111-122
Bowler, R.A., *Logistics and the Failure of the British Army in America 1775-1783* (Princeton: Princeton University Press, 1975)
Bowler, R.A., 'The American Revolution and British Army Administrative Reform', *Journal of the Society for Army Historical Research*, vol.58, 1980, pp.66-77
Brown, S., *The Duke of York's Flanders Campaign. Fighting the French Revolution 1793-1795* (Barnsley: Frontline Books, 2018)
Browning, R., 'The Duke of Newcastle and the Financial Management of the Seven Years War in Germany', *Journal of the Society for Army Historical Research*, vol.49, 1971, pp.20-35
Brumwell, S., *Redcoats: The British Soldier and War in the Americas, 1755-1763* (Cambridge: Cambridge University Press, 2002)
Burne, A., *The Noble Duke of York. The Military Life of Frederick Duke of York and Albany* (London: Staples Press, 1949)
Cannon, R., *Historical Record of The Sixth Regiment of Dragoon Guards or The Carbineers* (London: Longman, Orme and Co, 1839)
Cantlie, N., *A History of the Army Medical Department* (London: Churchill Livingstone, 1974)
Carman, W.Y., 'Sir William Congreve, 1741-1814', *Journal of the Society for Army Historical Research*, vol.51, 1973, pp.63-68
Chaplin, T.H.A., *Medicine in England during the Reign of George III: The Fitzpatrick Lectures Delivered at the Royal College of Physicians 1917-1918* (London: Henry Kimpton, 1919)
Charters, E., *Disease, War, and the Imperial State. The Welfare of the British Armed Forces During the Seven Years War* (London: The University of Chicago Press, 2014)
Clode, C.M., *The Military Forces of the Crown; their Administration and Government* (London: John Murray, 1869)
Conway, S., *The British Army, 1714-1783. An Institutional History* (Barnsley: Pen & Sword, 2021)
Crooks, J.J., *History of the Royal Irish Regiment of Artillery* (Dublin: Browne and Nolan, 1914)
Cunliffe, M., *The Royal Irish Fusiliers 1793-1950* (Oxford: Oxford University Press, 1952)
Curtis, E.E., *The Organization of the British Army in the American Revolution* (New Haven: Yale University Press, 1926, reprinted by EP Publishing, 1972)
Demet, P., *'We Are Accustomed to do Our Duty.' German Auxiliaries with the British Army 1793-95* (Warwick: Helion, 2018)
Duffy, C., *Fire and Stone. The Science of Fortress Warfare 1660-1860* (Newton Abbot: David & Charles, 1975)
Duffy, C., *The Fortress in the Age of Vauban and Frederick the Great, 1660-1789* (London: Routledge & Kegan Paul, 1985)
Duffy, C., *The Military Experience in the Age of Reason* (London: Routledge & Kegan Paul, 1987)
Duffy, M., *Soldiers, Sugar and Seapower. The British Expeditions to the West Indies and the War Against Revolutionary France* (Oxford: Clarendon Press, 1987)
Duncan, F., *History of the Royal Regiment of Artillery Compiled from the Original Records* (London: John Murray, 1874)
Duncan, L.C., *Medical Men in the American Revolution* (New York: Kelley, 1970)
Ehrman, J., *The Younger Pitt. The Years of Acclaim* (London: Constable, 1969)
Emsley, C., *British Society and the French Wars 1793-1815* (London: Macmillan, 1979)

Esdaile, C.J., *The Wars of the French Revolution 1792-1801* (Abingdon: Routledge, 2019)
Espírito Santo, G., and de Brito, P., *A logística do exército Anglo-Luso na guerra Peninsular* (Parede: Principia Editora, 2012)
Evelyn, G.J., "'I learned what not to do': The British Army in Flanders and Holland 1793-95', in Guy, A.J. (ed.), *The Road to Waterloo. The British Army and the Struggle against Revolutionary and Napoleonic France, 1793-1815* (London: National Army Museum, 1990), pp.16-22
Fatherly, S., 'Tending the Army: Women and the British General Hospital in North America, 1754-1763', *Early American Studies*, vol.10:3, 2012, pp.569-578
ffoulkes, C., 'Notes on the Development of Signals used for Military Purposes', *Journal of the Society for Army Historical Research*, vol.22, 1943, p.20-27
Ford, W.C., *British Officers Serving in the American Revolution 1774-1783* (Brooklyn: Historical Printing Club, 1897)
Fortescue, J.W., *A History of the British Army* (London: Macmillan, 1899-1930)
Franklin, C.E., *British Napoleonic Field Artillery* (Stroud: Spellmount, 2008)
Frederick, J.B.M., *Lineage Book of British Land Forces 1660-1978* (Wakefield: Microform Academic Publishers, 1984)
Frey, S.R., *The British Soldier in America. A Social History of Military Life in America During the Revolutionary Period* (Austin: University of Texas Press, 1981)
Glover, R., *Peninsular Preparation. The Reform of the British Army 1795-1809* (Cambridge: Ken Trotman, 1988)
Graham, J.J., *Memoir of General Graham with Notices of the Campaigns in which he was Engaged from 1779 to 1801* (Edinburgh: R. & R. Clark, 1862)
Griffith, P., *The Vauban Fortifications of France* (Oxford: Osprey Publishing, 2006)
Gruber, I., *Books and the British Army in the Age of the American Revolution* (Chapel Hill: University of North Carolina Press, 2010)
Gruber von Arni, E.E., *Hospital Care and the British Standing Army, 1660-1714* (Aldershot: Ashgate, 2006)
Guy, A., *Œconomy and Discipline. Officership and Administration in the British Army 1714-63* (Manchester: Manchester University Press, 1985)
Hagist, D.N., *Noble Volunteers. The British Soldiers who Fought the American Revolution* (Yardley, Pennsylvania: Westholme, 2020)
Hamilton, F.W., *The Origin and History of the First or Grenadier Guards* (London: Murray, 1874)
Harding, D.F., *Smallarms of the East India Company 1600-1856. Volume 1: Procurement and Design* (London: Foresight Books, 1997)
Howard, M., 'The Forgotten Dimensions of Strategy', *Foreign Affairs*, vol.57:5, 1979, pp.975-986
Houlding, J.A., *Fit for Service. The Training of the British Army, 1715-1795*, (Oxford: Clarendon Press, 1981)
Hurl-Eamon, J., *Marriage and the British Army in the Long Eighteenth Century* (Oxford: Oxford University Press, 2014)
Kaufmann, M.H., *Surgeons at War: Medical Arrangements for the Treatment of the Sick and Wounded in the British Army during the late 18th and 19th Centuries* (Westport: Greenwood Press, 2000)
Kelly, C., *War and the Militarization of British Army Medicine, 1793-1830* (London: Routledge, 2011)
King, L.S., *The Medical World of the Eighteenth Century* (New York: Krieger, 1958)
Kopperman, P.E., 'Medical Services in the British Army, 1742-1783', *Journal of the History of Medicine and Allied Sciences*, vol.34:4, 1979, pp.428-455
Kopperman, P.E., 'The British High Command and Soldiers' Wives in America, 1755-1783', *Journal of the Society for Army Historical Research*, vol.60, 1982, pp.14-34
Kopperman P.E., 'The British Army in North America and the West Indies, 1755-83: A Medical Perspective', in G.L. Hudson (ed.), *British Military and Naval Medicine, 1600-1830* (Amsterdam: Editions Rodopi, 2007), pp.51-86
Lenihan, P., *Fluxes, Fevers and Fighting men. War and Disease in Ancien Regime Europe 1648-1789* (Warwick: Helion, 2019)
Little, H.M., 'The Emergence of a Commissariat during the Seven Years War in Germany', *Journal of the Society for Army Historical Research*, vol.61, 1983, pp.201-214
Little, H.M., 'Thomas Pownall and Army Supply, 1761-1766', *Journal of the Society for Army Historical Research*, vol.65, 1987, pp.92-104
Lynn, J.A., *The Bayonets of the Republic. Motivation and Tactics in the Army of Revolutionary France 1791-94* (Urbana and Chicago: University of Illinois Press, 1984)
Lynn, J.A. (ed.), *Feeding Mars: Logistics in Western Warfare from the Middle Ages to the Present* (Colorado: Westview Press, 1993)

MacDonagh, O., *The Inspector General. Sir Jeremiah Fitzpatrick and the Politics of Social Reform, 1783–1802* (London: Croom Helm, 1981)
Mackinnon, D., *Origin and Services of the Coldstream Guards* (London: Bentley, 1833)
Massé, C.H., *The Predecessors of the Royal Army Service Corps* (Aldershot: Gale & Polden, 1948)
Matheson, C., *The Life of Henry Dundas First Viscount Melville 1742–1811* (London: Constable, 1933)
Mauskopf, S.H., 'Chemistry in the Arsenal: State Regulation and Scientific Methodology of Gunpowder in Eighteenth-Century England and France', in B.D. Steele and T. Dorland (eds), *The Heirs of Archimedes. Science and the Art of War through the Age of Enlightenment* (Cambridge, Massachusetts: The MIT Press, 2005), pp.293–330
Mauskopf, S.H., 'The Crisis of English Gunpowder in the Eighteenth Century', in U. Klein and E.C. Spary (eds), *Materials and Expertise in Early Modern Europe* (Chicago: University of Chicago Press, 2009) pp.288–320
Oatts, L.B., *I Serve. Regimental History of the 3rd Carabineers (Prince of Wales's Dragoon Guards)* (Chester: Privately published, 1966)
O'Donnell, H., *Historical Records of the 14th Regiment, now the Prince of Wales's Own (West Yorkshire Regiment), from its formation in 1685, to 1892* (Devonport: Swiss, 1893)
Olson, A.G., *The Radical Duke. The Career and Correspondence of Charles Lennox, third Duke of Richmond* (Oxford: Oxford University Press, 1961)
Peterkin, A., and Johnston, W., *Commissioned Officers in the Medical Services of the British Army 1660–1960* (London: The Wellcome Historical Medical Library, 1968)
Phelan, I.P., 'Marlborough as Logistician', *Journal of the Society for Army Historical Research*, vol.67, 1989, pp.253–257 and vol.68, 1990, pp.36–48 and 103–119
Rodger, N.A.M., *The Wooden World: An Anatomy of the Georgian Navy* (London: Collins, 1986)
Rogers, H.C.B., *The British Army of the Eighteenth Century* (London: George Allen & Unwin, 1977)
Roider, K.A., *Baron Thugut and Austria's Response to the French Revolution* (Princeton: Princeton University Press, 1987)
Schama, S., *Patriots and Liberators. Revolution in the Netherlands 1780–1813* (London: Collins, 1977)
Scouller, R.E., *The Armies of Queen Anne* (Oxford: Oxford University Press, 1966)
Shy, J., *Toward Lexington. The Role of the British Army in the Coming of the American Revolution* (Princeton: Princeton University Press, 1965)
Spring, M.H., *With Zeal and Bayonets Only. The British Army on Campaign in North America, 1775–1783* (Norman: University of Oklahoma Press, 2008)
Stansfield, S., *Early Modern Systems of Command. Queen Anne's Generals, Staff Officers and the Direction of Allied Warfare in the Low Countries and Germany, 1702–1711* (Solihull: Helion, 2015)
Steppler, G.A., 'The British Army on the Eve of War', in Guy, A.J. (ed.), *The Road to Waterloo. The British Army and the Struggle against Revolutionary and Napoleonic France, 1793–1815* (London: National Army Museum, 1990), pp.6–15
Stevenson, L.G., 'John Hunter, Surgeon-General 1790–1793', *Journal of the History of Medicine*, vol.19, 1964, pp.239–266
Syrett, D., *Shipping and the American War 1775–83* (London: The Athlone Press, 1970)
Thomas, R.N.W., 'Wellington in the Low Countries 1794–1795', *The International History Review*, vol.11, 1989, pp.14–30
Thomas, R.N.W., 'Command and Control in the First Coalition: The Duke of York in the Low Countries, 1793–1794', in K.A. Roider, & J.C. Horgan (eds), *The Consortium on Revolutionary Europe 1750–1850, Proceedings, 1991* (Tallahassee: Florida State University, 1992), pp.267–273
Thomas, R.N.W., 'The Corps of Royal Waggoners and Army Transport During the Campaign in the Low Countries, 1794–1795', *Journal of the Society for Army Historical Research*, vol.76, 1998, pp.157–162
Van Creveld, M.L., *Supplying War: Logistics from Wallenstein to Patton* (Cambridge: Cambridge University Press, 1977)
Ward, S.G.P., *Wellington's Headquarters. A Study of the Administrative Problems in the Peninsula* (Oxford: Oxford University Press, 1957)
Ward, S.G.P., 'The Author of the 'Accurate and Impartial Narrative'', *Journal of the Society for Army Historical Research*, vol.70, 1992, pp. 211–223
Whitworth, R., *Field Marshal Lord Ligonier. A Story of the British Army, 1702–1770* (Oxford: Clarendon Press, 1958)
West, J., *Gunpowder, Government and War in the Mid-Eighteenth Century* (London: Boydell Press, 1991)
Witzleben, A. von, *Prinz Friedrich Josias von Coburg-Saalfeld, Herzog zu Sachsen* (Berlin: R. Decker, 1859)
Zwitzer, H.L. 'The British and Netherlands Armies in Relation to the Anglo-Dutch Alliance, 1688–1795', in G.J.A. Raven and N.A.M. Rodger (eds), *Navies and Armies: The Anglo-Dutch Relationship in War and Peace, 1688–1988* (Edinburgh: John Donald, 1990)

Internet Sources

Rev War 75, <http://www.revwar75.com>
The Dictionary of Canadian Biography, <http://www.biographi.ca>
The Gazette, <https://www.thegazette.co.uk/>
The History of Parliament online, <https://www.historyofparliamentonline.org/research>
The Peerage, < https://www.thepeerage.com>
The Oxford Dictionary of National Biography, <https://www.oxforddnb.com>

Theses

Bailey, D.W., *The Board of Ordnance and Small Arms Supply* (Unpublished PhD thesis. King's College London, 1988)
Bartlett, K.J., *The Development of the British Army during the Wars with France, 1793–1815* (Unpublished PhD thesis. Durham University, 1997)
Chilcott, C., *Maintaining the British Army, 1793 to 1820* (Unpublished PhD thesis. Bath Spa University. 2006)
Ferguson, K.P., *The Army in Ireland from the Restoration to the Act of Union* (Unpublished PhD thesis. University College Dublin, 1980)
Kirby, T., *The Duke of Wellington and the Supply System during the Peninsula War* (Unpublished Master's thesis. Fort Leavenworth, 2011)
Limm, A., *'Fairly Out-Generalled and Disgracefully Beaten': the British Army in the Low Countries, 1793–1814* (Unpublished PhD thesis. Birmingham University, 2014)
McLauchlan, T., *Wellington's Supply System during the Peninsular War, 1809–1814* (Unpublished Master's thesis. McGill University, 1997)
Morgan, G.W., *The Impact of War on the Administration of the Army, Navy and Ordnance in Britain, 1739–1754* (Unpublished PhD thesis. Leicester University, 1977)
Pimlott, J.L., *The Administration of the British Army 1783–1793* (Unpublished PhD thesis. Leicester University, 1975)
Redgrave, T.M.O., *Wellington's Logistical Arrangements in the Peninsular War, 1809–1814* (Unpublished PhD thesis. University of London, 1979)
Steppler, G.A., *The Common Soldier in the Reign of George III, 1760–1793* (Unpublished PhD thesis. University of Oxford, 1984)
Western, J.R., *The Recruitment of the Land Forces of Great Britain, 1793–1798* (Unpublished PhD thesis. University of Edinburgh, 1953)

Index

Abercromby, Major General Ralph 26, 39, 49, 95, 153, 189–191, 201, 252
Admiralty, the 16, 18, 174
Amherst, Jeffrey, General Lord 18, 40, 136, 138, 145–147, 149, 174, 180–181, 215–216, 264–265, 267
Antwerp 28–29, 33, 49, 88, 112, 115, 121, 124, 158, 189, 201, 204, 223
Army Medical Board 136, 138–140, 145–149, 153, 158, 160–161, 168, 171
Army Medical Department 65, 137–139, 141, 144–146, 262–263
Arnhem 87, 160, 167, 233
Auckland, William Eden, Lord 26, 28–29, 44, 67, 71, 242
Austrian Netherlands, the 23–24, 27–31, 33, 43, 45, 84, 88, 98, 113, 116, 121–123, 127, 234, 269

Bentinck, Captain Lord William 30, 34, 63–64, 66, 71, 95, 248
Bergen-op-Zoom 49, 162, 169, 192, 230, 264
Board of General Officers 17, 174
Board of Ordnance xiii, 16, 19–20, 23, 53, 172, 174, 217–219, 223, 236, 238, 242, 255, 257, 259, 262, 264–265, 267–268
Board of Ordnance, corps of; **Royal Artillery** 23, 37, 45, 80, 83, 93, 141, 152, 154, 210, 217–218, 225–232, 234, 239, 242, 251–252, 255, 257–258, 261, 263; **Royal Irish Artillery** 227–230, 255; **Royal Engineers** 20, 79, 82, 219, 241–243, 247, 259, 261; **Royal Military Artificers** 83, 152, 154, 210, 219, 231, 236, 241–245, 248, 251, 255, 259
Boxtel 49, 244
Breda 24, 131
Bremen 132, 155, 158, 161
British Army, cavalry regiments of; **1st Life Guards** 203; **Royal Horse Guards** xii, 183–184; **1st Dragoon Guards** xi, 61, 80, 142, 183–184, 209–210; **2nd Dragoon Guards** 39, 58, 61–62, 64–65, 70, 141; **3rd Dragoon Guards** 196; **5th Dragoon Guards** 93, 184; **6th Dragoon Guards** 184, 209–210; **1st Dragoons** 114, 183, 203, 209–210; **2nd Dragoons** 63, 93, 105, 119; **6th Dragoons** 74, 93, 209–210; **15th Dragoons** 141; **7th Light Dragoons** 114; **8th Light Dragoons** 30, 154, 205; **11th Light Dragoons** 63–65; **12th Light Dragoons** 81, 205; **14th Light Dragoons** 154; **15th Light Dragoons** 212, 244; **16th Light Dragoons** 93, 117, 119, 184, 213, 222; **24th Light Dragoons** 63
British Army, infantry regiments of; **1st Foot Guards** 25, 39, 62, 69, 92–93, 186, 188, 194, 209, 233, 251; **Coldstream Guards** xi, 35, 38–39, 63–65, 119, 186–187, 190, 203, 209, 212, 224, 226, 245, 252, 255, 258, 268; **3rd Foot Guards** 71, 74, 78, 80, 93–94, 146, 186, 188, 209, 246, 252, 258; **3rd** 158, 161, 163, 169, 202–203, 207; **8th** 93, 164, 197, 201–202, 204; **10th** 135, 187, 208; **11th** 62; **12th** 30, 164, 191–192, 200, 202, 204, 206, 222; **14th** 26, 45, 73, 90, 93, 146, 151–152, 153, 185, 189–191, 193, 195–199, 202, 205, 209–210, 212, 226, 252; **15th** 62; **16th** 71; **19th** 66–67, 193, 202, 205; **23rd** 63; **25th** 142; **27th** 202–203; **28th** 45, 63, 87, 164, 202–203, 246; **30th** 64, 66, 70, 197, 209; **31st** 192, 205; **33rd** 151, 155, 164, 201–202, 204–205, 215, 260; **34th** 192; **37th** 26, 65, 93, 119, 144, 151–152, 155, 185, 189–191, 193, 195–196, 198–199, 202, 205, 215, 232, 264; **38th** 30, 73, 80, 191–192, 200–202, 205, 220, 258, 264; **42nd** 169, 193, 202, 204, 206; **44th** 90, 132, 164, 201–202, 204, 210, **47th** 70; **49th** 80; **53rd** 26, 93, 119, 141, 151–153, 155, 185, 189–191, 193, 195, 197–199, 202, 206, 246; **55th** 30, 69, 191–192, 197, 200–202, 205, 220, 258; **56th** 59; **57th** 87, 124, 164, 193, 202, 204, 233; **60th** 105, 202; **63rd** 141, 202, 205, 207,

210, 215; **66th** 62; **71st** 59; **78th** 233; **79th** 182, 192–193, 199, 233; **80th** 154, 163, 202, 233; **82nd** 71, 204–205; **84th** 182, 192–193, 202, 233; **85th** 163, 182, 193, 233; **87th** 76, 182, 185, 192, 210, 264; **88th** 81, 85, 162, 182, 185, 192, 202, 206, 210, 233; **89th** 182, 185, 202
British Army, other units and formations; **Guards Brigade** 24, 31, 188, 209–210, 235, 239, 244–246, 250, 252, 263; **Guards Flank Battalion** 39, 73, 188, 211, 232, 235, 258; Line Flank Battalion 189–190, 232; **Corps of Royal Waggoners** 83–84, 118, 238; **independent companies** 85, 179–183, 185, 189–190, 192, 263–264; for **Royal Artillery**, **Royal Engineers**, and **Royal Military Artificers** see Board of Ordnance
Brownrigg, Lieutenant Colonel Robert 57, 81, 95, 206
Bruges 45, 105, 114–116, 120–121, 123–124, 145, 157–158, 165–166, 190, 193, 228
Brunswick, Duke of 24, 28, 44, 55, 59–60, 62–63, 242, 269
Brussels 40, 43, 46, 131, 161, 213

Calvert, Major Harry 35–36, 43–44, 62–63, 65–67, 81, 94–95, 190–191, 193, 200, 202–204, 231, 233–234, 243, 256, 266
Cambrai 33, 35, 42
Camp de César 35–36, 42
Cathcart, Major General Lord 59, 200–201, 205
Childers, Captain John Walbanke 63, 66, 71, 95
Clerfayt, *Feldzeugmeister* François de Croix, Count von 41–43, 46–47, 246
Clinton, Lieutenant and Captain Henry 25–26, 28, 34, 36, 61–63, 66, 94–95, 102, 200, 203–204, 248
Coburg, Prince Friedrich Josias von Coburg-Saalfeld 27–30, 34–35, 40–43, 46–47, 49, 62, 123, 268
Coevorden 124
Condé 29, 49, 121, 238, 252, 255, 257
Condé-sur-l'Escaut 33, 50
Congreve, Lieutenant Colonel William 221, 227–229, 236, 239, 247, 251, 257
Cornwallis, General Charles, Marquis 41, 43–44, 47, 218, 269
Craig, Colonel Sir James 38, 60, 66, 70–71, 76, 95, 145, 163–164, 166, 189, 192, 200, 205, 231, 236–237
Craufurd, Major Charles 40, 57, 61–64, 66, 70–71, 94
Cumberland, Duke of 16–17, 39, 138, 237, 269

Dalrymple, Colonel Sir Hew 43, 65, 191, 204, 206, 251, 266
De Lancey, Colonel Oliver 89, 111
Dickson, Assistant Surgeon James 114, 159, 161–162
Diksmuide 105, 115
Don, Lieutenant Colonel George 47, 71, 127, 164, 202
Dordrecht 45, 79, 103, 116, 159, 226, 242
Druten 190, 196, 215
Dundas, Major General David 59, 71, 201
Dundas, Henry, 1st Viscount Melville 18–19, 27–29, 31, 34, 38–41, 49–50, 66, 69–71, 74, 95, 159, 164, 174, 180–182, 214–215, 223–224, 230, 235, 243–244, 255, 264, 268
Dundas, Major General Ralph 93, 184, 201
Dunkirk xiii, 29–30, 32–36, 74, 76, 80, 82, 91, 115, 120, 125–126, 165, 189–190, 193, 199, 227, 229, 232, 243, 245, 253–257, 259, 264, 269

Emmerich 104, 115
Erskine, Lieutenant General Sir William 39–40, 58–59, 74, 81, 126, 231

Famars 36, 61, 122, 190
Fawcett, Lieutenant General Sir William 17, 184, 186, 189
Fenwick, First Lieutenant Thomas 37, 45, 80, 232, 251, 255, 258
FitzPatrick, Dr Jeremiah 167–168
Fleurus, Battle of 33, 43, 50
Fox, Colonel the Hon Henry 37, 57–58, 60, 80–81, 95, 166, 173, 175, 202, 205, 262
Francis II, Emperor of Austria 41–42
Frederick-William, King of Prussia 44–45, 47
Freytag, *Feldmarschall* Wilhelm von 30, 40–41, 74, 94, 126, 256

Ghent 37, 70, 78, 83, 87, 90, 105, 112, 114–116, 123–124, 131–132, 143, 157–158, 160, 229, 233
Gravendeel 159, 162
Grenville, William, Lord 19, 29, 34, 39–41, 50, 122, 174, 180–181, 214–215, 223–224, 264
Gunning, John 138–140, 145, 149, 167, 170–171

Harcourt, Lieutenant General the Hon William 38–39, 50, 89, 124, 146, 157, 161–162, 170, 187, 213, 235
Helvoetsluys 26, 28, 88, 103, 159, 167, 226, 242

Hesse Cassel 29, 31, 44, 60, 109
Hesse Darmstadt 31, 60, 109
Home, Sir Everard 145, 149, 165, 167
Hondschoote 30, 34, 36, 50, 67, 256, 269
Hunter, John 137–142, 144–146, 165–166, 168, 201

Jackson, Dr Robert 153, 158, 161, 163, 169, 267
Johnstone, Colonel Robert 78–81, 94, 247, 262

Karl, Archduke 41, 74
Kaunitz, *Feldmarschall-Lieutenant* Count Franz von 41–42
Keate, Thomas 138–140, 145, 148–150
Kennedy, Dr Hugh 105, 129, 142, 144–146, 149–150, 157, 165, 168, 170–171, 262
Kerr, Major John Charles 85, 118
Kortrijk 23, 41–42, 73, 90, 105, 115–116, 131, 233, 258

La Vendée 39, 49, 107, 195, 215
Lake, Major General Gerard 26, 39, 74, 80, 188
Landrécies 22, 33, 42, 50, 245–246
Le Cateau-Cambrésis 41–42, 212, 245, 259
Le Mesurier, Havilland 105, 109, 120, 129
Le Quesnoy 22, 33–35, 49
Leigh, Colonel Charles 188, 252
Lille 23, 28–30, 33, 36, 253
Lys, River 22, 41, 119

Maastricht 27, 49, 131
Mack, *Oberst* Karl Mack von Lieberich 35, 40–42
Mainz 33, 36, 47
Marlborough, Duke of 16, 53, 55, 98–99, 131, 269
Maubeuge 29, 33–34, 36, 269
McGrigor, Surgeon James 162, 192, 267
Menen 23, 29, 33, 41–42, 45, 68, 103, 131, 158, 165, 193, 247
Meuse. River 22, 33, 43, 49, 111, 158, 169
Moira, Earl of 48–49, 59, 63, 71, 76, 87, 107, 119, 192–195, 201, 204, 210, 212, 221, 228, 230, 232–234, 243–244
Moncrieff, Colonel Sir James 30, 39, 60, 79–80, 95, 219, 242–243, 248, 250, 252, 256–257, 259, 262
Mons 32, 42
Motz, Henry 103–106, 108, 119, 129
Mouscron 42, 246
Mulgrave, Colonel Henry, Lord 192, 233, 257, 264
Murray, Colonel Sir James 27–29, 31, 34, 37, 39, 60, 64–65, 67–70, 94–95, 230, 235, 244, 255, 262

Nepean, Evan 164, 192
Nieuwpoort 41, 59, 105, 114–115, 120, 152, 243, 255–257
Nijmegen 49, 104, 115, 160, 247–248

Oosterhout 46, 247, 259
Orange, Prince of 26, 29, 34, 40, 45–47, 60, 260
Ostend 28–29, 41, 49, 59, 76–77, 87, 105, 110–111, 114–117, 119, 121–124, 127, 144, 148–150, 158, 163, 166, 190–191, 193, 200–201, 203, 213, 220, 228, 232, 234, 238, 243–244, 255, 264, 268
Oudenaarde 105, 115, 193

Paget, Lieutenant Colonel the Hon Edward 203, 207, 215
Pennington, Captain and Lieutenant Colonel Lowther 39, 64
Pepys, Sir Lucas 138–139, 148
Pitt, William 19, 34, 39–41, 43, 50, 101–103, 125–126, 174, 180–181, 215–216, 223–224, 255, 264–265
Poole, Captain James 105, 118
Portland, Duke of 18, 63

Quiverain 117, 121

Richmond, Duke of 20–21, 216, 221–224, 227, 230, 235, 238, 242–244, 257, 265–266
Royal Navy 16, 20, 122, 137, 220, 264
Royal Military College 53, 217, 267

Sambre, River 34, 41–43
Sargent, John 21, 119
Scheldt, River 24, 41, 119, 122, 150, 246
Sontag, Captain John 81, 83–84
St Ghislain 78, 160
St Leger, Colonel John Hayes 37, 69–71, 89–90, 257
Stahremberg, Count 29, 40, 43
Stanhope, Captain and Lieutenant Colonel the Hon Fitzroy 93, 188
Stewart, Major General Alexander, 77, 200–203
Stewart, Lieutenant Charles 45, 246
Stewart, Lieutenant Colonel John 228, 230, 235
Sutherland, Captain Alexander 242–244, 252

Taylor, Herbert 57–58, 60–61, 64–66, 69–70, 79–80, 94–95, 103, 114, 144, 211, 233, 241, 250, 258
Thugut, Franz Maria, Baron von 40, 43, 47

Toulon 39–40, 168, 215
Tourcoing xi, 30, 42, 50, 193, 195, 199, 210–212, 258
Treasury, the xii–xiii, 17, 20, 54, 90, 99–101, 103–113, 117–118, 120–123, 125–127, 129, 161, 166, 236, 262, 268

United Provinces, the 24–28, 30–31, 44, 49, 60, 67, 73, 84, 98, 103, 110, 112–114, 122–124, 150, 159, 163, 185, 232, 234, 238, 242, 262–263, 269

Valenciennes xiii, 28–30, 33, 35–36, 41, 49, 62–63, 73, 82, 87, 117, 120, 144, 232, 234, 237, 239–240, 245, 248–250, 252–253, 255–257, 259
Valmy 24, 47
Vaux 42, 62, 234, 239, 258
Veurne 22, 29, 115, 120, 126

Waal, River 49–50, 85, 111, 158, 160, 169, 247–248, 259
Wallmoden, *General der Cavallerie* Count Ludwig von 41, 50, 58, 73, 125
Watson, Brook 31, 90, 101–127, 129, 161, 166, 236, 240, 262, 266
Wattignies 34, 36, 50, 269

Wesley, Lieutenant Colonel the Hon Arthur 204–205, 215, 260
West Flanders 29, 37, 41–42
West Indies 39, 67, 79, 141, 163, 168, 176, 192, 201, 215, 223, 227, 230, 244, 261, 264
Whyte, Major General Richard 191, 193, 195, 257, 264
Willems 42, 62
Willemstad 24, 45
Windham, William 18, 37, 43, 46, 49, 231, 268
Woolwich, Arsenal 23, 59, 79, 217, 226–228
Wright, Major Jesse 45, 226, 242, 258
Wynyard, Lieutenant and Captain William 63–64, 66, 92, 95

Yonge, Sir George 18, 140, 142, 267
York, HRH Frederick, Duke of xi–xiv, 17, 25–28, 30–31, 33–47, 49, 51, 53, 56–61, 63, 65–67, 69, 74, 76, 80–82, 90–91, 93–95, 102, 108–109, 112–113, 115, 119–121, 123–128, 133, 135, 142, 145, 147, 149, 152–153, 155, 157, 159, 162–165, 167–168, 170–171, 175, 180, 182, 184, 189, 191, 193, 196, 200–201, 207, 209, 211, 215, 220, 224, 227–228, 236–238, 240, 243, 245–246, 248, 251, 253, 255–262, 265–269
Ypres 33, 41, 105, 115–116, 120–121

From Reason to Revolution – Warfare 1721-1815

http://www.helion.co.uk/series/from-reason-to-revolution-1721-1815.php

The 'From Reason to Revolution' series covers the period of military history 1721–1815, an era in which fortress-based strategy and linear battles gave way to the nation-in-arms and the beginnings of total war.

This era saw the evolution and growth of light troops of all arms, and of increasingly flexible command systems to cope with the growing armies fielded by nations able to mobilise far greater proportions of their manpower than ever before. Many of these developments were fired by the great political upheavals of the era, with revolutions in America and France bringing about social change which in turn fed back into the military sphere as whole nations readied themselves for war. Only in the closing years of the period, as the reactionary powers began to regain the upper hand, did a military synthesis of the best of the old and the new become possible.

The series will examine the military and naval history of the period in a greater degree of detail than has hitherto been attempted, and has a very wide brief, with the intention of covering all aspects from the battles, campaigns, logistics, and tactics, to the personalities, armies, uniforms, and equipment.

Submissions

The publishers would be pleased to receive submissions for this series. Please contact series editor Andrew Bamford via email (andrewbamford@helion.co.uk), or in writing to Helion & Company Limited, Unit 8 Amherst Business Centre, Budbrooke Road, Warwick, CV34 5WE

Titles

No 1 *Lobositz to Leuthen: Horace St Paul and the Campaigns of the Austrian Army in the Seven Years War 1756-57* (Neil Cogswell)

No 2 *Glories to Useless Heroism: The Seven Years War in North America from the French journals of Comte Maurés de Malartic, 1755-1760* (William Raffle (ed.))

No 3 *Reminiscences 1808-1815 Under Wellington: The Peninsular and Waterloo Memoirs of William Hay* (Andrew Bamford (ed.))

No 4 *Far Distant Ships: The Royal Navy and the Blockade of Brest 1793-1815* (Quintin Barry)

No 5 *Godoy's Army: Spanish Regiments and Uniforms from the Estado Militar of 1800* (Charles Esdaile and Alan Perry)

No 6 *On Gladsmuir Shall the Battle Be! The Battle of Prestonpans 1745* (Arran Johnston)

No 7 *The French Army of the Orient 1798-1801: Napoleon's Beloved 'Egyptians'* (Yves Martin)

No 8 *The Autobiography, or Narrative of a Soldier: The Peninsular War Memoirs of William Brown of the 45th Foot* (Steve Brown (ed.))

No 9 *Recollections from the Ranks: Three Russian Soldiers' Autobiographies from the Napoleonic Wars* (Darrin Boland)

No 10 *By Fire and Bayonet: Grey's West Indies Campaign of 1794* (Steve Brown)

No 11 *Olmütz to Torgau: Horace St Paul and the Campaigns of the Austrian Army in the Seven Years War 1758-60* (Neil Cogswell)

No 12 *Murat's Army: The Army of the Kingdom of Naples 1806-1815* (Digby Smith)

No 13 *The Veteran or 40 Years' Service in the British Army: The Scurrilous Recollections of Paymaster John Harley 47th Foot – 1798-1838* (Gareth Glover (ed.))

No 14 *Narrative of the Eventful Life of Thomas Jackson: Militiaman and Coldstream Sergeant, 1803-15* (Eamonn O'Keeffe (ed.))

No.15 *For Orange and the States: The Army of the Dutch Republic 1713-1772 Part I: Infantry* (Marc Geerdinck-Schaftenaar)

No 16 *Men Who Are Determined to be Free: The American Assault on Stony Point, 15 July 1779* (David C. Bonk)

No 17 *Next to Wellington: General Sir George Murray: The Story of a Scottish Soldier and Statesman, Wellington's Quartermaster General* (John Harding-Edgar)

No 18 *Between Scylla and Charybdis: The Army of Elector Friedrich August of Saxony 1733-1763 Part I: Staff and Cavalry* (Marco Pagan)

No 19 *The Secret Expedition: The Anglo-Russian Invasion of Holland 1799* (Geert van Uythoven)

No 20 *'We Are Accustomed to do our Duty': German Auxiliaries with the British Army 1793-95* (Paul Demet)

No 21 *With the Guards in Flanders: The Diary of Captain Roger Morris 1793-95* (Peter Harington (ed.))

No 22 *The British Army in Egypt 1801: An Underrated Army Comes of Age* (Carole Divall)

No 23 *Better is the Proud Plaid: The Clothing, Weapons, and Accoutrements of the Jacobites in the '45* (Jenn Scott)

No 24 *The Lilies and the Thistle: French Troops in the Jacobite '45* (Andrew Bamford)

No 25 *A Light Infantryman With Wellington: The Letters of Captain George Ulrich Barlow 52nd and 69th Foot 1808-15* (Gareth Glover (ed.))

No 26 *Swiss Regiments in the Service of France 1798-1815: Uniforms, Organisation, Campaigns* (Stephen Ede-Borrett)

No 27 *For Orange and the States! The Army of the Dutch Republic 1713-1772: Part II: Cavalry and Specialist Troops* (Marc Geerdinck-Schaftenaar)

No 28 *Fashioning Regulation, Regulating Fashion: Uniforms and Dress of the British Army 1800-1815 Volume I* (Ben Townsend)

No 29 *Riflemen: The History of the 5th Battalion 60th (Royal American) Regiment, 1797-1818* (Robert Griffith)

No 30 *The Key to Lisbon: The Third French Invasion of Portugal, 1810-11* (Kenton White)

No 31 *Command and Leadership: Proceedings of the 2018 Helion & Company 'From Reason to Revolution' Conference* (Andrew Bamford (ed.))

No 32 *Waterloo After the Glory: Hospital Sketches and Reports on the Wounded After the Battle* (Michael Crumplin and Gareth Glover)

No 33 *Fluxes, Fevers, and Fighting Men: War and Disease in Ancien Regime Europe 1648-1789* (Pádraig Lenihan)

No 34 *'They Were Good Soldiers': African-Americans Serving in the Continental Army, 1775-1783* (John U. Rees)

No 35 *A Redcoat in America: The Diaries of Lieutenant William Bamford, 1757-1765 and 1776* (John B. Hattendorf (ed.))

No 36 *Between Scylla and Charybdis: The Army of Friedrich August II of Saxony, 1733-1763: Part II: Infantry and Artillery* (Marco Pagan)

No 37 *Québec Under Siege: French Eye-Witness Accounts from the Campaign of 1759* (Charles A. Mayhood (ed.))

No 38 *King George's Hangman: Henry Hawley and the Battle of Falkirk 1746* (Jonathan D. Oates)

No 39 *Zweybrücken in Command: The Reichsarmee in the Campaign of 1758* (Neil Cogswell)

No 40 *So Bloody a Day: The 16th Light Dragoons in the Waterloo Campaign* (David J. Blackmore)

No 41 *Northern Tars in Southern Waters: The Russian Fleet in the Mediterranean 1806-1810* (Vladimir Bogdanovich Bronevskiy / Darrin Boland)

No 42 *Royal Navy Officers of the Seven Years War: A Biographical Dictionary of Commissioned Officers 1748-1763* (Cy Harrison)

No 43 *All at Sea: Naval Support for the British Army During the American Revolutionary War* (John Dillon)

No 44 *Glory is Fleeting: New Scholarship on the Napoleonic Wars* (Andrew Bamford (ed.))

No 45 *Fashioning Regulation, Regulating Fashion: Uniforms and Dress of the British Army 1800-1815 Vol. II* (Ben Townsend)

No 46 *Revenge in the Name of Honour: The Royal Navy's Quest for Vengeance in the Single Ship Actions of the War of 1812* (Nicholas James Kaizer)

No 47 *They Fought With Extraordinary Bravery: The III German (Saxon) Army Corps in the Southern Netherlands 1814* (Geert van Uythoven)

No 48 *The Danish Army of the Napoleonic Wars 1801-1814, Organisation, Uniforms & Equipment: Volume 1: High Command, Line and Light Infantry* (David Wilson)

No 49 *Neither Up Nor Down: The British Army and the Flanders Campaign 1793-1895* (Phillip Ball)

No 50 *Guerra Fantástica: The Portuguese Army and the Seven Years War* (António Barrento)

No 51 *From Across the Sea: North Americans in Nelson's Navy* (Sean M. Heuvel and John A. Rodgaard)

No 52 *Rebellious Scots to Crush: The Military Response to the Jacobite '45* (Andrew Bamford (ed.))

No 53 *The Army of George II 1727-1760: The Soldiers who Forged an Empire* (Peter Brown)

No 54 *Wellington at Bay: The Battle of Villamuriel, 25 October 1812* (Garry David Wills)

No 55 *Life in the Red Coat: The British Soldier 1721-1815* (Andrew Bamford (ed.))

No 56 *Wellington's Favourite Engineer. John Burgoyne: Operations, Engineering, and the Making of a Field Marshal* (Mark S. Thompson)

No 57 *Scharnhorst: The Formative Years, 1755-1801* (Charles Edward White)

No 58 *At the Point of the Bayonet: The Peninsular War Battles of Arroyomolinos and Almaraz 1811-1812* (Robert Griffith)

No 59 *Sieges of the '45: Siege Warfare during the Jacobite Rebellion of 1745-1746* (Jonathan D. Oates)

No 60 *Austrian Cavalry of the Revolutionary and Napoleonic Wars, 1792–1815* (Enrico Acerbi, András K. Molnár)

No 61 *The Danish Army of the Napoleonic Wars 1801-1814, Organisation, Uniforms & Equipment: Volume 2: Cavalry and Artillery* (David Wilson)

No 62 *Napoleon's Stolen Army: How the Royal Navy Rescued a Spanish Army in the Baltic* (John Marsden)

No 63 *Crisis at the Chesapeake: The Royal Navy and the Struggle for America 1775-1783* (Quintin Barry)

No 64 *Bullocks, Grain, and Good Madeira: The Maratha and Jat Campaigns 1803-1806 and the emergence of an Indian Army* (Joshua Provan)

No 65 *Sir James McGrigor: The Adventurous Life of Wellington's Chief Medical Officer* (Tom Scotland)

No 66 *Fashioning Regulation, Regulating Fashion: Uniforms and Dress of the British Army 1800-1815 Volume I* (Ben Townsend) (paperback edition)

No 67 *Fashioning Regulation, Regulating Fashion: Uniforms and Dress of the British Army 1800-1815 Volume II* (Ben Townsend) (paperback edition)

No 68 *The Secret Expedition: The Anglo-Russian Invasion of Holland 1799* (Geert van Uythoven) (paperback edition)

No 69 *The Sea is My Element: The Eventful Life of Admiral Sir Pulteney Malcolm 1768-1838* (Paul Martinovich)

No 70 *The Sword and the Spirit: Proceedings of the first 'War & Peace in the Age of Napoleon' Conference* (Zack White (ed.))

No 71 *Lobositz to Leuthen: Horace St Paul and the Campaigns of the Austrian Army in the Seven Years War 1756-57* (Neil Cogswell) (paperback edition)

No 72 *For God and King. A History of the Damas Legion 1793-1798: A Case Study of the Military Emigration during the French Revolution* (Hughes de Bazouges and Alistair Nichols)

No 73 *'Their Infantry and Guns Will Astonish You': The Army of Hindustan and European Mercenaries in Maratha service 1780-1803* (Andy Copestake)

No 74 *Like A Brazen Wall: The Battle of Minden, 1759, and its Place in the Seven Years War* (Ewan Carmichael)

No 75 *Wellington and the Lines of Torres Vedras: The Defence of Lisbon during the Peninsular War* (Mark Thompson)

No 76 *French Light Infantry 1784-1815: From the Chasseurs of Louis XVI to Napoleon's Grande Armée* (Terry Crowdy)

No 77 *Riflemen: The History of the 5th Battalion 60th (Royal American) Regiment, 1797-1818* (Robert Griffith) (paperback edition)

No 78 *Hastenbeck 1757: The French Army and the Opening Campaign of the Seven Years War* (Olivier Lapray)

No 79 *Napoleonic French Military Uniforms: As Depicted by Horace and Carle Vernet and Eugène Lami* (Guy Dempsey (trans. and ed.))

No 80 *These Distinguished Corps: British Grenadier and Light Infantry Battalions in the American Revolution* (Don N. Hagist)

No 81 *Rebellion, Invasion, and Occupation: The British Army in Ireland, 1793 -1815* (Wayne Stack)

No 82 *You Have to Die in Piedmont! The Battle of Assietta, 19 July 1747. The War of the Austrian Succession in the Alps* (Giovanni Cerino Badone)

No 83 *A Very Fine Regiment: the 47th Foot in the American War of Independence, 1773–1783* (Paul Knight)

No 84 *By Fire and Bayonet: Grey's West Indies Campaign of 1794* (Steve Brown) (paperback edition)

No 85 *No Want of Courage: The British Army in Flanders, 1793-1795* (R.N.W. Thomas)

No 86 *Far Distant Ships: The Royal Navy and the Blockade of Brest 1793-1815* (Quintin Barry) (paperback edition)